W9-COX-250

WHAT CHRISTIAN LEADERS ARE SAYING ABOUT THIS BOOK

TIM LAHAYE

Author of more than 50 books
including co-author of the *Left Behind* Series

"To suggest that the merciful, longsuffering, gracious and loving God of the Bible would invent a dreadful doctrine like Calvinism, which would have us believe it is an act of 'grace' to select only certain people for heaven and, by exclusion, others for hell, comes perilously close to blasphemy. And that is why I congratulate Dave Hunt for writing this excellent clarification of the doctrine that has its roots more in Greek humanism, from where it originated, than it does in Scripture. This book could well be the most important book written in the twenty-first century for all evangelical Christians to read. It will help you know and love the real God of the Bible who clearly says of Himself, 'It is not My will that *any* should perish but that *all* should come to repentance.' Calvinism is a far cry from the God of the Bible who loves mankind so much that He sent His only Son to save *whosoever* calls on Him for mercy in the name of His resurrected Son, Jesus Christ. Every evangelical minister should read this book. If they did, we would see a mighty revival of soul-winning passion that would turn this world upside down as multitudes saw the real God of the Bible, not the false God of Augustinianism and Calvinism."

CHUCK SMITH

Pastor, Calvary Chapel Costa Mesa

"Dave Hunt has done it again. Even as his books, *The Seduction of Christianity* and *A Woman Rides the Beast* have stirred the Christian community into taking a serious look at the aberrant teachings of some Pentecostals and the Roman Catholic church, so now in his latest book on Calvinism, he brings to the light the teachings of John Calvin, which are bound to cause ripples through the entire church, and send many back to a serious study of TULIP in light of God's Word. He has researched the origins of the teachings of Calvinism and thoroughly documents his findings. It is a must-read for those who are serious in their desire to understand the influence that Calvin has had and continues to have on the Evangelical church."

ELMER L. TOWNS

Dean, School of Religion, Liberty University

"Dave Hunt has given exact details to show the agonizing faults of Calvinistic abuses that most people have not considered. I would like for all of my students at Liberty University to read this in-depth analysis. It seems that each year Calvinism, like dandelions, comes in the spring. Students get wrapped up in arguing the issues of Calvinism. Those students who don't like aggressive soul-winning use their view of Calvinism to defend their position. Those who are aggressive soul winners attack the weaknesses of Calvinism. Very little of their discussions are grounded in the truth of the Word of God. In the final analysis, their arguments are like weeds, i.e., dandelions that bear no fruit. May many read this volume to 'be no more children, tossed to and fro, and carried about with every wind of doctrine, by the sleight of men, and cunning craftiness,' but may they be grounded in the Word of God."

WILLIAM MACDONALD

Author of more than 80 books in 100 languages including the *Believer's Bible Commentary* and *True Discipleship*

"This book exposes traditional Calvinism for portraying God in a totally unscriptural manner. Professed Calvinists will want to rethink their position when they realize the Biblical truths that are at stake. This book will stand as a definitive work on the subject."

DR. CHUCK MISSLER

Founder, Koinonia House

"The character of God has been totally misrepresented by our common denominational traditions. Dave Hunt continues his intrepid commitment to revealing the truth—however unfashionable or politically incorrect it may be deemed. Blindfold your prejudices and be ready for a stunning and desperately needed perspective on this highly controversial area. Here is another essential for the serious student of God's Word."

ARNO FROESE

Executive Director, Midnight Call Ministry • Editor, *Midnight Call*

"Rarely has anyone undertaken the exhaustive task of detailing and documenting the misconception of God's sovereign grace as has Dave Hunt. Reading this work should convince even the most staunch Calvinist to recognize the flawed philosophical theology of preselection as an attempt to eliminate man's capacity to exercise his free will, which reduces God's sovereign love to an act of a mere dictator. This book needs to be read by every communicator of the Gospel in defense of the fundamental principles of God's grace."

JOSEPH R. CHAMBERS, DD, DSL

Pastor, author, and radio host

"This incredible book by Dave Hunt is imperative in our generation of 'class warfare.' It is hard to believe that the Christian world has its own system of 'apartheid.' That's exactly what hyper-Calvinism represents, and this book exposes the horror of spiritual apartheid for what it really is. Calvinism makes our Heavenly Father look like the worst of despots and I join Dave in declaring Him: Not Guilty! The biblical revelation of redemption leaves no one uninvited."

JIM CUSTER

Right Start Ministries

"I am glad to see Dave deal with a tough subject, supply materials that many of us have not accessed until now, and challenge the Biblical basis for TULIP."

BOB WILKIN, PH.D.

Founder and Executive Director, Grace Evangelical Society

"Dave Hunt has given us a fascinating exposé of modern five-point Calvinism that is both highly readable and practical. I especially enjoyed the section on perseverance and assurance of salvation."

HARRY BOLLBACK

Co-founder with Jack Wyrtzen of Word of Life International

"As a biblicist, I find this to be a refreshing biblical review of things which for many years have brought confusion to believers. We've allowed words and ideas of men to determine our positions. This book reminds us to listen to what the Word of God has to say."

JOE JORDAN

Executive Director Word of Life Fellowship, Inc.

"Dave Hunt's treatment of the age-old controversy over election and predestination in his book, *What Love is This? Calvinism's Misrepresentation of God,* is not only thought-provoking but also brings the reader to focus on a scriptural viewpoint in this very thorny theological issue. Many times theology is approached philosophically and not biblically, and this approach will bring havoc in the Church. In Dave's book, we are challenged to go back to the Scriptures as we evaluate the workings of God on this all-important subject of salvation. This is definitely a book that causes us to reflect on how we formulate our doctrine."

WHAT LOVE IS THIS?

CALVINISM'S MISREPRESENTATION OF GOD

UPDATED AND EXPANDED

DAVE HUNT

BEND • OREGON
www.thebereancall.org

WHAT LOVE IS THIS?
Third Edition

Published by The Berean Call

ISBN-13: 978-1-928660-12-5
ISBN-10: 1-928660-12-6
Library of Congress Control Number: 2004107548

[First Edition published by Loyal Publishing
ISBN 1-929125-30-5]

Unless otherwise indicated, Scripture quotations are from
The Holy Bible, King James Version (KJV)
Used by Permission

The Berean Call
PO Box 7019
Bend, Oregon, 97708-7019

PRINTED IN THE UNITED STATES OF AMERICA

Contents

A Brief Word

DISCUSSIONS WITH NUMBERS of people around the world reveal that many sincere, Bible-believing Christians are "Calvinists" only by default. Thinking that the only choice is between Calvinism (with its presumed doctrine of eternal security) and Arminianism (with its teaching that salvation can be lost), and confident of Christ's promise to keep eternally those who believe in Him, they therefore consider themselves to be Calvinists.

It takes only a few simple questions to discover that most Christians are largely unaware of what John Calvin and his early followers of the sixteenth and seventeenth centuries actually believed and practiced. Nor do they fully understand what most of today's leading Calvinists believe.

Although there are disputed variations of the Calvinist doctrine, among its chief proponents (whom we quote extensively in context) there is general agreement on certain core beliefs. Many evangelicals who think they are Calvinists will be surprised to learn of Calvin's belief in salvation through infant baptism, and of his grossly un-Christian behavior, at times, as the "Protestant Pope" of Geneva, Switzerland.

Most shocking of all, however, is Calvinism's misrepresentation of God who "is love." It is our prayer that the following pages will enable readers to examine more carefully the vital issues involved and to follow God's Holy Word and not man.

THE FIRST EDITION of this book was greeted by fervent opposition and criticism from Calvinists. In this enlarged and revised edition I have endeavored to respond to the critics.

—Dave Hunt

PUBLISHER'S NOTE: This third edition also includes an extensive, newly expanded author/subject index to better assist readers and researchers.

CHAPTER

1

Why This Book?

CAN YOU ANSWER SOME QUESTIONS about Calvinism?" The query came to me from a young man sitting with me and several others at a restaurant in a city where I was speaking at a conference.[1]

"Why do you ask *me*?"

"We heard you were writing a book about Calvinism."

"Yes, I am—a book, in fact, that I didn't want to write. There are fine Christians on both sides. The last thing I want to do is create more controversy—but it's a topic that really has to be faced and dealt with thoroughly." Glancing around the table, I was surprised at the sudden interest reflected on each face. Everyone was listening intently.

"I had scarcely given Calvinism a thought for years. Then suddenly—or so it seemed to me—in the last few years Calvinism has emerged as an issue everywhere. Perhaps I'm just waking up, but it seems to me that this peculiar doctrine is being promoted far more widely and aggressively now than I was ever aware of in the past."

"Our church recently added a new associate pastor to the staff—a graduate of the Master's College and Seminary in Southern California," explained the young man. "He introduces Calvinism in almost every session in his Bible class."

"Let me suggest how he might do it," I responded. "He asks the class what they think comes first, faith or regeneration. Everyone says, 'Faith, of course—believe on the Lord Jesus Christ and thou shalt be saved.' Then he challenges them, 'But mankind is dead in trespasses and sins. How can a dead man believe?'"

I had the young man's total attention. "That's it exactly! How did you know?"

"Then he explains," I continued, "that God has to give life sovereignly to those who are spiritually dead before they can believe or even understand the gospel—that regeneration must precede faith."

"You're right! But it seems bizarre...like having to get saved before you can get saved!"

"The Calvinist wouldn't put it in those precise words," I responded, "but it's even a bit stranger than that. Without understanding or believing anything about God or Christ or the Bible—because the 'totally depraved' supposedly can't until they're regenerated—the 'elect' are made spiritually alive by a sovereign act of God without any desire or cooperation on their part, and without even knowing what is happening to them at the time."

"That's exactly what he's been teaching," added another member of the same church. "It doesn't make sense. I never read anything like that in the Bible."

"Are you the only ones who have expressed any concern?" I asked. "Do those who thought that faith came first accept this new concept immediately?"

"Most do. But it *has* caused some confusion. And a few people have left the church."

"No one challenges him," I asked, "with the obvious fact that spiritual death can't be equated with physical death? That *physically* dead people not only can't believe but can't sin or do anything else?"

"I guess none of us have thought of that."

"What does the senior pastor say?"

"He doesn't seem to know how to handle the confusion. We never heard anything like this from the pulpit before, but now hints of Calvinism are even finding their way into *his* sermons."

The conversation went on like this for some time. Every new aspect of Calvinism I explained was greeted with further exclamations of "Yes! That's exactly what we're hearing."

Others, from entirely different areas of the country, began to relate their experiences. One man had recently left a church that had split over Calvinism. The deacon board had voted that every member must sign a Calvinistic statement of faith. Someone else came from a church whose pastor and elders had taken a hard line against what they considered a divisive issue and had disfellowshiped a Sunday school teacher for influencing his junior high class with Calvinism, in spite of several warnings.

Another couple had visited a highly recommended church in a large city near their home, pastored by a well-known Calvinist author.

"We don't really know much about Calvinism," my dinner companions confessed. "But it was a strange experience. On the one hand, we had the impression that these people felt certain they were the *elect.* Yet there also seemed to be some insecurity, as though performance were a major evidence of one's salvation."

As we got up to leave, a young woman who had sat through the entire discussion in silence asked if she could have a private moment of my time. We sat down again, and she began a tale of grief. She was a pastor's wife. Their lives and ministry had been happy and fruitful until her husband and two close friends, also pastors, became interested in a new "truth." All three were very intellectual. As a result of reading current Calvinist authors they had been drawn into the writings of John Calvin, Jonathan Edwards, John Knox, and others.

Their study, taking them all the way back to Augustine, eventually became almost an obsession. Then each of them began to preach their new "light" from their pulpits. After being warned several times to desist, they were removed from their pastorates. Eventually, her husband began to worry whether he was really one of the elect. The nagging questions grew into full-blown doubts about his salvation. The Calvinism that had once seemed so satisfying began to haunt him with uncertainty. Was he one of the elect?

"You were never drawn into it?" I asked.

She shook her head. "I'm not an intellectual—which may be why it never appealed to me. But isn't God supposed to be a God of love? In my simple mind it didn't make sense that the God of the Bible didn't love everyone enough to want them all in heaven, that Christ hadn't died for everyone even though the Bible seemed to say that He had."

Tears came to her eyes. At last she continued, "I kept trying to tell my husband that the God he was now believing in—a God who predestined people before they were even born to spend eternity in the Lake of Fire—was not the God I knew and loved."

Troubling encounters such as these became more frequent and soon demanded deeper insight on my part into a system obviously embraced by a larger portion of the church than I had realized. It seemed so alien to everything I had believed about a God whose sovereignty did not diminish His mercy and love. For my own peace of mind, I was compelled to pursue the lengthy investigation that resulted in this book.

An Issue of Great Importance

Calvinism has never seemed biblical to me for a number of reasons that we will come to in due order. Over the years, my considerable objections have been discussed privately, in detail, with several friends who are staunch Calvinists. Thankfully, in spite of our serious differences and our inability to resolve them, there was never any loss of good will. We remain in close friendship to this day and simply avoid this subject.

It is true that "throughout history many of the great evangelists, missionaries, and stalwart theologians held to the...doctrines of grace known as Calvinism."[2] R. C. Sproul declares that "the titans of classical Christian scholarship" are Calvinists.[3] The additional claim is often made that, although many have not made it known publicly, most of today's leading evangelicals in America hold to some form of this doctrine. I soon discovered that there were far more books in print promoting Calvinism than I had ever imagined. Their number and influence are growing rapidly.

Like *John MacArthur's Study Bible*, the *New Geneva Study Bible* aggressively promotes Calvinism in its marginal explanations of key passages. It claims to present "Reformation truth." That bold phrase equates the Reformation with Calvinism—a proposition almost universally accepted among evangelicals today. The question of whether this is true, which we will deal with in the following pages, is surely one of great importance.

The significance of our concern is given further weight by the fact that its proponents even claim that "Calvinism is pure biblical Christianity in its clearest and purest expression."[4] D. James Kennedy has said, "I am a Presbyterian because I believe Presbyterianism is the purest form of Calvinism."[5] John Piper writes, "The doctrines of grace (Total depravity, Unconditional election, Limited atonement, Irresistible grace, Perseverance of the saints) are the warp and woof of the biblical gospel cherished by so many saints for centuries."[6]

Wouldn't this mean, then, that those who do not preach Calvinism do not preach the gospel? And how could evangelicals possibly be saved who reject the five points of Calvinism that Piper claims are "the warp and woof of the biblical gospel"? C. H. Spurgeon, who at times contradicted Calvinism, declared:

> ...those great truths, which are called Calvinism...are, I believe, the essential doctrines of the Gospel that is in Jesus Christ. Now I do not ask whether you believe all this [Calvinism]. It is possible you may not. But I believe you will before you enter heaven. I

> am persuaded that as God may have washed your hearts, He will wash your brains before you enter heaven.[7]

Such a strong statement is impressive, coming from Charles Haddon Spurgeon. John H. Gerstner writes, "We believe with the great Baptist preacher, Charles Haddon Spurgeon, that Calvinism is just another name for Christianity."[8] Again, if Calvinism is true Christianity, would that mean that non-Calvinists are not Christians? Surely, most Calvinists would not say so, but isn't the implication there?

Of course, there were many Christian leaders of equal stature in the history of the church, such as D. L. Moody, who were of the opposite opinion. Norman F. Douty lists more than seventy Christian leaders who, in whole or in part, opposed Calvinism (especially its doctrine of Limited Atonement)—among them such men as Richard Baxter, John Newton, John and Charles Wesley, John Bunyan, H. C. G. Moule, and others.[9] A study of early church history reveals that Calvinistic doctrines were unknown during the church's first three centuries. From his knowledge of ecclesiastical history, Bishop Davenant, present at Dort, declares:

> It may be truly affirmed that before the dispute between Augustine and Pelagius, there was no question concerning the death of Christ, whether it was to be extended to all mankind, or to be confined only to the elect. For the Fathers...not a word (that I know of) occurs among them of the exclusion of any person by the decree of God. They agree that it is actually beneficial to those only who believe, yet they everywhere confess that Christ died in behalf of all mankind....
>
> Augustine died in AD 429, and up to his time, at least, there is not the slightest evidence that any Christian ever dreamed of a propitiation for the elect alone. Even after him, the doctrine of a limited propitiation was but slowly propagated, and for long but partially received.[10]

Today there is growing division on this issue, most Calvinists insisting that Christ died only for the elect. On the other hand, IFCA International, a group of about 700 independent evangelical churches and 1,200 pastors (some of them Calvinists) declares in its doctrinal statement, "We believe that the Lord Jesus Christ died on the cross for all mankind...to accomplish the redemption of all who trust in him...."[11]

Spurgeon himself, so often quoted by Calvinists to support their view, was torn between his evangelist's heart that desired the salvation of all and his Calvinistic beliefs. At times he seemed to reject Limited Atonement, though he often firmly preached it. Sometimes he seemed to contradict himself almost within the same breath:

> I know there are some who think it necessary to their system of theology to limit the merit of the blood of Jesus: if my theological system needed such limitation, I would cast it to the winds. I cannot, I dare not, allow the thought to find lodging in my mind, it seems so near akin to blasphemy. In Christ's finished work I see an ocean of merit; my plummet finds no bottom, my eye discerns no shore. There must be sufficient efficacy in the blood of Christ, if God had so willed it to have saved not only all in this world, but all in ten thousand worlds....Having a divine Person for an offering, it is not consistent to conceive of limited value; bound and measure are terms inapplicable to the divine sacrifice. The intent of the divine purpose fixes the application of the infinite offering, but does not change it into a finite work.[12]

Merit and *value* must apply to the *effect* of the Cross. If the Cross is intended for a limited number (the elect), its merit and value are necessarily limited. "If God had so willed it" is the key clause—which Spurgeon clearly denied at times. On the other hand, that Spurgeon believed salvation was available to all mankind is evident from many of his sermons. The contradiction is clear—a fact that Calvinists are reluctant to admit. Thus I have been accused of misrepresenting, and even misquoting, C. H. Spurgeon. Sufficient further statements by Spurgeon (see index) will be presented herein to enable readers to come to their own conclusions.

Aggressive Promotion

Calvinists are increasingly insisting that their peculiar dogmas represent the faith of "the Reformers who led the Reformation" and should be accepted by all evangelical Christians as true Christianity, and as the biblical expression of the gospel. With respect to that...

- There is much they stand for with which all Christians would agree.
- There is much they stand for with which many evangelicals think they agree because of misunderstandings, but actually do not, which will be clarified in the following pages.

- There is much they stand for with regard to the church, Israel, and the return of Christ to which those who believe in the imminent rapture of the church would take strong exception. These latter views have nothing to do with the gospel and therefore will not be dealt with herein.

In the year 2000, the Alliance of Reformation Christians met in London in opposition to the influence of the Toronto Blessing in England and sent this message to evangelicals worldwide: "We therefore call upon those who bear the label 'evangelical' to affirm their faith once again in accordance with the witness of Scripture and in continuity with the historic testimony of the church."[13] By "historic testimony of the church," they mean the peculiar doctrines that come from Augustine, as interpreted and expanded by John Calvin and which were at one time forced by a state church upon all in England and Scotland and those parts of Europe where Calvinists were in control. Historic documentation is provided in chapters 5 and 6.

Today's Calvinists speak ever more earnestly and boldly about the need for a "new Reformation," by which they very clearly mean a revival of Calvinism as the dominant view in Christendom. Consider some of the resolutions that make up "The London Declaration 2000: Alliance of Reformation Christians—A vision for biblical unity in the modern church, 'The Evangelical Problem'":

Under "The Question of Truth"

> We therefore call upon evangelicals to return to the once-held biblical view...that to lay claim to a particular doctrine [Calvinism] as true is not spiritual arrogance but a biblical duty.

Under "A Vision for Reformation"

> We therefore call upon evangelicals to affirm a vision for reformation which is in accordance with the witness of Scripture and in continuity with the historic testimony of the [Calvinist] church. Such a vision is of a church which is both *Catholic* and *Reformed.* By "Catholic" we do *not* mean "Roman Catholic"... [See Chapter 4, "Calvinism's Surprising Catholic Connection."] By *Reformed,* we mean that we confess those doctrines about the authority of Scripture and salvation by grace alone which our Reformed [Calvinist] forefathers reaffirmed at the time of the Reformation [their emphasis].

Under "Four Affirmations"

> *Under 1:* We likewise affirm that we are *Augustinians* in our doctrine of man and in our doctrine of salvation. This is because we believe that Augustine and his successors, including the [Calvinist] Reformers, faithfully reflect the Bible's teaching regarding the total spiritual inability of fallen man to respond to God, God the Father's gracious unconditional election of a people to be saved, the design of the incarnate Son's atoning work as intended surely and certainly to secure the salvation of that people [the elect only], the monergistic grace of the Holy Spirit in regeneration [without understanding or faith on man's part], and the perseverance of the elect. Accordingly, we also reject all forms of synergism or Semi-Pelagianism in which man is accorded a cooperative role in his regeneration [even to believe], e.g. Arminianism. We reject equally any softening of Augustinian soteriology, e.g. Amyraldinianism ('four point' Calvinism), and any hardening of it, e.g. *Hyper-Calvinism*....The notion of one Catholic and Reformed [Calvinist] Church—one main, majestic stream of historic Christian orthodoxy [Augustinianism/Calvinism]—is thus integral to our understanding. This notion we affirm as true and foundational to any evangelical outlook worthy of the name.
>
> *Under 2:* Reformed Catholics affirm the importance of the church and its history in any authentic vision of God's redemptive work in space and time. Evangelicalism today is infected with a deadly amnesia with regard to the historic [Calvinist] church.... We specifically reject the subjective and often disorderly spectacle of charismatic-style worship, with its attendant practices, such as alleged tongues-speaking, prophecies, "slayings in the Spirit," etc.
>
> *Under 4:* We bemoan the influence among evangelicals of a pietistic dispensationalism in which the world is considered irredeemably wicked (and thus hardly worth the effort of influencing), and in which the only hope is supposed to be the imminent rapture of the saints.

A Challenge to Remain Silent

With the recent upsurge of Calvinism, a number of leading Calvinists have begun to take a far more aggressive stance in its public promotion. Both sides, in fact, are increasingly making this issue a matter of fellowship in the Lord, resulting in division in a number of otherwise sound churches.

In some churches, members are forbidden to promote Calvinism even privately. In others, only Calvinists are accepted as members. Of course, the latter has been true of pastors and mission candidates for centuries in nearly all Presbyterian churches and even in some Baptist churches—but now that position seems to be growing.

Almost daily I found that this subject was claiming a wider interest and greater importance than I had ever imagined. It seemed obvious that there was great need for further research and writing to deal with this important issue.

As it became known that I intended to write such a book, a number of pastors cautioned me to refrain from publicly expressing myself on this subject. Some claimed that, out of ignorance of its true teachings, I had already misrepresented "Reformed Doctrine." A typical response from the Calvinist friends to whom I sent an early manuscript for comment went like this: "The caricatures you present and the straw men you construct demonstrate to me that you have absolutely no understanding of the Reformed position, and until you do I would counsel that you refrain from putting anything in print."[14]

Letters began to pour into our ministry, The Berean Call, from around the world, many from pastors insisting that I was unqualified to address Calvinism and urging me to seal my lips and drop my pen regarding this topic. It was suggested that I would lose many friends and alienate myself from leading evangelicals, most of whom were said to be convinced Calvinists. Furthermore, who would publish such a book, since the major publishers had brought out many books supporting the other side?

What moved me most was the concern earnestly expressed by close friends that a book from me on this issue could cause division—the last thing I wanted. "We can just hear it now," several friends told me: "Here comes Dave Hunt again; this time he's attacking Calvinists!" That concern weighed heavily upon me.

One must be willing to accept wise counsel. But the advice to remain silent, though given by so many out of genuine concern, seemed, after much prayer and soul-searching on my part, to be ill-advised. Spurgeon called the debate over God's sovereignty and man's free will "a controversy which...I believe to have been really healthy and which has done us all a vast amount of good...."[15] My heart's desire is that this book will be only to God's eternal glory and to the blessing of His people.

---

1. Narration represents a composite of several of the author's recent actual experiences.
2. Duane Edward Spencer, *TULIP: The Five Points of Calvinism in the Light of Scripture* (Grand Rapids, MI: Baker Book House, 1979), 6.
3. R. C. Sproul, *Chosen by God* (Carol Stream, IL: Tyndale House, 1986), 15.
4. Leonard J. Coppes, *Are Five Points Enough? The Ten Points of Calvinism* (Denver, CO: self-published, 1980), xi.
5. D. James Kennedy, *Why I Am a Presbyterian* (Ft. Lauderdale, FL: Coral Ridge Ministries, n. d.), 1.
6. John Piper, *TULIP: The Pursuit of God's Glory in Salvation* (Minneapolis, MN: Bethlehem Baptist Church, 2000), back cover.
7. Spurgeon's Sermons, Vols 1 and 2, "The Peculiar Sleep of the Beloved" (Grand Rapids, MI: Baker Books, 1999), 48
8. John H. Gerstner, *Wrongly Dividing the Word of Truth: A Critique of Dispensationalism* (Brentwood, TN: Wolgemuth and Hyatt, Publishers, Inc., 1991), 107.
9. Norman F. Douty, *The Death of Christ* (Irving, TX: Williams and Watrous Publishing Company, n. d.), 136–63.
10. James Morrison, *The Extent of the Atonement* (London: Hamilton, Adams and Co., 1882), 114–17.
11. IFCA International, *What We Believe,* I: (3) b (www.ifca.org).
12. "Number One Thousand; Or, 'Bread Enough and to Spare'" http://www.blueletterbible.org/Comm/charles_spurgeon/sermons/1000.html.
13. "The London Declaration 2000: Alliance of Reformation Christians—a vision for biblical unity in the modern church, 'The Evangelical Problem.' "
14. Personal to Dave Hunt, dated October 19, 2000. On file.
15. Charles Haddon Spurgeon, "God's Will and Man's Will," No. 442 (Newington: Metropolitan Tabernacle, sermon delivered Sunday, March 30, 1862).

CHAPTER

2

Is Biblical Understanding Reserved for an Elite?

CALVINISTS EMPHASIZE that their theology rests upon solid biblical exegesis, being "firmly based...upon the Word of God."[1] Some have gone so far as to assert that "this teaching was held to be the truth by the apostles,"[2] and even that "Christ taught the doctrines that have come to be known as the five points of Calvinism."[3]

According to the Bible itself, however, no one should accept such claims without verifying them from Scripture. Any doctrine claiming to be based on the Bible must be carefully checked against the Bible—an option open to anyone who knows God's Word. Relying upon one supposed biblical expert for an evaluation of the opinions of another would be going in circles. No matter whose opinion one accepted, the end result would be the same: one would still be held hostage to human opinion. Each individual must personally check out all opinions directly from the Bible. Yet I was being advised to keep silent on the basis that only those with special qualifications were competent to check Calvinism against the Bible, an idea that in itself contradicted Scripture.

The inhabitants of the city of Berea, though not even Christians when Paul first preached the gospel to them, "searched the scriptures daily, [to see] whether those things [Paul preached] were so" (Acts 17:11)—and they were commended as "noble" for doing so. Yet leading Calvinists insist that it requires special (and apparently lengthy) preparation for anyone to become qualified to examine that peculiar doctrine in light of the Bible. Why?

After all, the Bible itself declares that a "young man" can understand its instructions and thereby "cleanse his way" (Psalm 119:9). Even a child can know the Holy Scriptures through home instruction from a mother and grandmother (2 Timothy 1:5; 3:15). Timothy was certainly not a seminary-trained theologian, yet Paul considered him competent to study and "rightly divide" God's Word. If special expertise were required to test Calvinism against Scripture, that would be proof enough that this peculiar doctrine did not come from valid biblical exegesis. Anything that enigmatic, by very definition, could not have been derived from the Bible, which itself claims to be written for the simple:

> For ye see your calling, brethren, how that not many wise men after the flesh, not many mighty, not many noble, are called: but God hath chosen the foolish things of the world to confound the wise; and God hath chosen the weak things of the world to confound the things which are mighty.... That no flesh should glory in his presence. (1 Corinthians 1:26–29)

Is Calvinism So Difficult to Understand?

Many friends, whose obvious sincerity was appreciated, were telling me that in spite of my quoting John Calvin directly from his writings, along with quoting leading Calvinists of today, I was still likely to misrepresent Calvinism because I didn't understand it. Even after a three-hour detailed discussion with Calvinist friends, they still told me, "You just don't understand Calvinism." Then what of the claim that Calvinism *is* the gospel and true Christianity? Could multitudes of mature and fruitful evangelicals have somehow misunderstood the gospel and Christianity?

Should Calvinism remain a mystery for the common Christian? That very fact, if true, would be additional proof that Calvinism was not derived from the Scriptures. How could something so complicated possibly come from that upon which every person is capable of meditating day and night (Psalm 1:1–2)? If the essential nourishment God's Word provides is to be every man's daily sustenance for spiritual life (Deuteronomy 8:3), could Calvinism really be the biblical gospel and biblical Christianity and yet be so difficult for the ordinary Christian to understand?

Why should Calvinism be such a complex and apparently esoteric subject that it would require years to comprehend? Such an attitude could very well intimidate many into accepting this belief simply because such a vast array of highly respected theologians and evangelical leaders espouse it. Surely the great majority of Calvinists are ordinary Christians. On what basis, then, without the expertise and intense study that I apparently lacked, were they able to understand and accept it?

As for familiarizing oneself with Calvinism, there are surely more than sufficient resources accessible to anyone genuinely interested in consulting them. Numerous books on that subject are available, both pro and con. *The five points of calvinism* by Edwin H. Palmer, along with books by R. C. Sproul, John Piper, John MacArthur, A. W. Pink, C. H. Spurgeon, and others, are highly recommended by leading Calvinists. Calvin's *Institutes of the Christian Religion,* as well as other of his writings and those of Augustine and John Knox, and other classics, are also readily available. On the other side, the books by Samuel Fisk are informative. Laurence M. Vance's *The Other Side of Calvinism* is an exhaustive treatment of more than 700 pages, with hundreds of footnotes documenting his quotations.

Making Certain of Accuracy and Fairness

To make certain that no mistaken interpretations of the doctrines under consideration survived in this book, a preliminary manuscript was submitted to a number of Calvinist friends and acquaintances for their critiques. Reading and discussing with them their valuable comments, for which I am deeply grateful, has been an education in itself. In that process, it became clearer than ever that Calvinists don't agree on everything even among themselves.

A number of critics have faulted me for not accepting the "corrections" offered by Calvinists, which they, of course, consider necessarily to be true. On the contrary, I have carefully considered (though not accepted) every suggestion—even though Calvinists often contradict each other (and even Calvin himself), and some accuse others of being "hyper-Calvinists." We must each arrive at our own conclusions—and this book is about the serious differences many of us have with Calvinists over the interpretation of key passages of Scripture.

Most Calvinists (but not all) agree upon five major points. Some insist that there are ten or even more relevant points. Palmer suggests, "Calvinism is not restricted to five points: it has thousands of points."[4] It's not likely that we can cover all those alleged points in these pages! Palmer himself deals with only five.

There are a number of disagreements between "five-point" and "four-point" Calvinists. For example, Lewis Sperry Chafer, founder of Dallas

Theological Seminary, called himself a "four-point" Calvinist because he rejected Limited Atonement.[5] Vance points out that "Many Baptists in the General Association of Regular Baptist Churches are four-point Calvinists."[6] To deny one point while accepting the other four, however, has been called by five-point Calvinists the "blessed inconsistency." They are correct. We shall see that each point is a logical consequence of those preceding it. It is not possible to be a Calvinist and hold *logically* and consistently to less than all five points.

We therefore agree with the widely declared statement that one "must hold all five points of Calvinism"[7] because "The Five Points of Calvinism all tie together. He who accepts one of the points will accept the other points."[8] Even those who agree on all five, however, have different ways of understanding and defending them.

Obviously, we cannot cover every variety of opinion in this book but must stick to what the majority would accept as a fair presentation of their beliefs. Some Calvinists accuse others of being hyper-Calvinistic, a label that is difficult to define. We will endeavor to establish the major Calvinist beliefs as clearly as we can.

In the further interest of accuracy, we quote extensively not only Calvin himself but from the writings of numerous Calvinists who are highly regarded by their colleagues. One book from which we quote a number of times is *The Potter's Freedom* by apologist James R. White, which is endorsed by a number of today's evangelical leaders. It is an especially valuable resource because it was written specifically to answer Norman Geisler's objections to certain points of Calvinism raised in his recent book, *Chosen But Free*. There should be more than sufficient citations from authoritative sources for the reader who is willing to go to these references to make absolutely certain that Calvinism is being fairly presented.

An Appeal for Open Discussion

God's foreknowledge, predestination/election, human choice, God's sovereignty, and man's responsibility are widely alleged to be mysteries beyond our ability to reconcile. Therefore, some insist that these concepts should be accepted without any attempt at understanding or reconciling apparent conflicts. The illustration is used repeatedly that as we approach heaven's gate we see written above it, "Whosoever will may come," but once we have entered we see from the inside the words, "Chosen in Him before the foundation of the world." We respect the many church leaders who continue to offer such an explanation as though that were sufficient. There are, however, several compelling reasons for not acquiescing to that popular position.

First of all, God intends for us to understand His Word rather than to plead "mystery" over vital portions of it. He has given it for our learning. Of God's Word the psalmist said, "it is a lamp unto my feet, and a light unto my path" (Psalms 119:105), and such it is intended to be for each of us today. Peter acknowledged that there are "things hard to be understood" and warned that Scripture is sometimes twisted by some, resulting in destruction to those who do so (2 Peter 3:16). God never suggests, however, that there is any part of His Word that we should not attempt to understand fully. Inasmuch as many passages in Scripture are devoted to the difficult themes we will address, we can confidently expect that the Bible itself will clarify the issues.

Second, the history of the church from its earliest beginnings has involved sharp differences of opinion on many vital subjects, including the gospel itself. Numerous destructive heresies have developed and have been vigorously opposed. Neither Christ nor His apostles considered divergent views on the essentials of the gospel to be normal or acceptable, but commanded the believers to "earnestly contend for the faith which was once delivered to the saints" (Jude 3). That command applies to us today.

Third, it hardly seems that our Lord would have us draw back from seriously considering and understanding foreknowledge and election/predestination, as well as man's responsibility and how it all fits together in God's sovereign grace. Although we may never see the entire body of Christ in perfect agreement, each of us is responsible to understand these issues as clearly as each one is able, through diligent study—and to help one another in the process.

Finally, God calls upon us to seek Him in order that we may know Him, though His ways and His thoughts are as far above ours as "the heavens are higher than the earth" (Isaiah 55:8–9). Surely, as we come to know God better, we will understand His Word and His will more fully. God is our Savior; to know Him is life eternal (John 17:3). Knowing God must include a deepening understanding of all He has revealed to us in His Word.

We are to live, as Christ said (quoting His own declaration as the *I AM* to Israel through Moses in Deuteronomy 8:3), not "by bread alone, but by *every* word that proceedeth out of the mouth of God" (Matthew 4:4). Solomon said, "*Every* word of God is pure" (Proverbs 30:5; emphases added).

Then we must carefully consider and seek to understand *every word.*

The Most Compelling Reason

It is a general assumption that, whatever other disagreements we may have, when it comes to the gospel of our salvation both Calvinists and non-Calvinists are in full agreement. Some Calvinists, however, disagree, claiming (as we have already seen) that the biblical gospel *is Calvinism.* For example: "God's plan of salvation revealed in the Scriptures consists of what is popularly known as the Five Points of Calvinism."[9] Loraine Boettner declares, "The great advantage of the Reformed Faith is that in the framework of the Five Points of Calvinism it sets forth clearly what the Bible teaches concerning the way of salvation."[10] Others insist that "if you do not know the Five Points of Calvinism, you do not know the gospel, but some perversion of it...."[11] B. B. Warfield claimed, "Calvinism is evangelicalism in its purest and only stable expression."[12]

Such claims that the Five Points of Calvinism make up the gospel raise the concerns about Calvinism to a new level! If much special study is required to understand Calvinism, and if years of Bible study still leave one ignorant on this subject, and if Calvinism *is the gospel of our salvation*—then where does that leave the multitudes who think they are saved but are ignorant of Calvinism? This question may seem divisive but it cannot be ignored.

Another grave question is raised concerning the proclamation of the gospel to the whole world as Christ commanded. Calvinists insist that their doctrine does not diminish the zeal with which the gospel is to be preached. To support this assertion, they name some of the great preachers and missionaries who were staunch Calvinists, such as George Whitefield, Adoniram Judson, William Carey, and others. And it is true that, although they know that many to whom they preach are not among the elect, some Calvinists nevertheless preach earnestly so that the elect may hear and believe.

Certainly, however, the zeal of such men and women in bringing the gospel to the world could not be *because* of their Calvinism but only *in spite* of it. To believe that those who will be saved have been predestined to salvation by God's decree, that no others can be saved, and that the elect must be regenerated by God's sovereign act without the gospel or any persuasion by any preacher, or by any faith in God on their part, could hardly provide motivation for earnestly preaching the gospel. No matter how the Calvinist tries to argue to the contrary, such a belief can only lessen the zeal a reasonable person might otherwise have, to reach the lost with the gospel of God's grace in Christ.

Facing a Real Dilemma

The gospel that Peter and Paul and the other apostles preached was for everyone in the audiences they faced, wherever they went. It was not a message that only the elect could believe. Peter told Cornelius and his family and friends, "And he [Christ] commanded us to preach unto the people [not to a select group]...that whosoever [among the people to whom He preached] believeth in him shall receive remission of sins" (Acts 10:42–43).

In contrast, Calvin's gospel says that Christ died, and His blood atones, for only the elect. Could this be the same gospel Paul preached? Paul proclaimed to audiences, "We declare unto [all of] you glad tidings..." (Acts 13:32). The "glad tidings" of the gospel that Paul preached echoed what the angel of the Lord had said to the shepherds at the time of Christ's birth: "I bring you tidings of great joy, which shall be to all people..." (Luke 2:10). These tidings of great joy concerned the fact that "the Savior of the world" (Luke 2:11; John 4:42) had been born.

Calvin's gospel, however, says that Christ is not the Savior of the world, but only of the elect. How could that message be "tidings of great joy" to those whom the Savior did not come to save and for whose sins He refused to die?

Paul could and did honestly say to everyone he met, "Christ died for you." In complete contrast, a book on biblical counseling that we have long recommended to readers declares, "As a reformed Christian, the writer [author] believes that counselors must not tell any unsaved counselee that Christ died for him, for *they cannot say that.* No man knows except Christ himself who are his elect for whom he died" (emphasis added).[13]

The author calls himself a "*reformed* Christian." What might *that* mean? Obviously, Calvin's message of salvation for a select group *does not* bring "great joy" to "all people."

Palmer writes, "But thank God that Christ's death was an absolute guarantee that every single one of the elect would be saved."[14] So great joy comes to the elect alone! As for the rest, Calvin's doctrine that God had predestined their damnation could hardly be "tidings of great joy"! This is the way Calvin put it:

> To many this seems a perplexing subject, because they deem it most incongruous that of the great body of mankind some should be predestinated to salvation, and others to destruction.... From

> this we infer, that all who know not that they are the peculiar people of God, must be wretched from perpetual trepidation....[15]

What gospel is this that is cause for joy to only some? It cannot be the biblical gospel that the angels announced! Because of the eternal importance of that question for the whole world to whom Christ commanded us to take the gospel, we are compelled to examine Calvinism closely in light of Scripture. Could it really be true, as Arthur C. Custance insists, that "Calvinism is the Gospel and to teach Calvinism is in fact to preach the Gospel"?[16]

Is Calvinism founded upon the plain text of Scripture? Or does it require interpreting common words and phrases such as *all, all men, world, everyone that thirsteth, any man,* and *whosoever will* to mean "the elect"? Is a peculiar interpretation of Scripture required to sustain this doctrine?

Our concern is for the defense of the character of the true God, the God of mercy and love whose "tender mercies are over all his works" (Psalms 145:9). The Bible declares that He is "not willing that any should perish, but that all should come to repentance" (2 Peter 3:9); "who will have all men to be saved, and to come unto the knowledge of the truth" (1 Timothy 2:4). Such is the God of the Bible, from Genesis to Revelation.

Open examination and discussion of important issues—especially the gospel and the very nature and character of God—can only be healthy for the body of Christ. It is my prayer that our investigation of Calvinism and its comparison with God's Holy Word, as expressed in the following pages, will bring helpful and needed clarification.

---

1. W. J. Seaton, *The Five Points of Calvinism* (Carlisle, PA: The Banner of Truth Trust, 1970), 8.
2. Jimmie B. Davis, *The Berea Baptist Banner*, February 5, 1995, 30.
3. Mark Duncan, *The Five Points of Christian Reconstruction from the Lips of Our Lord* (Edmonton, AB: Still Waters Revival Books, 1990), 10.
4. Edwin H. Palmer, foreword to *the five points of calvinism* (Grand Rapids, MI: Baker Books, enlarged ed., 20th prtg. 1999), 1.
5. Lewis Sperry Chafer, *Systematic Theology* (Dallas, TX: Dallas Seminary Press, 1948), 3:184.
6. Laurence M. Vance, *The Other Side of Calvinism* (Pensacola, FL: Vance Publications, rev. ed. 1999), 147.
7. Charles W. Bronson, *The Extent of the Atonement* (Pasadena, TX: Pilgrim Publications, 1992), 19.
8. Palmer, *five points*, 27.
9. Leonard J. Coppes, *Are Five Points Enough? The Ten Points of Calvinism* (Denver, CO: self-published, 1980), 55.
10. Loraine Boettner, *The Reformed Faith* (Phillipsburg, NJ: Presbyterian and Reformed Publishing Co., 1983), 24.
11. Fred Phelps, "The Five Points of Calvinism" (*The Berea Baptist Banner*, February 5, 1990), 21.
12. Benjamin B. Warfield, *Calvin and Augustine,* ed. Samuel G. Craig (Phillipsburg, NJ: Presbyterian and Reformed Publishing Co., 1956), 497.
13. Jay E. Adams, *Competent to Counsel* (Grand Rapids, MI: Baker Book House, 1970), 70.
14. Palmer, *five points*, 92.
15. John Calvin, *Institutes of the Christian Religion,* trans. Henry Beveridge (Grand Rapids, MI: Wm. Eerdmans Publishing Company, 1998 ed.), III: xxi, 1.
16. Arthur C. Custance, *The Sovereignty of Grace* (Phillipsburg, NJ: Presbyterian and Reformed Publishing Co., 1979), 302.

CHAPTER

3

John Calvin and His Institutes

CALVINISM AND THE CONTROVERSIES surrounding it have confronted Protestants for more than four hundred years.

Of course, the whole dispute in the church goes back long before John Calvin, to Augustine, Pelagius, and others. Aurelius Augustinus was born November 13, 354, at Tagaste, a small town near the eastern border of modern Algeria. His father was a Roman official and a pagan; his mother, Monica, a Christian. In 386, after studies in philosophy, law, and the classics (he was greatly inspired by Plato), a year of teaching grammar, and a brief career as a rhetorician, Augustine embraced Christianity. He entered what was essentially the Roman Catholic Church of his day, and established a monastery, which he moved to Hippo, Africa, upon being appointed its bishop. Often called the father of Roman Catholicism's major doctrines, Augustine, as we shall see, heavily influenced later philosophers and even exerts a strong influence among evangelicals today, much of it through Calvinism.

Although the Roman Catholic Church had not yet assumed its present form and power, the foundations were being laid in which Augustine played a leading role. Already, on February 27, 380, the "Edict of the Emperor Gratian, Valentinian II, and Theodosius I" declared:

> We order those who follow this doctrine to receive the title of Catholic Christians, but others we judge to be mad and raving and worthy of incurring the disgrace of heretical teaching, nor

> are their assemblies to receive the name of churches. They are to be punished not only by Divine retribution but also by our own measures, which we have decided in accordance with Divine inspiration.[1]

Born in Britain near the end of the fourth century, Pelagius rose to prominence after the fall of Rome in August 410 forced him to flee to North Africa. There he came into open conflict with Augustine for his views that there had been sinless beings before Christ and that it was possible through human effort, aided by grace, for anyone to live above sin. He claimed that Adam was mortal when created and that his sin did not bring death upon mankind but affected only himself. Consequently, infants are born in the same state Adam was in before he sinned. Moreover, good works were essential to salvation, especially for the rich to give their goods to the poor to help effect the moral transformation of society, which he believed possible. He considered "forgive us our sins" to be a prayer involving false humility and unsuitable for Christians, inasmuch as sin is not a necessity but man's own fault.

Semi-Pelagianism was developed a few years later by a French monk, John Cassianus, who modified Pelagianism by denying its extreme views on human merit and accepting the necessity of the power of the Holy Spirit but retaining the belief that man can do good, that he can resist God's grace, that he must cooperate in election, does have the will to choose between good and evil, and can lose his salvation. Those who reject Calvinism are often accused of promoting semi-Pelagianism, which is a broad label and often not true. Such labels can be misleading—including the label "Calvinist," because of the many shades and variations of Calvinism.

Although generally recognizing that Augustine was the source of most of what Calvin taught, Calvinists disagree among themselves over the exact composition of this doctrine. Nor would Calvin himself agree completely with many of his followers today. An attempt is made in the following pages to quote those who represent the current view among most Calvinists.

Even without the growing controversy, however, John Calvin is worthy of study because of the enormous impact he has had, and continues to have, in the Christian world. The Scottish Reformer, John Knox, credited with founding the Presbyterian Church, spent several years in Geneva and brought Calvinism to Scotland and to the Presbyterian movement. Daniel Gerdes said, "Calvin's labors were so highly useful to the Church of Christ, that there is hardly any department of the Christian world to be found that is not full of them.[2] It has been said that "No man in the history of the Church has been more admired and ridiculed, loved and hated, blessed and cursed."[3] Vance claims that "the prodigious impact of Calvin upon Christianity has yet to be fathomed." He goes on to refer to

> ...such institutions and organizations as Calvin College, Calvin Seminary, the *Calvin Theological Journal*, the International Congress on Calvin Research, the Calvin Translation Society, the Calvin Foundation, and the H. Henry Meeter Center for Calvin Studies, which contains over 3,000 books and 12,000 articles concerning John Calvin. The majority of Calvin's writings are still available today, which is quite an exploit considering that he lived over 400 years ago. There are extant over 2,000 of Calvin's sermons, while Calvin's complete works occupy fifty-nine volumes in the *Corpus Reformatorum*. College and seminary students at both Presbyterian and Reformed schools have the option of taking a whole course on John Calvin. Moreover, Calvin has the eminence of being mentioned in every dictionary, encyclopedia, and history book, both sacred and secular.[4]

How Much Calvin in Calvinism?

There is an attempt by many Calvinists today to disassociate Calvin from Calvinism, in view of its earlier origins in Augustine and the Latin Vulgate Bible. Moreover, it was not until the Great Synod of Dort (Dordrecht), more than fifty years after Calvin's death, that the five points of Calvinism were first set forth in order. Ironically, this declaration came about only as an expression of opposition to the five points of Arminianism. Nevertheless, this system of thought continues to be universally known as "Calvinism." Loraine Boettner says, "It was Calvin who wrought out this system of theological thought with such logical clearness and emphasis that it has ever since borne his name."[5] Where it really came from, as we shall see in the next chapter, is admitted by Custance who says that Augustine was "perhaps the first after Paul to realize the Total Depravity of man."[6] Farrar agrees: "To him [Augustine]...[is] due the exaggerated doctrine of total human depravity...."[7]

In spite of its long and varied origins and development, the term "Calvinism" remains as the commonly used identification. As Engelsma says, speaking in agreement with the overwhelming majority of Calvinists, "It was Calvin who developed these truths, systematically and fully; and therefore, they came to be called by his name."[8] B. B. Warfield declares, "It was he who gave the Evangelical movement a theology."[9] Timothy George writes that it was Calvin who "presented more clearly and more masterfully than anyone before him the essential elements of Protestant theology."[10] R. Tudor Jones calls Calvin's *Institutes* "one of the seminal works of Christian theology...his thinking was to be the motive force behind revolutionary changes in several European countries."[11] Edwin H. Palmer expresses an admiration for Calvin that seems to grow ever stronger among his followers:

> The name Calvinism has often been used, not because Calvin was the first or sole teacher, but because after the long silence of the Middle Ages, he was the most eloquent and systematic expositor of these truths. To the novitiate, however, it seemed as if Calvin originated them.[12]

Of course, Calvinists are convinced that the Bible itself is the true source of this religious system. C. H. Spurgeon declared, "I believe nothing because Calvin taught it, but because I have found his teaching in the Word of God.[13] ... We hold and assert again and again that the truth which Calvin preached was the very truth which the apostle Paul had long before written in his inspired epistles, and which is most clearly revealed in the discourses of our blessed Lord Himself."[14]

We respectfully disagree with this great preacher. Certainly, Spurgeon had to pick and choose which of Calvin's beliefs to embrace. In fact, as we shall see, especially in his later years, Spurgeon often made statements that were in direct conflict with Calvinism. His favorite sermon, the one through which he said more souls had come to Christ than through any other, was criticized by many Calvinists as being Arminian!

How Much Catholicism in Calvinism?

In the following pages we shall document that the wide praise heaped upon Calvin as a great exegete is badly misplaced. He taught much that was clearly wrong, and which many of his evangelical followers of today either don't know or perhaps don't want to know. There is much serious error contained in Calvin's writings—infant baptism, baptismal regeneration, reprobation for God's pleasure, enforcing doctrine with the secular sword, etc.

On account of such doctrines alone, Calvin's expertise as an outstanding exegete of God's Word is suspect. Much of his teaching is recognized today in Roman Catholicism. Let those evangelicals who praise Calvin as thoroughly biblical justify, for example, the following from his *Institutes*:

> I believe in the Holy Catholic Church...whence flow perpetual remission of sins, and full restoration to eternal life.[15] But as it is now our purpose to discourse of the visible Church, let us learn, from her single title of Mother, how useful, nay, how necessary the knowledge of her is, since there is no other means of entering into life unless she conceive us in the womb and give us birth, unless she nourish us at her breasts, and, in short, keep us under her charge and government, until, divested of mortal flesh, we become like the angels.... Moreover, beyond the pale of the Church no forgiveness of sins, no salvation, can be hoped for, as Isaiah and Joel testify (Isaiah 37:32, Joel 2:32).... Hence the abandonment of the Church is always fatal.[16]

Of course, by "Catholic Church" he did not mean *Roman* Catholic, but the true church universal. Nowhere in Scripture, however, is the church called "Mother" or credited with conceiving us in her womb to spiritual life. Nor is the true church ever referred to as the means of "entering into life" or forgiveness of sins. Calvin is simply reflecting dogmas that he absorbed as a devout Roman Catholic during the first twenty-four years of his life, and especially through the writings of Augustine, the greatest of all Catholics.

As for Isaiah 37:32 and the entire book of Joel, few Bible students would make such an application to the church. Isaiah refers to a remnant of Israel escaping out of Mount Zion during a coming judgment, while Joel refers to a remnant being preserved in Zion. Even if one erroneously equated Israel with the church, these passages do not support Calvin's statements.

Of course, in becoming a Protestant, Calvin rejected the papacy as representing the true church. He declared that "in declining fatal participation in such wickedness, we run no risk of being dissevered from the Church of Christ."[17]

Nevertheless, while condemning Romanism as false, he carried over into Protestantism much of her structure and false views, such as infant baptism, a clergy with special powers, and efficacy of sacraments performed only by such clergy. More of that later.

Early Life and Conversion

The man known today throughout the world as John Calvin, who is generally credited as the founder of the system of Protestantism named after him, was born July 10, 1509, in Noyon, France, as *Jean Chauvin.* His was a devoutly religious Roman Catholic family of prominence in an ecclesiastical town dominated by the local bishop and his assisting priests. As secretary and legal advisor to the bishop, Jean's father, Gerald, was an inside participant in a corrupt, religion-based political system.

In a bit of old-fashioned and quite common nepotism, young Jean was put on the Church payroll at the age of twelve, remaining on it for thirteen years—until one year after his apparent conversion to Luther's Protestantism. From his earliest years, Jean was the beneficiary of an ungodly partnership between the civil and religious authorities, who held the common people in bondage—a partnership dominated by the Church. It was a pattern that he would later implement as a "Protestant" with even greater efficiency in Geneva, Switzerland, including church dominance in civil affairs, and persecution and even execution of those accused of heresy.

Upon entering the Collège de La Marche at the University of Paris, Jean's love of Latin was reflected in his registration as *Johannes Calvinus.* There he diligently spent excessively long hours in compulsive study that had ill effects upon his health in later years and possibly shortened his life. He was known for his deep Catholic piety and blunt rebukes of his friends' morals.

Quite unexpectedly, in 1528, Jean's father, Gerald, was excommunicated from the Roman Catholic Church. Shortly thereafter, Calvin's brother, a priest, was also excommunicated for heresy. As a result, Gerald ordered Jean/Johannes, who was studying for the priesthood, to Orléans for the study of law.

Calvin later explained, "My father had intended me for theology from my childhood. But [since] the law proved everywhere very lucrative for its practitioners, the prospect suddenly made him change his mind."[18] This new pursuit became the young man's passion and possibly laid some of the foundation for the legalism that was later to become so pervasive in the system of theology that he would thereafter develop.

After earning a Bachelor of Laws in 1531 (he would later be granted a doctorate in law), Jean—now Johannes (John)—returned to Paris, immersed himself in a passionate study of classical literature, and published his first piece of writing, a Latin essay on Seneca's *De Clementia*. Historian Will Durant says that John, still a devout Roman Catholic, "seemed dedicated to humanism, when some sermons of Luther reached him and stirred him with their audacity."[19] Secret discussions of daring dissension soon swept Calvin into a circle of young humanist intellectuals who were urging reform of the Church along the lines of Luther's bold rebellion against the Pope.

By January 1534, though not yet a full-fledged Protestant, Calvin had become vocal enough in support of Luther's ideas that he was forced to flee Paris. Finding refuge in the town of Angoulême, he began to write his voluminous classic, *Institutes of the Christian Religion*, and quite remarkably finished the first and smaller edition the following year. Boettner acknowledges:

> The first [Latin] edition contained in brief outline all the essential elements of his system, and, considering the youthfulness of the author, was a marvel of intellectual precocity. It was later enlarged to five times the size of the original and published in French, but never did he make any radical departure from any of the doctrines set forth in the first edition.[20]

Today's Calvinists avoid the uncomfortable fact that in all of his voluminous writings, Calvin never tells of being born again through faith in Christ. He considered himself to have been a Christian from the moment of his Roman Catholic infant baptism: "...at whatever time we are baptised, we are washed and purified once for the whole of life...we must recall...our baptism...so as to feel certain and secure of the remission of sins...it wipes and washes away all our defilements."[21] He trusted in that baptism as proof that he was one of the elect[22] and denounced all who, like today's evangelical ex-Catholics, were baptized after believing the gospel.

Those saved out of Catholicism and baptized as believers were known as Anabaptists and were persecuted by Catholics, Lutherans, and Calvinists. Of such, near the time of his conversion to Luther's Protestantism, Calvin wrote, "One should not be content with simply killing such people, but should burn them cruelly."[23] Calvin banished them from Geneva in 1537.[24] How could today's born-again and baptized former Catholics consider Calvin as one of them? They couldn't—and wouldn't.

Calvin's *Institutes*

In his *Institutes,* Calvin masterfully developed his own brand of Christianity. It was without a doubt an expansion upon Augustinianism and was heavily influenced by the Latin Vulgate—the official Bible of the Roman Catholic Church and the one Calvin had long studied in its original Latin. The *Institutes*, arising from these two primary sources, has influenced succeeding generations to an extent far beyond anything its young author could have imagined at the time.

Most of those today, including evangelical leaders who hold Calvin in great esteem, are not aware that they have been captivated by the writings of a devout Roman Catholic, newly converted to Luther's Protestantism, who had broken with Rome only a year before.

Oddly, Calvin kept himself on the payroll of the Roman Catholic Church for nearly a year after he claimed to have been miraculously delivered from the "deep slough" of "obstinate addiction to the superstitions of the papacy."[25] Not until May 4, 1534, did he return to his hometown of Noyon to resign from the Bishop's employ, where he was arrested, imprisoned, managed to escape, and fled.[26] Although he was on the run and changing his place of residence, Calvin finished his original *Institutes* in August 1535. The first edition was published in March 1536.[27]

By any standard, this young man was far from mature in the Christian faith. Calvin himself said, "I was greatly astonished that, before a year passed [after he left the Roman church], all those who had some desire for pure doctrine betook themselves to me in order to learn, *although I myself had done little more than begin*" (emphasis added).[28]

Unquestionably, his *Institutes* could not possibly have come from a deep and fully developed evangelical understanding of Scripture. Instead, they came from the energetic enthusiasm of a recent law graduate and fervent student of philosophy and religion, a young zealot devoted to Augustine and a newly adopted cause. Durant says:

> [As] a lad of twenty-six, he completed the most eloquent, fervent, lucid, logical, influential, and terrible work in all the literature of the religious revolution.... He carried into theology and ethics the logic, precision, and severity of Justinian's *Institutes* and gave his own masterpiece a similar name.[29]

Commendably, like Luther and the other Reformers, Calvin was determined that Scripture would be his sole authority. Early in the *Institutes* he laid down that foundation, affirming that "if we look at it [the Bible] with clear eyes and unbiased judgment, it will forthwith present itself with a divine majesty which will subdue our presumptuous opposition and force us to do it homage."[30]

Calvin revered God's Word as so far surpassing anything man had ever or could ever produce that "compared with its energetic influence, the beauties of rhetoricians and philosophers will almost entirely disappear; so that it is easy to perceive something divine in the sacred Scriptures...."[31] No one can question Calvin's zeal to follow the Bible, or his sincere conviction that what he conceived and taught was true to God's Word. Nevertheless, just as the Bereans searched the Scriptures daily to determine whether Paul's teaching was true to God's Word, so we must do with Calvin's teaching.

At the time of writing his *Institutes,* Calvin, far from being an apostle like Paul, was at best a brand-new convert. Therefore, in writing the *Institutes,* Calvin sought, with his brilliant legal mind, to make up for what he lacked in spiritual maturity and guidance of the Holy Spirit. Despite his natural intelligence, however, this young zealot seemed blind to the fact that the partnership he later forged in Geneva between church and state (as Luther also did) was one of Roman Catholicism's major wrongs all over again, and the very antithesis of Christ's life and teaching. The remnants of that error still plague Europe today in the form of state churches.

Basic Elements: Sovereignty and Predestination

A basic foundation of Calvin's religious system was an extremist view of God's sovereignty that denied the human will and considered the church to be God's kingdom on earth—both views inspired by Augustine's writings. Verduin writes of Augustine, "Here we have an early representation of the notion that the Church of Christ was intended by its Founder to enter into a situation radically different from the one depicted in the New Testament.... This idea set forth by Augustine...led to all sorts of theological absurdities."[32]

Augustine taught that foreknowledge was the same as predestination: "Consequently, sometimes the same predestination is signified also under the name of foreknowledge."[33] Thus, God's foreknowledge *causes* future events. Interestingly, R. C. Sproul writes that "virtually nothing in John Calvin's view of predestination...was not first in Martin Luther, and before Luther in Augustine."[34] Calvin saw God as the author of every event, including all sin:

> If God merely foresaw human events, and did not also arrange and dispose of them at his pleasure, there might be room for agitating the question, how far his foreknowledge amounts to necessity; but since...He has decreed that they are so to happen...it is clear that all events take place by his sovereign appointment.[35]

R. C. Sproul states plainly, "God wills all things that come to pass... God created sin."[36] Out of this extreme view of God's sovereignty came Calvin's understanding of predestination. According to him (following the teaching of Augustine), in eternity past God decided to save only a fraction of the human race and consigned the rest to eternal torment—simply because it pleased Him to do so:

> Those, therefore, whom God passes by he reprobates, and that for no other cause but because he is pleased to exclude them from the inheritance which he predestines to his children....[37]
>
> But if all whom the Lord predestines to death are naturally liable to sentence of death, of what injustice, pray, do they complain...because by his eternal providence they were before their birth doomed to perpetual destruction...what will they be able to mutter against this defense?[38]
>
> Of this no other cause can be adduced than reprobation, which is hidden in the secret counsel of God.[39] Now since the arrangement of all things is in the hand of God...He arranges... that individuals are born, who are doomed from the womb to certain death, and are to glorify him by their destruction....[40]
>
> God, according to the good pleasure of his will, without any regard to merit, elects those whom he chooses for sons, while he rejects and reprobates others.... It is right for him to show by punishing that he is a just judge.... Here the words of Augustine most admirably apply.... When other vessels are made unto dishonor, it must be imputed not to injustice, but to judgment.[41]

In his *Institutes*, Calvin emphasizes sovereignty but scarcely mentions God's love for sinners. Luther, too, was convinced that God, by His own sovereign choice and independent of anything in man, had from eternity past determined whom He would save and whom He would damn. Calvin (like Augustine and most Calvinists today) said God could foresee the future only because He had willed it.[42] Here we have the horrible doctrine of reprobation from Calvin's own pen, echoing once again his mentor, Augustine:

> We say, then that Scripture clearly proves this much, that God by his eternal and immutable counsel determined once for all those whom it was his pleasure one day to admit to salvation and those whom, on the other hand, it was his pleasure to doom to destruction. We maintain that this counsel as regards the elect is founded on his free mercy, without any respect to human worth, while those whom he dooms to destruction are excluded from access to life by a just and blameless...incomprehensible judgment.... By excluding the reprobate...he by these marks in a manner discloses the judgment which awaits them.[43]

Depravity and "Mystery"

God's mercy as Calvin understood it was very limited. He majors upon God's justice; unquestionably, God would be just in damning the entire human race. The real question, however, is whether God who *is love* would neglect to make salvation available to *anyone*—much less predestine to damnation multitudes whom He *could* save if He so desired. The Bible clearly declares God's love for all mankind and His desire that all should be saved. It is in defense of God's love and character that we propose to test Calvinism against God's Word.

According to Calvin, rather than salvation depending upon whether a person freely believed the gospel, it depended upon whether God had predestined him to salvation. No one could believe unto salvation without God regenerating and then producing in those whom He had chosen the faith to believe. This conclusion followed logically from Calvin's extreme view of human depravity, which he laid out in his first writings:

> The mind of man is so completely alienated from the righteousness of God that it conceives, desires, and undertakes everything that is impious, perverse, base, impure, and flagitious. His heart is so thoroughly infected by the poison of sin that it cannot produce anything but what is corrupt; and if at any time men do anything apparently good, yet the mind always remains involved in hypocrisy and deceit, and the heart enslaved by its inward perversity.[44]

By *Total Depravity*, Calvinism means total *inability*. Left to themselves, all men not only do not seek God but are *totally unable* to seek Him, much less to believe in Jesus Christ to the saving of their souls. As a consequence of this total inability, God *causes some* to believe just as He causes *all* to sin.

We must then conclude that God, who *is love*, doesn't love all men enough to rescue them from eternal punishment but reserves His love for a select group called the elect.

Some Calvinists attempt to deny that Calvin taught that God decreed the damnation of the lost from whom He withheld the Irresistible Grace that He bestowed upon the elect. Instead, they say that He simply "leaves the non-elect in his just judgment to their own wickedness and obduracy."[45]

Like Augustine, however, Calvin says it both ways. Clearly, to *allow* anyone whom God *could* rescue to go to hell (no matter how much they deserved it) is the same as *consigning* them to that fate, which Calvin called "reprobation." Nor is there any question that, through Calvinism's Irresistible Grace, God *could* save the entire human race if He desired to do so. Surely, Infinite Love would not allow those loved to suffer eternal torment—yet God, according to Calvinism, is pleased to damn billions. Such teaching misrepresents the God of the Bible, as we shall document from Scripture.

In the final analysis, no rationalization can explain away the bluntness of Calvin's language—that some were by God's "pleasure [in] his eternal providence...before their birth doomed to perpetual destruction...." This sovereign consigning of some to bliss and others to torment was a display of God's power that would, according to Calvin, "promote our admiration of His glory."[46]

Even non-Christians find it a shocking doctrine that God is glorified in predestinating some to salvation and others to damnation, though there is no difference in merit between the saved and lost. That God would leave *anyone* to eternal torment who could be rescued, however, would demean God, since to do so is repugnant to the conscience and compassion that God has placed within all mankind!

Calvin himself admitted that this doctrine was repulsive to intelligent reason. As in Roman Catholicism, Calvin sought to escape the obvious contradictions in his system by pleading "mystery":

> Paul...rising to the sublime mystery of predestination....[47]
>
> How sinful it is to insist on knowing the causes of the divine will, since it is itself, and justly ought to be, the cause of all that exists.... Therefore, when it is asked why the Lord did so, we must answer, because he pleased.... Of this no other cause can be adduced than reprobation, which is hidden in the secret counsel of God.[48]

Calvin claims to derive from the Bible the teaching that God, to His glory, predestined vast multitudes to eternal damnation without allowing them any choice. In fact, while he was still a Roman Catholic he had doubtless already come to such a conclusion from his immersion in the writings of Augustine and the official (and badly corrupted) Roman Catholic Bible, the Latin Vulgate.

Spurgeon, though a Calvinist (whom Calvinists love to quote in their support) who at times confirmed Limited Atonement, was unable to escape his God-given conscience. His evangelist's heart often betrayed itself in statements expressing a compassion for the lost and a desire for their salvation—a compassion that contradicted the Calvinism he preached at other times. For example:

> As it is *my* wish [and] *your* wish…so it is God's wish that all men should be saved…he is no less benevolent than we are.[49]

It is impossible to reconcile that statement with the doctrine of Limited Atonement, which Spurgeon at other times affirmed. It is irrational to say that God sincerely desires the salvation of all, yet sent His Son to die for only some. But this, as we shall see, is just one of many contradictions in which Calvinism traps its adherents.

---

1. Sidney Z. Ehler and John B. Morrall, *Church and State Through the Centuries: A Collection of Historic Documents and Commentaries* (London, 1954) 7.
2. Cited in Philip Schaff, *History of the Christian Church* (New York: Charles Scribner, 1910; Grand Rapids, MI: Wm B. Eerdmans Publishing Co., reprint 1959), 8:281.
3. Georgia Harkness, *John Calvin: The Man and His Ethics* (Nashville, TN: Abingdon Press, 1958), 3.
4. Laurence M. Vance, *The Other Side of Calvinism* (Pensacola, FL; Vance Publications, rev. ed. 1999), 69–70.
5. Loraine Boettner, *The Reformed Doctrine of Predestination* (Philipsburg, NJ: Presbyterian and Reformed Publishing Co., 1932), 3–4.
6. Arthur C. Custance, *The Sovereignty of Grace* (Phillipsburg, NJ: Presbyterian and Reformed Publishing Co., 1979), 18.
7. Frederic W. Farrar, *History of Interpretation* (New York: E. P. Dutton and Co., 1886), 24.
8. David J. Engelsma, *A Defense of Calvinism as the Gospel* (The Evangelism Committee, Protestant Reformed Church, n. d.), 22.
9. Benjamin B. Warfield, *Calvin and Augustine*, ed. Samuel G. Craig (Phillipsburg, NJ: Presbyterian and Reformed Publishing Co., 1956), 22.
10. Timothy George, *Theology of the Reformers* (Nashville, TN: Broadman Press, 1988), 179.

11. R. Tudor Jones, *The Great Reformation* (Downer's Grove, IL: InterVarsity Press, n. d.), 133.
12. Edwin H. Palmer, foreword to *the five points of calvinism* (Grand Rapids, MI: Baker Books, enlarged ed., 20th prtg. 1999), 2.
13. Charles Haddon Spurgeon, *Autobiography of Charles H. Spurgeon* (Philadelphia, PA: American Baptist Society, n. d.), 44:402.
14. Spurgeon, *Autobiography,* 47:398.
15. John Calvin, "Method and Arrangement," in *Institutes of the Christian Religion*, trans. Henry Beveridge (Grand Rapids, MI: Wm. Eerdmans Publishing Company, 1998 ed.), 29.
16. Ibid., IV: i, 4.
17. Ibid., IV: ii, 2.
18. William J. Bouwsma, *John Calvin: A Sixteenth Century Portrait* (United Kingdom: Oxford University Press, 1988), 10.
19. Will Durant, "The Reformation," Pt. VI of *The Story of Civilization* (New York: Simon and Schuster, 1957), 460.
20. Boettner, *Reformed*, 403.
21. Calvin, *Institutes*, IV: xv, 3.
22. Ibid., 1–6; xvi, 24, etc.
23. Roland Bainton, *Michel Servet, heretique et martyr* (Geneva: Iroz 1953), 152-153, quoting letter of February 26, 1533, now lost.
24. Bernard Cottret, *Calvin: A Biography* (Grand Rapids, MI: William B. Eerdmans, 2000), 129; Calvin, *Institutes*, IV: xv, 16; IV: xvi, 31.
25. John Calvin, *Commentary on Psalms—Volume 1*, Author's Preface, www.cal.org/c/calvin/comment3/comm_vol08/htm/TOC.htm.
26. J. D. Douglas, *Who's Who In Christian History*, 128–29; cited in Henry R. Pike, *The Other Side of John Calvin* (Head to Heart, n. d.), 9–10. See also Alister E. McGrath, *A Life of John Calvin* (Cambridge, MA: Blackwell Publishers, 1990), 73; and Jones, *Reformation*, 127.
27. Jones, *Reformation*, 127.
28. Calvin, *Commentary on Psalms*, Preface.
29. Durant, "Reformation," VI: *Civilization*, 459–60.
30. Calvin, *Institutes*, I:vii,4.
31. Ibid., viii,1.
32. Leonard Verduin, *The Reformers and Their Stepchildren* (Sarasota, FL: Christian Hymnary Publishers, 1991), 66.
33. Augustine, *On the Gift of Perseverance*, chapter 47, http://whitefield.freeservices.com/augustine06.html.
34. R. C. Sproul, *Grace Unknown* (Grand Rapids, MI: Baker Books, 1997), 189.
35. Calvin, *Institutes*, III: xxiii, 6.
36. R. C. Sproul, Jr., *Almighty Over All* (Grand Rapids, MI: Baker Books, 1999), 54.
37. Calvin, *Institutes*, III: xxiii, 1.
38. Ibid., 3.
39. Ibid., 4.
40. Ibid., 6.
41. Ibid., 10-11.

42. Ibid., xxi–xxii.
43. Ibid., xxi 7.
44. Ibid., II: v,19.
45. Canons of Dort (Dordrecht, Holland, 1619), 1,6.
46. Calvin, *Institutes*, III: xxi, 1.
47. Ibid., II: xii, 5.
48. Ibid., III: xxiii, 2,4.
49. C. H. Spurgeon, *Metropolitan Tabernacle Pulpit*, Vol. 26:49–52.

CHAPTER

4

Calvinism's Surprising Catholic Connection

THERE IS NO QUESTION that Calvin imposed upon the Bible certain erroneous interpretations from his Roman Catholic background. Many leading Calvinists agree that the writings of Augustine were the actual source of most of what is known as Calvinism today. Calvinists David Steele and Curtis Thomas point out that "The basic doctrines of the Calvinistic position had been vigorously defended by Augustine against Pelagius during the fifth century."[1]

In his eye-opening book, *The Other Side of Calvinism*, Laurence M. Vance thoroughly documents that "John Calvin did not originate the doctrines that bear his name...."[2] Vance quotes numerous well-known Calvinists to this effect. For example, Kenneth G. Talbot and W. Gary Crampton write, "The system of doctrine which bears the name of John Calvin was in no way originated by him...."[3] B. B. Warfield declared, "The system of doctrine taught by Calvin is just the Augustinianism common to the whole body of the Reformers."[4] Thus the debt that the creeds coming out of the Reformation owe to Augustine is also acknowledged. This is not surprising in view of the fact that most of the Reformers had been part of the Roman Catholic Church, of which Augustine was one of the most highly regarded "saints." John Piper acknowledges that Augustine was the major influence upon both Calvin and Luther, who continued to revere him and his doctrines even after they broke away from Roman Catholicism.[5]

C. H. Spurgeon admitted that "perhaps Calvin himself derived it [Calvinism] mainly from the writings of Augustine."[6] Alvin L. Baker wrote, "There is hardly a doctrine of Calvin that does not bear the marks of Augustine's influence."[7] For example, the following from Augustine sounds like an echo reverberating through the writings of Calvin:

> Even as he has appointed them to be regenerated...whom he predestinated to everlasting life, as the most merciful bestower of grace, whilst to those whom he has predestinated to eternal death, he is also the most righteous awarder of punishment.[8]

C. Gregg Singer said, "The main features of Calvin's theology are found in the writings of St. Augustine to such an extent that many theologians regard Calvinism as a more fully developed form of Augustinianism."[9] Such statements are staggering declarations in view of the undisputed fact that, as Vance points out, the Roman Catholic Church itself has a better claim on Augustine than do the Calvinists.[10] Calvin himself said:

> Augustine is so wholly with me, that if I wished to write a confession of my faith, I could do so with all fulness and satisfaction to myself out of his writings."[11]

Augustine and the Use of Force

The fourth century Donatists believed that the church should be a pure communion of true believers who demonstrated the truth of the gospel in their lives. They abhorred the apostasy that had come into the church when Constantine wedded Christianity to paganism in order to unify the empire. Compromising clergy were "evil priests working hand in glove with the kings of the earth, who show that they have no king but Caesar." To the Donatists, the church was a "small body of saved surrounded by the unregenerate mass."[12] This is, of course, the biblical view.

Augustine, on the other hand, saw the church of his day as a mixture of believers and unbelievers, in which purity and evil should be allowed to exist side by side for the sake of unity. He used the power of the state to compel church attendance (as Calvin also would 1,200 years later): "Whoever was not found within the Church was not asked the reason, but was to be corrected and converted...."[13] Calvin followed his mentor Augustine in enforcing church attendance and participation in the sacraments by threats (and worse) against the citizens of Geneva. Augustine "identified the Donatists as heretics...who could be subjected to imperial legislation [and force] in exactly the same way as other criminals and misbelievers, including poisoners and pagans."[14] Frend says of Augustine, "The questing, sensitive youth had become the father of the inquisition."[15]

Though he preferred persuasion if possible, Augustine supported military force against those who were rebaptized as believers after conversion to Christ and for other alleged heretics. In his controversy with the Donatists, using a distorted and un-Christian interpretation of Luke 14:23,[16] Augustine declared:

> Why therefore should not the Church use force in compelling her lost sons to return?... The Lord Himself said, "Go out into the highways and hedges and compel them to come in...." Wherefore is the power which the Church has received...through the religious character and faith of kings...the instrument by which those who are found in the highways and hedges—that is, in heresies and schisms—are compelled to come in, and let them not find fault with being compelled.[17]

Sadly, Calvin put into effect in Geneva the very principles of punishment, coercion, and death that Augustine advocated and that the Roman Catholic Church followed consistently for centuries. Henry H. Milman writes: "Augustinianism was worked up into a still more rigid and uncompromising system by the severe intellect of Calvin."[18] And he justified himself by Augustine's erroneous interpretation of Luke 14:23. How could any who today hail Calvin as a great exegete accept such abuse of this passage?

Compel? Isn't that God's job through Unconditional Election and Irresistible Grace? *Compel* those for whom Christ didn't die and whom God has predestined to eternal torment? This verse refutes Calvinism no matter how it is intepreted!

Augustine's Dominant Influence

There is no question as to the important role Augustine played in molding Calvin's thinking, theology, and actions. This is particularly true concerning the key foundations of Calvinism. Warfield refers to Calvin and Augustine as "two extraordinarily gifted men [who] tower like pyramids over the scene of history."[19] Calvin's *Institutes of the Christian Religion* make repeated favorable references to Augustine, frequently citing his writings as authoritative and using the expression, "Confirmed by the authority of Augustine."[20] Calvin often credits Augustine with having formulated key concepts, which he then expounds in his *Institutes*. The following are but a very small sampling of such references:

- "We have come into the way of faith," says Augustine: "Let us constantly adhere to it...."[21]
- The truth of God is too powerful, both here and everywhere, to dread the slanders of the ungodly, as Augustine powerfully maintains.... Augustine disguises not that...he was often charged with preaching the doctrine of predestination too freely, but... he abundantly refutes the charge.... For it has been shrewdly observed by Augustine (De Genesi ad litteram, Lib V) that we can safely follow Scripture....[22]
- For Augustine, rightly expounding this passage, says....[23]
- I say with Augustine, that the Lord has created those who, as he certainly foreknew, were to go to destruction, and he did so because he so willed.[24]
- If your mind is troubled, decline not to embrace the counsel of Augustine....[25]
- I will not hesitate, therefore, simply to confess with Augustine that...those things will certainly happen which he [God] has foreseen [and] that the destruction [of the non-elect] consequent upon predestination is also most just.[26]
- Augustine, in two passages in particular, gives a [favorable] portraiture of the form of ancient monasticism. [Calvin then proceeds to quote Augustine's commendation of the early monks.][27]
- Here the words of Augustine most admirably apply....[28]
- This is a faithful saying from Augustine; but because his words will perhaps have more authority than mine, let us adduce the following passage from his treatise....[29]
- Wherefore, Augustine not undeservedly orders such, as senseless teachers or sinister and ill-omened prophets, to retire from the Church.[30]

We could multiply many times over the above examples of Augustine's influence upon Calvin from the scores of times Calvin quotes extensively from Augustine's writings. Leading Calvinists admit that Calvin's basic beliefs were already formed while he was still a devout Roman Catholic, through the writings of Augustine—an influence that remained with him throughout his life.

Augustinian teachings that Calvin presented in his *Institutes* included the sovereignty that made God the cause of all (including sin), the predestination of some to salvation and of others to damnation, election and reprobation, faith as an irresistible gift from God—in fact, the key concepts at the heart of Calvinism.

We search in vain for evidence that Calvin ever disapproved of any of Augustine's heresies. Calvinist Richard A. Muller admits, "John Calvin was part of a long line of thinkers who based their doctrine of predestination on the Augustinian interpretation of St. Paul."[31] In each expanded edition of his *Institutes*, Calvin quotes and relies upon Augustine more than ever.

Is Calvinism Really a Protestant Belief?

That many prominent evangelicals today are still under the spell of Augustine is evident—and astonishing, considering his numerous heresies. Norm Geisler has said, "St. Augustine was one of the greatest Christian thinkers of all time."[32] Yet Augustine said, "I should not believe the gospel unless I were moved to do so by the authority of the [Catholic] Church."[33] That statement was quoted with great satisfaction by Pope John Paul II in his 1986 celebration of the 1600th anniversary of Augustine's conversion. The Pope went on to say:

> Augustine's legacy...is the theological methods to which he remained absolutely faithful...full adherence to the authority of the faith...revealed through Scripture, Tradition and the Church.... Likewise the profound sense of mystery—"for it is better," he exclaims, "to have a faithful ignorance than a presumptuous knowledge...." I express once again my fervent desire...that the authoritative teaching of such a great doctor and pastor may flourish ever more happily in the Church....[34]

In my debate with him, James White claims that "Calvin refuted this very passage in *Institutes,* and any fair reading of Augustine's own writings disproves this misrepresentation by Hunt."[35] In fact, Calvin acknowledged the authenticity of the statement and attempted to defend it as legitimate reasoning for those who had not the assurance of faith by the Holy Spirit.[36]

Vance provides numerous astonishing quotations from Calvinists praising Augustine: "One of the greatest theological and philosophical minds that God has ever so seen fit to give to His church."[37] "The greatest Christian since New Testament times...greatest man that ever wrote Latin."[38] "[His] labors and writings, more than those of any other man in the age in which he lived, contributed to the promotion of sound doctrine and the revival of true religion."[39]

Warfield adds, "Augustine determined for all time the doctrine of grace."[40] Yet he [Augustine] believed that grace came through the Roman Catholic sacraments. That Calvinists shower such praise upon Augustine makes it easier to comprehend why they heap the same praise on Calvin.

As for the formation of Roman Catholicism's doctrines and practices, Augustine's influence was the greatest in history. Vance reminds us that Augustine was "one of Catholicism's original four 'Doctors of the Church' [with] a feast day [dedicated to him] in the Catholic Church on August 28, the day of his death."[41] Pope John Paul II has called Augustine "the common father of our Christian civilization."[42] William P. Grady, on the other hand, writes, "The deluded Augustine (354–430) went so far as to announce (through his book, *The City of God*) that Rome had been privileged to usher in the millennial kingdom (otherwise known as the 'Dark Ages')."[43]

Drawing from a Polluted Stream

Sir Robert Anderson reminds us that "the Roman [Catholic] Church was molded by Augustine into the form it has ever since maintained. Of all the errors that later centuries developed in the teachings of the church, scarcely one cannot be found in embryo in his writings."[44] Those errors include infant baptism for regeneration (infants who die unbaptized are damned), the necessity of baptism for the remission of sins (martyrdom, as in Islam, does the same), purgatory, salvation in the Church alone through its sacraments, and persecution of those who reject Catholic dogmas. Augustine also fathered acceptance of the Apocrypha (which he admitted even the Jews rejected), allegorical interpretation of the Bible (thus the creation account, the six days, and other details in Genesis are not necessarily literal), and rejection of the literal personal reign of Christ on earth for a thousand years (we are now supposedly in the millennial reign of Christ with the Church reigning and the devil presently bound).

Augustine insists that Satan is now "bound" on the basis that "even now men are, and doubtless to the end of the world shall be, converted to the faith from the unbelief in which he [Satan] held them." That he views the promised binding of Satan in the "bottomless pit" (Revelation 20:1–3) allegorically is clear. Amazingly, Satan "is bound in each instance in which he is spoiled of one of his goods [i.e., someone believes in Christ]." And even more amazing, "the abyss in which he is shut up" is somehow construed by Augustine to be "in the depths" of Christ-rejecters' "blind hearts." It is thus that Satan is continually shut up as in an abyss.[45]

Augustine doesn't attempt to explain how he arrived at such an astonishing idea, much less how one abyss could exist in millions of hearts or how, being "bound" there, Satan would still be free to blind those within whose "hearts" he is supposedly bound (2 Corinthians 4:4). Nor does he explain how or why, in spite of Satan's being bound,

- Christ commissioned Paul to turn Jew and Gentile "from the power of Satan unto God" (Acts 26:18)
- Paul could deliver the Corinthian fornicator to Satan (1 Corinthians 5:5)
- Satan can transform himself "into an angel of light" (2 Corinthians 11:14)
- Paul would warn the Ephesian believers not to "give place to the devil" (Ephesians 4:27) and urge them and us today to "stand against the wiles of the devil" (6:11)
- Satan could still be going about "like a roaring lion...seeking whom he may devour" (1 Peter 5:8)
- Satan could still be able to continually accuse Christians before God and, with his angels, yet wage war in heaven against "Michael and his angels" and at last be cast out of heaven to earth (Revelation 12:7–10)

Augustine was one of the first to place the authority of tradition on a level with the Bible, and to incorporate much philosophy, especially Platonism, into his theology. Exposing the folly of those who praise Augustine, Vance writes:

> He believed in apostolic succession from Peter as one of the marks of the true church, taught that Mary was sinless and promoted her worship. He was the first who defined the so-called sacraments as a visible sign of invisible grace.... The memorial of the Lord's supper became that of the spiritual presence of Christ's body and blood. To Augustine the only true church was the Catholic Church. Writing against the Donatists, he asserted: "The Catholic Church alone is the body of Christ.... Outside this body the Holy Spirit giveth life to no one...[and] he is not a partaker of divine love who is the enemy of unity. Therefore they have not the Holy Ghost who are outside the Church.[46]

And this is the man whom Geisler calls "one of the greatest Christian thinkers of all time." On the contrary, Calvin drew from a badly polluted stream when he embraced the teachings of Augustine! How could one dip into such contaminating heresy without becoming confused and infected? Yet this bewildering muddle of speculation and formative Roman Catholicism is acknowledged to be the source of Calvinism—and is praised by leading evangelicals. One comes away dumbfounded at the acclaim heaped upon both Calvin and Augustine by otherwise sound Christian leaders.

An Amazing Contradiction

Calvin's almost complete agreement with and repeated praise of Augustine cannot be denied. Calvin called himself "an Augustinian theologian."[47] Of Augustine he said, "whom we quote frequently, as being the best and most faithful witness of all antiquity."[48]

Calvinists themselves insist upon the connection between Calvin and Augustine. McGrath writes, "Above all, Calvin regarded his thought as a faithful exposition of the leading ideas of Augustine of Hippo."[49] Wendel concedes, "Upon points of doctrine he borrows from St. Augustine with both hands."[50] Vance writes:

> Howbeit, to prove conclusively that Calvin was a disciple of Augustine, we need look no further than Calvin himself. One can't read five pages in Calvin's *Institutes* without seeing the name of Augustine. Calvin quotes Augustine over four hundred times in the *Institutes* alone. He called Augustine by such titles as "holy man" and "holy father."[51]

As Vance further points out, "Calvinists admit that Calvin was heavily influenced by Augustine in forming his doctrine of predestination."[52] How could one of the leaders of the Reformation embrace so fully the doctrines of one who has been called the "principal theological creator of the Latin-Catholic system as distinct from...Evangelical Protestantism..."?[53]

Calvin's admiration of Augustine and his embracing of much of his teaching is only one of several major contradictions in his life, which will be fully documented in this book. The situation is contradictory on the Roman Catholic side as well. Their dogmas reject some of the most important doctrines held by the most famous of their saints—the very Augustinian doctrines that Calvin embraced.

Here we confront a strange anomaly. Warfield declares that "it is Augustine who gave us the Reformation"[54]—yet at the same time, he also acknowledges that Augustine was "in a true sense the founder of Roman Catholicism"[55] and "the creator of the Holy Roman Empire."[56]

Strangely, Calvin apparently failed to recognize that Augustine never understood salvation by grace alone through faith alone in Christ alone. Philip F. Congdon writes, "Another curious parallel is evident between Classical Calvinist theology and Roman Catholic theology. The two share an inclusion of works in the gospel message, and an impossibility of assurance of salvation.... Both hold to the primacy of God's grace; both include the necessity of our works."[57] Augustine's heresies, especially his Romanist view of faith in Christ being supplemented by good works and the sacraments, were not lost on Luther, who wrote: "In the beginning, I devoured Augustine, but when...I knew what justification by faith really was, then it was out with him."[58]

Yet leading Calvinists suggest that I side with Roman Catholicism by rejecting Calvinism, even though it comes largely from the ultimate Roman Catholic, Augustine. Here is how one writer expressed it to me:

> And given that the position you espouse is, in fact, utterly opposed to the very heart of the message of the Reformers, and is instead in line with Rome's view of man's will and the nature of grace, I find it *tremendously* inconsistent on your part. You speak often of opposing the traditions of men, yet, in this case, you embrace the very traditions that lie at the heart of Rome's "gospel."[59]

On the contrary, the Reformers and their creeds are infected with ideas that came from the greatest Roman Catholic, Augustine himself. Furthermore, a rejection of Election, Predestination, and the Preservation of the Saints as defined by Calvinists is hardly embracing "the heart of Rome's 'gospel.'" The real heart of Rome's gospel is good works and sacraments. Certainly Calvin's retention of sacramentalism, baptismal regeneration for infants, and honoring the Roman Catholic priesthood as valid is a more serious embrace of Catholicism's false gospel. The rejection of Calvinism requires no agreement with Rome whatsoever on any part of its heretical doctrines of salvation.

It seems incomprehensible that the predominant influence upon Reformed theology and creeds could be so closely related to the very Roman Catholicism against which the Reformers rebelled. Yet those who fail to bow to these creeds are allegedly "in error." How the Protestant creeds came to be dominated by Calvinistic doctrine is an interesting story.

The Role of the Latin Vulgate

Along with the writings of Augustine, the Latin Vulgate also molded Calvin's thoughts as expressed in his *Institutes of the Christian Religion.* Fluent in Latin, Calvin had long used that corrupted translation of the Bible, which, since its composition by Jerome at the beginning of the fifth century, was the official Bible of Roman Catholics. It was again so declared by the Council of Trent in 1546, when Calvin was 37 years of age. More than that, its influence reached into the Protestant movement: "For one thousand years the Vulgate was practically the only Bible known and read in Western Europe. All commentaries were based upon the Vulgate text.... Preachers based their sermons on it."[60]

The Vulgate was permeated with Augustinian views on predestination and the rejection of free will. According to Philip Schaff, "The Vulgate can be charged, indeed, with innumerable faults, inaccuracies, inconsistencies, and arbitrary dealing in particulars."[61] Others have expressed the same opinion. Samuel Fisk quotes Samuel Berger, who in the *Cambridge History of the English Bible, Vol. 3* (S. L. Greenslade, ed., Cambridge, England: University Press, 1963, 414), called the Vulgate "the most vulgarized and bastardized text imaginable."[62] Grady says, "Damasus commissioned Jerome to revive the archaic Old Latin Bible in A.D. 382...the completed monstrosity became known as the Latin 'Vulgate'...and was used of the devil to usher in the Dark Ages."[63] Fisk reminds us:

> Well-known examples of far-reaching errors include the whole system of Catholic "penance," drawn from the Vulgate's "do penance"...when the Latin should have followed the Greek—*repent.*

> Likewise the word "sacrament" was a mis-reading from the Vulgate of the original word for *mystery*. Even more significant, perhaps, was the rendering of the word *presbyter* (elder) as "priest."[64]

Augustine described the problem that led to the production of the Vulgate: "In the earliest days of the faith, when a Greek manuscript came into anyone's hands, and he thought he possessed a little facility in both languages, he ventured to make a translation [into Latin]."[65] As a consequence of such individual endeavor, Bruce says, "The time came, however, when the multiplicity of [Latin] texts [of Scripture] became too inconvenient to be tolerated any longer, and Pope Damasus...commissioned his secretary, Jerome, to undertake the work" of revision to produce one authorized Latin version.

Bruce continues: "He [Jerome] was told to be cautious for the sake of 'weaker brethren' who did not like to see their favorite texts tampered with, even in the interests of greater accuracy. Even so, he went much too far for the taste of many, while he himself knew that he was not going far enough."[66] *Unger's Bible Dictionary* comments:

> For many centuries it [Vulgate] was the only Bible generally used.... In the age of the Reformation the Vulgate [influenced] popular versions. That of Luther (N. T. in 1523) was the most important and in this the Vulgate had great weight. From Luther the influence of the Latin passed to our own Authorized Version [KJV]....[67]

The Geneva and King James Bibles and Protestant Creeds

Of no small importance to our study is the fact that this corrupt translation had an influence upon the Protestant churches in Europe, England, and America. That influence carried over into the Geneva Bible (which has further problems; see below) as well as into other early versions of the English Bible, and even into the King James Bible of today.

As the Vulgate was filled with Augustinianisms, the Geneva Bible was filled with Calvinism, in the text as well as in voluminous notes. H. S. Miller's *General Biblical Introduction* says, "It was a revision of Tyndale's, with an Introduction by Calvin...the work of English reformers, assisted by Beza, Calvin, and possibly others." J. R. Dore, in *Old Bibles: An Account of the Early Versions of the English Bible*, 2nd edition, adds that "almost every chapter [of the Geneva Bible] has voluminous notes full of Calvinistic doctrine." Andrew Edgar, in *The Bibles of England*, declares, "At the time the Geneva Bible was first published, Calvin was the ruling spirit in Geneva. All the features of his theological, ecclesiastical, political, and social system are accordingly reflected in the marginal annotations.... The doctrine of predestination is proclaimed to be the head cornerstone of the gospel."[68]

W. Hoare says in *The Evolution of the English Bible*, "Considered as a literary whole it [the Geneva Bible] has about it the character of a Calvinist manifesto...a book with a special purpose." F. F. Bruce adds,

> "The notes of the Geneva Bible...are, to be sure, unashamedly Calvinistic in doctrine.... The people of England and Scotland... learned much of their biblical exegesis from these notes.... The Geneva Bible immediately won, and retained, widespread popularity. It became the household Bible of English-speaking Protestants.... This became the authorized Bible in Scotland and was brought to America where it had a strong influence."[69]

Butterworth points out: "In the lineage of the King James Bible this [Geneva Bible] is by all means the most important single volume.... The Geneva Bible...had a very great influence in the shaping of the King James Bible."[70] Robinson is even more emphatic:

> A large part of its [Geneva Bible] innovations are included in the Authorized Version [KJV].... Sometimes the Geneva text and the Geneva margin are taken over intact, sometimes the text becomes the margin and the margin the text. Sometimes the margin becomes the text and no alternative is offered. Very often the Genevan margin becomes the Authorized Version text with or without verbal change."[71]

Further documentation could be given, but this should be sufficient to trace briefly the influence from that ultimate Roman Catholic, Augustine, through the Latin Vulgate and his writings, upon Calvin—and through Calvin, into the Geneva Bible and on into the King James Bible. And thus into the pulpits and homes of Protestants throughout Europe, England, and America. It is small wonder, then, that those who, like Arminius, dared to question Calvinism, were overwhelmed with opposition. Of course, various synods and assemblies were held to formulate accepted creeds and to punish the dissenters, but the decks were stacked in favor of Calvinism, and no influence to mitigate this error was allowed. This will be documented in chapters 5 and 6.

The New Geneva Study Bible and Reformation Truth

Today's *New Geneva Study Bible* (recently reprinted as *The Reformation Study Bible*) is being widely distributed in an effort to indoctrinate the readers into Calvinism. Its New King James translation is appealing. As with the original Geneva Bible, however, the notes are Calvinistic treatises. In his foreword, R. C. Sproul writes,

> The New Geneva Study Bible is so called because it stands in the tradition of the original Geneva Bible.... The light of the Reformation was the light of the Bible.... The Geneva Bible was published in 1560...[and] dominated the English-speaking world for a hundred years.... Pilgrims and Puritans carried the Geneva Bible to the shores of the New World. American colonists were reared on the Geneva Bible.... The New Geneva Study Bible contains a modern restatement of Reformation truth in its comments and theological notes. Its purpose is to present the light of the Reformation afresh.

In fact, its purpose is to indoctrinate the reader into Calvinism, which inaccurately is marketed as "Reformation truth"—as though Calvinism and Protestantism are identical. There was, in fact, much more to the Reformation than Calvinism, Calvinists' claims notwithstanding.

The Necessity to Clarify Confusion

Calvinism is experiencing resurgence today. Yet there is widespread ignorance of what both Augustine and Calvin really taught and practiced. Has the truth been suppressed to further a particular theology? Consider Boettner's declaration that "Calvin and Augustine easily rank as the two outstanding systematic expounders of the Christian system since Saint Paul."[72] Spurgeon, also declared: "Augustine obtained his views, without doubt, through the Spirit of God, from the diligent study of the writings of Paul, and Paul received them of the Holy Ghost, from Jesus Christ".[73]

One cannot but view such statements with astonishment. How incredible that Loraine Boettner, one of the foremost apologists opposing the Roman Catholic Church, praised Augustine, who gave the Roman Catholic Church so many of its basic doctrines that he is among the most highly honored of its "saints" to this day.

As for Spurgeon, would he have considered that Augustine's teaching of salvation by the Roman Catholic Church, through its sacraments alone, beginning with regeneration by infant baptism; the use of force even to the death against "heretics"; acceptance of the Apocrypha; allegorical interpretation of creation and the prophecies concerning Israel; a rejection of the literal reign of Christ on David's throne; and so much other false doctrine, had also all been received from the Holy Spirit? How could Augustine—and Calvin, who embraced and passed on many of his major errors—be so wrong on so much and yet be biblically sound as regards predestination, election, sovereignty, etc.? Is there not ample cause to examine carefully these foundational teachings of Calvinism?

One can only respond in the affirmative. For that reason, the key Calvinist doctrines will be presented in the following pages and compared carefully with God's Word.

---

1. David N. Steele and Curtis C. Thomas, *The Five Points of Calvinism* (Phillipsburg, NJ: Presbyterian and Reformed Publishing Co., 1963), 19.
2. Laurence M. Vance, *The Other Side of Calvinism* (Pensacola, FL: Vance Publications, rev. ed., 1999), 37.
3. Kenneth G. Talbot and W. Gary Crampton, *Calvinism, Hyper-Calvinism and Arminianism* (Edmonton, AB: Still Water Revival Books, 1990), 78.
4. Benjamin B. Warfield, *Calvin and Augustine*, ed. Samuel G. Craig (Phillipsburg, NJ: Presbyterian and Reformed Publishing Co., 1956), 22.
5. John Piper, *The Legacy of Sovereign Joy: God's Triumphant Grace in the Lives of Augustine, Luther, and Calvin* (Wheaton, IL: Crossway Books, 2000), 24-25.
6. Charles Haddon Spurgeon, ed., *Exposition of the Doctrine of Grace* (Pasadena, CA: Pilgrim Publications, n. d.), 298.
7. Alvin L. Baker, *Berkouwer's Doctrine of Election: Balance or Imbalance?* (Phillipsburg, NJ: Presbyterian and Reformed Publishing Co., 1981), 25.
8. St. Augustine, *A Treatment On the Soul and its Origins*, Book IV, 16.
9. C. Gregg Singer, *John Calvin: His Roots and Fruits* (Abingdon Press, 1989), vii.
10. Vance, *Other Side*, 40.
11. John Calvin, "A Treatise on the Eternal Predestination of God," in *John Calvin, Calvin's Calvinism*, trans. Henry Cole (Grandville, MI: Reformed Free Publishing Association, 1987), 38; cited in Vance, *Other Side*, 38.
12. Leonard Verduin, *The Reformers and Their Stepchildren* (Sarasota, FL: Christian Hymnary Publishers, 1991), 33.

13. *Petilian* II.85.189; cited in W. H. C. Frend, *The Rise of Christianity* (Philadelphia, PA: Fortress Press, 1984), 671.
14. Frend, *Rise*, 671.
15. Ibid., 672.
16. F.F. Bruce, *Light in the West, Vol 3 in The Spreading Flame* (Grand Rapids, MI: Wm. B. Eerdmans Publishing Co, 1956), 60-61.
17. E. H. Broadbent, *The Pilgrim Church* (Port Colborne, ON: Gospel Folio Press, reprint 1999), 49.
18. Henry H. Milman, *History of Christianity* (New York: A. C. Armstrong and Son, 1886), 3:176.
19. Warfield, *Calvin*, v.
20. John Calvin, contents page of *Institutes of the Christian Religion*, trans. Henry Beveridge (Grand Rapids, MI: Wm. B. Eerdmans Publishing Co., 1998 ed.), III: xxiii, IV: xvii, etc.
21. Calvin, *Institutes*, III: xxi, 2.
22. Ibid., xxi, 4.
23. Ibid., xxiii, 1.
24. Ibid., 5.
25. Ibid.
26. Ibid., 8.
27. Ibid., IV: xiii, 9.
28. Ibid., III: xxiii, 11.
29. Ibid., 13.
30. Ibid., 14.
31. Richard A. Muller, *Christ and the Decree* (Grand Rapids, MI: Baker Book House, 1988), 22.
32. Norman L. Geisler, *What Augustine Says* (Grand Rapids, MI: Baker Book House, 1982), 9.
33. Aug. Cont. Epist. Fundament c.v.
34. John Paul II, Sovereign Pontiff, *Augustineum Hyponensem* (Apostolic Letter, August 28, 1986. Available at: www. cin.org/jp2.ency/augustin.html).
35. Dave Hunt and James White, *Debating Calvinism*, (Sisters, OR: Multnomah Publishers, 2004), 244.
36. Calvin, *Institutes*, I: vii, 3.
37. Talbot and Crampton, *Calvinism, Hyper-Calvinism*, 78; cited in Vance, *Other Side*, 39.
38. Alexander Souter, *The Earliest Latin Commentaries on the Epistles* of St. Paul (n. p., 1927), 139.
39. N. L. Rice, *God Sovereign and Man Free* (Harrisonburg, VA: Sprinkle Publications, 1985), 13.
40. Benjamin B. Warfield, "The Idea of Systematic Theology," in *The Princeton Theology*, ed. Mark A. Noll (Phillipsburg, NJ: Presbyterian and Reformed Publishing Co., 1983), 258.
41. Vance, *Other Side*, 41.
42. Richard N. Ostling, "The Second Founder of the Faith" (*Time*, September 29, 1986).
43. William P. Grady, *Final Authority: A Christian's Guide to the King James Bible* (Knoxville, TN: Grady Publications, 1993), 54.
44. Sir Robert Anderson, *The Bible or the Church?* (London: Pickering and Inglis, 2nd ed., n. d.), 53.

45. Augustine, *The City of God*, trans. Marcus Dods. In *Great Books of the Western World,* ed. Robert Maynard Hutchins and Mortimer J. Adler (Encyclopaedia Brittanica, Inc., 1952), XX:7, 8.
46. Vance, *Other Side*, 55.
47. Talbot and Crampton, *Calvinism, Hyper-Calvinism*, 79.
48. Calvin, *Institutes*, IV:xiv, 26.
49. Alister E. McGrath, *The Life of John Calvin* (Cambridge, MA: Blackwell Publishers, 1990), 151.
50. Francois Wendel, *Calvin: Origins and Development of His Religious Thought* (Grand Rapids, MI: Baker Books, 1997), 124.
51. Vance, *Other Side*; citing Calvin, *Institutes*, 139, 146, 148–49.
52. Vance, *Other Side*, 113; citing Wendel, *Origins*, 264, and Timothy George, *Theology of the Reformers* (Nashville, TN: Broadman Press, 1988), 232.
53. Philip Schaff, *History of the Christian Church* (New York: Charles Scribner's Sons, 1910; Grand Rapids, MI: Wm B. Eerdmans Publishing Co., reprint 1959), III: 1018.
54. Warfield, *Calvin*, 322.
55. Ibid., 313.
56. Ibid., 318.
57. Philip F. Congdon, "Soteriological Implications of Five-point Calvinism," *Journal of the Grace Evangelical Society*, Autumn 1995, 8:15, 55–68.
58. George, *Theology*, 68.
59. James R. White to Dave Hunt, August 4, 2000. On file.
60. David Schaff, *Our Father's Faith and Ours*, 172; cited in Samuel Fisk, *Calvinistic Paths Retraced* (Raleigh, NC: Biblical Evangelism Press, 1985), 68.
61. Philip Schaff, *History*, II:975–76.
62. Samuel Fisk, *Calvinistic Paths Retraced* (Raleigh, NC: Biblical Evangelism Press, 1985), 68.
63. Grady, *Final Authority*, 35.
64. Fisk, *Calvinistic*, 67.
65. F. F. Bruce, *The Books and the Parchments* (London: Pickering and Inglis, Ltd., 1950), 191.
66. Bruce, *Books*, 194–95.
67. Merrill F. Unger, *Unger's Bible Dictionary* (Chicago, IL: Moody Press, 1969), 1151–54.
68. Fisk, *Calvinistic*, 70–75.
69. F.F. Bruce, *The English Bible: A History of Translations* (New York: Oxford University Press, 1961), 90-91.
70. Charles C. Butterworth, *The Literary Lineage of the King James Bible* (Philadelphia: University of Pennsylvania Press, 1941), 163.
71. H. Wheeler Robinson, *The Bible In Its Ancient and English Versions* (Oxford: Clarendon Press, 1940), 186, 206–207.
72. Loraine Boettner, *The Reformed Doctrine of Predestination* (Phillipsburg, NJ : Presbyterian and Reformed Publishing Co., 1932), 405.
73. Spurgeon, *Exposition*, 298; cited in Vance, *Other Side*, 38.

CHAPTER

5

Irresistibly Imposed "Christianity"

ONE OF SATAN'S CLEVEREST and most effective strategies was to delude the Emperor Constantine with a false conversion. The influence of that one event upon subsequent history, both religious and secular, is incalculable. Accounts differ, but whether this came about through a vision or a dream as recounted by Eusebius and Lactantius,[1] Constantine saw a "cross" in the sky and heard a "voice" proclaiming (by some accounts the words were inscribed on the cross), "In this sign thou shalt conquer." In the prior year, the god Apollo had also promised him victory.

Constantine's edicts of toleration gave every man "a right to choose his religion according to the dictates of his own conscience and honest conviction, without compulsion and interference from the government."[2] Schaff views Constantine's conversion as a wonderful advance for Christianity: "The church ascends the throne of the Caesars under the banner of the cross, and gives new vigor and lustre to the hoary empire of Rome."[3] In fact, that "conversion" accelerated the corruption of the church through its marriage to the world.[4]

How could a true follower of the Christ, whose kingdom is not of this world and whose servants do not wage war, proceed to wage war in His name? How could a true follower, under the banner of His cross, proceed to conquer with the sword? Of course, the Crusaders later did the same, slaughtering both Muslims and Jews to retake the "holy land" under Pope Urban II's pledge (matching Muhammad's and the Qur'an's promise to Muslims) of full forgiveness of sins for those who died in this holy war

(Muslims call it *jihad*). The Crusades, of course, like all of the popes' wars, were very Augustinian. The City of God had to be defended!

From Constantine to Augustine

As Durant and other historians have pointed out, Constantine never renounced his loyalty to the pagan gods. He abolished neither the Altar of Victory in the Senate nor the Vestal Virgins who tended the sacred fire of the goddess Vesta. The Sun-god, not Christ, continued to be honored on the imperial coins. In spite of the "cross" (actually the cross of the god Mithras) on his shields and military banners, Constantine had a medallion created honoring the Sun for the "liberation" of Rome; and when he prescribed a day of rest, it was again in the name of the Sun-god ("the day celebrated by the veneration of the Sun"[5]) and not the Son of God.[6] Durant reminds us that throughout his "Christian" life, Constantine used pagan as well as Christian rites and continued to rely upon "pagan magic formulas to protect crops and heal disease."[7]

That Constantine murdered those who might have had a claim to his throne, including his son Crispus, a nephew, and brother-in-law, is further indication that his "conversion" was, as many historians agree, a clever political maneuver to unite the empire. Historian Philip Hughes, himself a Catholic priest, reminds us, "in his manners he [Constantine] remained, to the end, very much the Pagan of his early life. His furious tempers, the cruelty which, once aroused, spared not the lives even of his wife and son, are...an unpleasing witness to the imperfection of his conversion."[8]

It was not long after the new tolerance that Constantine found himself faced with a problem he had never anticipated: division within the Christian church to which he had given freedom. As we noted in the last chapter, it came to a head in North Africa with the Donatists, who, concerned for purity of the faith, separated from the official state churches, rejected their ordinances, and insisted on rebaptizing clergy who had repented after having denied the faith during the persecutions that arose when the Emperor Diocletian demanded that he be worshiped as a god.[9] After years of futile efforts to reestablish unity through discussion, pleadings, councils, and decrees, Constantine finally resorted to force. Frend explains:

> In the spring of 317 he [Constantine] followed up his decision by publishing a "most severe" edict against the Donatists, confiscating their property and exiling their leaders. Within four years the

> universal freedom of conscience proclaimed at Milan had been abrogated, and the state had become a persecutor once more, only this time in favor of Christian orthodoxy.... [The Donatists] neither understood nor cared about Constantine's conversion. For them it was a case of the Devil insisting that "Christ was a lover of unity".... In their view, the fundamental hostility of the state toward the [true] church had not been altered.[10]

In his own day and way, Augustine followed Constantine's lead in his treatment of the Donatists, who were still a thorn in the side of the Roman Church. "While Augustine and the Catholics emphasized the unity of the Church, the Donatists insisted upon the purity of the Church and rebaptized all those who came to them from the Catholics—considering the Catholics corrupt."[11] Constantine had been "relentless [as would be Augustine and his disciple Calvin] in his pursuit of 'heretics' [forbidding] those outside of the Catholic church to assemble...and confiscated their property.... The very things Christians had endured themselves were now being practiced in the name of Christianity."[12]

As a good citizen enjoying the blessing of the Emperor, and believing in the state church Constantine had established, Augustine persecuted and even sanctioned the killing of the Donatists and other schismatics, as we have already seen. Gibbon tells us that the severe measures against the Donatists "obtained the warmest approbation of St. Augustine [and thereby] great numbers of the Donatists were reconciled to [forced back into] the Catholic Church."[13]

Of Augustine it has been said that "the very greatness of his name has been the means of perpetuating the grossest errors which he himself propagated. More than anyone else, Augustine has encouraged the pernicious doctrine of salvation through the sacraments of an organized earthly Church, which brought with it priestcraft with all the evil and miseries that has entailed down through the centuries."[14]

From Augustine to Calvin

There is no question that John Calvin still viewed the church of Christ through Roman Catholic eyes. He saw the church (as Constantine had molded it and Augustine had cemented it) as a partner of the state, with the state enforcing orthodoxy (as the state church defined it) upon all its citizens. Calvin applied his legal training and zeal to the development of a *system* of Christianity based upon an extreme view of God's sovereignty, which, by the sheer force of its logic, would compel kings and all mankind to conform all affairs to righteousness. In partnership with the church, kings and other civil rulers would enforce Calvinistic Christianity.

Of those who believed in a thousand-year reign of Christ upon earth, Calvin said their "fiction is too puerile to need or to deserve refutation."[15] As far as Calvin was concerned, Christ's kingdom began with His advent upon earth and had been in process ever since. Rejecting the literal future reign of Christ upon the earth through His Second Coming to establish an earthly kingdom upon David's throne in Jerusalem, Calvin apparently felt obliged to establish the kingdom by his own efforts in Christ's absence.

The Bible makes it clear that one must be "born again" even to "see the kingdom of God" (John 3:3) and that "flesh and blood cannot inherit the kingdom of God" (1 Corinthians 15:50). Ignoring this biblical truth and following Augustine's error, Calvin determined (along with Guillaume Farel) to establish the kingdom of God on earth in Geneva, Switzerland.

On November 10, 1536, the Confession of Faith, which all the bourgeoisie and inhabitants of Geneva and subjects in its territories should swear to adhere to, and which Farel had drafted in consultation with Calvin, was officially presented to the city. It was a lengthy document with detailed rules covering everything from church membership, attendance, preaching, and obedience of the flock, to expulsion of offenders. Geneva's authorities approved the document on January 16, 1537. "In March the Anabaptists were banished. In April, at Calvin's instigation [a house-to-house inspection was launched] to ensure that the inhabitants subscribed to the Confession of Faith.... On October 30 there was an attempt to wring a profession of faith from all those hesitating. Finally, on November 12, an edict was issued declaring that all recalcitrants '[who] do not wish to swear to the Reformation are commanded to leave the city'...."[16]

"The Reformation"? There were variations and differences among the several factions in the budding Reformation, from Luther to Zwingli. But in Geneva, Calvinism alone was to be known as "The Reformation" and "Reformed Theology." That presumptuous claim is still insisted upon by Calvinists today all over the world.

Calvin's first attempt failed. Boettner acknowledges, "Due to an attempt of Calvin and Farel to enforce a too severe system of discipline in Geneva, it became necessary for them to leave the city temporarily."[17]

Calvin's Triumphant Return

Three years later, however, facing Catholic opposition from within and the threat of armed intervention by Roman Catholics from without, Geneva's city council decided that they needed Calvin's strong measures and invited him back. He reentered the city on September 13, 1541. This time, he would eventually succeed in imposing his version of the Reformation upon Geneva's citizens with an iron hand. His first act was to hand the city council his *Ecclesiastical Ordinances*, which were adopted November 20, 1541. Stefan Zweig tells us:

> One of the most momentous experiments of all time began when this lean and harsh man entered the Cornavian Gate [of Geneva]. A State [the walled city-state of Geneva] was to be converted into a rigid mechanism; innumerable souls, people with countless feelings and thoughts, were to be compacted into an all-embracing and unique system. This was the first [Protestant] attempt made in Europe to impose...a uniform subordination upon an entire populace.
>
> With systematic thoroughness, Calvin set to work for the realization of his plan to convert Geneva into the first Kingdom of God on earth. It was to be a community without corruption, disorder, vice or sin; it was to be the New Jerusalem, a centre from which the salvation of the world would radiate.... The whole of his life was devoted to the service of this one idea.[18]

Calvin's intention to establish ecclesiastical rule would occupy most of the rest of his life. Though recognizing Calvin's influence and power, the Small Council of Sixty and the Large Council of Two Hundred, responsible for civil affairs, resisted being taken over by the religious authority (consistory) over which Calvin held sway. The power struggle continued for years, the councils even seeking to retain control over some church disciplines such as excommunications, with Calvin defiantly refusing to yield.

Finally, in February 1555, Calvin's supporters gained the absolute majority on the council. On May 16th there was an attempted uprising against Calvin's exclusion from the Lord's Supper of certain libertarian civic officials.[19] Riot leaders who fled Geneva to Bern were sentenced to death in absentia. Four who failed to escape were beheaded and quartered, and their body parts were hung in strategic locations as a warning.[20] Evoking the phrase "henchmen of Satan" that he had years before used against

Anabaptists, Calvin justified this barbarity: "Those who do not correct evil when they can do so and their office requires it are guilty of it."[21]

From early 1554 until his death in 1564, "no one any longer dared oppose the Reformer openly."[22] Calvin's opponents had either been silenced, expelled, or had fled to save their lives. Calvin's "control of the city continued without weakening." He was determined to make Geneva the base for building Augustine's City of God everywhere. "Geneva became the symbol and incarnation of that 'other' Reformation...,"[23] but which Calvinists today claim was *the* Reformation.

Tyranny in Geneva

Perhaps Calvin thought he was God's instrument to force Irresistible Grace (a key doctrine in Calvinism) upon the citizens of Geneva, Switzerland—even upon those who proved their unworthiness by resisting to the death. He unquestionably did his best to be irresistible in imposing "righteousness," but what he imposed and the manner in which he imposed it was far from grace and the teachings and example of Christ.

Some of those who profess a "Reformed" faith today, especially those known as Reconstructionists such as the late Rousas J. Rushdoony, Gary North, Jay Grimstead, and others (including organizations such as the Coalition on Revival), take Calvin's Geneva as their model and thus hope to Christianize the United States and then the world. Many Christian activists of looser attachment to Calvin hope, in their own way, through protest marches and the organizing of large enough voting blocks, to force an ungodly American citizenry into godly living. No one ever worked so hard at attempting to do this and for so long a time as Calvin. Durant reports:

> To regulate lay conduct a system of domiciliary visits was established...and questioned the occupants on all phases of their lives.... The allowable color and quantity of clothing, and the number of dishes permissible at a meal, were specified by law. Jewelry and lace were frowned upon. A woman was jailed for arranging her hair to an immoral height....
>
> Censorship of the press was taken over from Catholic and secular precedents and enlarged: books...of immoral tendency were banned.... To speak disrespectfully of Calvin or the clergy was a crime. A first violation of these ordinances was punished with a reprimand, further violation with fines, persistent violation with imprisonment or banishment. Fornication was to be punished with exile or drowning; adultery, blasphemy, or idolatry,

> with death...a child was beheaded for striking its parents. In the years 1558–59 there were 414 prosecutions for moral offenses; between 1542 and 1564 there were seventy-six banishments and fifty-eight executions; the total population of Geneva was then about 20,000.[24]

The oppression of Geneva could not have come from the Holy Spirit's guidance ("...where the Spirit of the Lord is, there is liberty" [2 Corinthians 3:17]), but rather from Calvin's powerful personality and extreme view of God's sovereignty that denied free will to man. Thus "grace" had to be irresistibly imposed in an unbiblical attempt to inflict "godliness" upon the citizens of Geneva. In contrast to the humility, mercy, love, compassion, and longsuffering of Christ, whom he loved and tried to serve, Calvin exerted authority much like the papacy he despised. Moreover, he criticized other Protestant leaders for not doing the same:

> Seeing that the defenders of the Papacy are so bitter and bold in behalf of their superstitions, that in their atrocious fury they shed the blood of the innocent, it should shame Christian magistrates that in the protection of certain truth, they are entirely destitute of spirit.[25]

Calvin's defenders deny the facts and attempt to exonerate him by blaming what he did on the civil authorities. Boettner even insists that "Calvin was the first of the Reformers to demand complete separation between Church and State."[26] In fact, Calvin not only established ecclesiastical law, but he codified the civil legislation.[27] He held the civil authorities responsible to "foster and maintain the external worship of God, to defend sound doctrine and the condition of the church"[28] and to see that "no idolatry, no blasphemy against God's name, no calumnies against his truth, nor other offenses to religion break out and be disseminated among the people...[but] to prevent the true religion...from being with impunity openly violated and polluted by public blasphemy."[29]

Calvin used the civil arm to impose his peculiar doctrines upon the citizens of Geneva, and to enforce them. Zweig, who pored over the official records of the City Council for Calvin's day, tells us, "There is hardly a day, in the records of the settings of the Town Council, in which we do not find the remark: 'Better consult Master Calvin about this.'"[30] Pike reminds us that Calvin was given a "consultant's chair" in every meeting of the city authorities and "when he was sick the authorities would come to his house for their sessions."[31] Rather than diminishing with time, Calvin's power only grew. John McNeil, a Calvinist, admits that "in Calvin's latter years, and under his influence, the laws of Geneva became more detailed and more stringent."[32]

Don't Cross Dr. Calvin!

With dictatorial control over the populace ("he ruled as few sovereigns have done"[33]), Calvin imposed his brand of Christianity upon the citizenry with floggings, imprisonments, banishments, and burnings at the stake. Calvin has been called "the Protestant Pope" and "the Genevese dictator" who "would tolerate in Geneva the opinions of only one person, his own."[34] Concerning the adoption in Geneva of a confession of faith that was made mandatory for all citizens, the historian Philip Schaff comments:

> It was a glaring inconsistency that those who had just shaken off the yoke of popery as an intolerable burden, should subject their conscience and intellect to a human creed; in other words, substitute for the old Roman popery a modern Protestant popery.[35]

Durant says that "Calvin held power as the head of this consistory; from 1541 till his death in 1564, his voice was the most influential in Geneva."[36] Vance reminds us that:

> Calvin was involved in every conceivable aspect of city life: safety regulations to protect children, laws against recruiting mercenaries, new inventions, the introduction of cloth manufacturing, and even dentistry. He was consulted not only on all important state affairs, but on the supervision of the markets and assistance for the poor.[37]

Calvin's efforts were often laudable, but matters of faith were legislated as well. A confession of faith drawn up by Calvin was made mandatory for all citizens. It was a crime for anyone to disagree with this Protestant pope. Durant comments:

> All the claims of the popes for the supremacy of the church over the state were renewed by Calvin for his church....[Calvin] was as thorough as any pope in rejecting individualism of belief; this greatest legislator of Protestantism completely repudiated that principle of private judgment with which the new religion

> had begun.... In Geneva...those...who could not accept it would have to seek other habitats. Persistent absence from Protestant [Calvinist] services, or continued refusal to take the Eucharist was a punishable offense.
>
> Heresy again became...treason to the state, and was to be punished with death.... In one year, on the advice of the Consistory, fourteen alleged witches were sent to the stake on the charge that they had persuaded Satan to afflict Geneva with plague.[38]

Calvin was again following in the footsteps of Augustine, who had enforced "unity...through common participation in the Sacraments...."[39] A medical doctor named Jerome Bolsec dared to disagree with Calvin's doctrine of predestination. He was arrested for saying that "those who posit an eternal decree in God by which he has ordained some to life and the rest to death make of Him a tyrant...."[40] Bolsec was arrested and banished from Geneva with the warning that if he ever returned he would be flogged.[41] John Trolliet, a city notary, criticized Calvin's view of predestination for "making God the author of sin."[42] In fact, the charge was true, as we shall see in chapters 9 and 10. The court decreed that "thenceforward no one should dare to speak against this book [*Institutes*] and its doctrine."[43] So much for the freedom of conscience that had been promised would replace the popes' intolerable oppression!

Calvin's power was so great that it was tantamount to treason against the state to oppose him. A citizen named Jacques Gruet was arrested on suspicion of having placed a placard on Calvin's pulpit which read in part, "Gross hypocrite...! After people have suffered long, they avenge themselves.... Take care that you are not served like M. Verle [who had been killed]...."[44]

Gruet was tortured twice daily in a manner similar to which Rome, rightly condemned by the Reformers for doing so, tortured the victims of her inquisitions who were accused of daring to disagree with her dogmas. The use of torture for extracting "confessions" was approved by Calvin.[45] After thirty days of severe suffering, Gruet finally confessed—whether truthfully, or in desperation to end the torture, no one knows. On July 16, 1547, "half dead, he was tied to a stake, his feet were nailed to it, and his head was cut off."[46] Beheading was the penalty for *civil* crimes; burning at the stake was the penalty for *theological heresy*. Here we see disagreement with Calvin was treated as a capital offense against the *state*.

Irrational Behavior

Calvin followed the principles of punishment, coercion, and death that Augustine had advocated. Concerning just one period of panic in the face of plague and famine, Cottret describes "an irrational determination to punish the fomenters of the evil." He tells of a man who "died under torture in February 1545, without admitting his crime…the body was dragged to the middle of town, in order not to deprive the inhabitants of the fine burning they had a right to. Sorcerers, like heretics…were characterized by their combustible qualities…. The executions continued. Yet those detained refused to confess; the tortures were combined skillfully to avoid killing the guilty foolishly…[some] were decapitated…. Some committed suicide in their cells to avoid torture…. One of the arrested women threw herself from a window…. Seven men and twenty-four women died in the affair; others fled. "[47]

In a letter, Calvin advised a friend: "The Lord tests us in a surprising manner. A conspiracy has just been discovered of men and women who for three years employed themselves in spreading the plague in the city by means of sorcery…. Fifteen women have already been burned, and the men have been punished still more rigorously. Twenty-five of these criminals are still shut up in the prisons…. So far God has preserved our house."

Cottret continues: "Calvin therefore shares in all respects the fantasies of his entourage. He found occasion to exhort his contemporaries to pursue sorcerers in order to 'extirpate such a race'…. A pair of these henchmen of Satan had just been burned the previous month…."[48] Calvin even believed that the devil, on at least one occasion, helped rid Geneva of evil, "for in October 1546 he [the devil] bore away through the air (so Calvin himself testifies) a man who was ill with the plague, and who was known for his misconduct and impiety."[49]

Good Intentions Gone Astray

No one has ever been as successful as John Calvin at totalitarian imposition of "godliness" upon a whole society. And therefore, no one has proved as clearly as he that coercion cannot succeed because it can never change the *hearts* of men. Calvin's theology, as laid out in his *Institutes*, denied that unregenerate man could choose to believe and obey God. Apparently, he was ignorant of the commonsense fact that genuine choice is essential if man is to love and obey God or show love and real compassion to his fellows.

By his determined efforts to make Geneva's citizens obey, Calvin disproved his own theories of Unconditional Election and Irresistible Grace.

What he did prove, seemingly, by years of totalitarian intimidation and force, was the first of Calvinism's Five Points, Total Depravity. Try as he might, there were many whom he simply could not persuade to live as he decreed, no matter how severe the penalty for failing to do so. He did succeed in creating many hypocrites who outwardly conformed to the law so long as the authorities were looking, but in their hearts longed for and practiced, when possible, the same old sins of the past.

Yes, there were reports from visitors that "cursing and swearing, unchastity, sacrilege, adultery, and impure living" such as were found elsewhere were absent from Geneva.[50] John Knox, of course, was enthusiastic. He called Geneva "the most perfect school of Christ that ever was in the earth since the days of the Apostles."[51] A visiting Lutheran minister, who thought Calvin's coercion was commendable, wrote in 1610, "When I was in Geneva I observed something great which I shall remember and desire as long as I live." He praised the "weekly investigations into the conduct, and even the smallest transgressions, of the citizens" and concluded, "If it were not for the difference of religion, I would have been chained to Geneva forever."[52]

Difference of religion? Yes, Calvinism was not Lutheranism, although both persecuted the Anabaptists. Protestantism involved several rival factions, to say nothing of millions of true Christians who had never given allegiance to Rome and thus had not come out of her as "Protestants." Untold multitudes of these believers had been martyred by Roman Catholics at the instigations of numerous popes for a thousand years before Luther and Calvin were born. Thus today's representation of Calvinism as "Reformation theology" that supposedly revived true Christianity is grossly inaccurate.

Admirers of John Calvin cite favorable stories as proof of the godly influence he and his theories exerted in changing a godless society into one that honored God. His methods, however, often far from Christlike, could not be justified by *any* results. Nor could Calvin's means, as we have already noted, be justified by the fact that torture, imprisonment, and execution had been employed by Luther and the popes and other Roman Catholic clergy to force their religious views upon those under their power. A true follower of Christ is not to be conformed to this world but in his behavior is to follow Christ's example, no matter in what culture or time in history he finds himself.

Calvin's followers boast that he was the greatest of exegetes, who obeyed Scripture meticulously both in formulating his theology and in guiding his life. Supposedly, Calvin "was willing to break sharply with tradition where it was contrary to the Word of God."[53] At the same time, he is defended with the excuse that he was only conforming to the traditions long established by Rome, which began with Constantine. Otto Scott says, "In the early years of the Reformation, censorship of manners and morals remained a settled, accepted part of existing, ancient police regulations not only in Geneva, but in all Europe."[54]

This is true. Such curbs discouraged rebellious attempts to leave one's "class," etc. But that was not Christianity as taught and exemplified by Christ and His apostles.

There is no way to defend Calvin's conduct from Scripture. Yes, he was loving and caring toward those who agreed with him. Yes, he expended himself and shortened his life through visiting the sick, caring for the flock, and preaching continually. But in his treatment of those who disagreed with him, he did not follow but violated both the teachings and the example of Christ and His apostles.

The Hopelessness of Imposed "Godliness"

Sadly, in spite of threats and torture, Calvin's Geneva was not as righteous a city as the selected optimistic stories seem to indicate. The surviving records of the Council of Geneva unveil a city more similar to the rest of the world than Calvin's admirers like to admit. These documents reveal "a high percentage of illegitimate children, abandoned infants, forced marriages, and sentences of death."[55] The stepdaughter and son-in-law of Calvin were among the many condemned for adultery.[56] Calvin had done his best but had failed. He had not been able to produce among sinners the ideal society—Augustine's City of God—which he had envisioned when he wrote his *Institutes*.

Calvinists teach that the totally depraved unsaved can respond to God *only* in unbelief, rebellion, and opposition. White explains: "Unregenerate men who are enemies of God most assuredly respond to God: in a universally negative fashion."[57] That being the case, by his own theory, Calvin's efforts at Geneva were doomed before they began!

Speaking for most Calvinists, R. C. Sproul explains that according to the "Reformed view of predestination before a person can choose Christ he must be born again"[58] by a sovereign act of God. How could Calvin be sure that God had done this work in the hearts of all in Geneva? If God had not predestined every citizen of Geneva to salvation, then Calvin was wrong in trying to force them into a Christian mold. Yet coercion even by force was an integral part of the system as practiced by Calvin himself and his immediate successors.

If Calvinists today do not approve of such conduct, might not the Calvinism that produced such tyranny also be wrong in other respects?

How many of the "elect" were there in Geneva? As Jay Adams points out, no one, not even Calvin, could know. Calvinism has no explanation for how the elect could have been identified with certainty among the hypocrites who acted as though they were among the elect by behaving themselves, but did so only out of fear of the temporal consequences. No matter how hard Calvin tried, if God (according to Calvin's doctrine) had not elected every citizen in Geneva to salvation (and He apparently had not), then evil would still persist—though not as blatantly as in other cities of that day.

Considering Calvin's abysmal record of failure, one wonders why today's Reconstructionists, who hold to the same dogma, nevertheless believe they will be able to impose righteous living upon entire nations. Or why evangelicals continue to praise Calvin, the oppressor of Geneva.

Servetus: The Arch Heretic

Born Miguel Serveto in Villanova in 1511, the man known to the world as Michael Servetus "discovered the pulmonary circulation of the blood—the passage of the blood from the right chamber of the heart along the pulmonary artery to and through the lungs, its purification there by aeration, and its return via the pulmonary vein to the left chamber of the heart." He was in some ways "a bit more insane than the average of his time," announcing the end of the world in which "the Archangel Michael would lead a holy war against both the papal and Genevese Antichrists."[59]

Unquestionably, he was a rank heretic whose ravings about Christ reflected a combination of Islam and Judaism, both of which intrigued him. He was, however, right about some things: that God does not predestine souls to hell and that God is love. His otherwise outrageous ideas might have passed unnoticed had he not published them and attempted to force them upon Calvin and his fellow ministers in Geneva with aggressive, contemptuous, and blasphemous railings. That Servetus titled one of his published works *The Restitution of Christianity* could only be taken as an intentional personal affront by the author of the *Institutes of the Christian Religion.*

Servetus wrote at least thirty unwelcome letters to Calvin, which must have irritated the latter greatly. On February 13, 1546, Calvin wrote to Farel, "Servetus has just sent me a long volume of his ravings. If I consent he will come here, but I will not give my word, for should he come, if my authority is of any avail, I will not suffer him to get out alive."[60] Servetus made the mistake of passing through Geneva seven years later on his way to Naples and was recognized when he attended church (possibly out of fear of arrest for nonattendance) by someone who saw through his disguise and notified Calvin, who in turn ordered his arrest.

The Torture and Burning of Servetus

Early in the trial, which lasted two months, Calvin wrote to Farel, "I hope that sentence of death will be passed upon him."[61] Obviously, if the God one believes in predestines billions to a burning hell (all of whom He *could* rescue), then to burn at the stake a totally depraved heretic would seem quite mild and easily justifiable. That logic, however, seems somehow to escape many of today's evangelical Christians who admire the man and call themselves Calvinists.

The indictment, drawn up by Calvin the lawyer, contained thirty-eight charges supported by quotations from Servetus's writings. Calvin personally appeared in court as the accuser and as "chief witness for the prosecution."[62] Calvin's personal reports of the trial matched Servetus's railings with such epithets as "the dirty dog wiped his snout...the perfidious scamp soils each page with impious ravings," etc.[63]

Geneva's Council consulted the other churches of Protestant Switzerland, and six weeks later their reply was received: Servetus should be condemned but not executed. Nevertheless, under Calvin's leadership, He was sentenced to death on two counts of heresy: Unitarianism (rejection of the Trinity) and rejection of infant baptism. Durant gives the horrifying details:

> He asked to be beheaded rather than burned; Calvin was inclined to support this plea, but the aged Farel...reproved him for such tolerance; and the Council voted that Servetus should be burned alive.

> The sentence was carried out the next morning, October 17, 1553.... On the way [to the burning] Farel importuned Servetus to earn divine mercy by confessing the crime of heresy; according to Farel the condemned man replied, "I am not guilty, I have not merited death"; and he besought God to pardon his accusers. He was fastened to a stake by iron chains, and his last book was bound to his side. When the flames reached his face he shrieked with agony. After half an hour of burning he died.[64]

Calvin accused Servetus of "specious arguments" against infant baptism. But the latter's main objections (in spite of his other faults) were actually quite sound. Calvin's derisive response, purged of that unchristian "biting and mocking tone of ridicule that would never leave him"[65] is condensed as follows:

> Servetus [argues] that no man becomes our brother unless by the Spirit of adoption...only conferred by the hearing of faith.... Who will presume...that [God] may not ingraft infants into Christ by some other secret method...? Again he objects, that infants cannot be...begotten by the word. But what I have said again and again I now repeat...God takes his own methods of regenerating...to consecrate infants to himself, and initiate them by a sacred symbol.... Circumcision was common to infants before they received understanding.... Doubtless the design of Satan in assaulting paedobaptism with all his forces is to...efface, that attestation of divine grace...that from their birth they have been...acknowledged by him as his children.....[66]

In spite of his other false views, Servetus was correct in his objections to infant baptism and was therefore, in that respect, burned at the stake for a biblical belief that opposed Calvin's heresy of baptismal regeneration of infants practiced in many Calvinist churches to this day.

The Failure of Attempted Exonerations

Many attempts have been made by his modern followers to exonerate Calvin for the unconscionably cruel death of Michael Servetus. It is said that Calvin visited him in prison and pleaded with him to recant. At the same time, Calvin's willingness for Servetus to be beheaded rather than burned at the stake was not necessarily motivated by kindness, but was an attempt to transfer responsibility to the civil authority. Beheading was the penalty for civil crimes; burning at the stake was for heresy. The charges, however, were clearly theological, not civil, and were brought by Calvin himself.

The civil authority only acted at the behest of the church. According to the laws of Geneva, Servetus, as a traveler passing through, should have been expelled from the city, not executed. It was only his heresy that doomed him—and only because Calvin pressed the charges. Calvin did exactly what his view of God required, in keeping with what he had written to Farel seven years before.

Here again, over Calvin's shoulder, we see the long shadow of Augustine. To justify his actions, Calvin borrowed the same perverted interpretation of Luke 14:23 that Augustine had used. Frend said, "Seldom have gospel words been given so unexpected a meaning."[67] Farrar writes:

> To him [Augustine] are due…above all the bitter spirit of theological hatred and persecution. His writings became the Bible of the Inquisition. His name was adduced—and could there be a more terrible Nemesis on his errors?—to justify the murder of Servetus.[68]

There was wide acclaim from Catholics and Protestants alike for the burning of Servetus. The Inquisition in Vienna burned him in effigy. Melanchthon wrote Calvin a letter in which he called the burning "a pious and memorable example to all posterity" and gave "thanks to the Son of God" for the just "punishment of this blasphemous man." Others, however, disagreed; and Calvin became the target of criticism.

Many living in Calvin's time recognized the wickedness of using force to promote "Christianity." Full approval was lacking even among Calvin's closest friends.[69] Rebuking Calvin for the burning of Servetus, Chancellor Nicholas Zurkinden, a magistrate, said the sword was inappropriate for enforcing faith.[70] In spite of many such rebukes, Calvin insisted that the civil sword must keep the faith pure. His conduct was in line with his rejection of God's love toward all, and his denial of human choice to believe the gospel.

Calvin's Self-Justifications

Some critics argued that burning Servetus would only encourage the Roman Catholics of France to do the same to the Huguenots (70,000 would be slaughtered in one night in 1572). Stung by such opposition, in

February 1554, Calvin published a broadside aimed at his critics: *Defensio orthodoxae fidei de sacra Trinitate contra prodigiosos errores Michaelis Serveti.* He argued that all who oppose God's truth are worse than murderers, because murder merely kills the body whereas heresy damns the soul for eternity (was that worse than predestination by God to eternal damnation?), and that God had explicitly instructed Christians to kill heretics and even to smite with the sword any city that abandoned the true faith:

> Whoever shall maintain that wrong is done to heretics and blasphemers in punishing them [with death] makes himself an accomplice in their crime.... It is God who speaks, and it is clear what law He would have kept in the Church even to the end of the world...so that we spare not kin nor blood of any, and forget all humanity when the matter is to combat for His glory.[71]

Historian R. Tudor Jones declares that this tract, which Calvin wrote in defense of the burning of Michael Servetus, "is Calvin at his most chilling...as frightening in its way as Luther's tract against the rebellious peasants."[72] Eight years later, Calvin was still defending himself against criticism and still advocating the burning of heretics. In a 1561 letter to the Marquis de Poet, high chamberlain to the King of Navarre, Calvin advises sternly:

> Do not fail to rid the country of those zealous scoundrels who stir up the people to revolt against us. Such monsters should be exterminated, as I have exterminated Michael Servetus the Spaniard.[73]

A year later (just two years before his own death), Calvin again justifies Servetus's death, while at the same time acknowledging that he was responsible: "And what crime was it of mine if our Council *at my exhortation*... took vengeance upon his execrable blasphemies (emphasis added)?"[74]

Calvinists today still persist in offering one excuse after another to exonerate their hero. Nevertheless, even such a staunch Calvinist as William Cunningham writes:

> There can be no doubt that Calvin beforehand, at the time, and after the event, explicitly approved and defended the putting him [Servetus] to death, and assumed the responsibility of the transaction.[75]

Does the Christian Life Conform to Culture?

Today Calvin's supporters complain, "No Christian leader has ever been so often condemned by so many. And the usual grounds for condemnation are the execution of Servetus and the doctrine of predestination."[76] In fact, Servetus was only one of many such victims of Calvinism carried to its logical conclusion. Defenders usually plead that what Calvin did was common practice and that he should be judged by the standard of his time. Are "new creatures in Christ Jesus" to rise no higher than the conventions of their culture and their moment in history? Surely not!

God's sovereignty in controlling and causing everything that occurs is the very heart of Calvinism. Staunch Calvinist C. Gregg Singer declares that "the secret grandeur of Calvin's theology lies in his grasp of the biblical teaching of the sovereignty of God."[77] Could Calvin truly have believed that he was God's instrument chosen from past eternity to coerce, torture, and kill in order to force Geneva's citizens into behavior that God had predestined and would *cause*?

Calvin has been acclaimed as a godly example who based his theology and actions upon Scripture alone. But much that he did was unbiblical in the extreme, though consistent with his theology. Is not that fact sufficient reason to examine Calvinism carefully from Scripture? That the Pope and Luther joined in unholy alliances with civil rulers to imprison, flog, torture, and kill dissenters in the name of Christ does not justify Calvin. Is it not possible that some of Calvin's theology was just as unscriptural as the principles that drove his conduct? William Jones declares:

> And with respect to Calvin, it is manifest, that...the most hateful feature in all the multiform character of popery adhered to him through life—I mean the *spirit of persecution*.[78]

Is not Christ alone the standard for His followers? And is He not always the same, unchanged by time or culture? How can the popes be condemned (and rightly so) for the evil they did under the banner of the Cross, while Calvin is excused for doing much the same, though on a smaller scale? The following are just two passages among many that condemn Calvin:

- But the wisdom that is from above is first pure, then peaceable, gentle, and easy to be intreated, full of mercy and good fruits, without partiality, and without hypocrisy. (James 3:17)

- He that saith he abideth in him [Christ] ought himself also so to walk, even as he [Christ] walked. (1 John 2:6)

One wonders how so many of today's Christian leaders can continue to laud a man whose behavior was often so far removed from the biblical exemplar reflected above.

---

1. W. H. C. Frend, *The Rise of Christianity* (Philadelphia, PA: Fortress Press, 1984), 482.
2. Philip Schaff, *History of the Christian Church* (New York: Charles Scribner's Sons, 1910; Wm. B. Eerdmans Publishing Company, reprint 1959), II:72–73.
3. Ibid.
4. F. F. Bruce, *Light in the West*, Bk. III of *The Spreading Flame* (Grand Rapids, MI: Wm B. Eerdmans Publishing Co., 1956), 11–13.
5. *Codex Theodosianus*, (July 3, A.D. 321), XVI:8.1.
6. Frend, *Rise*, 484.
7. Will Durant, "Caesar and Christ," Pt. III of *The Story of Civilization* (New York: Simon and Schuster, 1950), 656.
8. Philip Hughes, *A History of the Church* (London, 1934), 1:198.
9. E. H. Broadbent, *The Pilgrim Church* (Port Colborne, ON: Gospel Folio Press, reprint 1999), 38–39.
10. Frend, *Rise*, 492.
11. John Laurence Mosheim, *An Ecclesiastical History, Ancient and Modern*, trans. Archibald MacLaine (Cincinnati: Applegate and Co., 1854), 101; and many other historians.
12. Laurence M. Vance, *The Other Side of Calvinism* (Pensacola, FL: Vance Publications, rev. ed. 1999), 45.
13. Edward Gibbon, *The History of the Decline and Fall of the Roman Empire* (New York: Modern Library, n. d.), 2:233.
14. John W. Kennedy, *The Torch of the Testimony* (Christian Books Publishing House, 1963), 68.
15. John Calvin, *Institutes of the Christian Religion,* trans. Henry Beveridge (Grand Rapids, MI: Wm. B. Eerdmans Publishing Company, 1998 ed.), III: xxv, 5.
16. Bernard Cottret, *Calvin: A Biography* (Grand Rapids, MI: William B. Eerdmans Publishing Company, 2000), 128-130.
17. Loraine Boettner, *The Reformed Doctrine of Predestination* (Phillipsburg, NJ: Presbyterian and Reformed Publishing Co., 1932), 408.
18. Stefan Zweig, Eden Paul and Cedar Paul, trans., *The Right to Heresy* (London: Cassell and Company, 1936), 57; cited in Henry R. Pike, *The Other Side of John Calvin* (Head to Heart, n. d.), 21–22.
19. Francois Wendel, *Calvin: Origins and Development of His Religious Thought* (Grand Rapids, MI: Baker Books, 1997), 98-101; Cottret, *Calvin*, 195-198.
20. Wendel, *Calvin*, 100; Cottret, *Calvin*, 198-200.

21. Cottret, *Calvin*, 200.
22. Roget Amédée, *L'Église et l'État a Genève du temps de Calvin. Étude d'histoire politico-ecclésiastique* (Geneva: J. Jullien, 1867).
23. Bernard Cottret, *Calvin: A Biography*, tr. M. Wallace McDonald (Grand Rapids, MI: William B. Eerdmans Publishing Company, 2000) 250.
24. Durant, *Civilization*, III: 474.
25. George Park Fisher, *The Reformation* (New York: Scribner, Armstrong and Co., 1873), 224.
26. Boettner, *Reformed*, 410.
27. Ronald S. Wallace, *Calvin, Geneva, and the Reformation* (Grand Rapids, MI: Baker Book House, 1990), 29.
28. Calvin, *Institutes*, IV: xx, 2.
29. Ibid., 3.
30. Zweig, *Erasmus*, 217.
31. Pike, *John Calvin*, 26.
32. John T. McNeil, *The History and Character of Calvinism* (Oxford: Oxford University Press, 1966), 189.
33. Williston Walker, *John Calvin: The Organizer of Reformed Protestantism* (New York: Schocken Books, 1969), 259.
34. Walker, *Organizer*, 107.
35. Schaff, *History*, 8:357.
36. Durant, *Civilization*, VI: 473.
37. Vance, *Other Side*, 85.
38. Durant, *Civilization*, IV: 465.
39. Frend, *Rise*, 669.
40. *The Register of the Company of Pastors of Geneva in the Time of Calvin*, trans. and ed. Philip E. Hughes (Grand Rapids, MI: Wm B. Eerdmans Publishing Co., 1966), 137–38; cited in Vance, *Other Side*, 84.
41. Schaff, *History*, 8:618.
42. G. R. Potter and M. Greengrass, *John Calvin* (New York: St. Martin's Press, 1983), 92–93.
43. *Register of Geneva*, cited in Vance, *Other Side*, 201.
44. Schaff, *History*, 502.
45. Fisher, *Reformation*, 222.
46. J. M. Robertson, *Short History of Freethought* (London, 1914), I:443–44.
47. Cottret, *Biography*, 180-181.
48. Ibid.
49. Wendel, *Calvin*, 85.
50. Schaff, *History*, 644.
51. Bard Thompson, *Humanists and Reformers: A History of the Renaissance and Reformation* (Grand Rapids, MI: Wm B. Eerdmans Publishing Co., 1996), 501.
52. Schaff, *History*, 519.
53. C. Gregg Singer, *John Calvin: His Roots and Fruits* (Abingdon Press, 1989), 19.
54. Otto Scott, *The Great Christian Revolution* (Windsor, NY: The Reformer Library, 1994), 46.

55. Charles Beard, *The Reformation of the Sixteenth Century in Relation to Modern Thought and Knowledge* (London, 1885), 353; also see Edwin Muir, John Knox (London, 1920), 108.
56. Preserved Smith, *The Age of the Reformation* (New York, 1920), 174.
57. James R. White, *The Potter's Freedom* (Amityville, NY: Calvary Press Publishing, 2000), 98.
58. R. C. Sproul, *Chosen by God* (Carol Stream, IL: Tyndale House Publishers, Inc., 1986), 72.
59. Durant, *Civilization*, VI:481.
60. Roland Bainton, *Hunted Heretic: The Life of Michael Servetus* (Boston: The Beacon Press, 1953), 144; cited in Durant, *Civilization*, VI:481. See also John Calvin, *The Letters of John Calvin* (Carlisle, PA: The Banner of Truth Trust, 1980), 159.
61. John Calvin, dated August 20, 1553; quoted in Calvin, *Letters*.
62. Wallace, *Calvin, Geneva*, 77.
63. Durant, *Civilization*, VI: 483.
64. Ibid., 484.
65. Cottret, *Biography*, 78.
66. Calvin, *Institutes*, IV: xvi, 31.
67. Frend, *Rise*, 672.
68. Frederic W. Farrar, *History of Interpretation* (New York: E. P. Dutton and Co., 1886), 235–38.
69. Ferdinand Buisson, Sebastien Castellion. *Sa Vie et son oeuvre* (1515-1563) (Paris: Hachette, 1892), I:354.
70. Letter from N. Zurkinden to Calvin, February 10, 1554, cited in Cottret, 227.
71. J. W. Allen, *History of Political Thought in the Sixteenth Century* (London, 1951), 87.
72. R. Tudor Jones, *The Great Reformation* (Downer's Grove, IL: InterVarsity Press, n. d.), 140.
73. John Calvin to the Marquis de Poet, in *The Works of Voltaire* (Chicago: E. R. Dumont, 1901), 4:89; quoted in Vance, *Other Side*, 95, who gives two other sources for this quote.
74. Schaff, *History*, 8:690–91.
75. William Cunningham, *The Reformers and the Theology of the Reformation* (Carlisle, PA: The Banner of Truth Trust, 1967), 316–17.
76. Scott, *Revolution*, 100.
77. Singer, *Roots*, 32.
78. William Jones, *The History of the Christian Church* (Church History Research and Archives, 5th ed. 1983), 2:238.

CHAPTER

6

Arminius, Dort, Westminster, and Five Points

CALVINISM IS OFTEN contrasted with Arminianism, so named after Jacobus Arminius (1560–1609). All those who do not fully agree with Calvinists on all five points of TULIP (see below) are almost automatically accused of being Arminians (not to be confused with ethnic Armenians), yet many against whom this charge is laid have never heard the term. Moreover, many Calvinists who malign Arminius have never read his works and know nothing more than hearsay about him and his beliefs.

Ironically, this Dutch theologian started out as a Calvinist and even studied under Beza in Calvin's seminary in Geneva. He was a devout follower of Christ and suffered much for his faith. His entire family was murdered in his absence when Spanish Catholic troops enforcing the Inquisition massacred the population of his hometown of Oudewater in Holland.

Arminius was wrongfully charged with nearly every false doctrine ever invented, from Socinianism (denial of predestination, of the true nature of the Atonement and of the Trinity) to Pelagianism (the denial that Adam's sin affected his posterity, an undue emphasis upon free will, salvation by grace plus works, and the possibility of sinless perfection). Thus to be called an Arminian is a more serious charge than many of either the accusers or the accused realize. So strong was Calvinism in certain parts of Europe in Arminius's day that to disagree with it was tantamount to a denial of the gospel and even of God's entire Word—and it could cost one's life. In England, for example, a 1648 Act of Parliament made a rejection of Calvinistic infant baptism punishable by death.[1]

Arminius had to bear the special onus that came upon any Protestant of his day, especially in Holland, who dared to take a second look at Calvinism from the Scriptures, a guilt sometimes attached to non-Calvinists today. He was accused of having secret leanings toward Roman Catholicism, in spite of his open denunciation of Catholic sacraments and of the papacy as the kingdom of Antichrist. Upon visiting Rome to see the Vatican for himself, Arminius reported that he saw "'the mystery of iniquity' in a more foul, ugly, and detestable form than his imagination could ever have conceived."[2] Some of those who have called themselves Arminians promote serious heresy, having "adopted views quite contrary" to what he taught,[3] but Arminius himself was actually biblical in his beliefs and far more Christlike in his life than was Calvin. Vance rightly declares that "Arminius was just as orthodox on the cardinal doctrines of the Christian Faith as any Calvinist, ancient or modern."[4]

Character and Conduct Comparisons

Some Calvinists have criticized the first edition of this book for what they call my alleged "caricature of Calvin [and] adoring portrait of Arminius...." On the contrary, I have simply given the historic facts, which none of my critics have been able to refute. In *Debating Calvinism* (Multnomah, 2004), James White said he would "refute the calumnies [I] launched at...Calvin [and] Augustine." I'm still waiting. It is unconscionable that Calvinists have swept under the rug Calvin's un-Christlike conduct—and have refused to acknowledge the facts when confronted with them.

There is no denying that Calvin was abusive, derisive, contemptuous, insulting, disparaging, harsh, and sarcastic in his writings and opinions expressed of others. Nor was this only in his language but frequently in his actual treatment of many who dared to disagree with him—as we have briefly shown.

In contrast, Arminius was a consistent Christian in his writings and kind and considerate in his treatment of others. Nowhere in his writings or actions does one find anything of the sarcasm, derision, and contempt for contrary opinions that characterize Calvin's writings. There was nothing about Arminius to suggest revenge against one's enemies or the use of violence in the cause of Christ—much less the death sentence for heresy that was enforced in Calvin's Geneva.

In evaluating either of these two strong leaders, one must also remember that, just as the Five Points of Calvinism were not formulated by Calvin but by the Synod of Dort, so neither was it Arminius who articulated the five points of Arminianism, but the Remonstrants who did so after his death.

Arminius and His Teachings

Arminius stood uncompromisingly for sound doctrine and believed in the infallibility and inerrancy of the Bible as inspired by God. He rejected the Mass as a denial of "the truth and excellence of the sacrifice of Christ."[5] He joined in calling the pope "the adulterer and pimp of the Church, the false prophet...the enemy of God...the Antichrist...[6] the man of sin, the son of perdition, that most notorious outlaw[7]...[who] shall be destroyed at the glorious advent of Christ,"[8] and urged all true believers to "engage in... the destruction of Popery, as they would...the kingdom of Antichrist...."[9] And he endeavored to "destroy Popery" by his lucid and powerful preaching of the gospel and sound doctrine from God's Word.

Arminius recognized and rejected the false doctrines of Augustine for what they were. In contrast to Augustine, Arminius also rejected the Apocrypha and authority of tradition. He believed in the eternal Sonship of Christ, co-equal and co-eternal with the Father and the Holy Spirit,[10] that Christ came to this earth as a man,[11] that He was Jehovah of the Old Testament[12] who died for our sins, paying the full penalty by His one sacrifice of Himself on the cross,[13] that He was buried, rose again, and ascended to heaven,[14] that man is hopelessly lost and bound by sin, and that salvation is by grace alone through faith alone in Christ alone.[15]

Arminius preached that salvation was entirely through Christ as a work of grace, which God alone could do in the heart. He categorically denied the false charges made against him of Pelagianism and Socinianism.[16] He also, with these words, defended himself against the false charge that he taught the doctrine of falling away:

> For I never...taught any thing contrary to the word of God, or to the Confession and Catechism of the Belgic Churches. At no period have I ceased to make this avowal, and I repeat it on this occasion....Yet since a sinister report, has for a long time been industriously and extensively circulated about me...and since this unfounded rumor has already operated most injuriously against me, I importunately entreat to be favored with your gracious permission to make an ingenuous and open declaration....

[Articles were circulated] as if they had been my composition: when, in reality…they had neither proceeded from me, nor accorded with my sentiments, and, as well as I could form a judgment they appeared to me to be at variance with the word of God….

Twice I repeated this solemn asservation, and besought the brethren "not so readily to attach credit to reports that were circulated concerning me, nor so easily to listen to any thing that was represented as proceeding from me or that had been rumored abroad to my manifest injury…."

My sentiments respecting the perseverance of the saints are, that those persons who have been grafted into Christ by true faith, and have thus been made partakers of his life-giving Spirit, possess sufficient powers [or strength] to fight against Satan, sin, the world and their own flesh, and to gain the victory over these enemies—yet not without the assistance of the grace of the same Holy Spirit. Jesus Christ also by his Spirit assists them in all their temptations, and affords them the ready aid of his hand; and, provided they stand prepared for the battle, implore his help, and be not wanting to themselves, Christ preserves them from falling. So that it is not possible for them, by any of the cunning craftiness or power of Satan, to be either seduced or dragged out of the hands of Christ….

Though I here openly and ingenuously affirm, I never taught that a true believer can, either totally or finally fall away from the faith, and perish; yet I will not conceal, that there are passages of scripture which seem to me to wear this aspect; and those answers to them which I have been permitted to see, are not of such a kind as to approve themselves on all points to my understanding. On the other hand, certain passages are produced for the contrary doctrine [of unconditional perseverance] which are worthy of much consideration….

I am not conscious to myself, of having taught or entertained any other sentiments concerning the justification of man before God, than those which are held unanimously by the Reformed and Protestant Churches, and which are in complete agreement with their expressed opinions…yet my opinion is not so widely different from [Calvin's] as to prevent me from employing the signature of my own hand in subscribing to those things which he has delivered on this subject [of justification], in the third book of his Institutes; this I am prepared to do at any time, and to give them my full approval…. For I am not of the congregation of those who wish to have dominion over the faith of another man, but am only a minister to believers, with the design of promoting in them an increase of knowledge, truth, piety, peace and joy in Jesus Christ our Lord."[17]

Staunch Calvinist R. K. McGregor Wright acknowledges that Arminius solidly affirmed the eternal security of the saints, although that doctrine was "...abandoned by his followers...a few years after his death."[18] Arminius is maligned and denounced today by Calvinists, while Augustine is praised. Even while admitting that Arminius "affirmed dogmatically that it is impossible for believers to decline from salvation," Dillow insists that "Arminius believes salvation can be lost.[19] J. I. Packer quotes with approval "Robert Traill, the Scottish Puritan, [who] wrote in 1692, 'The principles of Arminianism are the natural dictates of a carnal mind, which is enmity both to the law of God, and to the gospel of Christ, and, next to the dead sea of Popery (into which also this stream runs), have, since Pelagius to this day, been the greatest plague of the Church of Christ, and it is like will be till his second coming.'"[20] Sheldon, however, says, "The doctrinal system of Arminius, who is confessed on all hands to have been a man of most exemplary spirit and life, was the Calvinistic system with no further modification than necessarily resulted from rejecting the tenet of absolute predestination."[21] A leading Arminian of the nineteenth century summarized his understanding of that doctrine:

> Arminianism teaches that God in Jesus Christ made provision fully for the salvation of all those who, by repentance towards God and faith in our Lord Jesus Christ, accept the terms [of the gospel], and all who do thus accept are eternally saved.[22]

One could hardly argue with that statement. Yet Calvinists continue to accuse Arminius of teaching that salvation could be lost—and to label as "Arminians" anyone who disagrees with them. The same is often the case today.

The Break with Calvinism

Arminius was as determined as Calvin to follow only the Lord and His Word. That sincere desire got him into trouble because he considered himself no more "bound to adopt all the private interpretations of the Reformed"[23] than those of the Roman Catholic Church.[24] He concluded from earnest study of the Scriptures that in some respects Calvinism was simply not biblical. And he suffered false accusations and persecution for that careful and prayerful opinion—as do non-Calvinists today.

Arminius was convinced from the Scriptures that those who will be in heaven will be there because they believed the gospel, not because God elected them to be saved, and regenerated them without any faith on their part. He firmly believed and taught predestination as "an eternal and gracious decree of God in Christ, by which He determines to justify and adopt believers, and to endow them with life eternal, but to condemn unbelievers and impenitent persons."[25] What E. H. Broadbent in his classic *The Pilgrim Church* had to say about Arminius stands in stark contrast to the slander the latter still suffers from Calvinists:

> Brought up under the influence of Calvin's teaching, Arminius—acknowledged by all as a man of spotless character, in ability and learning unexcelled—was chosen to write in defense of Calvinism of the less extreme kind, which was felt to be endangered by the attacks made upon it. Studying the subject, however, he came to see that much that he held was indefensible; that it made God the author of sin, set limits to His saving grace, left the majority of mankind without hope or possibility of salvation.
>
> He saw from the Scriptures that the atoning work of Christ was for all, and that man's freedom of choice is a part of the divine decree. Coming back to the original teaching of Scripture and faith of the Church, he avoided the extremes into which both parties to the long controversy had fallen. His statement of what he had come to believe involved him personally in conflicts which so affected his spirit as to shorten his life [he died at the age of 49, Calvin at 55]. His teaching took a vivid and evangelical form later, in the Methodist revival.[26]

Fisk agrees that "Arminianism comes from the name of a man who first embraced the Calvinistic system, was called upon to defend it against the opposition, and who upon further study came around to a more moderate position."[27] McNeill, himself a Presbyterian, is honest enough to say that Arminius "does not repudiate predestination, but condemns supralapsarianism [that God from eternity past predestined the non-elect to sin and to suffer eternal damnation] as subversive of the gospel."[28] Earle E. Cairns explains the major differences between the two systems:

> His [Arminius's] attempt to modify Calvinism so that...God might not be considered the author of sin, nor man an automaton in the hands of God, brought down upon him the opposition.... Both Arminius and Calvin taught that man, who inherited Adam's sin, is under the wrath of God. But Arminius believed that man

> was able to initiate his salvation after God had granted him the primary grace to enable his will to cooperate with God....[29] Arminius accepted election but believed that the decree to save some and damn others had "its foundation in the foreknowledge of God."[30] Thus election was conditional rather than unconditional.... Arminius also believed that Christ's death was sufficient for all but that it was efficient only for believers.[31] Calvin limited the atonement to those elected to salvation. Arminius also taught that men might resist the saving grace of God,[32] whereas Calvin maintained that grace was irresistible.[33]

The earnest desire of Arminius had simply been to mitigate Calvinism's extremes. Of Arminius, Newman says, "He was recognized as among the ablest and most learned men of his time. His expository sermons were so lucid, eloquent, and well delivered as to attract large audiences. He was called upon from time to time to write against opponents of Calvinism, which he did in a moderate and satisfactory way. When pestilence was raging in 1602, he distinguished himself by heroic service."[34]

In the early days, no one lashed out more viciously at "Arminians" than John Owen, who referred to "the poison of Arminianism...hewing at the very root of Christianity."[35] This effort reached its peak in his lengthy treatise against "the doctrines of Arminius" titled *A Display of Arminianism*, first published in 1642 by order of the Committee of the House of Commons in Parliament for the Regulating of Printing and Publishing of Books. Seemingly lost in the earnest polemics was one cautionary word in the "Prefatory Note," which went unheeded then as now: "It may be questioned if Owen sufficiently discriminates the doctrine of Arminius from the full development which his system, after his death, received in the hands of his followers."[36]

Arminianism and State Churches

Arminius's moderate view attracted a large following. Many Protestant pastors, uncomfortable with the extremes of Calvinism and with its militancy against those who disagreed, began to preach the same modified Calvinism as Arminius and received considerable opposition from Calvinists. The latter, following Augustine's teaching and the practice of Rome, saw church and state as partners, with the state enforcing sanctions against whomever the church considered to be heretics—an intolerance that Arminius and his followers opposed. McGregor writes that "the entire process of the Reformation took place in the context of state churches, with secular power supporting the Reformers and protecting their gains.[37]

This great error was the legacy of Constantine, the first to forbid anyone outside the established church to meet for religious purposes and the first to confiscate the property of those who did. Believing that baptism was "the salvation of God...the seal which confers immortality...the seal of salvation,"[38] he had waited until just before his death to be baptized so as not to risk sinning thereafter and losing his salvation. Later, Emperor Theodosius issued an edict making "the religion which was taught by St. Peter to the Romans, which has been faithfully preserved by tradition"[39] the official faith of the empire. As noted earlier; adherents were to be called "Catholic Christians," and all others were forbidden to meet in their churches.[40] One historian has explained the tragic effect for the church:

> The Scriptures were now no longer the standard of the Christian faith...[but] the decisions of fathers and councils...religion propagated not by the apostolic methods of persuasion, accompanied with the meekness and gentleness of Christ, but by imperial edicts and decrees; nor were gainsayers to be brought to conviction by...reason and scripture, but persecuted and destroyed.[41]

Such was the official relationship between church and state that Calvin inherited from Augustine, enforced in Geneva, and which the Calvinists, wherever possible, carried on and used to enforce their will upon those who differed with them. In league with princes, kings, and emperors, the Roman Catholic Church had for centuries controlled all of Europe. The Reformation created a new state church across Europe, in competition with Rome, which was either Lutheran or Calvinist. The latter claim the name "Reformed."

The Presbyterian Church in Scotland, the Church of England, and the Dutch Reformed Church, which persecuted the Arminians in Holland, were all Calvinistic state churches. Tragically, they followed Constantine, Augustine, and Calvin in the unbiblical and grandiose ambition of imposing their brand of Christianity upon all, in partnership with the state. As David Gay points out:

> In the *Institutes* Calvin said that civil government is assigned to foster and maintain the external worship of God, to defend sound doctrine and the condition of the church. He dismissed the Anabaptists as stupid fanatics because they argued that these

> matters are the business of the church, not the civil authorities. Nevertheless, Calvin was wrong; they were right.... He was writing from the viewpoint of Constantine, not the New Testament....[42]

Synods, Assemblies, Councils, and Confessions

Those who disagree with Calvinism today on the basis of their understanding of God's Word are accused of abandoning, ignoring, or even defying the great confessions and established creeds of the church. We must ask, "Which church?" Roman Catholics also refer to "the Church" in a similar manner, but millions of true believers were not part of it for centuries before the Reformation, refusing to bow to the popes or to submit to Rome's heresies. Calvinists today, looking back upon the first century or so of the Reformation, refer to "the church" in much the same way, meaning state churches carrying on what Calvin began in Geneva, with those who disagree looked down upon as heretics who reject "the Reformed faith"— thus equating Calvinism with the Reformation.

Calvin diligently persecuted even to the death those who disagreed with his extreme views on sovereignty and predestination. Yet he tolerated the many heresies of Augustine—and even adopted some. We find only praise in his writings for this man who held to so much that was unbiblical. In fact, Calvin looked to Augustine as the authority justifying his own erroneous beliefs and practices.

It must be remembered that the Reformation creeds and confessions were formulated not by agreement among all Christians but by either the Lutheran or the Calvinist segment alone. The Synod of Dort and the Westminster Assembly, referred to by Calvinists as authoritative declarations of Christian truth, were dominated by Calvinists and forced Calvinism as the official state religion upon everyone.

So the accusation that one fails to follow these "great Reformed confessions" is merely another way of saying that one disagrees with Calvinism! It also furthers the false impression that Calvinism was the official belief held by all of the Reformers. Concerning the five points of Calvinism, Hodges writes, "None of these ideas has any right to be called normative Protestant theology. None has ever been held by a wide cross-section of Christendom. Most importantly, none of them is biblical...all of them lie outside the proper parameters of Christian orthodoxy."[43]

The Five Arminian Points

Arminius was part of the state Dutch Reformed Church, as were the leaders who carried on his beliefs after his premature death in 1609. Inevitably, open controversy developed over predestination and whether the Belgic Confession and Heidelberg Catechism should be reviewed for possible revision. To discuss the issues, forty-six Arminian ministers met privately in Gouda, Holland, on January 14, 1610. They drew up and signed a Remonstrance (protest) against Calvinism, stating that its doctrines were "not contained in the Word of God nor in the Heidelberg Catechism, and are unedifying—yea, dangerous—and should not be preached to Christian people."[44]

The Remonstrance comprised five brief paragraphs that became known as the five points of Arminianism. In summary they stated:

> 1. That God from eternity past determined to save all who believe in Jesus and to "leave the incorrigible and unbelieving in sin and under wrath...."
>
> 2. That Christ died for and obtained redemption and forgiveness of sins for all, but these benefits are effective only for those who believe on Christ.
>
> 3. That man cannot "think, will or do anything that is truly good," and that includes "saving faith," but must be regenerated.
>
> 4. That God's grace is absolutely essential for salvation, but that it may be resisted.
>
> 5. That those truly saved through faith in Christ are empowered by the Holy Spirit to resist sin; but whether they could fall away from the faith "must be more particularly determined out of the Holy Scripture, before we ourselves can teach it with full persuasion of our minds."

The Calvinist response came a few months later in the form of a Counter-Remonstrance, which contained seven articles. The second and third points have been combined under the heading of Unconditional Election, with the sixth and seventh points combined under Perseverance of the Saints, resulting in what has become known as the Five Points of Calvinism.

Vance summarizes this declaration well as follows:

1. Because the whole race has fallen in Adam and become corrupt and powerless to believe, God draws out of condemnation those whom he has chosen unto salvation, passing by the others.
2. The children of believers, as long as they do not manifest the contrary, are to be reckoned among God's elect.
3. God has decreed to bestow faith and perseverance and thus save those whom he has chosen to salvation.
4. God delivered up his Son Jesus Christ to die on the cross to save only the elect.
5. The Holy Spirit, externally through the preaching of the Gospel, works a special grace internally in the hearts of the elect, giving them power to believe.
6. Those whom God has decreed to save are supported and preserved by the Holy Spirit so that they cannot finally lose their true faith.
7. True believers do not carelessly pursue the lusts of the flesh, but work out their own salvation in the fear of the Lord.[45]

The Growing Controversy

The Counter-Remonstrance was in turn answered by The Opinion of the Remonstrants. This was a far more lengthy document which went into great detail to establish what the Remonstrants "in conscience have thus far considered and still consider to be in harmony with the Word of God...." It contained lengthy objections to Calvinism under four headings, the main points of which are summarized in the following excerpts:

From Section I (10 paragraphs):

3. God...has not ordained the fall...has not deprived Adam of the necessary and sufficient grace, does also not...bring some [men] unto [eternal] life, but deprive others of the benefit of life....
4. God has not decreed without intervening actual sins to leave by far the greater part of men, excluded from all hope of salvation, in the fall.

5. God has ordained that Christ should be the atonement for the sins of the whole world, and by virtue of this decree He has decided to justify and to save those who believe in Him, and to provide men with the means necessary and sufficient unto faith...

6. No one is rejected from eternal life nor from the means sufficient thereto by any antecedent absolute decree....

From Section II (4 paragraphs):

1. The price of salvation, which Christ offered to God...paid for all and every man, according to...the grace of God the Father; and therefore no one is definitely excluded from... the benefits of the death of Christ by an absolute and antecedent decree of God.

3. Although Christ has merited reconciliation with God and the forgiveness of sins for all men...no one becomes an actual partaker of the benefits of the death of Christ except by faith....

From Section III (12 paragraphs):

5. The efficacious grace by which anyone is converted is not irresistible, and although God through the Word and the inner operation of His Spirit so influences the will that He both bestows the power to believe and...indeed causes man to believe, nevertheless man is able of himself to despise this grace, not to believe, and thus to perish through his own fault.

6. Although according to the altogether free will of God the disparity of divine grace may be very great, nevertheless the Holy Spirit bestows, or is ready to bestow, as much grace upon all men and every man to whom God's Word is preached as is sufficient for the furtherance of the sufficient grace unto faith and conversion whom God is said to be willing to save according to the decree of absolute election, but also they who are not actually converted.

12. We also hold to be false and horrible that God should in a hidden manner incite men to the sin which He openly forbids; that those who sin do not act contrary to the true will of God...that it is according to justice a crime worthy of death to do God's will.

From Section IV (8 paragraphs):

3. True believers can fall from true faith and fall into such sins as cannot be consistent with true and justifying faith, and not only can this happen, but it also not infrequently occurs.

4. True believers can through their own fault...finally fall away and go lost.

5. Nevertheless we do not believe, though true believers sometimes fall into grave and conscience-devastating sins, that they immediately fall from all hope of conversion, but we acknowledge that it can happen that God according to His abundant mercy, again calls them to conversion through His grace....

6. Therefore we heartily reject the following doctrines, which are daily spread abroad among the people in public writings, as being harmful to piety and good morals; namely: 1) That true believers cannot sin deliberately, but only out of ignorance and weakness. 2) That true believers through no sins can fall from the grace of God. 3) That a thousand sins, yea, all the sins of the whole world, cannot render election invalid; when it is added to this that all men are obligated to believe that they are chosen unto salvation, and therefore cannot fall from election, we present for consideration what a wide door that opens for carnal certainty. 4) That to believers and to the elect no sins, however great and grave they may be, are imputed....5) That true believers, having fallen into corrupt heresies, into grave and shameful sins, such as adultery and murder, on account of which the Church, according to the institution of Christ, is obligated to testify that she cannot tolerate them in her external fellowship, and that they shall have no part in the kingdom of Christ, unless they repent, nevertheless cannot totally and finally fall from the faith.

8. A true believer can and must be certain for the future that he, granted intervening, watching, praying, and other holy exercises, can persevere in the true faith, and that the grace of God to persevere will never be lacking to him; but we do not see how he may be assured that he will never neglect his duty in the future, but in the works of faith, piety and love, as befits a believer, persevere in this school of Christian warfare. Neither do we deem it necessary that the believer should be certain of this.[46]

These four headings (which clearly departed from what Arminius had taught) were understood to contain five points, which the Calvinists at the Synod of Dort answered with what has become known as the Five Points of Calvinism. The major difference is obvious: the Arminians put the blame for man's eternal punishment upon man himself for rejecting the gospel by his own free will, though he could have accepted it through God's gracious enabling; whereas the Calvinists laid sin itself and the damnation of man totally upon God, who simply predestined everything to turn out that way. A. W. Tozer, respected by many Calvinists, declared, "So when man exercises his freedom [of choice], he is fulfilling the sovereignty of God, not canceling it out."[47]

The State of the Netherlands, in its concern for unity among its citizens, ordered both parties to meet to iron out their differences. Six leaders from each side met in the Hague on March 31, 1611, but failed to reach an agreement. While the Arminians pleaded for tolerance, the Calvinists were determined to convene a national conference to have their opponents declared heretics. Of course, the view at that time was that the state would exact the prescribed penalties upon heretics, up to and including death.

The Great Synod of Dort (Dordrecht)

The persisting theological differences eventually involved the government in an internal battle between political rivals. The Calvinists won out, Prince Maurice siding with them. Magistrates sympathetic to the Arminians were replaced. This later paved the way for the national synod, which, after letters sent inviting foreign representatives, was then convened at Dordrecht on November 13, 1618, and lasted into May of the following year.

Convinced that they were standing for truth, each Calvinist delegate took an oath to follow only the Word of God and to "aim at the glory of God, the peace of the Church, and especially the preservation of the purity of doctrine. So help me, my Savior, Jesus Christ! I beseech him to assist me by his Holy Spirit."[48]

Calvinists ever since have hailed Dort as a gathering of history's most godly leaders, who sincerely followed their oath. In John Wesley's opinion, however, Dort was as impartial as the Council of Trent.[49] In fact, Dort had been called by state officials favoring the Calvinists for the sole purpose of supporting the Calvinists and condemning the Arminians, so it can hardly be considered an impartial tribunal, and certainly did not represent a consensus among true believers.

Moreover, Baptists who today point to Dort as the articulation of what they believe are, as Vance points out,[50] "not only conforming to a Dutch Reformed State-Church creed, they are following Augustine, for as the Reformed theologian Herman Hanko asserts, 'Our fathers at Dordrecht knew well that these truths set forth in the Canons could not only be traced back to the Calvin Reformation; they could be traced back to the theology of St. Augustine.... For it was Augustine who had originally defined these truths.'[51] Custance insists that the Five Points were 'formulated implicitly by Augustine.'"[52]

The Arminians were not allowed to plead their case as equals, but were removed from the status of delegates to that of defendants, and were summarily expelled from the synod and publicly denounced. After Dort, the Remonstrants were asked to recant or be banished. More than 200 Arminian ministers were removed from their pulpits and many were exiled. There was an attempt to establish a harsh Calvinistic theocracy where only Calvinism could be publicly proclaimed, but it lasted only a short time. It was not, however, until 1625 that persecution of Arminians officially ceased.[53]

Cairns calls the Great Synod of Dort "an international Calvinistic assembly" in which the Arminians "came before the meeting in the role of defendants." Calvinists have called Dort "a symbol of the triumph of orthodox Calvinism in the Netherlands."[54] Louis Berkhof declares, "Five thoroughly Calvinistic Canons, in which the doctrines of the Reformation, and particularly of Calvin, on the disputed points are set forth with clearness and precision."[55]

Ever since Dort, Calvinists have hailed these Canons as "a bulwark, a defense, of the truth of God's Word concerning our salvation."[56] We have already quoted a variety of Calvinist leaders, to the effect that Calvinism's Five Points are the gospel. Such opinions should cause concern in the church today in view of the resurgence of Calvinism through the efforts of esteemed evangelical leaders.

Fruits of the Synod of Dort

In evaluating the Synod of Dort and the Five Points of Calvinism that it pronounced, one cannot avoid recognition of the political nature of the gathering. Christ had drawn a clear line of separation between the things that are Caesar's and…"the things that are God's" (Mark 12:17). In tragic contrast, Calvinistic church leaders were acting as instruments of Caesar (the state)—and the state acted on their behalf to punish their opponents. That

Calvinists together with the state falsely charged, persecuted, imprisoned, and executed some of the Arminian leaders must also be a consideration in evaluating this entire procedure and its fruits—as well as Calvinism itself.

Although both the Arminians and Calvinists at this time were in agreement as to the church-state alliance, the Arminians had no desire to use the state to enforce their views upon their opponents, but only to protect their own freedom of conscience and practice. Even Calvinists admit that "the divines who composed the Synod of Dort generally held that the civil magistrate was entitled to inflict pains and penalties as a punishment for heresy" and that, in contrast, the Arminians advocated "toleration and forbearance in regard to differences of opinion upon religious subjects."[57]

Consider, for example, the fate of the four main leaders of the Arminian movement. John Uytenbogaert, who had studied at Geneva under Calvin's successor, Beza, and served as chaplain to Prince Maurice (son and successor of William of Orange), was exiled after the Synod of Dort and had his goods confiscated. Simon Episcopius, a professor of theology and chief spokesman for the Arminians at Dort, was banished. John Van Oldenbarnevelt, who was advocate-general of Holland and a national hero for helping William of Orange negotiate the Union of Utrecht, was falsely charged with treason and was beheaded. Hugo Grotius, a famed lawyer known worldwide for his expertise in international law, was sentenced to life in prison but escaped and later became Swedish ambassador to Paris.

What biblical basis could anyone propose for exacting such penalties for a disagreement over doctrine? If the Calvinists could be so wrong in so much that is so important, might they not also be wrong in some basic theological assumptions? Yet in spite of a complete misunderstanding of and disobedience concerning such vital and fundamental New Testament teachings as separation of church and state (John 15:14–21; 16:33; 1 John 2:15–17) and nonimposition of belief by force, these men are hailed as "great divines" and the doctrine they forcefully imposed on others is embraced as the truth of God—now called "the Reformed faith" and "the doctrines of grace"—to be accepted by all today. The church, once persecuted, now persecuted fellow believers!

The Westminster Assembly

Dort was followed in 1643 by a similar prestigious gathering of "divines" in England. The Westminster Assembly was also under the auspices of the state. That Assembly formulated The Westminster Confession of

Faith, which has been called "the most systematically complete statement of Calvinism ever devised."[58] Vance reminds us that "Due to the close relationship between Church and state that existed at the time, the acceptance of Calvinism in England, culminating in the Westminster Assembly, is deeply intertwined with the civil and religious history of England."[59] A brief word about that history is therefore in order.

In the two preceding centuries, England had gone through a long struggle to escape Rome. At times she made progress, at other times she fell back into bondage. Henry VII had been proclaimed king in 1486 by a papal bull of Pope Innocent VIII. The Latin Vulgate was the official Bible. Wycliffe's Bible was suppressed, and the Provincial Council at Oxford in 1408 had forbidden the translation and printing of "any text of Holy Scripture into the English or other language...."[60] Henry VIII, who had written to Erasmus from London in 1511 that "many heretics furnish a daily holocaust,"[61] at the behest of Cromwell reversed himself and encouraged the Bible in English to be opened in every house and parish church—but a year before his death banned "the New Testament of Tyndale's or Coverdale's translation."[62]

During his brief reign, King Edward VI turned England away from Rome and welcomed Reformed theologians from the Continent into England, giving Calvinism a foothold there that it would never relinquish. In the late sixteenth century, the University of Cambridge became a Calvinist stronghold. Edward's sister, Mary I, daughter of Henry VIII, known as "Bloody Mary," succeeding him, brought England back under popery, forbade possession of any Protestant books, and burned at the stake hundreds who would not accept Rome's doctrines.

After Mary's death, the Geneva Bible came into use. Elizabeth I expelled the Jesuits from England. Under her, the Thirty-Nine Articles of the Church of England (mildly Calvinistic, but rejecting limited atonement) were formulated; they remain the official creed of that church to this day. John Knox held forth in Scotland, while the Puritans rose in England, only to be forced to conform by King James I, who gave us the King James Bible in 1611.

Charles I succeeded James. There were debates in Parliament over Calvinism, with its proponents gaining the upper hand. The Long Parliament ordered the printing of *A Display of Arminianism* by John Owen, which denounced Arminianism and upheld Limited Atonement. In the context of this tumultuous background and the continued partnership of the church with the state, the Westminster Assembly was convened by Parliament. The Parliament "waged a civil war against the king...abolished episcopacy, ejected two thousand royalist ministers... summoned the Westminster Assembly, executed Archbishop Laud, and eventually executed the king himself in 1649."[63]

Once again the deck was stacked. Westminster was not a gathering of those representing all true believers, but only of the Calvinists, who had gained the upper hand in Parliament. Today's boast is that "all of the Westminster divines were Calvinists."[64] Furthermore, as Vance wisely comments, "...like the Synod of Dort, the presence of government officials at an ostensibly religious assembly raises some questions about its legitimacy."[65] Expenses of the members were borne by the State. Even Calvinists admit, "The Assembly was the creature of Parliament and was never able to escape from Parliamentary supervision."[66]

Logan confesses, "The Assembly...was clearly and completely subservient to the political authority of Parliament."[67] De Witt also declares that the Assembly "was answerable, not to the King of Kings, but to the Lords and Commons of the English Parliament."[68] Schaff points out that "the Assembly...clung to the idea of a national state church, with a uniform system of doctrine, worship, and discipline, to which every man, woman, and child in three kingdoms should conform."[69] Bettany writes:

> In 1643 also the Westminster Assembly of divines was convened by Parliament to reform the Church of England "on the basis of the word of God, and to bring it into a nearer agreement with the Church of Scotland and the Reformed Churches on the Continent." The Scotch commissioners now required, as the price of their co-operation with the English Parliament against Charles, the adoption of the Solemn League and Covenant [drawn by a Scottish revolutionary committee requiring signers to extirpate prelacy in all its forms in Scotland, Ireland and England]....
>
> With this weapon...and the test of loyalty to the king, ejections of Episcopalians from their livings...amounted to some thousands.... So many vacancies were created that they could not be filled.... Finally the Westminster Assembly was ordered to draw up a scheme for ordination.... The Westminster Assembly laboured to evolve an acceptable scheme of Presbyterianism, the Independent members, however...proposing toleration for all sects....
>
> The question soon arose...should presbyteries have the power of including or excluding members, or should each Independent congregation wield that power? Parliament undertook to settle the whole matter by ordaining that all persons aggrieved by the

> action of a presbytery might appeal to Parliament.... Cromwell in vain tried to reconcile Independents and Presbyterians. The latter predominated in Parliament, and in 1648 showed their continued intolerance by enacting that all who denied God, or the Trinity, or the atonement, or the canonical books of Scripture, or the resurrection of the dead and a final judgment were to 'suffer the pains of death, as in case of felony, without benefit of clergy.'... A long catalogue of heresies of the second class was specified, to be punished by imprisonment....[70]

Lessons to Be Learned

The so-called Reformation synods and councils and the confessions and decrees they generated, which many Calvinists today honor as stating the true doctrine of Christ, were promoted by an established state church in partnership with the civil rulers—contrary to the Word of God. Always the overriding concern was for unity, and those who did not agree with the majority position were silenced, persecuted, imprisoned, banished, and sometimes executed.

Just as the Roman Catholic Church had persecuted and killed those who did not agree with her down through the centuries, so the newly established Protestant churches began to do the same. Anabaptists, for example, were persecuted and killed by both Catholics and Protestants because the latter still believed in Augustine's baptism of infants into the family of God, with its magical powers of regeneration—a Roman Catholic heresy that clung to Luther and Calvin and that clings to most of their followers to this day.

History clearly records that these were the men and the motives behind the established creeds and confessions. Unquestionably, their *modus operandi* followed in the footsteps of Constantine. Not a true Christian, and thus not interested in truth but in the "unity" of the empire, Constantine used "Christianity" to that end. Under him, the church, once persecuted by the world, became the persecutor. True Christians were still the ones being persecuted. The only change was that an oppressive church had joined the world to persecute those not subscribing to its dogmas.

The new persecution was done in the name of Christ but was the very antithesis of all Christ taught and lived, and for which He died. Following in the footsteps of Rome, which in most matters they opposed, the Protestant churches continued the same practice. We cannot, and dare not, ignore these facts in evaluating "Reformation" creeds and statements of faith that came from councils and synods called by the state for the sake of unity.

Augustine had been happy to use the state in an unbiblical partnership to enforce "faith" upon heretics. Driven by the same belief, Calvin used the same system in Geneva. Nor can one deny the obvious relationship between this forcing of "faith" upon the unwilling, and the two major doctrines of both Augustine and Calvin—Total Depravity and double Predestination with their concomitant denial of any genuine choice for mankind with regard to God and salvation. Freedom of conscience was the natural victim, a form of oppression that even the unsaved can tolerate only for so long.

Defining Calvinism

In spite of many differences of opinion among Calvinists today, Calvinism is generally explained by the acronym, **TULIP**. Philip F. Congdon writes that "a tulip is a beautiful flower, but bad theology. The fruit of the flower is appealing; the fruit of the theology is appalling...works, as an *inevitable result*, are necessary for salvation. To be fair, Classical Calvinists usually object to this by describing the gospel message as *not* 'faith + works = justification,' but 'faith = justification + works'.... This is no more than a word game. It is best seen in the old Calvinist saying: 'You are saved by faith alone, but the faith that saves you is never alone....'"[71]

Some readers may have never heard of **TULIP**. Others, though knowing that it has something to do with Calvinism, find it difficult to remember what each letter stands for. Here, in brief, is a summary of common explanations. In each case, in order to avoid the charge that they are not properly stated, they are presented in the words of the major Calvinistic creeds or confessions:

> **"T" stands for Total Depravity:** that man, because he is spiritually dead to God "in trespasses and in sins" (Ephesians 2:1; Colossians 2:13), is incapable of responding to the gospel, though able to make other moral choices.
>
> The Westminster Confession of Faith declares, "Our first parents...became dead in sin, and wholly defiled in all the faculties and parts of soul and body...wholly inclined to all evil.... Man, by his fall into a state of sin, hath wholly lost all ability of will to any spiritual good accompanying salvation...being altogether averse from that good, and dead to sin, is not able by his own strength,

to convert himself, or to prepare himself thereunto."[72]

"U" stands for Unconditional Election: that God decides on no basis whatsoever but by the mystery of His will to save some, called the elect, and to allow all others to go to hell, even though He *could* save *all* mankind if He so desired.

The Canons of Dort declare, "That some receive the gift of faith from God, and others do not receive it proceeds from God's eternal decree...[by] which decree, he graciously softens the hearts of the elect, however obstinate, and inclines them to believe, while he leaves the non-elect in his just judgment to their own wickedness and obduracy."[73]

"L" stands for Limited Atonement: that the elect are the only ones for whom Christ died in payment of the penalty for their sins, and that His death is efficacious for no others, nor was intended to be.

Dort declares: "For this was the sovereign counsel, and most gracious will and purpose of God the Father, that…the most precious death of his Son should extend to all the elect…all those, and those only, who were from eternity chosen to salvation…he purchased by his death."[74]

"I" stands for Irresistible Grace: that God is able to cause whomever He will to respond to the gospel; that without this enabling, no one could do so; and that He only provides this Irresistible Grace to the elect and damns the rest.

The Westminster Confession states: "All those whom God hath predestinated unto life, and those only, he is pleased, in his appointed and accepted time, effectually to call, by his Word and Spirit, out of that state of sin and death…effectually drawing them to Jesus Christ; yet so, as they come most freely, being made willing by his grace."[75]

"P" stands for Perseverance of the Saints: that God will not allow any of the elect to fail to persevere in living a life consistent with the salvation that He has sovereignly given them.

The Westminster Confession states: "They, whom God hath accepted in his Beloved, effectually called, and sanctified by His Spirit, can neither totally nor finally fall away from the state of grace, but shall certainly persevere therein to the end, and be eternally saved. This perseverance of the saints depends not upon their own free will, but upon the immutability of the decree of election.[76]

William Cunningham speaks for most Calvinists when he writes that "No synod or council was ever held in the church, whose decisions, all things considered, are entitled to more deference and respect [than the Synod of Dort]."[77]

With all due respect, I would suggest that the Bible alone is our authority, not the beliefs of either John Calvin or Jacobus Arminius, or any council, synod, assembly, or creed. In the following pages, the points of TULIP are compared with the Bible, one point at a time, and in order.

---

1. George Park Fisher, *History of the Christian Church*, (New York: Charles Scribner's Sons, 1902), 406.
2. Jacobus Arminius, *The Works of James Arminius,* trans. James and William Nichols (Grand Rapids, MI: Baker Book House, 1986), I:26.
3. From the old *Edinburgh Encyclopedia* (Scotland: n. p.,n. d.); quoted in Arminius, *Works*, 1:306.
4. Laurence M. Vance, *The Other Side of Calvinism* (Pensacola, FL: Vance Publications, rev. ed., 1999), 126.
5. Arminius, *Works*, 2:243–44.
6. Ibid., 2:264–65.
7. Ibid., 1:298.
8. Ibid., 299.
9. Ibid.,644.
10. Ibid., 2:115–18, 138, 141–43, 145, etc.
11. Ibid.,379.
12. Ibid., 141.
13. Ibid., 443
14. Ibid., 387–88.
15. Ibid., 157, 256; 1:659–60.
16. Ibid., 1:102.
17. *The Works of James Arminius, Vols. 1 & 2*, Translated from the Latin by James Nichols: "The Apology or Defense of James Arminius, against certain theological articles extensively distributed and currently circulated…in the low countries and beyond…in which both Arminius, and Adrian Borrius, a minister of Leyden, are rendered suspected of novelty and heterodoxy, of error and heresy, on the subject of religion," probably published early in 1609 shortly before his death. See also, *A Declaration of the Sentiments of Arminius—on Predestination, Divine Providence, the freedom of the will, the grace of God, the Divinity of the Son of God, and the justification of man before God.* Delivered before the states of Holland, at the Hague, on the thirtieth of October, 1608.
18. R. K. McGregor Wright, *No Place for Sovereignty: What's Wrong with Freewill Theism* (Downer's Grove, IL: InterVarsity Press, 1996), 29.
19. Joseph C. Dillow, *The Reign of the Servant Kings: A Study of Eternal Security and the Final Significance of Man* (Haysville, NC: Schoettle Publishing Co., 2nd ed. 1993), 266

20. J. I. Packer, "*Sola Fide*: The Reformed Doctrine of Justification" (http://www.the-highway.com/Justification_Packer.html).
21. Henry C. Sheldon, *History of Christian Doctrine* (New York: Harper and Bros., 2nd ed. 1895), 2:34–35.
22. George L. Curtiss, *Arminianism in History* (New York: Cranston and Curts, 1894), 10.
23. Arminius, *Works*, 1:103.
24. Ibid., 2:81.
25. Ibid., 623.
26. E. H. Broadbent, *The Pilgrim Church* (Port Colborne, ON: Gospel Folio Press, reprint 1999), 255.
27. Samuel Fisk, *Calvinistic Paths Retraced* (Raleigh, NC: Biblical Evangelism Press, 1985), 120.
28. John T. McNeil, *Makers of the Christian Tradition* (San Francisco: Harper and Row, 1964), 221.
29. Arminius, *Works*, 1:329; 2:472–73.
30. Ibid., 1:248.
31. Ibid., 316–17.
32. Ibid., 1:254; 2:497.
33. Earle E. Cairns, *Christianity Through the Centuries: A History of the Christian Church,* revised and enlarged ed. (Grand Rapids, MI: Zondervan, 1981), 325.
34. Albert H. Newman, *A Manual of Church History* (Philadelphia, PA: American Baptist Publication Society, 1933), 2:340.
35. John Owen, *A Display of Arminianism*, "To the right honourable, The Lords and Gentlemen of the Committee for Religion," and "To the Christian Reader" in *The Works of John Owen*, ed. William Goold (The Banner of Truth Trust, 1978) X: 7-8.
36. Ibid., 4
37. McGregor, *No Place*, 28
38. Eusebius Pamphilius of Caesaria, advisor to Constantine, *The Life of Constantine* (n. p., c. A.D. 335), 3.62.
39. Philip Schaff, *History of the Christian Church* (New York: Charles Scribner, 1910; Grand Rapids, MI: Wm B. Eerdmans Publishing Co., reprint 1959), 142.
40. Ibid.
41. William Jones, *The History of the Christian Church* (Church History Research and Archives, 5th ed. 1983), 1:306.
42. David Gay, *Battle for the Church: 1517–1644* (Lowestoft, UK: Brachus, 1997), 44.
43. Zane C. Hodges, "The New Puritanism, Pt. 2: Michael S. Horton: Holy War with Unholy Weapons," *Journal of the Grace Evangelical Society*, Spring 1994, 6:11.
44. Curtiss, *Arminianism.*, 69.
45. Vance, *Other Side*, 151–52.
46. From "The Opinions of the Remonstrants" (presented at Dordrecht, Holland), 1619.
47. A. W. Tozer, "The Sovereignty of God" (Camp Hill, PA: Christian Publications, 1997), Audiotape.
48. Quoted in full in Vance, *Other Side*, 153–54.
49. Quoted in Arminius, *Works*, I: lxiii.
50. Vance, *Other Side*, 158–59.

51. Herman Hanko, "Total Depravity," in Herman Hanko, Homer C. Hoeksema, and Gise J. Van Baren, *The Five Points of Calvinism* (Grandville, MI: Reformed Free Publishing Association, 1976), 10.
52. Arthur C. Custance, *The Sovereignty of Grace* (Phillipsburg, NJ: Presbyterian and Reformed Publishing Co., 1979), 71.
53. Cairns, *Christianity,* 325.
54. Cited in Vance, *Other Side*, 148.
55. Louis Berkhof, *The History of Christian Doctrines* (Grand Rapids, MI: Baker Book House, 1937), 152.
56. Homer Hoeksema, *The Voice of Our Fathers* (Grandville, MI: Reformed Free Publishing Association, 1980), 114.
57. William Cunningham, *The Reformers and the Theology of the Reformation* (Carlisle, PA: Banner of Truth Trust, 1967), 2:381; cited in Vance, *Other Side*, 153.
58. M. Howard Rienstra, "The History and Development of Calvinism in Scotland and England," in Bratt, ed., *The Rise and Development of Calvinism*, 110; cited in Vance, *Other Side*, 159.
59. Vance, *Other Side*.
60. Alfred W. Pollard, ed., *Records of the English Bible* (Oxford: Oxford University Press, 1911), 1.
61. H. Maynard Smith, *Pre-Reformation England* (New York: Russell and Russell, 1963), 289.
62. Paul L. Hughes and James F. Larkin, eds., *Tudor Royal Proclamations* (New Haven, CT: Yale University Press, 1964), 1:374.
63. Vance, *Other Side*, 167.
64. William S. Barker, "The Men and Parties of the Assembly," in John L. Carson and David W. Hall, eds., *To Glorify and Enjoy God: A Commemoration of the 350th Anniversary of the Westminster Assembly*, 52; cited in Vance, *Other Side*, 171.
65. Vance, *Other Side*, 172.
66. John T. McNeil, *The History and Character of Calvinism* (Oxford: Oxford University Press, 1966), 324.
67. Samuel T. Logan, "The Context and Work of the Assembly," in Carson and Hall, *To Glorify*, 36.
68. John R. de Witt, "The Form of Church Government," in Carson and Hall, *To Glorify*, 148.
69. Philip Schaff, *The Creeds of Christendom* (Grand Rapids, MI: Baker Book House, 1990), 1:730.
70. G. T. Bettany, *A Popular History of the Reformation and Modern Protestantism* (London: Ward, Lock and Bowden, Ltd, 1895), 414–20.
71. Philip F. Congdon, "Soteriological Implications of Five-point Calvinism," *Journal of the Grace Evangelical Society*, Autumn 1995, 8:15, 55–68.
72. Westminster Confession of Faith (London: n. p., 1643), VI: i, ii, iv; IX: iii.
73. Canons of Dort (Dordrecht, Holland, 1619), 1:6.
74. Ibid., II:8.
75. Westminster, X:I.
76. Ibid., XVII: i, ii.
77. William Cunningham, *Historical Theology* (Edmonton, AB: Still Waters Revival Books, n. d.), 2:379.

CHAPTER 7

Total Depravity

OF THE TEN WORDS making up the acronym TULIP, four (total, depravity, unconditional, and irresistible) are not even found in the Bible, and two (limited and perseverance) are each found only once. As for the phrases expressed by each letter (Total Depravity, Unconditional Election, Limited Atonement, Irresistible Grace, and Perseverance of the Saints), *none* of them appears anywhere from the beginning of Genesis to the end of Revelation.

We have, therefore, good cause to be at least cautious in approaching these key Calvinist concepts. The burden is upon their promoters to show that these ideas, in spite of their absence from Scripture, are indeed taught there. "Trinity" likewise does not occur, but it is clearly taught.

Calvinism offers a special definition of human depravity: that depravity equals inability—and this special definition necessitates both Unconditional Election and Irresistible Grace. As the Canons of Dort declare, "Therefore all men...without the regenerating grace of the Holy Spirit...are neither able nor willing to return to God...nor to dispose themselves to reformation."[1] That declaration expresses human opinion—it is never stated in the Bible.

Calvinism insists that all men, being totally depraved by nature, are *unable* to repent and believe the gospel, yet holds us accountable for failing to do so. How can it reasonably be said that a person is unwilling to do what he is unable to do? There is no way either to prove or to disprove the statement.

Can we say that a man is *unwilling* to fly like a bird? If he were able, he might very well be willing. Certainly his alleged unwillingness to fly like a bird cannot be blamed as the reason he doesn't do so! Nor can he be held accountable for failing to fly so long as flying is impossible for him. Isn't Calvinism guilty of both absurdity and injustice by declaring man to be incapable of repentance and faith, then condemning him for failing to repent and believe?

Calvinism's Undeniable Irrationality

Such glaring contradictions are innate within Calvinism and have caused divisions even among Calvinists, who cannot all agree among themselves. Consider the controversy in 1945 over the fitness for ordination of Gordon H. Clark. "Cornelius Van Til led the seminary faculty in a *Complaint* against Clark's understanding of the Confession of Faith."[2] Clark was accused of "rationalism" for his unwillingness to declare (as so-called "moderate" Calvinists do) that salvation was sincerely offered by God to those for whom Christ, according to Calvinism, did not die and whom God had from eternity past predestined to eternal torment. Clark considered it to be a direct contradiction that God could seek the salvation of those "He has from eternity determined not to save."

Clark was accused by so-called moderates of being a "hyper-Calvinist"—but such labels are misleading. Both Clark and his "moderate" opponents believed exactly the same—that God had predestined some to heaven and others to hell. Clark was simply being honest in admitting that it could not rationally be said that God "loves" those He could save but doesn't. "Moderate" Calvinism is thus guilty of an undeniable contradiction, yet John MacArthur spends an entire book trying to support this contradiction.[3] As we shall see, the "moderates" hide their irrationality behind the idea that God is "free" to love different people with different kinds of love—forgetting that any kind of genuine love is loving, and that it is not loving to damn those who could be saved.

A similar controversy, which originated among the faculty at Calvin Seminary, "had plagued the Christian Reformed Church during the 1920s...[and in 1924] ended with the exodus of the Calvinists from the Christian Reformed Church under the leadership of Herman Hoeksema, and the formation of a new church, the Protestant Reformed Church."[4] Van Til, in disagreement with the Westminster Confession, argued that Clark was making "logic rule over Scripture...." Van Til insisted that

Scripture contains irreconcilable paradoxes that "have of necessity the appearance of being contradictory."[5]

If that is the case, then Scripture is irrational and cannot be defended reasonably; yet God offers to reason with man (Isaiah 1:18). Peter tells us that we must always be ready to give an answer to everyone who asks a *reason* for our faith (1 Peter 3:15) and Paul "reasoned" with the Jews (Acts 18:4,19).

Attempting to escape the irrationality of blaming the non-elect for failing to do what they can't do, some Calvinists insist that man is able but simply not willing to turn to Christ. This is a minority view that contradicts Total Depravity and it is partially correct. The problem with sinners is indeed unwillingness. For a person to be unwilling, however, he must have a will, and thus by an act of that will could become willing—a fact that Calvinism denies. Furthermore, Calvin and his followers have declared in the clearest language that man is unable to believe the gospel, to turn to Christ, or to seek God or good: "He is free to turn to Christ, but not able."[6] Inability is certainly the major view.

There is not a verse in the Bible, however, that presents Calvinism's radical idea that the sinner is incapable of believing the very gospel that offers him forgiveness and salvation, and yet he is condemned by God for failing to believe. In fact, as we shall see, the Bible declares otherwise. "All men everywhere" (Acts 17:30) are repeatedly called upon to repent and to believe on Christ. One would never derive from Scripture the idea that the unregenerate are unable to believe. Dave Breese, highly respected and brilliant author and expositor of Scripture, declared that it "cannot be shown that 'total depravity' is in fact a scriptural truth."[7]

Yet Talbot and Crampton write, "The Bible stresses the total inability of fallen man to respond to the things of God.... This is what the Calvinist refers to as 'total depravity.'"[8] Palmer calls this doctrine "the most central issue between the Arminian and the Calvinist, what Martin Luther even said was the hinge on which the whole Reformation turned."[9]

Consequently, the Calvinist insists that regeneration must precede faith—and thus it must precede salvation, which is by faith alone: "once he [the sinner] is born again, he can for the first time turn to Jesus...asking Jesus to save him" (emphasis added).[10] What strange and unbiblical doctrine is this, that a sinner must be born again before he can believe the gospel! Is it not through believing the gospel that we are born again (1 Peter 1:23-25)? R. C. Sproul declares, "A cardinal point of Reformed theology is the maxim, 'Regeneration precedes faith.'"[11]

Nowhere in Scripture, however, is there a suggestion that man must be *regenerated before* he can be saved by faith in Christ. Indeed, many scriptures declare the opposite, for example: "...to make thee wise unto salvation through faith which is in Christ Jesus" (2 Timothy 3:15), and "ye are all the children of God by faith in Christ Jesus" (Galatians 3:26). Faith *always* precedes salvation/regeneration. There is not one scripture that states clearly the doctrine that regeneration comes first and then faith follows—*not one.* We will deal with this key doctrine in more depth later.

Spurgeon, though a Calvinist, said, "A man who is regenerated is saved."[12] John MacArthur also equates being saved and regenerated.[13] Calvin correctly declared, "Every man from the commencement of his faith, becomes a Christian...."[14] But if the elect must be regenerated before they have faith, their regeneration still leaves them non-Christians, since a man is saved by faith and thereby becomes a Christian (John 6:47; 11:25; 20:31; Acts 16:31; Romans 1:16; 10:9; 1 Corinthians 1:21; Hebrews 10:39; etc.). What "regeneration" is this that doesn't save? Spurgeon did not accept this part of Calvinism and therefore said it was "ridiculous" to preach Christ to the regenerate.[15] Of course. Contradicting the teaching of "regeneration precedes faith" so popular among Calvinists today, Calvin even titled a chapter, "Regeneration by Faith."[16]

Nevertheless, viewing depravity as inability, which necessitates regeneration before salvation, is the very foundation of most of today's Calvinism. Engelsma acknowledges, "Deny this doctrine and the whole of Calvinism is demolished."[17] To be fair, we must, says Engelsma, "let Calvinism speak for itself."[18] That is why we so extensively quote so many Calvinists.

Inasmuch as Total Depravity requires regeneration *before* faith or salvation, many Calvinists assume it could take place—and probably does—in infancy. Thus Hoeksema reasons that "regeneration can take place in the smallest of infants...in the sphere of the covenant of God, He usually regenerates His elect children from infancy."[19] Do the children of Calvinists then behave in a sanctified way far different from other children? Hardly.

There we have one more declaration that regeneration leaves a person still unsaved, insomuch as salvation is by faith, and infants neither can understand nor believe the gospel, which is a clear requirement for salvation. We ask Calvinists, in all sincereity, where this strange doctrine is stated in the Bible. None of them has ever answered that question.

Depravity Equals Inability?

Most Christians, if asked whether man is by nature totally depraved, would likely respond in the affirmative. However, the Calvinists' view of the obvious sinfulness of mankind goes far beyond the average Christian's ordinary understanding of depravity. As another leading Calvinist states, "Paul's assessment of persons apart from Christ may justly be summed up in the theological categories of 'total depravity' and 'total inability.'"[20]

"Inability"? A person may be unable to walk, or to think properly, or to enter a restricted area. In each case the person is prevented in some way from doing what he otherwise could do. Calvinism, however, does not admit to a normal ability that some are prevented from using. It asserts a universal and unique incapacity: that *no one* can believe the gospel without being sovereignly regenerated by God. Nowhere in the Bible, however, is this proposition clearly stated. Yet this is Calvinism's very foundation, from which the other four points flow.

The Bible repeatedly presents man's sinfulness and warns that rejecting the salvation God has provided in Christ leaves the sinner to suffer eternal punishment under the wrath of God. Never, however, does the Bible suggest that because of Adam's original sin all of his descendants lack the capacity to turn to God through faith in Christ. Much less does Scripture teach that God only gives the "ability" to believe the gospel to a certain select group. Instead, the Bible is filled with invitations to all men to repent and believe on Christ to the saving of their souls—and warnings that if they refuse to do so they will suffer God's wrath eternally. Paul went everywhere, preaching to everyone he encountered throughout the Roman Empire "repentance toward God, and faith toward our Lord Jesus Christ" (Acts 20:21). Apparently, he believed that anyone could respond—not just a certain elect whom God had sovereignly regenerated and then given them faith to believe.

Clearly, *all* are *commanded* to repent and turn to Christ. As Paul declared on Mars' Hill in Athens, God "commandeth all men everywhere to repent" (Acts 17:30). To say that God commands men to do what they cannot do without His grace, then withholds the grace they need and punishes them eternally for failing to obey, is to make a mockery of God's Word, of His mercy and love, and is to libel His character. Not inability but unwillingness is man's problem: "The wicked, through the pride of his countenance, will not seek after God" (Psalm 10:4). Christ rebuked the rabbis, "And ye *will not* come to me, that ye might have life" (John 5:40)

—an unjust accusation to level at those who *could not* come unless God caused them to do so.

It is neither stated in Scripture, nor does it follow reasonably, that anyone, as a result of his depravity, even if his every thought is evil, is thereby unable to believe the glad tidings of the gospel and receive Christ as his Savior. Here, once again, we find Augustine's influence. As noted earlier, it is claimed that Augustine was "perhaps the first after Paul to realize the Total Depravity of man;"[21] indeed, that Augustine invented "the exaggerated doctrine of total human depravity...."[22] One often wonders whether Calvin relied more upon Augustine than upon the Bible.

Turning depravity into inability leads inevitably to points 2 and 4: that God must unconditionally elect those who will be saved; and that He must effect that work through Irresistible Grace. Yet even the claim of inability turns out to be misleading.

What Ability Is Needed to Receive a Gift?

The Bible makes it clear that salvation is the *gift* of God through Jesus Christ, and that it is offered to all mankind: "...by the righteousness of one [Christ] the *free gift* came upon *all men* unto justification of life" (Romans 5:18). No one can purchase, earn, or merit salvation. It must be (and need only be) received as a *free* gift. What ability is required to accept a gift? Only the capacity to choose—something that daily experience proves is normal to every human being, even to the smallest child. How, then, is it possible for any sinner to lack the "ability" to be saved?

Of course, the natural mind is at enmity with God. We are rebellious sinners bent upon taking our own way and blinded by the deceitfulness of our own lusts. But not one of the many scriptures that describe man's depravity state that he is impervious to the convicting power of the Holy Spirit—or *no one* could be saved. Nor does any scripture declare that God convicts and convinces only an elect group. Rather, the Spirit of truth convinces "the world of sin, and of righteousness, and of judgment..." (John 16:8).

Unquestionably, to receive the gift of salvation one must simply believe the gospel. Moreover, the very command, "Go ye into all the world, and preach the gospel to every creature" (Mark 16:15) implies the ability of *every* person to believe the gospel. Indeed, that everyone knows the truth of God's existence, his moral responsibility to God, and his breach of the moral laws, is stated repeatedly in Scripture:

- The heavens declare the glory of God; and the firmament sheweth his handywork.... There is no speech nor language, where their voice is not heard. (Psalm 19:1–3)
- If any man thirst, let him come unto me, and drink. (John 7:37)
- Whosoever will, let him take the water of life freely. (Revelation 22:17)
- For the wrath of God is revealed from heaven against all ungodliness and unrighteousness of men, who hold the truth in unrighteousness; because that which may be known of God is manifest in them; for God hath shewed it unto them. For the invisible things of him from the creation of the world are clearly seen, being understood by the things that are made, even his eternal power and Godhead; so that they are without excuse.... (Romans 1:18–22)
- For when the Gentiles, which have not the law, do by nature the things contained in the law, these, having not the law [i.e., given to the Jews through Moses],...shew the work of the law written in their hearts, their conscience also bearing witness, and their thoughts the mean while accusing or else excusing one another.... (Romans 2:14–15)
- Believe on the Lord Jesus Christ, and thou shalt be saved... (Acts 16:31)

In 1 Corinthians 2:7–16, Paul refers to "the things of the Spirit of God [which] are spiritually discerned...the hidden wisdom [concerning] the things which God hath prepared for them that love him...the deep things of God...which the Holy Ghost teacheth [which] are spiritually discerned." The Calvinist uses this passage to support his idea of "total depravity"—i.e., that only the elect who have been regenerated can understand and believe the gospel. Paul, however, is here speaking of more than the simple gospel; he is referring to the deeper understanding of spiritual truth that comes with maturity in Christ. That fact, if not understood from what we have just quoted, is crystal clear from his next words: "And I, brethren, could not speak unto you as unto spiritual, but as unto carnal, even as unto babes in Christ. I have fed you with milk, and not with meat: for hitherto ye were not able to bear it..." (1 Corinthians 3:1–2).

Nevertheless, even if he were speaking only of the gospel, this passage could not be used to support the teaching of total inability of the natural man to believe. Of course, no one can understand the gospel except by the enlightening of the Holy Spirit. But neither here nor elsewhere does Paul even hint (much less state plainly) that the Holy Spirit only reveals the gospel to an elect group. He declares that the "gospel is hid to them that are lost" because "the god of this world [Satan] hath blinded the minds of them which believe not..." (2 Corinthians 4:3,4)—an effort Satan would not need to expend if all men were totally depraved and thus totally unable to believe the gospel.

Furthermore, Paul clearly states that "the grace of God that bringeth salvation hath appeared to all men" (Titus 2:11). Similarly, Christ (as just noted), declared that the Holy Spirit, "the Spirit of truth," would "reprove the world of sin, and of righteousness, and of judgment" (John 16:8). The New King James translates "reprove" as "convict." John MacArthur explains this as "conviction of the need for the Savior."[23] It is clear from the context that Christ means the entire world of sinners, not that the conviction of the need of a Savior is only for an elect whom He has predestined for eternity in heaven.

Just as no special ability is required on the part of the endangered person to be rescued from drowning or from a burning building, or on the part of the imprisoned criminal who is pardoned to accept his release, so no unusual ability is required of the person whom Christ rescues from eternal condemnation. Thus, Calvinism's very foundation in its special definition of human depravity as inability is as unreasonable as it is unbiblical.

Born Again Before Salvation?

Explaining Calvinism carefully, Palmer reiterates that no man can understand the gospel and that this "lack of understanding is also a part of man's depravity...all minds are blind, unless they are regenerated."[24] The thoroughly Calvinistic London Baptist Confession of 1689 stated, "As a consequence of his fall into a state of sin, man...is not able, by any strength of his own, to turn himself to God, or even to prepare himself to turn to God."[25] On the contrary, man's problem is *not* inability but unwillingness: "ye will not hear...will not believe...(Habakkuk 1:5; Acts 3:23). There are too many scriptures to list, but here are several more: Isaiah 7:9; Zechariah 14:17; Malachi 2:2; Matthew 18:16; Luke 9:5, 19:14, 22:67; John 4:48; Acts 22:18; 2 Timothy 4:3, and others.

James White devotes an entire chapter to "The Inabilities of Man." He recites a long list of man's sins, of his evil, of his depravity, and explains that he is a "*fallen creature*, a slave to sin, spiritually dead, incapable of doing what is pleasing to God." He cites many scriptures concerning man's estrangement from God and the deceitfulness of his heart, that he can no more change his heart than the leopard can change his spots, that his mind is hostile toward God, that no man can come to Christ except the Father draw him, and so forth. White declares, "The Reformed assertion is that man cannot understand *and embrace* the gospel nor respond in *faith and repentance* toward Christ without God first freeing him from sin and giving him spiritual life (regeneration)."[26] Nowhere, however, does he cite a scripture that declares the most wretched sinner's *inability* to believe the gospel or to receive the free gift of eternal life that God offers to all.

There are, of course, many scriptures describing man's evil heart and practices. None, however, states that a man cannot believe the gospel unless he is one of the elect and has been given that faith by a sovereign act of God. Pink declares that "the sinner, of himself, *cannot* repent and believe."[27]

Here the Calvinist comes dangerously close to teaching salvation by works. If there is no *work* I must do to be saved, then how can I lack the *ability* to do it? And surely no one lacks the ability simply to believe!

For all of their insistence upon man's inability to believe the gospel and to receive Christ, however, Calvinists cannot agree among themselves. J. I. Packer contradicts his fellow Calvinists (and what he himself says elsewhere) in declaring that adoption (i.e., regeneration) *follows* faith and justification: "God elected men from eternity in order that in due time they might be justified, upon their believing. Their adoption as God's sons follows upon their justification; it is, indeed, no more than the positive outworking of God's justifying sentence."[28]

Of course, Packer, like other Calvinists, would deny that he is contradicting himself. How? He would argue that "regeneration" (as Calvinism defines it) is not the same as justification, or being adopted as sons and daughters into God's family. But if "regeneration" is not being "born again" as Christ described it to Nicodemus, but leaves the sinner, though regenerated, still unjustified before God, we demand to know where in Scripture this Calvinist "regeneration" is presented. In fact, it is not biblical at all.

As we have seen, defining depravity as inability requires God to sovereignly *regenerate* man, and without any recognition, understanding, or faith on man's part, raise him from being "dead in trespasses and sins" (Ephesians 2:1) to spiritual life. Only then can He give man the faith to believe the gospel. As Dort, quoted above, says, "Without the regenerating grace of the Holy Spirit, they are neither able nor willing to return to God...."[29]

Enabling grace is needed for faith, but not *"regenerating* grace." Where does the Bible say one must be *regenerated* before one can believe the gospel? Not one verse can be cited in which that proposition is stated clearly.

Most non-Calvinists have thought that being "born again," as Christ presented it to Nicodemus in John 3, is the same as being saved. Therefore, they are surprised to learn that Calvinism teaches that one must experience the new birth, which Christ describes in John 3, *before* one can believe the gospel and be saved. As Sproul emphasizes once again, "The Reformed view of predestination teaches that before a person can choose Christ...he must be born again...one does not first believe, then become reborn...."[30]

On the contrary, we are "born again" by believing "the word which by the gospel is preached…" (1 Peter: 1:23–25). In fact, the Bible always presents faith as the condition of salvation.

The Disturbing Consequences

Sadly, the acceptance of this theory leads to a corollary that is even more unbiblical as well as contradictory to the innate sense of compassion that God has placed within even unregenerate man: that God *could* save all mankind but deliberately withholds from multitudes the salvation He gives to the elect. Obviously, what God does for the elect (who likewise were "totally depraved" by nature) He could do for all, if He so desired. That He doesn't would prove that the One who *is love* lacks love for all mankind—which is contrary to *all* Scripture: "Who will have all men to be saved, and to come unto the knowledge of the truth" (1 Timothy 2:4).

If lost sinners suffer from such an inability that they can be saved only by God's sovereign act of regeneration (and all men are not saved), it follows that God limits His mercy and grace to a *select group*. As one of the most fervent Calvinists, Arthur W. Pink, writes to the elect, "Then do you not see that it is due to no lack of power in God...that *other rebels* are not saved too? If God was able to subdue *your* will and win *your* heart, and that *without* interfering with your moral responsibility, then is He not able to do the same for others [i.e., the non-elect]? Assuredly He is."[31]

Here we confront a major problem with Calvinism: its denial of God's infinite love for all. That God, who repeatedly declares His love for all mankind, would choose to save only some and leave all others to suffer eternal damnation would be contrary to His very nature of infinite love and mercy as the Bible presents Him. Yet the very damnation of perhaps billions is said by the Calvinist to have been foreordained from eternity past because it pleases and glorifies God! The Westminster Confession of Faith, paraphrasing Calvin himself, declares that God ordains to eternal punishment multitudes whom He *could* just as well ordain to eternal life and joy in heaven:

> By the decree of God, for the manifestation of his glory, some men and angels are predestinated unto everlasting life; and others foreordained to everlasting death.... Those of mankind that are predestinated unto life, God...hath chosen in Christ unto everlasting glory...to the praise of his glorious grace.... The rest of mankind, God was pleased, according to the unsearchable counsel of his own will...for the glory of his sovereign power over his creatures...to ordain them to dishonor and wrath for their sin, to the praise of his glorious justice.[32]

Even Sproul admits, "If some people are not elected unto salvation then it would seem that God is not at all that loving toward them. Further, it seems that it would have been more loving of God not to have allowed them to be born. That may indeed be the case."[33] God's love, however, is infinite and perfect. It is therefore an oxymoron to suggest that God was ever toward anyone "not all that loving" and might "have been more loving." No Calvinist has ever satisfactorily explained the lack of love with which they charge God. Who could fail to be gravely concerned for this gross misrepresentation of our loving Creator?!

The great Apostle Paul could declare unequivocally, "I am not ashamed of the gospel of Christ!" It almost sounds as though Sproul has some reservations concerning the gospel according to Calvinism. If the gospel is not good news to everyone, but only to the elect, is that cause for us to be ashamed of a God who is less than loving to all? Paul did not have the problem of believing that God was "not all that loving."

By now it should be clear that Calvinism is founded upon the premise that God does not love everyone, is not merciful to all, does not want all to be saved, but in fact is pleased to damn billions whom, by sovereign regeneration, He could have saved had He so desired. If that is the God of the Bible, Calvinism is true. If that is not the God of the Bible, who "is love" (1 John 4:8), Calvinism is false. The central issue is God's love and character in relation to mankind, as presented in Scripture. The very title of this book, *What Love Is This?*, asks of Calvinism a question to which it has no answer.

As we have already pointed out, Spurgeon (whom Calvinists love to quote when he supports Calvinism) found himself in deep conflict.

He urged everyone to come to Christ—yet to do so contradicted his affirmation of Limited Atonement. In effect, Spurgeon was urging men to come to Christ, even though he didn't believe Christ had died for them. Yet conscience and knowledge of God would not allow him to escape the fact that, just as God commands all mankind to "love your neighbor as yourself," so God must genuinely love all mankind.

As we have previously noted, in reference to 1 Timothy 2:4, Spurgeon declared: "As it is *my* wish…[and] *your* wish…so it is God's wish that all men should be saved….. He is no less benevolent than we are."[34] Spurgeon was caught in the web of contradictions woven by Calvinism. How could God, whose sovereignty enables Him to do anything He desires (a cornerstone of Calvinism), fail to save those He "wishes" to be saved?

Which Comes First, Salvation or Faith?

Nowhere, from Genesis to Revelation, does the Bible teach that sinful man, without first being regenerated, is incapable of repenting of his sins, turning to God, and believing the gospel to the saving of his soul. On the contrary, it is all too clear that faith precedes salvation and is in fact a *condition* of salvation. There are scores of verses declaring that we are saved through faith, through believing on the Lord Jesus Christ as He is presented in the gospel. This sequence of events is undeniable:

- He that believeth...shall be saved.... (Mark 16:16)
- Then cometh the devil, and taketh away the word out of their hearts, lest they should believe and be saved.... (Luke 8:12)
- Believe on the Lord Jesus Christ, and thou shalt be saved.... (Acts 16:31)
- I am not ashamed of the gospel of Christ: for it is the power of God unto salvation to every one that believeth.... (Romans 1:16)
- Moreover, brethren, I declare unto you the gospel...by which also ye are saved...unless ye have believed in vain. (1 Corinthians 15:1–2)
- For by grace are ye saved through faith.... (Ephesians 2:8)
- ...them which should hereafter believe on him to life everlasting. (1 Timothy 1:16)

These scriptures are clear. Therefore, in order to support "regeneration before faith," it must be proved that regeneration leaves one still unsaved and thus under God's judgment. But that view is both unbiblical and irrational.

In numerous places, the Bible declares that upon believing in Christ according to the gospel (and *only* by believing), we receive eternal life from God as a free gift: "That whosoever believeth in him should...have everlasting life (John 3:16); He that heareth...and believeth...hath everlasting life...(5:24); That ye might believe that Jesus is the Christ, the Son of God; and that believing ye might have life through his name" (20:31). Believing is obviously a condition for receiving the gift of eternal life. Could one be "regenerated" and remain unsaved and without "life through his name," which is received by faith alone? Not according to the Bible! How, then, could regeneration precede faith?

The Bible clearly teaches that the very moment (and not a moment before) one believes in and receives the Lord Jesus Christ as the Savior who died for one's sins, that person has been born (regenerated of the Spirit of God) into the family of God and has thereby become a child of God. Surely there are not two kinds of life that God freely gives to sinners: one through a special Calvinist "regeneration" and the other at salvation by faith. The eternal life received as a free gift through believing in Christ can only be the same life one receives upon being born again.

Certainly, Christ gives Nicodemus no reason to believe that the life of God received from the Holy Spirit through the new birth differs in any way from the eternal life one receives by faith in Him. How could "regeneration" be something else? The fact that eternal life comes through faith and that eternal life is only by the new birth indicates quite clearly that faith is the requirement for and therefore precedes regeneration. Believing in Christ unto salvation is not the *result* of regeneration but the essential *requirement* for it to take place.

Verse after verse, in the plainest possible language, the Bible puts believing the gospel *before* regeneration. Paul tells his children in the faith, "in Christ Jesus I have begotten you through the gospel" (1 Corinthians 4:15), while Peter declares that we are "born again...by the word of God... the word which by the gospel is preached..." (1 Peter 1:23–25).

Being born again by the Word of God can refer only to regeneration, but the Word of God is effectual only to those who believe. Paul declares under the inspiration of God, "faith cometh by hearing, and hearing by the word of God" (Romans 10:17) and he even calls it "the word of faith which we preach" (verse 8). Of those who are lost, we are told that "the word preached did not profit them, not being mixed with faith" (Hebrews 4:2).

On the basis of abundant testimony from Scripture, we can only conclude that faith in Christ through the gospel precedes regeneration. Therefore, the new birth does not take place by an act of God apart from a person's understanding of and faith in the gospel but as a result thereof. The doctrine that one must be born again (regenerated) before one can believe is simply not biblical.

Even Spurgeon, in spite of his claim of being a staunch Calvinist, could not accept the teaching that regeneration came before faith in Christ through the gospel. Calvinists quote him when he supports them, but they ignore statements such as the following:

> If I am to preach faith in Christ to a man who is regenerated, then the man, being regenerated, is saved already, and it is an unnecessary and ridiculous thing for me to preach Christ to him, and bid him to believe in order to be saved when he is saved already, being regenerate. Am I only to preach faith to those who have it? Absurd, indeed! Is not this waiting till the man is cured and then bringing him the medicine? This is preaching Christ to the righteous and not to sinners.[35]

Who can deny that Spurgeon's argument is both biblical and reasonable? Nor can it be denied that he was at the same time, though unwittingly, denying the very heart of the Calvinism he at other times stoutly affirmed.

Biblical Support for Total Depravity?

To show that the Bible does indeed teach total depravity as inability, the Calvinist cites such scriptures as "And GOD saw that the wickedness of man was great in the earth, and that every imagination of the thoughts of his heart was only evil continually" (Genesis 6:5; 8:21). Other verses offered in alleged proof of this doctrine include Jeremiah 17:9, "The heart is deceitful above all things, and desperately wicked," and Romans 3:10–18, "There is none righteous...none that seeketh after God...none that doeth good...no fear of God before their eyes," and so forth.

Obviously, however, the fact that man's thoughts are only evil continually, that his heart is desperately wicked and deceitful, and that he neither seeks nor fears God, does not say that he is therefore *unable*, unless first of all regenerated by God, to *believe* the gospel even if convicted and convinced thereof by the Holy Spirit. Paul teaches otherwise: "ye were the servants of sin, but ye have obeyed from the heart that form of doctrine which was delivered you" (Romans 6:17). Clearly, servants of sin responded to the command to repent and believe in Christ, and as a result they were regenerated—born of the Spirit of God into the family of God, and thus saved.

Nor does the statement that "none seeks after God" deny that any man, no matter how depraved, can respond by intelligent choice without first being regenerated if God seeks and draws him. Neither does the Bible teach that God only seeks and draws an "elect" but no others. Indeed, many passages affirm that under the drawing of the Holy Spirit sinful man *can* make a moral response: "Draw me, we will run after thee" (Song of Solomon 1:4); "And ye shall seek me, and find me, when ye shall search for me with all your heart" (Jeremiah 29:13); "He [God] is a rewarder of them that diligently seek him" (Hebrews 11:6). Everyone that thirsteth, no matter how wicked, is commanded to turn unto the Lord, with never so much as a hint that this is impossible until God first regenerates them (Isaiah 55:1–7).

Furthermore, the offer of salvation is extended to "all the ends of the earth" (Isaiah 45:22). That this offer is not just for a select elect is clear. The "everyone that thirsteth" reminds one of Christ's cry, "If any man thirst, let him come unto me, and drink" (John 7:37). All those who thirst are offered the same "living water" that Christ offered to the woman at the well (John 4:10). And it is with this same promise to *whosoever will* that the Bible ends: "And whosoever will, let him take of the water of life freely" (Revelation 22:17).

The universality of God's offer of salvation is presented repeatedly throughout the Bible; for example: "preach the gospel to every creature" (Mark 16:15); and "For God so loved the world, that he gave his only begotten Son, that whosoever believeth in him should not perish, but have everlasting life" (John 3:16), etc. Surely, "every creature," "the world," and "whosoever" must include *all,* no matter how badly depraved.

It would take considerable manipulation to maintain that the offer of salvation is extended only to the elect, or even that only the elect could respond, and even then, not until they had been sovereignly regenerated. Paul confirms this desire of God for all nations when he declares to the Greek philosophers on Mars' Hill:

> God that made the world and all things therein...hath made of one blood all nations of men for to dwell on all the face of the earth, and hath determined the times before appointed, and the bounds of their habitation; That they should seek the Lord, if haply they might feel after him, and find him, though he be not far from every one of us: For in him we live, and move, and have our being; as certain also of your own poets have said.... (Acts 17:24–28)

Is it really possible that Paul's "all nations of men" and "every one of us" and "we" referred to an elect of whom the Greeks had never heard? On the contrary, Paul is clearly including his listeners and antagonists on Mars' Hill as among those who have their physical life and being from God and who may seek and find Him. This was what the Greek poets to whom he refers had said (surely these philosophers were not referring to the elect), and Paul is affirming that general understanding and declaring the person of the true God to them, a God who is "not far from every one of us," who commands all men to seek Him, and who may be found by all. There is no suggestion that anyone's depravity and bondage to sin makes it impossible to believe in Christ without first being sovereignly regenerated.

Is There a Bias at Work?

If God intends that all mankind (no matter how depraved) seek Him, and if He must be sought before He is found, then we can only conclude that those who have not yet found God and thus are not yet regenerated are capable of a genuine seeking after God as He draws *all men* unto Him (John 12:32). Calvinism's conclusion (that because of his depravity, man must be regenerated before he can believe or even seek God) is thus contrary to the clear teaching of Scripture—a fact that will be dealt with in more depth in subsequent chapters.

Calvinists often cite John 1:13 as proof that man's alleged inability due to his total depravity requires that he must first be regenerated before he can believe the gospel or receive Christ as his Savior. It speaks of those "Which were born, not of blood, nor of the will of the flesh, nor of the will of man, but of God." Commenting on this verse, Calvin writes, "Hence it follows, first, that faith does not proceed from ourselves, but is the fruit of spiritual regeneration; for the Evangelist affirms that no man can believe, unless he be begotten of God; and therefore faith is a heavenly gift."[36] In fact, Calvin's conclusion doesn't follow at all from this passage. He is reading into the text something not there in order to support his own doctrine. Indeed, he has the context backwards.

The context makes John's meaning quite clear: "He came unto his own, and his own received him not. But as many as received him, to them gave he power [the right or privilege] to become the sons of God, even to them that believe on his name" (verses 11–12). His own people, the Jews, rejected Christ. In contrast to those who did not receive Him, however, all those who did receive Him and believe on His name are, *as a result of receiving Him and believing*, given the right to *become* the sons of God. This new birth (verse 13) by an act of God regenerating them into His family through His Spirit is for those who have received Christ and believed "on his name" (verse 12). We deal with this in more depth in Chapter 21.

Is God Sincere?

If the doctrine of Total Depravity as defined in **TULIP** were true, then from Genesis to Revelation we would have the contradiction of God pleading year after year, century after century, for repentance from a seemingly endless procession of billions of individuals who (being totally depraved) were incapable of repenting and whom He had already predestined to eternal torment from a past eternity. He would be presented in Scripture as pleading with those to repent and turn to Him whom He had created so hopelessly depraved that they could not possibly repent unless He first regenerated them, and from whom He was withholding the very regeneration and grace they needed to turn to Him, and whom He had no intention of saving. Such a scenario turns most of the Bible into a charade and mocks the rational intelligence and conscience with which God has bestowed mankind.

Yet the "moderate" Calvinist claims to affirm, in contrast to the "hyper-Calvinist," that God sincerely offers salvation to all. *Sincerely* offers salvation to those for whom Christ did not die and whom He predestined to eternal torment? This is madness. Yet Calvinists who honestly admit that the God of Calvinism does *not* love all mankind and does *not* genuinely offer salvation to all through the gospel are called "hyper-Calvinists." That label is a ploy by "moderates" to escape the horrible truth!

If because of "total depravity" man lacks the ability to respond without God's sovereign act of regeneration, then all of God's pleas are obviously both useless and senseless. There is no question that if Calvinism were true, there would be no reason for God to urge men to repent—yet He does. God's sovereign act of regeneration is alleged to require no faith or participation of any kind on man's part. Thus, the entire history of God's dealings with man as recorded in the Bible loses credibility.

Calvinism drives us into an irrational dead end. There would be no need for God to plead with the elect, whom He has already predestined to salvation, a salvation which He allegedly effects sovereignly *before* any faith is exercised on their part. Nor does it make any better sense for God to present the gospel to and plead with the non-elect who *cannot* believe it until they have been sovereignly regenerated, but whom He will not regenerate, having already damned them by His eternal decree. Yet He continues to plead and blame them for not repenting, even while He withholds from them the essential grace that He gives only to the elect! And this is only one of Calvinism's gross misrepresentations of God.

Calvin's Inconsistency

In his discussions of Total Depravity, Calvin sometimes seemed confused and unable to articulate his ideas well. He theorized that totally depraved man naturally loves truth, *but not enough*; still, he has great gifts from his Creator, and whatever truth he has comes from God—yet he cannot fully know the truth and thus be saved. One is left to wonder about the exact meaning of this terminology and where it is stated in Scripture. At other times, Calvin further contradicts himself concerning this key doctrine, and in some places even indicates that "total" doesn't *really* mean total. For example, Calvin engaged in the following confusing speculation, which seems to teeter on the brink of Total Depravity, fall over the edge at times, then recover itself:

> The human mind...is naturally influenced by the love of truth [but] this love of truth fails before it reaches the goal [yet] man's efforts are not always so utterly fruitless as not to lead to some result...and intelligence naturally implanted...should lead every individual for himself to recognize it as a special gift of God....
>
> Therefore...the human mind, however much fallen and perverted from its original integrity, is still adorned and invested with admirable gifts from its Creator.
>
> He...by the virtue of the Spirit...has been pleased to assist us...with great talents for the investigation of truth [but] not based on a solid foundation of truth.... The Lord has bestowed on [philosophers] some slight perception of his Godhead, that they might not plead ignorance as an excuse for their impiety, and has,

> at times, instigated them to deliver some truths, the confession of which should be their own condemnation.... Their discernment was not such as to direct them to the truth, far less to enable them to attain it, but resembled that of the bewildered traveler....
>
> An Apostle declares, "When the Gentiles...do by nature the things contained in the law, these...shew the work of the law written in their hearts..." (Romans 2:14–15) [so] we certainly cannot say that they are altogether blind.[37]

Confusion and contradictions reign here. Is man totally depraved or isn't he? And if he is, exactly what does that mean? The belief that the natural man doesn't understand the things of God unless they are revealed to him by God cannot be denied—the Bible says so. That is true of everything we have; it all comes from God:

- He giveth to all life, and breath, and all things...for in him we live, and move, and have our being.... (Acts 17:25, 28)
- Every good gift and every perfect gift is from above, and cometh down from the Father of lights, with whom is no variableness, neither shadow of turning. (James 1:17)

But without biblical warrant, Calvin introduces the idea of degrees: All men by nature receive much truth from God, but in varying degrees. Most of them just don't receive enough—such a quantity and quality of grace is only for the elect. Unregenerate man can see, yet he is blind—but not *totally* blind. What exactly does Calvin mean? We are left to wonder.

Faced with a Choice

Calvinists object to the assertion that the natural man is "not *so* totally depraved that he can't hear God's voice and come to Christ." They respond, "Totally depraved is totally depraved. It makes no sense to say man isn't *so* totally depraved." Not only is Total Depravity not a biblical concept, but as the quote above shows, Calvin *himself* said that man is not *so* totally depraved that he cannot receive much truth from God; he just doesn't get enough truth, because God withholds it. Why? And where does the Bible say *that?* Calvin says God withholds truth in order "to render man inexcusable...." That is like crippling a man in order to render him inexcusable for failing to run fast enough or jump high enough!

Calvin says that truth comes only from the Spirit of truth, so whatever truth man has is received from God. Then if God gives all men some truth, why doesn't He give them enough to know and seek Him? Surely God can give all mankind as much truth as He desires to give. Calvin cannot show us that man naturally has a capacity for *this* much truth but not for *that* much. How was *depravity* redefined as an *incapacity*, which isn't total but is just enough to damn the soul? There is nothing anywhere in Scripture to support such speculation.

When Peter confessed to Jesus, "Thou art the Christ," Jesus told him, "Flesh and blood hath not revealed it unto thee, but my Father which is in heaven" (Matthew 16:15–17). Peter must have been a totally depraved natural man when the Father revealed Christ to him. Surely he hadn't yet been born of the Spirit. Though he acknowledged Jesus as the Christ, he still lacked any understanding about Christ dying for his sins. Could not the Father, therefore, reveal Christ to everyone as He did to Peter? Why not? Clearly, Peter had a revelation from the Father concerning Christ *before* he was regenerated.

For all the importance Calvinism places upon the doctrine of Total Depravity, inasmuch as that is the supposed condition of all mankind and the elect are delivered out of it, being totally depraved is not what keeps men in darkness after all, but God's withholding the needed light. The lost are kept out of heaven not only by their sin (for which there is a remedy) but by God's withholding the grace they need for salvation, because He has already predestined them to eternal torment—a condition impossible to remedy!

Given what the Bible tells us of God's dealings with man and Calvinism's doctrine of man's inability to believe, there are only two choices: either to charge the Infinite God with acting insincerely and in limited love and limited grace, or to admit that Calvinism is in error. In fact, this leads to another conclusion just as devastating to Calvinism, to be considered in the next chapter.

---

1. Canons of Dort (Dordrecht, Holland, 1619), III, IV:3.
2. Garrett P. Johnson, "The Myth of Common Grace," *The Trinity Review*, March/April 1987, 1.
3. John MacArthur, Jr., *The Love of God* (Dallas, TX: Word Publishing, 1996).
4. Johnson, "Myth."
5. Cornelius Van Til, *Common Grace and the Gospel* (Phillipsburg, NJ: Presbyterian and Reformed Publishing Company, 1973), 165–66; cited in Johnson, "Myth".
6. Frank B. Beck, *The Five Points of Calvinism* (Lithgow, Australia: Covenanter Press, 2nd Australian ed., 1986), 9.
7. Dave Breese, "The Five Points of Calvinism" (self-published paper, n. d.).
8. Kenneth G. Talbot and W. Gary Crampton, *Calvinism, Hyper-Calvinism and Arminianism* (Edmonton, AB: Still Waters Revival Books, 1990), 20.
9. Edwin H. Palmer, *the five points of calvinism* (Grand Rapids, MI: Baker Books, enlarged ed., 20th prtg. 1999), 19; citing Martin Luther, *The Bondage of the Will*, trans. J. I. Packer and O. R. Johnston (Grand Rapids, MI: Fleming H. Revell, 1957), 319.
10. Ibid., 19.
11. R. C. Sproul, *Chosen by God* (Carol Stream, IL: Tyndale House Publishers, Inc., 1986), 10.
12. C. H. Spurgeon, "The Warrant of Faith" (Pasadena, TX: Pilgrim Publications, 1978), 3. One-sermon booklet from 63-volume set.
13. John MacArthur, audiotape, "The Love of God, Part 5, Romans 9" (Grace To You, 90–81, 1995).
14. John Calvin, *Institutes of the Christian Religion*, trans. Henry Beveridge (Grand Rapids, MI: Wm. B. Eerdmans Publishing Company, 1998 ed.), II: xvii, 1.
15. Spurgeon, "The Warrant of Faith," 3.
16. Calvin, *Institutes*, III: iii.
17. David J. Engelsma, "The Death of Confessional Calvinism in Scottish Presbyterianism," *The Standard Bearer*, December 1, 1992, 103.
18. David J. Engelsma, *A Defense of Calvinism as the Gospel* (The Evangelism Committee, Protestant Reformed Church, n. d.), 18.
19. Homer Hoeksema, *Reformed Dogmatics* (Grandville, MI: Reformed Free Publishing Association, 1966), 464.
20. Douglas Moo, *The Epistle to the Romans* (Grand Rapids, MI: Wm B. Eerdmans Publishing Co., 1996), 488.
21. Arthur C. Custance, *The Sovereignty of Grace* (Phillipsburg, NJ: Presbyterian and Reformed Publishing Co., 1979), 18.
22. Frederic W. Farrar, *History of Interpretation* (New York: E. P. Dutton and Co., 1886), 24.
23. John MacArthur, *The MacArthur Study Bible* (Dallas, TX: Word Publishing, 1997), 1617.
24. Palmer, *five points*, 16.
25. Quoted in *A Faith to Confess: The Baptist Confession of Faith of 1689, Rewritten in Modern English* (Carey Publications, 1986); cited in James R. White, The Potter's Freedom (Amityville, NY: Calvary Press Publishing, 2000), 78.
26. White, *Potter's*, 101.
27. Arthur W. Pink, *The Sovereignty of God* (Grand Rapids, MI: Baker Book House, 2nd prtg. 1986), 149.

28. J. I. Packer, "*Sola Fide:* The Reformed Doctrine of Justification" (www.the-highway.com/Justification_Packer.html).
29. Dort, Canons, III,IV:3.
30. Sproul, *Chosen*, 72.
31. Pink, *Sovereignty*, 50.
32. Westminster Confession of Faith (London: n. p. 1643), III: iii, v, vii.
33. Sproul, *Chosen*, 32.
34. C. H. Spurgeon, *Metropolitan Tabernacle Pulpit*, vol 26, 49–52.
35. C. H. Spurgeon, "The Warrant of Faith" (Pasadena, TX: Pilgrim Publications, 1978), 3. One-sermon booklet from 63–volume set.
36. John Calvin, *Commentary on the Gospel According to John* (Grand Rapids, MI: Baker Book House, 1984), 43; cited in White, *Potter's*, 182–83.
37. Calvin, *Institutes*, II: ii, 12–22.

CHAPTER

8

The Solemn Issue: God's Character

WHY DOES GOD WASTE His time and effort and the time and effort of His many prophets pleading with those who, according to Calvinism, cannot hear Him and who—even if they could, being totally depraved—would never respond to His appeal by believing and obeying Him? Would it not be the worst kind of hypocrisy for God to express concern for the eternal welfare of those He has predestined to eternal torment? Why create this elaborate fiction of mourning and weeping over multitudes who God knows will not only refuse to repent but who, unless He regenerates them, *cannot* repent because of their total inability to do so?

On the contrary, God must be appealing to human conscience and will—something that Calvinism cannot allow for the non-elect. Pink argues that "to affirm that he [man] is a free agent is *to deny that he is totally depraved.*"[1] But man is a free agent, as we shall see.

Why does the Holy Spirit, through Scripture, repeatedly give the impression that God desires all men to repent and commands them and pleads with them to do so, while at the same time He withholds from all but a select group the essential means of repenting? Why would God weep over and plead with those for whom He couldn't possibly have either love or genuine concern, having already predestined them to eternal damnation? Beck declares, "He [man] is free to turn to Christ but not able."[2] That is like saying that man is free to go to Mars any time he pleases.

Is this a joke? The Calvinist seems unaware of the contradiction in what he is saying. Bryson raises a logical question:

> And since the unregenerate are reprobate [predestined to damnation by God's decree] as a result of a choice made by God alone, how could they be responsible for their lostness...and inevitable damnation?[3]

It would be a mocking taunt for God to promise man that if he would earnestly and sincerely seek Him he would find Him, if in fact it were impossible for man to do so unless God regenerated him. As inspired by the Holy Spirit, however, the entire Bible from Genesis to Revelation gives the clear impression that those with whom God pleads could of their own volition repent and turn to Him if they so desired. Taking Scripture at face value, H. A. Ironside said:

> The gospel preacher can declare without any kind of mental reservation the blessed fact that whosoever will, may take the water of life freely (Revelation 22:17). This is not at all a question of being *allowed* to take Christ as Saviour. It is an earnest entreaty to do so. (Emphasis added)[4]

Choice and Human Responsibility

Frederic Farrar has rightly said that what God commands "must be in the power of the will, since ability is the measurement of obligation."[5] G. Campbell Morgan stated firmly, "We cannot study this Bible without being brought face to face with personal responsibility.... When the voice of God speaks, man's will is free to obey or to disobey."[6] Kenneth Foreman said, "If there is anything the Bible shows it is that God does hold men responsible for their actions. God's 'thou shalt' is spoken to free persons, not to puppets."[7]

Yet Gerstner insists upon the contradiction that is innate in Calvinism: "It is your decision to choose or reject Christ, but it is not of your own free will."[8] How it can be my decision, when I am not free to choose, is meaningful only to Calvinists. To all others such a statement is outrageously irrational and contradictory.

Calvinism clearly requires its own peculiar definition of words. Pink wrote, "Those who speak of man's 'free will,' and insist upon his inherent power to either accept or reject the Saviour, do but voice their ignorance of the real condition of Adam's fallen children."[9] Yet Jesus clearly taught that the unregenerated man can indeed make a willing choice to do God's will and thereby know the truth: "If any man will do [i.e., wills to do] his [God's] will, he shall know of the doctrine, whether it be of God, or whether I speak of myself" (John 7:17). He offered "if any man will" not to a special elect but to the unregenerated multitude and rabbis who would soon crucify Him. Bishop J. C. Ryle, who stood so firmly against Romanism in England in the nineteenth century, commented:

> The English language here fails to give the full force of the Greek. It is literally, "If any man is willing to do—has a mind and desire and inclination to do God's will...." It should never be forgotten that God deals with us as moral beings, and not as beasts or stones.[10]

Through the centuries, a non-Calvinist understanding of Scripture concerning human responsibility and ability has been ably expressed by many Christian leaders. Calvinists, however, are often ambivalent. A prominent Baptist wrote, "The individual not only must act for himself; he is the only one who can. God has made him competent."[11] While seeming to affirm "inability" due to total depravity, at the same time A. H. Strong insisted, "The sinner can...seek God from motives of self-interest...the sinner can...give attention to divine truth."[12] Griffith Thomas wrote, "Total depravity does not mean the absolute loss of...the freedom of the soul in choosing…conscious action. In this sense our freedom is real and the Fall has not affected it.... Fallen man has the faculty of will, as he has other faculties...."[13] In the same vein, W. L. Pettingill argued from Scripture, "Whosoever will may come. He is only to come, and God does all the rest."[14]

What God Is This?

For God to act as Calvinism teaches would be inconsistent with the repeated assurance in His Word that He is merciful and loving toward *all.* The committed Calvinist W. G. T. Shedd wrote, "The charges that have been made...from time immemorial are, that Calvinism represents God as a tyrannical sovereign who is destitute of love and mercy for any but an elect few, that it attributes to man the depravity of devils, deprives him of moral freedom, and subjects him to the arbitrary cruelty of a Being who creates some men in order to damn them."[15] As we are amply documenting, this accusation is true. In fact, Shedd admitted that this charge had been made even by some Calvinists against what they called hyper-Calvinism.[16] As we have already seen, however, and will demonstrate more fully, Calvinists who accuse others of being "hyper" actually believe the same thing, but attempt to cover up that fact with double-talk.

In defending his misrepresentation of God, the Calvinist argues that for God to graciously regenerate all mankind instead of only the elect "would violate His justice, which requires just punishment for sin."[17] On the contrary, if saving and regenerating the elect is no violation of His character or justice, neither would it be a violation for Him to do the same for all mankind. Why must God's infinite mercy be limited to a select group? By this extreme view of sovereignty, Calvinism blames God rather than the sinner for the sinner's rejection of Christ and his eternal doom.

To justify his beliefs, the Calvinist falsely argues that imploring those who cannot respond "is a just and necessary way for God to act if man is to be held accountable as a fallen and sinful creature, regardless of his inability to respond."[18] The very suggestion is offensive to common sense and man's God-given conscience. God does not implore men to do what, by his immutable decree, they cannot do, in order to hold them accountable! Yet Calvin, a lawyer, claimed this was God's justice in action.

After declaring that God only regenerates an elect group, Palmer exults, "What a good God!"[19] Good to Calvinism's elect, but certainly *not* good to those whom He could save but instead damns to eternal suffering. In fact, the God of the Bible is good to all:

- For thou, Lord, art good, and ready to forgive; and plenteous in mercy unto all them that call upon thee. (Psalms 86:5)
- The hand of our God is upon all them for good that seek him.... (Ezra 8:22)
- Jesus of Nazareth...went about doing good, and healing all that were oppressed of the devil; for God was with him. (Acts 10:38) [Were only the elect "oppressed of the devil"?]
- The Lord is good to all: and his tender mercies are over all his works. (Psalms 145:9)

How could it increase the responsibility of those who are incapable of responding to plead with and warn them? Instead, whoever withheld the help that someone needed would be accountable. Yet this immoral, deliberate withholding of salvation is attributed to God under the excuse that it is "God's good pleasure to do so." Would someone who stood by and watched a person drown, whom he could have saved, be exonerated if he explained that it had been his "good pleasure" to do so? Doesn't God have an even higher—yes, a perfect—standard of love and concern? To attribute such callousness to God is to grossly misrepresent and malign Him!

A Question not of Sovereignty but of Character

God, because of our guilt as sinners, certainly has the right to damn us all. However, His justice does not require Him to damn some sinners but not others, the non-elect but not the elect, since all are equally depraved and guilty. Nor is it rational or biblical that God, who is infinite in love and mercy, would allow *anyone* to be damned whom He *could* justly deliver. Many scriptures clearly declare that God sent His Son "to be the Saviour of the world" (John 4:42; 1 John 4:14) and that Christ on the cross paid the penalty for the sins of the whole world so that God "might be just, and the justifier of him which believeth in Jesus" (Romans 3:25–26). Tragically, Calvinism limits Christ's redemption and God's infinite mercy and love.

Amazingly, however, most Calvinists claim to see no contradiction between the God of love presented in Scripture "who will have all men to be saved" (1 Timothy 2:4) and the God who "saves whom he wills of his mere good pleasure"[20] and leaves the rest of mankind without His mercy and grace because "it was his good pleasure to doom [them] to destruction."[21]

In attempting to escape the clear implications of this lamentable doctrine, Calvinists argue that although totally depraved man can do nothing but reject the gospel, God is nevertheless perfectly just in holding him accountable and damning him. Paul explains how God can justly forgive sinners (Romans 3:21–30), but nowhere does Scripture explain how God could justly condemn for sinning those incapable of anything else, whom He predestined to sin and to eternal destruction before they were born.

With no apparent sense of irony, a Calvinist friend who critiqued the first rough draft of the manuscript for this book, claiming I didn't "understand Calvinism," wrote:

> Nor do Calvinists deny that men can respond to the gospel or [teach] that God withholds the ability to respond. They do

> respond...negatively. And this response has nothing to do with God withholding anything.... God does not prevent man from coming to Him. They are free to come to Him if they want to. What God does withhold is His mercy, which He is under no obligation to give since it is man's desire not to know God.[22]

Not a Question of Obligation

Of course, Calvinism's God prevents the non-elect from coming to Him by withholding the grace without which no one can believe. Furthermore, He has predestined them to eternal damnation—nor did He give His Son to die for them, according to the doctrine of Limited Atonement. Could there be any stronger means of preventing the non-elect from being saved through faith in Christ? What this friend apparently means is that God withholds nothing that He is under *obligation* to bestow.

Of course God is under no obligation to extend mercy or grace to *anyone*. By very definition, mercy and grace are completely without obligation. Thus one cannot excuse the Calvinistic God's failure to extend grace and mercy to all by simply saying He is under no obligation to do so. Obligation is not the basis for extending grace and mercy, but rather, love and the desire to meet the sinner's need.

All of God's qualities are infinite and in perfect balance. Among those qualities is mercy: "But thou, O Lord, art a God full of compassion, and gracious, longsuffering, and plenteous in mercy and truth" (Psalms 86:15). All through Scripture, it is made clear that God is infinite in mercy. He requires of us that we "love mercy," and He "delighteth in mercy" (Micah 7:18; 6:8). Paul tells us that God "is rich in mercy" (Ephesians 2:4), and that He has pronounced both Jews and Gentiles "all in unbelief, that he might have mercy upon all" (Romans 11:32).

Do any of these scriptures even hint that God limits His grace and mercy to a select group? Not one scripture says so!

Contrary to Calvinism, the biblical accounts of God's dealings with man demonstrate that God both desires and lovingly, graciously, and mercifully extends a genuine offer of repentance and salvation to all mankind. The plain language of Scripture proclaims that God truly desires to convince, to convict, and to save all who are lost—and that they all have the capacity to turn to Him if they so desire. That conclusion is impressed upon the reader by hundreds of clear statements in the Bible, calling upon men to repent and turn to God. Calvinism, however, denies the plain meaning of these scriptures.

Why Does God Strive?

The Calvinist insists that being spiritually dead in sin means that man can no more hear the gospel or respond to God than if he were physically dead. Yet in the very context of the first exposé of man's wicked heart, which the Calvinist offers as proof of Total Depravity, we hear God saying, "My spirit shall not always strive with man" (Genesis 6:3).

How can there be a real "striving" if man is dead in sin and therefore cannot even hear, much less be persuaded? Why would the Spirit of God *strive* with a *corpse*? And how could God be sincerely striving to convince those to believe for whom Christ did not die, and from whom He withholds the faith to believe? The entire teaching of Calvinism denies *sincerity* on God's part in seemingly offering salvation to those He has no intention of saving.

All through the Bible, we see God striving and pleading with man until, at various times and with various persons, we are told that because of man's continued rebellion God ceased to strive with him: "so [He] gave them up unto their own hearts' lust" (Psalms 81:12); "Wherefore God also gave them up to uncleanness through the lusts of their own hearts" (Romans 1:24).

To "give them up" indicates there was a time when God was genuinely striving to convince and win them and had not given them up. But a change has come in God's actions toward them, a change *not in God's heart or desire*—which are unchangeable—but a change in His *dealings* with those who have so hardened their hearts toward Him that there is no point for Him to further strive with them.

If Calvinism were true, however, there could be no genuine striving at all, no bona fide offer of repentance and faith and redemption, no sincere desire on God's part to see the non-elect saved. Indeed, for the Calvinist, God strives with no one, because the salvation or doom of all is a matter of His having predestined them to one or the other. There would be neither purpose nor need for God to strive or plead with man if the eternal destiny of both elect and non-elect has been fixed from a past eternity by God's decree.

If Calvinism were true, it would be meaningless for God to say that His Spirit will no longer strive with man.

Caught in a Maze of Contradictions

Trying to deny this obvious inconsistency and thereby to distinguish himself from "hyper-Calvinists," John MacArthur, Jr., says, "God's love is for the world in general, the human race, all humanity."[23] As evidence, he says, "…the fact that God promises to forgive…and even pleads with sinners to repent—proves His love toward them."[24] Can MacArthur be serious?! It proves God's love for Him to plead with spiritual corpses who can neither hear nor respond, whom He has not sovereignly chosen to believe in Him,[25] from whom He withholds the grace to believe and for whom Christ did not die?

To show that they are not "hyper-Calvinists," the "moderates" such as MacArthur dare to say that God loves those who "by his eternal and immutable counsel…it was his pleasure to doom to destruction"![26] Attempting to justify this clear contradiction, MacArthur proposes a difference between "God's will of decree (His eternal purpose) [and] God's will of desire. There is a distinction between God's desire and His eternal saving purpose, which must transcend His desires." Where does the Bible say that God's purpose "must transcend His desires"? Such inner conflict between purpose and desire is impossible for God! How could God "desire" all men to be saved, yet not purpose or decree it?

Commenting on "desires all men to be saved" in 1 Timothy 2:4, MacArthur writes, "In His eternal purpose, He chose only the elect out of the world (John 17:6) and passed over the rest, leaving them to the consequences of their sin…."[27] In attempting to escape the stigma of hyper-Calvinism, however, MacArthur entraps himself in the theory that God desires something that He doesn't bring to pass, though He could—a clear contradiction as well as a denial of God's omnipotence and a retreat from a major Calvinist text, "who worketh all things after the counsel of his own will" (Ephesians 1:11).

Is there a distinction between hyper- and moderate Calvinists? If so, Calvin himself, who repeatedly made such statements as "by his eternal providence they were before their birth doomed to eternal destruction,"[28] was "hyper." But the founder of Calvinism can no more be a hyper-Calvinist than the founder of Islam can be an extremist Muslim. As Muhammad defines Islam, so Calvin defines Calvinism—otherwise it should not be called Calvinism.

In fact, as we shall see, the predestination of the non-elect to eternal torment, far from being hyper-Calvinism, is a basic tenet that flows inevitably from its five points. Nor is it rational to claim that God really loves those He never intended to save and for whom Christ did not die.

John Piper attempts to absolve moderates of being "hyper" by claiming (like MacArthur) that God has "two wills" and that it is not "divine schizophrenia" for God to will that all persons be saved (1 Timothy 2:4) and "...to elect [only] those who will actually be saved...."[29] This is double-talk! He goes so far as to say, "Every time the gospel is preached to unbelievers it is a mercy of God that gives this opportunity for salvation."[30] That preaching the gospel gives opportunity for salvation to those for whom Christ did not die, whom God never had any intention of saving and whom He in fact has already predestined to eternity in the Lake of Fire, is the height of contradiction. It is, however, only one of many impossible irrationalities which moderates attempt to maintain in order to distance themselves from those they disparage as hyper-Calvinists!

---

1. Arthur W. Pink, *The Sovereignty of God* (Grand Rapids, MI: Baker Book House, 2nd prtg. 1984), 138.
2. Frank B. Beck, *The Five Points of Calvinism* (Lithgow, Australia: Covenanter Press, 2nd Australian ed., 1986), 10.
3. George L. Bryson, *The Five Points of Calvinism: "Weighed and Found Wanting"* (Costa Mesa, CA: The Word for Today, 1996), 36.
4. H. A. Ironside, *What's the Answer?* (Grand Rapids, MI: Zondervan, 1944), 43–44.
5. Frederic W. Farrar, *A Manual of Christian Doctrine* (The Alliance Press, n. d.), 76.
6. G. Campbell Morgan, *The Westminster Pulpit* (Grand Rapids, MI: Fleming H. Revell, 1954), II:306–307.
7. Kenneth J. Foreman, *God's Will and Ours* (Richmond, VA: Outlook Publishers, 1954), 42.
8. John H. Gerstner, *A Primer on Free Will* (Phillipsburg, NJ: Presbyterian and Reformed Publishing Co., 1982), 10.
9. Pink, *Sovereignty*, foreword to first edition, unnumbered first page.
10. John C. Ryle, *Expository Thoughts on the Gospel of John* (Wm. Hunt and Co., 1883), III:16,22.
11. W. R. White, *Baptist Distinctives* (Sunday School Board, SBC, 1946), 24–25.
12. Augustus H. Strong, *Systematic Theology* (Valley Forge, PA: Judson Press, 1907), 640.
13. W. H. Griffith Thomas, *The Principles of Theology* (London: Longmans, Green and Co., 1930), 165, 180.
14. William L. Pettingill, *Bible Questions Answered* (Just A Word Inc., 3rd ed. 1935), 374.
15. William G. T. Shedd, *Calvinism: Pure and Mixed* (Carlisle, PA: The Banner of Truth Trust, 1999), 15.
16. Ibid.
17. Calvinist friend to Dave Hunt, critical comment in manuscript draft margin. On file.

18. Calvinist reviewer to Dave Hunt, note in manuscript draft margin. On file.
19. Edwin H. Palmer, *the five points of calvinism* (Grand Rapids, MI: Baker Books, enlarged ed. 20th prtg. 1980), 21.
20. John Calvin, *Institutes of the Christian Religion*, trans. Henry Beveridge (Grand Rapids, MI: Wm. B. Eerdmans Publishing Company, 1998 ed.), III: xxi, 1.
21. Ibid., III:xxi,7.
22. Reviewer to Dave Hunt, marginal comment, n. d. On file.
23. John MacArthur, Jr., *The Love of God* (Dallas, TX: Word Publishing, 1997), 86.
24. Ibid., 15.
25. John MacArthur, Jr., *Saved Without a Doubt—MacArthur Study Series* (Colorado Springs, CO: Chariot Victor Publishing, 1992), 58–59.
26. Calvin, *Institutes*, III:xxi, 7.
27. John MacArthur, *The MacArthur Study Bible* (Nashville, TN: Word Publishing, 1997), 1862.
28. Calvin, *Institutes*, III: xxi, 7.
29. John Piper, "Are There Two Wills in God?" in *Still Sovereign: Contemporary Perspectives on Election, Foreknowledge, and Grace*, ed. Thomas R. Schreiner and Bruce A. Ware (Grand Rapids, MI: Baker Books, 2000), 107.
30. John Piper and Pastoral Staff, "TULIP: What We Believe About the Five Points of Calvinism: Position Paper of the Pastoral Staff" (Minneapolis, MN: Desiring God Ministries, 1997), 14.

CHAPTER

9

The Truth About Human Depravity

CALVINISM NOT ONLY presents a feigned pleading and striving by God for repentance from those whom He has already doomed. In addition, it confronts us with the alleged "mystery" of a God of infinite mercy and love who, nevertheless, doesn't manifest love toward everyone and therefore lets multitudes perish whom He could save. In fact, Calvin himself declared that it is to God's glory that He fills hell with those whom He could just as well bring into heaven. This repulsive doctrine, Calvin admits, comes from Augustine:

> There is nothing inconsistent with this when we say, that God, according to the good pleasure of his will...elects those whom he chooses for sons, while he rejects and reprobates others. For fuller satisfaction...see Augustine Epist. 115, et ad Bonif., Lib. ii, cap. 7.... The Lord therefore may show favour to whom he will, because he is merciful; not show it to all, because he is a just judge.[1]

On the contrary, not showing mercy *at all* could accompany justice; but not showing mercy *to* all when all are equally guilty is a perversion of justice. Mercy can only be shown to the *guilty* on a righteous basis; and if not, then justice has been corrupted. This fact poses a serious problem for Calvinism, which John Piper, in his major attempt to justify Calvinism's God, fails to consider in its entire 220 pages.[2] In revealing His glory to Moses as "merciful and gracious, longsuffering and abundant in goodness and truth," God declares that He "will by no means clear the guilty" (Exodus 34:6–7).

When Does "All" Not Include "All?"

Since God is both just and merciful, neither of these qualities can triumph over the other. God can only be merciful justly, not in spite of His justice. Thus God could only forgive sinners because the penalty for sin was fully paid (Romans 3:19–31). And that the penalty was paid for all, making it possible for God to justly and mercifully forgive all, and not just an elect class, is declared repeatedly in Scripture—as the conscience God has given us affirms. Surely all must agree with Spurgeon's statement that we have already quoted: "As it is *my* wish…[and] *your* wish…so it is God's wish that all men should be saved…. He is no less benevolent than we are."[3]

Would God undermine His own sincere desire for all to be saved by predestining multitudes to eternal torment and withholding from them the Irresistible Grace and regeneration without which His desire cannot be fulfilled? Of course not! We can only conclude that God does not prevent His own desire from being fulfilled. His desire is expressed in the gospel, which man can believe or not believe, accept or reject.

The Bible's clear language compels the reader to conclude that God loves all, desires the salvation of all, and genuinely strives to convince wicked men to repent and to accept His offer of salvation. Then why are all not saved? Clearly, men have the capability of responding when drawn by the Holy Spirit and convicted of their guilt and need, but though all are drawn, some willingly repent and believe while others refuse.

The Bible repeatedly presents a God who so loves the whole world that He sent His Son that "the *world* through him might be saved" (John 3:16; 1 John 4:14), who "will have *all men* to be saved" (1 Timothy 2:4) and who "is not willing that *any* should perish" (2 Peter 3:9). The Bible repeatedly presents Christ as the One "who gave himself a ransom for *all*" (1 Timothy 2:6), who is "the Saviour of *all men*, specially of those that believe" (1 Timothy 4:10), and Whose death provided a propitiation "for the sins of the *whole world*" (1 John 2:2). Christ calls unto *all* who are spiritually thirsty, hungry and weary of their sin's heavy load, "come unto me and I will give you rest," living water, the bread of life, eternal life. That invitation has touched the hearts of the thirsty, hungry, weary, and heavy laden for two thousand years. Yet Calvinism attempts to make all such promises apply to only a preordained elect.

Two Conflicting Views

Calvinism presents us with the alleged "mystery" of why God who *is love,* and who is infinite in mercy toward all, lets billions go to hell whom He *could* rescue. The Bible, on the other hand, confronts us with quite another mystery: why anyone who is offered salvation as a free gift of God's grace chooses to reject it.

The answer to the first mystery is said to lie in the secret of God's will. The answer to the second is hidden in the hearts of those who reject God and the salvation He offers. Why would any man reject Christ and thereby consign himself to eternal torment? Ask *him*. The reason is hidden in *his* will, not in God's. Pusey writes:

> There is something wonderfully impressive in the respect shown by the Creator to the freedom of choice which has been bestowed upon the human race. In the Christian scheme of salvation God becomes the suitor striving by extraordinary means to win the affections of men. Christ stands at the door and knocks.... He respects the moral freedom of man, and does not put forth His hand to destroy that high prerogative.[4]

Viewed from the biblical perspective, no one who spends eternity in the Lake of Fire can complain that he is there because God didn't want him in heaven. All of the damned will be tormented by the knowledge that they are not there by God's predestination but by their own irrational and stubborn refusal to receive the salvation God provided and freely offered. And God will be glorified by their eternal punishment, because He did not pervert His justice by unjustly forgiving those who refused salvation on His righteous terms.

The Bible presents a God whose justice, not lack of love, fills a hell with those for whom He provided salvation but who refused to receive it. Of the rich young ruler (Mark 10:17–22) we are clearly told that Christ "beholding him loved him," yet this one who was loved "went away grieved," unable to give up his possessions to follow Christ. From the cross, Christ cried concerning those who crucified and rejected Him, "Father, forgive them..." (Luke 23:34).

In direct contrast, Calvinism presents a God who fills hell with those whom He could save but instead damns because He doesn't love them.

These two different views of God are the major point of separation between Calvinists and biblical non-Calvinists.

Here is the real issue that must be confronted in consideration of TULIP: *Is Calvinism or is it not a misrepresentation of the God of the Bible, who is love?* H. A. Ironside argued:

> Turn to your Bible and read for yourself in the only two chapters in which this word "predestinate" or "predestinated" is found. The first is Romans 8:29–30. The other chapter is Ephesians 1:5,11. You will note that there is no reference in these four verses to either Heaven or Hell, but to Christlikeness eventually. Nowhere are we told in Scripture that God predestinated one man to be saved and another to be lost. Men are to be saved or lost eternally because of their attitude toward the Lord Jesus Christ.[5]

When Is Depravity Not Total?

To maintain their doctrine of Total Depravity, Calvinists must reconcile it with the obvious fact that the most ungodly people are capable of some morally good thoughts and deeds. Nor can that fact be explained away by always attributing the ungodly's good deeds to selfish motives. Some unsaved soldiers have selflessly thrown themselves upon hand grenades to save their buddies' lives—an act of heroic compassion from which many Christians would shrink.

Unquestionably, all human beings are capable of summoning a worldly altruism that can be widely admired. Acknowledging this natural goodness, a Calvinist author writes, "Total Depravity...does not mean that man is as evil as he could be."[6] Yet how much more evil could one be than for *every thought* of one's heart to be *only evil continually*? And how can the so-called totally depraved have good thoughts and do good deeds? Calvinists contradict themselves continually in this regard. For example, just before stating that "it is impossible for him [the non-Christian] to do good...he is not even able to understand the good,"[7] Palmer has acknowledged what seems to be the opposite:

> Albert Schweitzer is an example of one who denied biblical Christianity and yet who put to shame many an orthodox Christian by his love and kindness. For other examples of relative good, consider...the non-Christian who risks his life by dashing before an oncoming truck to rescue a child...a blaspheming pagan who helps a beggar...the Jew who donates his large estate for public recreation....[8]

Another Calvinist writer admits that even the most ungodly persons "are able to love their children…sacrifice their own lives for the sake of family...sometimes even for strangers...are honest...good people who do good deeds."[9] Even some Nazi guards who had spent the day in torturing and killing would come home in the evening and exhibit love and kindness to their wives and children. Multitudes of ungodly people at times exhibit much tenderness and honesty. Of many unsaved businessmen it can be said, "His word is his bond," even that he "sweareth to his own hurt, and changeth not" (Psalm 15:4).

The Bible clearly teaches that the natural, unregenerated man *can* do good, and it offers many examples. We have already quoted from Romans 2 how unsaved Gentiles recognize God's moral laws in their consciences, seek to obey them, have guilt when they don't, and even judge one another by that standard. Yes, it says "there is none that doeth good, no, not one" (Romans 3:12). But Jesus also said, "Ye do good to them which do good to you...sinners also do even the same" (Luke 6:33). We must take Scripture as a whole.

Can a single verse be found in Scripture that clearly declares that man must be regenerated before he can believe the gospel? We are still waiting for Calvinists to point out even one.

The examples both given in Scripture and seen in daily experience force us to conclude that the declaration that "every imagination of the thoughts of his heart was only evil continually" describes the general attitude of the heart, not what it must produce at every moment of every day—the propensity but not the necessity. Similar statements that sound absolute, but are not, are found in *praise* of man. For example, God says of David that he walked before Him with a "perfect heart," and that he was a "man after mine own heart, which shall fulfill all my will" (1Kings 15:3; Acts 13:22, etc.). Yet David displeased God a number of times, even committing adultery and murder. In the same fashion, we must understand the statements about man's wickedness and sin as describing his natural tendency but not his irresistible necessity.

The Emperor's Clothes Again?

Many of the verses Calvinists use to support "T" (such as John 1:13 and Romans 9:16) have nothing to do with the concept of Total Depravity. In such passages we are simply told that by our own will we cannot force ourselves upon God. He is the author of salvation, and it is all by His mercy and grace, not by our effort or will, that we are saved. None of such passages, however, declares that anyone is unable to believe the gospel when it is presented to him with the convincing and convicting power of the Holy Spirit.

Philippians 2:13 is also cited, but this is clearly talking about the Christian working out in his life the salvation he has been given; it has nothing to do with either total depravity or believing the gospel.

Calvinists consider the "T" in TULIP to be of paramount importance. One of their writers argues that "the doctrine of total depravity [is] one of the most important truths that needs to be re-emphasized in our day." He begins his booklet by associating those who reject the Calvinist definition of total depravity with the remarks of professional wrestler Macho Comacho who has no conviction of sin; with those who deny that we are "sinners saved by grace"; with those who try to attract sinners with excitement and avoid dealing with sin; with those who try to build up the sinner's self-esteem; with those who preach "a steady diet of positive inspiration...reminiscent of Norman Vincent Peale and Dale Carnegie," etc.[10] Yet these are all errors against which non-Calvinists write and preach from scripture, just as much as Calvinists do, while rejecting the unbiblical theory of Total Depravity.

The writer being quoted then credits the doctrine of Total Depravity with uniquely 1) causing us to despair of ourselves and to cast ourselves completely upon Christ alone for salvation, 2) humbling our pride, 3) helping us to witness to sinners as a fellow sinner, 4) causing us to fear trusting ourselves and driving us to trust totally in the Lord, 5) causing us to bear up under suffering without complaint, 6) giving us greater love and forgiveness toward those who wrong us, and 7) moving us to greater love and devotion to God for His amazing grace.[11]

One wonders how that author could seriously believe that those of us who reject Calvinism's peculiar definition of Total Depravity are therefore lacking in these supposedly unique benefits, which he credits exclusively to the doctrine of Total Depravity!

When You're Dead, Are You Dead?

Another major argument the Calvinist uses for Total Depravity is that by nature we are all "dead in trespasses and in sins" (Ephesians 2:1; Colossians 2:13). Sproul calls this statement "A predestination passage par excellence."[12] Continuing the fallacious equating of spiritual death to physical death, Gordon H. Clark writes, "A dead man cannot exercise faith in Jesus Christ."[13] Of course, but neither can a dead man reject Christ, nor can he even sin. Nevertheless, James R. White, quoted above, whose book is endorsed by a host of evangelical leaders, continuing this analogy, writes:

> The fallen sons of Adam are dead in sin, incapable of even the first move toward God...filled with the effect of depravity and alienation from God....[14]

Where does the Bible say "incapable of even the first move toward God"? It doesn't! We are just as clearly told that Christians are "dead to sin" (Romans 6:2,7,11, etc.). Does that mean that they are therefore "incapable of the first move toward" sin? Certainly not. Take a human understanding of "dead," mix it together with the young John Calvin's immature understanding of God's Word, tainted by Augustinian philosophy, stir it all up, and out comes the theory of Total Depravity. Such humanistic reasoning leads to absurdities like the following from Palmer:

> The biblical picture, however, is of a man at the bottom of the ocean.... He has been there for a thousand years and the sharks have eaten his heart.... The man is dead and is totally unable to ask any lifeguard to save him. If he is to be saved, then a miracle must occur. He must be brought back to life and to the surface, and then ask the guard to rescue him....
>
> When Christ called to Lazarus to come out of the grave, Lazarus had no life in him so that he could hear, sit up, and emerge.... If he was to be able to hear Jesus calling him and to go to Him, then Jesus would have to make him alive. Jesus did resurrect him and then Lazarus could respond.
>
> These illustrations reveal the most central issue between the Arminian and the Calvinist.... The Arminian has the cart before the horse. Man is dead in sins...unable to ask for help unless God...makes him alive spiritually (Ephesians 2:5). Then, once he is born again, he can for the first time turn to Jesus, expressing sorrow for his sins and asking Jesus to save him.[15]

Such reasoning may be emotionally appealing but it is neither biblical nor rational. Sproul himself admits that "Spiritually dead people are still biologically alive."[16] Even though Pink's brand of Calvinism is too extreme for many Calvinists, he rejects the fallacy of using physical death to explain what it means to be dead in trespasses and sins:

> A corpse in the cemetery is no suitable analogy of the natural man. A corpse in the cemetery is incapable of performing evil! A corpse cannot "despise and reject" Christ (Isaiah 53:3), cannot "resist the Holy Spirit" (Acts 7:51), cannot disobey the gospel (2 Thessalonians 1:8); but the natural man can and does do these things! [17]

When we come to the Calvinist's interpretation of what it means for man to be dead in sin and dead to God, the "T" of **TULIP** begins to overlap with the teaching on Irresistible Grace. Therefore, the remainder of the discussion concerning man's spiritual death, and his alleged inability to respond to the gospel, will be deferred until we reach the "I".

Leopard's Spots, Man's Skin Color–Like Sin?

That such reasoned deductions are the Calvinist's main weapons may explain why their doctrines are so appealing to intellectuals. Yet this is in spite of the fact that so many of Calvinism's arguments are contradictory to both the Bible and logic. White reasons:

> Just as a person cannot change the color of their [*sic*] skin, or the leopard its spots, so the one who practices evil cannot break the bondage of sin and start doing good.... The New Testament continues the testimony of the radical depravity of man...Paul begins with a dreadfully long discussion of the universal sinfulness of man...Jew and Gentile alike.[18]

That no sinner can "break the bondage of sin" cannot be disputed. But it is a quantum leap beyond that fact to declare that the prisoner of sin cannot with great joy receive the deliverance Christ freely gives. What prisoner would not welcome freedom? Ah, but to be truly free one must be convicted of sin and believe the gospel. Granted. And where does it say in Scripture that the Holy Spirit neglects to bring that conviction and understanding to *anyone*? He does that for the elect—why not for all? In fact, He does.

That one cannot change the color of his skin does not mean that one cannot gladly receive the cleansing of sin through Christ's blood. Such analogies do not fit the actual situation any more than does the equating of physical and spiritual death. Instead of allegorical examples, we need clear teaching from God's Word. Scripture, however, does not support Calvinism.

The natural man is indeed enslaved by sin and would not of his own initiative seek after God. But incapable of being convicted of his sin and the judgment to come, or of believing the good news of the gospel? Not a single verse in Scripture clearly states that proposition.

"Thy Faith Hath Saved Thee"

Calvinists are concerned that if man could do anything toward his salvation, that fact would rob God of some of the credit for saving him. Confusion arises through failing to recognize the obvious distinction between man's inability to do anything for his salvation (which is biblical) and an alleged inability to believe the gospel (which is not biblical). To believe the gospel and to receive Christ requires no work or worth on man's part, contributes nothing to his salvation, gives no credit to man, and detracts in no way from God's glory.

Failing to make this distinction, Hanko earnestly states that "the truth of total depravity [i.e., inability to believe the gospel] is the only truth which preserves intact the glory of God."[19] In the same way, Ross writes, "The teaching of the natural man's total inability concerning salvation is not only scriptural, but it is a doctrine that gives all the glory to God in the salvation of sinners."[20] Storms argues, "By making election conditional upon something that man does, even if what he does is simply to repent and believe the gospel, God's grace is seriously compromised."[21]

On the contrary, it is clearly not true that believing in and receiving Christ gives any credit to man or detracts at all from the fact that it is Christ alone who procures our redemption. Faith is not a work, nor does any credit accrue to the person who simply believes.

The phrase "thy faith" is found eleven times in Scripture, while "your faith" is found twenty-four times. Individuals are given credit that the faith is their own. Never is there any indication that the person was regenerated and then given faith to believe—or that the faith was a gift from God as Calvinism insists it must be. Nor is there the least suggestion that the exercise of faith by any of these individuals has detracted at all from God's glory.

Christ said "*thy faith* hath made thee whole" to the woman who was healed by touching the hem of His garment (Matthew 9:22; Mark 5:34; Luke 8:48), to the blind man outside Jericho (Mark 10:52), and to the Samaritan healed of leprosy (Luke 17:19). Christ said, "*Thy faith* hath saved thee," to the sinful woman who washed His feet with her tears (Luke 7:50) and to the blind man outside Jericho (Luke 18:42). "Great *is thy faith,*" He said to the Canaanite woman who desired just a "crumb" of blessing (Matthew 15:28). And to Peter, before he was converted, He said, "I have prayed for thee, that *thy faith* fail not" (Luke 22:32). Each of these statements is made to the unregenerate.

For Christians as well, one's faith is still said to be that of the individual: James says, "shew me *thy faith*" (James 2:18). Peter writes, "that the trial of *your faith*, being much more precious than gold that perisheth..." (1Peter 1:7). Otherwise, what would be the point of rewards?

One cannot escape the countless times in the Bible when both unsaved (for their salvation) and saved (for their walk with Christ and fruitfulness) are commanded to believe in God, in His promises, in Christ, and in His Word. Man has no relationship with God apart from faith. If faith exercised by man detracts from God's glory, it would be impossible for man to have any relationship with God without lessening His glory. Obviously, that is not the case.

Simple Confusion Over Inability

Yes, man is totally unable to contribute one iota to his salvation. It does not follow, however, that he therefore cannot by faith receive the salvation freely offered in Christ. It is confusion at this point that creates the doctrine of Total Depravity and leads to the remainder of the Five Points.

Spurgeon labored under no such delusion. Calvinists eagerly cite Spurgeon for support, and there is no doubt that Spurgeon often declared himself to be a Calvinist. Yet he frequently made statements that contradicted Calvinism. The following is from a British scholar who thoroughly knew Spurgeon's writings and sermons:

> Charles Haddon Spurgeon always claimed to be a Calvinist.... His mind was soaked in the writings of the Puritan divines; but his intense zeal for the conversion of souls led him to step outside the bounds of the creed he had inherited. His sermon on "Compel them to come in" was criticized as Arminian and unsound. To his critics he replied: "My Master set His seal on that message. I never preached a sermon by which so many souls were won to God.... If it be thought an evil thing to bid the sinner lay hold of eternal life, I will yet be more evil in this respect and herein imitate my Lord and His apostles."
>
> More than once Spurgeon prayed, "Lord, hasten to bring

> in all Thine elect, and then elect some more." He seems to have used that phrase often in conversation, and on his lips it was no mere badinage. With its definite rejection of a limited atonement, it would have horrified John Calvin.... The truth seems to be that the old Calvinistic phrases were often on Spurgeon's lips but the genuine Calvinistic meaning had gone out of them.
>
> J. C. Carlile admits that "illogical as it may seem, Spurgeon's Calvinism was of such a character that while he proclaimed the majesty of God *he did not hesitate to ascribe freedom of will to man and to insist that any man might find in Jesus Christ deliverance from the power of sin* (emphasis added)."[22]

Scripture repeatedly states that man is dead in sin and in bondage to sin, that his heart is desperately wicked, that his thoughts are evil from his youth, and that he is a rebel against God by nature and practice. There is no statement, however, that he is totally depraved as defined by the "T" in TULIP. No matter how horrifyingly the Bible presents the evil of the human heart, never does it teach Calvinism's peculiar Total Depravity. That will be seen more clearly as we move on to the other four points of Calvinism and contrast them with Scripture.

---

1. John Calvin, *Institutes of the Christian Religion*, trans. Henry Beveridge (Grand Rapids, MI: Wm. B. Eerdmans Publishing Company, 1998 ed.), III:xxiii, 10–11.
2. John Piper, *The Justification of God: An Exegetical and Theological Study of Romans* 9:1–23 (Grand Rapids, MI: Baker Books, 2000).
3. C. H. Spurgeon, *Metropolitan Tabernacle Pulpet*, vol 26, 49-52.
4. Edward B. Pusey, *What Is Of Faith As To Everlasting Punishment?* (England: James Parker and Co., 1881), 103–104.
5. H. A. Ironside, *Full Assurance* (Chicago, IL: Moody Press, 1937), 93–94.
6. James R. White, *The Potter's Freedom* (Amityville, NY: Calvary Press Publishing, 2000), 39.
7. Edwin H. Palmer, *the five points of calvinism* (Grand Rapids, MI: Baker Books, enlarged ed. 20th prtg. 1980), 15.
8. Ibid., 11.
9. Steven J. Cole, *Total Depravity* (Flagstaff AZ, 1999), 3.
10. Ibid., 1–3.
11. Ibid., 9–13.
12. R. C. Sproul, *Chosen by God* (Carol Stream, IL: Tyndale House Publishers Inc., 1986), 113.
13. Gordon H. Clark, *The Biblical Doctrine of Man* (Jefferson, MD: The Trinity Foundation, 1984), 102.
14. White, *Potter's*, 75.

15. Palmer, *five points*, 18–19.

16. Sproul, *Chosen*, 120.

17. Arthur W. Pink, *Studies in the Scriptures* (n. p., 1927), 250–61; cited in Samuel Fisk, *Election and Predestination* (England: Penfold Book and Bible House, 1997), 155.

18. White, *Potter's*, 80–81.

19. Herman Hanko, in Herman Hanko, Homer C. Hoeksema, and Gise J. Van Baren, *The Five Points of Calvinism* (Grandville, MI: Reformed Free Publishing Association, 1976), 23.

20. Tom Ross, *Abandoned Truth: The Doctrines of Grace* (Providence Baptist Church, 1991), 45.

21. C. Samuel Storms, *Chosen for Life* (Grand Rapids, MI: Baker Book House, 1987), 55.

22. A. C. Underwood, *A History of the English Baptists* (The Baptist Union of Great Britain and Ireland, 1947), 203–206; cited in Fisk, *Election and Predestination* (England: Penfold Book and Bible House, 1997), 69–70.

CHAPTER

10

A Distorted Sovereignty

HAVING SEEN that Total Depravity is a key doctrine of Calvinism, we need to understand that behind this belief is something even more fundamental: a grave misunderstanding concerning the sovereignty of God. Singer boasts, "The secret grandeur of Calvin's theology lies in his grasp of the biblical teaching of the sovereignty of God."[1]

In fact, Calvin did not grasp the biblical teaching, but distorted it. Calvinism places such an exaggerated emphasis on sovereignty that it does away with any real choice for man: "No person since Adam has ever had a free will.... Every unsaved person is...free to go in only one direction...free to go down."[2] One can, however, argue biblically, "Unless a man is free to will there is no basis for believing that truth [exists] in any field—science, theology, or philosophy.... Unless there is free will there is no meaning to praise or blame [and] there is no sin."[3]

The apparent tension between God's sovereignty and man's free will has been a point of study and discussion—and, sadly, of contention—among sincere Christians for centuries. Some have taken the approach of C. I. Scofield, that these are two truths that must both be accepted but that cannot be reconciled. "Both are wholly true, but the connecting and reconciling truth has not been revealed."[4] In apparent agreement, James M. Gray, a past president of Moody Bible Institute, suggested that "no one finite mind could hold God's...sovereignty and man's free agency... both equally at the same time. How necessary, however, that both be duly emphasized!"[5]

Likewise, William L. Pettingill wrote, "God insists upon His sovereignty and also upon man's responsibility. Believe both and preach both, leaving the task of 'harmonizing' with Him."[6] In a similar vein, A. T. Pierson, although a leading Presbyterian, declared that both "the sovereign will of God and the freedom of man" are taught in Scripture and that "if we cannot reconcile these two, it is because the subject is so infinitely lifted up above us. Man is free.... Thus the last great invitation in God's Book is an appeal to the *will*."[7] R. A. Torrey agreed that we should not "try to explain away the clear teaching of the Word of God as to the sovereignty of God [and] the freedom of the human will...."[8]

Unfortunately, neither Calvin nor many of his followers today have been willing to accept both sides of this biblical teaching. The result has been devastating in its consequences for the gospel: that man can only reject Christ; he cannot accept and believe in Him unless he is sovereignly regenerated by God. Calvinism refuses to accept what so many great evangelists have recognized is vital. Edgar Mullins expresses very well the essential balance that is missing:

> Free will in man is as fundamental a truth as any other in the gospel and must never be canceled in our doctrinal statements. Man would not be man without it and God never robs us of our true moral manhood in saving us.... The decree of salvation must be looked at as a whole to understand it. Some have looked at God's choice alone and ignored the means and the necessary choice on man's part.[9]

A Commendable but Mistaken Zeal

Talbot and Crampton assure us that "The sovereignty of God is...the most basic principle of Calvinism...the foundation upon which all [including Christianity itself] is built."[10] Boettner agrees: "The basic principle of Calvinism is the sovereignty of God."[11] Such fervor for God's sovereignty is commendable. However, Calvinists have mistakenly made God the effective *cause* of every event that occurs: "Whatever is done in time is according to his [God's] decree in eternity."[12] But would a Holy God decree the evil that fills man's heart and the world today? Surely not!

Calvinism denies to man any real choice concerning *anything* he thinks or does. Spurgeon referred to "a class of strong-minded hard-headed men who magnify sovereignty at the expense of [human] responsibility."[13]

The Calvinist mistakenly believes that if man could make a genuine choice, even in his rebellion against God, it would be a denial that God is sovereign. Thus God must be the cause of all sin, beginning with Adam and Eve. Boettner argues, "Even the fall of Adam, and through him the fall of the race, was not by chance or accident, but was so ordained in the secret counsels of God."[14] That unhappy conclusion is necessitated by a concept of sovereignty that is required neither by the Bible nor by logic.

We have noted the admission by some Calvinists that man is free to respond to God. At the same time, however, the doctrine of Total Depravity requires that he can respond only negatively and in opposition to God. Of course, that is not freedom at all. Congdon points out:

> Classical Calvinists may talk about man having a "free will," but it is a very limited freedom! That is, a person may choose to reject Christ—all people do—but only those who have been elected may choose to accept Him. This is no "free will"! Are the open invitations to trust Christ in the Bible actually a cruel hoax? I don't think so. Are all people free to put their trust in the Lord Jesus Christ as personal Savior for their sin? Yes. That is why the call to missions is so urgent.[15]

Freedom to Rebel but Not to Repent?

How can there be any real freedom of choice if only one kind of choice can be made, and one, at that, which has been decreed eternally? To call this "free choice" is a fraud. It is, however, the only "freedom" Calvinism can allow. Pink favorably quotes J. Denham Smith, whom he honors as a "deeply taught servant of God":

> I believe in free will; but then it is a will only free to act according to nature.... The sinner in his sinful nature could never have a will according to God. For this he must be born again.[16]

Nowhere does the Bible support such a statement; and this is one of Calvinism's most grievous errors. Were Abraham and Moses "born again," i.e., regenerated? Isn't that a New Testament term? What does Smith mean by "a will according to God"? Even Christians don't always do God's will. A desire to know God? Surely all men are expected to seek the Lord while He may be found. That God promises to be found by those who seek Him must imply that the unregenerate can seek Him.

Nor does it help the Calvinist to say that man can only will and act according to his sinful nature and against God. How could it be God's will that man defy His law? If sinful acts are admitted to come from genuine choice, then we have the same challenge to God's sovereignty that the Calvinist cannot allow. Either man has a free will, or his sin is all according to God's will. As we have seen, the latter is exactly what Calvin himself taught and many Calvinists still believe, making God the author of evil.

Could it be that Adam's nature was actually sinful, though God pronounced him "good" when He created him? How else, except by free will, can his sin be explained? The Calvinist escapes free will by declaring that even the sin of Adam and Eve was foreordained and decreed by God. Pink argues, "God foreordains everything which comes to pass. His sovereign rule extends throughout the entire Universe and is over every creature.... God initiates all things, regulates all things...."[17] Then why did Christ tell us to pray, "Thy will be done on earth..." if all is already according to God's will and decree?

It is fallacious to imagine that for God to be in control of His universe He must foreordain and initiate everything. In fact, it would deny His omniscience and omnipotence to suggest that God cannot foreknow and control what He doesn't foreordain, decree, and cause. Here again, Calvinists are trapped in contradictions. Though he was a leading Presbyterian theologian, A. A. Hodge recognized the severe consequences of that extremist view of God's sovereignty: "Everything is gone if free-will is gone; the moral system is gone if free-will is gone...."[18] At the same time, however, he declared: "Foreordination is an act of the...benevolent will of God from all eternity determining...all events...that come to pass."[19]

Confronting a Vital Distinction

For the Calvinist to uphold his extreme view of control, God must be the cause of man's total depravity and the negative response it produces. There is no way to escape this conclusion. If God were not the cause of man's sin, man would be acting independently of God, and that cannot be allowed for *anything* in the Calvinist scheme. It follows, then, that "He [God] could...have prevented it [the fall and entrance of sin into the world], but He did not prevent it: ergo, He willed it."[20] Thus one must conclude, "It is even biblical to say that God has foreordained sin."[21]

The only way, however, to defend God's integrity, love, and compassion in a world filled with sin and suffering is to acknowledge that He has granted to man the power to choose for himself. It is thus man's fault and by his own free choice that sin and suffering are the common experience of all mankind. God has provided full forgiveness of sins on a righteous basis, and will eventually create a new universe into which sin can never enter—a universe to be inhabited by all those who have received the Lord Jesus Christ as Savior. God is exonerated and man alone is to blame for sin and suffering. Such is the teaching of the Bible, as we shall see in depth.

Calvinism rests upon a mistaken view of what it means for God to be sovereign. Palmer tells us that God predestines untold multitudes to everlasting torment "for the glory of His sovereign power over His creatures...."[22] Obviously, God could show His sovereign power over His creatures in many ways other than by decreeing their eternal damnation, a fate surely not required by sovereignty.

The Bible teaches that God sovereignly—without diminishing His sovereignty—gave man the power to rebel against Him. Thus, sin is man's responsibility alone, by his free choice, not by God's decree. Calvinism's basic error is a failure to see that God could sovereignly give to man the power of genuine choice and still remain in control of the universe. To acknowledge both sovereignty and free will would destroy the very foundations of the entire Calvinist system.

This false view of God's sovereignty is the Calvinists' only justification for God's saving only a select group and damning the rest. If one asks how a loving God could damn millions or perhaps billions whom He could have saved, the answer is that it "pleased Him so to do." If one persists and asks *why* it pleased Him, the response is that the reason is hidden "in the mystery of His will."

Free will does not diminish God's control over His universe. Being omnipotent and omniscient, God can so arrange circumstances as to keep man's rebellion from frustrating His purposes. In fact, God can use man's free will to help fulfill His own plans, and He is thereby even more glorified than if He decreed everything man does.

Hear it from Calvin and Calvinists

In his classic, *the five points of calvinism*, Edwin H. Palmer writes, "Although sin and unbelief are contrary to what God commands (His perceptive will), God has included them in His sovereign decree (ordained them, caused them to certainly come to pass).... How is it that a holy God, who hates sin, not only passively permits sin but also certainly and efficaciously decrees that sin shall be? Our infinite God presents us with some astounding truths...."[23]

"Astounding" is the wrong adjective. What Palmer admits astounds even him, a man who dogmatically defends this doctrine, is *appalling* to non-Calvinists, including even non-Christians. Palmer expounds further upon this outrageous doctrine:

> All things that happen in all the world at any time and in all history—whether with inorganic matter, vegetation, animals, man, or angels (both the good and evil ones)—come to pass because God ordained them. Even sin—the fall of the devil from heaven, the fall of Adam, and every evil thought, word, and deed in all of history, including the worst sin of all, Judas' betrayal of Christ—is included in the eternal decree of our holy God.
>
> [If] sin is outside the decree of God, then the vast percentage of human actions...are removed from God's plan. God's power is reduced to the forces of nature.... Sin is not only foreknown by God, it is also foreordained by God. In fact, because God foreordained it, He foreknew it. Calvin is very clear on this point: "Man wills with an evil will what God wills with a good will...."[24]

There is neither biblical nor rational support for such dogma. Surely God in His infinite power and foreknowledge could fit into His plan even the most rebellious thoughts and deeds of mankind. He is perfectly able to frustrate, prevent, or use man's plans and deeds to fulfill His will, and He can do so without destroying man's ability to exercise free choice. To make God the author of sin is to blasphemously misrepresent Him.

Why would an infinitely holy God ruin his own creation by purposely creating sin? Why invent the elaborate story of "casting fallen angels out of heaven"? Why cause mankind to sin in order to "forgive" them? How would that glorify God? Instead, in Calvinism God becomes like the person who sets a forest fire so he can "discover" it, put it out, and be a hero. It also turns God into a fraud who pretends that Satan, though God's own intentional creation, was His enemy. How absurd!

Limiting God

Furthermore, why would God need to foreordain something in order to foreknow it? Obviously, if God can only know what He himself has decreed, and would be taken by surprise if man had free choice, then His knowledge would not be infinite (i.e., God would not be omniscient).

Yet Calvinists persist in this unbiblical and irrational doctrine, which they imagine defends God's sovereignty, but actually diminishes it: "If God did not foreordain all things, then He could not know the future. God foreknows and knows all things because He decreed all things to be."[25] On the contrary, God does not have to decree human thoughts and actions to foreknow them. He knows all beforehand because He is omniscient.

The contemporary Calvinists we are quoting are expressing the very heart of Calvinism. They are being true to John Calvin, who in turn reminds us that the same was taught by Augustine. The latter has been described as the first of the early so-called Church Fathers who "taught the absolute sovereignty of God."[26]

In his *Institutes,* Calvin acknowledged his debt to Augustine concerning God's predetermination of mankind's every thought, word, and deed, good or bad, including all evil committed:

> [W]e hold that God is the disposer and ruler of all things—that from the remotest eternity, according to his own wisdom, he decreed...that, by his providence, not heaven and earth and inanimate creatures only, but also the counsels and wills of men are so governed as to move exactly in the course which he has destined....
>
> In short, Augustine everywhere teaches...that there cannot be a greater absurdity than to hold that anything is done without the ordination of God; because it would happen at random. For which reason, he also excludes the contingency which depends on human will, maintaining a little further on, in clearer terms, that no cause must be sought for but the will of God.... I say, then, that...the order, method, end, and necessity of events, are...produced by the will of God....[27]

An Irrational Position

Augustine did say that all wills are subject to the will of God, but he did not go as far as Calvin carries him. Moreover, Calvin leaps further into a number of fallacies that have been perpetuated to this day. Obviously, contrary to Calvin, actions by the free will of humans do not happen at random. If they did, our entire judicial system would break down, since rape, murder, robbery, and all other crimes would have to be viewed as random events beyond their perpetrators' moral responsibility or control. This is, of course, nonsense.

Ironically, Pink attempts to avoid the intolerable consequences of Calvin's strong statements by also appealing to Augustine: "Let it be emphatically said that God does not *produce* the sinful dispositions of any of His creatures, though He does *restrain* and *direct* them to the accomplishing of His own purposes. Hence He is neither the Author nor the Approver of sin. This distinction was expressed thus by Augustine: 'that men's sin proceeds from themselves; that in sinning they perform this or that action, is from the power of God who divideth the darkness according to His pleasure.'"[28]

Yet Calvin himself is already on record, and echoed by many of his followers today, that God is the *cause* and thus the author of every thought, word, and deed. Pink, like Palmer, has often said the same! Without that conclusion, though it is repugnant to man's God-given conscience, Calvinism's sovereignty won't hold up, nor will its five points.

Is This the God of the Bible?

The human conscience and sense of right and wrong—which man has received from God himself—cry out in revulsion against such teaching. Have not Calvin and Augustine misrepresented the loving, merciful God of the Bible? Did God create us to be mere puppets, with Him pulling the strings? Is our innate sense of making genuine choices of our own volition, sometimes rationally and at other times impulsively or even out of lust, a total delusion?

God appeals to human reason: "Come now and let us reason together, saith the Lord" (Isaiah 1:18). No one can engage in reason without making choices between differing opinions, theories, options, or possible courses of action. Thus, without the power of choice, man is not a rational being. And surely, without the power to make genuine choices man could not be a morally responsible being, accountable to his Creator.

All through the Bible, man is called upon to choose between time and eternity, between Satan and God, between evil and good, between self and Christ. Jonathan Edwards affirmed that "an act of the will is the same as an act of choosing or choice."[29] Nor is there any reason biblically, scientifically, or logically why man—who makes choices of all kinds daily—could not also, without first being regenerated, choose between good and evil, God and Satan, and genuinely open his heart to Christ.

Palmer calls it a paradox that "although man is totally depraved and unable to believe, and that although faith is a gift of God produced by the irresistible work of the Holy Spirit, nevertheless, it is up to man to believe. He has the duty to obey God's command to believe."[30] This is no paradox; it is an absurdity. No one can justly be held accountable for failing to do what it is impossible for him to do.

Could it be true that we really have no choice, but that God causes us to do whatever we do, having predestined our every thought, word, and deed? That certainly is not a perception held in ordinary experience, as Augustine himself argued. Yet, though so contrary to common sense, the Calvinist is forced to accept this view in order to support his system.

Augustine, as will be shown in the next chapter, believed in man's free will, while Luther taught that man's will is in bondage to sin. Calvin says that the sin to which we are in bondage was decreed by God, and thus there is no escape except by God's sovereign act. If such is the case, then it is God who holds man in sin's bondage!

Nowhere does the Bible state that God's sovereignty requires that man has no power to make a genuine choice, moral or otherwise. Obviously, if God's sovereignty makes man totally incapable of any moral choice, then God must sovereignly cause him to believe the gospel. Thus, the five points of Calvinism actually flow from this erroneous view of sovereignty.

A Merciless Sovereignty

Calvin's God plays into the hands of atheists who justly charge that an all-powerful "God" who causes men to sin and then condemns them for doing so is a monster. Will Durant was not a Christian, but one must take his complaint about Calvin seriously: "...we will agree that even error lives because it serves some vital need. But we shall always find it hard to love the man who darkened the human soul with the most absurd and blasphemous conception of God in all the long and honored history of nonsense."[31]

Following Calvin's lead, and with no apparent realization of the blasphemy he expresses against the God who *is love*, Palmer writes:

> The Bible has well over a hundred examples in which God brought sin to pass.... This is the awesome biblical asymmetry: God ordains sin, and man is to blame. We cannot comprehend this. If all things are ordained by God—including sin and unbelief—then God has ordained who will be unbelievers.... It is essential to establish the biblical data on the foreordination of sin.[32]

This is not "awesome" but repugnant to conscience and a libel upon God's character—nor is it biblical. Palmer quotes "scores of texts that [allegedly] indicate sin is foreordained by God."[33] In fact, none of the biblical passages he cites supports that horrifying thesis.

James Orr, editor of the original *International Standard Bible Encyclopedia*, called this doctrine "one which no plea of logical consistency will ever get the human mind to accept and which is bound to provoke revolt against the whole system with which it is associated."[34] King James, who had sent a delegation to the Synod of Dort, referred to "that infamous decree of the late Synod, and the decision of that detestable formulary, by which the far greater part of the human race are condemned to hell for no other reason, *than the mere will of God, without any regard to sin,* the necessity of sinning, as well as that of being damned, being fastened on them by that great nail of the decree before-mentioned"[35] [emphasis in original].

Attempting to justify this doctrine, so many Calvinists have responded to me in discussions, in letters, and in comments written in the margin of preliminary manuscripts I sent to them for review, "God is under no obligation to extend His grace to those whom He predestines to eternal judgment." Of course God is under no obligation to any man for anything. As we have already noted, however, grace and mercy do not flow from obligation but rather from God's love. Nor can God's perfect holiness and justice be compromised in the process. Evaluating a popular Calvinist author, Zane Hodges writes,

> The result of [Michael S.] Horton's theology is that non-elect people are hopelessly bound for hell because God declines to regenerate them.... The picture of God that emerges from this is a hideous distortion of His loving character and nature. It is not surprising, therefore, to find Horton also writing: "He [God] cannot love us directly because of our sinfulness, but he can love us in union with Christ, because Christ is the one the Father loves."[36] What this amounts to is that God does not "directly" love *anyone* unless *first* He regenerates him or her, since "regeneration is the commencement of union." In other words, God does not love the elect until they are regenerated, and He *never* loves the non-elect at all.[37]

---

1. C. Gregg Singer, *John Calvin: His Roots and Fruits* (Abingdon Press, 1989), 32.
2. W. E. Best, *Free Grace Versus Free Will* (Houston, TX: W. E. Best Books Missionary Trust, 1977], 20.
3. Peter A. Bertocci, *Free Will, Responsibility, and Grace* (Nashville, TN: Abingdon Press, 1957), 22, 96.
4. C. I. Scofield, *Scofield Bible Correspondence Course* (Chicago, IL: Moody Bible Institute, 1907), III:445.
5. James M. Gray, *Bible Problems Explained* (Grand Rapids, MI: Fleming H. Revell, 3rd ed. 1913), 45.
6. William L. Pettingill, *Bible Questions Answered* (Just A Word Inc., 3rd ed. 1935), 209.
7. Arthur T. Pierson, *The Believer's Life: Its Past, Present, and Future Tenses* (London: Morgan and Scott, 1905), 24–30.
8. Reuben A. Torrey, *The Importance and Value of Proper Bible Study* (Chicago, IL: Moody Press, 1921), 80–81.
9. Edgar Y. Mullins, *Baptist Beliefs* (Valley Forge, PA: Judson Press, 4th ed. 1925), 27.
10. Kenneth G. Talbot and W. Gary Crampton, *Calvinism, Hyper-Calvinism and Arminianism* (Edmonton, AB: Still Waters Revival Books, 1990), 14.
11. Loraine Boettner, *The Reformed Faith* (Phillipsburg, NJ: Presbyterian and Reformed Publishing Co., 1983), 2.
12. John Gill, *A Body of Doctrinal and Practical Divinity* (Paris, AR: Baptist Standard Bearer, 1987), 173.
13. Charles Haddon Spurgeon, "God's Will and Man's Will," No. 442 (Newington, Metropolitan Tabernacle; sermon delivered Sunday morning, March 30, 1862).
14. Loraine Boettner, *The Reformed Doctrine of Predestination* (Phillipsburg, NJ: Presbyterian and Reformed Publishing Co., 1932), 234.
15. Philip F. Congdon, "Soteriological Implications of Five-point Calvinism," *Journal of the Grace Evangelical Society,* Autumn 1995, 8:15, 55–68.
16. Arthur W. Pink, *The Sovereignty of God* (Grand Rapids, MI: Baker Book House, 2nd prtg. 1986), 138–39.
17. Ibid., 240.
18. A. A. Hodge, quoted in D. A. Carson, *Divine Sovereignty and Human Responsibility* (Atlanta, GA: John Knox Press, 1981), 207.
19. A. A. Hodge, *Outlines of Theology* (Grand Rapids, MI: Zondervan, 1972), 201-202.
20. Jerom Zanchius, *The Doctrine of Absolute Predestination*, trans. Augustus M. Toplady (Grand Rapids, MI: Baker Book House, 1977), 88.
21. Edwin H. Palmer, *the five points of calvinism* (Grand Rapids, MI: Baker Books, enlarged ed., 20th prtg. 1999), 82.
22. Ibid., 95, 124–35.
23. Ibid., 95, 97–100, 116.
24. Ibid.
25. David S. West, *The Baptist Examiner*, March 18, 1989, 5; cited in Laurence M. Vance, *The Other Side of Calvinism* (Pensacola, FL: Vance Publications, rev. ed. 1999), 255.
26. C. Norman Sellers, *Election and Perseverance* (Haysville, NC: Schoettle Publishing Co., 1987), 3.

27. John Calvin, *Institutes of the Christian Religion*, trans. Henry Beveridge (Grand Rapids, MI: Wm. B. Eerdmans Publishing Company, 1998 ed.), I: xvi, 6,8,9.
28. Pink, *Sovereignty*, 156.
29. Jonathan Edwards, *Freedom of the Will*, ed. Paul Ramsey (New Haven, Ct: Yale University Press, 1957), 137.
30. Palmer, *Sovereignty*, 87.
31. Will Durant, "The Reformation," Pt. VI of *The Story of Civilization* (New York: Simon and Schuster, 1957), 90.
32. Palmer, *Sovereignty*, 97–100,116.
33. Ibid., 16.
34. Quoted in Alan P. F. Sell, *The Great Debate* (Grand Rapids, MI: Baker Book House, 1982), 7.
35. In Jacobus Arminius, *The Works of James Arminius*, trans. James and William Nichols (Grand Rapids, MI: Baker Book House, 1986), 1:213.
36. Quoting from Michael S. Horton, ed., *Christ the Lord: The Reformation and Lordship Salvation* (Grand Rapids, MI: Baker Book House, 1992), 111.
37. Zane C. Hodges, "The New Puritanism, Pt 3: Michael S. Horton: Holy War With Unholy Weapons," *Journal of the Grace Evangelical Society*," Spring 1994, 7:12, 17–29.

CHAPTER

11

Sovereignty and Free Will

ONE OFTEN HEARS Christians say, "God is in control; He's still on the throne." But what does that mean? Was God not in control when Satan rebelled and when Adam and Eve disobeyed, but now He is? Does God's being in control mean that all rape, murder, war, famine, suffering, and evil is exactly what He planned and desires—as Palmer says, "— even the moving of a finger...the mistake of a typist..."?[1]

That God is absolutely sovereign does not require that everything man chooses to do or not to do is not his own choice at all but was foreordained by God from eternity past. There is neither logical nor biblical reason why a sovereign God by His own sovereign design could not allow creatures made in His image the freedom of moral choice. Indeed, He must, if man is to be more than a cardboard puppet!

In a chapter titled "the great mystery," Palmer insists that the non-Calvinist denies the sovereignty of God while insisting upon man's power of choice, while the "hyper-Calvinist denies the responsibility of man." He then suggests that the true

> Calvinist…accepts both sides of the antinomy. He realizes that what he advocates is ridiculous...impossible for man to harmonize these two sets of data. To say on the one hand that God has made certain all that ever happens, and yet to say that man is responsible for what he does? Nonsense! It must be one or the other. To say that God foreordains the sin of Judas, and yet Judas is to blame? Foolishness...! This is in accord with Paul, who

> said, "The word of the cross is to them that perish foolishness" (1 Corinthians 1:18). The Greeks seek after wisdom and logic, and to them the Calvinist is irrational.... So the Calvinist has to make up his mind: what is his authority? His own human reason or the Word of God? If he answers, the human reasoning powers, then, like the Arminian and hyper-Calvinist, he will have to exclude one of the two parallel forces. But...he believes the Bible is God's Word...infallible and inerrant...[T]he apparent paradox of the sovereignty of God and the responsibility of man...belongs to the Lord our God, and we should leave it there. We ought not to probe into the secret counsel of God."[2]

On the contrary, there is no contradiction between God's sovereignty and man's free will. That God can be sovereign and man be free to choose is not an unfathomable mystery. But Calvinism denies free will by its definition of sovereignty, making God the cause of all, including sin—yet man is accountable for what God *causes* him to do. That proposition is irrational. The confusion here should be obvious.

The "paradox" has been created by Calvinism's distortion of sovereignty. Accepting this manmade contradiction, J. I. Packer says we must "refuse to regard the apparent inconsistency as real."[3] That pronouncement sounds more like Christian Science, Positive Thinking, or Positive Confession than biblical exegesis!

On the contrary, as Reimensnyder has said, "The free-will of man is the most marvelous of the Creator's works."[4] It is indeed the gift that makes possible every other gift from God—for without the power to choose, man could not consciously receive any moral or spiritual gift from God. That fact, of course, is self-evident—and biblical. Repeatedly men and women are called upon to make moral choices, to love and obey God, to believe the gospel, and to receive Christ: "choose you this day whom ye will serve" (Joshua 24:15); "if ye be willing and obedient, ye shall eat the good of the land" (Isaiah 1:19); "Daniel purposed in his heart that he would not defile himself" (Daniel 1:8), etc.

A Serious Contradiction

Unquestionably, men by their own choice can and do defy and disobey God. The knowledge that men continually break God's laws is common to every human conscience and experience. In spite of the fact that He is sovereign, and, obviously, without violating or lessening His sovereignty,

God's will is continually being resisted and rejected as a result of the rebellion of Satan and man. That both citizens and foreigners often violate its laws does not deny a country's sovereignty. Indeed, lawbreakers will be punished if apprehended.

Even Christians do not always perfectly fulfill God's will. If so, they would have no sin to confess, and there would have been no need for the Epistles or Christ's letters to the seven churches of Asia or for the judgment seat of Christ—or any other correction from God. Rewards, too, would be meaningless without freewill.

The Bible itself contains many examples of men defying and disobeying God in spite of His being sovereign and in control of His universe. Through Isaiah the prophet, God laments, "I have nourished and brought up children, and they have rebelled against me" (Isaiah 1:2). They are offering sacrifices that He abhors, obviously not according to His will, and they are living lives that dishonor Him. We are told that "the Pharisees and lawyers [continuing the tradition of those before them] rejected the counsel of God against themselves" (Luke 7:30). Quite clearly, everything that happens in human affairs is *not* according to God's will.

Throughout the Old Testament, God pleads with Israel to repent of her rebellion, to return to Him and obey Him. Of Israel He says, "All day long I have stretched forth my hands unto a disobedient and gainsaying people" (Romans 10:21). Israel's history provides more than ample proof that in spite of His absolute sovereignty, man can and does rebel, and that the sin he commits is not God's will, much less His decree. Typical of His continual lament is the following:

> I sent unto you all my servants the prophets, rising early and sending them, saying, Oh, do not this abominable thing that I hate. But they hearkened not, nor inclined their ear to turn from their wickedness, to burn no incense unto other gods. Wherefore my fury and mine anger was poured forth, and was kindled in the cities of Judah and in the streets of Jerusalem; and they are wasted and desolate, as at this day. (Jeremiah 44:4–6)

Surely, the idolatry that God calls "this abominable thing that I hate" could not be according to His will. That His will is rejected by man's rebellion, however, just as the Ten Commandments are broken millions of times each day around the world, does not in the least deny or weaken His sovereignty.

What About Ephesians 1:11?

In light of such scriptures, how can we understand the statement that God works "all things according to the counsel of His own will" (Ephesians 1:11)? Alvin Baker claims that this passage proves that "God works 'all things,' including sin, according to His eternal will."[5] However, the word "worketh" (KJV) is *energeo*, which doesn't convey the idea of controlled manipulation but of stimulation. See Colossians 1:29 and 2 Thessalonians 2:7,9; see also "work out your own salvation...for it is God which worketh in [energizes] you" (Philippians 2:12–13).

Nor does Paul say that God works all according to His will, but according to the *counsel* of His will. There is a huge difference. Obviously, the eternal "counsel" of His will must have allowed man the freedom to love and obey, or to defy, his Creator—otherwise sin would be God's will. We could never conclude from this passage (and particularly not in light of the many scriptures stating that men defy God's will) that mankind's every thought, word, and deed is according to God's perfect will, exactly the way God desired and decreed it. Yet that is what Calvinists erroneously conclude from Ephesians 1:11. To make that the case, as Calvin did, portrays God as the effective cause of every sin ever committed.

Christ asks us to pray, "Thy kingdom come Thy will be done in earth, as it is in heaven" (Matthew 6:10; Luke 11:2). Why would Christ suggest such a prayer, if everything is already according to God's will and His eternal decree—and if we are already in the kingdom of God with Satan bound, as both Calvin and Augustine taught?

The objection is raised: "How dare you suggest that the omnipotent God cannot effect His will!" Of course He can and does, but that in itself does not say that God wills everything that happens. Without freedom to do his own will, man would not be a morally responsible being, nor could he be guilty of sin. That much is axiomatic.

Christ's special commendation of "whosoever shall do the will of my Father" (Matthew 12:50; Mark 3:35), and such statements from His lips as "Not every one that saith unto me, Lord, Lord, shall enter into the kingdom of heaven; but he that doeth the will of my Father" (Matthew 7:21), show very clearly that everyone doesn't always fulfill God's will. The same truth is found in Isaiah 65:12, 1 Thessalonians 5:17–22, Hebrews 10:36, 1 Peter 2:15–16, 1 John 2:17 and elsewhere. Clearly, there is a distinction between what God desires and wills, and what He *allows*.

An Important Distinction

Many scriptures show that God's will can be, and is, defied by man. Nor does Scripture ever suggest that there is any will or plan of God with which man's will and actions are by nature in perfect accord. Forster and Marston point out, however, that "Some Christian writers seem to have been unable to accept this.... If, as they believe, everything that happens is God's will, then the unrepentance and perishing of the wicked must also be God's will. Yet God himself says it is *not* his will...."[6]

On the fact of human rebellion and disobedience in defiance of God, both Calvinists and non-Calvinists agree. The disagreement comes in the explanation. The former say that even man's rebellion has been decreed sovereignly by God and that God's will is the effective cause of it. The latter explain sin as the result of man's own selfish and evil desires and deeds in defiance of God. Thereby man is justly held morally accountable, because it is in the power of his will either to intend to obey or to deliberately disobey God. The Calvinist, however, denies that man, because he is "totally depraved," has such a choice—yet holds him accountable in spite of his alleged inability to act in any way except as God has decreed.

Thus any independent choice on man's part—even to sin—must be denied in order to maintain TULIP. This is especially true when it comes to salvation. Pink writes, "To say that the sinner's salvation turns upon the action of his own will, is another form of the God-dishonoring dogma of salvation by human efforts.... Any movement of the will is a work...."[7]

On the contrary, there is a huge difference between deciding or willing to do something and actually doing it—something that every lazy person and procrastinator repeatedly demonstrates. Merely to will is not a work at all. Paul clearly makes that distinction when he says, "To will is present with me; but how to perform that which is good I find not" (Romans 7:18). Indeed, Paul's will is not the major problem but rather his inability *even as a regenerated person* to do the good he wills and to refrain from the evil that his will rejects.

The gospel is "the power of God unto salvation to every one that believeth" (Romans 1:16). The effective power that saves man is all of God, but man receives salvation by faith—and only by faith. For the condemned sinner simply to receive by faith the salvation that Christ purchased on the Cross is no work on man's part at all. Yet the Calvinist insists that it is. For Pink to call receiving Christ by faith "human effort" is to invent his own meaning of words.

The distinction between faith and works is so clear in Scripture that we need not belabor the point.

It is the Calvinists' extreme view of God's sovereignty that causes them to reject the biblical teaching that salvation is offered freely to all. Instead, they limit salvation to the elect. Otherwise, they argue, if man is free either to accept or reject salvation, that leaves the final decision up to man and places God at his mercy.

"So are you suggesting," they object, "that God wants to save all mankind but lacks the power to do so? It is a denial of God's omnipotence and sovereignty if there is anything He desires but can't accomplish." Yet MacArthur, Packer, Piper, and others say that God desires the salvation of all yet doesn't decree it. This is a real contradiction, whereas it is no contradiction at all to say that God has given man the free choice of whether to receive Christ or not.

In fact, power has no relationship to grace and love, which provide salvation. Moreover, as we shall see, there are many things God cannot do, and a lack of "power" is not the reason for any of them, nor is His sovereignty mitigated in the least.

What a Sovereign God *Cannot Do*

Vance points out, "The Calvinist perception of God as being absolutely sovereign is very much accurate; however, that doesn't mean that it takes precedence over his other attributes."[8] Clearly, God's ability and even His right to act in His sovereignty are only exercised in harmony with His other attributes, which must all remain in perfect balance. Calvinism destroys that balance. It puts such emphasis upon sovereignty that God's other qualities are made inconsequential by comparison, and God is presented as acting out of character. That is why this book is subtitled, *Calvinism's Misrepresentation of God.*

Throughout history, sovereign despots have misused their sovereignty for their own evil purposes. Obviously, however, God employs His sovereignty not as a despot but in love, grace, mercy, kindness, justice, and truth—all in perfect symmetry with His total character and all of His attributes. Indeed, He cannot act despotically or use His sovereignty for evil. Cannot? Yes, *cannot.*

"Heresy!" cries someone. "God is infinite in power; there is nothing He cannot do." Really? The very fact that He is infinite in power means He *cannot* fail. There is much else that finite beings routinely do but that the infinite, absolutely sovereign God *cannot do because He is God.* He cannot travel because He is omnipresent. He cannot lie, cheat, steal, be mistaken, contradict Himself, act contrary to His character, etc. Nor did God will any of this in man. To will sin in others would be the same as to practice it Himself—a fact that Calvinists overlook.

What God cannot do is not *in spite of who He is*, but *because of who He is*. Thus Augustine wrote, "Wherefore, He cannot do some things for the very reason that He is omnipotent."[9] There are things God cannot do, because to do them would violate His very character. He cannot deny or contradict Himself. He cannot change. He cannot go back on His Word.

God Can Neither Tempt Nor Be Tempted

Scripture must be taken in context and compared with Scripture; one isolated verse cannot become the rule. Jesus said, "With God all things are possible" (Matthew 19:26). Yet it is impossible for God to do evil, to cause others to do evil, or even to entice anyone into evil. This is clearly stated in Scripture: "Let no man say when he is tempted, I am tempted of God: for God cannot be tempted with evil, neither tempteth he any man..." (James 1:13–14).

What about instances in Scripture where the Bible says God tempted someone, or was tempted Himself—for example, "God did tempt Abraham" (Genesis 22:1)? The Hebrew word there and throughout the Old Testament is *nacah*, which means to test or prove, as in assaying the purity of a metal. It has nothing to do with tempting *to sin*. God was testing Abraham's faith and obedience.

As for God being tempted, Israel was warned, "Ye shall not tempt the Lord your God" (Deuteronomy 6:16). They had done so at Massah, in demanding water: "they tempted the Lord, saying, Is the Lord among us, or not?" (Exodus 17:7). Later they "tempted God in their heart by asking meat for their lust...they said, Can God furnish a table in the wilderness? Yea...they tempted and provoked the most high God" (Psalms 78:18,41,56).

Clearly, God was not being tempted to do *evil*—an impossibility. But instead of waiting upon Him in patient trust to meet their needs, His people were demanding that He prove His power by giving them what they wanted to satisfy their lusts. Their "temptation" of God was a provocation that put Him in the position either of giving in to their desire or of punishing them for rebellion.

When Jesus was "tempted of the devil" to cast himself from the pinnacle of the temple to prove the promise of God that angels would bear Him up in their hands, He quoted Deuteronomy 6:16—"Thou shalt not tempt the Lord thy God" (Matthew 4:1–11). In other words, it is one thing to rely upon God to meet our needs as they arise and as He sees fit, but it is something else to put ourselves deliberately in a situation where we demand that God *must* act if we are to be rescued or protected.

In the quotation above, James goes on to say, "every man is tempted, when he is drawn away of his own lust and enticed." Temptation to evil comes from within, not from without. The man who would never be "tempted" by an opportunity to be dishonest in business may succumb to the temptation to commit adultery and thus be dishonest with his wife.

God was not tempting Adam and Eve to sin when He told them not to eat of a particular tree; He was testing them. Eve was tempted by her own natural lust, her selfish desire. Even in innocence, mankind became selfish and disobedient. We see this in very young infants, who as yet presumably do not know the difference between right and wrong.

What God Cannot Do to Save Man

Furthermore, when it comes to salvation, there are three specific things God cannot do. First of all, He cannot forgive sin without the penalty being paid. In the Garden of Gethsemane the night before the cross, Christ cried out in agony, "O my Father, if it be possible, let this cup pass from me..." (Matthew 26:39). Surely had it been possible to provide salvation without Christ paying the penalty demanded by His justice, the Father would have allowed Him to escape the cross. We know, therefore, that it was not possible for God to save man any other way. Even God's sovereign, omnipotent power cannot simply decree that sinners be forgiven. This fact destroys the very foundation of Calvinism's salvation for the elect alone by sovereign decree.

Secondly, God cannot force a gift upon anyone. That fact also shows that salvation for the elect cannot be by predestination. Salvation can neither be earned nor merited—it can only be *received* as a gift from God. And the recipient must be willing; the gift cannot be imposed by the giver against the recipient's will.

Finally, even God cannot force anyone to love Him or to accept His love. Force cannot produce love. True love can only come voluntarily from the heart.

By the very nature of giving and receiving, and of loving and receiving love, man must have the power to choose freely from his heart as God has sovereignly ordained—"if thou shalt...believe in thine heart...thou shalt be saved" (Romans 10:9). The reception of God's gift of salvation and of God's love (all in and through Jesus Christ and His sacrifice for our sins) can only be by a free choice.

Christ repeatedly gave such invitations as "Come unto me, all ye that labour and are heavy laden, and I will give you rest" (Matthew 11:28), or "If any man thirst, let him come unto me, and drink" (John 7:37); and "whosoever will, let him take the water of life freely" (Revelation 22:17). Relying upon the ordinary meaning of words, we can only conclude from Scripture that Christ is offering to all a gift that may be accepted or rejected.

There is no question that salvation is a free gift of God's grace: "For God so loved the world, that he gave his only begotten Son" (John 3:16); "If thou knewest the gift of God" (John 4:10); "But not as the offence, so also is the free gift" (Romans 5:15); "For the wages of sin is death, but the gift of God is eternal life through Jesus Christ our Lord" (Romans 6:23); "For by grace are ye saved...it is the gift of God" (Ephesians 2:8); "God hath given to us eternal life" (1 John 5:11), etc. By its very nature, a gift must be received by an act of the will. If forced upon the recipient, it is not a gift.

Tragically, Calvinism undermines the very foundation of salvation and man's loving, trusting relationship with God through Christ.

Free Will Does Not Conflict With God's Sovereignty

Literally hundreds of verses throughout the Bible offer salvation to all who will believe and receive. The Calvinist objects that if man had the choice of saying yes or no to Christ, he would have the final say in his salvation, his destiny would be in his own hands, and God would be at his mercy. Therefore, where the Bible seems to say that God desires all to be saved and is offering salvation to all either to be accepted or rejected, the Calvinist must limit the application only to the elect—and they must have no choice. Thus Scripture's clear meaning is changed to make it conform to TULIP.

God's sovereignty is not in question. The issue is what that means biblically. The Calvinist argues that if God's desire is for all men to be saved—and obviously they are *not* all saved—then God's will is frustrated by rebellious, sinful men who by their wills have been able to overturn God's sovereignty.

As a consequence of this mistaken view of sovereignty, the plain meaning of numerous passages must be changed in order to support TULIP. The Calvinist insists, "The heresy of free will dethrones God and enthrones man."[10] In fact, this error was rejected by Augustine himself.

Setting the Record Straight

Clearly, there are a number of things a sovereign God *cannot* do, yet none of these limitations impinges in the least upon His sovereignty. God is not the less sovereign because He cannot lie or sin or change or deny Himself, etc. These follow *because* of His sinless, holy, perfect character.

Nor is God any the less sovereign or lacking in power because He cannot force anyone to love Him or to receive the gift of eternal life through Jesus Christ. Power and love (and love's gift) do not belong in the same discussion. In fact, of the many things we have seen that God cannot do, a lack of "power" or a lessening of sovereignty is not the reason for any of them. Pusey points out that "It would be self-contradictory, that Almighty God should create a free agent capable of loving Him, without also being capable of rejecting His love.... Without free-will we could not freely love God. Freedom is a condition of love."[11]

Far from denying God's sovereignty, to recognize that mankind has been given by God the capacity to choose to love Him or not, and to receive or reject the free gift of salvation, is to admit what God's sovereignty itself has lovingly and wonderfully provided. In His sovereignty, God has so constituted the nature of a gift and of love that man must have the power of choice or he cannot experience either one from God's gracious hand.

Nor could the power of choice challenge God's sovereignty, since it is God's sovereignty that has bestowed this gift upon man and set the conditions for loving, for receiving love, and for giving and receiving a gift. Yet as Zane Hodges points out:

> If there is one thing five-point Calvinists hold with vigorous tenacity, it is the belief that there can be no human *free will* at all. With surprising illogic, they usually argue that God cannot be sovereign if man is granted any degree of free will. But this view of God actually *diminishes* the greatness of His sovereign power. For if God cannot control a universe in which there is genuine free will, and is reduced to the creation of "robots," then such a God is of truly limited power indeed.[12]

It is foolish to suggest that if man could reject Christ, that would put him in control of either his own destiny or of God. God is in control. It is He who makes the rules, sets the requirements for salvation, and determines the consequences of either acceptance or rejection. God is no less sovereign over those who reject Christ than He is over those who accept Him. He is the one who has determined the conditions of salvation and what will happen both to those who accept and to those who reject His offer.

But the Calvinist, because of his extreme view of sovereignty, can no more allow any man to say yes to Christ than he can allow him to say no. This error, having destroyed the foundation for a genuine salvation, creates a false one. And in order to support this false salvation that, allegedly, God imposes upon an elect, Calvinism has had to invent its five points. This fact will become ever more clear as we proceed.

1. Edwin H. Palmer, *the five points of calvinism* (Grand Rapids, MI: Baker Books, enlarged ed., 20th prtg. 1999), 25.
2. Ibid., 85–87.
3. J. I. Packer, *Evangelism and the Sovereignty of God* (Downer's Grove, IL: InterVarsity Press, 1961), 212.
4. Junius B. Reimensnyder, *Doom Eternal* (N. S. Quiney, 1880), 357; cited in Samuel Fisk, *Calvinistic Paths Retraced* (Raleigh, NC: Biblical Evangelism Press, 1985), 223.
5. Alvin L. Baker, *Berkower's Doctrine of Election: Balance or Imbalance*? (Phillipsburg, NJ: Presbyterian and Reformed Publishing Co., 1981), 174.
6. Roger T. Forster and V. Paul Marston, *God's Strategy in Human History* (Bloomington, MN: Bethany House Publishers, 1973), 32.
7. Arthur W. Pink, *The Sovereignty of God* (Grand Rapids, MI: Baker Book House, 2nd prtg. 1986), 218.
8. David S. West, *The Baptist Examiner*, March 18, 1989, 5; cited in Laurence M. Vance, *The Other Side of Calvinism* (Pensacola, FL: Vance Publications, rev. ed. 1999), 256–57.
9. Augustine, *The City of God*, trans. Marcus Dods; in *Great Books of the Western World*, ed. Robert Maynard Hutchins and Mortimer J. Adler (Encyclopaedia Britannica, Inc., 1952), 18: V.10.
10. W. E. Best, *Free Grace Versus Free Will* (Houston, TX: W. E. Best Books Missionary Trust, 1977), 35.
11. Edward B. Pusey, *What Is Of Faith As To Everlasting Punishment?* (James Parker and Co., 1881), 22–24; cited in Fisk, *Calvinistic*, 222.
12. Zane C. Hodges, "The New Puritanism, Pt 3: Michael S. Horton: Holy War With Unholy Weapons," *Journal of the Grace Evangelical Society*, Spring 1994, 7:12.

CHAPTER

12

Foreknowledge and Man's Will

MANY THEOLOGIANS and philosophers seem to find a conflict also between God's foreknowledge and man's free will. If God knows what will happen before it happens, then it must happen as He foreknew, or His foreknowledge would be wrong. That being the case, how could anyone be free to make a choice? To consider that question, we must define some terms.

The biblical doctrine of foreknowledge simply states that God knows everything that will happen before it happens. The psalmist's statement, "For there is not a word in my tongue, but, lo, O LORD, thou knowest it altogether" (Psalm 139:4), tells us that God knows every thought and word before we speak it—and has known it from eternity past—but does not say that God's foreknowledge *causes* these thoughts and words. At the council of apostles and elders in Jerusalem, James stated clearly, "Known unto God are all his works from the beginning of the world" (Acts 15:18). To know everything He would do, God must have known every thought, word, and event that would ever occur. This biblical truth is clearly necessary if God is to be omnipotent, omniscient, and omnipresent, the Creator and Sustainer of all.

Unquestionably, from eternity past, God must have known everything. That includes the motions of the stars and electrons, and the exact location at any nanosecond of each atom and the earthly bodies they comprise, large and small, animate and inanimate. God knew everything that would happen to each one and how each would function. Before He created the universe or men or angels, God knew every event that would ever occur in heaven or in the physical universe, and thus necessarily every thought, word, and deed of every human or angel that would ever exist. This is what it means to be God and therefore to be omniscient.

Creator and Creation

This cornerstone truth of Scripture was stated well by Augustine: "For to confess that God exists, and at the same time to deny that He has foreknowledge of future things, is the most manifest folly.... But...we [who] confess the most high and true God Himself, do confess His will, supreme power, and prescience."[1] No one, however, stated God's foreknowledge more fully than the much defamed Arminius:

> [God] knows all things possible, whether they be in the capability of God or of the creature...imagination or enunciation...all things that could have an existence...those which are necessary and contingent, good and bad, universal and particular, future, present and past, excellent and vile; He knows things substantial and accidental of every kind; the actions and passions, the modes and circumstances...external words and deeds, internal thoughts, deliberations, counsels, and determinations, and the entities of reason, whether complex or simple.[2]

Calvinism, unfortunately, takes a far different view of foreknowledge, which actually denigrates God's omniscience: "If God did not foreordain all things, then he could not know the future."[3] Without scriptural support, Calvin declared that God "foresees the things which are to happen, simply because he has decreed that they are so to happen...."[4] Going even further, another author says, "The idea that God knows the future without having planned it and without controlling it is totally foreign to Scripture."[5] In fact, the opposite is the case. Nowhere does Scripture say or even imply that God knows all beforehand *only because He has foreordained and caused it.*

How, then, can God be sure that what He foreknows will happen and that something will not intervene to change the future? Simply because He is all-knowing, and therefore the future is as plain to Him as the past. If God had to plan and cause something to happen or even to control its occurrence in order to know it would take place, He would be limited in His foreknowledge and therefore not the infinite, omniscient God that He is. If the Calvinistic view is correct, then every detail of every crime and disease and of the destruction to property and the human suffering and loss of life and limb caused by natural disasters would be foreordained and caused by God; otherwise, He would be ignorant of the future.

We are told that "one day is with the Lord as a thousand years, and a thousand years as one day" (2 Peter 3:8); and that "a thousand years in thy sight are but as yesterday when it is past, and as a watch in the night" (Psalm 90:4). Some have attempted to find a hidden meaning in these statements, but there is none.

The phrases "with the Lord" and "in thy sight" are the key to understanding this rather simple and straightforward declaration. Time is part of the physical universe, which God created out of nothing. God himself is therefore outside of time. That is the simple truth in these two scriptures.

As one scientist recently explained, "The actual existence of past, present, and future is required by Einstein's theory of relativity. All space and time form a four-dimensional continuum that simply exists; the theory does not permit time to be treated as a dimension in which the future is open or incomplete." He further explained:

> From a Christian point of view, it is reasonable to conclude that the temporal and the spatial extent of our universe were created together, and thus the entire four-dimensional structure resides before [in the view of] its Creator in an eternal present. Thus our modern scientific understanding of the nature of time fits quite well with the Christian tradition that God has knowledge of all time, past, present, and future: "Before Abraham was, I am."[6]

Note that God does not say, "I was," or "I will be." He says, "I *am*." He is the self-existent One ever present to all events, whether past, present, or future from our point of view.

God's Continual Protection

God knows the future without His foreknowledge influencing it because He views it as an outside observer. God is totally separate and distinct from space, time, and matter. Therefore, just as He looks at the universe from outside, so He sees past, present, and future from outside, knowing it all at once.

We are finite and God is infinite; therefore, we could not possibly understand *how* He knows the future. He has given us enough intelligence, however, to understand that He *must* know it. As David said, speaking for all mankind, "Such knowledge is too wonderful for me; it is high, I cannot attain unto it" (Psalm 139:6).

Scripture makes it equally clear that God is no passive observer entirely disinterested in events taking their own course. Keeping a watchful eye and playing an active part, He fulfills His eternal purpose for all creation. As the psalmist declared, "Say unto God, How terrible [awesome] art thou in thy works...! Come and see the works of God: he is terrible in his doing toward the children of men.... He ruleth by his power for ever..." (Psalm 66:3,5,7).

God exerts His influence upon men and events (exactly as He has foreknown He would from eternity past) in order to create the future for us that He desires and has willed. In light of man's willful intentions and actions, whatever influence or action God has foreknown would be necessary on His part to implement His plans would obviously also be part of God's foreknowledge—eliminating any necessity of emergency adjustment.

At times all Christians have an awareness of God's marvelous and gracious intervention in their lives. "Just in time" intervention (the way God, from our perspective, so often works) may seem like a last-minute thought and action on His part, but that is clearly not the case. No doubt, His good hand is always upon His people, but in ways beyond human comprehension. As David said again:

> Thou has beset me behind and before, and laid thine hand upon me.... Whither shall I go from thy spirit? or whither shall I flee from thy presence?... Into heaven...in hell...the uttermost part of the sea; even there shall thy hand lead me, and thy right hand shall hold me....
>
> How precious also are thy thoughts unto me, O God! how great is the sum of them! If I should count them, they are more in number than the sand: when I awake, I am still with thee. (Psalm 139:5–18)

The Problem of Evil

It is an inescapable fact that, in spite of God's foreknowledge and sovereignty, evil predominates in human affairs. That God is not the author of evil is clearly stated in the Bible, as we have already seen. Therefore, we can only conclude that He has, in His sovereignty, given man moral responsibility to be exercised with free choice. That men choose wickedness is not what

God desires for mankind. Total Depravity, as defined by Calvinism, eliminates man's faculty of free will:

> Inasmuch as Adam's offspring are born with sinful natures, they do not have the ability to choose spiritual good over evil. Consequently, man's will is no longer free...from the dominion of sin...as Adam's will was free before the fall.[7]

The Bible presents evil as the result of man's free will choosing for self instead of for God. The Calvinist, however, in denying human moral freedom, makes God the *cause* of all evil, insisting that He "creates the very thoughts and intents of the soul."[8] As Calvin declared:

> The first man fell because the Lord deemed it meet that he should...because he saw that his own glory would thereby be displayed.... Man therefore falls, divine providence so ordaining, but he falls by his own fault.... I will not hesitate, therefore, simply to confess with Augustine...that the destruction consequent upon predestination is also most just."[9]

This idea, however, is so contradictory to man's God-given conscience and sense of justice that Calvin spent much of his *Institutes* struggling unsuccessfully to justify it. Calvin digs a hole from which no Calvinist to this day has been able to escape. He does this by irrationally and unbiblically insisting that God can only foreknow what He foreordains:

> The decree, I admit, is dreadful; and yet it is impossible to deny that God foreknew what the end of man was to be before he made him, and foreknew, because he had so ordained by his decree.[10]

In defending God's sovereignty, another Calvinist, at the same time that he denies that man has a free will, implies that man's will must exist after all: "Free will is the invention of man, instigated by the devil."[11] How can free will be man's invention by an act of his will if his will doesn't exist? Calvin struggles with the problem of man's will and is forced to acknowledge that man is not rational without it:

> I feel pleased with the well-known saying which has been borrowed from the writings of Augustine, that man's natural gifts were corrupted by sin, and his supernatural gifts withdrawn.... [In fact, being a creature and not the Creator, man never had "supernatural" gifts.]

> For although there is still [after Adam's fall] some residue of intelligence and judgment as well as will [because] reason, by which man discerns between good and evil...could not be entirely destroyed; but...a shapeless ruin is all that remains...the will, because inseparable from the nature of man, did not perish, but was so enslaved by depraved lusts as to be incapable of one righteous desire....
>
> To charge the intellect with perpetual blindness so as to leave it no intelligence of any description whatever, is repugnant not only to the Word of God, but to common experience...the human mind [retains] a certain desire of investigating truth...[but it] fails before it reaches the goal...falling away into vanity...unable, from dulness, to pursue the right path...and, after various wanderings, stumbling every now and then like one groping in darkness, at length gets so completely bewildered....
>
> Still, however, man's efforts are not always so utterly fruitless as not to lead to some results....[12]

Calvin carries on in this fashion page after page. Man has *some* intelligence for discerning "between good and evil," but that ability is "a shapeless ruin...." What does that mean? He can't tell us. The will did not *perish* but was so enslaved as to be morally useless in desiring the good which it dimly perceives. Man has *some* desire after truth, but is unable due to "dulness" to pursue it fully, so that he becomes "completely bewildered," yet his efforts are not "so utterly fruitless as not to lead to *some* results...." Every effort to extricate himself only causes Calvin to sink deeper into the bog of his own contriving.

Far from supporting such assertions by careful exegesis of Scripture, Calvin can't provide one verse that even comes close to what he theorizes. Indeed, what does he assert? He hedges, qualifies, and contradicts himself so often that he really offers nothing but useless double-talk.

Why Doesn't God Stop Evil and Suffering?

Of course, sinful man and rebellious Satan must be blamed and God, who is perfect in holiness, must be exonerated—but this is impossible if God has predestined everything. Many pages and even chapters of the *Institutes* are given to attempting to prove that everything man does, including all evil, is foreordained of God, but that man is nevertheless guilty and is justly punished by God for doing the very evil that God has ordained. (See for example *Institutes* I: xv-xviii; III: xxi-xxiv.)

Many of today's Calvinists deny that Calvinism teaches that God *causes* evil. Yet that is clearly what Calvin himself insisted upon: "That men do nothing save at the secret instigation of God, and do not discuss and deliberate on anything, but what he has previously decreed with himself, and brings to pass by his secret direction, is proved by numberless clear passages of Scripture."[13] In fact, there is no such Scripture—and Calvin's examples apply only to some men, not to all.

Could not the sinner blame for his sin and eternal suffering in the Lake of Fire a God who allows him to choose only evil and not good? Who, by eternal decree, sovereignly originated his evil thoughts and caused his evil deeds and then in punishment for that evil predestined him to eternal torment? But wait! Doesn't Romans 9:19–22 declare that no man has the right to complain against God? Paul asks: "Shall the thing formed say to him that formed it, Why hast thou made me thus? Hath not the potter power over the clay, of the same lump to make one vessel unto honour, and the other unto dishonour?" That important question will be dealt with in depth later.

Why, if God is sovereign and all-powerful, doesn't He intervene to stop all evil? That is a meaningless question, however, if (as is claimed) God has decreed the rampant evil and suffering that plague mankind. Why would He undo what He has foreordained? Yet Calvinists insist that God *could* stop all evil if He so desired, because He controls everything. But how could God reverse what He has predestined? He cannot change His mind or go back on His Word. Therefore, if He foreordained evil, He cannot stop it. Here we uncover another contradiction.

The question cannot be escaped: Why would a good God who *is love* decree evil and suffering for billions not only in this life but for eternity in the Lake of Fire? That question is an embarrassment to at least some Calvinists, such as R. C. Sproul and John Piper, because there is no rational (much less biblical) answer within that system of theology. This was admitted by Calvin himself: "I again ask how it is that the fall of Adam involves so many nations with their infant children in eternal death without remedy, unless that is so meet to God? Here the most loquacious tongues must be dumb."[14]

There is, of course, a biblical answer to the question of sin that satisfies man's God-given conscience. Man has genuine moral responsibility to God because, beginning with Adam and Eve and coming down to the present, "all have sinned" by their own free will, not by an imposed divine decree. Therefore, any sovereign intervention short of wiping out the human race would not solve the problem of evil, because evil comes from within the heart of man.

Jesus said that from the human heart itself "proceed...evil thoughts, murders, adulteries, fornications, thefts, false witness, blasphemies..." (Matthew 15:19). The only solution short of destroying mankind, as God almost did with the flood, is to completely change the heart. Calvinism claims that God can do this through a sovereign "regeneration" of whomever He pleases without any faith or understanding on man's part. If that were the case, He could have done so with Adam and Eve and with all mankind, eliminating the sin and suffering in man's entire history. If the problem of sin is all God's doing, then He could undo it as well—but not if He has foreordained it!

On the contrary, because it was by *man* that sin entered the world, the biblical solution is found in the man Christ Jesus alone (Romans 5:12–21). Only through His death in payment of the just penalty for our sins, and in His resurrection to live His life in believers can man be forgiven and born again of the Spirit of God.

This wonderful salvation cannot be forced upon anyone but is God's gracious gift for all who will receive it through believing the gospel of Jesus Christ. It is by faith that we are saved and created in Christ Jesus "unto good works, which God hath before ordained that we should walk in them" (Ephesians 2:8–10). To believe the gospel and to receive Christ requires the exercise of a free choice on man's part, a choice that Calvinism will not allow. As Oxford professor Andrew Fairbairn explained,

> While Freedom reigned in Heaven, Necessity governed on earth; and men were but pawns in the hands of the Almighty who moved them whithersoever He willed. This was the principle common to theologies like those of Augustine and Calvin.... It made illusions of our most common experience.[15]

Practical Consequences of Denying Free Will

Sadly, many of those who deny that God allows any free choice to man have been prone to act like the Deity they believed in by denying choice to those who disagreed with them and attempting to coerce everyone into conformity. In this they were following Calvin, who "demanded that the state must consent to be the servant of the church.... Liberty of conscience was not granted. Heretics and dissenters were executed or banished, and the people were compelled by the arms of the magistracy to perform what was considered their religious duties."[16]

As we have already seen, setting up a state church in the early days of the Reformation, Calvinists forced their views on others whenever possible. One historian writes, "A majority of the framers of the new creeds [in England and Scotland] believed in the divine right of Presbyterianism. They considered it a duty of the state to enforce uniformity, and were not prepared to make concessions of any importance to the Independents [i.e., the "free churches" that rejected the state church system]. In 1648, Parliament passed an act of extremely intolerant character. Eight [theological] errors [were] made punishable with death."[17]

As we have also observed, the Westminster Assembly was called and financed by Parliament and was controlled by Presbyterians; Baptists and Independents were excluded as "mortal enemies of the State Church."[18] Tolerance for any religious belief other than Calvinism "was denounced by leading members of the [Westminster] Assembly as the 'last and strongest hold of Satan....'" The Assembly was determined to enforce its brand of religion "upon the entire population."[19]

The Horrible Consequences of Calvinistic "Sovereignty"

This small segment of history provides hundreds of examples of men who loved the Lord with their whole heart and were willing to suffer imprisonment and death in His service, yet because of some of their religious beliefs, they treated other Christians in a most un-Christian manner. Samuel Rutherford was such a man. His letters from prison contained such deep spiritual insights and were so moving that nearly 400 editions were eventually published. Robert Murray McCheyne said that "the *Letters of Samuel Rutherford* were often in his hand." Richard Baxter held these letters in such regard that he said that, apart from the Bible, "such a book as *Mr. Rutherford's Letters* the world never saw the like." Spurgeon considered them "the nearest thing to inspiration which can be found in all the writings of mere men."[20]

Historians described Rutherford as a "gracious and godly man." Yet, because of his Calvinist beliefs, he "denied absolutely the moral principles underlying religious toleration."[21] Sounding like the popes he despised, he even went so far as to declare that "there is but one true Church and all who are outside it are heretics who must be destroyed!"[22]

Never did Christ or His apostles or the early church attempt to force anyone to believe the gospel. The tolerance the early church had for the ungodly around them was not an acceptance of their errors. It was a recognition that no one could be forced against his will into the kingdom of God. They attempted to persuade the heathen to believe the gospel, but never did they attempt to force them to do so (as Islam requires)—nor did they believe in a God who could or would. The gospel is the good news of God's love in Christ and can only be received *willingly* from the heart. Since Calvinism denies the necessity of choice, it was only natural that its adherents would seek to force their views on all dissenters.

Roger Williams, one of the best-known advocates of religious freedom in his day, published a protest titled *The Bloudy Tenent [Bloody Tenet] of Persecution for Cause and Conscience*. He fled England for America, where he was badly treated by the Puritans. In England, the Westminster Assembly had his book publicly burned.[23] In 1648, the Presbyterians succeeded in enacting the "gag law...to punish the Baptists as 'blasphemers and heretics'.... Under this infamous law four hundred Baptists were thrown into prison."[24]

In fact, dissenters had been suffering persecution and imprisonment for years—Protestants suffering at the hands of fellow Protestants for not being Calvinists. Nearly thirty years before, the following entreaty, titled "A most Humble Supplication of many of the King's Majesty's loyal subjects...who are persecuted (only for differing in religion) contrary to Divine and human testimonies," had been smuggled out of a prison:

> Our miseries are long and lingering imprisonments for many years in divers counties of England, in which many have died and left behind them widows, and many small children; taking away our goods...not for any disloyalty to your Majesty, nor hurt to any mortal man...but only because we dare not assent unto, and practise in the worship of God, such things as we have not faith in, because it is sin against the Most High.[25]

Many Calvinists would deplore the persecution perpetrated by the early proponents of this doctrine. They would not approve of that side of the Westminster Assembly. Yet they praise its Calvinistic Confession, seemingly blind to the connection between the two. And they zealously promote Calvinism as "Reformation theology," as though the Calvinists had alone carried the Reformation on their shoulders. There were hundreds of thousands of others who were just as sincere in their faith (and we believe far more biblical) as were Calvin and Luther; and they suffered for Christ at the hands not only of the Roman Catholics but of Calvinists and Lutherans as well.

Love: The Missing Ingredient

God's love for the lost and the love of Christians for the lost—two major interrelated themes of Scripture—have no part in Calvinism. We know many would take offense at that statement who, indeed, are lovingly concerned for the lost. This is, however, *in spite* of and contrary to their Calvinism and not because of it. Though a Presbyterian theological professor and one-time Moderator of the General Assembly, Herrick Johnson acknowledged:

> Across the Westminster Confession could justly be written: "The Gospel for the elect only." That Confession was written under the absolute dominion of one idea, the doctrine of predestination. It does not contain one of the three truths: God's love for a lost world; Christ's compassion for a lost world; and the gospel universal for a lost world.[26]

In Calvin's entire *Institutes of the Christian Religion* there is *not one mention* of God's love for the lost! Nor is that surprising in view of the fact that Calvin's God can only love the elect.[27] Does that not bother today's evangelical leaders who praise Calvin as the great exegete and call themselves Calvinists?

Furthermore, Calvin's concept of love is defective. He says that God "requires that the love which we bear to Him be diffused among all mankind, so that our fundamental principle must ever be, Let a man be what he may, he is still to be loved, because God is loved."[28] This is one of several places where Calvin says the Christian is to love "all mankind." Should not God, then, who *is love,* love all men also? Calvin never says so, but at least here he seems to imply an agreement with that principle—though his idea of God's love is strange indeed.

He tells us that God's "boundless goodness is displayed" to everyone, "but not so as to bring all to salvation."[29] How could a "goodness" that stops short of what it could do be seriously described as "goodness," much less as "boundless"? This goodness (in spite of stopping short) is said by Calvin to be "evidence of his [God's] love." Again we ask, how can failing to do all the good that God is able to do be evidence of His love?

And evidence to whom? And how can it be said that God loves those whom He predestined to eternal torment before they were born?

This warped view of God's love is further revealed in Calvin's statement that this alleged display of God's "goodness" is not for the purpose of helping all mankind. Instead, God's intention is to bring "a heavier judgment...[upon] the reprobate for rejecting the evidence of his [God's] love."[30] This argument leaves one stunned. Can a "goodness" that doesn't do all the good it could be evidence of God's love? Would it not, instead, be evidence of a *lack* of love? And for using the common sense and conscience God has given us, are we to be condemned for rejecting what Calvin mistakenly called the "evidence of God's love"?

The Failure of Attempted "Explanations"

Follow Calvin's reasoning. God loves and saves only the elect; He neglects to save those whom He hasn't elected to salvation. Incredibly, through "shin[ing] the light of his word on the undeserving," he reveals His goodness and love by withholding it from them, the better to damn them for "rejecting the evidence of his love."

Such warped reasoning is an integral part of Calvinism that attempts to show that God loves those whom He could have saved but instead damns. Hear it from pastor and author John Piper, one of today's most respected Calvinist apologists:

> We do not deny that all men are the intended beneficiaries of the cross *in some sense*.... What we deny is that all men are intended as the beneficiaries of the death of Christ *in the same way*. All of God's mercy toward unbelievers—from the rising sun (Matthew 5:45) to the worldwide preaching of the gospel (John 3:16)—is made possible because of the cross.... Every time the gospel is preached to unbelievers it is the mercy of God that gives this opportunity for salvation.[31] (Emphasis in original)

Trying to reason with those who espouse such obviously contradictory statements leaves one with a sense of complete frustration. Proclaiming the gospel to those He has predestined to damnation is an act of God's mercy, by which He is giving "opportunity for salvation" to those who can't be saved?! And the gospel being preached to the doomed non-elect stems from God's "mercy toward unbelievers" flowing from the Cross?

Words such as love, grace, and mercy seem to have lost what was once their meaning. It is impossible to reason with those for whom the above seems reasonable. Are we talking about two different "Gods" and two different "gospels"—one described in the Bible, the other invented by Calvin and Augustine?

Differentiating Foreknowledge from Predestination

Calvinism's view of predestination, which for Calvin was seemingly empty of genuine love, is a large part of the problem. As we have seen, Pink says, "God foreknows what will be because He has decreed what shall be."[32] He was following Calvin, who said that "God foreknew what the end of man was to be...because he had so ordained by his decree."[33] Central to that belief is the denial that God's foreknowledge has anything to do with knowing something in advance. Instead, foreknowledge is defined as "foreordaining" and is equated with predestination.

Thus when Paul writes, "For whom he did foreknow, he also did predestinate" (Romans 8:29), Calvin insisted that it must be read, "For whom He predestinated He also did predestinate"—an obvious redundancy. This will be discussed further when we come to Predestination. It is mentioned here only to show why this view was adopted by Calvin, a view that is followed loyally by his followers today.

To know something in advance is not the same as predetermining that it will happen. Foreordination and foreknowledge are not the same, but they can overlap. Whatever God has predestined, He obviously knows will happen. His foreknowledge, however, is not limited to what He has predestined. He does not need to predestine something in order to know it will happen. Were that the case, as we have already observed, God would not be omniscient.

An unbiblical view of predestination, as we shall see in more detail later, is foundational to Calvinism. Arthur W. Pink claims that "God *decreed* from all eternity that Judas should betray the Lord Jesus" because through Zechariah "God declared that His Son should be sold for 'thirty pieces of silver' (Zechariah 11:12).... In prophecy God makes known what *will* be, and in making known what will be, He is but revealing to us what He has ordained *shall be*." Pink goes on to argue that in spite of all he did, being foreordained, Judas was nevertheless "a *responsible agent* in fulfilling this decree of God."[34]

Pink is best known for his strong views on God's sovereignty, especially through his book *The Sovereignty of God*. Vance points out that "Pink's

Calvinism upset some Calvinists so bad[ly] that an attempt was made to tone it down by The Banner of Truth Trust, by issuing, in 1961, a 'British Revised Edition' of *The Sovereignty of God* in which three chapters and the four appendices were expunged. For this they have been severely criticized (and rightly so) by other Calvinists."[35]

Philosophers and theologians have long speculated about how God could know the future without *causing* the future. The consequences of whether this is true are serious. We have already given two reasons why God's foreknowledge of what will happen need have no influence upon what to man are future events. Even Calvin wrote, "I, for my part, am willing to admit, that mere prescience lays no necessity on the creatures; though some do not assent to this, but hold that it is itself the cause of things."[36] Calvin's reason, however, was that he held foreknowledge and predestination to be one and the same: "but since he foresees the things which are to happen, simply because he has decreed that they are so to happen, it is vain to debate about prescience, while it is clear that all events take place by his sovereign appointment."[37]

Of course, "all events" must include every evil thought, word, and deed. So here again, as elsewhere, Calvin clearly declares that God is the cause of evil. Yet in the face of undeniable evidence, so-called "moderate Calvinists" today deny that Calvinism teaches that God is the cause, and thus the author, of evil. There is obviously a vast difference between saying that God fully *foresees* everything that will happen and *allows* much that is not His perfect will (which Calvin would not permit)—and in saying that God *predetermines* everything that occurs and thus is the *cause* of it (which Calvin insisted is the case). The latter view, which is Calvinism's foundational doctrine, makes man a mere automaton and reveals God as the effective cause behind all evil, wickedness, and sin. Thus a terrible blemish is imposed upon God's holy character!

Like Calvin, Luther asserts that "God foreknows and wills all things." And he argues that if this is not true, then "how can you believe, trust and rely on His promises?"[38] The answer is, "Quite easily. We rely upon God's promises because He is God, knows all, and cannot lie."

Luther is simply mistaken here, as he was on much else. Scripture nowhere indicates that God must *will* all things in order to *know* them—or in order to make and keep promises. What God promises to do, He *will* do, regardless of the will or actions of man or nature, yet without violating human will. That He is able to protect us and bring us to heaven does not require that He must will every event that swirls about us—much less that

He must be the direct cause of every sin we commit or of which we may become the victims.

Foreknowledge as Proof

More than simply claiming that God knows the future in advance, Scripture proves this fact by revealing His infinite foreknowledge in the hundreds of supernatural prophecies recorded therein. God foretells the future through His prophets for a number of reasons, the greatest being to prove that He is the one true God, as opposed to false gods, and to prove beyond question that, in contrast to all other sacred books of world religions, the Bible is His only and infallible written Word to mankind. Thus God declares:

- Behold, the former things [which I foretold] are come to pass, and new things do I declare: before they spring forth I tell you of them. (Isaiah 42:9)
- I am God, and there is none like me, declaring the end from the beginning, and from ancient times the things that are not yet done, saying, My counsel shall stand, and I will do all my pleasure.... (Isaiah 46:9–10)
- I have even from the beginning declared it to thee; before it came to pass I shewed it thee: lest thou shouldest say, Mine idol hath done them, and my graven image, and my molten image, hath commanded them. (Isaiah 48:5)

For at least two reasons, one cannot deny God's complete foreknowledge of the future. First of all, one would be denying God as He necessarily is and as the Bible presents Him. Second, one would be denying the very foundation of Christianity. Old Testament prophecies comprise the major evidence God offers to man's faith that Jesus of Nazareth is the Christ, the Messiah of Israel. Without Him there is no Christianity. So complete is this proof—solely on the basis of numerous clear prophecies—that no one who makes a careful investigation can honestly deny that the Lord Jesus Christ is the prophesied Messiah, the Savior of the world.

The Apostle Paul firmly links the gospel of our salvation in Christ with God's foreknowledge expressed through His prophets: "...the gospel of God (which he had promised afore by his prophets in the holy scriptures), concerning his Son Jesus Christ our Lord..." (Romans 1:1–3).

Paul validates the gospel of salvation with the phrase, "according to the scriptures," meaning, of course, Old Testament prophecies:

> Moreover, brethren, I declare unto you the gospel which I preached unto you, which also ye have received, and wherein ye stand... How that Christ died for our sins *according to the scriptures*; and that he was buried, and that he rose again the third day *according to the scriptures....* (1 Corinthians 15:1–4; emphasis added)

Unless God's prophets, through His foreknowledge, had told us how, where, and when the Messiah would be born, and of His sinless life and miracles, His betrayal for thirty pieces of silver by one of His disciples, His rejection by His people the Jews, and many other specifics including His cruel crucifixion and His glorious resurrection, we would have had no way of identifying the Messiah when He came. Had the precise details not been foretold by prophets who had already been proved to be inspired of God, His betrayal, rejection, and crucifixion would have been enough to convince us (as most Jews are convinced to this day) that He could not have been the Messiah. The detailed identification leaves those who reject Christ without excuse.

None of the world's religions has such prophetic evidence for its validity. There are no prophecies for Buddha, Confucius, Muhammad, or any other leader of the world's religions, whereas there are literally hundreds of prophecies proving that Jesus Christ is the Messiah.

And here we confront another odd contradiction (beyond the scope of this book, but which we have dealt with in other writings): that those of the so-called Reformed position (in general) who put such emphasis upon foreknowledge and predestination have, following Augustine's lead yet further, rejected the premillennial rapture of the church, the literal thousand-year reign of Christ on David's throne, and the literal fulfillment of all of God's promises to His chosen people, Israel, along with so much else that is clearly prophesied for the future. Instead, like Augustine, to their own harm they allegorize and spiritualize away this massive and vital portion of God's revealed foreknowledge—the very prophecies about Israel that constitute the major proofs God has provided for His existence and that the Bible is His Word.

What About Man's Will?

As surely as we recognize that God is sovereign, we also recognize that we have at least limited freedom to act within whatever bounds He may have established for human actions. This recognition seems to be continually validated by daily experience. What L. S. Keyser says could hardly be disputed: "That man has a conscience which distinguishes between right and wrong, and free will by which he is able to choose between them, scarcely seems to require any argument.... His whole experience tells him that he is a free moral being."[39] Alexander Maclaren, one of England's great Baptist preachers, put it in similar terms:

> If I cannot trust my sense that I can do this or not do it, as I choose, there is nothing that I can trust. Will is the power of determining which of two [or more] roads I shall go.... God, the infinite Will, has given to men, whom He made in His own image, this inexplicable and awful power of coinciding with or opposing His purpose and His voice....[40]

It is not only Calvinists and Lutherans who deny free will, but for thousands of years atheists and skeptics have also argued against this belief. Even Arminius declared that "the Free Will of man towards the True Good is...imprisoned, destroyed, and lost...it has no powers whatsoever except such as are excited by Divine grace."[41] Of course, neither can man think rationally or even breathe except by God's grace—but we do think and breathe, and we make choices by our own wills as well as by God's grace.

It hardly seems reasonable that our perception of making choices, some of which we agonize over for days, could simply be an illusion and that we are mere puppets of God's foreordination. In his *Confessions*, Augustine, supposed originator of "absolute sovereignty," wrote:

> I knew as well that I had a will as that I lived: when then I did will or nill anything, I was most sure that no other than myself did will and nill: and I all but saw that there was the cause of my sin."[42]

The very fact that John tells us that the redeemed are born again "not of the will of man" indicates that there must be much else for which the will of man is to be credited and blamed. Peter's statement that men "willingly are ignorant" (2 Peter 3:5) of God's truth indicates that depravity is not something beyond man's control, but the product of his willing choice. That God says to Israel, "If ye be willing and obedient...but if ye refuse and rebel..." (Isaiah 1:19–20), indicates again that man can be reasoned with and can choose by an act of his will either to obey or to disobey God. There are numerous statements in Scripture indicating that God has given man a free will to make moral and spiritual choices for which he alone bears responsibility and is to be blamed.

While God works "all things after [according to] the *counsel* of His own will" (Ephesians 1:11), this does not state that God *causes* everything that happens in the universe. It is perfectly compatible with God's sovereignty for Him (by His own *counsel*) to allow man to disobey Him. Without free will, man could not receive God's love, love Him in return, and receive the gift of salvation.

Confusion Where Clarity Is Needed

Although Calvinism rejects free will, its adherents can't agree upon what this means. Some allow man freedom in the sphere of earthly matters and deny it only when it comes to believing in Christ. Palmer defines "free will" as "the kind of freedom that no man has," not only "to believe on Christ or to reject Him," but even "the ability or freedom to choose either good or evil."[43] Spencer further explains, "*Total Depravity* insists that man does not have a 'free will' in the sense that he is *free* to trust Jesus Christ as his Lord and Saviour."[44] Vance counters that "No philosopher who denies to man a free will does so on the basis of man's depravity."[45] Nor did (or could) Calvin produce any scripture to support his undefined assertions that man can choose *some* good but *not enough* good, or that he is therefore unable to believe in Christ to the saving of his soul.

Even defining terms divides Calvinists. Charles Hodge insists that "the [Calvinist] doctrine of man's inability, therefore, does not assume that man has ceased to be a free moral agent."[46] Pink, however, declares that "'free moral agency' is an expression of human invention[47] [which denies] that he [man] is totally depraved...[48] the sinner's will is...free in only one direction, namely in the direction of evil."[49] Spurgeon said, "Free will is nonsense."[50] Pink quotes J. N. Darby in another *non sequitur*: "If Christ came to save that which is lost, free will has no place."[51]

On the other hand, equally strong Calvinists Talbot and Crampton rightfully insist that to deny that man has "free moral agency would be to allege that he could never make a choice about anything at all. That would be absurd."[52] Another Calvinist points out that "Calvin retains [to man] so little of the will...that he cannot explain adequately the moral character of human action [in] choices between good and evil."[53] Each of us must come to his own conclusion based upon Scripture.

What Scripture Says About Free Will

The words "will," "free-will," "willing," "freewill," "free will," along with related words such as "voluntary," "choose," etc., are found nearly 4,000 times in Scripture. The requirement of willing obedience from the heart is a theme that runs all through the Bible: "If ye be willing and obedient..." (Isaiah 1:19), "If any man will do his [God's] will..." (John 7:17), "If thou believest with all thine heart" (Acts 8:37), etc.

God wants our hearts, and the very concept of "heart" used throughout Scripture is meaningless without free will. That "the king's heart is in the hand of the Lord, as the rivers of water: he turneth it whithersoever he will" (Proverbs 21:1) does not say that the king has no choice as Calvinism insists. At the least, this is Solomon's declaration of submission as Israel's King to God; and at the most, it says that God can turn any king's heart when He so desires. But it does not declare that everything any king thinks, speaks, and does is according to God's will and by His pre-ordination. That proposition, again, would make God the author of evil.

The phrase, "freewill offering" is found nine times (Leviticus 22:21, 23; Numbers 15:3; Deuteronomy 16:10; 23:23; Ezra 1:4; 3:5; 7:16; 8:28), and "freewill offerings" is found seven times (Leviticus 22:18, 38; Numbers 29:39; Deuteronomy 12:6, 17; 2 Chronicles 31:14, Psalm 119:108). Those numbers, however, do not tell the full story. There were countless freewill offerings as the following indicates: "And Kore the son of Imnah the Levite...was over the freewill offerings of God, to distribute the oblations of the LORD, and the most holy things (2 Chronicles 31:14). The phrase "willingly offered" is found five times, such as "the people willingly offered themselves" (Judges 5:2). Both phrases are even used together: "willingly offered a freewill offering unto the LORD (Ezra 3:5). Could the fact that God gave man free will—and a major reason why—be stated more clearly?

Do Outside Influences Destroy Free Will?

In order to support the doctrine of Total Depravity, the Calvinist must show that man's will is totally enslaved by sin. The argument has been used that no choice could be made without some influence. Of course, whatever choice one makes is affected to some extent by multiple factors: health or mental mood, the weather, financial pressures, temptations, lust, timing, opportunity, and so forth. And many if not most of these almost numberless influences would seem to be beyond the control of the chooser. How then can the will ever be free?

In pressing this point, Talbot and Crampton write, "If this Arminian concept of free will is taken to its logical conclusion, then it would be sinful to preach the gospel to fallen man. Why? Because it would be an attempt to *cause* him to turn to Christ, which would be a violation of his free will."[54] In other words, it would be wrong to attempt to influence man to believe the gospel, because his choice would not have been made freely.

Then Paul was wrong. He said, "we persuade men..." (2 Corinthians 5:11). What were Isaiah, Jeremiah, Ezekiel, and the prophets trying to do but to persuade Israel to turn from her evil back to God in full repentance?

Echoing this same argument, Pink imagines he delivers a death blow to free will with this broadside: "There is something which *influences* the choice; something which *determines* the decision."[55] Not so. Influences *influence*; they don't *determine*.

Nor is free will an "Arminian concept." For thousands of years, many non-Christian philosophers have marshaled excellent arguments in favor of man's free will. Further, the very fact that various influences are brought to bear while man arrives at any choice is in itself evidence that man has a free will. If man had no will, there would be nothing for these "influences" to influence. Influences don't make decisions. The will takes into consideration all factors, and no matter how compelling any influences (i.e., facts, reasons, circumstances, emergencies, contingencies, etc.) may have been, the will still makes its own choice—often irrationally.

That it may have been influenced to some extent in no way proves that the will did not take all factors into consideration and make its own decision. No matter how it reached a resolution, only the will could have decided. Although the Calvinist looks to Augustine for so much, and avidly quotes him for support, here again Augustine is ignored, for he argued persuasively on this very point:

> ...we do many things which, if we were not willing, we should certainly not do. This is primarily true of the act of willing itself—for if we will, it *is*; if we will not, it *is* not—for we should not will if we were unwilling.[56]

Influences can be powerful. Many of today's preachers deliberately employ psychological and salesmanship techniques, entrapping multitudes in false professions of faith. God does not use psychological techniques but truth to convince and persuade. This is the purpose of prophecy. Paul "confounded the Jews...proving that this is very Christ" (Acts 9:22). Apollos did the same, "publickly, shewing by the scriptures that Jesus was Christ" (Acts 18:28). We should do the same today.

There is obviously a godly persuasion that does not employ deceptive techniques. Moreover, as we have already seen, if Calvinism were true, Paul's use of persuasion would be misguided for other reasons: the elect would need no persuasion and the non-elect, being totally depraved and predestined to eternal damnation, could not be persuaded.

Foreknowledge and Man's Will

Given the above, a central issue has engaged philosophers, skeptics, and theologians in debate for thousands of years: *How* can God's foreknowledge and man's free will both be true? Inasmuch as God knows what everyone will ever think or do, isn't everything therefore predetermined? And wouldn't that fact rule out any possibility that man could make a free choice concerning anything at all?

We have already seen why God's foreknowledge has no causative effect upon man's free choice. God, being timeless, sees from outside—as though they had already happened—what to us are future events. Thus His foreknowledge has no effect on man's will. There is no reason why in His omniscience God cannot know what man will freely choose to do before he chooses to do it—and have that knowledge without *causing* the event to occur.

There is yet another question that troubles many: If man is free to choose between options, would that not in itself deny both God's sovereignty and His foreknowledge? Luther claimed that this question was the very heart of the Reformation and of the gospel itself. In fact, Luther dogmatically insisted that it was impossible for God to foreknow the future and for man at the same time to be a free agent to act as he wills.

Believing firmly in God's foreknowledge, Luther wrote an entire book titled *The Bondage of the Will,* to prove that the very idea of man's free will is a fallacy and an illusion. Several reasons have already been given as to why Luther was wrong on this point, and that issue will be dealt with further in the next chapter.

Though Calvin took so much from Augustine, like Luther he also rejected the Augustinian belief that God could foreknow the future, while at the same time man could have a free will. According to Calvin, foreknowledge leaves no room whatsoever for free will, because foreknowledge is the same as predestination:

> If God merely foresaw human events, and did not also arrange and dispose of them at his pleasure, there might be room for agitating the question [of free will]...but since he foresees the things which are to happen, simply because he has decreed them, they are so to happen, it is vain to debate about prescience....
>
> If this frigid fiction [of free will] is received, where will be the omnipotence of God, by which, according to his secret counsel on which everything depends, he rules over all?[57]

Calvin repeatedly uses such unbiblical and utterly fallacious reasoning. The Calvinist assumes a contradiction between sovereignty and free will that doesn't exist. The fact that God is able to allow man freedom of choice, while still effecting His purposes unhindered, is all the more glorifying to His sovereign wisdom, power, and foreknowledge.

Augustine on Free Will

In taking so much else from him, the Calvinist overlooks the fact that Augustine clearly affirmed the free will of man.[58] Moreover, Augustine argued that there *is no incompatibility* between God's absolute sovereignty and man's free will; and that to deny that fact, as did Luther and Calvin, would be "impious"! Augustine writes persuasively:

> ...we assert both that God knows all things before they come to pass and that we do by our free will whatsoever we know and feel to be done by us only because we will it....
>
> He Who foreknew all the causes of things would certainly among those causes not have been ignorant of our wills.... Wherefore our wills also have just so much power as God willed and foreknew that they should have.[59]

> Therefore we are by no means compelled, either, retaining the prescience of God to take away the freedom of the will, or, retaining the freedom of the will, to deny that He is prescient of future things, which is impious. But we…faithfully and sincerely confess both.[60]

Augustine holds to freedom of the human will even into the eternal state: "Neither are we to suppose that, because sin shall have no power to delight them, free will must be withdrawn. It will, on the contrary, be all the more truly free, because set free from delight in sinning to take unfailing delight in not sinning."[61]

When it came to free will, Calvin ignored Augustine, as did Luther—and to maintain their theories, ignored many scriptures.

Nowhere is the failure to use sound reason in exegeting Scripture more apparent than in Luther's debate with Erasmus over free will. This will be considered next.

---

1. Augustine, *The City of God*, trans. Marcus Dobs. In *Great Books of the Western World*, ed. Robert Maynard Hutchins and Mortimer J. Adler (Encyclopaedia Brittanica, Inc., 1952), V.9.
2. Jacobus Arminius, *The Works of James Arminius*, trans. James and William Nichols (Grand Rapids, MI: Baker Book House, 1986), 2:120.
3. David S. West, *The Baptist Examiner*, March 18, 1989, 5.
4. John Calvin, *Institutes of the Christian Religion*, trans. Henry Beveridge (Grand Rapids, MI: Wm. Eerdmans Publishing Company, 1998 ed.), III: xxiii, 6.
5. Grover E. Gunn, *The Doctrine of Grace* (Memphis, TN: Footstool Publications, 1987), 13.
6. Michael J. Kane, Ph. D., "Letters," *Christianity Today*, July 9, 2001, 9.
7. David N. Steele and Curtis C. Thomas, *The Five Points of Calvinism* (Phillipsburg, NJ: Presbyterian and Reformed Publishing Co., 1963), 25.
8. Loraine Boettner, *The Reformed Doctrine of Predestination* (Phillipsburg, NJ: Presbyterian and Reformed Publishing Co., 1932), 32.
9. Calvin, *Institutes*, III: xxiii, 8.
10. Ibid., 7.
11. David O. Wilmouth, *The Baptist Examiner*, September 16, 1989, 5.
12. Calvin, *Institutes*, II: ii, 12–13.
13. Ibid., I: xviii, 1.
14. Ibid., III: xxiii, 7.
15. Andrew M. Fairbairn, *The Philosophy of the Christian Religion* (New York: The MacMillan Co., 1923), 179.
16. John Horsch, *History of Christianity* (Scottsdale, PA: John Horsch, 1903), 270.

17. George Park Fisher, *History of the Christian Church* (New York: Charles Scribner's Sons, 1902), 406.

18. A. C. Underwood, *A History of the English Baptists* (The Baptist Union of Great Britain and Ireland, 1970), 72.

19. Albert H. Newman, *A Manual of Church History* (Philadelphia, PA: American Baptist Publication Society, 1933), II: 286–87.

20. *Letters of Samuel Rutherford* (Carlisle, PA: The Banner of Truth Trust, 1996; 1st ed. 1664), back cover.

21. David Gay, *Battle for the Church, 1517–1644* (Lowestoft, UK: Brachus, 1997), 438.

22. Underwood, *English Baptists*, 72.

23. C. Sylvester Horne, *A Popular History of the Free Churches* (Cambridge, UK: James Clarke and Co., 1903), 124–27.

24. John T. Christian, *A History of the Baptists* (Sunday School Board of the Southern Baptist Convention, 1922), I: 296–97.

25. Gay, *Battle*, 367.

26. Quoted in Augustus H. Strong, *Systematic Theology* (Valley Forge, PA: Judson Press, 1907), 779.

27. Calvin, *Institutes*, II: xvi, 3–4; II: xvii, 2–5.

28. Ibid., II: viii, 55.

29. Ibid., III: xxiv, 2.

30. Ibid.

31. John Piper and Pastoral Staff, "TULIP: What We Believe about the Five Points of Calvinism: Position Paper of the Pastoral Staff" (Minneapolis, MN: Desiring God Ministries, 1997), 14.

32. Arthur W. Pink, *The Doctrine of Election and Justification* (Grand Rapids, MI: Baker Book House, 1974), 172.

33. Calvin, *Institutes*, III: xxiii, 7.

34. Pink, *Election*, 155.

35. Marc D. Carpenter, Pt. 1 of "The Banner of Truth Versus Calvinism," *The Trinity Review*, May 1997, 1–4; cited in Vance, *Other Side*, 24.

36. Calvin, *Institutes*, III: xxiii, 6.

37. Ibid.

38. Martin Luther, *The Bondage of the Will*, trans. J. I. Packer and O. R. Johnston (Grand Rapids, MI: Fleming H. Revell, 1957, 11th prtg. 1999), 83–84.

39. Leander S. Keyser, *Election and Conversion* (Burlington, IA: Literary Board, 1914), 96.

40. Alexander Maclaren, *Expositions of Holy Scripture* (London: Hodder and Stoughton, n. d.), II: 333–34.

41. Jacobus Arminius, *The Works of James Arminius*, trans. James and Williams Nichols (Grand Rapids, MI: Baker Book House, 1986), 2:192.

42. Augustine, *The Confessions*, VII:5; in *Great Books of the Western World*, ed. Robert Maynard Hutchins and Mortimer J. Adler, trans. Edward Bouverie Pusey (Encyclopaedia Britannica, Inc., 1952), vol. 18.

43. Edwin H. Palmer, *the five points of calvinism* (Grand Rapids, MI: Baker Books, enlarged ed., 20th prtg. 1980), 36.

44. Duane Edward Spencer, *TULIP: The Five Points of Calvinism in the Light of Scripture* (Grand Rapids, MI: Baker Book House, 1979), 27.

45. Laurence M. Vance, *The Other Side of Calvinism* (Pensacola, FL: Vance Publications, rev. ed. 1999), 201.
46. Charles Hodge, *Systematic Theology* (Grand Rapids, MI: Wm B. Eerdmans Publishing Co., 1986), 2:260.
47. Arthur W. Pink, *The Sovereignty of God* (Grand Rapids, MI: Baker Book House, 2nd prtg. 1986), 143.
48. Ibid., 138.
49. Ibid., 135.
50. Charles H. Spurgeon, *Free Will—A Slave* (McDonough, GA: Free Grace Publications, 1977), 3.
51. Pink, *Sovereignty*, 138.
52. Kenneth G. Talbot and W. Gary Crampton, *Calvinism, Hyper-Calvinism and Arminianism* (Edmonton, AB: Still Waters Revival Books, 1990), 18.
53. Dewey J. Hoitenga, *John Calvin and the Will: A Critique and Corrective* (Grand Rapids, MI: Baker Books, 1997), 70.
54. Talbot and Crampton, *Calvinism*, 21.
55. Cited in Vance, *Other Side*, 202.
56. Augustine, *City of God*, V.10.
57. Calvin, *Institutes*, III: xxiii, 6–7.
58. Augustine, *Confessions*, VII: iii, 5; and *City of God*, V.9–10.
59. Augustine, *City of God*, V.9.
60. Ibid., 10.
61. Ibid., XXII.30.

CHAPTER

13

Erasmus and Luther in Debate

NEARLY ANY IN-DEPTH discussion with Calvinists eventually touches on the issue of free will. And, nearly always, reference will be made to Martin Luther's *Bondage of the Will.* John Armstrong declares, "This is what the Reformation is ultimately all about...*The Bondage of the Will...* Luther said this is the important book because it...takes us back where the real battle is."[1]

Calvinists are not alone in their high regard for this lengthy treatise. Many evangelicals, even without having read *Bondage,* hold it and Luther in high regard simply because of the key role he played in the Reformation. Yes, the entire Western world owes Martin Luther a debt of gratitude for his stalwart stand against the tyranny of Roman Catholicism, which ruled the world without challenge at that time. That does not mean, however, that we ought to accept everything that came from his pen without comparing it carefully to God's Word.

Appalled by the licentiousness he had seen in the Vatican and among the clergy in his visit to Rome, and by the sale of indulgences as tickets to heaven (financing the ongoing construction and remodeling of St. Peter's Basilica), on October 31, 1517, Luther nailed his *Disputation on the power and efficacy of Indulgences* (known as *The Ninety-five Theses*[2]) to the door of the Wittenberg Castle Chapel. (John Calvin was then eight years old.) Copies translated from the original Latin were widely distributed in many languages, inciting heated debate all across Europe and arousing hope among multitudes that the yoke of Rome could at last be loosened, if not broken.

When one studies his 95 theses, however, it seems that Luther was not entirely opposed to indulgences—only to their abuses. At this point he was still a Roman Catholic in his heart, not desiring to leave that false and corrupt Church, but rather to reform it. Instead of leaving, he would be excommunicated.

He rejected the sale of indulgences for money and the false proclamation that an indulgence of any kind could purchase salvation. That he did, however, still believe in purgatory and accepted the value of indulgences of a limited kind is quite clear from the following excerpts of his 95 Theses:

> **Paragraphs 17-22**
> Furthermore, it does not seem proved, either by reason or by Scripture, that souls in purgatory are outside the state of merit.... Nor does it seem proved that souls in purgatory, at least not all of them, are certain and assured of their own salvation.... [I]ndulgence preachers are in error who say that a man is absolved from every penalty and saved by papal indulgences. As a matter of fact, the pope remits to souls in purgatory no penalty which, according to canon law, they should have paid in this life.
>
> **Paragraph 26**
> The pope does very well when he grants remission to souls in purgatory, not by the power of the keys, which he does not have, but by way of intercession for them.
>
> **Paragraph 29**
> Who knows whether all souls in purgatory wish to be redeemed, since we have exceptions in St. Severinus and St. Paschal, as related in a legend.
>
> **Paragraphs 38-41**
> Nevertheless, papal remission and blessing are by no means to be disregarded...[but] must be preached with caution, lest people erroneously think that they are preferable to other good works of love.[3]

It is quite clear that Luther, far from having renounced all of Rome's abominations, was only cautiously groping his way. The same would be true of Calvin, who followed Luther's footsteps some years later. Nor were either of these Reformers ever delivered completely from Rome's errors. Tragically, much unbiblical baggage was thereby carried over from Catholicism into Lutheranism and Calvinism, which remains to this day. For example, millions of Lutherans and Calvinists around the world remain under the deadly delusion that their baptism as infants made them children of God fit for heaven. Their subsequent "confirmation" only reinforces that deadly delusion.

A Few Relevant Facts

On October 12, 1518, Luther was summoned to Rome by order of Pope Leo X. Arrested, he was held at Augsburg for trial before Cardinal Cajetan. Refused an impartial tribunal, Luther fled for his life by night. On January 3, 1521, a formal bull was issued by the Pope consigning Luther to hell if he did not recant. The Emperor, pledging Luther's safety, summoned him to appear before the Imperial Diet in Worms on April 17, 1521. The Chancellor of Treves, orator of the Diet, demanded that he retract his writings. Luther made this fearless and famous reply:

> I cannot submit my faith either to the pope or to the councils, because it is clear as day that they have frequently erred and contradicted each other. Unless therefore I am convinced by the testimony of Scripture, or by the clearest reasoning...I cannot and I will not retract.... Here I stand; I can do no other; may God help me. Amen! [4]

Now an outlaw by papal edict, Luther fled again and was "kidnapped" on his way back to Wittenberg by friends who took him for safekeeping to Wartburg Castle. From there he disseminated more "heresy" in writings that further shook all Europe. Rome's determination to eliminate Lutheran infidelity, as expressed by the Catholic authorities in March 1529 at the second Diet of Speyer, provoked a number of independent princes to assert the right to live according to the Bible. They expressed this firm resolve in the famous "Protest" of April 19, 1529, from which the term "Protestant" was coined.

The Imperial Diet was convened in Augsburg for a thorough examination of Protestant heresies. (Luther, having been excommunicated in 1521, was a wanted man and dared not appear.) On June 25, 1530, the Augsburg Confession (prepared by Melanchthon in consultation with Luther) was read before about 200 dignitaries. It delineated the clear differences between Lutheranism and Catholicism. In particular, Article IV affirmed that men "are freely justified...their sins are forgiven for Christ's sake, who, by His death, has made satisfaction for our sins." Article XIII declared that "the Sacraments were ordained...to be signs and testimonies" and condemned "those who teach that the Sacraments justify by the outward act...." Article XV admonished "that human traditions instituted to propitiate God, to merit grace, and to make satisfaction for sins, are opposed to the Gospel and the doctrine of faith. Wherefore vows and traditions concerning meats and days, etc., instituted to merit grace and to make satisfaction for sins, are useless and contrary to the Gospel."[5]

Luther still hoped that the Church could be reformed from within. Thus the Augsburg Confession still viewed the Roman Catholic Church as the true Church, and those signing it claimed to be true Catholics. Several times that document refers to the steadfastness of the preparers' traditional Catholic faith, particularly in their stand for the real presence of Christ in the Eucharist (still accepted by Lutherans today) and for the regenerative power of infant baptism in opposition to the "heretical Anabaptists."

Amazingly, that rather Catholic document has been the creed of most Lutherans ever since, officially incorporating some of Rome's errors into modern-day Lutheranism. Thus, it is not surprising that in Augsburg on October 31, 1999 (the date and place could hardly be a coincidence), in what can only be construed as a slap at Martin Luther and the Reformation—the Lutheran World Federation and representatives of the Roman Catholic Church signed a Joint Declaration on Justification By Faith, claiming agreement on the major point that had divided Lutherans and Catholics for nearly 470 years.

Contradictions, Contradictions . . .

While this "agreement" was being reached to heal a theological schism which had begun over indulgences, Pope John Paul II was defiantly offering special indulgences for the year 2000: forgiveness of sins for giving up cigarettes for a day, for making a pilgrimage to Rome, for walking through one or more of four "Holy Doors" he would open, and so forth. In spite of this new "agreement" between Lutherans and Catholics, not one change could be noted in Roman Catholic beliefs and practices. Everything that Martin Luther had so vigorously opposed was still fully in place—including the wearing of scapulars promising that "Whosoever dies wearing this scapular shall not suffer eternal fire" (John Paul II, whom many evangelicals call a "fine Christian," has worn one since childhood); the wearing of supposedly miraculous medals for protection; the use of "Holy Water;" prayers to saints, and especially to Mary, for help and even salvation; pilgrimages to shrines (some pilgrims walking on bloodied knees, the better to earn forgiveness of their sins); and too many other unbiblical and superstitious practices to enumerate. Never had the justification by faith, which Luther preached, been so thoroughly denied—and that by Lutherans eager to heal the essential breach with Rome for which thousands were burned at the stake.

The Pope even had the impertinence to remind the world that the practice of Holy Pilgrimages for forgiveness of sins had been initiated in 1300 by Pope Boniface VIII, whom he lauded as "of blessed memory." Apparently John Paul II thought it had been forgotten that Boniface was a murderous, anti-Christian, openly fornicating (a mother and her daughter were both among his mistresses) pope who had been so evil (though hardly more evil than many of both his predecessor and successor popes) that Dante's *Inferno* had him "buried" upside down in the deepest crevasse of hell.

Slaying its 6,000 inhabitants, Boniface "of blessed memory" to John Paul II, had utterly destroyed the beautiful Colonna city of Palestrina, Italy (with all its art and historic structures dating back to Julius Caesar) reducing it to a plowed field that he sowed with salt—giving indulgences to those who did this wanton evil.

Boniface had issued *Unam Sanctam,* an "infallible" Papal Bull, in 1302 (still in full force and effect today) declaring that there was no salvation outside the Roman Catholic Church and that for anyone to be saved it was "altogether necessary...to be subject to the Roman Pontiff."

Less than a year after the Joint Declaration, John Paul II, not to be outdone by Boniface, confirmed again that there was no salvation outside his Church. Lutherans were offended, as though this were something new. Yet the Pope had made such pronouncements before, and the same dogma has long been stated in Catholic catechisms and numerous other official documents. Nor had the new "agreement" between Lutherans and Catholics even addressed (much less corrected) numerous other Romish heresies.

Credit Where Credit Is Due

Unquestionably, Martin Luther was a great reformer to whom we owe (by God's grace) much of the freedom of worship, conscience, and speech that exists throughout the Western world today, in contrast, for example, to the almost total absence of such blessings in the Muslim and Communist worlds. However, much took place prior to Luther that made possible what he accomplished. That fact must be taken into account in evaluating his contributions.

Luther himself said, "We are not the first to declare the papacy to be the kingdom of Antichrist, since for many years before us so many and so great men...have undertaken to express the same thing so clearly...."[6] For example, in a full council at Rheims in the tenth century, the Bishop of Orléans called the Pope the Antichrist. In the eleventh century, Rome was denounced as "the See of Satan" by Berenger of Tours. The Waldensians identified the Pope as Antichrist in an A.D. 1100 treatise titled "The Noble Lesson." In 1206 an Albigensian conference in Montréal, France, indicted the Vatican as the woman "drunk with the blood of the martyrs," which she has continued to prove to this day in spite of shameful new "agreements" such as Evangelicals and Catholics Together and the more recent Joint Declaration.

A movement among priests and monks calling for a return to the Bible began many centuries before Luther. The reformation movement within the Roman Church can be traced as far back as Priscillian, Bishop of Avila. Falsely accused of heresy, witchcraft, and immorality by a Synod in Bordeaux, France, in A.D. 384 (seven of his writings proving these charges false were recently discovered in Germany's University of Wurzburg library), Priscillian and six others were beheaded at Trier in 385. Millions of true Christians were martyred at the hands of the Roman Catholic Church in the succeeding centuries prior to the Reformation.

Jumping ahead to the late 1300s, John Wycliff, called the "morning star of the Reformation," championed the authority of the Scriptures, translated and published them in English (while, almost as fast, Roman Catholics burned them), and preached and wrote against the evils of the popes and Catholic dogmas, especially transubstantiation. Influenced by Wycliff, Jan Hus, a fervent Catholic priest and rector of Prague University, was excommunicated in 1410. He was burned as a "heretic" in 1415—100 years before Luther and the Protestant Reformation—for calling a corrupt church to holiness and the authority of God's Word. In 1429, Pope Martin V commanded the King of Poland to exterminate the Hussites.

Many others who lived even closer to Luther's time played an important part in preparing Europe for the Reformation. One of these was Erasmus of Rotterdam. Because of his role in provoking Luther to write what some have called his masterpiece, *The Bondage of the Will*, this fascinating man, called by some historians "the bridge to the Reformation," must occupy some of our attention. At the height of the Reformation, it was popularly said in Paris that "Luther had only opened the door, after Erasmus had picked the lock."[7]

Erasmus of Rotterdam

Erasmus is one of the most interesting and enigmatic—and in many ways tragic—figures in history. He was born out of wedlock, a fact unknown to his father, Gerard, who, having fled in guilt from Holland to Rome, was told that his lover, Margaret, had died. Consumed with grief and remorse, Gerard entered the priesthood. Upon later returning to Holland, he discovered to his great joy that Margaret was alive, as was the son she had borne. Gerard would not, however, break his sacerdotal vows, nor would Margaret marry any other. Together they devoted themselves to their child, Erasmus, whom they put into school at the early age of four.

Despite being orphaned in his teens and living for years in desperate poverty, Erasmus pursued the study of Greek, Latin, and the classics and became possibly the most eloquent scholar of his day. Ordained an Augustinian priest at the age of 24, the year Columbus sailed to America, his splendid intellect and unusual clarity of expression eventually made Erasmus famous. He was courted by the powerful and rich, including kings, princes, prelates, and even popes, who curried his favor. Henry VIII invited Erasmus to England, where he lectured at Cambridge University and was a friend of luminaries such as Archbishop Warham, John Colet, and Sir Thomas More. All the while, Erasmus made no secret of his dislike of many of his Church's practices.

Both Erasmus's rejection of Rome's central doctrine of transubstantiation and his sense of humor (and no less his ability to remain in the good graces of important people in spite of offending them) are illustrated by a famous incident. Sir Thomas had loaned Erasmus a horse to carry him to the ship that would take him back across the Channel to the continent. The ever irascible Erasmus took the horse with him aboardship and, reaching shore, rode it all the way home. When More complained, Erasmus wrote back (reflecting the many times More had attempted to convince him of transubstantiation) a brief jingle as follows:

> You said of the bodily presence of Christ:
> Believe that you have, and you have him.
> Of the nag that I took my reply is the same:
> Believe that you have, and you have him.[8]

Erasmus the renegade had already channeled his keen wit into the most cutting satire, which he used to "unveil and combat the vices of the [Roman Catholic] Church...[he] attacked the monks and the prevailing abuses

[with] elegant and biting sarcasms against the theology and devotion of his age...he immolated...those schoolmen and those ignorant monks against whom he had declared war."[9] As one of his devices, Erasmus cleverly used fiction as a weapon. In *The Praise of Folly*, written largely at More's home, he personified the goddess Folly as Moria, to whom he gave such lines as

> Do we not see every country claiming its peculiar *saint*? Each trouble has its saint, and every saint his candle. This cures the toothache; that assists women in childbed, a third restores what a thief has stolen.... Especially [virtuous is] the virgin-mother of God, in whom the people place more confidence than in her Son....[10]

Moria attacks the bishops "who run more after gold than after souls." Even the highest officials in Rome cannot escape. She asks, "Can there be any greater enemies to the Church than these unholy pontiffs, who...allow Jesus Christ to be forgotten; who bind him by their mercenary regulations; who falsify his doctrine by forced interpretations; and crucify him a second time by their scandalous lives?"[11]

The Forerunner of the Reformation

The Praise of Folly appeared in 27 editions and in every European language during the lifetime of Erasmus, and "contributed more than any other [writing] to confirm the anti-sacerdotal tendency of the age." He urged men to get back to the "Christianity of the Bible" and pointed out that the *Vulgate* "swarmed with errors." One year before Luther nailed his 95 theses to the Wittenberg Chapel Door, Erasmus published his own critical edition of the New Testament in Greek, which contributed immensely to Luther's later success by opening a clearer picture of God's truth to many serious students of Scripture.

Erasmus raised his voice "against that mass of church regulations about dress, fasting, feast-days, vows, marriage and confessions which oppressed the people and enriched the priests." Eloquently he pressed his attack, of which the following is representative:

> In the churches they scarcely ever think of the gospel. The greater part of their sermons must be drawn up to please the commissaries of indulgences. The most holy doctrine of Christ must be suppressed or perverted to their profit. There is no longer any hope of cure, unless Christ himself should turn the hearts of rulers and of

> pontiffs, and excite them to seek for real piety.[12]

From today's perspective, it is almost impossible to appreciate the courage it took for Erasmus and a few others of influence to make such public declarations. There are so many unsung heroes of the Reformation, it is a pity that we cannot give them all due credit. Perhaps the meekest and least appreciated was Oecolampadius, who had declared himself in favor of Luther at Augsburg in late 1518. Later, when Oecolampadius took refuge in Basel, crowds filled St. Martin's Church whenever he took the pulpit. Erasmus fled to Basel also and the two fugitives became friends. Fearing that Erasmus's friendship with Oecolampadius would soften the latter's stand against Rome, Luther wrote to warn him with these guarded words: "I much fear that Erasmus, like Moses, will die in the country of Moab, and never lead us into the land of promise."[13]

In spite of their serious differences, however, "the friends of Luther, and even the reformer himself had long hoped to see Erasmus unite with them against Rome."[14] Unfortunately, in his heart, Erasmus (like some of the equally tragic Jewish religious leaders in Christ's day and some evangelical leaders in our own) was willing to displease God in order to gain praise from men. In the growing controversy, he attempted to remain in the good graces of the Church hierarchy while "endeavouring to obtain concessions from [Rome] that would unite the extreme parties. The vacillations and inconsistency of Erasmus disgusted Luther. 'You desire to walk upon eggs without crushing them,'"[15] complained Rome's fearless and uncompromising enemy.

Finally, the Open Antagonism

As the breach grew between him and Luther, Erasmus "was applied to from all quarters; the Pope, the emperor, kings, princes, scholars, and even his most intimate friends, entreated him to write against the reformer. 'No work,' wrote the Pope, 'can be more acceptable to God, and worthier of yourself and of your genius.'"[16]

In spite of his own opposition to Rome's corruptions that he had so often and eloquently expressed, he had remained in good standing within the Church. She had the power to provide him with great honors. Erasmus could not bring himself to make the sacrifice of coming out fully on the side of what he felt was Luther's extremism. Yet he preferred not to oppose Luther. "It is a very easy thing to say, 'Write against Luther,' replied he to a Romish theologian; but it is a matter full of peril...."

This indecision on the part of Erasmus "drew on him the attacks of the most violent men of both parties. Luther himself knew not how to reconcile the respect he felt for Erasmus's learning with the indignation he felt at his timidity."[17] Finally, desiring to free himself from any lingering hope of gaining Erasmus's half-hearted help, Luther wrote to Erasmus in April 1524. The letter revealed both his impatience and continued respect for the man seventeen years his elder, and seemingly offered an olive branch so uncharacteristic of Luther. In part he said:

> You have not yet received from the Lord the courage necessary to walk with us against the papists. We put up with your weakness.... But do not...pass over to our camp.... Since you are wanting in courage, remain where you are. I could wish that our people would allow your old age to fall asleep peacefully in the Lord. The greatness of our cause has long since gone beyond your strength. But on the other hand, my dear Erasmus, refrain from scattering over us with such profusion that pungent salt which you know so well how to conceal under the flowers of rhetoric; for it is more dangerous to be slightly wounded by Erasmus than to be ground to powder by all the papists put together. Be satisfied to remain a spectator of our tragedy; and publish no books against me; and for my part, I will write none against you.[18]

Luther must have known the reaction that such patronizing words would arouse from Erasmus. The master rhetorician was a proud man who took Luther's condescension as an insult to his genius and integrity. Now the die was cast. D'Aubigné comments, "Thus did Luther, the man of strife, ask for peace; it was Erasmus, the man of peace, who began the conflict.... If he had not yet determined to write against Luther, he probably did so then.... He had other motives besides."

Henry VIII and other nobility "earnestly pressed him to declare himself openly against the Reformation. Erasmus...suffered the promise to be wrung from him.... He was fond of glory, and already men were accusing him of fearing Luther, and of being too weak to answer him; he was accustomed to the highest seat, and the little monk of Wittenberg had dethroned the mighty philosopher of Rotterdam.... All Christendom that adhered to the old worship implored him...a capacious genius and the greatest reputation of the age were wanted to oppose the Reformation. Erasmus answered the call."[19]

Erasmus had once rejoiced in Luther's fulminations against Rome.

While cautioning the reformer to be more moderate and prudent, he had defended Luther with these words: "God has given men a physician who cuts deep into the flesh, because the malady would otherwise be incurable." On another occasion he had told the Elector of Saxony, "I am not at all surprised that it [Luther's criticism] has made so much noise; for he has committed two unpardonable crimes; he has attacked the pope's tiara and the monks' bellies."[20]

Erasmus's greatest weakness was the love of praise from those in high authority, and he cherished telling friends of the latest flatteries sent his way. Coming out openly against Luther would bring more praise than remaining on the sidelines. "'The pope,' wrote he with childish vanity to a friend... when he declared himself the opponent of Luther, 'has sent me a diploma full of kindness and honourable testimonials. His secretary declares that this is an unprecedented honour, and that the pope dictated every word himself.' "[21] In the final analysis, vanity had won out over truth.

The epitaph that Scripture has written over the life of Erasmus applies equally to the evangelical leaders and churches who in our day are making similar compromises with Rome and even with Islam: "For they loved the praise of men more than the praise of God" (John 12:43). May God deliver us from such leadership and grant repentance and a return to biblical truth.

A Hopeless Strategy

Erasmus could not in good conscience defend Rome's heresies and abuses. Neither could he call for the strong measures Luther was pressing, though he had once commended them. What should he do; what tack should he take? He chose to attack Luther, not on his opposition to Rome, which he could not honestly do, but on what Erasmus thought was an obscure point.

In the autumn of 1524, Erasmus published his now famous *Dissertation on the Freedom of the Will,* known thereafter to Luther and his supporters as the *Diatribe.* He wrote to Henry VIII, "Trust me, this is a daring act. I expect to be stoned for it."[22] Yet what did that really matter, when those with the most power and greatest rewards were fully on his side? The works of Erasmus had long before been listed on Pope Paul IV's *Index of Prohibited Books*, along with those of Calvin, Luther, and Zwingli. Now he received nothing but praise from every corner of the Church.

Luther's first reaction was anger that Erasmus would consider insignificant an issue of such great importance as whether man's will was free to act in response to the gospel. Nevertheless, at first he disdained to reply to a polemic that he considered so weak as to be unworthy of the battle. His silence brought exclamations of triumph from Rome's clergy: "Well, where is your Luther now...? Ah, ah! He has met with his match at last! He has learnt now to remain in the background; he has found out how to hold his tongue."[23]

Luther's Provoked Response

With uncharacteristic reluctance, Luther finally forced himself to prepare an answer, which he began to work on toward the end of 1525 (ten years before Calvin would write his *Institutes of the Christian Religion*). Melanchthon wrote to assure Erasmus that Luther's reply would be moderate, which Erasmus knew was an impossibility. Perhaps God had to choose men with defiant and even proud personalities to stand up to the pressure that Rome brought to bear upon those who dared to oppose her vaunted authority, a pitiless authority that had remained almost unchallenged for more than a thousand years.

The language in Calvin's *Institutes* reveals a man the equal of Rome in his utter contempt of and lack of patience or sympathy for those whose opinions diverged from his. Luther's writings reveal much the same, and he was brutal in his sarcastic put-down of Erasmus. The following is just a small sample of his *ad hominem* reply:

> By so doing, you merely let us see that in your heart you cherish a Lucian, or some other hog of Epicurus' herd.... Surely at this point you are either playing tricks with someone else's words, or practising a literary effect![24] You ooze Lucian from every pore; you swill Epicurius by the gallon.[25]
>
> Here again, as usual, you muddle everything up...and so you fall once more to insulting and dishonouring Scripture and God... let them blather who will.... The truth is, you fetch from afar and rake together all these irrelevancies simply because you are embarrassed.... Since you cannot overthrow...foreknowledge...by any argument, you try meantime to tire out the reader with a flow of empty verbiage....[26]
>
> See, I pray you, what abundance of by-ways and bolt-holes a slippery mind will seek out in its flight from truth! Yet it does not escape....[27]
>
> I'll be hanged if the Diatribe itself knows what it is talking

> about! Perhaps we have here the rhetorical trick of obscuring your meaning when danger is at hand, lest you be trapped in your words.[28]

Luther had not thought this subject through as thoroughly as he was forced now to do. He was willing to concede that man could indeed exercise his will in making choices with regard to earthly matters. But when it came to the question of man exercising any freedom of will toward his salvation, Luther laid the ground for what Calvin (who was about fifteen years old at this time) would ten years later present in his *Institutes* after his conversion to Luther's Protestantism. In his much admired *The Bondage of the Will*, Luther pompously chides and browbeats Erasmus:

> In this book of mine…I shall harry you and all the Sophists till you tell me exactly what "free-will" can and does do; and I hope to harry you (Christ helping me) as to make you repent of ever publishing your Diatribe…. God foreknows nothing contingently [i.e., no events depend upon something other than His will]…he foresees, purposes, and does all things according to His own immutable, eternal and infallible will. This bombshell knocks "free will" flat, and utterly shatters it…. You insist that we should learn the immutability of God's will, while forbidding us to know the immutability of His foreknowledge! Do you suppose that He does not will what He foreknows, or that He does not foreknow what He wills? If he wills what He foreknows, His will is eternal and changeless, because His nature is so. From which it follows, by resistless logic, that all we do, however it may appear to us to be done mutably and contingently, is in reality done necessarily and immutably in respect to God's will….[29]

Here, as often elsewhere in *Bondage*, Luther boasts of his conclusion without giving any valid supporting arguments. He secures his thesis by his own mere definition, not by logic or Scripture. His assertions above do not follow. Nor does he provide sufficient biblical support in this entire work to make his case for the will being in bondage. In bondage to what or to whom? He often implies the answer but fails to develop it fully or to face the consequences.

Luther is arguing that God's sovereignty *ipso facto* eliminates any possibility that man could exercise a free will: "This bombshell knocks 'free will' flat, and utterly shatters it…." That God foreknows the future, Luther argues, means the future is already predetermined, and that in itself proves that man could not act freely. Augustine considers the same problem far more carefully than Luther and comes to the opposite conclusion. We've already shown why Luther's idea is false. That God *knows* something will happen does not *cause* it to happen.

It is true that, because God knows what Mr. Jones will decide and do in the future, the latter will surely do so (or God would be wrong, which is impossible). But that does not mean Mr. Jones cannot exercise a genuine choice in thought, word, and deed; God simply knows in advance what Mr. Jones's free choice will be.

Is the will in bondage because God is sovereign and He has already determined all that will occur? Luther seems to argue as much. Ten years later, Calvin would come to the same conclusion, no doubt influenced by Luther, though he would word his thesis somewhat differently and avoid giving Luther any credit. If God's sovereignty and foreknowledge eliminated man's free will, however, we would face a far worse dilemma: man's will would be in bondage to God's will, making God the effective cause of every evil thought, word, and deed. The current dark state of our world would be exactly as God wills, rendering meaningless what Christ told us to pray: "Thy Kingdom come, Thy will be done, on earth as it is in heaven."

In vain, Luther tried to escape the obvious, uncomfortable quandary that if man cannot do anything except as God wills it, then God is the author of evil. That unhappy conclusion is forced upon us by an extreme view of sovereignty, which we have already seen is contradicted both by Scripture and reason. There is no way to assert that man can only do what God wills without admitting that God is therefore the invisible Hand effecting all the evil that man commits. That assertion is blasphemy—yet it lies at the very foundation of Calvinism as well as Lutheranism.

Is the Will Really in Bondage?

The defense of Calvinism traps even the best minds into hopeless contradictions. Spurgeon himself couldn't seem to make up his mind. In spite of referring to "the equally sure doctrine, that the will of man has its proper position in the work of salvation and is not to be ignored," Spurgeon also claimed that the idea of free will "left the whole economy of Grace and mercy to be the gathering together of fortuitous atoms impelled by man's own will!"[30] That, obviously, is not true. "Fortuitous atoms" have nothing to do with "Grace and mercy," nor does anyone who believes in man's power to make moral choices imagine that he can control atoms with his will! Spurgeon should have stayed with biblical exegesis.

He went on to lament, "We cannot tell on that theory whether God will be glorified or sin will triumph." Hardly. That we finite beings wouldn't know how something would turn out means nothing. The outcome always was known to God from eternity past.

Sadly, great preacher that he was, in that sermon Spurgeon erected and destroyed one straw man after another: "It must either be as God wills, or as man wills.... If not God, then you put man there, to say, 'I will,' or 'I will not.' If I will it, I will enter Heaven. If I will it, I will...conquer the Holy Spirit, for I am stronger than God and stronger than Omnipotence. If I will it, I will make the blood of Christ of no effect...it shall be *my* purpose that shall make His purpose stand, or make it fall."[31]

With all respect to Spurgeon, this is nonsense. Even the rankest Arminian would never imagine he could "conquer the Holy Spirit" or that he was "stronger than God" or that man's will could ever "make the blood of Christ of no effect" or force an entrance into heaven! God has set the rules for entering heaven. Man either accepts or rejects the salvation God offers in Christ—but he is certainly not in charge.

Like so many other Calvinists in their zeal to defend God's sovereignty to the exclusion of human will, Spurgeon stooped to twisting scripture to his own ends. For example, he quotes Christ's indictment of the rabbis, "You *will not* come to Me that you might have life." He then declares, "Where is free will after such a text as that? When Christ affirms that they will not, who dares say they will...? Man is so depraved, so set on mischief, the way of salvation is so obnoxious to his pride, so hateful to his lusts, that he cannot like it and will not like it, unless he who ordained the plan shall change his nature and subdue his will."[32]

Spurgeon misses the Lord's point. Christ is making this statement specifically to the rabbis, not to all men. Secondly, the statement itself says that they have a will, that by their own will they are rejecting Him: "You *will not* come to Me...." Nor does Christ say that they cannot will to do otherwise. Indeed, Christ's statement would be meaningless unless they *could* of their own will repent and come to Him. Only two chapters later Christ declares, "If any man will do His [God's] will, he shall know of the doctrine, whether it be of God..." (John 7:17). Spurgeon himself in this same sermon quotes this scripture as proof that man's will has a part to play in man's coming to Christ.[33]

Is the will really in bondage? If so, to what or to whom—and is it possible to set the captive will free from its bondage? If so, how can this be done? We must consider those questions carefully—and we will do so in the context of a further examination of Luther's treatise.

---

1. John Armstrong, "Reflections from Jonathan Edwards on the Current Debate over Justification by Faith Alone" (quoted in speech delivered at Annapolis 2000: A Passion for Truth conference). Transcript available from The Jonathan Edwards Institute, P. O. Box 2410, Princeton NJ 08542.
2. http://www.iclnet.org/pub/resources/text/wittenberg/wittenberg-luther.html.
3. Ibid.
4. J. H. Merle d'Aubigné, *History of the Reformations of the Sixteenth Century* (London: n. p., 1846; rev. ed. by Hartland Institute, Rapidan VA, n. d.), 245.
5. Ibid.
6. Ewald Plass, *What Luther Says* (St. Louis, MO: Concordia Publishing House, 1987), 1:35.
7. S. Fontaine, *Histoire Catholique de Notre Temps* (Paris: Pordre de St. Francois, 1562); cited in d'Aubigné, *History*, 411.
8. Cited in d'Aubigné, *History*, 414.
9. Ibid.
10. Ibid.
11. Ibid.
12. Ibid., 42.
13. Ibid., 412.
14. Ibid., 414.
15. Ibid., 413.
16. Ibid., 14.
17. Ibid., 414.
18. Ibid.
19. Ibid., 414–15.
20. Ibid., 101.
21. Ibid., 43.
22. Ibid., 415.
23. Ibid., 416.
24. Martin Luther, *The Bondage of the Will,* trans. J. I. Packer and O. R. Johnston (Grand Rapids, MI: Fleming H. Revell, 1957, 11th prtg. 1999), 70.
25. Ibid., 44.
26. Ibid., 86–87.
27. Ibid., 223.
28. Ibid., 228.

29. Ibid., 80–81.
30. Charles Haddon Spurgeon, "God's Will and Man's Will," No. 442 (Newington: Metropolitan Tabernacle; sermon delivered Sunday morning, March 30, 1862).
31. Ibid.
32. Ibid.
33. Ibid.

CHAPTER 14

The Bondage of the Will?

LUTHER WAS UNQUESTIONABLY the leading figure in the Reformation at this time, and the one to whom Protestants today owe the largest debt. Although many others before him had opposed Rome, Luther was the first to publish and distribute his challenge throughout Europe. Rome had always been able to silence her critics with bribery or death; now she faced a man who could not be bought and whose telling arguments had aroused so many powerful local rulers in his favor that her vengeful grasp could not reach him.

The Pope had one last hope: that the arguments put forth by Erasmus and widely published by Luther's enemies would persuade the masses who had defected to return to the shelter of the one true Church. After all, although Erasmus had criticized the Church, he had not been martyred, had not left her fold, and was still on the best of terms with the Pope. And it was he who was pointing out Dr. Luther's errors. That a reformation was needed, even the Church was willing to concede, but it was the kind Erasmus and others favored—a correction of acknowledged abuses, not a trashing of the traditions of centuries to start all over again from nothing!

The arguments Erasmus presented were powerfully persuasive to those who wanted to remain within the ancient fold. He was writing from a Roman Catholic perspective, defending Catholic dogma, a tactic calculated to strengthen Catholics in their beliefs, but which would hardly be effective for those who had already embraced Luther's rebellion. Perhaps all Erasmus intended to accomplish was to flatter those who could reward him the most.

We do not defend Erasmus, for much that he says is even less biblical than some of Luther's irrationalities. Although he had rejected the efficacy of sacraments and her other pagan practices in his past satires, Erasmus is still bound to Rome's heresy that grace aids man in achieving salvation by works. He writes, "...it does not...follow that man cannot...prepare himself by morally good works for God's favour."[1]

Sadly, Erasmus was wrong when it came to salvation, no matter how insightful his other criticisms of Rome. It is because man has already morally failed to keep God's law (and cannot mend that breach by keeping it thereafter, no matter how perfectly) that he needs grace—God's *unmerited* favor for which no preparation is required or effective.

An Awkward Duel

Luther lunges mercilessly to attack his foe at every turn. There is no point in dueling with the Pope. Neither he nor his cardinals and bishops will listen. At least in Erasmus, Luther has an antagonist who will listen and respond, and he vents his pent-up anger against Rome upon this man who dares to defend her blasphemous sacraments.

At times neither antagonist argues to the point. Though Luther is so clearly his master when it comes to exegesis of Scripture, it is often Erasmus who is the more reasonable of the two. The latter points out, for example, what we are arguing for in these pages: "If it is not in the power of every man to keep what is commanded, all the exhortations in the Scriptures, and all the promises, threats, expostulations, reproofs, adjurations, blessings, curses and hosts of precepts, are of necessity useless."[2]

Luther responds with much ridicule but little substance. He argues that the Old Testament passages Erasmus cites "only demand duty" but say nothing concerning free will.[3] Of course, that was all Erasmus intended to show, since the implication of free will necessarily follows. Nor can Luther cite one verse in Scripture that refers to "the bondage of the will."

Luther then demands of Erasmus why, if man can will to keep the law, he (Luther) must "labour so hard...? What need now of Christ? What need of the Spirit?"[4]

Erasmus had not even implied that there was no need of Christ or of the Holy Spirit. He simply suggested that it would be reasonable to conclude from God's many commands and appeals to reason and obedience that man must be capable of a willing response. But Luther doesn't deal with that; he is simply bombastic in arguing beside the point, even ridiculing Erasmus for correctly admitting that free will can only operate by God's grace.[5]

Luther pounces like a tiger on that admission, rather than agreeing with Erasmus and reasonably admitting the obvious: the fact that free will needs grace no more nullifies free will than breathing is nullified by the fact that it, too, is dependent upon God's grace. Surely man has both the ability and responsibility to cooperate with God's grace and power in whatever he does!

Throughout *Bondage,* Luther is like a bully who will not listen to reason. Yet Packer and other Calvinists praise the "dialectical strength of Luther's powerful Latin."[6] B. B. Warfield calls *Bondage* "a dialectic and polemic masterpiece."[7] In fact, *Bondage* contains so many contradictions and so much fallacious reasoning that one wonders how it obtained its reputation as such a logically drawn treatise.

One wonders, also, how evangelicals in their praise of Luther seemingly overlook the extent to which he was still deceived by his Roman Catholic background. This was especially evident in his view of the efficacy of the sacraments. In his *Small Catechism,* he declares that through the sacraments, "God *offers, gives,* and *seals* unto us *the forgiveness of sins* which Christ has earned for us" (emphasis in original).[8] This Catechism is used in nearly all Lutheran churches today (including the Missouri Synod) as their basic book of doctrine.

In answer to the question, "*What does Baptism give or profit?*" the *Catechism* declares, "It works forgiveness of sins, delivers from death and the devil, and gives eternal salvation to all who believe this, as the words and promises of God declare."[9] As for the Lord's Supper or Communion, Luther states, "It is the true body and blood of our Lord Jesus Christ under the bread and wine, for us Christians to eat and to drink[10].... In, with, and under the *bread* Christ gives us His *true body*; in, with, and under the *wine* He gives us His *true blood*[11]...in the Sacrament forgiveness of sins, life, and salvation are given..." (emphasis in original).[12]

Thus Rome's false gospel of sacramentalism survived the Reformation and is still honored in many Lutheran and Calvinist churches. Protestants who trust in their modified version of infant baptism and the Lord's Supper for their salvation are just as lost as Roman Catholics who trust in Rome's sacraments. Recognizing Luther's mistaken view of salvation may help some to realize that his view of free will and human responsibility could be equally wrong.

To What Is the Will in Bondage?

That the will—contrary to what Luther argues in his greatest treatise—is not bound is clear. We have already refuted the argument that, because the will is always beset with influences, that proves it is not free. Man, as Paul admits in his case (Romans 7:7-25), often fails to do what he would like to do—but not always. Paul doesn't say that he *never* can do what he wills—much less that his will is in bondage.

Luther imagines he does away with freedom of human will by arguing, "For if it is not we, but God alone, who works salvation in us, it follows that, willy-nilly, nothing we do has any saving significance prior to His working in us."[13] Of course salvation is not our doing; but that does not prove that we cannot freely receive the salvation Christ wrought as a gift of God's love. Throughout his entire treatise, Luther confuses the ability to *will* with the ability to *perform*, and mistakenly imagines he has disproved the former by disproving the latter.

Erasmus argues that for God to command man to do what he cannot do would be like asking a man whose arms are bound to use them. Luther responds that the man is "commanded to stretch forth his hand...to disprove his false assumption of freedom and power...."[14] Luther wins that small skirmish, but neither man even comes close to the Bible.

That God would not just command but earnestly plead, persuade, and beseech man endlessly through His prophets, promising and giving blessing for obedience and warning of and bringing destruction for disobedience, cannot be explained away by Luther's clever but trite rejoinder. Furthermore, we have numerous examples throughout Scripture of prophets and kings and ordinary persons, from Enoch to Noah to Abraham to David and onward, who, though not perfect, were indeed willingly obedient to God and pleased Him. What happened to Luther's "bondage of the will" in those cases?

The Book of Proverbs is one huge treatise refuting Luther's thesis. Solomon is appealing to his son to "know wisdom and instruction; to perceive the words of understanding; to receive the instruction of wisdom, justice, and judgment, and equity..." (Proverbs 1:2–3). He declares that "A wise man will hear, and will increase learning" (verse 5), and he admonishes his son, "if sinners entice thee, consent thou not" (verse 10). He exhorts, "My son, despise not the chastening of the LORD; neither be weary of his correction: for whom the LORD loveth he correcteth; even as a father the son in whom he delighteth" (3:11–12). Are these persuasive urgings not appeals to the will?

Everything Solomon writes is to persuade his son that wisdom is to be desired in place of folly and that the reward for serving God and righteousness far exceeds the reward for serving selfish lusts and desires. One must willingly heed the voice of wisdom. That the Lord corrects as an earthly father corrects is not, as Luther insists, simply to show that no correction is possible, but because the wise son will heed instruction—which is obviously only possible by an act of the will. Luther fails either to prove the bondage of the will or to demonstrate what it is that has the will bound.

The Will Must Be *Willing*

One searches *Bondage* in vain to find where it deals with the literally hundreds of biblical passages, from Genesis 24:58 to 1 Samuel 1:11 to 2 Samuel 6:21–22 to Psalms 4:8; 5:2–3; 9:1–2; 18:1; 30:1; to John 7:17, etc., which clearly indicate that man can indeed will to do God's will. The many passages where men express their willingness to obey and please God, and actually prove it in their performance, are conspicuous by their absence. Nor does Luther acknowledge, much less deal with, the fact that of the dozens of times the words "bondage" and "bound" occur in Scripture, not once are they used in reference to the human will.

Luther's argument that the will is bound admits the existence of the will, but does not explain why, or how, or to what or whom the will is in bondage. Nor does Luther, any better than Calvin, explain how the will is supposedly *unbound* so that man may believe the gospel. He argues that because, even in Christians, "human nature" lusts against the spirit, "how could it endeavor after good in those who are not yet born again of the Spirit...?"[15] This is no proof of *bondage* of the will.

Even the drunkard at times determines with his will to be sober. The will is not in bondage. Man's bodily desires at times overcome his will. But even many non-Christians have willed to be free of addiction to alcohol or tobacco and have been successful. Others tried with their will and failed—but not because the *will* was bound by sin; *they* were.

The Westminster Confession says that the elect come to Christ "most freely, being made willing by his [God's] grace." No one, however, is made willing against his will, but must have been willing to be made willing. God continually appeals to man's will ("whosoever will," etc).

There is no explaining away the fact that man has a will, as Augustine and even Calvin admitted and everyone experiences countless times each day. No one can persuade man to believe or do anything without his will being involved—unless he has been drugged or hypnotized. At this point we uncover the Achilles heel in Luther's argument (and we will see the same problem with Calvin when we come to Unconditional Election).

Once it is acknowledged that man has a will, there is no escape from it. Whatever change takes place in a man must involve his will, and for that to happen, the will must be willing. If the will was in bondage and has been delivered, the will must have been willing to be delivered. We deal with this further in the next chapter.

A Prejudicial Misuse of Scripture

Unfortunately, Luther often twists Scripture to prove his point. For example, taking a statement by a psalmist concerning a temporary state of mind from which he has repented—"I was as a beast before thee" (Psalm 73:22)—he likens man's will to a beast and launches into an analogy that has nothing to do with what the psalmist says: "So man's will is like a beast standing between two riders. If God rides, it wills and goes where God wills.... If Satan rides, it wills and goes where Satan wills. Nor may it choose to which rider it will run, or which it will seek; but the riders themselves fight to decide who shall have and hold it."[16]

So Satan can defeat God? And man has no choice whose servant he will be? Then why does God say, "Choose you this day whom ye will serve" (Joshua 24:15)? And why does God not defeat Satan in every case? Luther (like Calvin) forces us to conclude that those who will spend eternity in the Lake of Fire will be there because God did not want them in heaven—this falsity is a libel upon God's character and love!

Luther's attempted analogy doesn't follow from this or any other scripture. The psalmist admits comparing the prosperity of the wicked to his own troubles, and being envious of them. He realized that in so doing he had become as foolish *as* a beast—not that his will *was* a beast. Yet this same mistaken metaphor is used repeatedly by Calvinists. And both Luther and Calvin ignored the psalmist's repentance and the scores of other verses throughout Scripture, which make it clear that man responds to God in obedience by an act of his will.

Luther fails to distinguish between man's freedom to will and his lack of ability to carry out what he wills. Paul says, "To will is present with me; but how to perform that which is good I find not" (Romans 7:18). Obviously, man is free to believe the gospel and to receive Christ, which requires no special ability on his part.

Forcing Scripture to Say What it Doesn't

Luther quotes, "For the wrath of God is revealed from heaven against all ungodliness, and unrighteousness of men..." (Romans 1:18). He then claims that Paul's statement proves that man cannot will to do any good.[17] On the contrary, that God's wrath is aroused against man's ungodliness shows that God is angry with them for failing to do what they *could* have done had they been willing.

Luther goes on to quote Paul's quotation of Psalm 14:4: "There is none that doeth good, no, not one" (Romans 3:10–12). Like Calvin ten years later, he makes this an absolute statement about man's necessity when, in fact, it refers to his propensity.[18] That it must be the latter is clear from the abundance of scriptures telling us of good done even by the heathen and the exhortations even to the ungodly to do good. Nowhere does the Scripture tell us that man is in such total bondage to evil that he cannot respond obediently to God. Otherwise he could not be held accountable. We covered this earlier in regard to Total Depravity, but now offer several more examples from Scripture.

Abimelech, a pagan idol-worshiping king of the Philistines, could say to Isaac, "we have done unto thee nothing but good" (Genesis 26:10–11,29). Laban, another idol worshiper, in obedience to God, refrained from harming Jacob (Genesis 31:25–29). The Psalms are filled with exhortations to "do good" (Psalms 34:14; 37:3, etc.). Of a virtuous wife, it is said that she will do her husband "good and not evil all the days of her life" (Proverbs 31:12). Jesus counsels the Jews to "do good to them that hate you" (Matthew 5:44). There are literally scores of other verses in the Bible indicating that even the ungodly can do good at times.

Luther argues, "To say: man does not seek God, is the same as saying: man cannot seek God...."[19] He repeatedly makes such elementary mistakes, frequently offending both Scripture and reason. To say that Mr. Brown never goes into town is obviously not the same as saying that Mr. Brown *cannot* go into town. It could be that for some valid or imagined reason Mr. Brown doesn't want to or may even be afraid to go into town.

Not only does God call upon men repeatedly throughout the Bible to seek Him, as we have already seen—implying that man could and does seek God—but many scriptures commend those who have sought and found. For example, "every one that sought the LORD went out unto the tabernacle" (Exodus 33:7). Asa said, "we have sought the LORD our God" (2 Chronicles 14:7). We are told that when Israel did "turn unto the LORD

God of Israel, and sought him, he was found of them" (15:4). Ezra told the king, "The hand of our God is upon all them for good that seek him..." (Ezra 8:22). Asaph says, "In the day of my trouble I sought the Lord" (Psalm 77:2). Zephaniah refers to them "that have not sought the Lord," (Zephaniah 1:6), surely implying that there were some who did seek Him, and that all could if they would.

We could offer many more references showing that men have sought and found the Lord. Therefore we must conclude that Psalm 14, and Paul's quotation thereof in Romans 3, do not mean that no man ever has, ever will, or ever could seek the Lord. Rather, the general attitude of mankind is being described.

Luther goes on to argue that "the doctrine of salvation by faith in Christ disproves 'free-will.'"[20] That is absurd. In fact, salvation by faith *requires* a genuine choice by the will. The gospel promises salvation as a gift to those who will receive it; and one must have the power of choice or one cannot receive the gift. The gospel is an invitation to come to Christ, to receive Him, to believe on Him, to accept His death in one's place in payment of the penalty for one's sins. The gospel is an appeal to man's will: "Come unto me all...whosoever will, let him take the water of life freely" (Matthew 11:28; Revelation 22:17).

Confusing the Issue

Many of the scriptures and arguments Luther marshals for support throughout *Bondage* are irrelevant to the question of free will. Consider his reasoning from Romans 3:

> Here Paul utters very thunderbolts against "free-will." First: "The righteousness of God without the law," he says, "is manifested." He distinguishes the righteousness of God from the righteousness of the law; because the righteousness of faith comes by grace...without the works of the law (v. 28)....
>
> From all this it is very plain that the endeavour and effort of "free-will" are simply null; for if the righteousness of God exists without the law, and without the works of the law, how shall it not much more exist without "free-will"? For the supreme concern of "free-will" is to exercise itself in moral righteousness, the works of that law by which its blindness and impotence are "assisted." But this word "without" does away with morally good works, and the moral righteousness, and preparations for grace. Imagine any power you can think of as belonging to "free-will," and Paul will still

> stand firm and say: "the righteousness of God exists without it...!" And what will the guardians of "free-will" say to what follows: "being justified freely by His grace"...? How will endeavour, and merit, accord with freely given righteousness...? The Diatribe itself argued and expostulated throughout in this strain: "*If there is no freedom of will, what place is there for merit? If there is no place for merit, what place is there for reward? To what will it be ascribed if man is justified without merit?*" Paul here gives the answer—there is no such thing as merit at all, but all that are justified are justified freely, and this is ascribed to nothing but the grace of God.[21]

On the contrary, that the righteousness of God "exists without the law, and without works" has nothing to do with whether man has a free will or not. Of course, God's righteousness is independent of man's free will. That God is righteous neither proves nor disproves that man has free will. Luther's "very thunderbolts against 'free-will'" are irrelevant to the subject.

Furthermore, that righteousness cannot come by works is also irrelevant to free will. Those who believe in free will also affirm that man is "justified freely by His grace." But grace cannot be forced upon anyone or it would not be grace. Thus, it takes the power of choice for man to assent to God's grace and to receive the gift of salvation God graciously offers.

Erasmus is also wrong in asserting that human merit aids in justification. Human effort has no part in justification, as many scriptures declare—but that fact has no bearing on the question of free will. This section is typical of the confused reasoning Luther engages in throughout this entire book that Packer and others praise as Luther's greatest treatise.

More Irrelevancy

Luther presents some excellent biblical arguments against salvation by works, but that has nothing to do with whether man has a free will. Nor is there anything inherent in the gospel that requires that the will be in bondage. No Christian who believes that man has the power of choice sovereignly bestowed by God upon him as a moral agent imagines that this power has been given to man so that he could become righteous enough to merit salvation or even to contribute to his salvation in any way. Furthermore, the very fact that Paul refers to the righteousness that comes by the law indicates that man has some power to choose to keep the law, and to actually do so in at least some respects. Nor could he otherwise be held accountable.

Paul does not deny that man can do good works; he denies that good works can justify a sinner. Luther is clearly confused. One breach of the law dooms man forever. Keeping the law perfectly in the future, even if possible, could not make up for having broken the law in the past. Moreover, that Paul says, "by the deeds of the law there shall no flesh be justified in his sight" (Romans 3:20), indicates that it is possible for man to keep some provisions of the law some of the time. Paul's argument is not that it is impossible to keep for one moment any provision of the law, but that even to keep the law perfectly would not be enough. In his determination to prove the alleged bondage of the will, Luther misses Paul's whole point.

J. I. Packer says, "*The Bondage of the Will* is the greatest piece of theological writing that ever came from Luther's pen. This was his [Luther's] own opinion."[22] Warfield called *Bondage* "the embodiment of Luther's reformation conceptions, the nearest thing to a systematic statement of them that he ever made...in a true sense the manifesto of the Reformation."[23] Packer described it as "a major treatment of what Luther saw as the very heart of the gospel."[24] Such praise is incomprehensible!

If *Bondage* presents "the very heart of the gospels," one wonders who could be saved, because it encompasses some 300 pages of obtuse arguments, many of which the average person would find difficult to follow. One wonders, too, how Paul's simple "Believe on the Lord Jesus Christ, and thou shalt be saved" (Acts 16:31) has become so complicated. And how would proving that man *cannot* choose to believe (if that were indeed the case) encourage him to believe the gospel?

In contrast to the confusing arguments of Luther and the contradictory statements of Calvin, A. W. Tozer declared:

> *God sovereignly decreed that man should be free to exercise moral choice, and man from the beginning has fulfilled that decree by making his choice between good and evil.* When he chooses to do evil, he does not thereby countervail the sovereign will of God but fulfills it, inasmuch as the eternal decree decided not which choice the man should make but that he should be free to make it.... Man's will is free because God is sovereign. A God less than sovereign could not bestow moral freedom upon His creatures. He would be afraid to do so....
>
> God moves undisturbed and unhindered toward the fulfillment of those eternal purposes which He purposed in Christ Jesus before the world began.... Since He is omniscient, there can be no unforeseen circumstances, no accidents...[but] within the

broad field of God's sovereign, permissive will the deadly conflict of good and evil continues with increasing fury.

There is freedom to choose which side we shall be on but no freedom to negotiate the results of the choice once it is made.... Our choice is our own, but the consequences of the choice have already been determined by the sovereign will of God, and from this there is no appeal.[25]

---

1. Martin Luther, *The Bondage of the Will*, trans. J. I. Packer and O. R. Johnston (Grand Rapids, MI: Fleming H. Revell, 1957, 11th prtg. 1999), 246.
2. Luther, *Bondage*, 171; quoting Erasmus.
3. Ibid.
4. Ibid., 172.
5. Ibid., 173.
6. Ibid., "Translators' Note," 11.
7. Benjamin B. Warfield, "The Theology of the Reformation," in *Studies in Theology* (n. p., n. d.), 471; quoted in "Historical and Theological Introduction" to *The Bondage of the Will* by Packer and Johnston, 40–41.
8. *A Short Explanation of Dr. Martin Luther's Small Catechism: A Handbook of Christian Doctrine* (St. Louis, MO: Concordia Publishing House, 1971 ed.), 169.
9. Ibid., 174.
10. Ibid., 194.
11. Ibid., 195.
12. Ibid., 200.
13. Luther, *Bondage*, 102.
14. Ibid., 161.
15. Ibid., 313.
16. Ibid., 103–104.
17. Ibid., 273–275.
18. Ibid., 279–280.
19. Ibid., 281.
20. Ibid., 288–95.
21. Ibid., 289, 292.
22. Packer, Luther, *Bondage*, 40.
23. Warfield, "Theology," 471; cited in Luther, *Bondage*, 41.
24. Packer, Luther, *Bondage*, 41.
25. A. W. Tozer, *The Knowledge of the Holy* (San Francisco: Harper & Row, 1961), 117-119.

CHAPTER

15

Unconditional Election

UNCONDITIONAL ELECTION—another phrase that is not found in the Bible—"necessarily follows from total depravity."[1] This doctrine is declared to be the heart of Calvinism. Herman Hanko writes, "No man can claim ever to be either Calvinistic or Reformed without a firm and abiding commitment to this precious truth."[2] Sproul, though a staunch Calvinist, fears that the term "can be misleading and grossly abused."[3]

The Canons of Dort explained this tenet as "the unchangeable purpose of God, whereby, before the foundation of the world, he hath out of mere grace, according to the sovereign good pleasure of his own will, chosen, from the whole human race...a certain number of persons to redemption in Christ...."[4] Unconditional Election is the outworking of Calvinism's extreme view of sovereignty, which allows man no freedom of choice or action even to sin. That being the case, if anyone is to be saved, God must choose for them. Out of Unconditional Election, then, comes predestination to salvation.

Why so few were chosen by the God who "is love" (1 John 4:8), and the rest damned is, as we have already seen, a major problem that Calvin himself recognized. Yet throughout his *Institutes* he offered no satisfactory explanation. "That is a question for which I have no answer," admitted one of the staunchest critics of an early draft of this book. Unable to find any place for God's love in the theory of predestination arising out of unconditional election, Calvin struck back caustically at his critics in his usual manner, while pleading Augustine's authority:

> I admit that profane men lay hold of the subject of predestination to carp, or cavil, or snarl, or scoff. But if their petulance frightens us, it will be necessary to conceal all the principal articles of faith, because they and their fellows leave scarcely one of them unassailed with blasphemy....
>
> The truth of God is too powerful, both here and everywhere, to dread the slanders of the ungodly, as Augustine powerfully maintains.... Augustine disguises not that...he was often charged with preaching the doctrine of predestination too freely, but, as it was easy for him to do, he abundantly refutes the charge....
>
> The predestination by which God adopts some to the hope of life, and adjudges others to eternal death...is greatly cavilled at, especially by those who make prescience its cause.[5]

Calvin offers neither biblical nor rational proof for his (Augustine's) theory. In typical fashion, he mocks what he calls "the slanders of the ungodly" as though anyone who disagrees with him and Augustine is necessarily ungodly. Such would be his attitude toward many today who, professing a more moderate position, call themselves four-point or three-point Calvinists. As uncompromising as Calvin himself, Palmer declares,

> The first word that Calvinism suggests to most people is predestination; and if they have a modicum of theological knowledge, the other four points follow.... The Five Points of Calvinism all tie together. He who accepts one of the points will accept the other points. Unconditional election necessarily follows from total depravity."[6]

Many others agree:

> If any one of the five points of Calvinism is denied, the Reformed heritage is completely lost.... The truth of unconditional election stands at the foundation of them all [five points]. This truth is the touchstone of the Reformed faith. It is the very heart and core of the gospel.[7]

If the gospel is the power of God unto salvation to everyone who believes it (Romans 1:16), and if the five points of Calvinism comprise the very heart of the gospel, non-Calvinists cannot be saved. While many Calvinists would deny such a conclusion, it follows logically from the many statements we have already quoted by its leaders that Calvinism is the gospel and true Christianity.

Unconditional Election: The Heart of Calvinism

The term "unconditional election" was chosen by Calvinists because it allegedly conveys the meaning that "salvation is of the Lord and not of man." Spurgeon declared, "All true theology is summed in these two short sentences: Salvation is all of the grace of God. Damnation is all of the will of man."[8] There is a confusion, however, between (1) salvation, which could only be effected through the sacrifice of Christ for our sins, and (2) our acceptance thereof, which the Bible clearly states is a *condition*: "as many as *received him*...become the sons of God" (John 1:12). Calvinists insist, however, in misguided attempts to protect their extreme view of God's sovereignty, that salvation cannot be conditioned upon any act or belief on man's part. George L. Bryson rightly states:

> Calvinistic Election says to the unregenerate elect, "Don't worry, your Depravity is no obstacle to salvation," and to the unelect, "Too bad, you have not been predestined for salvation but [to] damnation."[9]

R. C. Sproul writes, "The term *election* refers specifically to one aspect of divine predestination. God's choosing of certain individuals to be saved."[10] Sproul continues, "The Reformed view teaches that God positively or actively intervenes in the lives of the elect to ensure their salvation."[11]

Man's acceptance or rejection of Christ plays no part: "By making election conditional upon something that man does, even if what he does is simply to repent and believe the gospel, God's grace is seriously compromised."[12] How the acceptance of God's grace by faith can compromise that grace is not explained, nor could it be. Paul declares that God's grace is received by faith alone (Ephesians 2:8). But Calvinism rejects faith as essential to regeneration and thus to salvation.

The Calvinist insists that God must "intervene" sovereignly to "regenerate" the elect without their having any faith in Christ or understanding of the gospel. Indeed, "faith" is declared to be a "work." "To reject [Calvinistic] election is to reject salvation by grace and promote salvation by works."[13] Thus by the erroneous view that faith is a work, the very faith God requires is denied as the means by which God's grace is received by man!

In the Bible, however, faith and works are contrasted as opposites. "By grace are ye saved, through faith;...not of works" (Ephesians 2:8–9); "But to him that worketh not, but believeth..." (Romans 4:5). To support Calvinism, the Bible must be contradicted in many places.

Calvinism's Unbiblical View of Sovereignty AGAIN

Unconditional Election is demanded by the distorted view of God's sovereignty, which we have earlier discussed and which undergirds all of Calvinism: that every thought, word, and deed is decreed by God—including all sin. We have already shown that this perspective is both irrational and unbiblical, but to the Calvinist it is a major foundation of his belief: "The all-out emphasis on the almighty sovereignty of Jehovah God is the truth and beauty of Calvinism."[14] Another writer adds, "Only the Calvinist...recognizes God's absolute sovereignty."[15]

On the contrary, all Christians believe that God is absolutely sovereign, but many recognize that sovereignty is not incompatible with freedom of choice. God is no less sovereign because Satan and mankind have rebelled and disobey Him continually.

Palmer declares with no apparent sense of contradiction that "God...has foreordained...even sin."[16] In fact, sin is rebellion against God, so it could hardly be willed by Him. Nevertheless, like Palmer, Gordon H. Clark insists that

> ...every event is foreordained because God is omniscient.... Of everything God says, 'Thus it must be....' Must not they who say that God does not foreordain evil acts now hang their heads in shame?[17]

Clark, Palmer, Pink, et al., are simply echoing Calvin, who said that God "foresees the things which are to happen, simply because he has decreed that they are so to happen...." How, then, can Calvinists today deny that Calvinism teaches that God causes sin? As we have noted, Calvin goes on to reason that it is therefore "vain to debate about prescience, while it is clear that all events take place by his [God's] sovereign appointment."[18] Following their leader, many Calvinists argue, "If a single event can happen outside of God's sovereignty, then He is not totally sovereign, and we cannot be assured that His plan for the ages will be accomplished."[19]

This theory, as we have seen, cannot be found in Scripture, nor is it reasonable. Deliverance from this false view comes by simply recognizing that there is a vast difference between what God decrees and what He allows, between what God desires and what His creatures do in disobedience of His will and rejection of His love. John R. Cross, who made the revealing New Tribes Mission video, *Delivered from the Power of Darkness*, has said it well:

> From the third chapter of Genesis on, the scriptures shout "free will." The whole volume talks about choices, and the associated consequences. God saw fit to write an entire book on choices, the Book of Wisdom (Proverbs). Having a free will makes sense of God's free love....
>
> Suppose you met someone who...showed real love for you—going out of his way to do special things for you...telling you they loved you. Then you found out that they had no choice—they were programmed to "be loving"...well, it would be a terrible disappointment. It would all seem so artificial, so meaningless, so empty. And it would be.
>
> Man was given a choice.... Having this choice defined man as a human being: to eat or not to eat, to obey or disobey, to love or not to love. Man was not a robot. Man was able to love by his own free choice [without which love is not love].[20]

Does God Cause Man to Sin?

It is true that God, being omniscient, knows all before it happens, and therefore nothing can happen that He doesn't know. For the omniscient God to know all, however, it is clearly not necessary that He must *decree and cause* all. Yet Calvin, limiting foreknowledge, insisted that God knows only what He has decreed; therefore, for God to know all, He must be the cause of all, including all evil. The doctrine of Unconditional Election then follows: that just as evil is God's doing, so election, too, must be all of God without even faith on man's part. Pink readily confesses the logical conclusion to which Calvinism's view of sovereignty and omniscience ultimately lead:

> ...to deny God's foreknowledge is to deny His omniscience.... But we must go further: not only...did His omniscient eye see Adam eating of the forbidden fruit, but He *decreed* beforehand that he *should* do so. (Emphasis in original)[21]

On the contrary, we have already seen that God, being separate from the time-space-matter universe He created, observes it from outside of time; thus His foreknowledge of the future leaves man free to choose. For God there is no time. Past, present, and future are meaningful only to man as part of his temporary existence in this physical universe.

God's knowledge of what to Him is one eternal present would have no effect upon what to man is still future. Calvin himself accepted this view without realizing its devastating impact upon his denial of man's ability to make genuine choices:

> When we ascribe prescience to God, we mean...that to his knowledge there is no past or future, but all things are present, and indeed so present, that...he truly sees and contemplates them as actually under his immediate inspection.[22]

Are "Tempting" and "Testing" Meaningless Terms?

Calvinism reasons that God, having foreordained from eternity past that Adam and Eve would eat of the Tree of Knowledge, forbids them to eat of it so He can punish them for doing what He foreordained and caused them to do! Then, by Unconditional Election, He saves a select number of their descendants to show His grace. That incredible scenario is contrary to the very character of a holy and just God who "cannot be tempted with evil, neither tempteth he any man" (James 1:13). Far from *causing* sin, God doesn't even *tempt* man to sin, as we have already seen.

We have noted that the Hebrew word translated "tempt" is *nacah*. It means to test or prove, not to entice to sin. When God asked Abraham to sacrifice Isaac, He was not enticing Abraham to commit murder but was testing Abraham's faith and obedience. To suggest that Abraham's every thought, word, and deed had already been foreordained by God makes any "test" of Abraham's faith meaningless. The same would be true of the hundreds of times God tested the faith and obedience of individuals and nations in the Bible.

Peter declares that the testing "of your faith [is] much more precious than of gold" (1 Peter 1:7). How can he speak of "*your* faith" if faith is all of God? And how can there be any meaningful "test" if man has no will and all has been predetermined by God from eternity past?

God gave Adam and Eve the easiest possible command. There must have been hundreds if not thousands of trees in the Garden bearing delicious fruit of many kinds. They could eat of any or all of them—except one: "Of every tree of the garden thou mayest freely eat: but of the tree of the knowledge of good and evil, thou shalt not eat of it: for in the day that thou eatest thereof, thou shalt surely die" (Genesis 2:16–17). This command was a necessary test of obedience and of love for their Creator.

God was *testing,* not *tempting,* His creatures. But this whole concept of warning man not to tempt God, and God testing man's obedience and faith, which occupies so many pages of Scripture, is meaningless if all has been eternally foreordained by God. This doctrine makes a mockery of all of God's pleadings through His prophets for man to repent, and renders the gospel itself redundant. Why plead with or warn or preach to those whose response has been foreordained from eternity past?

Incapable and Predestined, Yet Accountable?

According to the "T" in TULIP, man is unable to respond to God in any way except rebellion. He is free to pursue sin and to reject the gospel, but because he is totally incapable of seeking or pleasing God by the Calvinist definition, he cannot believe the gospel or have any faith in God. He can respond to God only in unbelief and disobedience. Palmer declares that "the non-Christian is hostile to God...he is not even able to understand the good."[23] White says he can understand but not embrace it.

Allegedly, by His eternal decree God has predestined man's every thought, word, and deed, including the most heinous atrocities committed by the world's worst criminals. Man's rebellion is only the acting out of what God has predetermined man will and must do—so man isn't a rebel but a puppet.

How can that which God foreordained and causes man to do be condemned as sinful rebellion against God's will? How can it be disobedience to do what God has willed? How could God complain when man does what He predestined him to do? And how could man then be justly punished for doing what he has no capability of *not* doing?

Such doctrine defames the God of love and justice who reveals Himself to mankind in the Scriptures. In defense of the character of the true God, John Wesley argued reasonably and biblically:

> He [God] will punish no man for doing anything he could not possibly avoid; neither for omitting anything which he could not possibly do. Every punishment supposes the offender might have avoided the offence for which he is punished. Otherwise, to punish him would be palpably unjust, and inconsistent with the character of God....[24]

Astonishingly, Calvinists see neither injustice nor contradiction in God foreordaining man's sin and then punishing him for what he could not avoid doing. This extreme view of sovereignty and predestination is applied to salvation by the doctrine of Unconditional Election. Although the Bible declares clearly and repeatedly that faith is the condition for salvation ("believe...and thou shalt be saved...he that believeth not shall be damned," etc.), Calvinism's Unconditional Election will not even allow faith unto salvation. God simply decides to save some, called "the elect," sovereignly regenerates them, and only thereafter gives them faith to believe on Christ, and damns the rest by His eternal decree. And God allegedly foreordains all this before He brings the doomed and damned into existence.

Scripture and conscience, however, impose upon *man* the duty to rescue everyone possible. But the Calvinist insists that it glorifies God for *Him* to rescue only a limited "elect." John MacArthur calls the elect "those chosen by God for salvation...."[25] That He chooses to damn the rest is said to show how wonderful it was that He saved at least some, thus causing the elect to be exceedingly grateful. The Calvinist attempts to escape the question of why God who *is love* saves so few by saying that the real wonder is that God would save *any*—which is no answer at all.

By this doctrine, if anyone is to be saved God must, through Irresistible Grace (which we will come to later), sovereignly *effect* within the sinner a saving response to the offer of salvation. Clark admitted, "The two theses most unacceptable to the Arminians are that God is the cause of sin and that God is the cause of salvation...."[26] Referring to the pronouncement of this doctrine at the Synod of Dort, England's King James (who gave us the King James Bible), though he was no Arminian and hardly a "saint," expressed his repugnance:

> This doctrine is so horrible, that I am persuaded, if there were a council of unclean spirits assembled in hell, and their prince the devil were to [ask] their opinion about the most likely means of stirring up the hatred of men against God their Maker; nothing could be invented by them that would be more efficacious for this purpose, or that could put a greater affront upon God's love for mankind than that infamous decree of the late Synod....[27]

A Strained and Unwarranted Redefinition of Words

Who could argue with the king's condemnation? Nevertheless, the attempt is made to muster biblical support by redefining certain words and phrases, such as "world," "whosoever," "any," "all men," and even "sinners" to mean only the elect. For example, Paul's statement that "Christ Jesus came into the world to save sinners" (1 Timothy 1:15) seems on its face to mean that His desire was for all sinners to be saved. That understanding would, of course, refute Calvinism. Therefore, the word "sinners" is redefined to mean only "the elect among sinners."

There is nothing anywhere in the Bible, however, to suggest that "sinners" really means the elect. The words "sinner" and "sinners" are found nearly seventy times in the Bible: "the men of Sodom were wicked and sinners" (Genesis 13:13); "the wealth of the sinner is laid up for the just" (Proverbs 13:22); "behold, the Son of man is betrayed into the hands of sinners" (Mark 14:41); "for sinners also love those that love them" (Luke 6:32); "we know that this man is a sinner" (John 9:24); "we know that God heareth not sinners" (John 9:31); "the law is not made for a righteous man, but for...the ungodly and for sinners" (1 Timothy 1:9); "but this man [Christ]...is holy, harmless, undefiled, separate from sinners" (Hebrews 7:24–26), etc. There is not one place in the Bible where "sinners" could be construed to mean "the elect."

Yet when the salvation of sinners, or God's love for sinners, is spoken of, then the Calvinist insists that "sinners" means the elect, such as in the following statements: "I am not come to call the righteous, but sinners to repentance" (Matthew 11:19; Luke 7:34), "This man receiveth sinners" (Luke 15:2); "while we were yet sinners, Christ died for us" (Romans 5:8), and so forth. Such redefinitions are required all through Scripture in order to support Calvinism.

Throughout the New Testament, the same Greek word is always used for "sinners." Thus there is no license whatsoever to give it a different meaning in certain cases in order to rescue Calvinism. Clearly, Calvinism would collapse if the Bible really meant that Christ came to save *all* sinners without discrimination, instead of only *some* sinners, i.e., the elect among them.

Who Are the Elect, and Why?

The Bible uses the term "elect" in a variety of ways: for Israel, Christ, a lady, a church, and angels. Never, however, is this word used to indicate that there is a select group who alone have been predestined to be saved. *Never.* Ironside declared, "Nowhere in the Bible are people ever predestinated to go to hell, and nowhere are people simply predestinated to go to Heaven... predestination is always to some special place of blessing."[28]

Calvinism defines the elect as that select group whom, alone, God has from eternity past appointed to salvation. All others are predestined by God to eternal damnation. The gospel can be preached day and night to the latter, yet to no avail, because they are totally incapable of believing it. God allegedly has no desire whatsoever to open their blind eyes and give them the faith to believe. He does that for the elect alone (through Unconditional Election), though He could do so for all. Yet *never* is this repugnant doctrine taught in Scripture!

"Moderate" Calvinists would claim that we have just described hyper-Calvinism. Attempting to deny "reprobation" or "double-predestination" (which Calvin clearly taught), the moderates would say that God merely left the non-elect to the just consequences of their sin. Left to their doom those He *could have rescued*, or predestined them to that fate—what is the difference? The so-called "hyper-Calvinist" simply admits the truth about Calvinism.

What "moderates" try to distance themselves from as "hyper" was taught by Calvin and has been part of mainstream Calvinism from the beginning. The Westminster Confession of Faith states, "By the decree of God, for the manifestation of His own glory, some men and angels are predestinated unto everlasting life, and others foreordained to everlasting death."[29] Yet having taught this belief, Calvin admitted:

> ...many...deem it most incongruous that of the great body of mankind some should be predestinated to salvation and others to destruction.[30]
>
> The decree, I admit, is dreadful; and yet it is impossible to deny that God foreknew what the end of man was to be before he made him, and foreknew, because he had so ordained by his decree.[31]

Calvin is forced to maintain what he admits is a "dreadful" decree. Why? Not by Scripture but by his unbiblical insistence that God can only foreknow what He decrees. From that error, it follows that since God knows everything that will occur, He must have decreed everything that would ever happen—from Adam's fall to the final doom of billions. Thank God that the Bible says the opposite: that "God so loved the *world,* that he gave his only begotten Son, that *whosoever* believeth in him should not perish, but have eternal life" (John 3:16). Both "world" and "whosoever" must be changed to "elect" for Calvinism to be sustained.

Perplexing Indeed!

Calvinism's "elect" are unconditionally (i.e., without any faith, understanding or choice on their part) elected to salvation simply because, in the mystery of His sovereign will, God decided, for no reason at all, to save them and *only* them. The Calvinist objects when we say, "for no reason at all." It is claimed that God needs no reason, that it simply pleased Him so to do, or that the reason is hidden in the mystery of His will: "We do not know what God bases His choice on...."[32]

Even God, however, must have a reason for saving some and damning others. Otherwise He would be acting unreasonably, and thus contrary to His Being. In fact, election/predestination is always said in the Bible to result from God's foreknowledge.[33] Those *whom He foreknew would believe* He predestined to special blessings, which He decided would accompany salvation from sin's penalty—"the things which God hath prepared for them that love him" (1 Corinthians 2:9).

God continually explains why man is separated from Him and what the solution is, and He offers to reason with man about this matter: "Come now, and let us reason together" (Isaiah 1:18). He reasons with Israel, sends His prophets to warn His chosen people, and explains repeatedly why, though reluctantly, He punishes them: "because of the wickedness of thy doings" (Deuteronomy 28:20); "they have forsaken the covenant of the Lord" (Deuteronomy 29:25); "because they have forsaken my law" (Jeremiah 9:13), etc. God explains that He gave His Son to die for the sins of the world because of His great love for all mankind: "For God sent not his Son into the world to condemn the world; but that the world through him might be saved" (John 3:17); "And we have seen and do testify that the Father sent the Son to be the Saviour of the world" (1 John 4:14).

Yet God never declares in Scripture a reason for saving a select group and damning all others. Surely such an important doctrine would be clearly explained, in defense of God's character, yet it isn't even mentioned. We can only conclude that Unconditional Election is but a human invention.

Scripture and Conscience Are United Against It

In fact, man's God-given conscience and Scripture cry out in protest against this doctrine. God is entirely "without partiality" (James 3:17), is "no respecter of persons" (Acts 10:34), and all men are equally worthy of

His condemnation and equally unworthy of His grace. Calvinists admit that the "elect," like all mankind by their view, were once totally depraved, incurably set against God and incapable of believing the gospel, with no more to commend them to God's grace than the "non-elect." Then why did He select them to salvation and damn all the rest? No reason can be found either in God or in man, or anywhere in Scripture.

There is no escaping the haunting question: Why did Calvin's God choose to save so few when He could have saved all? Without apology, James White informs us, "Why is one man raised to eternal life and another left to eternal destruction...? It is 'according to the kind intention of His will.'"[34] So it is God's *kindness* that causes Him to save so few and to damn so many! We are aghast at such a concept, and we are offended on behalf of our God.

Biblically, there is no question that God has the right to save whom He will and no one could complain. We are all deserving of the eternal punishment required by God's holiness against sin. But we are repeatedly told that God *is love* and that He is merciful to *all*, exactly what we would expect of Him in view of His command to us to love our neighbors as ourselves and to do good to all. We surely would not expect the "Father of mercies, and the God of all comfort" (2 Corinthians 1:3) to withhold mercy from *any* who so desperately need it—much less that He would take pleasure in doing so. Calvin hides behind Augustine's authority to justify this contradiction, but the effort falls short. For example:

> Now...he [God] arranges all things by his sovereign counsel, in such a way that individuals are born, who are doomed from the womb to certain death, and are to glorify him by their destruction.... If your mind is troubled, decline not to embrace the counsel of Augustine....[35]
>
> We admit that the guilt is common, but we say, that God in mercy succours some. Let him (they say) succour all. We object, that it is right for him to show by punishing that he is a just judge.... Here the words of Augustine most admirably apply.... Since God inflicts due punishment on those whom he reprobates, and bestows unmerited favour on those whom he calls, he is free from every accusation....[36]
>
> I will not hesitate...to confess with Augustine that the will of God is necessity...[and] that the destruction consequent upon predestination is also most just.... The first man fell because the Lord deemed it meet that he should...because he saw that his own glory would thereby be displayed....[37]

What "Justice" Is This?

God does not resort to judgment in order to demonstrate that He is a just judge. He *is* perfectly just, and His judgment falls upon those who deserve it and who reject His pardon through Christ—not upon a vast multitude whom He predestines to eternal torment because it pleases and glorifies Him! That belief of Calvin and Augustine libels the God of the Bible.

That God would impose "the necessity of sinning" upon man, then condemn him for sinning, cannot be called "just" by any semantic maneuver. Yet this is exactly what Calvin taught and defended:

> The [predestined to damnation] reprobate would excuse their sins...because a necessity of this nature is laid upon them by the ordination of God. We deny that they can thus be validly excused...every evil which they bear is inflicted by the most just judgment of God.[38]

The heartlessness that Calvin attributes to God is appalling. Surely, as Wesley argues, to punish for failure to do what it is impossible to do, or for having done what one could only do, is the opposite of justice. If that were not bad enough, that God would predestine man to sin so that He would have someone to judge is abhorrent even to the ungodly. It is offensive to the conscience God has given all mankind. Calvin attributes evil to God, then calls it just because "everything which he [God] wills must be held to be righteous."[39]

Scripture tells us the opposite—that God commands all men to repent, pleads with mankind to do so, is ready to pardon and promises salvation to all who believe on Christ. The following passages, in which God pleads with mankind to accept the salvation He offers in Christ, are only a few among many similar scriptures that refute Calvinism's Unconditional Election:

> Let the wicked forsake his way, and the unrighteous man his thoughts: and let him return unto the LORD, and he will have mercy upon him; and to our God, for he will abundantly pardon (Isaiah 55:7); Ye shall seek me and find me, when ye shall search for me with all your heart" (Jeremiah 29:13); Therefore, whosoever heareth these sayings of mine, and doeth them, I will liken him unto a wise man, which built his house upon a rock (Matthew 7:24); Come unto me, all ye that labour and are heavy laden, and I will give you rest (Matthew 11:28); If any man thirst,

> let him come unto me, and drink (John 7:37); And whosoever will, let him take the water of life freely (Revelation 22:17).

Each of the above very clearly includes two facts that refute Unconditional Election:

1) The command and invitation are given to all, not just to a select group. The words "wicked" and "unrighteous" and "whosoever" and "all" clearly mean what they say and cannot be turned into "elect."
2) There are conditions that must be met. There is both a command and an invitation to meet certain requirements: to "forsake" one's sin, to seek God with the whole heart, to "hear and do" what Christ commands, to "come" to Him, and to "take and drink" the water of life that Christ gives.

Evading the Issues

In all of his talk about God's sovereignty and justice, Calvin takes no account of God's other attributes such as His love and mercy. Not once in the nearly 1,300 pages of his *Institutes* does Calvin expound upon God's love for mankind or attempt to explain how God, who *is* love, could take pleasure in damning billions whom He could save if He so desired. How, indeed! Here is the great question that the very conscience God has implanted in all mankind finds so troubling—but Calvin never addresses it!

Biblically, God's sovereignty is exercised only in perfect unity with His total character. He is not a despotic sovereign. His sovereignty is enforced in harmony with His love, grace, mercy, kindness, justice and truth—but Calvin has almost nothing to say about these attributes, because they cannot be reconciled with his theory.

It is only reasonable to ask why God, who *is love*, lacks the love and compassion to save all whom He could save, and instead predestines billions to eternal torment. Calvin repeatedly hides his lack of an answer behind the word "mystery." But pleading "mystery" cannot cover up the horror of this doctrine. Yet that is the best Calvin can do, along with repeatedly appealing to Augustine's authority. He argues:

> Let us not be ashamed to be ignorant in a matter in which ignorance is learning. Rather let us willingly abstain from the search after knowledge, to which it is both foolish as well as perilous, and even fatal to aspire.[40]

> How sinful it is to insist on knowing the causes of the divine will, since it is itself, and justly ought to be, the cause of all that exists.... God, whose pleasure it is to inflict punishment on fools and transgressors...no other cause can be adduced...than the secret counsel of God.... Ignorance of things which we are not able, or which it is not lawful to know, is learning, while the desire to know them is a species of madness.[41]

Pleading "mystery" and exalting ignorance is contrary to God's Word, which tells us that we must "be ready always to give an answer to every man that asketh you a *reason*..." (1 Peter 3:15). Yet Calvin said it was wrong to seek a reason.

The only Greek word translated "mystery" is *musterion*. It is *never* used as Calvin used it to denote a secret not to be revealed. Rather, it *always* refers to knowledge that is being revealed. For example: "I would not...that ye should be ignorant of this mystery..." (Romans 11:25); "I shew you a mystery..." (1 Corinthians 15:51); "made known unto me the mystery..." (Ephesians 3:3); "Even the mystery which hath been hid...but now is made manifest..." (Colossians 1:26); "I will tell thee the mystery..." (Revelation 17:7), etc. The word is *never* used as Calvin uses it in relation to salvation, predestination, or sovereignty, and certainly not concerning some being saved and others damned.

No Escape by Semantics

According to the doctrine of Unconditional Election, both the faith to believe and the salvation the elect receive are imposed upon them by God's sovereignty, overriding entirely their alleged human incapacity to choose and their depraved will's rejection of the gospel. The Calvinist objects to the phrase "imposed upon them" and insists that God simply removed from the elect their natural resistance to the gospel.

Any removal, however, of the alleged natural rejection would have to change a rebellious sinner's desire. Palmer admits, "He even *makes* me, who really did not love Jesus, want to love Him and believe in Him (emphasis added)."[42] On the contrary, no one can be *made* either to love or to accept a gift, much less to change his mind without the willingness to do so. That willingness must come from the heart; it can't be created out of thin air.

No one can be forced to change his mind. No matter how he attempts to explain Unconditional Election, the Calvinist cannot escape a basic fact recognized by all mankind: that in any meaningful change of attitude or belief, the human will must consent for reasons that it accepts willingly. But that commonsense fact undermines God's sovereignty, according to Calvinism. On the contrary, it is a fact, and it refutes Calvinism.

The Calvinist claims that, according to Ephesians 2:8–10, faith is bestowed as a gift (we discuss that error in depth later). The Greek construction, however, demands that salvation, not faith, is the gift of God. Moreover, even if faith were the gift, it would have to be received—an act in itself requiring faith and the exercise of one's will. Saving faith is an absolutely essential element in any relationship and transaction between man and God, as many scriptures declare unequivocally: "He that *cometh* to God must *believe* that he is..." (Hebrews 11:6).

Jesus said, "According to *your* faith be it unto you" (Matthew 9:29). We have already pointed this out, but it bears repeating. The expression "your faith" is found twenty-four times: "your faith is spoken of..." (Romans 1:8); "if Christ be not raised, your faith is vain... (1 Corinthians 15:17), etc. "Thy faith" is found eleven times: "thy faith hath made thee whole..." (Mark 5:34; Luke 8:48); "the communication of thy faith..." (Philemon 6), etc. "His faith" is found twice: ("his faith is counted for righteousness" (Romans 4:5), etc., and "their faith" three times: "Jesus saw their faith" (Mark 2:5), etc. These are odd expressions if no one can have faith unless God sovereignly regenerates him—then gives him a faith that is not his own but totally of God.

Such teaching is clearly not biblical. Scripture repeatedly depicts God as appealing to man's reason, conscience, and will in order to persuade him to repent and believe. The entire history of God's dealing with man—past, present, and future, as revealed in Scripture—is a meaningless charade if Unconditional Election is true. And so it is with all of TULIP.

In Summary

It is love's essential ingredient—the power of choice—that Calvinism's misguided defense of a false view of God's sovereignty will not allow. And it is right here on Unconditional Election, the second of its five points, that Calvinism stubs its toe again on a huge contradiction over which its adherents cannot agree. Its perversion of sovereignty demands that whether one goes to heaven or hell depends solely upon God's will and decree; a man's receiving or rejecting Christ is not by his free choice but is irresistibly imposed upon him by God. As a result, the atheist feels justified in rejecting a God who, contrary to basic human compassion, predestines multitudes to eternal torment whom He could just as well have predestined to eternal joy in His presence.

Why wouldn't the God who *is love* exercise the absolute control Calvinism attributes to Him over every thought, word, and deed to eliminate sin, disease, suffering, and death and to bring all mankind into heaven? This contradiction of the basic standards that God has put in every human conscience raises an obvious question—and it is a question in response to which Calvinists themselves cannot agree upon an answer.

Some, like John Calvin, unashamedly say that God doesn't want everyone saved—indeed, that it is his "good pleasure" to damn so many. Others, realizing the revulsion that idea creates in anyone with a normal sense of mercy and kindness, call this "hyper-Calvinism" and attempt to find other explanations for God's alleged failure to irresistibly elect everyone. The necessity to overcome non-Calvinists' objections to God's apparent callousness (in predestining multitudes to eternal torment before they were even born) has been the mother of invention to a number of attempted rationalizations.

As we have seen, some try to escape the moral disaster by simply saying that the answer is hidden in the secret of God's will—an obvious copout. Others, while admitting the monstrous contradiction, insist that what to us seems abhorrent is not so to God—that we cannot impose our standards upon Him. That argument, however, is demolished by the fact that God has written His standards in every conscience and reasons with mankind upon that very basis (Isaiah 1:10–20).

All through Scripture, God appeals to man's conscience to do what he knows is right and to refrain from evil. Christ's teaching, "And as ye would that men should do to you, do ye also to them likewise" (Luke 6:31), clearly expresses the common sympathy that every normal person, though a sinner, realizes he ought to have for those in need. That this compassion comes from God and reflects His own kind desire toward mankind cannot be denied, and is acknowledged to be so by Spurgeon.

Calvinists cannot agree on how to handle Paul's clear declaration that God desires "all men to be saved" (1 Timothy 2:4). As we shall see later in more detail, like James White, many Calvinists argue that Paul doesn't mean "all men" but "all classes of men."[43] Calvin himself adopted this devious idea for escaping the truth concerning God's love for all.[44] Yet Spurgeon rejected this ploy. Instead, he honestly declared (as we have already noted):

> As it is my wish that it should be so, as it is your wish that it might be so, so it is God's wish that all men should be saved; for assuredly, he is not less benevolent than we are.[45]

This un-Calvinistic belief, however, got Spurgeon in trouble. Wasn't he contradicting the Limited Atonement he otherwise professed to accept? How could God sincerely wish for the salvation of those for whom Christ did not die and whom He had predestined to everlasting torment? And here—like Sproul, Piper, MacArthur, and others—Spurgeon fell back upon the idea that God apparently has two wills, "God's will of decree (His eternal purpose)...[and] God's will of desire."[46]

This sermon is apparently the origin of MacArthur's assertion of the same contradiction. How could God have two conflicting wills? Instead of finding a biblical and rational solution to this unbiblical and irrational idea (which must be maintained in order to defend Calvinism), Spurgeon pleaded ignorance:

> Then comes the question, "But if he wishes it to be so, why does he not make it so...[God] has an infinite benevolence which, nevertheless, is not in all points worked out by his infinite omnipotence; and if anybody asked me why it is not, I cannot tell. I have never set out to be an explainer of all difficulties, and I have no desire to do so."[47]

In fact, Calvinism itself creates this "difficulty"! The dilemma dissolves and the unanswerable question is answered by one simple admission: God in His sovereignty has given man the genuine power of choice. Thus God's sincere and loving desire for all mankind to be saved is not contradicted by His justice but is rejected by the free will of many. No one is *predestined* either to eternal bliss in God's presence or to eternal torment in separation from Him. Eternal destiny depends upon one's acceptance or rejection of Christ through the gospel.

Those who receive Christ have nothing to glory in but in Christ alone who paid the penalty for their sins. And those who suffer the just penalty for their sins have only themselves to blame for having willfully rejected the salvation God graciously provided and freely offered as a gift of His love.

Such is the clear teaching of Scripture from Genesis to Revelation. But to face that fact, the Calvinist would have to abandon the dogmas to which he has devoted his life and reputation. Many have done so. It is our prayer that this book will help many more to be delivered from TULIP.

1. Edwin H. Palmer, *the five points of calvinism* (Grand Rapids, MI: Baker Books, enlarged ed., 20th prtg., 1999), 27.
2. Herman Hanko, Homer C. Hoeksema, and Gise J. Van Baren, *The Five Points of Calvinism* (Grand Rapids, MI: Reformed Free Publishing Association, 1976), 28.
3. R. C. Sproul, *Chosen by God* (Carol Stream, IL: Tyndale House Publishers, Inc., 1986), 155.
4. Canons of Dort (Dordrecht, Holland, 1619), 1:7.
5. John Calvin, *Institutes of the Christian Religion*, trans. Henry Beveridge (Grand Rapids, MI: Wm. Eerdmans Publishing Company, 1998 ed.), III: xxi, 4,5.
6. Palmer, foreword to *five points*, 27.
7. Herman Hanko; cited in Laurence M. Vance, *The Other Side of Calvinism* (Pensacola, FL: Vance Publications, rev. ed. 1999), 245.
8. Charles Haddon Spurgeon, *Spurgeon at His Best,* ed. Tom Carter (Grand Rapids, MI: Baker Book House, 1988), 122.
9. George L. Bryson, *The Five Points of Calvinism "Weighed and Found Wanting"* (Costa Mesa, CA: The Word For Today, 1996), 36.
10. R. C. Sproul, *Grace Unknown* (Grand Rapids, MI: Baker Books, 1997), 141.
11. Sproul, *Chosen*, 142.
12. C. Samuel Storms, *Chosen for Life* (Grand Rapids, MI: Baker Book House, 1987), 55.
13. Carl Morton, in *The Berea Baptist Banner*, January 5, 1995, 19.
14. David J. Engelsma, *Hyper-Calvinism and the Call of the Gospel* (Grandville, MI: Reformed Free Publishing Association, 1980), 133.
15. Leonard J. Coppes, *Are Five Points Enough? The Ten Points of Calvinism* (Denver CO: self-published, 1980), 15.
16. Palmer, *five points*, 25.
17. Gordon H. Clark, *Predestination* (Phillipsburg, PA: Presbyterian and Reformed Publishing Co., 1987), 63–64; cited in Vance, *Other Side*, 265.
18. Calvin, *Institutes*, III: xxiii, 6.
19. Calvinist pastor in Arizona to Dave Hunt, August 11, 2000. On file.
20. John R. Cross, *The Stranger on the Road to Emmaus* (Olds, AB: Good Seed International, 1997), 56–57.
21. Arthur W. Pink, *The Sovereignty of God* (Grand Rapids, MI: Baker Book House, 2nd prtg. 1986), 249.
22. Calvin, *Institutes*, III: xxi, 5.
23. Palmer, *five points*, 15.
24. In Vance, *Other Side*, 236.
25. John MacArthur, *The MacArthur Study Bible* (Nashville, TN: Word Publishing, 1997), 1939.
26. Clark, *Predestination*, 185.
27. King James I; in Jacobus Arminius, *The Works of James Arminius*, trans. James and William Nichols (Grand Rapids, MI: Baker Book House, 1986), 1:213.
28. H. A. Ironside, *In the Heavenlies, Addresses on Ephesians* (Neptune, NJ: Loizeaux Brothers, 1937), 34.
29. Westminster Confession of Faith (London: 1643), III:3.

30. Calvin, *Institutes*, III: xxi, 1.
31. Calvin, *Institutes*, III: xxiii, 7.
32. Palmer, *five points*, 26.
33. See, for example, Romans 8:29 and 1 Peter 1:2.
34. James R. White, *The Potter's Freedom* (Amityville, NY: Calvary Press Publishing, 2000), 177.
35. Calvin, *Institutes*, III: xxiii, 5,6.
36. Ibid., 11.
37. Ibid., 8,9.
38. Ibid.
39. Ibid., 2.
40. Ibid., xxi, 2.
41. Ibid., xxiii, 4,8.
42. Palmer, *five points*, 21.
43. James R. White, *The Potter's Freedom* (Amityville, NY: Calvary Press Publishing, 2000), 139–143.
44. John Calvin, *Calvin's New Testament Commentaries* (Grand Rapids, MI: Wm. B. Eerdman's Publishing Co., 1994), 10:209.
45. C. H. Spurgeon, sermon preached January 16, 1880, "Salvation by Knowing the Truth," [www.apibs.org/chs/1516.htm].
46. Ibid.
47. Ibid.

CHAPTER

16

Is Salvation Available to All?

GOD DETERMINED of His own will to provide salvation. He devised the plan and set the rules to satisfy His love and justice. It is folly for anyone to imagine that man can set the requirements for salvation and impose them upon God. It is no less obvious that God, because He is God, has the prerogative of offering salvation to whomever He will. Yet Calvinists claim that their critics deny such "freedom" to God. We do not.

God declared, "[I] will be gracious to whom I will be gracious, and will shew mercy on whom I will shew mercy" (Exodus 33:19). He does not say, however, that He will be gracious and merciful to some and not to others—but that grace and mercy are by His initiative. He is under no obligation to be gracious and merciful to *anyone*.

Only by God's grace and mercy can anyone be saved: "By grace are ye saved....According to his mercy he saved us" (Ephesians 2:8; Titus 3:5). Since salvation is by grace, it cannot be earned, merited, or demanded on any basis whatsoever.

Grace and mercy can be given to whomever God should decide. However, far from indicating that His grace is limited because He has decided to save only a select group, the Bible clearly states that "God so loved the world" that He gave His Son to die "that the world through him might be saved" (John 3:16–17). Christ the Lamb of God came to take "away the sin of the world" (John 1:29), and He became the propitiation "for the sins of the whole world" (1 John 2:2).

God repeatedly declares that He is gracious and merciful to all. And so it is with God's love, from which His grace and mercy flow—without partiality it reaches out to all mankind.

Furthermore, in contrast to the literally hundreds of places where God's love is clearly expressed for all of Israel (most of whom rejected Him) and for the whole world (most of whom also reject Him), nowhere does the Bible declare that God doesn't love and desire the salvation of all. No Scripture indicates that God's love and salvation are limited to a select number. If this were the case, surely it would be stated clearly—but it is not. Instead, God's grace and mercy are repeatedly offered to all mankind.

The Calvinist therefore attempts to take the hundreds of declarations of God's love for all and "interpret" them to say the opposite. Thus, in expressions of God's desire for and offer of salvation to all, words such as "world" or "any" or "whosoever" or "sinners" or "all men" are interpreted to mean "the elect."

Sovereignty and Salvation

God is not in any way obligated to provide salvation for *anyone*. Yet the Bible repeatedly makes it clear that God's gracious purpose is for all mankind to be saved: "Who will have all men to be saved, and to come unto the knowledge of the truth.... Christ Jesus...gave himself a ransom for all..." (1 Timothy 2:4–6). "Whosoever believeth in him.... Whosoever will, let him take of the water of life freely" (John 3:16; Revelation 22:17), etc. Scripture could not declare more clearly that salvation is offered to *all* as a free gift of God's grace to be accepted or rejected.

Yet everyone is not saved. Why not, if the sovereign God truly wants all to be saved? Could the God who "worketh all things after the counsel of his own will" (Ephesians 1:11) merely express His will in an *offer* that man could by *his* will accept or reject?

Why not? Surely a command is stronger than an offer, and the Ten Commandments are not "Ten Suggestions." Yet this universal declaration of His desire for mankind, which God gave from Mount Sinai to Moses and has written in every human conscience, is broken billions of times every day by man's rebellious self-will. God's sovereignty is no more undermined by some accepting the offer of salvation and others rejecting it, than by man's continual disobedience of the Ten Commandments.

The word "whosoever" is defined in *Webster's New Universal Unabridged Dictionary* as "whoever; whatever person: an emphatic form." There are no alternate meanings—it *always* means whoever or whatever person. Yet Calvinism requires that in certain places "whosoever" actually means "the elect alone."

In truth, the correct meaning for "whosoever" completely contradicts Calvinism. The word "whosoever" is found 183 times in 163 verses in the Bible, beginning with "whosoever slayeth Cain" (Genesis 4:15) and ending with "whosoever will, let him take of the water of life freely" (Revelation 22:17). "Whosoever" clearly means everyone without exception. It is found in warnings ("whosoever eateth leavened bread"—Exodus 12:15) and in promises of reward ("whosoever smiteth the Jebusites first shall be chief"—1 Chronicles 11:6). Among the scores of other examples are "whosoever heareth, his ears shall tingle" (Jeremiah 19:3) and "whosoever shall call on the name of the Lord shall be delivered" (Joel 2:32). Not once in its 183 occurrences in the Bible could the word "whosoever" mean anything except "whosoever"! But wherever salvation is offered to whosoever will believe and receive Christ, the Calvinist changes the same Hebrew or Greek word to mean the "elect." He must in order to hold onto Calvinism. But isn't submission to God's Word more important than loyalty to a dogma?

Christ Defines "Whosoever"

The best-known Bible verse promises eternal life to "whosoever believeth in him" (John 3:16). Christ's last recorded words in Scripture are, "And let him that heareth say, Come. And let him that is athirst come. And whosoever will, let him take the water of life freely" (Revelation 22:16–17). There is nothing in these passages or in any other context to suggest that Christ *ever* offers salvation to anyone less than "whosoever."

Yet the doctrine of Unconditional Election declares that this offer is effective for only a select group, who alone have been unconditionally elected to salvation—a reinterpretation of God's clearly declared will that has no basis except the need to salvage Calvinism.

We have shown elsewhere that Christ left no question concerning the meaning of "whosoever" in John 3:16. In verses 14-15, He likened His being lifted up on the Cross for our sins to when the fiery serpents bit the Israelites because of their rebellion, and all who looked in faith to the uplifted brass serpent were healed. Numbers 21:8-9 is unequivocal: "... *everyone* that is bitten, when he looketh upon it [the brazen serpent], shall live...if a serpent had bitten *any man*, when he beheld the serpent of brass, he lived."

The healing from the poisonous snakebite was not for a select group within Israel whom God had predestined to be healed, but for "everyone...

any man." The only limitation was to look in faith to the upraised serpent. Likewise, everyone who has been bitten by "that old serpent, called the Devil, and Satan" (Revelation 12:9) is healed if they will but look in faith to Christ lifted up on the Cross. No wonder Calvinist apologists, such as James White, avoid the passages in the Old Testament that point to the sacrifice of Christ for the sins of the world.

Scripture clearly declares that there is "no difference" between Jew and Gentile, "all have sinned...all the world [is] guilty before God"—and that God is the God "of the Gentiles" as well as of the Jews. Thus salvation is for "all them that believe" (Romans 3:9-31).

If salvation is not genuinely available to all, why did Christ command His disciples to go into all the world and preach the gospel to every creature" (Mark 16:15)? Is that not giving a false impression, both to His disciples and to all who would read their account of Christ's teachings in the four Gospels? Christ repeatedly offered salvation to all who would believe and receive Him: "He that heareth my word, and believeth on him that sent me, hath everlasting life" (John 5:24); "If *any* man thirst, let him come unto me and drink" (7:37); "I am the door...by me if *any* man enter in, he shall be saved" (John 10:7-9), and so forth.

How would His disciples, or the common people who heard Him who had never heard of Augustine's and Calvin's theories, come to the conclusion that salvation was only for a limited number who had been unconditionally elected? Complicated reasoning and a system of "Five Points" are required to arrive at that conclusion. And if that were the case, would it not be misrepresentation of the worst sort to offer salvation to *whosoever will*? If Calvinism were true, Christ could have chosen words to convey that fact rather than seeming to offer salvation to whosoever would believe on and receive Him.

The Calvinist, of course, explains that he preaches the gospel to all because he doesn't *know* who is among the elect. Could it really be God's will for the gospel to be preached to those for whom Christ did not die, and for multitudes to be urged to believe from whom God withholds the necessary faith? Isn't this not only dishonest but cruel? Peter told the Jews gathered at Pentecost, "for the promise is unto you and to your children..." (Acts 2:39). Calvinism turns this promise into a lie, and the preaching of the gospel becomes a cruel hoax to multitudes!

Illustrating a Point

The God of the Bible declares repeatedly throughout His Word that He is not willing that anyone should perish but wills for "all men to be saved" (1 Timothy 2:4). Continually, and in the most urgent and solemn language possible, He calls upon all men to repent and to believe on His Son as the Savior of all mankind. Christ holds out His nail-pierced hands and pleads, "Come unto me, *all* ye that labour and are heavy laden, and I will give you rest" (Matthew 11:28). This is a promise that *all* who labor and are heavy laden with sin have every reason to believe is extended to *them*.

Believing the Bible, one must conclude that just as "*all* have sinned" (Romans 3:23), so *all* are offered deliverance from sin and its penalty through the gospel. Surely the "all" in "all we like sheep have gone astray" must be the same as the "all" in "the Lord hath laid on him the iniquity of us all" (Isaiah 53:6). Unquestionably, *all Israel* went astray. Therefore, Christ suffered for the sins of all Israel. Since Israel is a picture of the relationship God desires for all mankind, and since "all have sinned and come short of the glory of God" (Romans 3:23), we may thus be confident that God laid on Christ the sins of the whole world. As John the Baptist declared, "Behold the Lamb of God, which taketh away the sin of the world" (John 1:29).

To claim that "all" and "world" mean only a select group called "the elect" does violence to the plain meaning of language and impugns the character of God. In our newsletter, I likened Calvinism to the following scenario:

> If I should hold a rope 30 feet above a man at the bottom of a well and plead with him earnestly to take hold of it so that I could pull him out, wouldn't he think that I was mocking him? And if, in addition, I berate him for not grabbing the rope, would he not begin to wish he could grab me by the throat? And how could I maintain to any reasonable persons that I really wanted to bring the man up out of the well but he was the one who wasn't willing? So how can God really want to save those to whom He doesn't extend irresistible grace, that being the only means whereby they can believe the Gospel?

Misunderstanding a Biblical Illustration

In a radio discussion with me,[1] James White countered that the man at the bottom of the well was dead and couldn't grab the rope. The point of the illustration, however, had nothing to do with grabbing a rope. No illustration is perfect. Salvation is not by any effort on our part, nor do we hang onto Christ to be saved. He keeps us secure.

The point was that the rope was held so high above the man in the well that the professed rescuer couldn't be sincere. The would-be rescuer, of course, is not obligated to save the man below him. But if he does not desire to save him, why does he mock and chide the man at the bottom of the well for failing to grab the rope while continuing to hold it far beyond his reach?

The insincerity of the offer by the supposed rescuer was the point of the imperfect illustration. And so it is with our Lord's offer of salvation in the Bible: Calvinism turns it into an offer that, though it seems to be extended to all, really isn't.

Nor does it help to picture the man at the bottom of the well as dead. In that case, the supposed rescuer is pretending to call to a corpse that he knows cannot hear him. Furthermore, if the man at the top has the power to raise the dead man to life and take him out to safety but doesn't do so, how could he be sincere in his offer?

Such is the God of Calvinism: He pleads with men to repent, He sends forth His servants to preach a gospel that seems to offer salvation to every person, and He chides and damns those who do not believe, even though Christ did not die for them. Yet He neglects to elect them to salvation and does not give to them the essential faith without which they cannot respond to His pleadings. In fact, He has from eternity past irrevocably damned them eternally to the Lake of Fire!

Such insincerity cannot be explained away by the example of the potter and clay. The fact that the potter can do with the clay what he pleases could not explain the potter's promising perfection to each lump of clay and then discarding many, if not most, onto the rubbish heap.

Of course, God sovereignly has the right to save whom He will, and no one could complain. But His sovereignty is only one facet of His Being. God *is love* (i.e., love is the very essence of His character) and He is merciful to all—exactly what we would expect of Him. We surely would not expect the "Father of mercies, and the God of all comfort (2 Corinthians 1:3) to withhold mercy from any who so desperately need it—much less that He would take pleasure in doing so. Surely, God is being misrepresented by those who limit His love and mercy and grace to a select number.

"As Many as Were Ordained to Eternal Life Believed"

One of the Calvinists' favorite proof texts is Acts 13:48—"as many as were ordained to eternal life believed." Vance says, "Every Calvinist, no matter what else he believes, uses this verse to prove Unconditional Election...." Nettleton claims it is "this verse that made him a Calvinist."[2] White devotes four pages to it.[3] Palmer exults, "Here is another text with stunning clarity.... The stark simplicity of this text is astounding."[4]

Certainly, "*ordained* to eternal life" is the translation of the Greek word *tasso* (in this case *tetagmenoi*) found in all major translations (as White points out).[5] A number of paraphrases, however, give a decidedly non-Calvinistic rendering. *The Living Bible* puts it, "...as many as wanted eternal life, believed." *Rotherham's Emphasized Bible* says, "as many as had become disposed for life age-abiding...." The *Nazarene Translation 2000* by Mark Heber Miller has, "...all those who believed were disposed to ageless Life." Whatever the differing opinions of translators and commentators, this one verse cannot undo what hundreds of others establish.

The Calvinist, to support his beliefs, assumes that *tetagmenoi* must mean "predestined to salvation." Yet that is clearly not the meaning in any of the seven other usages of *tasso* in the New Testament. If that were the intent, why was *tasso* used and not *prooridzo* (predestinated)?

In fact, Adam Clarke declares rather dogmatically, "Whatever *tetagmenoi* may mean, which is the word we translate *ordained*, it includes no idea of *pre*ordination or *pre*destination of any kind.... [O]f all the meanings ever put on it, none agrees worse with its nature and known signification than that which represents it as intending those who were predestinated to eternal life; this is no meaning of the term and should never be applied to it."[6]

Nor does the context support the Calvinist rendering, as numerous commentaries declare. McGarvey comments that "the context has no allusion to anything like an *appointment* of one part, and a *rejection* of the other, but the writer draws a line of distinction between the *conduct* of certain Gentiles and that of the Jews addressed by Paul.... Luke says, many of the Gentiles '*were determined*' for everlasting life. It is an act of the mind to which Paul objects on the part of the Jews, and it is as clearly an act of mind in the Gentiles which Luke puts in contrast with it...."[7]

Several authorities trace the KJV's "ordained" to the corrupt Latin Vulgate, which, as T. E. Page points out, "has *praeordinati*, unfairly..."[8] *Cook's Commentary* reads, "The A.V. [KJV] has followed the Vulgate.

Rather, [it should read] were...disposed for eternal life, as in...Josephus...."[9] Likewise Dean Alford translated it, "as many as were *disposed* to eternal life believed."[10] *The Expositor's Greek Testament* says, "There is no countenance here for the *absolutum decretum* of the Calvinists."[11] A. T. Robertson likewise says: "The word *ordain* is not the *best* translation here. 'Appointed,' as Hacket shows, is better.... There is no evidence that Luke had in mind an *absolutum decretum*...of personal salvation."[12]

Greek grammarians tell us that *tetagemenoi*, a nominative case, perfect tense, passive middle voice participle of *tasso* is used, indicating an influence upon the Gentiles toward eternal life and believing the gospel. That this is a *present* influence and, as Barnes says, "not...an eternal decree," is generally agreed. It was at least in part Paul's persuasive preaching—which would fit the immediate context and the entire book of Acts: Paul and Barnabas "so spake, that a great multitude...believed (Acts 14:1). "The verb...is middle...thus implies personal action...among those who had ranged themselves for eternal life."[13]

Some claim that the Dead Sea Scrolls, as well as comments from early church writers, indicate that the first 15 chapters of Acts were probably written first in Hebrew. The Greek would be a translation. Some scholars claim that going back to a "redacted Hebrew" version, based upon word-for-word Greek-Hebrew equivalents, would render Acts 13:48 more like "as many as submitted to, needed, or wanted salvation, were saved." Furthermore, even if "ordained" were the correct meaning, these Greeks still would have had to believe the gospel and accept Christ by an act of their own faith and will, as all of Scripture testifies.

The Context Is Clear

Always salvation is promised to all ("Repent, and be baptized every one of you" [Acts 2:38]) contingent upon individual faith ("Believe on the Lord Jesus Christ, and thou shalt be saved" [Acts 16:31]). Never is there a hint of God's predestining certain ones to heaven whom He will sovereignly regenerate and irresistibly cause to believe the gospel while withholding that grace from others. It would be a clear contradiction of the rest of Acts and all of the Bible for 13:48 to mean that certain Gentiles, but not Jews, were foreordained by God to go to heaven and sovereignly given faith to believe the gospel.

The meaning depends upon: (1) comparative usages of *tasso* elsewhere, and (2) the context. Here are all other usages: "...into a mountain where Jesus had *appointed* them (Matthew 28:16); "For I also am a man *set* under authority" (Luke 7:8); "...they *determined* that Paul and Barnabas...should go up to Jerusalem" (Acts 15:2); "...all things which are *appointed* for thee to do" (Acts 22:10); "they had *appointed* him a day" (Acts 28:23); "...the powers that be are *ordained* of God" (Romans 13:1); "...they have *addicted* themselves to the ministry of the saints (1 Corinthians 16:15). In none of these other usages in the New Testament is there anything even close to a divine decree *causing* human action.

The context is clear. In verse 46, Paul tells the Jews, "seeing that ye put it [the gospel] from you...we turn to the Gentiles." That was their personal decision. Verse 48 presents the contrast between the Jews who had rejected the gospel and the Gentiles who believed it. The implication is of a personal decision by the Greeks, as well. There is no support for the Calvinists' claim that a sovereign decree was the sole reason.

Robertson comments,

> The *Jews* here had voluntarily *rejected* the word of *God*. On the other side were those Gentiles who gladly accepted what the *Jews* had *rejected*.... Why these Gentiles here ranged themselves on *God's* side as opposed to the *Jews*, Luke does not tell us. This verse does not solve the *vexed* problem of *divine* sovereignty and human free agency.[14]

The exact meaning of *tetagmenoi* is in dispute. Yet this is the best verse the Calvinist can point to for support. And to do so, he must arrive at a questionable meaning that contradicts literally hundreds of scriptures where the meaning is crystal clear.

Predestination to Salvation—or Not?

Predestination and election are biblical teachings—but they are *never* unto salvation. To the Calvinist, however, predestination/election is *always* and *only* unto salvation—a view that is imposed wrongly upon Scripture. In fact, election/predestination is always unto specific blessings that *accompany* salvation, but not to salvation itself.

Foreknowledge is always given as the reason for predestination (Romans 8:29; 1 Peter 1:2). Knowing who would believe the gospel is a valid *reason* for electing or predestinating those persons to certain blessings. But God's knowledge that He would extend Irresistible Grace to certain persons cannot be offered as the *reason* for doing so.

White has an entire chapter titled "Unconditional Election a Necessity." Indeed, it is a necessity for Calvinism, but not on any other basis. To define Unconditional Election, White quotes not from Scripture but from the 1689 London Baptist Confession of Faith, the Westminster Confession of Faith, and a number of leading Calvinists such as James P. Boyce:

> Before the world was made, God's eternal, immutable purpose, which originated in the secret counsel and good pleasure of His will, moved Him to choose (or to elect), in Christ, certain of mankind to everlasting glory.... (Baptist Confession) This decree...is made "independent" of all such foreknowledge God has of what will take place in time [and] predestines certain *specific individuals* to eternal life and others it leaves to justice. This is an election *unto salvation* and... is *utterly unconditional*... [of] either foreseen faith, actions, dispositions, or desires. (Westminster) [Salvation is conditioned upon faith: "*Believe*...and thou shalt be saved."] The latter theory [i.e., the Calvinistic theory] is that God...of his own purpose...has from Eternity...determined to save...a definite number of mankind (not the whole race...not for...their faith...) but of his own good pleasure (simply because he was pleased so to choose). (Boyce)[15]

These are fallible human opinions, which both Boyce and White admit express merely a "theory" that must be tested by Scripture. More quotations of men's opinions follow in the remainder of White's chapter. The final one is from Calvin himself:

> We shall never be clearly persuaded, as we ought to be, that our salvation flows from the wellspring of God's free mercy until we come to know his eternal election, which illumines God's grace by this contrast: that he does not indiscriminately adopt all into the hope of salvation but gives to some what he denies to others.[16]

Who ever imagined that God "indiscriminately adopt[s] into the hope of salvation"? Only those who believe the gospel are saved.

Giving God a Bad Name

One would think that, rather than quoting this statement, Calvinists would be embarrassed by it. How could God's withholding of salvation from billions to whom He *could* give it cause us to appreciate "the wellspring of

God's free mercy" and "illumine God's grace"? That is like praising a man's generosity by exposing his stinginess.

In their chapter on "Limited Atonement," after explaining that Christ died for only a select group and that all others have been damned by God for eternity, John Piper and his staff defy all logic with this statement: "Every time the gospel is preached to unbelievers it is the mercy of God that gives this opportunity for salvation."[17] Opportunity for salvation for those for whom Christ did not die, and who have been predestined to eternal damnation? What taunting, cruel mockery!

Far from glorifying God, Calvinism gives God a bad name. Atheists and other critics of the Bible ridicule this portrait of God as a monster who takes pleasure in imposing suffering on mankind. Calvin's God *could save the entire human race*—but only saves a relative few in order, allegedly, to demonstrate the greatness of His grace!

This continual emphasis upon God's sovereignty to the exclusion of His love, mercy, and grace pervades Calvinism. In the booklet that John Piper and his pastoral staff at Bethlehem Baptist Church in Minneapolis published, which promotes Calvinism, God's love to lost sinners is missing, while sovereignty is the repetitious, dominant theme. In the preface, Piper writes, "To know him [God] in his sovereignty is to become like an oak tree in the wind of adversity and confusion."[18] But entirely missing is *anything* about knowing God's love or loving Him.

The real issue is God's love and character. God's love for the world is missing from Calvin's *Institutes*. Indeed, God's love for anyone, including the elect, is scarcely mentioned—a stark contrast to the importance it is given in the Bible. In Calvinism, it is not love that brings salvation to mankind but God's sovereign choice for His good pleasure.

God expects us to love our enemies and to do good to all. Calvin admits that "God enjoins us to be merciful even to the unworthy...."[19] Yet He has a lesser standard for Himself? How could it glorify God for Him to be less gracious than He commands *mankind* to be? And where does God say that He limits His mercy—much less that He is thereby glorified?

Scripture declares, "The Lord is good to all" (Psalm 145:9), "plenteous in mercy unto all" that call upon Him (Psalm 86:5), and the "God of our salvation [is] the confidence of all the ends of the earth" (Psalm 65:5). How can God be "good" to those whom He, according to Calvinism, predestined to eternal torment? How can He be "plenteous in mercy" unto those whom He could have saved but didn't? And how can the God of salvation be the "confidence" of those He takes pleasure in damning?

Calvin refers to "our most merciful Father,"[20] yet he limits God's mercy to the elect.

Boyce offends the God-given conscience even of atheists in saying that God chose to save only a few and to let the others perish, because He "was *pleased* so to choose"! Where does God ever intimate that He is pleased to let *anyone* perish? In fact, He repeatedly states the opposite—that He has *no pleasure* in the wicked perishing.

A Strange "Mercy" and "Kindness"

The Baptist Confession declares that God's election, which is supposedly a manifestation of His mercy, "predestines certain *specific individuals* to eternal life and others it leaves to justice." How can it be a manifestation of mercy to leave the condemned to suffer the penalty that justice demands, when they could be justified and forgiven and rescued from eternal punishment? This is not a question of the guilt of sinners or of whether they deserve judgment, which we all do. The issue is mercy. Surely there can be no limit to the infinite mercy of the infinite God!

God solemnly warns man, "If thou forbear to deliver them that are drawn unto death...doth not he that pondereth the heart consider...and shall not he render to every man according to his works" (Proverbs 24:11–12)? Yet Calvin's God not only fails to deliver the lost but mercilessly decrees their doom! This cannot be the God of the Bible, of whom Jesus said, "it is not the will of your Father which is in heaven, that one of these little ones should perish" (Matthew 18:14)!

These "little ones" grow into adults. Is it then that God is pleased to damn many whom He formerly loved? But Calvinistic predestination refers to the ultimate torment even of children.

Calvin declares, "Hence the highest proof of Scripture is uniformly taken from the character of him whose word it is."[21] How can he dare to say this while impugning God's character? Calvin then goes on to extol God's mercy and grace as the pinnacle of His character:

> There are certain passages which contain more vivid descriptions of the divine character, setting it before us.... Moses, indeed, seems to have intended briefly to comprehend whatever may be known of God by man, when he said [actually God said], "The LORD, The LORD God, merciful and gracious, long-suffering, and abundant in goodness and truth, keeping mercy for thousands, forgiving iniquity and transgression and sin, and that will by no means clear the guilty...." (Exodus 34:6–7)

> In Jeremiah, where God proclaims the character in which he would have us to acknowledge him...it is substantially the same.... "I am the Lord which exercise loving-kindness, judgment, and righteousness in the earth...." (Jeremiah 9:24)[22]

Yet elsewhere Calvin claims that God's *withholding* of His grace, mercy, and love from all except the elect enhances the goodness of His character! In fact, Paul argues that God has found "all the world...guilty" (Romans 3:19) and has "concluded them all [Jew and Gentile] in unbelief, that he might have mercy upon all" (Romans 11:32). Unquestionably, the *all* who are guilty and in unbelief must be the whole world of sinners, Jews and Gentiles, *all* of whom are by nature rebels and in unbelief—and these are the *all* upon whom God is determined to have mercy. It could not be stated more clearly throughout Scripture that God's mercy extends to *all.*

Denying a Clear Contradiction

As we have already seen, White informs us, "Why is one man raised to eternal life and another left to eternal destruction...? It is 'according to the kind intention of His will.'"[23] So it is God's *kindness* that causes Him to damn so many! We are offended for our loving God!

The Calvinist, however, denies any contradiction in the idea that the God of infinite love is pleased to predestine billions to eternal torment. Calvin even castigates those who recognize this lie. He praises Augustine for throwing out of the Church any who suggest that God couldn't really love those He has predestined to eternal torment:

> Were anyone to address the people thus: If you do not believe, the reason is, because God has already doomed you to destruction: he would not only encourage sloth, but also give countenance to wickedness. Were any one to...say, that those who hear will not believe because they are reprobates [i.e., damned by God's foreordination], it were imprecation rather than doctrine.
>
> Wherefore, Augustine not undeservedly orders such, as senseless teachers or sinister and ill-omened prophets, to retire from the Church.[24]

Calvin is trying to escape the consequences of his own dogmas, but he can't. He repeatedly insists throughout his *Institutes* that "God saves whom he wills of his mere good pleasure"[25] and that some are "predestinated to salvation, and others to destruction."[26] Calvin says that the latter, whom it was God's good "pleasure to doom to destruction...are excluded from access to life...."[27] How those whom the omnipotent God has "excluded from access to life" could be responsible for their own doom and could be the beneficiaries of His infinite love is incomprehensible.

It is as if God has thrown into the ocean billions of people whom He has so created that they cannot swim a stroke. He "mercifully" rescues some of them and leaves the rest to drown in eternal death. How could anyone say to those whom God created to drown, "It is your own fault!"? How can Calvin (and Calvinists today) say it is "wickedness" and "imprecation" to say that the non-elect cannot believe the gospel because God has excluded them from faith, when, in fact, that is exactly what Calvinism teaches? It is outrageous to suggest that those whom God foreordains to eternal doom are not only to blame for their fate but are the objects of His love, mercy, and grace! *What Love Is This?!*

Biblical Mercy, Kindness, and Grace

All Scripture contradicts the false doctrine that God would withhold mercy from anyone. In fact, God is "ready to pardon, gracious and merciful, slow to anger, and of great kindness" (Nehemiah 9:17). Such statements are misleading if God intended to pardon only an elect group and predestined the rest (or simply left them) to eternal torment! Of the good and righteous man, the Bible says, "he is ever [always to all] merciful" (Psalm 37:26). Surely the very "gracious and merciful God" (Nehemiah 9:31) would be no less than always merciful to all. But Calvinism limits God's grace and mercy to a select group called the elect—a lower standard of mercy than He expects of us.

The Apostle James points out the hypocrisy of saying to someone who is "naked, and destitute of daily food...be ye warmed and filled" and then failing to meet his need (James 2:15–16). Yet the God who inspired James, according to Calvinism, tells a lost and perishing world, "Believe on the Lord Jesus Christ, and thou shalt be saved," but withholds the faith without which they cannot believe and be saved. Such a God sees those who are in greater need than physically naked and destitute, and He fails to rescue them from an eternal hell even though He could in His omnipotence and sovereignty do so—in fact, He has predestined them to this horrible fate. Is this really the God of the Bible, or a God that Calvin borrowed from Augustine?

The psalmist rejoices that God's "tender mercies are over all his works" (Psalm 145:9). The Calvinist, however, changes Scripture to limit God's mercy to "the elect." Christ exhorts us, "Be ye therefore merciful, as your Father also is merciful" (Luke 6:36). If our Father in heaven is merciful to only the elect, we could neglect helping multitudes and claim that so doing reveals how merciful we are!

Jesus illustrates the mercy of His Father in many ways. He tells us that after crying out, "God be merciful to me a sinner" (Luke 18:13), the publican was mercifully justified. Paul refers to "the Father of mercies and the God of all comfort" (2 Corinthians 1:3). Would the very "Father of mercies" be any less merciful *to all* than He expects mankind to be? "Blessed are the merciful: for they shall obtain mercy" (Matthew 5:7).

These scriptures, and scores more in the same vein, tell us that God's mercy is infinite, extending to all mankind without discrimination. The psalmist says, "I will sing of the mercies of the Lord for ever..." (Psalm 89:1). God's mercies are unto all who call upon Him. Indeed, the very glory of God is in His mercy to all mankind.

Of course, God has the right to limit His mercy. However, Scripture declares repeatedly and in many ways that God *does not* limit His mercy but extends it to all. One is forced to reject Calvinism on this basis if on no other, for it contradicts the very character of God that is consistently displayed throughout Scripture.

In contrast, the non-Calvinist believes that God offers salvation to all without discrimination, but He cannot *make* anyone believe, for that would violate their free will and eliminate love. Those who will spend eternity in the Lake of Fire will be there because of their own choice and won't be able to blame God.

Whether God loves all, is merciful to all, and provides salvation for all to accept or reject, is the real issue. The answer to that question should become increasingly clear to the reader in the following pages.

---

1. *Straight Talk Live* (KPXQ, Phoenix AZ, 11 August 2000). Audiotape AT073, available through The Berean Call, P. O. Box 7019, Bend OR 97708.
2. David Nettleton, *Chosen to Salvation* (Schaumburg, IL: Regular Baptist Press, 1983), 16; cited in Laurence M. Vance, *The Other Side of Calvinism* (Pensacola, FL: Vance Publications, rev. ed. 1999), 345.
3. James R. White, *The Potter's Freedom* (Amityville, NY: Calvary Press Publishing, 2000), 186–90.
4. Edwin H. Palmer, *the five points of calvinism* (Grand Rapids, MI: Baker Books, enlarged ed., 20th prtg. 1980) 29.
5. White, *Potter's*, 187–88.
6. Adam Clarke, *Adam Clarke's One-Volume Commentary*, (Cook Publications, 1989), 995.
7. J. W. McGarvey, *Commentary on Acts* (Lexington, KY: Transylvania Printing and Publishing Co. 1863).
8. T. E. Page, *The Acts of the Apostles, Greek Text with Explanatory Notes* (New York: Macmillan and Co., 1897), 169.
9. Frederic C. Cook, ed., *The Bible Commentary* (New York: Charles Scribner Sons, 1895).
10. Henry Alford, *The New Testament for English Readers* (Grand Rapids, MI: Baker Book House, 1983), I:745.
11. R. J. Knowling, *The Acts of the Apostles, The Expositor's Greek New Testament* (Pennsylvania: Dodd, Mead and Co., 1900), 300.
12. Archibald Thomas Robertson, *Word Pictures in the New Testament* (New York: Harper and Bros., 1930), III: 200.
13. *Acts, An Introduction and Commentary*, Tyndale New Testament Commentaries (Downer's Grove, IL: InterVarsity Press, 1974), additional notes 110.
14. A. T. Robertson, *Word Pictures in the New Testament*, (New York: Harper and Bros., 1930).
15. White, *Potter's*, 125–26.
16. John Calvin, *Institutes of the Christian Religion.* Trans. Henry Beveridge. (Grand Rapids, MI: Wm. B. Eerdmans, 1998 ed.) III:21:1.
17. John Piper and Pastoral Staff, "TULIP: What We Believe about the Five Points of Calvinism: Position Paper of the Pastoral Staff" (Minneapolis, MN: Desiring God Ministries, 1997), 14.
18. Ibid.
19. Calvin, *Institutes.*, III: xx, 15.
20. Ibid., 3.
21. Ibid., iii, 4.
22. Ibid., ii, 8, 2.
23. White, *Potter's*, 177.
24. Calvin, *Institutes*, III: xxiii, 14.
25. Ibid., xxi, 1.
26. Ibid.
27. Ibid., 7.

CHAPTER

17

Foreknowledge and Predestination/Election

IN SCRIPTURE, the basic meaning of the terms *predestination* and *election* is the same: to mark out beforehand for a special purpose and blessing. On what basis? The sole reason that is always given is *foreknowledge*. So declare both Peter and Paul: "For whom he did foreknow [Greek: *proginosko*], he also did predestinate [*proorizo*] to be conformed to the image of his Son..." (Romans 8:29); "Elect according to [*kata*] the foreknowledge [*prognosis*] of God the Father, through sanctification of the Spirit, unto obedience..." (1 Peter 1:2).

It seems that God predestined certain blessings for those He foreknew would believe the gospel and be saved. The heavenly Father planned from eternity past an inheritance for those who would become His children through faith in Christ Jesus: "That in the ages to come he might shew the exceeding riches of his grace in his kindness toward us through Christ Jesus" (Ephesians 2:7).

Never does election or predestination refer to salvation, but always and only to particular benefits. "What must be borne in mind is the fact that predestination is not God's predetermining from past ages who should and who should not be saved. Scripture does not teach this view."[1] Ironside declares: "...There is no reference in these four verses [the *only* four that refer to predestination] to either heaven or hell, but to Christlikeness eventually. Nowhere are we told in Scripture that God predestined one man to be saved and another to be lost."[2]

Perverting Predestination

Edward Hulme says of Calvin, "Predestination was his pivotal dogma.... 'Everything,' says Calvin, 'depends upon the mere will of God; if some are damned and others saved it is because God has created some for death and others for life.'"[3] Calvin declares: "I say with Augustine, that the Lord has created those who, as he certainly foreknew, were to go to destruction, and he did so because he so willed. Why he willed, it is not ours to ask...."[4]

Again, Palmer informs us, "The first word Calvinism suggests to most people is predestination; and...the other four points [of TULIP] follow."[5] John H. Leith writes, "Predestination can be taken as a special mark of Reformed theology."[6] Pink adds, "Not only has God the right to do as He wills with the creatures of His own hands, but *He exercises this right*, and nowhere is that seen more plainly than in His predestinating grace."[7] *Grace* preordains multitudes to eternal doom?

Predestination (according to Calvinism) is the "eternal decree of God, by which...some are preordained to eternal life, others to eternal damnation...."[8] Calvin reiterates: "Those, therefore, whom God passes by he reprobates, and that for no other cause but because he is pleased to exclude them from the inheritance which he predestines to his children...."[9] It is a libel on the character of God to say that damning billions pleases Him! Yet this distasteful doctrine is the inevitable result of Calvinism's extreme view of sovereignty.

The Calvinist "thrusts his doctrines of election and predestination into every conceivable Scripture text."[10] Vance goes on to say:

> Clark claims that "Isaiah has some two dozen verses that bear rather directly on the doctrine of predestination."[11] [Yet] the word neither occurs in Isaiah nor anywhere else in the Old Testament. Custance is even bolder: "Turning more specifically to the matter of Election to salvation, consider the following."[12] Then follows a list of twelve passages from the Old Testament in which election is not mentioned and salvation is not even in view.[13] Turning now to the New Testament, we find the same thing. Boettner audaciously declares: "There is hardly a chapter in the Gospel of John which does not either mention or imply election or reprobation.[14] But even after a statement like that he didn't give any verses. In answering the question, "I would like for you to list the scriptures which teach that God elected individuals to salvation before the world began," one Sovereign-Grace Baptist lists six scriptures where election is not even mentioned.[15]

The Role of Predestination in Calvinism

Calvin always limits God's mercy and love to the elect. As an Islamic expert says of that religious system: "The Divine will is irresistible, and has decreed in every detail the entire course of the universe which He governs, and the fate each moment of every creature therein.... Its dogma of predestination and of fate...leaves no room for human free-will...."[16] So it is with Calvinism.

Horsch comments, "According to Augustine's teaching, the history of mankind would, from a religious and spiritual point of view, be little more than a puppet show...."[17] R. C. Sproul writes, "God wills all things that come to pass...God desired for man to fall into sin…God created sin."[18] Sheldon agrees: "The Augustinian scheme...does represent Him [God] as foreordaining that the fall should involve, beyond every chance of rescue, the eternal ruin and damnation of the greater part of the race…"[19] Without any apparent embarrassment or regret, Palmer explains that by the teaching on predestination in Calvin's *Institutes* and echoed by most Calvinists to this day, God is the author of everything and therefore even of all sin:

> Foreordination means God's sovereign plan, whereby He decides all that is to happen in the entire universe. Nothing in this world happens by chance. God is in back of everything. He decides and causes all things to happen that do happen.... He has foreordained everything "after the counsel of his will" (Ephesians 1:11): the moving of a finger, the beating of a heart, the laughter of a girl, the mistake of a typist—even sin.[20]

No wonder Susanna Wesley wrote to her son John: "The doctrine of predestination as maintained by rigid Calvinists is very shocking, and ought utterly to be abhorred, because it charges the most holy God with being the author of sin."[21] This abhorrent doctrine is not biblical but is a human invention. Calvinism's five points require a sovereignty that allows man no freedom of the will, thereby necessitating that God be the predestinator and effective cause of all.

Consequently, mankind could blame God for everything, and Calvinists ought to acknowledge that fact. In a feature article as part of *Christianity Today's* "occasional series on doctrinal renewal, sponsored by a grant from Lilly Endowment Inc.," two Master of Divinity students at Princeton Theological Seminary recounted the joy of their conversion to Calvinism: "Blaming God for everything has been such a joy that we decided the least we could do...was to tell the world how we got here."[22]

Once again, looming over Calvin, is the long shadow of Augustine. Paul K. Jewett calls Augustine "the first true Predestinarian."[23] Of Calvinism's central doctrine of salvation through Irresistible Grace and Unconditional Election, Loraine Boettner declares, "This cardinal truth of Christianity was first clearly seen by Augustine."[24] Of that great Catholic "Saint" (another fallacy: in the Bible, all believers are saints), John Horsch commented:

> Augustine...was by theological speculation led to the belief in predestination...[that] God in his mercy selects and predestinates a [certain] number...for eternal life.... From the rest of mankind...God withholds his grace, and will condemn them even if they should die in infancy....[25]

This repugnant doctrine of punishing innocent infants mocks Christ's words, "Suffer the little children to come unto me, and forbid them not, for of such is the kingdom of God" (Mark 10:14).

Where Is God's Love?

Every biblical passage that mentions predestination/election will be searched in vain for any reference to anyone being predestined to damnation. How, then, does the Calvinist support such a doctrine? By implication only. Those whom God did not elect have been just as surely damned by His eternal decree. Calvin said it is "childish" to deny this, "since there could be no election without its opposite reprobation."[26] Boettner declares:

> The doctrine of absolute Predestination of course logically holds that some are foreordained to death as truly as others are foreordained to life. The very terms "elect" and "election" imply the terms "non-elect" and "reprobation".... We believe that from all eternity God has intended to leave some of Adam's posterity in their sins, and that the decisive factor...is to be found only in God's will.[27]

What a misrepresentation of God! We search the writings of Calvinists in vain to find some hint of regret or sympathy for those hopelessly doomed by God's eternal decree. How could the God who damns multitudes then profess His love for them—or regret His sovereign decrees?

Love and compassion—where shall we find these greatest of all virtues in Calvinism?

Calvinists propose various theories to make it seem that God really *does* love those He predestines to eternal torment. One of the most callous theories comes from Michael Horton in a book with a foreword by J. I. Packer. He argues, "This view intensifies God's love, by limiting it only to those who believe. That sure beats the indiscriminate, general benevolence we seem to be hearing much about today."[28]

For God to love all mankind would be a despicable "indiscriminate, general benevolence"? Limiting God's love to a select group intensifies God's love? What madness!

As noted, John Piper and his pastoral staff published a booklet titled "TULIP: What We Believe about the Five Points of Calvinism." Like Calvin's *Institutes*, it glorifies God's sovereignty (as we have already seen), but nowhere in its pages is there even a mention of God's love for sinners. John Calvin is presented as "the famous theologian and pastor of Geneva,"[29] with not a word about the floggings, imprisonments, tortures, banishments, and burnings at the stake that he encouraged there. Piper also praises Augustine,[30] but without a hint that he was the father of modern Roman Catholicism and held to numerous doctrines that evangelicals find repugnant. Is it honest to withhold vital facts in order to promote Calvinism?

Five times in the New Testament, Christ commands us, "Thou shalt love thy neighbour as thyself" (Matthew 19:19, etc.). Paul twice, and James once, reiterate this command that one must love one's neighbor as oneself (Romans 13:9; Galatians 5:14; James 2:8). Christ makes it clear that everyone who is in need is one's neighbor (Luke 10:29–37). Surely none are in greater need than the lost. Yet Calvinism tells us that the God who "is love," and who "so loved the world" and sent His Son "that the world through him might be saved" (John 3:17)—even though He could save *all*—damns billions for His "good pleasure" and to prove His justice. Aghast at such doctrine, one can only repeat in astonishment, *What Love Is This?*

Distorting a Metaphor

Calvinism negates God's love, mercy, and grace for any except the elect. "All who will finally be saved, were chosen to salvation by God the Father, before the foundation of the world, and given to Jesus Christ in the covenant of grace."[31] Piper writes, "Election refers to God's choosing whom to save. It is unconditional in that there is no condition man must meet before God chooses to save him. Man is dead in trespasses and sins. So there is no condition he can meet...."[32] John MacArthur, too, declares that unbelievers are "no more able to respond to God than a cadaver" and "are incapable of any spiritual activity...."[33] Vance points out the obvious error:

> And finally, if you make an exact parallel between a physically dead man and a spiritually dead man...then you likewise have to say...[if] he can't accept Christ because he is dead then he can't reject Christ either. A [physically] dead man cannot believe on Jesus Christ, but a [spiritually] dead man can."[34]

The physically dead can do nothing, not even commit sin; so they could hardly present a proper analogy of spiritual death. The spiritually "dead" are able to live active lives, get an education, earn a living, defy God, and continue to sin—or submit to the conviction of the Holy Spirit, repent of their sins, and believe on the Lord Jesus Christ as their Savior. Yet MacArthur reiterates:

> How can a person who is dead in sin, blinded by Satan, unable to understand the things of God, and continuously filled with evil suddenly exercise saving faith? A corpse could no sooner come out of a grave and walk.[35]

On the contrary, to the spiritually dead, Isaiah writes: "Ho, everyone that thirsteth, come ye to the waters.... Let the wicked forsake his way, and the unrighteous man his thoughts: and let him return unto the Lord, and he will have mercy upon him; and to our God, for he will abundantly pardon" (Isaiah 55:1,7). Surely the wicked are dead in trespasses and sins. Yet they are commanded to come, repent, and drink of Christ.

We agree that none would seek the Lord unless He first seeks them. Scripture declares, however, that God seeks *all.* He calls upon *all who thirst* to come to Him and drink, and upon *all who are wicked* to turn unto Him in reliance on His mercy. It must therefore be possible for those who are spiritually dead to hear God's voice, turn to the Lord, believe the gospel, and receive pardon by His grace.

Yet the insistent denial that the unregenerate can believe in Christ is a major point in Calvinism. Steele and Thomas argue that "The sinner is dead, blind, and deaf to the things of God.... Consequently...it takes regeneration by which the Spirit makes the sinner alive and gives him a new nature. Faith is not something man contributes to salvation...but is

God's gift to the sinner...."[36] Yet when Paul and Silas said, "Believe on the Lord Jesus Christ and thou shalt be saved" (Acts 16:31), were they suggesting that by believing the Philippian jailor would contribute faith to his salvation? Hardly.

And how could Paul and Silas even address the spiritually dead and invite them to believe on Christ? How could they know that those to whom they gave the invitation were going to be sovereignly regenerated and given faith to believe? Obviously Paul and Silas were not Calvinists.

A Simple Exegesis

Peter says we are "elect according to [kata]" God's foreknowledge (1 Peter 1:2). The Greek *kata* carries the meaning of homogeneity or harmony. Thus God's election/predestination was in agreement, or harmony, with something He foreknew about those whom He predestined to partake of the declared blessings. What could that have been?

Surely the most obvious possibility would be that God foreknew who would repent and believe the gospel, and on that basis He predestined them "to be conformed to the image of his Son" and "unto obedience." Apparently departing from his oft-professed Calvinism, Spurgeon declared:

> Mark, then, with care, that OUR CONFORMITY TO CHRIST IS THE SACRED OBJECT OF PREDESTINATION.... The Lord in boundless grace has resolved that a company whom no man can number... shall be restored to His image, in the particular form in which His Eternal Son displays it...the likeness of the Lord from Heaven. [Emphasis in original][37]

In order to escape foreknowledge as the basis of predestination, the Calvinist must establish another meaning for foreknow/foreknowledge that fits his theory. Generally, this attempt has taken two forms. Most try to maintain that foreknow/foreknowledge, instead of meaning to know in advance, means to determine in advance, or to foreordain. Piper writes, "he [God] foreknows—that is, elects—a people for himself...."[38] Others suggest that it means to love beforehand. There are, however, several reasons why neither of these stratagems will work.

Various Calvinist authors argue that "foreknowledge" is "the equivalent of a determined counsel...God's omniscient wisdom and intention... God's prerogative to 'choose beforehand.'"[39] MacArthur writes:

> God's foreknowledge, therefore, is not a reference to His omniscient foresight but to His foreordination. God does indeed foresee who is going to be a believer, but the faith He foresees is the faith He Himself creates. It's not that He merely sees what will happen in the future; rather He ordains it. The Bible clearly teaches that God sovereignly chooses people to believe in Him.[40]

He hasn't shown us from Scripture—he simply declares it to be so in order to support Calvinism. But this is not what Scripture says! Piper quotes C. E. B. Cranfield, who refers to the foreknowledge of Romans 8:29 as "that special taking knowledge of a person which is God's electing grace." Piper then comments that "foreknowledge is virtually the same as election.... He foreknows—that is, elects—a people for himself...."[41] But the Greek word is *proginosko*, which means to know beforehand in the sense of foreseeing. The Calvinist is desperately twisting the Scripture in order to maintain his theory.

Peter very clearly distinguishes counsel or determination as well as election *from* foreknowledge: "him [Christ], being delivered by the determinate [*horizo*] counsel [*boule*] *and* foreknowledge [*proginosko*] of God..." (Acts 2:23). If these are the same, then Peter is saying nonsensically that Christ was "delivered by the foreknowledge *and* foreknowledge," or by "the determined counsel *and* determined counsel" of God. Paul likewise makes a clear distinction: "For whom he [God] did foreknow, he *also* [*kai*] did predestinate...." The Greek *kai* denotes a differentiation, thus making it clear that foreknowledge could not be the same as predestination, or Paul, as already pointed out, would be redundantly saying, "whom he did predestinate he *also* did predestinate."

The Essential Function of Foreknowledge

This inspired statement by Peter on the Day of Pentecost reveals that in foretelling future events through His prophets and accomplishing them in history, God takes into account what He by His foreknowledge knows will be the actions and reactions of men. He did not *cause* Judas to betray Christ, nor did He *cause* the Jews to reject Him or the Romans to crucify Him—or predestine them to do so. He arranged that these particular individuals, who He knew would act in that manner, were on the scene at the right time to fulfill His will, though they were unaware that they were fulfilling prophecy. As Paul declared, "...because they knew him not, nor yet the voices of the prophets which are read every sabbath day, they fulfilled them in condemning him" (Acts 13:27).

To foreknow is simply to know in advance. And to know in advance is not the same as to foreordain. If God simply elected/predestined certain ones because He elected/predestined them, there would be no reason to mention foreknowledge at all. Clearly, that God foreknew certain persons would believe the gospel was the *reason* for electing/predestining them to the special *blessings*.

That foreknowledge means nothing more nor less than to know beforehand is clear not only in the particular scriptures above, but also in other places where the same Greek words are used in the New Testament. In referring to Jewish leaders of his acquaintance who he says "knew me from the beginning [i.e., before that day]" (Acts 26:4–5), Paul uses the same word, *progonisko,* translated at Romans 8:29 "for whom he did *foreknow.*" Peter uses the same word in a different context but with the identical meaning: "ye know [*proginosko*] these things before..." (2 Peter 3:17).

Other Calvinists point to the way sexual intercourse is expressed in the Old Testament: "Adam knew [*yada*] his wife" (Genesis 4:1), "Cain knew [*yada*] his wife" (verse 17), etc. They then suggest that "whom God foreknew" actually means "whom God loved beforehand." But that is nonsense.

While *yada* is at times used to denote a special relationship—"I did know thee in the wilderness" (Hosea 13:5), "You only have I known of all the families of the earth" (Amos 3:2)—never does it mean to know in advance, whereas that is the principle meaning of *proginosko* and *prognosis*. There is, therefore, no relationship between these words that would be of any help in supporting Calvinism.

Furthermore, to "know" one's wife in a sexual way could not be before the fact, nor does God "know" man in that manner. Therefore, the attempt to link love with foreknowledge through *yada*, to give the meaning "foreloved," won't work. That strained effort, however, reveals the lengths to which the Calvinist is both forced and willing to go to protect his theory.

Why Not Accept the Simplest Meaning?

Clearly, God in His omniscience has foreknown from eternity past who, when convicted of sin and drawn by His Holy Spirit, would willingly respond to the gospel. On the basis of that foreknowledge He predestined, or elected, those particular persons to special blessings: "...To be conformed to the image of his Son...unto obedience...." Paul adds another blessing: "According as he hath chosen us in him before the foundation of the world, that we should be holy and without blame before him in love" (Ephesians 1:4). Dave Breese writes, "We also notice that election in Scripture is not unto salvation, but 'unto obedience....' [In] Romans chapter 8... predestination is based upon the foreknowledge of God and its object is not salvation but conformity to the image of Christ."[42]

Paul and Peter are encouraging Christians with what God has in store for those who believe the gospel. As Paul declares, "Eye hath not seen, nor ear heard, neither have entered into the heart of man, the things which God hath prepared for them that love him. But God hath revealed them unto us by his Spirit..." (1 Corinthians 2:9–10).

Furthermore, not only is predestination/election never said to be unto salvation, but Paul carefully separates predestination from salvation whether in its call, its justification, or its glorification: "whom he did predestinate, them he *also* [*kai*] called...them he *also* [*kai*] justified...them he *also* [*kai*] glorified" (Romans 8:30). The Greek *kai* shows that a distinction is being made: predestination is not the same as calling, justification, or glorification. Hobbs comments, "Predestination...simply means that God has predetermined that those who respond affirmatively to His call...will be justified...and furthermore will be glorified. All of this is 'according to His purpose'...."[43] The plain meaning of the text is clear.

More Redundancies and Nonsense

There is a further problem with the Calvinist interpretation of "foreknowledge." Because it rejects knowing what man would do (i.e., repent and believe the gospel) it can involve nothing more than God knowing what He would do. To say that God foreknew what He had predestined would be nonsense.

Moreover, it would be impossible for God to "foreknow" what He purposed to do because His purposes have always existed. As James said, "Known unto God are all his works from the beginning of the world [*aion*]". (Acts 15:18). The Greek *aion*, rather, carries the meaning of "from all eternity."

Ironically, Rob Zins accuses non-Calvinists of teaching that "there was a time when God knew not [what man would do].... However, it is our contention that God knows all things because He wills all things."[44] On the contrary, we affirm that from eternity past God has known all that would happen in the universe and in the minds and affairs of men—*not* because He "wills all things" but because He knows all things, i.e., is omniscient.

Piper insists that "God does not foreknow the free decisions of people to believe in him because there aren't any such free decisions to know."[45] If so, man is a puppet with God pulling the strings, making foreknowledge meaningless. Without free choice man would not be morally responsible, could not love God, know God's love, receive the gift of salvation, have meaningful communion with God, or worship Him. Spurgeon asked: "Shall we never be able to drive into men's minds the truth that predestination and free agency are both facts?"[46]

Yet White writes, "In other words, the *foreknowledge* of God is based upon His decree, plan, or purpose which expresses His will, and not upon some foreseen act of *positive volition* on the part of man." Such a conclusion is not only unbiblical but assaults reason. There is no point in saying that God foreknew His eternal decrees—nor could He. Since His decrees have always been, and thus were never future to Him, there is no way in which He could know what they would be before they were decreed.

Neither could one say that God, because He knew in advance that He had decreed to save certain persons, therefore saved them. Foreknowledge is very clearly the *reason* given for election and predestination. God's knowing in advance what He would do could never be the *reason* for His doing it.

Clearly, knowing in advance who would believe the gospel, God made certain that those individuals heard the gospel, and He predestined them to partake of the many blessings He planned to bestow on the redeemed throughout eternity. Such is the reasonable and legitimate conclusion to be derived from the clear language expressed in these passages. Why go to such great lengths to find another meaning, except to support a theory?

A Closer Look at Election

The words "predestinate" and "predestinated" are used only four times in Scripture. The first three have already been considered. The fourth will be dealt with later. Election has a similar meaning, and the words "elect," "elected," "election," and "elect's" are together used twenty-seven times in the Bible.

The objects of God's election/predestination are called "the elect." The word "elect" (*bachiyr* in Hebrew, *eklektos* in Greek) is used in a variety of ways. It refers to the Messiah (Isaiah 42:1; 1 Peter 2:6), to Israel or

Jews (Isaiah 45:4; 65:9, 22; Matthew 24: 31; Mark 13:27), to the church (Romans 8:33; Colossians 3:12; Titus 1:1), to both Israel and the church (Matthew 24:24; Mark 13:22; Luke 18:7), to angels (1 Timothy 5:21), and to a lady (2 John 1,13).

These verses cover every mention of the word "elect" throughout the entire Bible. *Not once* is that word used to designate a special class of persons whom God has marked out for salvation and whom alone He loves. Contradicting Scripture (but agreeing with Calvin's *Institutes*), a minister of the Protestant Reformed Churches in America writes, "Thus it cannot be that God loves everyone. Since God's love is sovereign and therefore always a saving love, only those who experience the salvation of the Lord can be the objects of His love."[47] Again we must ask, *What love is this*? And where in the Scripture is this idea expressed?

The Five Pertinent Scriptures

The word "elect" is found four times in the Old Testament: once referring to the Messiah (Isaiah 42:1) and three times referring to Israel (Isaiah 45:4; 65:9, 22). None of these is pertinent to our inquiry. In the New Testament, the word "elect" is found seventeen times, the word "election" six times, the word "elect's" three times, and the word "elected" once.

Eliminating the one reference to angels, the one reference to Christ himself, the three references that could be both to Israel and the church, the three to a lady, the four to those Jews who have been preserved through the Great Tribulation and survived Armageddon, and the six that are simply a name for believers in Christ, we are left with five that pertain to the general subject of election:

1) That the purpose of God according to election might stand, not of works, but of him that calleth.... (Romans 9:11)
2) There is a remnant according to the election of grace. (Romans 11:5)
3) Knowing, brethren beloved, your election of God....(1 Thessalonians 1:4)
4) Elect according to the foreknowledge of God the Father, through sanctification of the Spirit, unto obedience and sprinkling of the blood of Jesus Christ: Grace unto you, and peace be multiplied. (1 Peter 1:2)

5) Wherefore the rather, brethren, give diligence to make your calling and election sure.... (2 Peter 1:10)

These scriptures present the following truths: (1) God works a definite purpose through election; (2) election involves not all mankind but a "remnant"; (3) election is according to God's grace; (4) election is "according to the foreknowledge of God the Father"; and (5) some responsibility rests upon the elect to make their "election sure."

If election is to salvation by Irresistible Grace without any intelligent or moral choice on man's part, it would be impossible to be sure of one's election. But if election is to service and blessing, Peter is reinforcing in different words Paul's exhortation to "walk worthy of the vocation wherewith ye are called" (Ephesians 4:1–6).

Thus, to make one's election sure is to fulfill the responsibility that comes with election, not to somehow be sure that one is among the elect and thus eternally saved. Marvin R. Vincent, an authority on biblical languages explains, "*Ekloge*, election [is] used of God's selection of men or agencies for special missions or attainments.... [Nowhere] in the New Testament is there any warrant for the revolting doctrine that God predestined a definite number of mankind to eternal life, and the rest to eternal destruction."[48]

Calvin's Fallacious Arguments

As already noted, election is determined by God's *foreknowledge*: "elect *according to the foreknowledge* of God the Father." In attempting to make predestination and election pertain to salvation so that it would fit his theory, Calvin entangled himself in fallacious reasoning and even heresy.

Of Ephesians 1:4–5, "According as he hath chosen us in him before the foundation of the world, that we should be holy and without blame before him in love: having predestinated us unto the adoption of children by Jesus Christ to himself, according to the good pleasure of his will," Calvin wrote:

> By saying they were elected before the foundation of the world, he [God] takes away all reference to worth.... In the additional statement that they were elected that they might be holy, the apostle openly refutes the error of those who deduce election from prescience, since he declares that whatever virtue appears in men is the result of election."[49]

His misunderstanding is obvious. That God would predestine to certain blessings those whom He foreknew would believe the gospel has nothing at all to do with their "worth." It is folly to suggest that some worth is ascribed to sinners if, by their own free choice, they believe the gospel and receive the Lord Jesus Christ as Savior. Indeed, it is because of their unworthiness and desperate need of salvation that sinners turn to Him.

And how could the blessings that are "the result of election" (as Calvin says above) be "virtues" for which those who receive them can take credit? In fact, the *why* of election is not even mentioned here. Therefore, this scripture cannot be used to dismiss what is so clearly stated in Romans 8:29 and 1 Peter 1:2—that God's foreknowledge is the *reason* behind His choosing certain ones to specific blessings.

The Calvinist argues that "elect according to the foreknowledge of God...whom he did foreknow them he also did predestinate" can't mean what it seems to mean, or God's sovereignty would be undermined. On the contrary, there is nothing inherent in the concept of sovereignty that requires that those to whom God sovereignly offers a gift cannot genuinely receive or reject it. And surely, God in His foreknowledge would know who those persons would be and could plan to bestow special blessings upon them.

That God, being outside of and independent of time, could know the future without *causing* it has been recognized for centuries by many who could not in good conscience accept the Calvinist definition of foreknowledge and predestination. For example, around 1780 John Wesley declared in a sermon that

> When we speak of God's foreknowledge we...speak...after the manner of men. For...there is no such thing as either foreknowledge or after knowledge in God. All...being present to him at once, he does not know one thing before another, or one thing after another; but sees all...from everlasting to everlasting. As all time, with everything that exists therein, is present with him at once, so he sees at once, whatever was, is or will be to the end of time. But observe; we must not think they are, because he knows them. No; he knows them, because they are.[50]

Some Important Distinctions

We could have been given eternal life, and even a place in heaven like the angels, without being made God's children and joint heirs with Christ of all the inheritance He has in the Father. But God, in His infinite love and grace, predestined believers to be part of His family—His very own children, who are called "unto his eternal glory by Christ Jesus" (1 Peter 5:10). As John Wesley said, "God decrees, from everlasting to everlasting, that all who believe in the Son of his love, shall be conformed to his image...."[51]

Salvation is clearly distinct from the blessings that accompany it—but Calvin had to make them one and the same or his cause was lost. Opposing this error, and echoing so many other biblical scholars, Andrew Telford wrote, "Nowhere in the Bible is Election connected with the salvation or the damnation of a human soul.... It has to do with service. It is God's elect who serve Him."[52] Sadly, in trying to make Scripture fit his theory, Calvin seems to have fallen deeply into error, once again relying upon Augustine:

> It is wisely observed by Augustine, that in the very head of the Church we have a bright mirror of free election...viz. that he [Christ] did not become the Son of God by living righteously, but was freely presented with this great honour, that he might afterwards make others partakers of his gifts. Should anyone here ask, why others are not what he was...if they are bent on depriving God of the free right of electing [to salvation] and reprobating [predestining to damnation], let them at the same time take away what has been given to Christ.[53]

Calvin seems to be denying the eternal Sonship of Christ and His eternal equality and oneness with the Father! He says that Christ *became* the Son of God, being "freely presented with this great honour...." Those who attempt to support Calvin often quote Psalm 2:7, as well as its quotation in Hebrews 1:5 and 5:5: "Thou art my Son; this day have I begotten thee." They claim this refers to a time when "Christ became the Son of God." When might that have been? It must have been in eternity past, because Christ was clearly the Son of God before He was born into the world: "and what is his son's name, if thou canst tell" (Proverbs 30:4)?

But there is no *time* in eternity—certainly nothing that could be called "this day." Time began with creation of the universe (Genesis 1:1). Furthermore, Christ, who is "the same yesterday, today and forever" (Hebrews 13:8), must therefore eternally be the Son of God. There was no point in eternity when "Christ *became* the Son of God" as Calvin alleges.

Is there a contradiction in Scripture? Of course not. Psalm 2:7 is not referring to Christ's *becoming* the Son of God at all. That never happened. He always *is* the Son of God. Paul tells us that "this day have I begotten thee" refers to Christ's resurrection: "God hath fulfilled the same unto us their children, in that he hath raised up Jesus again; as it is also written in the second psalm, Thou art my Son, this day have I begotten thee" (Acts 13:33). This agrees with His being called "the firstborn from the dead" (Colossians 1:18). Calvin was simply wrong on this point as on so many others.

Christ's alleged "election" to this honor apart from "living righteously" (i.e., without any merit) is then used by Calvin to establish the alleged election of humans to salvation apart from their worth or works. The comparison borders on blasphemy. Christ *is* the I AM from all eternity, one with the Father; and because of *who He is* it was He alone who could redeem us. Throughout the Old Testament, Yahweh, the God of Israel and great I AM, repeatedly says, "I, even I, am the LORD; and beside me there is no Saviour" (Isaiah 43:11 and many others). Jesus declares, "Before Abraham was, I am" (John 8:58).

Ridicule and "Mystery"

One of the sad features of Calvin's *Institutes* is the demeaning language he continually employs (much like Luther) to vilify all who disagree with him: "Hence it is, that in the present day so many dogs tear this doctrine [predestination] with envenomed teeth...assail it with their bark.... Since some feeling of shame restrains them from daring to belch forth their blasphemies against heaven, that they may give the freer vent to their rage, they pretend to pick a quarrel with us...this doctrine, which perverse men undeservedly assail because it is sometimes wickedly abused.... The profane make such a bluster with their foolish puerilities,"[54] and so forth, page after page.

Beneath Calvin's own bluster there is often little substance to his arguments, which he can support only by abusing Scripture. His obvious misunderstanding of opposing views, and the weak and unbiblical reasons Calvin adduces for rejecting foreknowledge as the basis of predestination, are reinforced with much ridicule:

> We, indeed, ascribe both prescience and predestination to God; but we say that it is absurd to make the latter subordinate to the former....[55] Others, who are neither versed in Scripture, nor entitled to any weight, assail sound doctrine with a petulance and

> improbity which it is impossible to tolerate... They ought at least to be restrained by feelings of awe from talking so confidently of this sublime mystery.[56]

The fact that foreknowledge is the *reason* for predestination, as Scripture declares, does not make the latter subordinate to the former. Both are among the many infinite qualities and abilities unique to God alone, none of which is either independent of or subordinate to any other. All of God's qualities are exercised in perfect harmony with each other. Thus, Calvin's argument entirely misses the point. And here, again, he pleads "mystery" when all else fails him.

What about 2 Thessalonians 2:13?

Calvinists often cite 2 Thessalonians 2:13 as proof of their position: "God hath from the beginning chosen you to salvation through sanctification of the Spirit and belief of the truth." Being "chosen to salvation," however, does not mean that one has been predestined for heaven. Numerous scriptures force us to conclude that all mankind have been "chosen to salvation" by the God who would "have all men to be saved..." (1 Timothy 2:4), who is "the savior of all men, specially of those that believe" (4:10), and whose Son "gave himself a ransom for all" (2:6).

If all have been chosen to salvation, why are all not saved? Christ said to His disciples, "Have not I chosen you twelve, and one of you is a devil? He spake of Judas...that should betray him..." (John 6:70-71). Judas was one of those chosen to be a disciple, but through his own choice he did not fulfill that calling and is now in hell.

God said to Israel, "The Lord thy God hath chosen thee to be a special people unto himself..." (Deuteronomy 7:6). That "choosing" did not automatically assure that all Israel would live the part. Unfortunately, Israel as a whole did not fulfill that calling but went into sin, and God had to cast her out of the land.

From these and other scriptures, it is clear that being "chosen" to salvation does not bring salvation: one must still believe the gospel in order to be saved. That fact is further made clear by the rest of the verse: "through sanctification of the Spirit and belief of the truth." Though "chosen to salvation," the means of salvation is not the choosing by God but the individual's "belief of the truth."

1. Herbert Lockyer, *All the Doctrines of the Bible* (Grand Rapids, MI: Zondervan, 1964), 153.
2. H. A. Ironside, *Full Assurance* (Chicago: Moody Press, 1937), 93–94.
3. Edward Maslin Hulme, *The Renaissance, the Protestant Reformation, and the Catholic Revolution* (New York: The Century Company, 1920), 299.
4. John Calvin, *Institutes of the Christian Religion*, trans. Henry Beveridge (Grand Rapids, MI: Wm. Eerdmans Publishing Company, 1998 ed.), III: xxiii, 5.
5. Edwin H. Palmer, foreword to *the five points of calvinism* (Grand Rapids, MI: Baker Books, enlarged ed., 20th prtg. 1980).
6. John H. Leith, *Introduction to the Reformed Tradition* (Atlanta, GA: John Knox Press, rev. ed. 1981), 103.
7. Arthur W. Pink, *The Sovereignty of God* (Grand Rapids, MI: Baker Book House, 2nd prtg. 1986), 52.
8. Calvin, *Institutes,* III: xxi, 5.
9. Ibid., xxiii, 1,4.
10. Laurence M. Vance, *The Other Side of Calvinism* (Pensacola, FL: Vance Publications, rev. ed. 1999), 248.
11. Gordon H. Clark, *Predestination* (Philipsburg, NJ: Presbyterian and Reformed Publishing Co., 1987), 181.
12. Arthur C. Custance, *The Sovereignty of Grace* (Phillipsburg, NJ: Presbyterian and Reformed Publishing Co., 1979), 7.
13. Numbers 16:5; 1 Kings 19:18, Psalms 65:4; 80:18–19; 110:3; Proverbs 16:1; Isaiah 26:12; Jeremiah 10:23; 31:18–19; 50:30; Lamentations 5:21.
14. Loraine Boettner, *The Reformed Doctrine of Predestination* (Phillipsburg, NJ: Presbyterian and Reformed Publishing Co., 1932), 346.
15. "Five Common Questions on the Doctrine of Election Simply and Clearly Answered," *The Baptist Examiner*, November 20, 1993, 5; cited in Vance, *Other Side*, 248.
16. Alfred S. Geden, *Comparative Religion* (London: Society for Promoting Christian Knowledge, 1917), 102–103.
17. John Horsch, *History of Christianity* (John Horsch, 1903), 104–105.
18. R. C. Sproul, Jr., *Almighty Over All* (Grand Rapids, MI: Baker Book House, 1999), 54.
19. Henry C. Sheldon, *History of Christian Doctrine* (New York: Harper and Bros., 2nd ed., 1895), II: 163.
20. Palmer, *five points*, 24–25.
21. A. W. Harrison, *Arminianism* (London: Duckworth, 1937), 189.
22. Jennifer L. Bayne and Sarah E. Hinlicky, "Free to be Creatures Again: How predestination descended like a dove on two unsuspecting seminarians, and *why* they are so grateful," *Christianity Today*, October 23, 2000, 38–44.
23. Paul K. Jewett, *Election and Predestination* (Grand Rapids, MI: Wm B. Eerdmans Publishing Co., 1985 ed.), 5.
24. Boettner, *Reformed*, 365.
25. Horsch, *History of Christianity*.
26. Calvin, *Institutes*, III: xxiii, 1.
27. Boettner, *Reformed*, 104.

28. Michael Scott Horton, *Putting Amazing Back Into Grace* (Nashville, TN: Thomas Nelson Publishers, 1991), 96.
29. John Piper and Pastoral Staff, "TULIP: What We Believe about the Five Points of Calvinism: Position Paper of the Pastoral Staff" (Minnepolis, MN: Desiring God Ministries, 1997), 3.
30. Ibid., 27–28.
31. John L. Dagg, *Manual of Theology and Church Order* (Harrisburg, VA: Sprinkle Publications, 1982), 309.
32. Piper and Staff, "TULIP," 19.
33. John F. MacArthur, Jr., *Faith Works: The Gospel According to the Apostles* (Dallas, TX: Word Publishing, 1993), 64–67.
34. Vance, *Other Side*, 522.
35. John MacArthur Jr., *Saved Without A Doubt—MacArthur Study Series* (Colorado Springs: Chariot Victor Books, 1992), 58.
36. David N. Steele and Curtis C. Thomas, *The Five Points of Calvinism* (Phillipsburg, NJ: Presbyterian and Reformed Publishing Co, 1963), 16.
37. Charles Haddon Spurgeon, *The Treasury of the New Testament* (Grand Rapids, MI: Zondervan, 1950), II: 72.
38. Piper and Staff, "TULIP".
39. S. Raymond Cox, "What Caused God To Choose His People?" (self-published paper, 1980), 3.
40. MacArthur, *Saved*, 59.
41. Piper and Staff, "TULIP," 22.
42. Dave Breese, "The Five Points of Calvinism" (self-published paper, n. d.).
43. Herschel H. Hobbs, *Fundamentals of our Faith* (Nashville: Broadman, 1960), 94–99.
44. Robert M. Zins, "A Believer's Guide to 2nd Peter 3:9" (self-published monograph, n. d.), 2–3.
45. Piper and Staff, "TULIP," 22.
46. Charles Haddon Spurgeon, *The Best Bread: Sermons Preached in 1887* (New York: Funk and Wagnalls, 1891), 109.
47. Steven R. Houck, "God's Sovereignty In Salvation" (The Evangelism Committee, Protestant Reformed Church, South Holland, IL, n. d.), 10.
48. Marvin R. Vincent, *Word Studies in the New Testament* (New York: Charles Scribner's Sons, 1924), IV: 16.
49. Calvin, *Institutes*, III: xxii, 2.
50. John Wesley, *Sermons on Several Occasions* (New York: J. Emory and B. Waugh, for the Methodist Episcopal Church at the Conference Office, 14 Crosby Street, 1831), II: 39.
51. Ibid.
52. Andrew Telford, *Subjects of Sovereignty* (Harvest Time Ministries, 1980), 55–56.
53. Calvin, *Institutes*, III: xxii, 1.
54. Ibid., I: xvii, 2,3.
55. Ibid., III: xxi, 5.
56. Ibid., xxii, 1.

CHAPTER

18

Limited Atonement

THE "L" IN TULIP represents one more integral theory in Calvin's scheme of salvation: "the doctrine which limits the atonement to...the elect."[1] This concept follows directly from the limitation Calvinists place upon God's love in spite of the fact that it, like every facet of His Being, is infinite. One of their prominent apologists declares, "The Bible teaches again and again that God does not love all people with the same love...'loved by God' is not applied to the world but only to the saints...(Romans 1:7)."[2]

Same love? But love is love—and "love…is kind" (1 Corinthians 13:4). Calvin himself declared, "All are not created on equal terms, but some are preordained to eternal life, others to eternal damnation...."[3] Is it loving or kind to "preordain to…eternal damnation"? Again we ask, *What Love Is This?*

A. A. Hodge confesses: "If they [critics] could prove that the love which prompted God to give his Son to die, as a sin offering...had for its objects all men...that Christ actually sacrificed his life with the purpose of saving all...on the condition of faith, then...the central principle of Arminianism is true [and Calvinism is false]...."[4] Boettner explained further:

> The Reformed Faith has held to the existence of an eternal, divine decree which, antecedently to any difference or desert in men themselves separates the human race into two portions and ordains one to everlasting life and the other to everlasting death.... Thus predestined and foreordained...their number is so certain and definite that it cannot be either increased or decreased.[5]

We protest that this doctrine is an outrageous misrepresentation of God. The God-given conscience of every person, saved and unsaved, recoils at the thought of creating beings simply in order to predestine them to eternal torment! Tragically, Calvinism forces its adherents to reject the normal human compassion that is otherwise held in common with all mankind.

Carson draws the line at Limited Atonement, arguing that this label "is singularly unfortunate for two reasons. *First,* it is a defensive, restrictive expression: here is atonement, and then someone wants to limit it. The notion of limiting something as glorious as the Atonement is intrinsically offensive. *Second,* even when inspected more coolly, 'limited atonement' is objectively misleading. Every view of the Atonement 'limits' it in some way, save for the unqualified universalist."[6]

His last sentence is a common Calvinist error—which accuses even those who say Christ died for all—of limiting the efficacy of the atonement because only those who believe are saved. On the contrary, the atonement is not limited by some rejecting Christ's sacrifice on their behalf. The inheritance left by the deceased is not reduced in value because some heirs refuse their share.

Honoring God's Love Is Heresy?

To the Calvinist, as Stanley Gower, a member of the Westminster Assembly, declared, there is no greater heresy than the suggestion that "God loveth all alike, Cain as well as Abel, Judas as the rest of the apostles."[7] Thus one must explain away that verse familiar to every Sunday-school child, "For God so loved the world, that he gave his only begotten Son, that whosoever believeth in him should not perish, but have everlasting life" (John 3:16). For Calvinism to stand, this verse (and many others expressing the same truth) cannot mean what the words seem to say: "world" and "whosoever" cannot signify all mankind but only the elect. Thus Calvinist children mean something else if ever they sing, "Jesus loves the little children, all the children of the world...." He only loves *some* of the children of the world!

Sproul writes, "The world for whom Christ died cannot mean the entire human family. It must refer to the universality of the elect (people from every tribe and nation)."[8] John Owen boldly states, "That the *world* here cannot signify all that ever were or should be, is as manifest as if it were written with the beams of the sun...."[9] How odd, then, that this bright sun is visible only to Calvinists—and that they disagree with one another on this key doctrine.

John MacArthur defends "The Love of God to Humanity."[10] He quotes Calvin that "the Father loves the human race,"[11] and that in John 3:16, God "useth the universal note [world] both that He may invite all men in general unto the participation of life, and that He may cut off all excuse from unbelievers."[12] But how can God invite "unto the participation of life" those whom He has predestined to eternal death in the Lake of Fire—and how can God "cut off all excuse from unbelievers," if Christ didn't die for them, and they were predestined to eternal torment from a past eternity? This is double talk!

MacArthur uses "humanity" in the generic sense, attempting thereby to deny God's love for every individual. Calvinists insist that God has a different kind of love for the elect than for the non-elect.[13] But love is love—and love of no kind predestines anyone to eternal torment who could be saved.

Calvinism's limitation upon the atonement of Christ ignores Old Testament types of the Cross, undermines the gospel, and limits God's boundless love. Owen, "after a more than seven years' serious inquiry... into the mind of God about these things..." asked earnestly, "To what purpose serves then general ransom [i.e., the alleged "heresy" that Christ loves all and died for all], but only to assert that Almighty God would have the precious blood of his dear Son poured out for innumerable souls whom he will not have to share in any drop thereof, and so, in respect of them, to be spilt in vain, or else to be shed for them only that they might be the deeper damned?"[14]

But it is Calvinism's predestination to damnation that creates this contradiction. Notice Owen's phrase, "whom he will not have to share in any drop thereof...." Of course it would be senseless for Christ to die for any whom God had determined to exclude from salvation. God did not exclude anyone. It is *man* who has rejected the salvation Christ provided for *all*.

No less sincere and earnestly concerned for truth, H. A. Ironside expressed the opposing common evangelical understanding in contrast to Calvinism's limited atonement for only a select number:

> No matter how far they [any sinners] have drifted from God; no matter what their sins may be, they do not have to peer into the book of the divine decrees in order to find out whether or not they are of the chosen or the elect. If they come in all their sin

> and guilt, confessing their iniquities and trusting in Christ, then they may have the assurance from His Word that they are saved. It has been well said that the "Whosoever *wills* are the elect, and the whosoever *won'ts* are the non-elect."[15]

Calvinists, however, firmly follow Calvin, who said of God, "for, (as he hates sin) he can only love those whom he justifies [i.e., the elect]."[16] Gerstner argues that if John 3:16 "is supposed to teach that God so loved everyone in the world that He gave His only son to provide them an opportunity to be saved by faith...such love on God's part...would be a refinement of cruelty.... Offering a gift of life to a spiritual corpse, a brilliant sunset to a blind man, and a reward to a legless cripple if only he will come and get it, are horrible mockeries."[17]

We agree that it would be cruel mockery to offer salvation to those whom God had no intention of saving and would not help to respond to the offer. But who says that all mankind cannot respond, if they so desire? Not the Bible, which offers salvation to "whosoever will," but Calvinism, which effectively changes "whosoever" into "elect"! So this "cruelty" is imposed by Calvinism itself, beginning with the very first of its five points. Yet "moderates," blaming all on "hyper-Calvinists," claim to believe that God sincerely loves and offers salvation to all, while in the same breath they say Christ did not die for all.[18]

By defining "total depravity" as "total inability," Calvinism says that none can respond to the gospel, not even the elect, until they have been sovereignly regenerated. Yet Christ commanded the gospel to be preached to everyone—and no one warns the non-elect that it isn't for them. Of course, how could they be warned, since no one knows who they are? So Christ commanded "cruelty and mockery"? And the Calvinist engages in it each time he preaches the gospel!

Why preach salvation to those already predestined to eternal damnation? "We must," says the Calvinist, "because no one knows who are the elect." So there is no escaping the fact that if Calvinism is true, then it is a cruel mockery to preach the gospel to anyone except the elect—but there is no way to identify them.

Would it lessen the non-elect's pain for the evangelist to explain, "This good news is only for the elect, so disregard it if you are not among them"? No, that would only add to the confusion. The cruelty is inherent in Calvinism's misrepresentation of God and His gospel.

The Doctrine Clearly Stated

Where does Scripture say that Christ's blood cannot be shed for those who would not benefit thereby? Nowhere. But this fiction is foundational to the doctrine of Limited Atonement: "that the cross of Christ provides a sure, secure and real salvation for everyone God intended it to save and for them alone."[19] Homer Hoeksema confesses the dire consequences of this belief, "If Christ died for the elect only, then there are no possible benefits in that death of Christ for anyone else...."[20] Steele and Thomas insist,

> Christ's redeeming work was intended to save the elect only and actually secured salvation for...certain specified sinners.... The gift of faith is infallibly applied by the Spirit to all for whom Christ died, thereby guaranteeing their salvation.[21]

This doctrine, however, is nowhere stated in the entire Bible in plain words, but is required by the rest of TULIP. Michael Horton argues, "If Jesus died for every person, but not every person is saved, His death did not actually save anybody.... If Christ died for people who will be in hell, His efforts cannot accurately be called a 'saving work' [and] there is no real saving power in the blood. Rather, the power would seem to be in the will of the creature."[22]

On the contrary, man's will has no power but can only accept or reject the salvation God offers in the gospel. The Calvinist complaint is like saying that the $1 million, which a father deposits in a bank in his estranged son's name, is of no value unless the son accepts it. Obviously, the sinner's acceptance of Christ no more gives the blood of Christ saving power than the son's acceptance of the $1 million would give it monetary value.

With no clear statement in all of Scripture to support this dogma, it must be defended by rationalizations: "If Christ died for all men and all men are not saved, the cross of Christ is of no effect. Calvary is a sham."[23] Of course, that doesn't follow. Otherwise, giving the Ten Commandments was a sham, because all men do not keep them.

Even Sproul acknowledges that "the value of Christ's atonement is sufficient to cover the sins of the world...."[24] It would have to be, because His perfect sacrifice must be of infinite value. Although "the cross is to them that perish foolishness" (1 Corinthians 1:18), it is not a sham but saves all who believe! As one of the most respected Bible teachers of recent years said, "The Bible teaches most strongly the doctrine of unlimited atonement.... The doctrine of limited atonement is specifically denied in Scripture...."[25]

But Calvinists persist: "Only Calvinism with its effective atonement limits man's power and exalts God's power and glory."[26] On the contrary, God offers salvation on His terms. That multitudes reject His offer only sends them to hell—hardly anything of which they could boast! Those who reject Christ are no more "in charge" than the multitudes who daily break God's commandments. Were Adam and Eve "in charge" when they rebelled? Was Satan? Of course not!

Did their rebellion give "power" to Satan, and to Adam and Eve? Of course not! Nor did it (any more than man's continued rebellion today) take anything away, in even the slightest degree, from either God's power or His glory. The Calvinist is driven to such fallacious and unbiblical arguments in his desperation to defend an indefensible dogma.

While some who call themselves Calvinists reject Limited Atonement, it is irrational to do so while accepting the other four points. A leading Calvinist author writes: "It is in this truth of limited atonement that the doctrine of sovereign election (and, in fact, sovereign predestination with its two aspects of election and reprobation), comes into focus."[27] In other words, the whole Calvinistic system collapses if Limited Atonement is not biblical, which indeed it is not.

Key, Yet Controversial, Even Among Calvinists

Limited Atonement is the one point that even Calvinists find difficult to accept. Certainly Spurgeon, at times, contradicted that which at other times he affirmed.

The book of Hebrews makes it clear that the Levitical system God gave to Israel for dealing with sin, involving the tabernacle, temple, priests and offerings, was "a figure for the time then present" (Hebrews 9:9), which pointed to the sacrifice of Christ that was to come. Indisputably, the Old Testament provision for sin and salvation was for *all Israel*, not for a special elect among them. Disobedience and unbelief were the only barriers separating every Israelite from God's grace. For example: "And the priests... made reconciliation...upon the altar...for *all Israel*...the burnt offering and the sin offering...for *all Israel*" (2 Chronicles 29:24); "offered burnt offerings...for *all Israel*" (Ezra 8:35); "the law of Moses... which I commanded... for *all Israel*, with the statutes and judgments" (Malachi 4:4), etc.

Spurgeon was accused of "Arminianism" for urging all unsaved to come to Christ, which he habitually did with great earnestness, thus contradicting Calvinism's claim that the number of those for whom Christ died was fixed and limited. Nor did he refrain from criticizing those whom he classified as hyper-Calvinists for their rejection of what was then called "duty-faith," meaning that it was the duty of all men to repent and believe the gospel.

It was over his persistent preaching of this message, in spite of much criticism, that the "duty-faith controversy" raged among "particular Baptists" in England. Spurgeon declared: "I cannot imagine a more ready instrument in the hands of Satan for the ruin of souls than a minister who tells sinners that it is not their duty to repent of their sins or to believe in Christ, and who has the arrogance to call himself a gospel minister, while he teaches that God hates some men infinitely and unchangeably for no reason whatever but simply because he chooses to do so."[28]

Spurgeon is criticizing the very heart of Calvinism—no wonder there was a furor! Many Calvinists of his day considered such statements to be a denial of Limited Atonement—which indeed they are. For pointing this out, I have been accused of misquoting and misrepresenting Spurgeon.

Some consider the doctrine of Limited Atonement to be "the Achilles Heel of Calvinism."[29] On the other hand, some Calvinists consider it to be their strongest point, "the hardest one of the *'Five Points of Calvinism'* for Arminians to cope with."[30] Most admit that it follows necessarily from Calvinism's view of predestination/reprobation: "If God has elected some and not others to eternal life, then plainly the primary purpose of Christ's work was to redeem the elect."[31]

We agree that it would be unreasonable for Christ to die for those whom God had from eternity past predestined to eternal torment, if there were such. But that problem is created by Calvinism's five points. "Give up this point [Calvinist election]," says another Calvinist, "and we have lost the battle on the sovereignty of God in salvation."[32]

The Calvinist recognizes that Unconditional Election and Limited Atonement "must stand or fall together. We cannot logically accept one and reject the other."[33] But the Bible repeatedly declares that Christ died for all mankind, that the gospel is offered and equally available to all, and that God wants all to be saved. Definitions of words must be changed to deny this clear biblical teaching.

Even John MacArthur acknowledges that God *desires* all men to be saved—but then he says that God inexplicably doesn't elect and predestine to salvation multitudes of those He desires to be saved. Odd, indeed, considering the emphasis Calvinists put on sovereignty, that God doesn't sovereignly fulfill His own desire![34]

Hodges notes that the God of Limited Atonement "is hardly the God of love whom we meet in the Bible. The deity of the determinist creates human beings for whom he has no direct love, and who have no free will, and thus they are created solely for…everlasting torment. Christ's death in no way affects them, and so they stand totally outside of any redemptive provision." He goes on to argue:

> The cruelty implicit in such a view is obvious to any observer outside of those who have been brought up in, or have bought into, this kind of theology. Despite specious arguments addressed to every text alleged against such theology, determinists of this type are bereft of true biblical support. It is absurd, for example, to claim (as they sometimes do) that when the Bible says, "God so loved the world," it means only "the world of the elect."[35]

In considering the scriptures bearing on this subject, it becomes clear that the only way Limited Atonement can be defended is to assign, arbitrarily, a restrictive Calvinist meaning to key words. Palmer boldly declares:

> It was just because God so loved the world of elect sinners that He sent His only begotten Son that the world [i.e., the elect by Calvinist definition] might be saved through Him (John 3:16–17). In this passage, "world" does not mean every single person, reprobate as well as elect, but the whole world in the sense of people [elected] from every tribe and nation....[36]

What evidence is there, either within this passage and its context or anywhere else in Scripture, that "world" has this restrictive Calvinist meaning? Palmer offers none, nor is there any.

Why Aren't All Men Saved?

In maintaining Limited Atonement, the Calvinist reasons, "If Christ paid the debt of sin, has saved, ransomed, given His life for *all* men, then *all* men will be saved."[37] In the same vein, Palmer writes, "But if the death of Jesus is what the Bible says it is—a substitutionary sacrifice for sins... whereby the sinner is really reconciled to God—then, obviously, it cannot be for every man...for then everybody would be saved, and obviously they are not."[38]

In a letter to John Wesley, George Whitefield reasoned, "You cannot make good the assertion 'that Christ died for them that perish,' without holding...'that all the damned souls would hereafter be brought out of hell....'"[39] This argument, however, rests upon the unbiblical theory that Christ's death immediately saved all of the elect, without any faith, understanding, or acceptance on their part. Contradicting many fellow Calvinists, Pink admitted, "A Saviour *provided* is not sufficient: he must be *received.* There must be '*faith* in His blood' (Romans 3:25) and faith is a *personal* thing. *I* must exercise faith."[40]

Though criticized by other Calvinists as an extremist on this point, Pink was right. That Christ "taste[d] death for every man" (Hebrews 2:9) does not automatically mean that all are delivered from eternal death, the penalty for sin. Nowhere does the Bible say so. Sinners are invited and urged to *come* to Christ and to *believe* on Him. Such is the sinner's responsibility—something he "*must*...do to be saved" (Acts 16:30).

That Christ died for our sins is the message preached in the gospel. It must, however, be believed to be of benefit to a sinner. Christ's death, though offered for "all men," is only efficacious for those who believe: He is "the Saviour of all men, specially of those that believe" (1 Timothy 4:10). Vance points out the obvious problem if the death of Christ automatically procures salvation for those for whom He died:

> But if the nature of the atonement was such that it actually in and of itself provided salvation for those for whom it was intended, then the "elect" could never have been born "dead in trespasses and sins" (Ephesians 2:1). And consequently, how could men who were saved, redeemed, reconciled, and justified be "by nature children of wrath" (Ephesians 2:3)...?[41]

The Passover, which Pink acknowledges as "one of the most striking and blessed foreshadowments of the Cross-work of Christ to be found anywhere in the Old Testament, is a clear example of the principle that the Atonement and its application are to be distinguished. The blood of the slain Passover lamb (Exodus 12:6,21) became efficacious only after it was applied to the doorpost per instructions (Exodus 12:7,22).... The death of the lamb saved no one: the blood had to be applied."[42] And so it is with Christ's death.

Calvinism bluntly blames God: "Because God has loved certain ones and not all, because He has sovereignly and immutably determined that these particular ones will be saved, He sent His Son to die for them, to save them, and not all the world."[43] Thus, all men are not saved because God doesn't want them to be and has predestined multitudes to suffer eternally.

According to the Bible, however, all are not saved because *they* (the lost) refuse to believe on Christ. Paul writes that salvation comes "unto all...that believe...for all have sinned" (Romans 3:22–23). Surely the "all have sinned" means all mankind. Thus the "all...that believe" must mean that all mankind *may* believe on Christ, if they will.

Salvation Is for All

Here are some of the many verses (with key words and phrases italicized) that declare that God (exactly as we would expect of the One who *is love* and the Father of mercies) loves everyone with infinite love and desires that all should be saved. He does not want anyone to perish and has made the death of Christ propitiatory for the sins of all mankind if they will only believe on Him:

- *All* we like sheep have gone astray; we have turned every one to his own way; and the LORD hath laid on him the iniquity of us all. (Isaiah 53:6) [Surely the "all" who went astray are the same "all" (i.e., all Israel and all mankind) whose iniquity was laid upon Christ.]
- Behold the Lamb of God, which taketh away the sin of *the world.*" (John 1:29) [Just as the Old Testament sacrifices were offered for all Israel and not for a select group of Israelites, so the fulfillment thereof in Christ's sacrifice as the Lamb of God was offered for the whole world of mankind and not for a limited "elect."]
- And as Moses lifted up the serpent in the wilderness, even so must the Son of man be lifted up: that *whosoever believeth* in him should not perish, but have eternal life. For God so loved *the world*, that he gave his only begotten Son, that *whosoever believeth* in him should not perish.... [F]or God sent not his Son into *the world* to condemn *the world;* but that *the world* through him might be saved. *He that believeth* on him is not condemned.... *He that believeth* on the Son hath everlasting life: and *he that believeth not* the Son shall not see life.... (John 3:14–18, 36) [Healing via the upraised serpent of brass, which Christ said pictured His being lifted up on the Cross, was for *all* who would look in faith.]

- Remember ye the law of Moses…which I commanded…for *all Israel….* (Malachi 4:4) [The law, with its accompanying sacrifices, was for *all* Israel—and the fulfillment in Christ is for *all* mankind.]
- If *any man* thirst, let him come unto me, and drink…. (John 7:37)
- For I am not ashamed of the gospel of Christ: for *it is the power of God unto salvation to every one that believeth*; to the Jew first, and also to the Greek. (Romans 1:16)
- Christ died for *the ungodly*. (Romans 5:6) [*All* are ungodly, not only the elect.]
- But the scripture hath concluded *all* under sin, that the promise by faith...might be given to *them that believe*. (Galatians 3:22)
- For the wages of sin is death; but the *gift of God* is eternal life through Jesus Christ our Lord. (Romans 6:23)
- Christ Jesus came into the world *to save sinners*. (1 Timothy 1:15) [Surely the elect are not the only sinners.]
- Who will have *all men* to be saved, and to come to the knowledge of the truth. (1 Timothy 2:4)
- Who gave himself a ransom *for all….* (1 Timothy 2:6)
- We trust in the living God, who is the *Saviour of all men*, specially of those that *believe*. (1 Timothy 4:10)
- That he by the grace of God should taste death *for every man*. (Hebrews 2:9)
- The Lord is...not willing that *any* should perish, but that *all* should come to repentance. (2 Peter 3:9)
- If we confess our sins, he is faithful and just to forgive us our sins, and to cleanse us from all unrighteousness…. And if *any man* sin, we have an advocate with the Father, Jesus Christ the righteous: And he is the propitiation for our sins: and *not for ours only; but also for the sins of the whole world*. (1 John 1:9–2:2)
- The Father sent the Son to be the *Saviour of the world*. (1 John 4:14)

To take these many (and the many others similar) clear declarations that salvation is for *all*, for the *world*, for *whosoever*, for *all Israel*, for *any man*, for *every one that believeth*, etc., and dare to say that only an elect group is in mind is to deliberately change God's Word!

Do only the elect go astray like lost sheep? Do only the elect thirst? Are only the elect ungodly and sinners? Are only the elect "under sin"? Obviously not. As surely as all men are sinners and have, like all of Israel, gone astray like lost sheep, so surely were the sins of all men laid upon Christ, and salvation is available to all through faith in Him.

These verses, and many more like them, clearly state in unambiguous language that Christ was sent to be "the Saviour of the world," that His death was "a ransom for all" and that He is therefore "the Saviour of all men" who will but believe. John Owen attempts to counter such scriptures and to support Limited Atonement with the following commentary upon 1 Timothy 1:15, "Christ Jesus came into the world to save sinners":

> Now, if you will ask who these sinners are towards whom he hath this gracious intent and purpose, himself tells you, Matthew 20:28, that he came to "give his life a ransom for *many*;" in other places called *us* believers distinguished from the world: for he "gave himself for *our* sins, that he might deliver *us* from this present evil *world*..." Galatians 1:4.... Ephesians 5:25–27, "He loved the church, and gave himself for *it*...." Titus 2:14, "He gave himself for *us*, that he might redeem *us* from all iniquity..." for through him "*we* have access into the grace wherein we stand," Romans 5:2, etc.[44]

An Unwarranted Assumption

Owen was brilliant, yet his argument is fallacious. His desire to defend Calvinism seemingly blinded him to the Scriptures and to simple reason. Obviously, the multitude of verses that state clearly that God loves all and is merciful to all and that Christ died for all are not nullified by other verses declaring that Christ died for the *church*, that His death was a ransom for *many*, or the assurance that He died for *us*, etc. These passages do not say that Christ died *only* for *many* sinners, *only* for the *church*, *only* for *us*, etc. By that interpretation, statements such as, "For if through the offense of one [Adam] many be dead...by one man's disobedience many were made sinners" (Romans 5:15, 19), etc., would indicate that only a limited number were made sinners and died through Adam's disobedience.

Of course, the apostles, writing to believers, would remind them that Christ died for *them*—but that statement cannot void the many clear declarations that He died for all. Yet this same argument is offered repeatedly by Calvinists to this day. Piper quotes the same inapplicable verses in which it is said that Christ was "a ransom for many," that He "bare the sin of many," and that He "loved the church and gave himself for her," etc. as "proof" that Christ's death was not propitiatory for all.[45]

By such reasoning, Paul wouldn't have been able to use "you," "ye," etc., in writing to the Corinthians because that would mean the benefits of Christ's death and resurrection were *only for them*. By the same argument, for David to say, "The Lord is *my* shepherd..." (Psalm 23:1) would mean that this was true only for David. Or when Israel's prophets wrote, "O God of *Israel*, the Saviour...their redeemer is strong, the Lord of hosts is his name..." (Isaiah 45:15; Jeremiah 50:34), it meant that God was the God and redeemer only of Israel.

Equally absurd, for Paul to say "the Son of God who loved *me*" (Galatians 2:20) would mean that Christ loved only Paul. Other arguments that Calvinists employ are equally unreasonable. Consider the following attempt by John Piper and his pastoral staff to explain away 1 Timothy 4:10:

> Christ's death so clearly demonstrates God's just abhorrence of sin that he is free to treat the world with mercy without compromising his righteousness. *In this sense* Christ is the savior of *all* men. But he is *especially* the Savior of those who believe. He did not die for all men in the same sense.... The death of Christ actually saves from *all* evil those for whom Christ died "especially."[46] [Emphasis in original]

Sense or Nonsense?

Can anyone make sense of "Christ did not die for all men in the *same* sense," yet He is the savior of all men "in *this* sense"? What is *this* sense? Because Christ's death "demonstrates God's just abhorrence of sin..." He is able to "treat the world with mercy without compromising his righteousness." But He doesn't treat all with mercy, because Christ "did not die for all men in the same sense...." Neither *this sense* nor *same sense* are defined, so we can't make *any sense* out of this nonsense. But it shows again the lengths to which one must go to defend Calvinism.

One is reminded of Spurgeon's objection (we've quoted it several times because it so clearly contradicts the Calvinism he otherwise affirmed) to such attempts to get around the clear words of Scripture. In commenting upon 1 Timothy 2:4 (contradicting his own defense of Limited Atonement at other times), he said:

> I was reading just now the exposition of [one] who explains the text so as to explain it away [as] if it read "Who will not have all men to be saved…." [In fact,] the passage should run thus—"whose wish it is that all men should be saved…." As it is my wish…as it is your wish…so it is God's wish that all men should be saved; for, assuredly, he is not less benevolent than we are.[47]

Yet Spurgeon contradicted himself again in saying that God is able to save all He desires to save. Since all are not saved, God's wish that all men should be saved cannot be sincere. Consequently, He *is* less benevolent than Spurgeon, who desired all men to be saved—and surely less benevolent than Paul, who was willing to be "accursed from Christ" if that would save his brethren the Jews (Romans 9:1–5). How could God desire all men to be saved, be able to save all He desires to save, yet all are not saved?

As we have just seen, John MacArthur, Jr. (like Spurgeon) tries to escape the obvious contradiction by saying that God has a "will of decree" and a "will of desire."[48] In the process of escaping one contradiction, he falls into another. How could God, given Calvinism's extreme view of sovereignty, fail to decree anything He truly desires? Calvinists boast that they exegete Scripture. But where in I Timothy 2:4 (or anywhere else) is there even a hint of "two wills," one of "decree" and one of "desire" as Piper and others also teach?

It is the imposition upon Scripture of an unbiblical theory that entraps the Calvinist in such contradictions. Obviously, the contradiction would disappear if free will were admitted—but that cannot be allowed, because it would destroy **TULIP**.

Boettner declares that "Calvinists hold that in the intention and secret plan of God, Christ died for the elect only…."[49] Otherwise, adds Boettner, "If Christ's death was intended to save all men, then we must say that God was either unable or unwilling to carry out His plans."[50] He forgets that Christ's death only benefits those who *receive* Christ (John 1:12) and that salvation, being "the gift of God" (Romans 6:23), must be willingly received. As for men being able to oppose God's plans, is the evil in the world God's plan? Why, then, are we to pray, "Thy will be done, on earth as it is in heaven"?

Remember Isaiah is speaking to all of Israel when he says, "all we like sheep have gone astray..." and when he declares that "the iniquity of us all" would be laid upon the coming Messiah. As surely as all went astray, so surely did God lay upon Christ the iniquity of *all*—yet many Israelites throughout history have not been saved. These and many other scriptures make it clear that the benefit of Christ's death, burial, and resurrection in full payment for the sins of the world is available to be received by whosoever believes the gospel, while the wrath of God abides upon all who reject Christ and the salvation genuinely offered to all in Him.

---

1. John Murray, *Redemption Accomplished and Applied* (Grand Rapids, MI: Wm B. Eerdmans Publishing Co., 1955), 64.
2. Edwin H. Palmer, *the five points of calvinism* (Grand Rapids, MI: Baker Books, enlarged ed., 20th prtg. 1999), 44.
3. John Calvin, *Institutes of the Christian Religion*, trans. Henry Beveridge (Grand Rapids, MI: Wm. Eerdmans Publishing Company, 1998 ed.), III: xxi, 5.
4. A. A. Hodge, *The Atonement* (Memphis, TN: Footstool Publishers, 1987), 348.
5. Loraine Boettner, *The Reformed Doctrine of Predestination* (Phillipsburg, NJ: Presbyterian and Reformed Publishing Co., 1932), 83–84.
6. D. A. Carson, *The Difficult Doctrine of the Love of God* (Wheaton, IL: Crossway Books, 2000), 73.
7. Stanley Gower, in the first of "Two Attestations" to John Owen, Bk. 1 of *The Death of Death in the Death of Christ* (n. p., 1647); in *The Works of John Owen*, ed. William H. Goold (Carlisle, PA: The Banner of Truth Trust, 3rd prtg. 1978), X:147.
8. R. C. Sproul, *Chosen by God* (Carol Stream, IL: Tyndale House Publishers, Inc., 1986), 207.
9. Gower, in *Owen, Works*, IV:338.
10. John MacArthur, Jr., *The Love of God* (Dallas, TX: Word Publishing, 1996), xv 85–86, 99–124.
11. John Calvin, *Commentary on a Harmony of the Evangelists, Matthew, Mark, and Luke*, William Pringle, trans. (Grand Rapids, MI: Baker, 1930), 314, cited in MacArthur, *Love of God*, 85.
12. MacArthur, *Love of God*, 195.
13. Ibid., 12–18.
14. Owen, *Works,* I:149.
15. H. A. Ironside, *Timothy, Titus and Philemon* (Neptune, NJ: Loizeaux Brothers, Inc., 1990), 55.
16. Calvin, *Institutes*, III: xi, 11.
17. John H. Gerstner, *Wrongly Dividing the Word of Truth: A Critique of Dispensationalism* (Brentwood, TN: Wolgemuth and Hyatt, Publishers, Inc., 1991), 124.
18. MacArthur, *Love of God*, 106–112.
19. Grover E. Gunn, *The Doctrine of Grace* (Memphis, TN: Footstool Publications), 1987, 17.
20. Cited in Laurence M. Vance, *The Other Side of Calvinism* (Pensacola, FL: Vance Publications, rev. ed. 1999), 423.
21. David N. Steele and Curtis C. Thomas, *The Five Points of Calvinism* (Phillipsburg, NJ: Presbyterian and Reformed Publishing Co., 1963), 17.
22. Michael Scott Horton, *Putting Amazing Back Into Grace* (Nashville, TN: Thomas Nelson Publishers, 1991), 89.

23. Herman Hanko, *God's Everlasting Covenant of Grace* (Grandville, MI: Reformed Free Publishing Association, 1988), 15.
24. R. C. Sproul, *Grace Unknown* (Grand Rapids, MI: Baker Books, 1997), 165.
25. Dave Breese, "The Five Points of Calvinism" (self-published paper, n. d.).
26. Leonard J. Coppes, *Are Five Points Enough? The Ten Points of Calvinism* (Denver CO: self-published, 1980), 49.
27. Homer Hoeksema, *Limited Atonement*, 151; cited in Vance, *Other Side*, 406.
28. C. H. Spurgeon, *New Park Street Pulpit* (London: Passmore and Alabaster), Vol 6, 28-29; sermon preached December 11, 1859.
29. Kenneth G. Talbot and W. Gary Crampton, *Calvinism, Hyper-Calvinism and Arminianism* (Edmonton, AB: Still Waters Revival Books, 1990), 11.
30. Ibid., 37.
31. Boettner, *Reformed*, 151.
32. Joseph M. Wilson, "How is the Atonement Limited?" *The Baptist Examiner*, December 9, 1989.
33. Boettner, *Reformed*, 151.
34. John MacArthur, *The MacArthur Study Bible* (Nashville: Word Publishing, 1997) 1862.
35. Zane C. Hodges, "The New Puritanism, Pt. 3: Michael S. Horton: Holy War With Unholy Weapons," *Journal of the Grace Evangelical Society,* Spring 1994, 7:12, 17–29.
36. Palmer, *five points*, 44–45.
37. W. J. Seaton, *The Five Points of Calvinism* (Carlisle, PA: The Banner of Truth Trust, 1970), 15.
38. Palmer, *five points*, 44.
39. Cited in Vance, *Other Side*, 423.
40. Arthur W. Pink, *Gleanings in Exodus* (Chicago: Moody Press, 1981), 84.
41. Vance, *Other Side*, 427.
42. Pink, *Gleanings*, 88.
43. Palmer, *five points*, 50.
44. Owen, *Works*, 1:157–58.
45. John Piper and Pastoral Staff, "TULIP: What We Believe about the Five Points of Calvinism: Position Paper of the Pastoral Staff" (Minneapolis, MN: Desiring God Ministries, 1997), 16–17.
46. Ibid., 14–15.
47. C. H. Spurgeon, *Metropolitan Tabernacle Pulpit*, vol. 26, "Salvation by Knowing the Truth," sermon preached on 1 Timothy 2:3–4, January 16, 1880.
48. John MacArthur, *The MacArthur Study Bible* (Nashville, TN: Word Publishing, 1997), 1862.
49. Boettner, *Reformed*, 150.
50. Ibid., 155.

CHAPTER

19

Abusing God's Word

ONE CAN ONLY conclude from Scripture that salvation is available to everyone in the entire world, Jew or Gentile, who will but believe in Christ "the Lamb of God, which taketh away the sin of the world" (John 1:29). How could such clear language be denied? Exactly as Palmer does: by changing the definition of words ("world" becomes "elect," etc.); and by rationalizations that at first seem to make sense but fail upon closer examination. One critic of what little I had written about Calvinism in our monthly newsletter argued, "If Christ died for all men, why aren't all men saved? Is believing necessary to make the blood of Christ efficacious for redemption? On the contrary, [it is not]."

This is Calvinistic reasoning: Christ must have died only for the elect; otherwise all would be saved. And the elect don't even need to believe on Christ in order to be born again, for they are sovereignly regenerated by God without any desire or understanding on their part. God simply wills it so. If man has any choice in the matter at all, Calvinism is refuted. As Palmer said sarcastically of the non-Calvinist view of the cross, "Christ not only shed His blood, He also spilled it. He intended to save all, but only some will be saved. Therefore, some of His blood was wasted: it was spilled."[1]

In the Calvinist scheme, believing the gospel is not the means of one's salvation and new birth. It supposedly proves that one is among the elect and was regenerated by God, and thereafter given the faith to believe. The same critic quoted above insisted that faith is not a prerequisite for salvation but "is simply the proof that the blood of Christ has saved a man."

Piper and his staff argue the same: "We do not think that faith precedes and causes new birth. Faith is the evidence that God has begotten us anew."[2] On the contrary, the Bible *always* puts faith *before* salvation—always—so Calvinism has man regenerated before he is saved, an unbiblical concept to which Spurgeon strongly objected.

Faith Is Essential

The Bible repeatedly says that we are "saved, *through faith*" (Ephesians 2:8). Paul told the Philippian jailor, "*Believe* on the Lord Jesus Christ, and thou *shalt be* saved..." (Acts 16:31). In the Greek, "believe" is always an active verb—something one does, not something done to him. But the Calvinist insists that, although the natural man can believe anything else, he is totally *unable* to believe in Christ. Therefore, God must regenerate him first and then *cause* him to believe by giving him the essential faith—something God supposedly does only for the elect, who alone He desires to save.

The many verses already quoted, however, some from the lips of Christ Himself, clearly make believing a *condition* of the new birth and salvation, which can only result from faith. The biblical reason all men are not saved, in spite of Christ having died for all, is that not all believe the gospel, which alone is "the power of God unto salvation to every one that believeth" (Romans 1:16). "Whosoever will," used repeatedly in Scripture, implies that while all *may*, many *won't*. Consider the following:

- To him give all the prophets witness, that...whosoever believeth in him shall receive remission of sins. (Acts 10:43)
- For the scripture saith, Whosoever believeth on him shall not be ashamed. (Romans 10:11)
- For whosoever shall call upon the name of the Lord shall be saved. (Romans 10:13)
- Whosoever will, let him take of the water of life freely. (Revelation 22:17)

The claim that "whosoever" means only the elect flies in the face of hundreds of scriptures. Nor can *one* verse be produced where this doctrine of Limited Atonement is clearly stated. Surely, such an important concept would be declared clearly and repeatedly. Yet it is not found *once* in clear language.

What About "Double Payment"?

Calvinists reason that for sinners to suffer eternally after Christ had suffered for them would mean that God was demanding double payment for their sins. Boettner insists that "Christ died not for an unorderly mass, but for His people, His Bride, His Church."[3] He argues elsewhere: "For God to have laid the sins of all men on Christ would mean that as regards the lost He would be punishing their sins twice, once in Christ, and then again in them."[4] Another author offers what he considers to be sound arguments against the possibility that John 3:16 and so many other verses could really mean what they say:

> [If] Jesus died, paying for the sins of all, God cannot legally or justly accuse and condemn anyone...regardless of whether they hear or accept the gospel, *sin cannot be justly paid for twice*.... For God not to pardon a sinner for whom Christ agonized would be a *travesty* of justice.... [Then] Jesus will never..."see of the travail of his soul and be satisfied" (Isaiah 53). Why? Because billions for whom He agonized, travailed and died, bearing their "sins in his own body on the tree," will suffer eternal hell. Jesus paid. They pay again. God is paid twice for one debt.[5] (Emphasis in original)

However, as we shall see in the next section, it was impossible for Christ to die for some sins and not for others. Christ had to die for sin itself, the sin which "by one man...entered into the world," and for the death that as a result "passed upon all men" (Romans 5:12). He had to pay the penalty owed by all. Christ's payment for sin cannot be divided up in order to apply it to individuals. Nor is Christ's "it is finished!" automatically credited to the account of anyone who does not acknowledge his guilt before God, repent, and accept Christ as his Savior.

As a result of Christ's death having paid the full penalty, no one will spend eternity in the Lake of Fire only because of his sins. The doom of those in hell was sealed by each of them rejecting Christ and the salvation He obtained and freely offers to all.

Furthermore, it is the sinner, not God, who creates any "double payment." God's justice has been fully satisfied in the death of His Son. The Father has proved His love by giving His Son, and Christ has proved His love by dying in the sinner's place. Therefore, even if double payment were involved, God could not be charged with injustice—it only occurs because of the refusal of some to admit their guilt and accept the full payment Christ made on their behalf.

Some go further and argue that it is a travesty of justice for Christ, an innocent party, to be punished in the place of the guilty and for the guilty thereby to go free. In fact, that is not the gospel according to Paul but according to Barabbas. The latter could say, "Christ died for me, in my place." That was true, but Christ's death in his place had neither an eternal nor even a moral effect on Barabbas. It merely set that criminal free to live for self again—and that is not the gospel.

The truth of the gospel was expressed by Paul: "I am crucified with Christ...[and now] Christ liveth in me" (Galatians 2:20). In fact, all those who believe in Christ, having given up life as they would have lived it, and having by faith accepted His death as their own, have been crucified with Him. Such was not the case with Barabbas even though Christ died in his place. Those who have *not* believed in Christ have not accepted His death as their death and thus will suffer "the second death" eternally (Revelation 20:14–15).

No one can complain that God created human beings for hell. He created them all for His glorious presence. Yes, He knew that all men would sin and come short of His glory, but He had a way whereby He could be just and yet justify *all* sinners (Romans 3:22–26) so they could be forgiven and spend eternity in His presence.

Even before Adam was created and sinned, God had planned redemption for him and for all his descendants. Anyone who will spend eternity in the Lake of Fire (Revelation 20:14) has sent himself there by rejecting the salvation God has provided for him as a free gift of His grace. God is exonerated. He has made salvation available for all, but He will not bend His justice to accommodate those who reject Christ. He cannot deny Himself.

Was "Some" of Christ's Blood Shed in Vain?

Acceptance of Limited Atonement by many seems to be based upon the sincere misunderstanding that if Christ's blood was shed for multitudes who didn't believe, some of it would have been shed in vain. Some Calvinists seem to believe that Christ's death was *potentially* redemptive of the whole world, but that the limiting factor was put upon it by God himself. Thus Gunn argues, "The cross could save everyone if God had only intended it to do so."[6] Spurgeon said the same.

It is argued that for anyone for whom Christ died to spend eternity in the Lake of Fire would not only be double payment and a violation of justice but would also mean that some of Christ's blood was needlessly shed. Sadly, C. H. Spurgeon lent his support on that very point in spite of his assertion that the value of Christ's atonement was unlimited:

> Some say that all men are Christ's by purchase. But, beloved, you and I do not believe in a sham redemption which does not redeem. We do not believe in a universal redemption which extends even to those who were in hell before the Savior died, and which includes...unrepentant men. We believe in an effectual redemption, and can never agree with those who would teach us that Christ's blood was shed in vain.[7]

The fact that Christ died for all, that He "tasted death for every man," is the clear teaching of Scripture. To suggest that Christ's blood would have been shed in vain if some of those for whom it was shed rejected Him and spent eternity in the Lake of Fire—or were already in hell—betrays a basic misunderstanding. Could such a great preacher as Spurgeon have missed the point here?

Redemption Through His Blood

How much of Christ's blood did it take to atone for those who will be in heaven? Obviously, all of it had to be shed to redeem even one person. There is no way to divide Christ's blood so that *this* part was shed for the redeemed and *that* part for those who are lost and thus *some* of it was shed in vain.

Even if no one believed on Him, Christ proved God's love, mercy and grace; He proved the sinfulness of sin, the justice of the penalty and glorified God in paying that penalty in full for all. Because of Christ's death on the cross, God has been fully vindicated in His creation of man and will be eternally glorified in those in hell. We will deal with that fact in more depth later.

We do not say that "all men are Christ's by purchase." Redemption, according to the Bible, becomes effectual only if and when a sinner believes the gospel. No one could escape hell apart from Christ having paid the full penalty for sin. And the rejection of Christ is one sin for which, by its very nature, Christ could not pay the penalty. This is the "sin against the Holy Ghost"—unpardonable in this life or in the life to come—because the pardon Christ purchased has been rejected. Indeed, that sin carries a far worse penalty of its own:

> Of how much sorer punishment...shall he be thought worthy, who hath trodden under foot the Son of God, and hath counted the blood of the covenant, wherewith he was sanctified, an unholy thing, and hath done despite unto the Spirit of grace? (Hebrews 10:29)

Here, again, we have a clear statement that the blood of Christ was not shed for the elect alone. It was shed even for those who despise it and tread underfoot the Son of God. The same truth is presented by Peter, that even those who go to destruction have been bought by Christ, obviously at the price of His blood shed for sin: "But there were false prophets also among the people, even as there shall be false teachers among you, who privily shall bring in damnable heresies, even denying the Lord that bought them, and bring upon themselves swift destruction" (2 Peter 2:1). Yes, false prophets condemned to hell were "bought" by Christ.

In view of these two scriptures, the Calvinist must either admit that one who was once saved lost his salvation through turning against Christ—or that one who "was sanctified" by Christ's blood and some whom "the Lord...bought" are not among the elect. Clearly, some for whom Christ's blood was shed will be lost. Thus the Calvinist has no basis for charging that believing that Christ's blood was shed for all leads inevitably to universalism, the teaching that all are saved.

Particular Atonement?

Calvinists contend that "It makes no sense for Christ to offer atonement for those the Father does not entrust to Him for salvation."[8] This is human reasoning without biblical support. Calvinists refer to "particular atonement"—the idea that the death of Christ had to be for a particular elect. Then Christ died only for particular sins—a belief that misunderstands the very nature of the atonement. Christ did not die for individual sins only, but for *sin itself*—a penalty that had to be paid for *anyone* to be saved. But His paying the penalty for sin itself required paying for all sins and providing salvation for all mankind.

Remember that to break one commandment is to be guilty of breaking all: "For whosoever shall keep the whole law, and yet offend in one point, he is guilty of all" (James 2:10). This is the case because of the very nature of sin. Sin is rebellion against God. Thus, however one rebels, no matter how insignificant it seems from a human viewpoint, one is a rebel. Sin is sin, and the penalty for what we might think is only the most trivial of sins is eternal separation from God in the Lake of Fire.

There is no way that Christ's death could be limited to paying for only the sin of the elect. To deliver even one person from eternal punishment, no matter how few or many the sins he may have committed, Christ had to pay the penalty demanded by His infinite justice for *sin*. Therefore, the death of Christ on the cross paid the penalty for sin itself (which includes *all* sin) that hangs over the heads of the entire human race. It could not be otherwise.

Christ is the "second man...the last Adam" (1 Corinthians 15:45–47), the representative not merely of the elect but of the entire human race. It couldn't be otherwise. What He did at Calvary was efficacious for all mankind. He paid for Adam's sin, which brought death upon all, so in paying that penalty He has freed all who willingly receive the salvation He offers.

Yes, we "confess our sins" (1 John 1:9) just as the Israelites were required to bring individual offerings for their individual sins. But there was "the sin offering," which made possible the forgiveness of all sin. "Sin offering" in the singular is mentioned in the Book of Leviticus far more than the offerings for sins.

That the blood of Christ was shed "for the remission of sins" is declared in Matthew 26:28; Luke 24:47; 1 Corinthians 15:3, and many other places. We are also told, however, that He died for sin. In fact, "sin" is mentioned more than twice as many times as "sins." Here are a few of those passages:

- When thou shalt make his soul an offering for sin...He bare the sin of many.... (Isaiah 53:10,12)
- Behold the Lamb of God, which taketh away the sin of the world. (John 1:29)
- Wherefore, as by one man sin entered into the world.... (Romans 5:12)
- For the wages of sin is death.... (Romans 6:23)
- For he hath made him to be sin for us...that we might be made the righteousness of God in him. (2 Corinthians 5:21)
- ...burnt offerings and sacrifices for sin.... (Hebrews 10:6,8; 13:11)

The Gospel Is *Personal*

To be consistent with his avowed Calvinism, Spurgeon could not offer salvation to each person to whom he preached, not knowing, as Jay Adams has said, who, if any, in his audience were among the elect. But in obedience to the Bible and in *denial* of Calvinism, Spurgeon preached the gospel as a call to *whosoever* would believe. Such preaching sparked the "Duty Faith" controversy in England, to which we have already referred. We can and must declare, to anyone and everyone, "That if *thou* shalt confess with *thy* mouth...and shalt believe in *thine* heart...*thou* shalt be saved.... For *whosoever* shall call upon the name of the Lord shall be saved" (Romans 10:9,13).

Salvation cannot be offered to anyone for whom Christ did not die, yet it is to be proclaimed to all: "Preach the gospel to every creature" (Mark 16:15). In contrast, the Calvinist cannot look an unsaved person in the eye and say with confidence, "Christ died for *you*!" That person may not be one of the elect, and such a statement could therefore be untrue. The Calvinist cannot, and dare not, assure a dying person that Christ died for him. Thus Calvinism denies the gospel of God's grace!

Paul could not tell the Philippian jailor, "Believe on the Lord Jesus Christ and *thou* shalt be saved, and *thy house*" if Christ had not died for him and his family. Did Paul have a special revelation that this entire family was among the elect—or is the gospel for all? How could Paul declare the same to large audiences everywhere, such as at Antioch in Pisidia: "...to *you* is the word of this salvation sent" (Acts 13:26), if Christ died only for a limited number known as the elect? Surely not everyone in the vast audiences he faced was among Calvinism's elect! How could Peter say to thousands of Jews gathered on Pentecost, "Repent, and be baptized *every one of you*..." (Acts 2:38), if Christ had not died for each and every one of them?

Just as Calvinists often contradict John Calvin and one another, Calvin contradicted himself at times. He made statements both supporting unlimited atonement and at other times in favor of limited atonement. Referring to Isaiah 53:12 he said, "on Him was laid the guilt of the whole world."[9] Concerning Mark 14:24, "This is my blood of the new testament, which is shed for many," Calvin said, "The word *many* does not mean a part of the world, but the whole human race."[10] Where is "limited atonement"?

When caught in such contradictions, the Calvinist resorts to double-talk. As we have seen, some Calvinists admit that God loves all, but claim that He loves the elect alone with "redeeming love" and others with a lesser love. MacArthur declares that God even "in some sense…loves his enemies."[11] *Some sense?* What does that mean? Love is love! It would not be love, *in any sense,* to fail to rescue from any disaster those who could be rescued—much less to predestine them to eternal doom.

Although even acknowledging that God loves the whole world of humanity, some Calvinists argue that this does not mean every individual but mankind in general. As we've seen, MacArthur uses this specious argument in his book, *The Love of God.*[12]

As we shall see when we come to Perseverance of the Saints, a major problem for Calvinists is how to be certain that one is among the elect, for whom alone, allegedly, Christ died. We see this uncertainty in Calvin himself. In his will, drawn up shortly before his death, Calvin wrote, "I humbly seek from God...to be washed and purified by the great Redeemer's blood, shed for the sins of the human race...."[13] How is it that this supposedly greatest of exegetes seemed uncertain of his salvation, in spite of Scripture's promise of absolute assurance: "These things have I written unto you that believe on the name of the Son of God; that ye may *know* that ye *have* eternal life..." (1 John 5:13)? Such assurance comes not by a special revelation that one is among the elect but by simple faith in Christ, "the Lamb of God, which taketh away the sin of the world" (John 1:29).

Changing the Meaning of "World"

Instead of acknowledging Calvin's apparent denial of Limited Atonement, which we have quoted above, White selectively quotes Calvin contradicting himself again: "In relation to John 1:29 and 1 John 2:2 the word 'world' is viewed as intending to transcend a nationalistic Jewish particularism."[14] There is nothing anywhere, however, either in John's gospel or epistle, to suggest that odd meaning. Yet Calvinism *must* interpret "world" as "the elect" in order to maintain itself. What did Calvin really believe, especially at the end of his life? It has been said that he began to have doubts, and the statement quoted from his will—"shed for the sins of the human race"—seems to confirm it.

Calvin is quoted when it suits today's Calvinists, and at other times he is ignored. Yet this confusing doctrine, upon which its adherents do not agree among themselves or even with Calvin, is still called "Calvinism" by everyone. At the same time, however, Calvinists continue to contradict Calvin, themselves, and each other.

Pink argued: "To say that God the Father has purposed the salvation of all mankind, that God the Son died with the express intention of saving the whole human race, and that God the Holy Spirit is now seeking to win the world to Christ; when...it is apparent that the great majority of our fellow-men are dying in sin, and passing into a hopeless eternity: is to say that God the Father is *disappointed*, that God the Son is *dissatisfied*, and that God the Holy Spirit is *defeated*."[15]

Such human reasoning is neither biblical nor rational but, unfortunately, is required to support Calvinism. To maintain this position, one would have to say that God was insincere in the hundreds of urgent and passionate pleadings and warnings for Israel to repent and obey Him, which are expressed through His prophets throughout the Old Testament. The fact is that Israel as a whole rebelled against Him continually during its entire existence, and continues in unbelief and rejection of her Messiah to this day. If such disobedience does not require God to be *disappointed, dissatisfied, and defeated* (emotions that He cannot have), then neither would that be God's reaction when Gentiles He loves, and for whom Christ died, reject the salvation He freely and lovingly offers.

Of course, the word "world" can have a variety of meanings, but the times that it does not mean either the physical world, the ungodly world system, or all mankind are exceedingly rare. Those instances could almost be counted on one hand out of the nearly 240 times "world" is found in the New Testament. Furthermore, we challenge any Calvinist to point out *one verse* where "world" explicitly means the elect. Please, *just one*!

Of the 80 times "world" occurs in 59 verses in John's gospel, *not once* does it mean "elect." That meaning has to be read into the text—and there is nothing in the usage to differentiate between those times when the Calvinist says it means "elect" and those times when he doesn't say so. Vance lists numerous examples from John's Gospel where "world" could not possibly mean the elect:

> The world knew not Christ (1:10). The world hates Christ (7:7). The world's works are evil (7:7). Unsaved Jews were of this world (8:23). Satan is the prince of this world (12:31; 14:30; 16:11). Christ's own are distinguished from the world (13:1; 14:19, 22). The world cannot receive the Holy Spirit (14:17). The world hates the disciples (15:18; 14:14) [and many more]....
>
> In arguing for limited atonement, Sproul inadvertently proves that the world does not refer to the "elect"...: "He [Jesus] explicitly excludes the non-elect from his great high priestly prayer, 'I do not pray for the world but for those whom you have given Me'

> (John 17:9)...."[16] So not only does the world *never* denote the "elect," it is unequivocally demeaned and condemned by God.[17]

Indeed, in Christ's high priestly prayer, He specifically distinguishes between the world of mankind for whom He died and those who have believed on Him out of the world. This is not a prayer for the salvation of the former, but for unity among the latter.

Each of us must, of course, go by the Bible, no matter what John Calvin or Charles H. Spurgeon or anyone else taught. The only justification for rejecting the ordinary meaning of "world" and assigning Calvinism's peculiar connotation (which certainly is nowhere plain from any text) is that Calvinism requires it. Richard Baxter argues persuasively:

> God telleth us as plain as can be spoken that Christ died for and tasted death for every man...others will deny these plain truths, because they think that [God cannot justly punish those for whom Christ hath paid the penalty].... But doth the Scripture speak...these opinions of theirs as plainly as it saith that Christ died for all and every man?
>
> Doth it say as plainly anywhere that He died not for all...? Doth it say anywhere that he died *only* for His Sheep, or His Elect, and exclude the Non-Elect? There is no such word in the Bible....[18]

Ingenious but Irrational

A favorite ploy of the Calvinist is to suggest that "world" does not mean "all people 'without exception,' but...'without distinction'...not [only] Jews, but also...Gentiles."[19] This is the same tactic as changing "all people" into "all *kinds* of people"—an irrational idea born of desperation. Such an idea is even more strained than to brazenly change "all people" or "world" into "elect." Under what circumstances would anyone understand "all" to mean all *kinds*?

A merchant advertises, "Giant Sale! All merchandise half price." Eager customers, however, discover that certain items are excluded from the sale. When they complain that the ad read *all* merchandise, the merchant says, "I didn't mean all 'without exception,' but all 'without distinction.' All *kinds* of products are indeed on sale, but not every item of every kind." This would be misleading advertising, and customers would have a legitimate complaint. Yet the Calvinist insists that God uses this same kind of deception in offering salvation to "whosovever will."

If a shepherd said, "I'm selling *all* of my sheep," would anyone think he meant *some* of all *kinds*, i.e., *some* males, *some* females, *some* newborn lambs, etc.? If headlines read, "All males between the ages of 20 and 45 are subject to military draft," who would imagine that it really meant *some* blacks, *some* whites, *some* from Illinois, *some* from Utah, etc.? Or if the announcement were made to a group of tourists stopping at an oasis near the Dead Sea in Israel that "Whoever is thirsty should get a drink now," would anyone imagine this meant *some* women, *some* men, *some* elderly among the thirsty, etc.?

Such a special meaning is *nowhere* found in all of Scripture. Yet Calvinism requires it for *every one* of the numerous statements concerning "all" and "world" and "whosoever," etc. that relates to the gospel throughout the entire Bible! Wouldn't the Calvinist meaning be stated clearly *at least once*? Yet it *never* is!

What About 1 John 2:2?

Lacking references in the Bible that plainly say that Christ died only for the elect, Calvinists somehow have to change those that say He died for all. First John 2:2 clearly states that Christ is "the propitiation for our sins and not for ours only, but for the sins of the whole world." Surely "our" and "ours" must refer to the elect. Therefore "the whole world," being in contrast to the elect, can only refer to the unsaved and would prove that Christ's death is propitiatory for all mankind.

To acknowledge what this passage declares would be the end of Calvinism. But how can that conclusion be avoided? Piper writes, "The 'whole world' refers to the children of God scattered throughout the whole world."[20] But isn't that what *our* and *ours* would refer to: everyone who is saved, no matter where or when they live—and isn't "whole world" placed in contrast to "our" and "ours"? White elaborates a bit further on this brazen eisegesis, which Calvinists have devised in order to rescue their Limited Atonement theory:

> The Reformed understanding is that Jesus Christ is the propitiation for the sins of all the Christians to which John was writing, and not only them, but for all Christians throughout the world, Jew and Gentile, at all times and in all places.[21]

Surely, "if any man sin, we have an advocate with the Father," refers to *all* Christians anywhere and at any time. Likewise, the "our" in "he is the propitiation for our sins" must refer to *all* Christians, not just John's contemporaries. It certainly is a true statement for all believers in Christ in every time, place, and culture. Furthermore, John's entire epistle, like all of the Bible of which it is a part, is addressed to all believers everywhere and in all ages. If the "our" thus refers to the redeemed, then "the whole world," being in contrast, could only represent those who are lost.

To escape the obvious, White claims that John was only writing to the Christians of his day, and, therefore, "our" means those who originally read the epistle; and "the whole world" means all other Christians not alive at the time when the epistle was written.[22] Nothing in the text even hints at such a conclusion. Nor would such a frivolous interpretation have been invented had it not been necessary in order to rescue Limited Atonement. Undeniably, in everything he says, John is writing under the inspiration of the Holy Spirit to all Christians everywhere and in all ages.

Piper reasons that "Propitiated sins cannot be punished.... Therefore it is very unlikely that 1 John 2:2 teaches that Jesus is the propitiation of every person in the world...."[23] Unlikely? Only because the plain declaration contradicts Calvinism. We have already shown that this argument doesn't work for at least two reasons: 1) Christ had to pay the penalty for all sin for even one person to be saved; and 2) the benefits of Christ's death do not come automatically, but only to those who believe and receive Him. Were this not the case, then the elect, for whom the Calvinist says Christ did die, would be saved without believing and before they were born.

Finally, Piper, following John Owens's lead, reasons that if Christ is really the propitiation for the sins of the whole world, then unbelief would not keep anyone out of heaven, because unbelief, being a sin, would have been propitiated as well.[24]

But propitiation does not occur when one believes in Christ. It must already have been accomplished on the Cross. Faith is the means of appropriating the benefits of Christ's sacrifice—a sacrifice that even the Calvinist acknowledges was of sufficient value to pay for the sins of all mankind. Either the elect were always saved and never needed to believe on Christ (a clear denial of the gospel), or there was a time when the propitiation Christ made on the Cross became effective for them through faith. John is simply saying with Paul that Christ "is the Saviour of all men, specially of those that believe" (1 Timothy 4:10).

Every Christian, by very definition, has been saved through faith in Christ, and His blood is the propitiation for their sins. This fact is so elementary and essential that one could hardly be a Christian without knowing it. It is therefore absurd to suggest that John is revealing something of importance by declaring that the blood of Christ avails not only for the people alive in his day but for all Christians in all ages. If this is what the Holy Spirit through John intended, why wasn't it stated clearly? Would the Holy Spirit use "world" to convey the meaning "all Christians in all times everywhere"? Hardly.

To Whom Did John Write?

Other Calvinists argue that "John would have been writing to a Jewish audience who had long believed that God was only the God of Israel. And so they needed to be taught and reminded that Christ died not only for the lost sheep of Israel but also for his lost sheep in all the world.... Thus, the 'whole world' is his lost sheep of Israel plus his lost sheep from among the other nations."[25] Surely, no one would even imagine such a far-fetched idea had Calvinism not been invented and an explanation required for "world" that would salvage the theory.

There is nothing in the entire epistle to suggest that John is addressing only Jewish believers. Indeed, when this was written there were more Gentile than Jewish believers. Furthermore, John tells us to whom he is speaking: "These things have I written unto you that believe on the name of the Son of God..." (1 John 5:13). That includes all Christians throughout history.

Moreover, not only is John writing to all believers in Christ, but he is doing so many years after the Jerusalem council of Acts 15, where the whole issue of salvation for Gentiles without their keeping the law of Moses had been settled. Paul's letter to the Galatian believers, which dealt with this issue in depth, had long been in circulation. John doesn't deal with this long-settled topic at all.

Who would have imagined, without the necessity to support a special theory, that John was writing only to the Christians of his day, or only to a Jewish audience? Furthermore, if John were not writing to all Christians in all ages, how could we apply his epistle to ourselves today? In fact, we know that he was writing to all believers in Christ, and Christians throughout the ages have read his gospel and epistles with that understanding.

When John writes, "He that saith, I know him, and keepeth not his commandments, is a liar.... [H]e that saith he is in the light, and hateth his brother, is in darkness.... [Y]e have an unction from the Holy One.... [T]he anointing which ye have received of him abideth in you..." (1 John 2:4,9,20,27), etc., throughout his epistle, could that only be intended for "Jewish believers" or for believers "of his own day"? Of course not! Surely all that he says is for all believers in Christ in every age.

What About the Meaning of "The Whole World"?

White quotes the song of the redeemed in Revelation 5:9–10. Because it says that Christ has redeemed by His blood men "out of every kindred, and tongue, and people, and nation," White reasons, "We suggest that this passage, then, sheds significant light upon 1 John 2:2..." *Significant light?* The passage is very straightforward. The only "light" White is searching so far afield for is something that will justify a Calvinist interpretation that is obviously not in the passage itself.

White continues, "...for it is obvious that the passage in Revelation is not saying that Christ purchased every man from every tribe, tongue, people and nation. Yet, obviously, this is a parallel concept to 'the world' in 1 John 2:2."

Parallel concept? What does that mean, and by what authority? The two statements are entirely different. One declares that Christ died for all; the other refers to those who accepted His sacrifice by faith. If White were truly looking for a parallel scripture, he couldn't find a clearer one than 1 Timothy 4:10, which we have already quoted: "...the Saviour of all men [the whole world], specially of those that believe" [the redeemed to whom John writes].

White then quotes the High Priest Caiaphas (John 11:49–52) that it is expedient "that one man die for the people, and that the whole nation perish not."[26] Surely Caiaphas really *meant* the people of Israel, the whole nation, a fact that contradicts Calvinism's Limited Atonement.

Sadly, this is one more example of how far Calvinists have to reach: to suggest that a future song in heaven and a statement by Caiaphas about the nation of Israel prove that "world" in 1 John 2:2 really means "all *Christians* throughout the world..."! The song in heaven is by the redeemed, those who make up the "our" in 1 John 2:2. They are redeemed "from" or "out of" every tribe and tongue and people and nation. In fact, White is helping us to see a contrast: John does not say "from" or "out of" the whole world; he clearly says "the whole world."

Why must White go so far afield? Within this very epistle there are many comparisons that define "world." In 1 John 3:1 we have the phrase, "...the world knoweth us not." Surely "us" refers to the redeemed; "world" is in contrast to them and cannot possibly mean some other group of Christians. In 3:13 we find, "Marvel not, my brethren, if the world hate you." Again, we have the same contrast between the redeemed brethren and the unsaved who hate them, making the meaning of "world" quite clear. In 4:5–6 we find, "They are of the world...we are of God." The distinction between the unsaved world and those who are saved—which is maintained consistently throughout the entire epistle—could not be clearer. Again, 1 John 5:19 declares, "We are of God, and the whole world lieth in wickedness."

To be consistent with his handling of 1 John 2:2, White must believe that "all Christians throughout the world, Jew and Gentile, at all times and in all places" are in wickedness and hate the believers to whom John was writing. In fact, nowhere in the entire epistle does "world" mean what the Calvinist tries to turn it into in 1 John 2:2!

There can be no doubt that throughout this entire epistle the word "world" consistently means exactly what a reasonable reader would expect: the world of mankind at large in contrast to the body of believers. One cannot claim that "world" in 1 John 2:2 is an exception and has a different meaning from everywhere else in the epistle. We can only conclude that Christ is the propitiation for the sins of the whole world, and therefore His death was not propitiatory for the elect only but for the sins of all mankind. Indeed, John says exactly that in so many words: "the Father sent the Son to be the Saviour of the world" (1 John 4:14).

Does that mean that all are automatically saved by Christ's death? No. The good news of the gospel is "the power of God unto salvation to everyone that believeth..." (Romans 1:16).

Clearly, without special definitions of words and much Scripture-twisting, the doctrine of Limited Atonement crumbles, and with it the rest of Calvinism.

---

1. Edwin H. Palmer, *the five points of calvinism* (Grand Rapids, MI: Baker Books, enlarged ed., 20th prtg. 1999). 42.
2. John Piper and Pastoral Staff, "TULIP: What We Believe about the Five Points of Calvinism: Position Paper of the Pastoral Staff" (Minneapolis, MN: Desiring God Ministries, 1997), 11.
3. Loraine Boettner, *Reformed Doctrine of Predestination* (Phillipsburg, NJ: Presbyterian and Reformed Publishing Company, 1998 ed.) 157.
4. Loraine Boettner, *The Reformed Faith* (Phillipsburg, NJ: Presbyterian and Reformed Publishing Co., 1983), 14.
5. Wm. Oosterman, "Take a Long Look at the Doctrine of Election" (Ottawa, Canada: The Lord's Library Publications, n. d.), 17. Available from Westboro Baptist Church, Ottawa.
6. Grover E. Gunn, *The Doctrine of Grace*, (Memphis, TN: Footstool Publications, 1987), 17.
7. *Sermons of C. H. Spurgeon* (available from Pilgrim Publications, Pasadena TX, n. d.), 48:303.
8. James R. White, *The Potter's Freedom* (Amityville, NY: Calvary Press Publishing, 2000), 231.
9. George Zeller, cited in "For Whom Did Christ Die?" (The Middletown Bible Church, 349 East Street, Middletown CT 06457, 1999), 23–24.
10. John Calvin, *Calvin's New Testament Commentaries* (Grand Rapids, MI: Wm B. Eerdmans Publishing Co., 1994), III:139.
11. John MacArthur, Jr., *The Love of God* (Dallas, TX: Word Publishing, 1996), 103.
12. Ibid., xv, 16–20, 99–124, etc.
13. Zeller, "For Whom," 23-24.
14. Cited in White, *Potter's*, 257.
15. Arthur W. Pink, *The Sovereignty of God* (Grand Rapids, MI: Baker Book House, 2nd prtg. 1986), 20.
16. Sproul, *Chosen,* 206.
17. Laurence M. Vance, *The Other Side of Calvinism* (Pensacola, FL: Vance Publications, rev. ed. 1999), 435.
18. Richard Baxter, *Universal Redemption of Mankind* (London: n. p., 1694), 282–83.
19. Thomas R. Schreiner, "Does Scripture Teach Prevenient Grace in the Wesleyan Sense?", ed. Thomas R. Schreiner and Bruce A. Ware, *Still Sovereign: Contemporary Perspectives on Election, Foreknowledge, and Grace* (Grand Rapids, MI: Baker Books, 2000), 240.
20. Piper and Staff, "TULIP," 16.
21. White, *Potter's*, 273–74.
22. Ibid., 274–75.
23. Piper and Staff, "TULIP," 16.
24. Ibid., 18.
25. Letter to Dave Hunt, dated September 3, 2000. On file.
26. White, *Potter's*, 275.

CHAPTER

20

Understanding Pivotal Scriptures

A MAJOR PASSAGE to which Calvinists look for support is Romans 9. R. C. Sproul declares that Romans 9:16 alone ("So then it is not of him that willeth, nor of him that runneth, but of God that sheweth mercy") "is absolutely fatal to Arminianism."[1] But the phrase "of him that willeth" credits man with a will that can desire to come to Christ. The verse is simply saying that human desire and effort are of no avail without God's grace. We are not defending Arminianism (whose adherents also do not agree among themselves); we are simply testing TULIP by God's Word.

Calvinists believe that Romans chapter 9 proves that man's choice has no role in salvation and that before birth, all men are predestined either to heaven or to damnation. White says, "It speaks of the inviolability of God's purpose in election and shows that His choices are not determined by anything in man [i.e., foreknowledge of an individual's eventual response to the gospel]."[2] Piper says that Jacob and Esau "were appointed for their respected [*sic*] destinies [for eternity] before they were born."[3] Hoeksema agrees: "We conclude, therefore, that the predestination of Jacob and Esau is a personal election and reprobation unto salvation and eternal desolation respectively."[4] In fact, this is not the case, as we shall see.

In Romans 9:13 ("As it is written, Jacob have I loved, but Esau have I hated"), Paul is quoting the prophet Malachi (Malachi 1:2). Such a statement is "written" nowhere else in Scripture. Nor is Malachi the prophet referring to Jacob and Esau as individuals but to the nations which descended from them: "The...word of the LORD to Israel by Malachi.

I have loved you...and I hated Esau, and laid his mountains and his heritage waste.... Edom...shall build, but I will throw down; and they shall call them...the people against whom the Lord hath indignation for ever.... I change not; therefore ye sons of Jacob are not consumed" (Malachi 1:1–4; 3:6).

Quite clearly, by "Esau" is meant the nation of Edom descended from him, and "Jacob" means Israel. Esau and Jacob *as individuals* are not in view.

Salvation Is Not the Subject

There is no reference in Malachi to the eternal salvation of either Jacob or Esau or their descendants, much less that Jacob and his descendants were predestined for heaven and Esau with his descendants for hell. No verse in Malachi even implies this! Clearly Paul's quotation of Malachi is improperly used in attempting to prove Calvinism's predestination and reprobation.

Furthermore, we know that many Israelites who descended from Jacob were lost eternally; conversely, one cannot prove that every descendant of Esau is or will be in hell. Even Calvinists would not say that every Israelite belonged to the elect in the Calvinist sense.

Commenting on the reference to Esau and Jacob in Romans, chapter 9, Broughton said, "Election is God choosing out a people through whom He is going to manifest Himself.... It is not...to salvation, but...to service...."[5] In full agreement, Professor H. H. Rowley declared, "Election is for service.... God chose Israel...not alone that He might reveal Himself to her, but that He might claim her for service."[6] Fisk comments, "Rowley, indeed, goes so far as to suggest that election is something which, if not fulfilled by the elect, may be withdrawn from them—a thought at which committed Calvinists would shudder."[7] Interestingly, Rowley's comments were part of a series of lectures he gave at Spurgeon's College in London.

Nor does Paul in Romans 9 even hint any more than does Malachi at the individual salvation of Esau, Jacob, or Pharaoh. Yet what Paul says about these individuals is used by Calvinists to "prove" their peculiar doctrine of election and predestination unto salvation or damnation. Vance points out that "the basic error of Calvinism is confounding election and predestination with salvation, which they never are in the Bible, but only in the philosophical speculations and theological implications of Calvinism...."[8] In fact, election and predestination always have to do with a particular purpose, ministry, or blessing to which one has been elected—not salvation.

"Two Nations...and Two Manner of People"

The fact that God was referring to nations and not to Jacob and Esau as individuals was clear from the very start. During her pregnancy, as the twins "struggled together within her," God told Rebekah, "Two nations are in thy womb, and two manner of people...the one...shall be stronger... and the elder shall serve the younger" (Genesis 25:23). If the *individuals* were in view, this would be a false prophecy, because Esau never served his brother, Jacob, nor could it be said that Jacob was stronger than Esau during their respective lifetimes.

The prophecy was, however, perfectly fulfilled in the nations (Edom and Israel) descended from Esau and Jacob. Yet Calvinists ignore that fact because it doesn't fit their theory, and they go to great lengths to make it apply to individual salvation or reprobation. For example, in all his "proof" of election to salvation from Romans 9, White, like most Calvinists, never mentions Genesis 25:23. Why does he avoid it? The reason is obvious.

Piper makes four oblique references to Genesis 25:23 but never exegetes it: 1) He quotes "the elder shall serve the younger" but not the essential statement that two nations are involved;[9] 2) He mentions in a footnote ("Luther denies Erasmus' interpretation of both Genesis 25:23 and Malachi 1:2"),[10] but fails to explain this denial or to show its validity; 3) He quotes Shrenk's statement in opposition to his own and in agreement with what we are saying, "The reference here is not to salvation, but to position and historical task, cf. the quotation from Genesis 25:23 in Romans 9:12: 'The elder shall serve the younger',"[11] but again, there is no recognition of God's statement that He was referring to nations; and 4) When he finally gives the full quote, he goes off on a tangent about how Israel became stronger than Edom and fails to make the obvious application to Romans 9: "The birth to Isaac and Rebecca of...Jacob and Esau was announced to Rebecca in Genesis 25:23, 'Two nations are in your womb, and two peoples born of you shall be divided.... The elder shall serve the younger.' How it became possible for Jacob and his descendants to gain the ascendancy over Esau and his descendants...is described in Genesis 25:29–34 and Genesis 27:18–29."[12]

In fact, the "ascendancy" did not occur during the lifetime of either Jacob or Esau but referred to their descendants only. Piper goes on to discuss that aspect, but gives no recognition whatsoever of the import of two nations being the subject of God's original prophecy and of Malachi's confirmation thereof. To do so would undermine the Calvinist interpretation of Romans 9, one of their key passages.

Luther, too, avoids facing the full impact of the fact that, in both Genesis and Malachi, God is ultimately referring to nations within which not every individual is either saved or lost.[13] Although he mentions that "two peoples are clearly distinguished,"[14] Luther erroneously applies it all to individual salvation to support his argument against free will.

God's clear statements in Genesis 25 have nothing to do with the eternal destiny of Esau and Jacob to heaven or to hell, but concern the "manner of people" their descendants would be and how they would fit into God's purposes. Thus, in quoting Genesis 25:23, Paul could not be speaking of individual salvation either, but rather of God's election of Israel to a preferred position of blessing and usefulness. The indisputable fact that two future nations are the subject of God's prophecy to Rebecca completely undermines Calvinistic arguments. Dick Sanford writes:

> Circle that word, "*Serve.*" It's not saying, "*The elder shall be saved and the younger shall not be.*" Never mix the scripture that is talking about *service* with scripture that is talking about *salvation*.... Service includes works that are rewarded. Salvation is grace apart from works....
>
> Here the Lord says that before they were ever born, He knew which one was going to be born first and.... I am going to switch this *service* pattern...[and] the inheritance is going to come through the younger instead of the older. That is a reversal also....
>
> Now it does not say, "Jacob have I saved [for] heaven and Esau...can't go to heaven....[but] I told you that...the blessing is not going to come through Esau...the children of Esau are not going to lead up to the Messiah; it's the children of Jacob that are going to lead up to the Messiah. (Emphasis in original)[15]

What About the Individuals?

Other than the two references in Malachi and Romans, we are told only once more that God loved Jacob (Psalm 47:4), and never again that He hated Esau. Moreover, "loved" and "hated" are comparative terms (as when Christ says we must hate father and mother in comparison to our love for Him—Matthew 10:37–38; Luke 14:26) and have nothing to do with salvation. As Forster and Marston point out,

> Malachi 1:2 does not mean that in a literal hatred of Esau and his descendants God has condemned every one of them to hell. It has reference simply to the higher position of the Hebrew race in the strategy of God.... In the original to which Paul is referring, Esau is simply a synonym for Edom [clear from the context: Malachi 1:2–5].... God's choice of Israel could not be a result of her merit or works.... [Paul's] introduction of the quotation from Malachi 1:2 is therefore of particular relevance here, and he uses it as he develops his theme....[16]

Calvinists emphasize the statement, "For the children being not yet born, neither having done any good or evil, that the purpose of God according to election might stand, not of works, but of him that calleth...." However, this statement is simply further proof that election is determined by foreknowledge. No one merits God's blessing, which is all of His grace—it is given to those who He foreknows will receive it.

Before these men were born, God knew that Jacob would turn to Him, that Esau would despise his birthright, and that his descendants would be the enemies of Israel. On that basis He hated Esau/Edom. If this were not the case, we would have God hating for no reason at all, which is contrary to all that the Bible tells us of the God who "*is love.*" Furthermore, if that were the case, it would render meaningless Christ's prophetic statement that "They hated me without a cause" (John 15:25).

It is clear that the election of Jacob and rejection of Esau had nothing to do with the salvation or damnation of either individual, or of their descendants. For Calvinists to use these passages to that end is simply faulty exegesis. Yet Palmer insists, "Thus, Romans 9 is clear in asserting that both election and preterition [passing over the non-elect] are unconditional...'Jacob I loved, but Esau I hated.'"[17]

What About Pharaoh?

Pharaoh's case, likewise, has nothing to do with his eternal destiny. God knew in advance the evil, self-willed heart of this tyrant, and that is why God raised him up at this particular time: "[F]or this cause have I raised thee up, for to shew in thee my power; and that my name may be declared throughout all the earth" (Exodus 9:16). God used Pharaoh's stubborn, proud heart to fully judge all the gods of Egypt, in the process of delivering His people from that pagan land.

God did not *cause* Pharaoh to sin, but arranged circumstances and events to put this particular man (whose every quirk and wicked impulse He foreknew in detail) to be in authority at that particular time, in order to use his evil to fulfill His will. We affirm as biblical and reasonable both God's ability and His sovereign right to arrange circumstances and to position on the stage of life those players whom He foreknows, so that His will is effected in human affairs—and to do so without violating their will or encouraging (much less becoming accessory to) their crimes.

For God to put Pharaoh at the right place and time to fit into His plans for Israel and Egypt has nothing to do with any of the elements in TULIP that affect personal salvation. Nor did God cause Pharaoh's actions; He simply allowed Pharaoh's evil to run its course, even strengthening Pharaoh's evil resolve to the extent to which it fulfilled God's own purpose.

There is only one biblical explanation for God taking some to heaven and sending others to hell: *Salvation is a genuine offer, and God, in His omniscient foreknowledge, knows how each person will respond.* The only cogent *reason* consistent with God's character for election and predestination of the redeemed to certain blessings is God's omniscient foreknowledge of who would believe. Concerning this entire passage dealing with Esau, Jacob, and Pharaoh, Ironside wrote:

> There is no question here of predestination to Heaven or reprobation to hell.... We are not told here, nor anywhere else, that before children are born it is God's purpose to send one to Heaven and another to hell.... The passage has to do entirely with privilege here on earth.[18]

Paul concludes this section by declaring that God, "to make his power known, endured with much longsuffering the vessels of wrath [such as Pharaoh] fitted to destruction" (Romans 9:22). Though *enduring* such vessels of wrath, God does not cause them to be or do evil. Rather, He sometimes purposes to use those whose hearts are evil, and endures their opposition and wickedness to the extent to which it fits into His will. In that way, God is able to make the wrath of man to praise Him (Psalm 76:10).

"Whom He Will He Hardeneth"

In relation to Pharaoh, Romans 9:18 states, "Therefore hath he mercy on whom he will have mercy, and whom he will he hardeneth." Calvinists make a great deal of the statement that God hardened Pharaoh's heart, as though that proves Unconditional Election and Limited Atonement. On the contrary, the hardening of his heart had nothing to do with whether Pharaoh would go to heaven, but with God's use of Pharaoh at the time of Israel's deliverance from Egypt. God says His purpose was "that I might shew these my signs before him: and that thou mayest tell in the ears of thy son, and of thy son's son, what things I have wrought in Egypt, and my signs which I have done among them; that ye may know how that I am the LORD" (Exodus 10:1).

When God hardened Pharaoh's heart to further His purposes for Israel and Egypt, to manifest His power more fully, and specifically to complete His judgment upon the gods of Egypt, He was, in fact, only helping Pharaoh to do what that tyrant wanted to do. When He sent Moses to Egypt, God declared, "I am sure that the king of Egypt will not let you go..." (Exodus 3:19). This was Pharaoh's disposition before a word was said about God's hardening of his heart.

Yet Calvinists are almost unanimous in their avoidance of this scripture. Passing it by, they begin their comments with Exodus 4:21, "I will harden his heart, that he shall not let the people go." Like the others, Pink ignores 3:19 and writes, "did not God harden his heart *before* the plagues were sent upon Egypt?—see Exodus 4:21!"[19] White, too, avoids 3:19 and also uses 4:21 as foundational.[20] So does Piper. In building his lengthy argument concerning the hardening of Pharaoh's heart, he relies heavily upon 4:21. Piper's many pages of erudite citations of the original Hebrew and Greek, with accompanying complicated arguments, lose their luster in view of his disregard of 3:19, which, had he noted it, would have changed the whole picture.[21]

Unfortunately, Piper flooded *The Justification of God* with Greek and Hebrew words in those alphabets without the English equivalents that authors usually supply. Thus, readers who are not Greek and Hebrew scholars must take his word for what he says. Nevertheless, his comments are revealing:

> [B]efore the first active assertion of God's hardening in Exodus 9:12 there are two assertions that he [Pharaoh] hardened his own heart [8:15,32] and after 9:12 there are two assertions that he

> hardened his own heart [9:34,35]. [Thus] Pharaoh's "self-hardening" is equally well attested before *and after* the first statement that God has hardened him…." (Emphasis added)[22]

Piper acknowledges that Pharaoh hardened his own heart, both before and after "the first active assertion of God's hardening…." It is important to understand that "God did not give Pharaoh the wicked desire to rebel against him. What God did was to give him the courage to carry out that desire. Thus God's action merely made the difference between a wicked act and the suppression of an evil desire through fear."[23] Furthermore, there is nothing in the story to indicate that Pharaoh was unable to obey God by a genuine response from his heart. Contradicting what he says elsewhere, and in a very un-Calvinistic statement that suggests free will, Calvin acknowledges that the ungodly *can* be moved to genuine repentance by God's warnings:

> Who does not now see that by threatenings of this kind [Jonah's prophecy of Nineveh's destruction, etc.], God wished to arouse those to repentance whom he terrified that they might escape the judgment which their sins deserved.[24]

In this case, however, through His foreknowledge God knew that Pharaoh, like Esau, would reject His will—just as He knew that Jacob would submit and obey (Genesis 28:7, 20–21; 32:9–11, 24–32; 49:28–33, etc.). Pharaoh was an evil man who had long abused the people of God. He selfishly desired to protect his own interests by keeping these people as slaves.

Yet the plagues became so terrifying that Pharaoh would have let Israel go—not from genuine repentance but from fear of further judgment. Yahweh, however, had not finished judging the gods of Egypt. Therefore, He hardened Pharaoh's heart by giving him the courage to persist in the resistance he really wanted to pursue, until God had fully executed His judgment upon Egypt's gods, bringing forth "the children of Israel, out of the land of Egypt by great judgments" (Exodus 7:4).

We gain a better understanding of God's dealings with Pharaoh through the Hebrew words translated "harden" or "hardened" in the King James. In the sense of hardening one's own heart, *kabed* is used four times: Exodus 7:14, 8:15, 9:7 and 9:34. *Qashah,* only used once (Exodus 7:3), means to become stiff-necked or stubborn. C*hazaq* (Exodus 4:21; 7:13,22; 8:15; 9:12,35; 10:20,27; 11:10; 14:4,8,17) means to strengthen or give courage, indicating that God was not causing Pharaoh to be an evil man or to do evil actions, but was giving Pharaoh the strength and courage to stand by his intent not to let Israel go, even when the plagues became overwhelmingly terrifying. As Forster and Marston explain after an in-depth word study:

> The Bible does not teach that God made Pharaoh unrepentant. The main word used for the hardening of Pharaoh's heart is *chazaq*, and it seems to mean that God emboldened or encouraged Pharaoh's heart so that he had the stubborn courage to stand even in the face of very frightening miracles.... *God never prevents anyone from repenting.* "Have I any pleasure in the death of the wicked? Says the Lord God: and not rather that he should return from his way and live?" (Emphasis added)[25]

Nor does the example of Pharaoh support the Calvinist view of Total Depravity. If Pharaoh had been totally depraved, why would God have to harden his heart? Piper says that four times Pharaoh hardened his own heart. Why even say so, if he could do nothing else? How could a totally depraved heart become harder than it already was?

Nor does it say that when Pharaoh at last let Israel go, God caused him to do so with Irresistible Grace. He was simply terrified, and on that basis submitted to Yahweh's will (Exodus 12:30–33), but still without true repentance.

Clay, the Potter, and Vessels of Wrath

As Paul's final commentary (White calls it a "crescendo")[26] in this important passage, he declares that no one can complain against God for what He does, because the clay has no right to demand of the potter,

> Why hast thou made me thus? Hath not the potter power over the clay, of the same lump to make one vessel unto honour, and another unto dishonour? What if God, willing to...make his power known, endured with much longsuffering the vessels of wrath fitted to destruction: And that he might make known the riches of his glory on the vessels of mercy, which he had afore prepared unto glory, even us, whom he hath called, not of the Jews only, but also of the Gentiles? (Romans 9:20–24)

Calvinists rely heavily upon this scripture passage. White declares:

> The Potter's freedom pulses through these words, flowing inexorably into the sea of sovereignty, rushing any would-be proponent

> of free will out of its path. God has the perfect right to do with His creation (including men) as He wishes, just as the Potter has utter sovereignty over the clay..."vessels of wrath....." Are these nations...? No, these are *sinners* upon whom God's wrath comes. They are said to have been specifically "prepared for destruction." That is their *purpose*.[27] (Emphasis in original)

That God the Potter 1) has the right to do with men as He pleases, and 2) endures with much longsuffering the vessels of wrath, we do not deny. That is all, however, that this passage tells us—it does not tell us what His desire is. Numerous other passages, however, do tell us in the clearest terms that God desires all to come to repentance and the knowledge of the truth, that He is not willing that any should perish, and that He takes no pleasure in the death of the wicked. We have cited many of these passages already.

There is *nothing* in Romans 9:20–24 to indicate that God the Potter causes anyone to be or do evil. Much less does this passage prove, as Calvinists claim, that God predestines some to heaven and others to hell. Paul is referring to God's use of the innate evil of wicked men such as Esau and Pharaoh, when it suits His purpose, to fulfill His will. In so doing, He endures "the contradiction of sinners" (Hebrews 12:3). Nor does the fact that God brings these vessels of wrath to the destruction they deserve prove that this is His will for them or that they have no choice, much less that they were predestined to destruction.

The Calvinist says God *could,* through Irresistible Grace, *cause* all mankind to believe in Christ and obey Him. If that be true, then the fact that He does not do so runs counter to all that the Bible says of His lovingkindness, mercy, and grace. There is no explanation for this glaring contradiction: the Calvinist is forced to plead "mystery."

In contrast, Scripture declares that God has given men the power of choice. Therefore, to force irresistible grace upon them would itself contradict that gift. God violates no one's will. Granted, He could have been gracious and suppressed the wickedness of Pharaoh and Judas had it suited His plans—but that would not have changed either their hearts or eternal destiny. As for these "vessels unto dishonor...fitted to destruction," however, He chose instead to strengthen their resolve to wickedness in order to effect His will. He did not cause them to choose evil, He used their wicked choice for His own purposes and in so doing "endured" their rebellion.

Herman Hoeksema claims that the example of the Potter teaches "God's absolute sovereignty to determine the final destiny of men, either to honor or dishonor, to salvation and glory or to damnation and desolation."[28] Likewise, Piper says, "It is clear that Paul still has in mind the issue of unconditional election [to salvation or damnation] raised in Romans 9:6–13."[29] We have just given a different explanation—which is both a reasonable exegesis and is in agreement with God's character of love and justice—and scores of other scriptures that declare God's love for all and His desire that all be saved. Paul is not at all dealing with the eternal destiny of Esau, Jacob, and Pharaoh.

John 3:16–17 Revisited

If there is one Bible verse that every child who ever attended an evangelical Sunday school is sure to know, that verse is John 3:16. What child encountering this verse for the first time, without a Calvinist teacher, would conclude that "world" did not mean the whole world of mankind but a limited number of individuals chosen by God? None would, of course.

Calvin himself, in his commentary on John 3:16, stated that "world" included "all men without exception." Luther also said it meant "the entire human race." But White, realizing that such an admission does away with Limited Atonement, manages a desperate end run around John 3:16. He suggests that sound exegesis requires "that whosoever believeth on him should not perish" actually means "in order that everyone believing in him should not perish...."[30] That slight twist allows White to suggest that Calvinism's elect *alone* believe (God having caused them to do so), and thus Christ died only for them. Even if that were true, Calvinism would still have to explain (in view of its insistence that men must be born again before God can give them faith) how *eternal* life can be received without faith. (Surely, sovereign "regeneration" is not to *temporary* life!) That question will be considered under Irresistible Grace.

To prevent such twisting of His Word, Christ himself explains this passage unequivocally: "And as Moses lifted up the serpent in the wilderness, even so must the Son of man be lifted up: that whosoever believeth on him should not perish, but have eternal life." (John 3:14–15). There is no question that just as the law and the entire Levitical sacrificial system were for "all Israel" (2 Chronicles 29:24; Ezra 6:17; Malachi 4:4, etc.), so was God's provision of the upraised serpent: "...*every one*...*any man*, when he beheld the serpent of brass, he lived" (Numbers 21:8–9).

In one look of simple faith, healing flowed to *each and every* Israelite without exception. The precise connection Christ reveals between this

Old Testament type and His crucifixion for sin ("as Moses lifted up the servant…so *must* the Son of man be lifted up") cannot be escaped. "… that whosoever believeth in him should not perish but have everlasting life" is a promise for all.

Every Old Testament type of the Cross was for every Israelite. There was no special elect among them to whom alone the Passover, manna, water out of the rock, the Day of Atonement, or general offerings for sin applied. Significantly, any check of the list of scriptures used in Calvinist books will reveal an avoidance of references to Old Testament types of Christ and His sacrifice on the Cross. The reason needs no explanation.

Like most other apologists for Calvinism, White avoids John 3:14-15 and doesn't even attempt to deal with the unequivocal statement in 3:17 "that the world through him might be saved" (to which his explanation of John 3:16 couldn't possibly apply). Obviously, this further comment by Christ explains the meaning of the entire section (John 3:14–18) pertaining to His death on the Cross, making it very clear that God gave His Son for the salvation of the entire world. Nor does White quote Calvin or anyone else concerning John 3:17. None of the thirteen contributors to *Still Sovereign* touches it. (We deal with this in more depth in chapter 27.)

Of course, White's interpretation of John 3:16 must agree with his argument that 1 John 2:2 couldn't possibly mean "that Christ's death is a satisfaction for the whole world." He justifies that view by the fact that John goes on to tell us "*not to love the world!*"[31] How does the fact that we are not to love the world prove that Christ did not die for the sins of the whole world? Obviously, John is using "world" in two different ways: the *people* of the world, and the world *system*.

Recognizing that fact, White rightly declares that in 1 John 2:15 "world" means "the *present evil system,* not the universal population of mankind" (emphasis in original). White is now caught in a web of his own making. If the fact that "world" in verse 15 means "the present evil system" refutes the claim that in verse 2 it means all the people in the world, why would it not also refute White's view that it means "all Christians throughout the world...at all times and in all places"?[32]

There is no way to escape the straightforward meaning: in 1 John 2:2, "world" means all unsaved mankind.

Christ Died for All

The scriptures declaring that Christ died to save all mankind are so numerous that only a few can be presented. In scriptures such as "For the Son of man is come to seek and to save that which was lost" (Luke 19:10), "Christ died for the ungodly" (Romans 5:6), and "Christ Jesus came into the world to save sinners" (1 Timothy 1:15), there is no suggestion that only a certain *elect* group among the "lost...ungodly...[and] sinners" is intended. There is simply no qualifier.

Surely the idea that such general language actually specifies a select "elect" would never be imagined without previous indoctrination into Calvinism. Yet White sees in such verses "the particularity that is so vehemently denied by the Arminian."[33]

White argues, "Is it not the message of the Bible that Christ *saves* sinners? By what warrant do we...change the meaning to 'wants to save'...?"

We, of course, could ask White, "What is the justification for changing 'sinners' to '*some* sinners'?"

He then quotes Paul's declaration, "I am crucified with Christ...the Son of God, who loved me, and gave himself for me" (Galatians 2:20), as proof that "sinners" and "ungodly, et al., mean *particular* sinners.[34] On the contrary, Paul is giving a *personal* testimony of his own faith in Christ; it cannot be used to place a limitation upon general nouns appearing elsewhere. Nor does he say, "I alone...for me alone." Every person who has the same relationship with Christ as Paul did can make the same statement: "the Son of God, who loved *me*, and gave himself for *me*," but that does not mean He doesn't love the world and did not die for all.

Naturally, at times the inspired writers of Scripture specifically applied what they said to those who were saved: "the LORD hath laid on him the iniquity of *us* all.... Christ died for *our* sins...that *we* might be made the righteousness of God in him...who gave himself for *our* sins...hast redeemed *us* to God by thy blood" (Isaiah 53:6; 1 Corinthians 15:3; 2 Corinthians 5:21; Galatians 1:4; Revelation 5:9, etc.). That fact does not in any way nullify the many verses that just as clearly say that Christ died for *all*.

Paul could not declare more clearly that Christ's purpose in coming into the world was to save sinners. That all sinners are not saved is not because Christ did not pay for their sins, but because all do not accept that payment. White argues that because all sinners don't get saved, this verse must therefore mean that the "sinners" Christ came to save could only be the elect.

To sustain that argument, however, one would have to change the meaning of hundreds of other Bible verses as well. Jesus himself declared, "I am not come to call the righteous, but sinners to repentance" (Matthew 9:13). Again, all sinners do not repent, so the Calvinist is compelled to say that Christ only calls *some* sinners to repentance, or else His call is in vain.

How could one perceive that meaning in this statement by Christ? Only Calvinists find it there—and only because Calvinism requires it. But it doesn't follow, because even the elect often fail to repent as thoroughly as they should. So to whatever extent they fail to give full honor and glory and obedience to God, are they not frustrating God's purposes just as surely as the non-elect are said to do by rejecting the gospel? Is it really God's will that multitudes of Christians live such shallow and even disobedient lives? Or is it because they so choose?

Repeatedly, the Bible states that God desires to rescue and bless all Israel and that her refusal to repent prevents Him from so doing. He sends His prophets day and night to plead with Israel to repent so He won't have to punish her. Yet God wants only *some* of Israel to repent? Many other similar examples could be given to show that Calvinism turns the loving and compassionate pleadings of God and Christ with sinners into a sham.

God Has Two Wills in Conflict?

Nothing could be clearer in refuting Limited Atonement than Paul's declaration, "who will have all men to be saved, and to come unto the knowledge of the truth" (1 Timothy 2:4). Piper admits that Paul is saying that "God does not delight in the perishing of the impenitent and that he has compassion on all people." But this sounds like "double-talk" if Calvinism is true (i.e., if God only elects some to heaven and sends the rest to hell), so he sets out to show that there are "'two wills' in God...that God decrees one state of affairs while also willing and teaching that a different state of affairs should come to pass."[35] This *is* double-talk.

John MacArthur, Jr., as we've seen, also tries to escape Paul's clear language and the message of all Scripture with the same astonishing idea that God has two conflicting wills. Here is the full text of his explanation:

> **2:4 desires all men to be saved.** The Gr. Word for "desires" is not that which normally expresses God's will of decree (His eternal purpose), but God's will of desire. There is a distinction between God's desire and His eternal saving purpose, which must transcend

> His desires. God does not want men to sin, He hates sin with all His being (Pss. 5:4; 45:7); thus, He hates its consequences—eternal wickedness in hell. God does not want people to remain wicked forever in eternal remorse and hatred of Himself. Yet, God, for His own glory, and to manifest that glory in wrath, chose to endure "vessels...prepared for destruction" for the supreme fulfillment of His will (Rom 9:22). In His eternal purpose, He chose only the elect out of the world (John 17:6) and passed over the rest, leaving them to the consequences of their sin, unbelief, and rejection of Christ (cf. Rom. 1:18-32). Ultimately, God's choices are determined by His sovereign, eternal purpose, not His desires.[36]

How could God have "desires" contrary to His "sovereign, eternal purpose"? That condition in a man is condemned as being double minded (James 1:8, 4:8). How could God's eternal purpose transcend His desire? Nowhere does the Bible say that God has two conflicting wills. That would be impossible for God "who worketh all things after the counsel of his own will" (Ephesians 1:11)—a favorite verse of Calvinists.

To be double minded would be inconceivable for God. The Calvinist insists that God *could* cause everyone to believe and be saved if He so desired. Then how could God desire all to be saved, a desire that He *could* cause to happen (according to Calvinism), yet not bring it to pass? Such a suggestion is neither biblical nor rational.

MacArthur adds to his error by equating God's alleged failure to fulfill His desire for all to be saved with His failure to prevent all men from sinning. Now we have a further problem. Either man has a genuine power of choice, or all sin must be attributed to God. In fact, the latter is what MacArthur implies and what leading Calvinists such as R. C. Sproul declare, as we have amply seen.

The Calvinist is caught on the horns of a dilemma. How can he maintain the position that God decrees and causes all, and yet exonerate God for the wickedness and eternal punishment of the vast majority of mankind? He falls back on the theory that God *really* doesn't want this state of affairs, and yet His eternal purpose and His decrees demand it. What a contradiction!

The biblical solution is so simple: that God indeed loves man, doesn't want any to perish, and has provided full pardon, redemption, eternal life, and the transformation of a new birth for all—but He has given man the power of choice so that man could love his fellows and, above all, love God. Sin, sorrow, and eternal judgment are thus on man's shoulders (fruit of his self-will), not on God's. But the Calvinist could not allow freedom of man's will, for that would destroy TULIP.

"All Men" Means "All Classes of Men"?

Contradicting fellow Calvinist MacArthur, White follows John Calvin in using a different ploy to get around this passage. He refers to other places wherein the expression "all men" isn't to be taken literally, such as Ananias's statement to Paul at his conversion, "For thou shalt be his witness unto all men..." (Acts 22:15). White reasons:

> Of course, Paul would not think that these words meant that he would witness of Christ to every single individual human being on the planet. Instead, he would have surely understood this to mean all *kinds* and *races* of men.... Paul speaks of *kinds* of people in other places as well.... Greek and Jew, circumcised and uncircumcised, barbarian, Scythian, slave and freeman....
>
> So it is perfectly consistent with the immediate and broader context of Paul's writings to recognize this use of "all men" in a generic fashion.[37]

On the contrary, Paul would never have understood Ananias to mean *kinds* and *races* of men. Obviously, "all *kinds* and *races*" is no more reasonable than "all men." Japanese? Australian aborigines? Siberian or North American Indians? If that is what Ananias meant, he was a false prophet. There are surely many kinds and races of men to whom Paul never did witness during his lifetime on Earth.

What would any of us understand such a statement addressed to ourselves to mean? Not all men everywhere (and certainly not *all kinds*) but all those with whom we would come in contact, and for Paul that would include through his testimony in Scripture as well. But what does White's strained interpretation of a statement by Ananias have to do with Paul's clear declaration that God wants "all men to be saved"?

White argues further that because Paul says prayer is to be made "for all men; for kings and for all that are in authority," he is referring to "classes of men" and that the following phrase, "who will have all men to be saved," therefore actually means "who will have *all classes of men* to be saved."[38] In fact, "kings...and all in authority" refers to only one class of men—that is, rulers. White is only echoing Calvin here: "For the apostle's meaning here is simply that...God regards all men as being equally worthy to share in salvation. But he is speaking of classes and not of individuals, and his only concern is to include princes and foreign nations in this number."[39]

Piper grasps at the same straw: "It is possible that careful exegesis of 1 Timothy 2:4 would lead us to believe that 'God's willing all persons to be saved' does not refer to every individual person in the world, but rather to all *sorts* of persons...."[40] The "careful exegesis," which he suggests would support this idea, is never revealed.

Calvinists love to quote Spurgeon for support, but here he accuses them (as do we) of altering the plain meaning of the text. The great preacher discussed this passage of Scripture in depth, and in the process, contradicted his own Calvinism as he expressed it at other times:

> What then? Shall we try to put another meaning into the text than that which it fairly bears? I trow not.... You must, most of you, be acquainted with the general method in which our older Calvinistic friends deal with this text. "All men" say they "that is, some men": as if the Holy Ghost could not have said "some men" if He meant some men. "All men," say they: "that is, some of all sorts of men": as if the Lord could not have said, "All sorts of men" if He had meant that. The Holy Ghost by the apostle has written, "All men," and unquestionably he means all men.... My love of consistency with my own doctrinal views is not great enough to allow me knowingly to alter a single text of Scripture.[41]

With Spurgeon, we ask again, if "all *classes*" is what the Holy Spirit meant to convey, why was it not stated clearly? The truth is that the Holy Spirit declared in unequivocal language that God is not willing for *any person to perish*—and they tamper with God's Word who put a Calvinist interpretation upon it!

"Kings and all that are in authority" are mentioned as special subjects of prayer for a definite reason: "that we may lead a quiet and peaceable life...." Can anyone seriously imagine that Paul urged prayer for kings and those in authority in order to convey to Timothy (and to us today) that *all classes of men* were meant to be the recipients of the gospel: tradesmen, sheep herders, soldiers, tinkers, tailors, robbers, etc.?

Wouldn't Paul be fearful that, unless he specifically mentioned them all, some despised classes such as prostitutes or slaves might be overlooked by Timothy and by us today? No. Christ had already told His disciples to "preach the gospel to every creature"! That Christ means *everyone*, every Christian knew then and knows now.

As for 1 Timothy 2:6 ("who gave himself a ransom for all"), White quotes R. K. Wright's reference to "the meticulous demonstration by John Gill that the Arminian exegesis of key passages (such as 2 Peter 3:9 and 1 Timothy 2:4–6) is fallacious."[42] Yet he fails to give us Gill's refutation. Why such effort to change the meaning of a clear text?

First Timothy 4:10 ("who is the Saviour of all men") is another scripture that states beyond doubt that Christ died for all. Yet White again has nothing to say about it. MacArthur comments: "The point is that He is the only Savior to whom anyone in the world can turn for forgiveness and eternal life—and therefore all are urged to embrace Him as Savior.... In setting forth His own Son as Savior of the world, God displays the same kind of love to the whole world that was manifest in the Old Testament to the rebellious Israelites. It is a sincere, tender-hearted, compassionate love that offers mercy and forgiveness."[43]

Can MacArthur be serious? This is typical "moderate Calvinist" double-speak, in contrast to the frankness of those whom they call "hyper-Calvinists" for not trying to hide the truth about Calvinism. *Sincere, tender-hearted, compassionate love that offers mercy and forgiveness* to those for whom both "moderates" and "hypers" agree Christ didn't die, who, as all Calvinists affirm, cannot respond to the offer without being sovereignly regenerated (a privilege that "moderates" agree is only for the elect), and who (again "moderates" agree) have been predestined to eternal torment, a fact that nothing can change?! Whom do the "moderates" think they are deceiving? Surely no one but themselves.

---

1. Cited in James White, *The Potter's Freedom* (Amityville, NY: Calvary Press Publishing, 2000), 222.
2. Ibid., 215.
3. John Piper, *The Justification of God: An Exegetical and Theological Study of Romans 9:1–23* (Grand Rapids, MI: Baker Books, 2000), 203–204.
4. Herman Hoeksema, *God's Eternal Good Pleasure*, ed. and rev., Homer C. Hoeksema (Grandville, MI: Reformed Free Publishing Association, 1979), 24.
5. Len G. Broughton, *Salvation and the Old Theology* (London: Hodder and Stoughton, n. d.), 152.
6. H. H. Rowley, *The Biblical Doctrine of Election* (Cambridge, UK: Lutterworth Press, 1952), 45.
7. Samuel Fisk, *Calvinistic Paths Retraced* (Raleigh, NC: Biblical Evangelism Press, 1985), 81.
8. Laurence M. Vance, *The Other Side of Calvinism* (Pensacola, FL: Vance Publications, rev. ed. 1999), 35.

9. Piper, *Justification*, 51.
10. Ibid., 56.
11. Ibid., 57.
12. Ibid., 61–62.
13. Martin Luther, *The Bondage of the Will*, trans. J. I. Packer and O. R. Johnston (Grand Rapids, MI: Fleming H. Revell, 1957, 11th prtg. 1999), 222–29.
14. Ibid., 225.
15. Dick Sanford, *Predestination and Election*, ed. John R. Cross (self-published monograph, n. d.), 11–12.
16. Roger T. Forster and V. Paul Marston, *God's Strategy in Human History* (Bloomington, MN: Bethany House Publishers, 1973), 75.
17. Edwin H. Palmer, *the five points of calvinism* (Grand Rapids, MI: Baker Books, enlarged ed., 20th prtg. 1999), 32–34, 105.
18. H. A. Ironside, *Lectures on the Epistle to the Romans* (Neptune, NJ: Loizeaux Brothers, 1926), 110, 116.
19. Arthur W. Pink, *The Sovereignty of God* (Grand Rapids, MI: Baker Book House, 2nd prtg. 1986), 96.
20. White, *Potter's*, 211, 221.
21. Piper, *Justification*, 155–81.
22. Ibid., 163.
23. Forster and Marston, *Strategy*, 75.
24. John Calvin, *Institutes of the Christian Religion*, trans. Henry Beveridge (Grand Rapids, MI: Wm. Eerdmans Publishing Company, 1998 ed.), V:xvii,14.
25. Forster and Marston, *Strategy*, 169–70.
26. White, *Potter's*, 213.
27. Ibid., 213–14.
28. Hoeksema, *Eternal*, 60.
29. Piper, *Justification*, 204.
30. White, *Potter's*, 194.
31. Ibid., 277.
32. Ibid., 274.
33. Ibid., 147.
34. Ibid., 247–49.
35. John Piper, "Are There Two Wills In God?" in *Still Sovereign*, ed. Thomas R. Schreiner and Bruce A. Ware (Grand Rapids, MI: Baker Books, 2000), 108–109.
36. John MacArthur, Author and General Editor, *The MacArthur Study Bible* (Nashville, TN: Word Publishing, 1997), 1862.
37. White, *Potter's*, 139–43.
38. Ibid.
39. John Calvin, *Calvin's New Testament Commentaries* (Grand Rapids, MI: Wm B. Eerdmans Publishing Co., 1994), 10:209.
40. Piper, "Two Wills," *Sovereign*, 108.
41. C. H. Spurgeon, *Metropolitan Tabernacle Pulpit,* vol. 26, pages 49–52.
42. White, *Potter's*, 25.
43. John MacArthur, Jr., *The Love of God* (Dallas, TX: Word Publishing, 1996), 116.

CHAPTER

21

More Pivotal Scriptures

THE FOLLOWING are a few more of the scriptures that Calvinists attempt to escape. Hebrews 2:9 ("that he by the grace of God should taste death for every man") is given the familiar Calvinist interpretation. White quotes verse 17: "made like His brethren...a merciful and faithful high priest...to make propitiation for the sins of the people." He goes on to "explain":

> What "people" is here in view? It is the "many sons" of 2:10, those He "sanctifies" (2:11), "My brethren" (2:12), "the children God gave Me" (2:13).... In light of this we understand the statement of Hebrews 2:9, "so that by the grace of God He might taste death for everyone." Another passage often cited without context by Arminians yet defined so plainly in the text.[1]

Let us consider the context. Even when the writer uses "we," he doesn't always refer only to believers: "How shall we escape, if we neglect so great salvation...?" (Hebrews 2:3). Surely this is addressed to all mankind, and not just to the elect, unless the Calvinist is willing to admit that the elect can neglect their salvation and thus be lost. That solemn admonition introduces this entire section of Hebrews 2, which continues in the same vein into chapters 3 and 4. Readers are given numerous warnings and exhortations to hold fast to the faith and not to harden their hearts lest they perish like the children of Israel perished in the wilderness through unbelief.

That this section contains references to those given to Christ by God through His sacrifice does not warrant interpreting "taste death for every man" to mean He tasted death only for the elect. Undoubtedly the entire epistle is addressed to believers, as are all epistles and the entire Bible—but much is also said both to and about the unsaved.

All of Israel was not saved and many perished, so Israel could hardly signify the Calvinist elect. The entire context surrounding Hebrews 2:9 contains some of the strongest verses Arminians cite in support of the belief that one's salvation can be lost, including the following:

- To day if ye will hear his voice, harden not your hearts.... (Hebrews 3:7–8)
- Take heed, brethren, lest there be in any of you an evil heart of unbelief, in departing from the living God. (Hebrews 3:12)
- For we are made partakers of Christ, if we hold the beginning of our confidence steadfast unto the end.... (Hebrews 3:14)
- Let us therefore fear, lest, a promise being left us of entering into his rest, any of you should seem to come short of it. (Hebrews 4:1)
- ...they to whom it [the gospel] was first preached entered not in because of unbelief. (Hebrews 4:6)

Oddly enough, in his book written to refute Arminianism and to defend Calvinism, White completely avoids these verses, which make up the entire context of Hebrews 2:9. And he does so in the process of chiding Arminians for avoiding the *context*!

What About 2 Peter 2:1?

Another important passage among those referred to briefly in the last chapter is 2 Peter 2:1 ("there shall be false teachers...denying the Lord that bought them"). Clearly these false teachers are lost—yet they have been "bought" with the blood of Christ. This is a clear denial of Limited Atonement. Though apparently accepted as "teachers" within the church, they were never saved, as is the case with those to whom Jude refers who have "crept in unawares…ungodly men...ordained to this condemnation" (Jude 4). This passage, too, is completely neglected by White and most other Calvinist apologists.

Very few Calvinists have attempted to deal with scriptures such as Hebrews 10:29 and 2 Peter 2:1, telling of the destruction upon those who despise the "blood of the covenant wherewith [they were] sanctified" and "despise the Lord that bought them...." Sproul's *Geneva Study Bible* attempts to escape by simply ignoring the obvious contradictions of Calvinism. Vance cites most of those who have made such attempts.[2]

> Charles Bronson insists that it "approaches blasphemy to say that Christ shed His precious blood for some and then, after all, they perished in hell."[3] Then what do these verses say? Dabney dismisses both verses because: "The language of Peter, and that of Hebrews...may receive an entirely adequate solution, without teaching that Christ actually 'bought' or 'sanctified' any apostate, by saying that the Apostles speak there '*ad hominem*.'"[4]

"*Ad hominem*"? What does *that* mean in this context?! There "*may*" be a solution that explains away such clear language? If there is, Calvinists haven't yet been able to agree upon it.

Concerning those who Hebrews 10:29 says were sanctified, Beck claims they were "sanctified but not saved."[5] But how can a Calvinist admit that any except the elect have been sanctified, as MacArthur clearly asserts in his *Study Bible*? That those described in both passages are lost eternally cannot be questioned. Thus we are left with only two choices: 1) they were once saved and lost their salvation; or 2) they were never saved, yet were purchased and sanctified by Christ's blood. Neither choice fits Calvinism! No wonder, then, that Calvinists generally avoid these two passages.

Gill maintains that Christ himself "is said here to be sanctified"[6]—which doesn't fit the context at all. Owen makes them mere "professors of the faith of the gospel,"[7] with which we would agree—but that doesn't explain how these non-elect "mere professors" could be "sanctified" with Christ's blood. Other than a few isolated comments, most Calvinists are strangely silent on these two passages. Even in his Hebrews commentary, Pink avoids Hebrews 10:29.

Surely Limited Atonement must be renounced. John 3:16 means what it says. Christ's blood was shed for the sins of the entire world and, in that sense, all are "sanctified." As Paul writes in 1 Timothy 4:10, Christ "is the savior of *all men*" inasmuch as salvation has been purchased for all, even for those who reject Him; and He is the savior "specially of those that believe," because they have believed the gospel, received Christ, and are thus saved eternally.

Understanding 2 Peter 3:9

With regard to 2 Peter 3:9, White refers again to John Gill's supposedly amazing but unrevealed refutation.[8] Twice he suggests that the "Reformed view" of this passage may be "a more consistent interpretation" than the one Geisler offers, but he fails to reveal it.[9] Next, he promises that "an exegetical interpretation of the passage" is coming.[10] Then we are told that Geisler fails to give "as meaningful and thorough a discussion" of the passage as "the Reformed exegesis"—yet neither Geisler's nor the "Reformed exegesis" is explained.[11]

Finally, we are given the Calvinistic interpretation of "The Lord is not slack...but is longsuffering to us-ward, not willing that any should perish, but that all should come to repentance." White declares that "the passage is not speaking about salvation as its topic." On that basis, he summarily rules out the possibility that Peter means what he states so clearly.

In fact, the passage speaks of a number of things: the last days; scoffers who would arise ridiculing the idea that Christ would return in judgment; a reminder of the flood that destroyed the world of that day, and that the present world will be destroyed by fire; that the Day of the Lord will come like a thief; that the entire universe will be dissolved; that we therefore ought to live godly lives; that unstable and unlearned persons twist the meaning of Paul's epistles; and finally there is an exhortation to keep from error and to "grow in grace and in the knowledge of our Lord and Saviour Jesus Christ."

Since Peter deals with so much in this final chapter of his epistle, there is no reason salvation could not be included. Surely he can address both saved and unsaved in this verse. If not, we have a serious contradiction. The phrase "longsuffering to us-ward" cannot be addressed to only the elect. It must include all mankind. If not, the phrase that follows ("not willing that any should perish") must apply to only the elect. But the latter can *only* mean all of mankind, since it refers to a perishing that surely does not imperil the elect.

There are only two possibilities: the reference is to 1) perishing under the penalty of sin or escaping that penalty by repenting; or 2) perishing in the fire that will destroy the world or escaping it. Certainly, perishing in the world-destroying fire of God's judgment is no more applicable to the elect than perishing under the penalty of sin. John Owen argued, "See, then, of whom the apostle is here speaking.... Such as had received 'great and precious promises'...whom he calls 'beloved'.... The text is clear, that it is all and only the elect whom he would not have to perish."[12] Likewise, John Gill writes, "It is not true that God is not willing that any one individual of the human race should perish, since he has made and appointed the wicked for the day of evil.... Nor is it his will that all men...should come to repentance, since he withholds from many both the means and grace of repentance...."[13]

Isn't Gill directly contradicting what God so clearly and repeatedly expresses of His desire for all to be saved? For example, the following is so unequivocal that Gill's contradiction thereof seems nothing short of blasphemy: "As I live, saith the Lord GOD, I have no pleasure in the death of the wicked; but that the wicked turn from his way and live: turn ye, turn ye from your evil ways; for why will ye die, O house of Israel?" (Ezekiel 33:11). There is no way to define "the wicked" and "house of Israel" as the elect!

Though a Calvinist, John Murray, former Westminster Seminary professor, whom Cornelius Van Til called "a great exegete of the Word of God,"[14] declared, "God does not wish that any men should perish. His wish is rather that all should enter upon life eternal by coming to repentance. The language in this part of the verse is so absolute that it is highly unnatural to envisage Peter as meaning merely that God does not wish that any believers should perish...."[15] Writing in the second century, Justin Martyr suggests that God is delaying the Last Judgment because "in His foreknowledge He sees that some will be saved by repentance, some who are, perhaps not yet in existence."[16]

Are the Elect in Danger of Perishing?

Let us assume that White is right and the subject is not salvation. "Perish," therefore, must refer to perishing in the fire of God's judgment that will, in the Day of the Lord, destroy the universe. That certainly is a valid possibility for unbelievers, but White claims the "any" and "all" refer to the elect. Now we have a new problem: how could there be any danger that the elect might perish in the final fire of God's judgment—and how would His longsuffering toward them prevent such an end?

White argues that since the epistle is addressed to believers it can only have reference to believers throughout. One of many letters received on this subject argues: "As in all of the epistles, 2 Peter is addressed to the *elect*.... Peter is not speaking to mankind in general here...."[17] We have shown, logically and biblically, that this argument, used frequently by Calvinists in other instances as well, is unfounded. The fact that believers are being addressed is no reason that Peter cannot make a statement about God's desire for the whole world, including the fate of unbelievers.

Although Peter is not speaking *to* mankind in general, but only *to* the elect, he is certainly not speaking only *about* the elect. Is it the elect who will be the last-days scoffers? Was it the elect who perished in the flood? Is it the elect who will perish in the coming fire that will destroy the world and the entire universe? Surely not. Nor could those to whom God is longsuffering, lest they perish in coming judgment, be the elect.

Moreover, salvation is undoubtedly the topic of at least this verse, since it refers to the repentance that God desires for all; and surely a repentance unto salvation is the only means of deliverance from the wrath to come. But the elect, being already saved, don't need to repent unto salvation, so how could "*any* should perish...*all* should come to repentance" refer to them?

Furthermore, the doctrine of Irresistible Grace claims that God can cause *anyone* to repent and believe the gospel at *any* time—so why would longsuffering be mentioned, if reference is to the elect? Whether the subject is salvation or not, Calvinism is in trouble. In spite of the contradictions we have just pointed out, the only escape is to insist that this does not refer to all mankind but only to the elect. Now we are faced with one more redundancy: God is not willing that any of those He has sovereignly elected not to perish should perish? And He is longsuffering to accomplish that goal? Such arguments are not sustainable.

The only consistent understanding of this verse is that the "us-ward" in the phrase "longsuffering to us-ward" is like an editorial "we" that includes everyone. It is true that in the only other place this expression is found in the New Testament, it clearly refers to the saved. But one use doesn't make a rule. "Us-ward" introduces the statements about "longsuffering" and "perish," which could only apply to the world at large.

Peter is referring to the destruction of the universe from which the elect have been delivered. The ungodly are the ones who will perish. The only consistent understanding of the verse is that God does not want *anyone* to perish, and, as He has done with Israel, is longsuffering in pleading with them and waiting upon them to repent and be saved—as all Scripture declares.

What About 1 Timothy 4:10?

Some further attention must be given to Paul's declaration that Christ "is the Saviour of all men, specially of those that believe." Surely "those that believe" must be the elect for whom Christ is the Saviour in a *special* way not true of "all men" in general. Thus "all men" can't possibly mean the elect. White omits reference to this passage, as do many other Calvinists.

There are, of course, similar contrasts made elsewhere in Scripture. Paul exhorts prayer "for all men...that we may lead a quiet and peaceable life..." (1 Timothy 2:1–2). Surely the "we" who are to pray must be Christians, and the "all men" must be everyone else. Again Paul writes, "Let us do good unto all men, especially unto...the household of faith" (Galatians 6:10). True believers must be the household of faith, again set in contrast to "all men."

Not only White and MacArthur, as we've seen, but other Calvinists adopt astonishing reasoning in order to escape the plain teaching of Scripture. Gary North explains that "Christ is indeed the Savior of all people prior to the day of judgment."[18] "Savior" in what way? North doesn't explain, nor can he. Calvin is no less irrational in his claim that Savior simply means that Christ shows "kindness" to all men.[19] Where is "Savior" ever used to signify "kindness"? And what kindness would bless in this life and predestine to torment for eternity as Calvinism teaches?

Calvin adds that by "Savior" the passage only means (for the non-elect) that Christ "guards and preserves."[20] Pink and Beck declare, somewhat like Calvin, that "Savior of all men" simply means that Christ is the "Preserver" of all men. *Temporarily*? Preserve from or to what?

In what way does God "preserve" those whom He has predestined to eternal damnation? And what could be meant by God's "kindness" to those He predestined before their birth to the Lake of Fire and from whom He withholds the salvation He *could* give them if He so desired? We are appalled at such outrageous efforts to escape the plain teaching of Scripture—and we are offended for our God at such boldness in perverting His Word and character!

Sproul explains: "**Savior of all men.** The general call to repentance and salvation is extended to all people" (emphasis in orginal).[21] How can salvation be "extended" to those for whom Christ did not die? And how can that supposed "call...to salvation" make Christ the Savior of those who are totally depraved and unable to respond to this call, and who have already been predestined to eternal damnation? Calvinism seems to pervert not only the Bible but men's minds, so that they are able to pretend that obvious contradictions make sense.

MacArthur goes into more depth in an attempt to remove the contradiction:

> Yet, the Gr. word translated "especially" must mean that all men enjoy God's salvation in some way like those who believe enjoy His salvation. The simple explanation is that God is the Savior of all men, only in a temporal sense, while of believers in an eternal sense...all men experience some earthly benefits from the goodness of God. Those benefits are: 1) common grace...God's goodness shown to all mankind universally...showering him with temporal blessings...; 2) compassion—the broken-hearted love of pity God shows to undeserving, unregenerate sinners...; 3) admonition... God constantly warns sinners of their fate, demonstrating the heart of a compassionate Creator who has no pleasure in the death of the wicked (Ezek 18:30-32; 33:11); 4) the gospel invitation—salvation in Christ is indiscriminately offered to all....[22]

Far from removing the scandalous contradiction, MacArthur only emphasizes it by accurately pointing out what the Bible teaches. That God has "broken-hearted love of pity" for and "constantly warns sinners of their fate" and that "salvation in Christ is indiscriminately offered to all" is the clear teaching of Scripture. But this is the very antithesis of Calvinism, which teaches that Christ died only for the elect and salvation is only for them.

MacArthur himself declares that "God chose only the elect out of the world"[23] and that "a corpse could no sooner come out of a grave and walk"[24] than for the non-elect even to hear the warnings and offers of salvation, let alone to respond in faith. Then how could salvation sincerely be "offered" to the non-elect? What deep holes Calvinists dig for themselves in trying to reconcile their theory with Scripture!

It is an insult to the God who *is love* to say that giving temporal blessings on this earth to those whom He predestined to eternal torment in the Lake of Fire before they were born is "God's salvation in some way..."! And it is a cruel mockery to tell those for whom Christ didn't even die that God is their Savior! Sproul and MacArthur very well know what Paul means by salvation—it isn't something temporary for this life only!

Grasping at Straws

The final verse listed previously, among those disproving Limited Atonement (though we could cite many others), is 1 John 4:14: "the Father sent the Son to be the Saviour of the world." This is one more scripture that White avoids (as does MacArthur in his study Bible). Instead, White focuses attention upon those passages that clearly refer to the blessings God has planned for His elect.

It is only to be expected that Paul and other inspired writers of Scripture would remind the redeemed that Christ died for them and that the Father delivered Christ to the cross for the sake of the elect. Such passages, however, as we have seen, do not in any way imply, much less declare, that Christ's death was *only* for them and not also for the sins of the whole world. If so, these passages would contradict the many others that declare in the plainest language that Christ did indeed die for all. But these are the only places to which the Calvinist can turn in positive support of his argument. Thus White tells us:

> The Father did not spare, or hold back, His very own Son, but delivered Him over *for us all* [Romans 8:32]. The word "delivered over" refers to the giving of the Son in sacrifice. The [same] Greek word is used in this context by Paul, as in Ephesians 5:2 (where Christ gives Himself up *for us*), and 5:25 (where Christ gives Himself *for the Church*). It is also used in Matthew 27:26 of the delivering up of Jesus to be crucified. The Father delivered over the Son to die upon the cross *for us*.... The Father gave the Son *in our place*, in the place of His *elect people*.
>
> In light of the tremendous price paid for our redemption in Christ, Paul then asks, "how will He (the Father) not also with Him (Christ) freely give us all things?" To whom is Paul speaking? God's elect. Surely these words could not be spoken of every single human for two reasons: Christ is not "given" to the person who endures God's wrath in eternity, and, God obviously does not give "all things" to those who spend eternity in hell...this is an empty passage [if it] says God *offers* all things, but very few actually *obtain* them. No, it is clear: God gives "all things" to those for whom He gave His Son as a sacrifice. That sacrifice was *for them;* it was made in their place. (Emphasis in original)[25]

Of course. Yet such passages as these have nothing to do with offering salvation to the world and, therefore, do not contradict the clear biblical teaching in many other places that Christ indeed died for all and that salvation is offered to all. That the elect should praise God for giving Christ to die for them (and that the Bible specifically reminds the elect of what Christ has done for them) does not in any way mean that Christ died *only* for them.

That Calvinists must grasp at such straws only exposes the bankruptcy of their theory. If the fact that the redeemed are grateful to Christ for dying for their sins proves that He died *only* for them, then the same reasoning would establish that Christ loved *only* Paul and died *only* for him. After all, Paul gratefully declares, "*I* am crucified with Christ...the Son of God, who loved *me*, and gave himself for *me*" (Galatians 2:20).

Hiding the Truth

MacArthur quotes an entire sermon that was preached in Scotland on June 7, 1724 by Calvinist pastor Thomas Boston on the text, 1 John 4:14. The following excerpt is sufficient to reveal the twisted thinking that is required to justify Calvinism in the face of scriptures that clearly declare His loving desire for all mankind to be saved:

> IT IS THE GREAT TRUTH AND TESTIMONY *of the gospel that the Father hath sent his Son Jesus Christ in the character of Savior of the world....* There is nothing wrong in the world but what there is a remedy to be found in Christ for [it].... The Savior of the world is certainly able to save the world; since He was sent of God in that character.... [*Character* but not actual...*able* to save but doesn't?]
>
> Our Lord Jesus is the *actual* Savior of the elect only, in whose room and stead only He died upon the cross.... Our Lord Jesus Christ is the *official* Savior, not of the elect only, but of the world of mankind indefinitely...God, looking on the ruined world of mankind, has constituted and appointed Jesus Christ His Son Savior of the world. Christ has Heaven's patent for this office, and wherever the gospel comes, He is held up as Savior by office.... So the matter lies here: in this official sense, Christ is Savior of the whole world...any of mankind's sinners may lay hold on this salvation.... [*Office...official sense...*all sinners may *lay hold* of what is *actual* for the elect alone? What perverse double talk!]
>
> If it were not so that Christ is Savior of the world, He could not warrantably be offered with His salvation to the world indefinitely; but to the elect only. If He were not commissioned to the office of Savior of all men, it would be no more appropriate to call all men to trust Him as Savior any more than He could be offered lawfully to fallen angels....
>
> How can you receive Him and lay hold of Him? Only by faith. Only by believing on Him, by being convinced of your sin and hopeless state, and by desiring to be saved from both. Believe Christ is *your* Savior by His Father's appointment; and so wholly trust on Him as a crucified Savior, for His whole salvation, on the ground of God's faithfulness in His Word. [The non-elect are

> supposed to *believe...lay hold of* and *receive* what God has reserved for the elect alone? What mockery!] (Emphasis in original)[26]

Here we see very clearly the schizophrenia into which the "moderate" Calvinist inevitably falls in his effort to distance himself from those he calls "hyper-Calvinists." The latter frankly admit that Calvinism teaches that God doesn't love everyone, never intended everyone to be saved, and has predestined all but the elect to eternal torment. Under the cover of much "moderate" verbiage, Thomas Boston tries to deny this fact—as does MacArthur, who quotes him for support. Yet, Boston admits that Christ is the "*actual* Savior of the elect only [and] died only for them." But to hide Calvinism's denial of "Saviour of all men," and its clear contradiction of God's love as the Bible presents it, Boston perversely declares that Christ has "the *character* of Savior of the world," has this *office* and is therefore the "*official* Savior of all mankind."

How Christ could be the *official* Savior of all and yet die for only the elect and never intend to save anyone else is not explained. Somehow, to assign to Christ the *character* of Savior of the world and to give him the title of *official* Savior of mankind allows Him not to provide salvation for everyone after all—and yet allows the Calvinist to pretend that no such limitation applies.

This is madness! And yet, this is the basis upon which the "moderate" Calvinist solemnly swears that he believes that God loves the whole world and wants the entire world to be saved and gave Christ to save all mankind. And we are supposed to believe that "moderates" mean what the Bible means, and what non-Calvinists mean by the same words!

Many non-Calvinists are deceived by such subterfuge, which moves them closer to becoming pseudo-Calvinists eventually. And the gospel? Of course, Boston cynically urges everyone to receive Christ by faith and says it is their own fault if they don't. He doesn't want to put an obstacle in the way of their faith by admitting that, according to Calvinism, faith is a gift of God given only to the elect after God has sovereignly regenerated them. But his reluctance to admit it, doesn't change the fact that this is the teaching of Calvinism. And tragically, learning this doctrine after the fact has been the undoing of many when they begin to examine themselves to determine whether they are actually among the elect.

God's Infinite Love Expressed through Paul

Limited Atonement cannot be supported from the Bible without avoiding many passages and adopting special interpretations for many others. Calvinists' arguments about the blood of Christ being wasted if shed for many who would not believe are specious. Then God wasted His time and the time and effort of His prophets who called, without success, upon millions of Jews for centuries to repent. From the cross Christ cried, "Father, forgive them," concerning those who were crucifying and mocking Him. Was He wasting His breath, since many if not most of those taunting and crucifying Him would never repent and thus not be forgiven? And how could He ask His Father to forgive them except on the basis of His blood, shed for their sin? But if that was shed only for the elect, how could Christ sincerely ask forgiveness for any non-elect?

Paul declares, in evident agony of soul, "I say the truth in Christ,... I have great heaviness and continual sorrow in my heart...for my brethren, my kinsmen according to the flesh" (Romans 9:1–3). He even wishes himself accursed of God if that would save the Jews. Surely, it is God's love for the lost that motivates Paul.

Yet Calvinism insists that God, who *is love,* has predestined billions to hell, while Paul, who surely is in touch with God, agonizes for their salvation! Is Paul more loving than God? Whence such love? Would it not be blasphemy for Paul to desire the salvation of those whom God does not desire to save? On the contrary, we are told that God desires "all men to be saved..."! Rob Zins writes to this author:

> Finally, you raise some philosophical problems with the *demand* of God that all men everywhere should repent and believe and the corresponding *will* of God which has determined that only some will be given the ability to do so. This is a difficult issue to face. But it is no more difficult to face than all men being condemned by the sin of one man, Adam. It is no more difficult to face than the fact of sin, corruption, evil and all other forms of sin *allowed* to continue when God could end them all.[27]

On the contrary, there is a huge difference between *allowing* men to sin and *causing* them to sin. There is a vast distinction between justly sentencing to eternal torment those who continue to defy God (rejecting the salvation He has graciously and lovingly provided for them) and in predestining them to the Lake of Fire without providing or offering any hope whatsoever.

As already noted, having given man the power of choice, God could end all evil only by destroying all men. Even "saved sinners" sometimes sin (1 John 1:9). But God is loving and longsuffering, calling upon men to repent, turn to Him, and receive the salvation He offers. Even though all sin and are justly condemned, God has provided salvation and made it available to all who will believe. He cannot force it upon anyone, however, without destroying man as a moral agent capable of loving and being loved. Yet Calvinism unbiblically claims that God *could save* everyone but refuses to do so because it is His "good pleasure" to damn multitudes.

Continually in Scripture, Christ and men of God from Moses to Paul expressed a fervent desire for the salvation of sinners. Obviously, not all are going to believe, yet the desire is sincerely expressed that they would do so. Calvinists change the straightforward language of such scriptures, even denying that God loves *all* in spite of the numerous clear statements that He does—while proposing a sham love that offers temporary "grace" to those it has predestined to eternal doom.

Yes, Christ in His prayer to the Father for His own says, "I pray not for the world" (John 17:9). That does not, however, nullify the Father's and Christ's love for the world, nor does it nullify the fact that He died for the sins of the whole world. This is not a prayer of salvation for the lost whom Christ repeatedly invited to come to Him, but a special prayer only for believers.

Unquestionably, there are difficult verses dealing with the whole subject of our salvation. They must be interpreted in the context of all of Scripture. In the final analysis, what we believe about God himself will determine our understanding of God's Holy Word.

The God of the Bible *is love*, His tender mercies are over all His works, He doesn't want anyone to be lost, and He so loved the world that He gave Christ to pay the penalty of sin for every man. Therefore, grace could not be irresistible or all would be saved—the fourth point of Calvinism, to which we now come.

---

1. James White, *The Potter's Freedom* (Amityville, NY: Calvary Press Publishing, 2000), 246–47.
2. Laurence M. Vance, *The Other Side of Calvinism* (Pensacola, FL: Vance Publications, rev. ed. 1999), 455–456.
3. Charles W. Bronson, *The Extent of the Atonement* (Pasadena, TX: Pilgrim Publications, 1992), 45.
4. Robert L. Dabney, *Systematic Theology* (Carlisle, PA: The Banner of Truth Trust, 2nd ed., 1985), 525.
5. Frank B. Beck, *The Five Points of Calvinism* (Lithgow, Australia: Covenanter Press, 2nd Australian ed. 1986), 53.
6. John A. Gill, *The Cause of God and Truth* (Paris, AR: The Baptist Standard Bearer, 1992), 58.
7. John Owen, *The Works of John Owen*, ed. William H. Goold (Carlisle, PA: The Banner of Truth Trust, 3rd prtg. 1978), X:365–66.
8. White, *Potter's*, 25.
9. Ibid., 135–36.
10. Ibid., 137.
11. Ibid., 143.
12. Owen, *Works*, X: 348–49.
13. Gill, *Cause*, (Paris, AR: The Baptist Standard Bearer, 1980), 62–63.
14. Quoted in Iain H. Murray, *The Life of John Murray* (Carlisle, PA: The Banner of Truth Trust, 1984), 93.
15. John Murray, *The Free Offer of the Gospel* (n. p., n. d.), 24.
16. St. Justin Martyr, Ch. 28 of *The First and Second Apologies, Ancient Christian Writers, No. 56* (New York: Paulist Press, 1997).
17. From England to Dave Hunt, dated September 8, 2000. On file.
18. Gary North, *Dominion and Common Grace* (Tyler, TX: Institute for Christian Economics, 1987), 44.
19. John Calvin, *Commentary on the Gospel of John, The Comprehensive John Calvin Collection* (Ages Digital Library, 1998) op. Cit., 3:245.
20. Ibid.
21. R. C. Sproul, General Editor, *New Geneva Study Bible* (Nashville, TN: Thomas Nelson Publishers, 1995), 1913.
22. John MacArthur, Author and General Editor, *The MacArthur Study Bible* (Nashville, TN: Word Publishing, 1997), 1867.
23. MacArthur, *Study Bible*, 1862.
24. John MacArthur Jr., *Saved Without A Doubt - MacArthur Study Series* (Colorado Springs: Chariot Victor Books, 1992), 58.
25. White, *Potter's*, 236–38.
26. John MacArthur, Jr., *The Love of God* (Dallas, TX: Word Publishing, 1996), 199-214.
27. Robert M. Zins to Dave Hunt, August 24, 2000. On file.

CHAPTER

22

Irresistible Grace

IN THE DOCTRINE of Irresistible Grace, we find once again the pervasive influence of Augustine. Boettner informs us, "This cardinal truth of Christianity [Irresistible Grace] was first clearly seen by Augustine."[1] Warfield says Augustine "recovered [it] for the Church."[2] Likewise, some Baptists agree that "Augustine may be regarded as the father of the soteriological system [called] 'Calvinism.'"[3] Sproul even says, "Augustinianism is presently called Calvinism or Reformed Theology."[4] Shedd declares:

> Augustine accounts for the fact that some men are renewed and some are not, by the unconditional decree (*decretum absolutum*), according to which God determines to select from the fallen mass of mankind (*massa perditionis*), the whole of whom are alike guilty and under condemnation, a portion upon whom he bestows renewing grace, and to leave the remainder to their own self-will and the operation of law and justice.[5]

Having once taught free will and that God desired to save all mankind,[6] Augustine later changed his view. Faith became something that God irresistibly bestowed upon the elect without their having believed anything or having made any decision or even having been aware that they were being regenerated.[7] By such reasoning, man (being by nature dead in sin) can't even *hear* the gospel—much less respond to the pleadings of Christ. Irresistible Grace is necessitated by this unbiblical premise, to which Calvinists cling in spite of the fact that our Lord calls to *all*, "Come unto me, *all* ye that labour and are heavy laden, and I will give you rest.... If *any* man thirst, let him come unto me, and drink" (Matthew 11:28; John 7:37), etc. Apparently *all*, even the spiritually dead, can hear and come and drink, as other passages make very clear. Dave Breese writes, "If grace were irresistible, one fails to understand even the reason for preaching the gospel...."[8] Certainly, it would be absurd for God to plead with men to repent and believe, if they *cannot* unless He irresistably causes them to do so.

The Serious Consequences of Sovereignty Misapplied

To recap Calvinism up to this point: because of Total Depravity, those whom God has unconditionally elected and predestined to eternal life and for whom alone Christ died are first sovereignly regenerated without faith, understanding, or even knowing it is happening to them. Thereafter (some would say simultaneously) the grace to believe on Christ as Savior and Lord is irresistibly imposed upon the newly regenerated elect, whom God from eternity past has predetermined to save, and they are given faith to believe on Christ. Piper says that man must first

> ...be born of God. Then, with the new nature of God, he immediately receives Christ. The two acts (regeneration and faith) are so closely connected that in experience we cannot distinguish them...new birth is the effect of irresistible grace...an act of sovereign creation....[9]

Irresistible Grace is essential in the Calvinist theory of salvation. No one can resist God's saving grace, irresistibly imposed upon those whom He has predestined to eternal life. As Piper says, "[T]here can be no salvation without the reality of irresistible grace. If we are dead in our sins, totally unable to submit to God, then we will never believe in Christ unless God overcomes our rebellion."[10]

Sadly, this doctrine, too—like all of TULIP—leads to a denial of God's love, mercy, and grace as revealed in Scripture. Piper declares, "God is sovereign and can overcome all resistance when he wills...irresistible grace refers to the sovereign work of God to overcome the rebellion of our hearts and bring us to faith in Christ so that we can be saved."[11] If that were true, God could have irresistibly imposed grace upon Adam and Eve and spared mankind the suffering and evil that resulted from their rebellion. Why didn't He? *What love is this?*

Does God actually love and have compassion not for the world (as the Bible says) but for a limited elect only (as Calvinists insist)? Piper says God chose to save the elect alone by irresistibly imposing His grace upon them and He predestined the remainder of mankind to eternal torment. Isn't such a scenario abhorrent to every conscience? And doesn't it malign the God of the Bible, whose "tender mercies are over all his works" (Psalm 145:9) and who "would have all men to be saved" (1 Timothy 2:4)?

If, as the Bible declares, God truly loves all and has given them the power of choice, then the lost are responsible for their own doom through willfully rejecting the salvation God lovingly and freely offers in Christ. Yet Hodge declares, "According to the Augustinian scheme, the non-elect have all the advantages and opportunities of securing their salvation...."[12] What advantages and opportunities for salvation do those have from whom God withholds the regeneration and irresistible grace without which Calvinists say no one can believe unto salvation, for whom Christ didn't die, and whom He predestined to eternal doom before they were born? This is mockery! Yet Sproul, Piper, MacArthur, and other leading "moderate" Calvinists of today persist in this obvious contradiction!

Furthermore, how can such persons be justly held accountable? Should a paraplegic be faulted for failing to become a world-class gymnast, or a man for failing to bear children or to breastfeed the children his wife bears? Absurd! Yet we are told that God's perfect justice operates in this fashion. Tragically, Calvinism's misrepresentation of God has caused many to turn away from God as from a monster.

Allegedly, God has created all men incapable of choosing to seek Him and of believing the gospel. The only hope is in God himself sovereignly regenerating the sinner—but He only does this for a limited elect and damns the rest in order to prove His sovereignty and justice. Such is the message of TULIP. Considering himself one of the elect, Piper finds great joy in TULIP and expresses no regrets for the predestined fate of those for whom this doctrine could only cause eternal anguish:

> We need to rethink our Reformed doctrine of salvation so that every limb and every branch in the tree is coursing with the sap of Augustinian delight. We need to make plain that *total depravity* is not just badness, but blindness...and *unconditional election* means that the completeness of our joy in Jesus was planned for us before we ever existed [never mind that eternal doom was also planned for others]; and that *limited atonement* is the assurance that indestructible joy in God is infallibly secured for us [the elect

> for whom alone Christ died] by the blood of the covenant; and *irresistible grace* is the commitment and power of God's love... the *perseverance of the saints* is the almighty work of God to keep us....[13] (Emphasis in original)

What Love, Compassion, and Grace Is This?

The elect alone enjoy the "Augustinian delight" of having been chosen to salvation. What delight is there for those who, before they came into existence, were already predestined to eternal torment? Nor can the Calvinist have the slightest sympathy for those whom God has, for His good pleasure, doomed eternally.

In contrast, consider the Bible's repeated assurance that God's love and grace toward all mankind are boundless and eternal. Here are just a few scriptures among many to that effect:

- For the LORD your God is gracious and merciful, and will not turn away his face from you, if ye return unto him. (2 Chronicles 30:9)
- Thou art a God ready to pardon, gracious and merciful, slow to anger, and of great kindness...for thou art a gracious and merciful God. (Nehemiah 9:17,31)
- But thou, O Lord, art a God full of compassion, and gracious, longsuffering, and plenteous in mercy and truth. (Psalm 86:15)
- The LORD is gracious and full of compassion. (Psalms 111:4; 112:4; 145:8, etc.)
- And rend your heart, and not your garments, and turn unto the LORD your God: for he is gracious and merciful.... (Joel 2:13)
- For I knew that thou art a gracious God, and merciful,...of great kindness. (Jonah 4:2)

Like hundreds of others, each of these scriptures is addressed to all of Israel, most of whom rejected God's grace. Never is there any hint that God's merciful compassion extends to less than all. "We love him because he first loved us" (1 John 4:19) declares that our love is in response to God's love. Nowhere does Scripture indicate that we love God, as Piper exults, because we are among a select group whom He predestined to salvation and sovereignly regenerated.

What about those allegedly not chosen to salvation, whom God never intended to save, for whom Christ did not die, and for whom there is no hope? Is it not sadistic to command *them* to love God? Yet this very first of the Ten Commandments, like all of them, is a command to all. How could the non-elect love God when God doesn't love them? Such teaching dishonors God and can only cause resentment toward Him.

Sadly, in reading scores of books by Calvinists, one finds much that extols God's sovereignty but almost nothing of His love. Packer admits, "In Reformation days as since, treatments of God's love in election were often...preempted by wrangles of an abstract sort about God's sovereignty in reprobation."[14] What else has Calvinism to offer!?

As Piper declares, "The doctrine of irresistible grace means that God is sovereign and can overcome all resistance when He wills."[15]

The Christian is to love others with God's love as his strength and example, for "love is of God" (1 John 4:7), "...the love of God is shed abroad in our hearts by the Holy Ghost, which is given unto us" (Romans 5:5), "Ye yourselves are taught of God to love one another" (1 Thessalonians 4:9).

God's love flowing through the believer has a practical effect: "But whoso hath this world's good, and seeth his brother have need, and shutteth up his bowels of compassion from him, how dwelleth the love of God in him?" (1 John 3:17). We are commanded to love our enemies and to do good to all, even to those who hate us (Matthew 5:44; Luke 6:35, etc.). How odd that God's love dwelling in us would unfailingly meet through us the needs of others—yet God himself sees billions in the direst of need and refuses to help them—indeed, damns those He could save. Surely this is not the God portrayed in the Bible!

A Longsuffering God

Sovereignty in Calvinism, as we have seen, is such that God is behind every emotion and act of every individual, causing each sin and causing each impulse of "love." Supposedly the heart of man is "made willing" in order to love God. But "made willing" is an oxymoron. One can be persuaded or convinced but not *made* willing, because the will must be willing in and of itself.

Again we are compelled to ask, "What love is this?" If Calvin's God can be said to love at all, it is with a love that allegedly can be imposed upon *anyone* and man's response is by that same imposition. But such is not the nature of love.

By contrast, in the Bible God's infinite love, grace, and mercy are demonstrated powerfully in His dealings with Israel. Moreover, the rejection and hatred against Him by disobedient Israel cause God's true love to shine all the brighter. Though himself a Calvinist, D. A. Carson expresses the contradiction of Calvinism clearly:

> The entire prophecy of Hosea is an astonishing portrayal of the love of God. Almighty God is likened to a betrayed and cuckolded husband. But the intensity of God's passion for the covenant nation comes to a climax in Hosea 11. "When Israel was a child," God declares, "I loved him, and out of Egypt I called my son: (11:1)...." But the more God loved Israel, the more they drifted away. God was the one who cared for them...the one who "led them with cords of love and human kindness" (11:4). Yet they... "Sacrificed to Baals and loved idolatry." So God promises judgment. They will return to "Egypt" and Assyria, i.e., to captivity and slavery, "because they refuse to repent" (11:5). Their cities will be destroyed (11:6).... Thus it sounds as if implacable judgment has been pronounced. But then it is almost as if God cannot endure the thought. In an agony of emotional intensity, God cries,
>
> "How can I give you up, Ephraim?
> How can I hand you over, Israel?...
> My heart is changed within me;
> all my compassion is aroused.
> I will not carry out my fierce anger....
> For I am God, and not man...
> I will not come in wrath....
> I will settle them in their homes,"
> declares the Lord.[16]

Yet if Calvinism be true, these pleadings are a sham. The elect don't need them, and the non-elect can't heed them. The totally depraved who are elected to salvation must be regenerated and infused with Irresistible Grace, while the rest of mankind are damned without remedy. Why pretend this love and concern when man has no choice and God can irresistably make anyone do whatever He wants?

Supposedly, to save only a select elect and to damn the rest was necessary to prove God's sovereignty and justice, and will eternally be to His greater glory. Obviously, however, God need not damn anyone in order to prove either His sovereignty or justice. If it is not a threat to God's sovereignty to save the elect, neither would it be for Him to save a million more, 100 million more—or more loving yet, to save all mankind.

Scores of Bible passages leave no doubt that God loves and desires to bless not just an elect who will be redeemed out of Israel, but all of Israel (and therefore all mankind as well), including those who refuse His love and gracious offer of blessing. God's very character is reflected in the commandments He gave to His chosen people. They were to restore even to an enemy his ox or ass that had wandered off (Exodus 23:4). Yet God himself won't give wandering mankind the kindness He commands that man give to beasts? Such teaching doesn't ring true to Scripture or to the conscience God has placed within each person (Romans 2:14–15).

A Foundational Misunderstanding

How does this grievous libel upon God's holy character arise among true Christians? Chiefly through an overemphasis upon the sovereignty of God to the exclusion of all else. It is imagined that if man can make a choice—if even with the wooing and winning of the Holy Spirit he can willingly, from his heart, respond to the love of God in the gospel—God's sovereignty has been nullified. Pink insists that if man could, by an act of his will, believe on and receive Christ, "then the Christian would have ground for boasting and self-glorying over *his* cooperation with the Spirit...."[17] Even Carson, in a book that has so much balanced truth to offer, falls into this error:

> If Christ died for all people with exactly the same intent...then surely it is impossible to avoid the conclusion that the *ultimate* distinguishing mark between those who are saved and those who are not is their own decision, their own will. That is surely ground for boasting.[18]

Only a Calvinist could fail to see the fallacy of this argument. Salvation is "the gift of God" (Romans 6:23). How could a gift be received without the ability to choose? The ability to say no—which is all Calvinism grants to the totally depraved—is meaningless without the accompanying ability to say yes.

Furthermore, how could accepting a gift provide a basis for boasting? If the gift is offered to all freely for the taking, those who receive the gift have no basis whatsoever for giving any credit to themselves. All has been provided in Christ, it is His work, to Him is all the glory, and it is absurd to suggest that the hopeless sinner who has been rescued without merit or effort on his part, but simply by receiving God's grace, could thereby boast of anything.

The Calvinist is so fearful that any response on man's part would challenge God's sovereignty that he invents ever more untenable arguments. Charles Hodge insists that "if efficacious grace is the exercise of almighty power it is irresistible."[19] Following the same reasoning, C. D. Cole writes, "The power of grace is the power of God. This makes it fitting to speak of irresistible grace. Surely we can speak of an irresistible God!"[20]

The flaw in such reasoning is elementary. Omnipotent power has nothing to do with grace or love or bestowing a gift. Indeed, just as God himself cannot force anyone to love Him (a coerced response is the opposite of love), so it would be the very opposite of grace to force any gift or benefit of "grace" upon anyone who did not want to receive it. To be a gift, it must be received willingly. *Power* has nothing to do with God's gracious, loving gift.

Beck, like so many Calvinists, echoes the same unsound argument: "I repeat, the Gospel of Christ *is* the power of God unto salvation! *Nothing* can stop it.... If God's grace can be *successfully* resisted, then *God* can be overcome...."[21] Such arguments are an embarrassment to sound reason. God's power in salvation refers to His ability to pay sin's penalty so that He can be just and yet justify sinners; it does not refer to His forcing salvation upon those who would otherwise reject it. Nowhere in Scripture is there such a concept. Always it is "whosoever *will* may come"—never the imposition of God's grace upon any unwilling person. Here we must agree with Arminius, who said, "Grace is not an omnipotent act of God, which cannot be resisted by the free-will of men."[22] It cannot be, or it would not be grace by very definition.

Yahweh sent His prophets generation after generation to plead for repentance from a people who steadfastly refused the offer of His grace. Why was that grace not "irresistible"? If God's omnipotent power can cause whomever He wills to receive the gift of His grace, then "gift" is no more gift, "grace" is no more grace, and man is not a morally responsible being.

In all of God's pleadings with Israel for her repentance and His promises of blessing if she would do so, there is *never* any suggestion that He could or would impose His grace upon her irresistibly. No Calvinist has ever given a biblical explanation for Irresistible Grace.

As only one of many examples, God cries, "Oh that my people had hearkened unto me...! I should soon have subdued their enemies, [and] have fed them also with the finest of the wheat" (Psalm 81:8–16). Instead, God's judgment fell upon Israel. Was judgment what He intended all along, and were His pleadings insincere? One is driven to such a conclusion by Calvinism—which undermines all of Scripture. Such pleadings with Israel, and with all mankind, are turned into a shameful pretense.

More Contradictions

This elementary but sincere misunderstanding of omnipotence is foundational to Calvinism. Tom Ross argues: "If every man possesses a free will that is powerful enough to resist the will of God in salvation, what would prevent that same man from choosing to resist the will of God in damnation at the great white throne of judgment?"[23] Ross is confused. Those gathered before the great white throne are there because they have repeatedly hardened themselves against God's love and gracious offer of salvation. Now they face His judgment. Grace is *offered* in love; judgment is *imposed* by justice and power.

Can Ross see no difference between salvation offered in God's grace, and judgment imposed by His justice? Can he be serious in suggesting that because the former could be rejected so could the latter? Not all Calvinists agree. Thus Carson writes that "God's unconditioned sovereignty and the responsibility of human beings are mutually compatible."[24]

We do not minimize God's sovereignty—but that must be balanced with His other attributes. Carson declares, "I do not think that what the Bible says about the love of God can long survive at the forefront of our thinking if it is abstracted from the sovereignty of God, the holiness of God, the wrath of God, the providence of God, or the personhood of God—to mention only a few nonnegotiable elements of basic Christianity."[25]

God's absolute sovereignty did not prevent rebellion by Satan and Adam, man's continual disobedience of the Ten Commandments, and his straying like a lost sheep in rejection of God's will. Much less does sovereignty mean that God is behind it all, *causing* every sin—as Calvinism requires. This error gave rise to the belief that grace must be irresistible.

Every conscience bears witness to Carson's un-Calvinistic statement that "The Scriptures do not mock us when they say, 'Like as a father pitieth his children, so the Lord pitieth them that fear him.'"[26] Yet Carson remains a Calvinist while contradicting in many ways what most of his colleagues believe.

Some Calvinists attempt to escape the horrifying consequences of their doctrine by suggesting that predestination unto damnation, and God's invitation to all to believe, are both true even though they contradict each other. Supposedly, we just don't know how to reconcile these apparent conflicts and should not attempt to, for all will be revealed in eternity.

The truth is that Calvinism itself has created this particular "mystery." Although there is much that finite beings cannot understand, we have been given a conscience with a keen sense of right and wrong, and of justice and injustice. God calls us to reason with Him about these things. He goes to great lengths to explain His justice and love, and has given even to unregenerate man the capacity to understand the gospel, and to believe in Christ or to reject Him. Calvinism, as we have repeatedly seen, is repugnant to the God-given conscience.

Irresistible Grace and the Gospel

Most Calvinists attempt to honor Christ's command to "preach the gospel to every creature." Yet it is difficult to uphold the importance of the gospel when the unregenerate are unable to believe it, and the elect are regenerated without it, then sovereignly and supernaturally given faith to believe. Seemingly unaware that he is contradicting the very "Reformed Theology" of which he is a major defender, R. C. Sproul, Jr., earnestly exhorts readers, "If we believe in the power of the gospel to effect our salvation, we must believe in the power of the Gospel preached to bring in His elect."[27] But Calvinism's elect have been predestined from a past eternity, and it is God's sovereign act of regeneration, *not the gospel,* which alone can "bring in His elect."

Given TULIP, how can the gospel effect the salvation of anyone? The unregenerate, elect or non-elect, cannot respond to or believe it. Nor would it benefit the non-elect to understand, because they have been predestined to eternal damnation from the beginning.

The elect are regenerated without the gospel and only then can they believe it. But once regenerated, they have already been saved unless one can be sovereignly regenerated (i.e., born again by the Spirit) and still not be saved. Having been regenerated without the gospel, subsequently hearing and believing it cannot save them, since they have already been saved in their regeneration.

Sproul is being faithful to God's Word, which clearly teaches that the gospel "is the power of God unto salvation to every one that believeth" it

(Romans 1:16). In being true to the Bible, however, he must ignore Calvinism's teaching that one cannot believe the gospel until one has been regenerated. So he talks as though the gospel, as the Bible says, must be believed for salvation—but he cannot truly believe this, or he would have to abandon Calvinism.

Sproul spends an entire book rightly rebuking the signers of "Evangelicals and Catholics Together: The Christian Mission in the Third Millennium." He argues correctly that "Justification by faith alone is essential to the gospel. The gospel is essential to Christianity and to salvation."[28] He ends the book with this un-Calvinistic quote from John Calvin: "Let it therefore remain settled...that we are justified by faith alone."[29]

But Sproul believes there is no faith until regeneration, so the new birth into God's family as a child of God leaves one still unjustified! Furthermore, since faith in Christ through the gospel is essential to salvation, we have the elect born again as children of God before they are saved.

When it deals with the gospel, Calvinism becomes very confusing. How can the gospel preached "bring in His elect" as Sproul declares? Even the elect can't believe it until they have been regenerated—and Calvinism is firm that regeneration is the way for God to "bring in His elect." Was it not the sovereign act of regeneration that brought the elect into the fold? Then the gospel was not involved, and Sproul is offering false motivation for preaching it.

The Calvinist apparently has two compartments in his mind: in one, he holds to Calvinism's dogmas faithfully, and in the other, he holds to the teaching of Scripture. It can't be easy or comfortable for the conscience. The fact that faith in Christ through the gospel precedes the new birth/salvation (in contradiction to the doctrine of regeneration before faith) is undeniably taught in scores of passages such as the following:

- The devil...taketh away the word out of their hearts, lest they should believe and be saved. (Luke 8:12)
- Believe on the Lord Jesus Christ, and thou shalt be saved.... (Acts 16:31)
- That if thou shalt...believe in thine heart...thou shalt be saved. (Romans 10:9)
- In whom [Christ] also ye trusted, *after* that ye heard the word of truth, the *gospel* of your *salvation*: in whom also *after that ye believed*, ye were sealed with that holy Spirit of promise....(Ephesians 1:13; emphasis added)

A Classic Oxymoron

On its very face, the phrase "Irresistible Grace" presents another irreconcilable contradiction. As far as grace is concerned, there are two possible meanings for the word "irresistible": irresistible in its appeal to all mankind; or irresistible in its imposition upon the elect alone. The former is, of course, vigorously denied by Calvinism. That system is founded upon the belief that grace and the gospel have no appeal at all to the totally depraved, spiritually dead sons and daughters of Adam. Nor does grace have any appeal even to the elect until they have been sovereignly regenerated.

Only one possibility remains: that grace is irresistibly imposed upon a chosen elect—and this is the teaching of Calvinism. But to impose anything upon anyone is the very antithesis of grace. Forcing even a most valuable and desirable gift upon someone who does not wish to receive it would be ungracious in the extreme. Thus the phrase "Irresistible Grace" is another oxymoron. Yet this is an integral element without which the other four points of TULIP collapse.

Moreover, this fourth point of TULIP, like the first three, confronts us with one more phrase unknown to Scripture—so how can it possibly be biblical? The word "irresistible" does not appear in the Bible. The wonderful grace of God, however, is one of the most precious truths presented in His Word. The word "grace" occurs 170 times in 159 verses. And *never* in *any* mention of it is there a suggestion that grace is irresistibly imposed. Always the inference is that God's grace is given freely and willingly received.

Consider a few examples:

- But Noah found grace in the eyes of the LORD. (Genesis 6:8)
- The LORD will give grace and glory.... (Psalm 84:11)
- By whom we have received grace and apostleship.... (Romans 1:5)
- Having then gifts differing according to the grace that is given to us.... (Romans 12:6)
- I thank my God...for the grace of God which is given you by Jesus Christ.... (1 Corinthians 1:4)
- Unto me, who am less than the least of all saints, is this grace given.... (Ephesians 3:8)

- But unto every one of us is given grace according to the measure of the gift of Christ. (Ephesians 4:7)
- Likewise, ye husbands...giving honour unto the wife...as being heirs together of the grace of life.... (1 Peter 3:7)

What about other scriptures, such as "And I will pour upon the house of David, and upon the inhabitants of Jerusalem, the spirit of grace and supplications..." (Zechariah 12:10); "And with great power gave the apostles witness...and great grace was upon them" (Acts 4:33); "And God is able to make all grace abound toward you..." (2 Corinthians 9:8), etc.? Although the indication seems stronger that God is sovereignly granting grace, there is no indication that God's grace is irresistibly imposed upon anyone. Each must, of his own will, choose to receive it.

The "Two Conflicting Wills" Theory Revisited

Many Calvinists, in upholding that system, make astonishing statements such as the following: "Because God's will is always done, the will of every creature must conform to the sovereign will of God."[30] Logically, then, *every thought, word, and deed* of mankind (including the most heinous wickedness) has been willed by God. Vance comments, "That fornication and unthankfulness are actually part of God's 'secret will' should come as no surprise in light of...the Calvinistic concept of God's all-encompassing decree."[31] But does not everyone's God-given conscience shrink in horror from this doctrine that all evil is according to God's will? Pink even rejects the distinction sometimes made between God's "perfect will" and His "permissive will," because "God only permits that which is according to His will."[32] He thus contradicts MacArthur's view of 1 Timothy 2:4 that God has two conflicting wills—a view with which Sproul, Piper, and other leading Calvinists are in full agreement.

Calvinists struggle to reconcile a sovereignty that causes every sinful thought, word, and deed and damns billions, with the repeated biblical assurances of God's goodness, compassion, and love for all. Much like MacArthur, John Piper proposes an unbiblical and irrational solution—the idea that God has *two wills* that contradict one another yet are not in conflict:

> Therefore I affirm with John 3:16 and 1 Timothy 2:4 that God loves the world with a deep compassion that desires the salvation

> of all men. Yet I also affirm that God has chosen from before the foundation of the world whom he will save from sin. Since not all people are saved we must choose whether we believe (with the Arminians) that God's will to save all people is restrained by his commitment to human self-determination or whether we believe (with the Calvinists) that God's will to save all people is restrained by his commitment to the glorification of his sovereign grace (Ephesians 1:6, 12, 14; Romans 9:22–23).... This book aims to show that the sovereignty of God's grace in salvation is taught in Scripture. My contribution has simply been to show that God's will for all people to be saved is not at odds with the sovereignty of God's grace in election. That is, my answer to the question about what restrains God's will to save all people is his supreme commitment to uphold and display the full range of his glory through the sovereign demonstration of his wrath and mercy for the enjoyment of his elect and believing people from every tribe and tongue and nation.[33]

Once again, we have an unblushing contradiction from Piper. In His great love and compassion, God "desires the salvation of all men." Yet to "display the full range of his glory" he doesn't save them all—and this in spite of the insistence that He could save all if he so desired. Let us get this straight: Piper's God desires the salvation of all men; in His sovereign imposition of irresistible grace, he *could* save all but doesn't in order to demonstrate his wrath.

Here we have the clearest contradiction possible. How can the Calvinist escape? Ah, Piper has found an ingenious way to affirm that God loves and really desires to save even those whom He has predestined to damnation from eternity past: God has *two wills* which, though they contradict each other, are really in secret agreement. Are we being led into madness where words have lost their meaning?

We are asked to believe that it is no contradiction for God to contradict himself if it furthers the "sovereign demonstration of his wrath and mercy"! Reason fails Piper once again. Damning billions would certainly demonstrate God's wrath—but how would that glorify Him in his mercy? And even if that somehow were the case, there is no way to reconcile reprobation with the clear expressions of God's love and desire for the salvation of all—expressions which Piper uncalvinistically claims to accept at face value.

Piper has yet another problem. God does not contradict Himself. Therefore, Piper must reconcile what he calls "two wills" of God to show that they are in agreement, even though they directly disagree with and invalidate each other. And this he fails to do, because it is impossible. A contradiction is a contradiction, and there is no honest way that two contradictory propositions can be massaged into agreement.

Piper is following Calvin, who fell into the same misconception. He said, "This is His wondrous love towards the human race, that He desires all men to be saved, and is prepared to bring even the perishing to safety.... God is prepared to receive all men into repentance, so that none may perish." [34] Could this be the same John Calvin who declared so often and so clearly that, from a past eternity, God had predestined billions to damnation? Is Calvin's God a schizophrenic?

Very much like Piper's "two wills," Calvin fell back upon a "secret will": "No mention is made here of the secret decree of God by which the wicked are doomed to their own ruin."[35] Sproul attempts to play the same broken string. Bryson responds reasonably and succinctly:

> Thus, Calvinists are in the rather awkward position of claiming to make a valid offer of salvation (to the unelect)...while denying [that] the only provision (i.e., Christ's death) of salvation is for the unelect...[and saying] that the unelect cannot possibly believe [the gospel].... To add insult to injury, they are claiming this is just the way God (from all eternity) wanted it to be.[36]

Calvinists claim that man's will and actions cannot be in conflict with God's will, for that would make man greater than God. That unbiblical position concerning God's sovereignty drives them to propose that the two wills in conflict are not God's will and man's will, but two wills of God's design. In other words, they claim that the battle is not between God and man, as the Bible says, but rather God against himself, as Calvinism insists. God is being misrepresented.

---

1. Loraine Boettner, *The Reformed Doctrine of Predestination* (Phillipsburg, NJ: Presbyterian and Reformed Publishing Co., 1932), 365.
2. Benjamin B. Warfield, *Calvin and Augustine*, ed. Samuel G. Craig (Phillipsburg, NJ: Presbyterian and Reformed Publishing Co., 1956), 321.
3. Kenneth H. Good, *Are Baptists Calvinists?* (Rochester, NY: Backus Book Publishers, 1988), 49.
4. R. C. Sproul, *The Holiness of God* (Carol Stream, IL: Tyndale House Publishers, Inc., 1993 ed.), 273.
5. William G. T. Shedd, *A History of Christian Doctrine* (New York: Charles Scribner and Co., 3rd ed. 1865), 70.
6. Augustine, *On the Spirit and the Letter.* In Laurence M. Vance, *The Other Side of Calvinism* (Pensacola, FL: Vance Publications, rev. ed. 1999), 57.
7. Augustine, *On the Predestination of the Saints*, op. cit., 7,8,16.
8. Dave Breese, "The Five Points of Calvinism" (self-published paper, n. d.), 3.
9. John Piper and Pastoral Staff, "TULIP: What We Believe about the Five Points of Calvinism: Position Paper of the Pastoral Staff" (Minneapolis, MN: Desiring God Ministries, 1997), 12.
10. Piper and Staff, "TULIP," 9.
11. Ibid.
12. Charles Hodge, *Systematic Theology* (Grand Rapids, MI: Wm B. Eerdmans Publishing Co., 1986), 2:643.
13. John Piper, *The Legacy of Sovereign Joy: God's Triumphant Grace in the Lives of Augustine, Luther, and Calvin* (Wheaton, IL: Crossway Books, 2000), 73.
14. J. I. Packer, "The Love of God: Universal and Particular," in *Still Sovereign,* ed. Thomas R. Schreiner and Bruce A. Ware (Grand Rapids, MI: Baker Books, 2000) 281.
15. Piper and Staff, "TULIP," 9.
16. D. A. Carson, *The Difficult Doctrine of the Love of God* (Wheaton, IL: Crossway Books, 2000), 46–47.
17. Arthur W. Pink, *The Sovereignty of God* (Grand Rapids, MI: Baker Book House, 2nd prtg. 1986), 128.
18. Carson, *Difficult*, 78–79.
19. Hodge, *Systematic*, II:687.
20. C. D. Cole, *Definitions of Doctrines* (Swengle, PA: Bible Truth Depot, n. d.), 84.
21. Frank B. Beck, *The Five Points of Calvinism* (Lithgow, Australia: Covenanter Press, 2nd Australian ed. 1986), 40.
22. Jacobus Arminius, *The Works of James Arminius*, trans. James and William Nichols (Grand Rapids, MI: Baker Book House, 1986), I:525.
23. Tom Ross, *Abandoned Truth: The Doctrines of Grace* (Providence Baptist Church, 1991), 56.
24. Carson, *Difficult*, 52.
25. Ibid., 11.
26. Ibid., 29.
27. R. C. Sproul, Jr., "The Authentic Message," *Tabletalk*, Ligonier Ministries, Inc., June 2001, 7.

28. R. C. Sproul, *Faith Alone: The Evangelical Doctrine of Justification* (Grand Rapids, MI: Baker Books, 1995), 19, and throughout the book.

29. Ibid., 192; citing Calvin, *The Epistles of Paul the Apostle* (a comment on Galatians 2:16), 39.

30. Steven R. Houck, *The Bondage of the Will* (Lansing, IL: Peace Protestant Reformed Church, n. d.), 3.

31. Laurence M. Vance, *The Other Side of Calvinism* (Pensacola, FL: Vance Publications, rev. ed. 1999), 481.

32. Pink, *Sovereignty*, 243.

33. John Piper, "Are There Two Wills In God?" In *Still Sovereign*, ed. Thomas R. Schreiner and Bruce A. Ware (Grand Rapids, MI: Baker Books, 2000), 130–31.

34. John Calvin, *Calvin's New Testament Commentaries* (Grand Rapids, MI: Wm B. Eerdmans Publishing Co., 1994), 12, 364.

35. Ibid.

36. George L. Bryson, *The Five Points of Calvinism: Weighed and Found Wanting* (Costa Mesa, CA: The Word For Today, 1996), 56.

CHAPTER 23

The Calvinist's Irresolvable Problem

EVEN CHRISTIANS at times disobey God. Consider the following: "For this is the will of God, even your sanctification..." (1 Thessalonians 4:3); "In every thing give thanks: for this is the will of God..." (1 Thessalonians 5:18). What Christian fulfills God's will by always living a perfectly sanctified life and giving thanks to God "in everything"?

God's will is violated continually by unbelievers disobeying the Law, and by believers failing to live as they should. "These things write I unto you, that ye sin not" (1 John 2:1) expresses the will of God for every Christian. Yet John also declares that no Christian fully lives up to this desire of God: "If we say that we have no sin, we deceive ourselves.... If we say that we have not sinned, we make him a liar, and his truth is not in us" (1 John 1:8,10).

Even God's grace requires faith and obedience. Many scriptures make it clear that while grace is unmerited, we must accept and respond to it. Paul declares, "I laboured more abundantly than they all: yet not I, but the grace of God which was with me" (1 Corinthians 15:10); "We...beseech you also that ye receive not the grace of God in vain" (2 Corinthians 6:1); "My son, be strong in the grace that is in Christ Jesus" (2 Timothy 2:1); "Let us therefore come boldly unto the throne of grace, that we may obtain mercy..." (Hebrews 4:16). Clearly Paul is declaring that God's grace is *not* irresistible but must be wedded to human will and effort.

Numerous scriptures teach that the reception of God's grace is not through irresistible imposition by an overwhelming, omnipotent sovereignty without willingness on man's part. One could even fail to accept (or accept in part and not fully cooperate with) God's grace. God sincerely desired to bless Israel. Nevertheless, she refused His grace and placed herself instead under His judgment by her rebellion and idolatry.

God's desire for Israel, as for all men, was good: "For I know the thoughts that I think toward you, saith the Lord, thoughts of peace, and not of evil..." (Jeremiah 29:11). Yet much evil befell Israel. Why? Because the blessings of His grace were contingent upon Israel's faith and obedience. By her disobedience, she reaped God's wrath.

We are even told that they "limited the Holy One of Israel" (Psalm 78:41). Think of that—limiting the omnipotent, sovereign God, which Calvinists say is impossible! Indeed, the rabbis "rejected the counsel of God against themselves" (Luke 7:30)—but there is no hint that they thereby annulled God's sovereignty or gained control over God.

The Christian life and victory is not only by sovereign power, but the believers' faith and obedience as "labourers together with God" (1 Corinthians 3:9) are essential: "Whereunto I also labour, striving according to his working, which worketh in me mightily" (Colossians 1:29); "work out your own salvation with fear and trembling. For it is God which worketh in you both to will and to do of his good pleasure" (Philippians 2:12–13).

God truly and powerfully works within the believer, and we can do nothing but by the leading and empowering of the Holy Spirit. At the same time, however, we must devote ourselves willingly to the work of God through us. Most Calvinists admit this cooperative effort when it comes to living the Christian life, but insist that there can be no such willingness in believing the gospel and accepting Christ.

Again we point out how unreasonable it is—that, if He so desired, God could sovereignly cause every totally depraved sinner to turn to him, yet His sovereignty seems to lose its Calvinistic power when it comes to causing Christians to live in victory and holiness and fruitfulness. It is certainly clear that once God has regenerated the elect, they do not all live to His glory as fully as they might and as His perfect will for them, as expressed in Scripture, desires.

Surely, God's desire for Christians goes far beyond their experience. If not, we would have to admit that the shallow and unfruitful lives of so many genuine believers are exactly what God desires for them. We ask again, what is the meaning of rewards and the Judgment Seat of Christ if each Christian's every thought, word, and deed is exactly as God wills? And if that is the case, why aren't Christians perfect? Surely the continual disobedience, both of unbelievers and believers, proves that God's grace is not "irresistible." Nor does man's disobedience diminish God's sovereignty in the least. Obviously, freedom of choice itself is part of God's plan.

Yet the idea of Irresistible Grace is predicated upon the belief that a human ability to accept or to reject the gospel would deny God's sovereignty. We have shown that reasoning to be fallacious and that the very concept is unbiblical and irrational.

In spite of its doctrine of "irresistible" grace, Calvinism denies that grace is "imposed" by God upon the elect. At this point, Calvinists begin to contradict themselves further. Sproul, for example, concedes that Irresistible Grace can be resisted but at the same time declares that "it is invincible."[1] We are left to wonder how something invincible can be resisted. Most Calvinists agree that Irresistible Grace produces an "effectual call" that is "ultimately irresistible." Vance quotes a number of Calvinists to this effect and explains that this concept is "derived from Chapter X in the Westminster Confession of Faith."[2]

Sproul says that for the elect, God takes away all that caused them in their total depravity to resist Him. The great problem is how to get a totally depraved man saved—a man who cannot even hear the gospel, much less understand and believe it. Remember, the Synod of Dort describes this process as not taking away man's "will and its properties" but "sweetly and powerfully bend[ing] it...."[3] But to "bend" the will of the totally depraved (rather than to destroy and create a new one) means that the original will must have yielded to God. Moreover, what does it mean to "bend" the will, and how is that done "sweetly" and at the same time "powerfully"? And if the human will is not destroyed and something else not put in its place, then it cannot be denied that the human will does, after all, decide and choose to be bent.

This is a knotty problem! After declaring that totally depraved man's will and its properties of self-determination are not taken away, Dort laid out its complaint against Arminians: "The true doctrine having been explained, the Synod *rejects* the errors of those: 1. Who teach...; 2. Who teach...;" and so forth, through nine numbered paragraphs. Much of what is listed as being rejected was not believed by the Arminians, nor is it believed by most non-Calvinists today.

Paragraph 8 wrestled with the difficult problem created by Calvinism itself: How can man's will be allowed any part in receiving Christ, when it is totally depraved, man is spiritually dead, and God's sovereignty must cause all, including sin, and salvation through faith in Christ? Here is the alleged non-Calvinist error denounced by that paragraph:

> 8. Who teach: That God in the regeneration of man does not use such powers of his omnipotence as potently and infallibly bend man's will to faith and conversion; but that all the works of grace having been accomplished, which God employs to convert man, man may yet so resist God and the Holy Spirit, when God intends man's regeneration and wills to regenerate him, and indeed that man often does so resist that he prevents entirely his regeneration, and that it therefore remains in man's power to be regenerated or not.[4]

Of course, it is not in man's power to be regenerated, nor would the rankest Arminian suggest that it was. Regeneration is entirely God's work—but it is also a *gift* that the recipient must willingly *receive*: "the gift of God is eternal life through Jesus Christ our Lord" (Romans 6:23). That man can accept or reject the offered salvation, however, does not mean that it is in his power to be regenerated.

While Ben Rose insists that "God does not bring anyone into the kingdom against his or her will,"[5] yet that statement is clearly contradicted by the phrase "irresistible grace." If, under the conviction of the Holy Spirit, man could make a genuine choice to believe and to receive, there would be no need for grace to be "irresistible." The Westminster Confession of Faith continues the double-talk:

> All those whom God hath predestinated unto life, and those alone, he is pleased...effectually to call...to grace and salvation by Jesus Christ; enlightening their minds spiritually and savingly to understand the things of God...renewing their wills, and, by his almighty power...effectually drawing them to Jesus Christ: yet so as they come most freely, being made willing by his grace.[6]

No Explaining Away

There is no escaping the mind and will. Even Calvinism's sovereign regeneration (supposedly without faith or consent) does not create a new man out of nothing—but it *regenerates* him. Consequently, Westminster must use phrases such as "enlightening their minds." Remember, this was allegedly a totally depraved sinner who could choose only evil. Yet his mind must have the inherent ability to understand truth, or how could it be "enlightened"?

And what about "renewing their wills"? Could that mean restoring some capacity once held but lost? Not if man is totally depraved. When was the will ever that to which it is *renewed* (i.e., restored) by this regeneration and enlightenment? "Renewal" does not fit Calvinism. How can those born spiritually dead be renewed to what they never were? The very language contradicts the foundational beliefs of Calvinism—but there are no other words available.

Of course, we need to be enlightened. How that happens is the question. For the Calvinist, enlightenment is irresistibly imposed upon a totally depraved sinner who has no capacity to be enlightened and never experienced any such state of mind or will to which he could be renewed. Therefore the process cannot be described as "enlightenment" or "renewal"—but Westminster can find no expression, either in Scripture or in language itself, to "explain" this false belief.

Men are without excuse, because all understand the law of God written in every conscience and fear the consequences of disobedience. Thus man is morally responsible to God. Biblically, the problem is not that man *cannot understand* the gospel or that he *cannot submit* to God, but that he *will not*: "Ye *will not* come to me, that ye might have life" (John 5:40); "Because...when they knew God, they glorified him not as God, neither were thankful; but became vain in their imaginations, and their foolish heart was darkened. Professing themselves to be wise, they became fools..." (Romans 1:21-22).

For that stubborn self-will to change, the Holy Spirit must, of course, work in heart and mind. But it is not an *irresistible* work upon hopelessly blind and dead creatures, but a persuasion with the truth of those who know what they are doing and could believe on Christ if they were willing. Scores of scriptures make it clear that those who are "willing and obedient" (Isaiah 1:19) receive God's salvation; that "whosoever will [may] take of the water of life freely" (Revelation 22:17). All are loved by God, sought and persuaded by God, and all have the choice either to accept or reject the salvation He offers. That fact is what makes eternal judgment just—and so tragic.

What Does Christ Teach?

Responding to the criticism of the Pharisees that He received sinners and ate with them, Christ gave the illustrations of the lost sheep, lost coin, and prodigal son to show that humans seek and have great joy in finding the lost, whether sheep, coin, or wayward son (Luke 15:1–32). It seems equally clear that these illustrations are intended also to tell us of God's love and joy in seeking and finding the lost. The vignettes Christ gives do not seem to represent true children of God who have wandered away and are being brought back by God but rather examples of lost mankind.

In telling the prodigal's story, Christ uses language that contradicts Calvinism. The "totally depraved" prodigal realizes his situation, comes to a decision, makes a choice, and acts upon it by his will: "And when he came to himself, he said.... I will arise and go to my father, and will say unto him, Father, I have sinned against heaven, and before thee...." Christ does not say that the prodigal, being totally incapable of understanding his situation, or of repenting and returning to the father, was irresistibly drawn by the father.

Although the prodigal "was dead," and was "lost" (Luke 15:24), that did not prevent him from being moved in his conscience and choosing to return of his own volition to the father. If the prodigal does not represent the unregenerate lost sinner dead in sin whom God welcomes in love, then the Calvinist must admit that salvation can be lost—which neither side believes.

Christ declared that all men are to act like the good Samaritan toward everyone in need (Luke 10:30–37); we are to love even our enemies and do good to those who hate us (Matthew 5:44). If this is the standard God sets for mankind, would He not behave even more benevolently toward all? If Paul did not want a single Jew to go to hell and was in continual agony of soul for their salvation, willing even to be accursed of God if that would save his "kinsmen according to the flesh" (Romans 9:1–3), would God, who must have put this selfless love in Paul's heart, be any *less* loving and concerned for lost humanity on its way to hell? Surely not the God of the Bible!

What About God's Love?

It is simply impossible to maintain that a God who damns those He *could* save (much less who takes pleasure in so doing!) is merciful and full of love. How then can the Calvinist escape the charge that he misrepresents the God of the Bible? Sovereignty can't excuse or justify callous neglect on God's part to rescue those He could save. That God has the right to damn everyone does not make it loving and merciful.

Our disagreement with Calvinism is not over God's sovereignty, which is biblical. The issue is whether God loves all without partiality and desires all to be saved. Unquestionably, Calvinism denies such love, no matter how the "moderate" Calvinists try to explain that fact away. Yet the Bible repeatedly declares God's love to all and His desire that all should be saved and none should be lost.

The God of the Bible is surely even more loving than He expects Christians to be. We may be certain, as Spurgeon said, that just as we desire the salvation of all, so that is God's desire—as Scripture so often and plainly declares. To say that the God who is not willing for any to perish provides salvation for only a limited number of elect does violence to Scripture and maligns God's character.

If grace is irresistible, why doesn't God, who is love and full of compassion, impose it upon everyone? But grace *cannot* be irresistible. God cannot *force* anyone to believe in Christ, much less to love Him. All who would be in God's presence for eternity must love Him sincerely, and love requires a genuine choice.

The Bible declares that multitudes will spend eternity in the Lake of Fire. Why? There are only two possible reasons: either God causes multitudes of men to go to hell because He doesn't love and has no desire to save them—or they willfully reject the salvation He offers. Nor can it be both, or God's will would coincide with that of rebels.

Was Paul Wrong in His Passionate Concern?

It seems reasonable that Paul, who was inspired of the Holy Spirit to provide the definitive teaching concerning foreknowledge, election/predestination, sovereignty, and salvation by grace through faith, would know these subjects even better than Calvin. Could Paul have been wrong in his continual agony for the salvation of Israel (and indeed of all men)? Yet if God himself, as Calvin sincerely believed, is not concerned over the lost (and how could He be, having predestined their eternal torment?), then we must conclude that Paul was badly out of touch with the Holy Spirit for being in continual, prayerful distress for the salvation of the Jews. Paul misunderstood the scriptures which he was inspired to write, but Calvin interpreted them correctly?!

Paul confesses, "Brethren, my heart's desire and prayer to God for Israel is, that they might be saved" (Romans 10:1). Surely he cannot be praying for Calvin's elect, for their salvation has been predestined from eternity past. Irresistible Grace will make certain they are saved, so there is no need to pray for them. And how could Paul dare to express deep concern for those whom God in His sovereignty has willed to be damned, and for whom God has no concern and Christ did not die—if that were indeed the case?

It is troubling that we hear no concern from Calvinists that so many will spend eternity in hell. That attitude, however, is perfectly consistent with their beliefs. Why should one be disappointed at that which is God's sovereign good pleasure? And wouldn't it be rebellion to be concerned for the salvation of those whom God refuses to save?

What God Is This?

Calvinism's God does not desire to save all mankind, and Calvinism's Christ had no intention of dying for the sins of all on the cross. At this point, we reach our ultimate objection to this system of religion, which young Calvin learned from Augustine and further developed and passed along to millions who follow it today. This doctrine is repugnant even to unbelievers, because it contradicts the conscience and the sense of obligation and fairness God has implanted in every one of us. Yet a Calvinist pastor insists, "To suggest that Christ came *actually* to save all men is 'universalism'...a heresy openly promoted by the ecumenical churches."[7] On the contrary, universalism teaches that all men will ultimately *be saved*, not that salvation is *offered* to all.

A Calvinist editor in England wrote to me earnestly, "The plain truth is that God does *not* wish to save all men. If He did, then He would save them... [why don't "moderates" admit this?]. If God wanted to save all men, why did He prevent Paul from preaching the gospel in certain areas?"[8] Such an argument makes sense only to a Calvinist, for whom salvation is not something man receives by faith in his heart but is imposed upon him contrary to his natural will and cannot be resisted. Hence the necessity for Irresistible Grace.

But what does this have to do with God preventing Paul from preaching in certain places? There could have been many reasons for redirecting Paul. Certainly he could not preach everywhere. Again Calvinists are grasping at straws.

Peter asked Christ, "Lord, how oft shall my brother sin against me, and I forgive him? till seven times?" The Lord responded that he ought to forgive "seventy times seven." Christ then told the story of the servant who, because he would not forgive a fellow servant, was "delivered...to the tormentors." In application, He said, "So likewise shall my heavenly Father do also unto you, if ye from your hearts forgive not every one his brother their trespasses" (Matthew 18:21–35).

Surely if our heavenly Father expects us to forgive those who sin against us, how much more can we be confident that He is ready to forgive all who sin against Him. This is God as the Bible portrays Him—infinite in love, grace, and mercy, ready to forgive all who call upon Him. Calvinism misrepresents Him as only loving and forgiving a limited number of sinners.

The Darkest Side of Calvinism

We consider TULIP to be a libel against our loving and merciful God as He reveals himself both in His Word and in human conscience. Because of the Lord's mercy to the rebellious house of Israel, Nehemiah praises Him: "...thou art a gracious and merciful God" (Nehemiah 9:31). In seeking to call His wayward people to himself, God says to disobedient Israel through the prophet Jeremiah, "I am merciful" (Jeremiah 3:12). In the spirit of all of the prophets, Joel begs Israel to repent: "[T]urn unto the LORD your God; for he is gracious and merciful, slow to anger, and of great kindness..." (Joel 2:13).

There is no way to reconcile with conscience or Scripture the lack of concern on the part of Calvinism's God for *all* of the lost. R. C. Sproul wrote, "How we understand the person and character of God the Father affects every aspect of our lives."[9] He is right, and what effect must it have upon those who believe in a God who limits His love, grace and mercy to a select group, takes pleasure in damning the rest of mankind, and tells us to be merciful as He is merciful!

David, who surely knew God at least as well as Calvin did, declared, "With the merciful thou wilt shew thyself merciful..." (2 Samuel 22:26). Not a word about being merciful to the elect only. The God of the Bible is merciful to those who have shown mercy to others. Is this not what Jesus also said in the Sermon on the Mount: "Blessed are the merciful: for they shall obtain mercy" (Matthew 5:7)? But we are to believe that those who show mercy would receive no mercy from God unless they were among the elect. Yet both Christ and David make it sound as though, even without the benefit of Irresistible Grace, some of the "totally depraved" show mercy to their fellows, and because of that God's mercy will be given to them. Apparently, showing mercy reveals a heart willing to receive (and to be grateful for) God's mercies.

This Is Election?

Calvin seemed to believe that nearly everyone in Geneva was one of the elect and treated them accordingly. Why? First of all, Calvin believed that baptism transformed an infant into one of the elect. In fact, to have been baptized at any age, even by the most wicked and unbelieving Roman Catholic priest, was to have entered into the kingdom of God if one thereafter believed in the efficacy of that sacrament:

> God in baptism promises the remission of sins, and will undoubtedly perform what he has promised to all believers. That promise was offered to us in baptism, let us therefore embrace it in faith.[10]

This is a remarkable statement. According to Calvin, the gospel is no certain way to bring people to Christ—but baptism is. Baptism gives certain entrance into the kingdom of God! Furthermore, Calvin taught that the children of believers, even though not baptized, are automatically among the elect:

> Children who happen to depart this life before an opportunity of immersing them in water are not excluded from the kingdom of heaven.... Hence it follows, that the children of believers are not baptised in order that though formerly aliens from the Church, they may then, for the first time, become children of God, but rather are received into the Church by a formal sign, because, in virtue of the promise, they *previously belonged* to the body of Christ (emphasis added).[11]

Apparently from Calvin's belief that everyone in Geneva, having been baptized, was one of the elect (though he might have to burn, behead, flog, torture, or banish some of them for heresy), attendance at church services was required of all. It was perhaps this rule that caused Servetus to risk drawing attention to himself by attending the service where he was recognized. Moreover, also mandatory for everyone (with few exceptions) was the partaking of the bread and wine at the celebration of the Lord's Supper.

Considering Paul's clear warning that "he that eateth and drinketh unworthily, eateth and drinketh damnation to himself" (1 Corinthians 11:29), what can be said in defense of Calvin's forcing of the Eucharist upon the unwilling? Could he have sincerely believed that every citizen in his holy "City of God" belonged to Christ? Wasn't this a worse sort of "universalism" than that which Calvinists attribute to those of us who believe Christ died for all?

There was at least one exception to this universalism that nevertheless hardly changes the picture. A notorious libertine named Berthelier had been forbidden by the Church Consistory to partake of the Lord's Supper. In 1553, together with others of his persuasion, he attempted to do so and was repulsed by Calvin.[12] This sparked the last uprising against Calvin (harshly put down by force with executions) to which we have earlier referred.

Left with Unanswered Questions

Calvinism's elect, chosen by God for salvation, must somehow be *made* to believe the gospel in spite of both their natural unwillingness and alleged inability. The gospel of God's grace, which seemingly is offered to whosoever will believe, must be imposed—but this "grace" is only for those whom God has elected. As White explains, this is why Irresistible Grace is an absolute necessity:

> Unregenerate man is fully capable of understanding the facts of the gospel: he is simply incapable, due to his corruption and enmity, to submit himself to that gospel....[13]

This is a terrible attack upon the gospel, rendering powerless what Paul declares is itself "the power of God unto salvation" (Romans 1:16)! With no clear support from the Bible, the "Reformed position" must be deduced from the fact that man is "dead in sin"[14]—erroneously ascribing (as we have already seen) the symptoms of physical death to the spiritually dead.

Once sovereignly regenerated, the person is presumably able, under the influence of Irresistible Grace, to believe the gospel and thereafter to serve Christ from the heart. Yet grace is evidently no longer imposed irresistibly upon the elect once they are regenerated, since they do not always behave as they should, much less to perfection. But Scripture describes in very clear terms the Christlike life that believers are to live:

> Therefore if any man be in Christ, he is a new creature: old things have passed away; behold, all things are become new. Christ liveth in me.... For we are his workmanship, created in Christ Jesus unto good works, which God hath before ordained that we should walk in them. For it is God which worketh in you both to will and to do of his good pleasure.... Every one that doeth righteousness is born of him.... Whosoever abideth in him sinneth not...greater is he that is in you than he that is in the world...." (2 Corinthians 5:17; Galatians 2:20; Ephesians 2:10; Philippians 2:13: 1 John 2:29; 3:6; 4:4)

The Calvinist cannot point to any passage in the Bible that clearly states that grace is irresistible or that God imposes it upon the elect who otherwise could not believe the gospel. Yet many passages such as the above clearly state that God intends Christ-likeness for those who are regenerated. Then why don't Christians perfectly perform the "good works, which God hath before ordained" for them (Ephesians 2:10)?

If God irresistibly imposes His grace upon the "totally depraved" to regenerate them, why doesn't He impose it upon the regenerated unto perfection in Christian living? There is no biblical answer to this question if we deny free will and accept the theory of Irresistible Grace.

Paul even gives the example of a true Christian, surely one of the elect, who does not have even *one good work* as evidence that he belongs to Christ. Yet "he himself shall be saved"(1 Corinthians 3:12–15). How could God's sovereignty completely override human moral responsibility and choice, as the Calvinist insists, to the extent that man has no choice when it comes to salvation—and yet the elect are able to resist God's grace and His will and thus often fail to do the good works that God has ordained for them?

If the elect, having been made spiritually alive by sovereign regeneration, nevertheless do not perfectly obey God, why is unbelief and rebellion equated by Calvinism with total depravity and spiritual death?

If God's sovereignty does not nullify for the elect the moral accountability to make choices, why would His sovereignty disallow a genuine choice on the part of the unsaved to accept or reject the gospel? If disobedience to God's will by the elect poses no threat to God's sovereignty, why would a rejection of the gospel by some of the unsaved pose such a threat?

And would not an irresistible imposition of grace turn it into no grace at all? Some of these questions are considered in the next chapter.

1. R. C. Sproul, *Grace Unknown* (Grand Rapids, MI: Baker Books, 1997), 189.
2. Laurence M. Vance, *The Other Side of Calvinism* (Pensacola, FL: Vance Publications, rev. ed. 1999), 478.
3. Canons of Dort (Dordrecht, Holland, 1619); reproduced in Vance, *Other Side*, 607–26.
4. Canons, III, IV, "Of the Corruptions of Man, His Conversion to God, and the Manner Thereof,", 17/8.
5. Ben Lacy Rose, *T. U. L. I. P.: The Five Disputed Points of Calvinism* (Franklin, TN: Providence House Publishers, 1996), 37.
6. Westminster Confession of Faith (London: n. p., 1643), X,1.
7. Pastor in Australia to Dave Hunt, September 8, 2000. On file.
8. Editor of British Christian publication, England, to Dave Hunt, September 8, 2000. On file.
9. R. C. Sproul, *The Holiness of God* (Carol Stream, IL: Tyndale House Publishers, Inc. 1993 ed.), 20.
10. John Calvin, *Institutes of the Christian Religion*, trans. Henry Beveridge (Grand Rapids, MI: Wm. B. Eerdmans Publishing Company, 1998 ed.), IV: xxv, 17.
11. Ibid., IV: xxv, 22.
12. Piper, *Legacy*, 135–47; citing Henry F. Henderson, *Calvin in His Letters* (London: J. M. Dent and Co., 1909), 77–79.
13. James R. White, *The Potter's Freedom* (Amityville, NY: Calvary Press Publishing, 2000), 101.
14. Ibid.

CHAPTER

24

When Grace Isn't Grace

WHAT CALVIN PRACTICED in imposing his Augustinian doctrine upon those who disagreed was in many instances far from Christianity and God's grace. It was, however, consistent with his view of *Irresistible* Grace and a God who sovereignly imposes it upon the elect.

If Calvinism were true, how else could God make certain that the blood of Christ, shed on the cross for sin, would actually bring salvation to the elect? How could a "totally depraved" sinner be made to believe, except irresistibly? In his dispute with Rome, Calvin insisted that "divine grace [acts] irresistibly...."[1]

White argues that because the Bible says *Christ saves* sinners, we can't change it to say that he "saves synergistically with the assistance of the sinner himself."[2] Simply *believing* the gospel and *receiving* its free gift of salvation, however, could hardly qualify as "assistance" to God. Yet Pink likewise argues:

> What impression is made upon the minds of those men of the world who, occasionally, attend a Gospel service...? Is it not that a *disappointed* God is the One whom Christians believe in? From what is heard from the average evangelist today, is not any serious hearer *obliged* to conclude that he professes to represent a God who is filled with benevolent intentions, yet unable to carry them out; that He is earnestly desirous of blessing men, but that they will not let Him?[3]

Has Pink forgotten that much of the Old Testament was written by weeping prophets who expressed God's disappointment and grief over Israel's rejection of His love and grace and proffered mercy? Nevertheless, to the Calvinist, if salvation is merely an offer that man can refuse, that puts man in charge rather than God. This argument is foolish. The recipient of a gift can only accept or reject what is offered. To sovereignly impose either a gift or love would destroy both. Man is *not* in charge. If he doesn't turn to God willingly with his whole heart, he is eternally doomed.

Calvin's mistaken belief that God's sovereignty would be destroyed by free will necessitated a God who elected some to salvation and predestined the rest of mankind to eternal hell. No human could have any choice in the matter. That abhorrent doctrine directly contradicts the hundreds of scriptures in which God calls upon all men to repent, to believe, and to receive eternal life as a gift of His grace. Calvinism blinds its followers to such scriptures. Thus Pink mourns:

> It is sad indeed to find one like the late Dr. [A. T.] Pierson—whose writings are generally so scriptural and helpful—saying, "It is a tremendous thought that even God Himself cannot...prevent me from defying and denying Him, and would not exercise His power in such a direction if He could, and could not if He would" (*A Spiritual Clinique*). It is sadder still to discover that many other respected and loved brethren are giving expression to the same sentiments. Sad, because directly at variance with the Holy Scriptures."[4]

In fact, Calvinism is "at variance with the Holy Scriptures."

God the Puppet Master

The insistence upon a sovereignty that necessarily disallows any choice to man became the foundation of that system of theology known as Calvinism today. God's sovereignty and man's inability to say, think, or do anything that God had not predestined has been the continuing emphasis, reducing man to a puppet with God pulling the strings.

Engelsma asserts, "The Apostle Paul was an avowed, ardent predestinarian, holding double predestination, election, and reprobation."[5] What Engelsma attributes to Paul, Jewett claims was the common belief of every theologian in history worth mentioning: "Every theologian of the first rank from Augustine to Barth has affirmed...that God's election is a righteous and holy decision that he makes according to his own good pleasure to redeem the objects of his electing love."[6] Man cannot even believe the gospel without God *causing* him to do so. And that He causes so few to believe and predestines so many to eternal torment is "according to his own good pleasure"! Is this really the "God and Father of our Lord Jesus Christ" (Ephesians 1:3)?

Piper writes an entire book "to defend the claim that God is not unrighteous in unconditionally predestining some Israelites to salvation and some to condemnation."[7]

What are we to make of God's pleadings with *all* Israel to repent? And what of the fact that *all* Israel killed the lamb, sprinkled the blood, were delivered from Egypt, ate the manna, and "did all drink the same spiritual drink...that spiritual Rock that followed them: and that Rock was Christ" (I Corinthians 10:4)? Yet God predestined many if not most of them to eternal condemnation? On the contrary, it was clear tht God desired the eternal salvation of *all* Israel.

We have no disagreement with Calvinism concerning God's righteousness or His justice—the issue is His love. Does He love the whole world and desire all men to be saved, or doesn't He? Calvinism limits God's infinite love to a select group; the Bible declares His love for all—and allows man the choice that love requires.

Packer explains the Calvinist position: "God loves all in some ways (everyone whom he creates...receives many undeserved good gifts...). He loves some in all ways (that is...He brings them to faith, to new life and to glory according to his predestinating purpose)."[8] But would it really be love "in some ways" for God to give temporary, earthly "undeserved good gifts" to those He has predestined to eternal torment? Love "in some ways"? Absolutely not! Love cannot stop short of giving all it possibly could to those who are loved.

What love is this that provides *temporal blessings* for those it predestines to *eternal doom*?" Christ said it was a bad bargain for a man to "gain the whole world, and lose his own soul" (Matthew 16:26). Thus it could not be love of *any kind* for God to give even "the whole world" to one whom He had predestined to "lose his own soul"! Yet Packer calls it a gift of the "love" that Calvinism attributes to God. Palmer declares:

> By the decree of God, for the manifestation of His glory, some men and angels are predestinated to everlasting life; and others foreordained to everlasting death.... God has appointed the elect to glory.... The rest of mankind God was pleased, according to

> the unsearchable counsel of His own will...for the glory of His sovereign power over His creatures...to ordain them to dishonor and wrath for their sin, to the praise of His glorious justice.[9]

How can we fail to denounce such a horrifying misrepresentation of God? Calvinism is driven to this God-dishonoring belief by its misunderstanding of sovereignty. And the solution is so simple: acknowledge that God sovereignly gave to man a genuine power of choice, and God is exonerated and honored.

A One-Sided Emphasis

Calvinism's continual emphasis is upon God's sovereignty, glory, justice, and wrath. Searching its literature, one finds very little, if anything, of God's mercy, grace, compassion, and love for anyone but the elect.

Irresistible Grace is a human invention imposed upon the Bible. White writes, " 'Irresistible grace' is a reference to God's sovereign regeneration of His elect: any other use of this phrase is in error."[10] He insists upon precise rules for handling a phrase that isn't even found in the Bible—a concept about which Paul and the other apostles obviously knew nothing.

When Moses asked for a revelation of God's glory, the response was, "I will make all my goodness pass before thee...[and] the Lord passed by before him, and proclaimed, The Lord, The Lord God, merciful and gracious, longsuffering, and abundant in goodness and truth, Keeping mercy for thousands, forgiving iniquity and transgression and sin, and that will by no means clear [i.e., forgive without the penalty being paid] the guilty...(Exodus 33:19; 34:6–7).

Calvinism places great emphasis upon God's statement, "[I] will be gracious to whom I will be gracious, and will shew mercy on whom I will shew mercy" (Exodus 33:19)—but always from the negative point of view, as though God were pronouncing limitations upon His grace and mercy, when He is actually declaring their limitless expanse. Piper writes, "In dispensing mercy and grace God is dependent on nothing but his own free and sovereign choice."[11]

That is true, but God declares repeatedly that His grace and mercy are for all. The Calvinist, however, sees in God's declaration to Moses a limiting of grace and mercy to the elect, whereas the whole tenor of Scripture tells us that His mercy and grace are boundless. The entire context of this passage requires the understanding that God is revealing the infinite expanse of His mercy and grace, and not its limitations—while at the same time making it clear that grace does not compromise justice: "and that will by no means clear the guilty" (Exodus 34:7).

A Continuing Cover-Up

Is it possible that Calvin's tyrannical influence over Geneva, which was often so un-Christlike, was a direct result of his view of God as a harsh Sovereign more ready to condemn than to save? Tragically, that view of God persists among many Calvinists today.

Calvinists have avoided the truth about John Calvin the man. The booklet put out by John Piper and his pastoral staff at Bethlehem Baptist Church in Minneapolis opens with "Historical Information." It begins, "John Calvin, the famous theologian and pastor of Geneva...."[12]—and that is it for the "historical information." There is not one word of the oppressive behavior of this "Protestant Pope," which we have documented in Chapter 5. Is it really fair to readers to praise Calvin without telling the truth? Doesn't that give a false impression? Isn't Calvin's conduct as important as his theology? Aren't the two ultimately related?

In a more recent book, Piper purports to tell the truth faithfully about Augustine, Luther, and Calvin, whom he calls "three famous and flawed fathers in the Christian church..." and thereby to show how "the faithfulness of God triumphs over the flaws of men."[13] Piper declares that his aim in this book "is that the glorious Gospel of God's all-satisfying, omnipotent grace will be savored, studied and spread for the joy of all peoples—in a never-ending legacy of Sovereign Joy."[14] *All peoples*—including the multitudes predestined to destruction? Can he be serious? And *Sovereign Joy*? What is that?

Calvinism's gospel of "omnipotent grace will be savored, studied and spread for the joy" of the non-elect, who have been foreordained to eternal doom and born into this world without any hope of changing their fate? What mockery! Yet the Calvinist seems blind to what his theory has done to the God who *is love* and to how it destroys any sense of urgency and responsibility to preach the gospel.

Piper reminds us that "The standard text on theology that Calvin and Luther drank from was *Sentences* by Peter Lombard. Nine-tenths of this book consists of quotations from Augustine.... Luther was an Augustinian monk, and Calvin immersed himself in the writings of Augustine, as we can see from the increased use of Augustine's writings in each new edition of the *Institutes*...paradoxically, one of the most esteemed fathers of the Roman Catholic Church 'gave us the Reformation.'"[15] Piper considers this paradox to be good; we do not, and for the many reasons we are giving—among them Rome's heresies that were carried over into the Reformation by Luther and Calvin. Why have I been so harshly criticized for pointing out the very "Catholic connection" that Piper admits?

His supposed exposé of Calvin's "flaws" is almost a whitewash. Piper admits that "fifteen women were burned at the stake" and that there were some cruelties. The full truth, as we have seen, is far worse. All is largely excused, however, as "Calvin's accommodation to brutal times" (as though Christians have no higher standard than current custom) and as having been done "in tribute and defense of Protestant martyrs in France."[16] Piper writes:

> The worst was his joining in the condemnation of the heretic, Michael Servetus, to burning at the stake in Geneva.... Calvin argued the case against him. He was sentenced to death. Calvin called for a swift execution, instead of burning, but he was burned at the stake on October 27, 1553.
>
> This has tarnished Calvin's name so severely that many cannot give his teaching a hearing. But it is not clear that most of us, given that milieu, would not have acted similarly under the circumstances...the times were harsh, immoral, and barbarous and had a contaminating effect on everyone.... There was in the life and ministry of John Calvin a grand God-centeredness, Bible-allegiance, and iron constancy.
>
> Under the banner of God's mercy to miserable sinners, we would do well to listen and learn.... The conviction behind this book is that the glory of God, however dimly, is mirrored in the flawed lives of his faithful servants.[17]

With those sweet words, Piper really means that "under the banner of God's mercy to *some* miserable sinners," the favored elect may "listen and learn." But the non-elect can't listen and learn; they are totally depraved and without understanding or hope, because Piper's "God" keeps them in blindness! And even if they could understand the message and wanted to believe, it would not be possible, because they have been damned from eternity past by an immutable decree of the Almighty. Is it really fair to readers to give such a false impression of "sovereign" joy to "all peoples"?

And was it really "a grand God-centeredness, Bible-allegiance, and iron constancy" that produced the ungodly and unbiblical tyranny under

Calvin at Geneva? Review Chapter 5 to see how Calvin is being protected by Piper. There were *dozens* of others burned at the stake, not just Servetus, and there were many Christians who did not practice torture and burning at the stake in Calvin's day, thus proving that no one needed to make "accommodation to brutal times." Would Paul have, or John, or Christ? Why Calvin?

Could it be that Calvin's view of God (as taking pleasure in damning billions He *could* save) fit right in with the "harshness of the times"? Given Calvin's doctrine, no "accommodation to brutal times" was necessary.

And why doesn't Piper explain that the reason Calvin pushed for beheading was because that type of execution was for civil crimes, and the onus would not be on himself? But the charges pressed against Servetus by Calvin in court were theological and required the flames. Calvin was simply trying to circumvent the law. Do we praise him for that? Eight years later, Calvin was still advising other rulers to exterminate heretics "like I exterminated Michael Servetus..."! Calvin was a victim of his times? No, a victim of his theology!

Unbiblical and Unreasonable

As we have already seen, the theory of Irresistible Grace (as with the rest of Calvinism) conflicts with both Scripture and reason. One of the most astonishing requirements of TULIP is "regeneration before faith." Sproul explains: "Reformed theology views regeneration as the immediate supernatural work of the Holy Spirit that effects the change of the soul's disposition.... Faith is a fruit of regeneration."[18]

Having already given some attention to this strange theory, we need to examine it in more depth. That this dogma is not produced by biblical exegesis but is necessitated by the other points in TULIP is clear. Nowhere does the Bible state that regeneration (i.e., the new birth, being born again, given eternal life, salvation) *precedes* faith, but there are scores of scriptures that tell us that *faith of necessity* comes first:

- He that believeth and is baptized shall be saved.... (Mark 16:16)
- To them gave he power to become [through the new birth] the sons of God, even to them that believe on his name. (John 1:12)
- He that believeth on me hath everlasting life. (John 6:47)

- He that believeth in me, though he were dead, yet shall he live.... (John 11:25)
- ...that believing ye might have life through his name. (John 20:31)
- Believe on the Lord Jesus Christ, and thou shalt be saved.... (Acts 16:31)
- And many of the Corinthians hearing believed, and were baptized. (Acts 18:8)
- The gospel of Christ...is the power of God unto salvation to everyone that believeth.... (Romans 1:16)
- That if thou shalt...believe in thine heart...thou shalt be saved. (Romans 10:9)
- It pleased God...to save them that believe. (1 Corinthians 1:21)
- ...them that believe to the saving of the soul. (Hebrews 10:39)

Indisputably, the above scriptures, and many others, declare that only upon believing in Christ, and as a result of that faith, is one "saved." But if faith only follows regeneration, one has become a "born-again" Christian *before* believing unto salvation—a concept directly contrary to Scripture. Sproul acknowledges that if one is a Christian, one is regenerate; and if one is regenerate, one is a Christian.[19] But how could one become a Christian by "regeneration" without believing on Christ through the Gospel?

Robert Morey claims there is one verse in the Bible that teaches regeneration before faith: John 3:3. He declares, "Christ places regeneration by the Spirit as a requirement before one can 'see,' i.e., believe or have faith in the Kingdom of God...a sinner who is born of the flesh can not believe the good news of the Kingdom until he is born by the Spirit."[20]

Such loose, wishful thinking is not typical of Morey. To "*see*" the kingdom means to "*believe* or have faith in the Kingdom..."? There is no such concept as "faith in the Kingdom" anywhere in Scripture: faith is in God and in Christ. And Christ explains "see" when He reiterates, "Except a man be born of water and of the Spirit, he cannot *enter into* the kingdom of God" (John 3:5). One must be *in* the kingdom of God to see it. Realizing that it is absurd to speak of "faith in the Kingdom," Morey rephrases it to "believe the good news of the Kingdom," which is equally far from what Christ says.

Christ commanded us as His disciples to go into all the world and preach the gospel to every person whom we encounter and who will listen. The Apostle Paul had a passion to get the gospel to everyone he could reach. He spent his life persuading Jews and Gentiles to believe in Christ, disputing in the synagogues and public places. But (as we have emphasized) if Calvinism is true, Paul wasted his time—and so would we. The elect need no persuasion, being sovereignly regenerated without believing on Christ. And the non-elect are totally depraved, even "dead," unable to believe unto salvation, no matter how persuasively we preach the gospel.

Demeaning the Great Commission

How can God's grace that brings regeneration reach Calvinism's "totally depraved" sinner who is incapable of believing the gospel? Only by turning grace into Irresistible Grace—a concept unknown in Scripture. Since man is allegedly unable to believe on Christ, salvation must be imposed upon him without his first believing the gospel. If Total Depravity means that no man can believe the gospel unto salvation, then not only the theory of Irresistible Grace follows but also that man must be regenerated and made alive before he can believe and be saved.

Yet a biblical view keeps slipping in, betrayed by un-Calvinistic admissions. For example, the following from Sproul: "Once Luther grasped the teaching of Paul in Romans, he was reborn."[21] This slip of the pen contradicts the claim that one must first be regenerated, and only then can the gospel be understood and believed. Which is it? We are reborn/regenerated before we can believe the gospel, or through believing the gospel? Or are we reborn twice, once by God's sovereign act before we believe, and then again after first being regenerated and given the faith to believe?

In contrast, the Bible repeatedly declares in the plainest language (and in numerous passages) that no man can be changed from unrepentant sinner to child of God without from the heart believing the gospel and, as a result of believing, being born of the Spirit of God. But if no one can believe the gospel without first being regenerated by the Spirit of God, as Calvinism declares, then not only the damnation of billions but also the continuance of evil must be God's will, inasmuch as He chooses to regenerate so few and to move upon so few hearts with Irresistible Grace. The Bible, reason, and conscience are all outraged. Dick Sanford has put it well:

> The teaching that [because of God's sovereignty] a man who's saved couldn't have done anything but be saved, and a man who's lost couldn't have done anything but be lost destroys the concept of grace. It changes grace to simple programming. Love is not required.... Man isn't responding to a loving God's grace, he is simply doing what he was programmed to do.[22]

Building Upon a "Dead" Foundation

It was a serious misunderstanding of "dead in sins" that gave birth to Irresistible Grace. While this issue was dealt with in Chapter 9, further discussion was promised under this heading. Inasmuch as White is recognized as an authority on Calvinism, let him elaborate further upon its assertions with regard to the "I" in TULIP:

> Reformed authors frequently point to the biblical teaching that man is "dead in sin" as substantiation of their belief that God *must* be absolutely sovereign and salvation *must* be completely of free grace and *not* a synergistic cooperation between God and man since man is not *capable* of cooperating any more than a corpse.[23] If men are dead in sin at all [i.e., by Calvinism's own peculiar definition], it follows that they must have spiritual life restored to them before they can do spiritually good things.... Spiritually dead men believe all sorts of things: just not those things that are pleasing to God.[24]

Where does the Bible make this distinction that the spiritually dead can "believe all sorts of things" but not "those things that are pleasing to God"? And what does this have to do with salvation, since salvation does not depend upon being "pleasing to God"? And if spiritual death is likened to physical death, then the spiritually dead shouldn't be able even to think or to believe *anything*. But if the analogy fails completely in that respect, how can it be valid with regard to the gospel?

White offers no direct teaching from the Bible. There is none. The doctrine of Irresistible Grace was deduced from the biblical statement that men are spiritually dead. The only way to make it fit TULIP was to equate "spiritual death" with "physical death." That error became a major pillar of Calvinism.

A Subtle Surrender to Materialism

Dabney argued, "The corpse does not restore life to itself; after life is restored it becomes a living agent."[25] What does that have to do with salvation? Who imagines that the sinner restores himself to life? All the sinner must do is believe the gospel; it is God who, in response to faith, creates spiritual life through the new birth.

Calvinists seemingly forget the soul and spirit, of which the body is only the temporary, earthly house. The physical body of a living person doesn't know it's alive. The soul and spirit constitute the real person who thinks and wills. Thus, likening spiritual death to a corpse misses the point and leads to confusion. The error in this analogy becomes even clearer when one remembers that regeneration unto spiritual life leaves the person physically unchanged.

In spite of the physical death of the body, the spirit of man continues to think and will. Christ tells of the rich man who, after his death, could think and speak and express desires "in hell" (Luke 16:22–31). The tissues of a living body, including even the brain, know nothing of the "issues of life" (Proverbs 4:23), yet the Calvinist founds his theory upon the materialistic fact that a corpse can't do anything. Piper embraces the same error: "God is the one who sovereignly decides who will be shown such mercy [as to be made spiritually alive]...."[26]

Likewise, Westblade calls spiritual death "a moral one that does not hinder us physically but clouds the eyes of the heart.... Moral corpses that we are, the only hope we have for a will that turns its passion toward God lies in the call of God [that] makes 'us alive together with Christ....'"[27] Here the error goes a bit deeper. Now morals are connected with the physical body, and because a corpse can't make moral choices (of course, neither could the physical body when it was alive)—the natural man, being spiritually dead, is therefore imagined to be morally dead.

Where does the Bible teach this? Aren't the Ten Commandments given to spiritually dead mankind, and don't the spiritually dead understand the moral issues and often keep some of the commandments? Paul says that even the spiritually dead Gentiles "shew the work of the law written in their hearts, their conscience also bearing witness, and their thoughts the mean while accusing or else excusing one another..." (Romans 2:14–15). Doesn't God appeal to every man's conscience?

Abraham reminds the rich man in hell of his past moral failure. Though his body is a corpse in the grave, the rich man knows his sin—that it is too late for him—and he expresses earnest moral concern that his living brothers be warned so that they will not join him in hell. The Calvinist has created a false analogy, far from both the Bible and common sense.

The Bible offers no justification whatsoever, from Genesis to Revelation, for concluding that man is morally a corpse. Prone to evil, yes; but unable to understand that he is a sinner and that Christ died for his sins? Unable to recognize his sin and incapable of believing the gospel? No. The Bible teaches that the spiritually dead *can* understand the gospel and believe on the Lord Jesus Christ unto salvation (John 5:24–25, etc.).

Adding to the Confusion

J. I. Packer affirms this same basic error: "'Dead' evidently signifies total unresponsiveness to God, total unawareness of his love, and total lack of the life he gives: no metaphor for spiritual inability and destitution could be stronger."[28]

Evidently? What does that mean? "Total unresponsiveness to God" and "total unawareness" of God's love, even in the God-given conscience? Why doesn't Scripture state the Calvinist position plainly, if it is biblical?

Packer offers no biblical support for his assertion. There is none. Here Calvinists become confused and contradict themselves and one another. Consider this admission from Schreiner:

> We are not saying that they [the totally depraved and spiritually dead] are as evil as they can possibly be. Jesus says, "...you then, though you are evil, know how to give good gifts to your children" (Luke 11:13). If people were as evil as they possibly could be, they would not desire to give good things to their children [but] Jesus still says that they are evil. Evil people still give good gifts...and do kind things...."[29]

If the totally depraved and spiritually dead are "moral corpses," how can they make any moral choices and do any good? That they can is undeniable. Yet the spiritually "dead" person, even though able to do *some* good, is unable to seek God or believe the gospel? That distinction is never made in Scripture.

White has already been quoted to the effect that although the spiritually dead man can believe other things, he cannot believe the right things and certainly not the gospel, though he can understand and reject it.[30] Calvinism thus hinges upon a peculiar definition of the word "dead."

Those who are "dead in sin" can do *this*, but they can't do *that*—yet these rules are found nowhere in Scripture.

The gospel is to be preached to "every creature" (Mark 16:15). It would be irrational for God to send His servants to suffer and die in preaching the gospel to those who were incapable of understanding and believing it. Yet Palmer reasons, "Only when the Holy Spirit regenerates man and makes him alive spiritually can man have faith in Christ and be saved."[31] In all of the Calvinist writing we have studied, not one verse from Scripture is cited that clearly states this doctrine. It never would have been invented were it not required by TULIP.

Irresistible Grace and Spiritual Death

The word "dead" is used several ways in Scripture. Even the saved who are both physically and spiritually alive are said to be "dead to sin" (Romans 6:2,7,11). Yet every Christian knows that "dead to sin" is not an absolute statement but must be experienced by faith. Christians are said to be dead in other ways as well: "dead with Christ" (Romans 6:8; Colossians 2:20); "dead to the law" (Galatians 2:19); "for ye are dead, and your life is hid with Christ in God" (Colossians 3:3); "For if we be dead with him..." (2 Timothy 2:11), etc. Yet none of these biblical analogies fits perfectly with being physically dead.

As for sinners, the Bible unquestionably teaches that they are spiritually dead to God. But what does that mean? Adam was spiritually dead from the moment he sinned, but he heard when God spoke to him and told him the consequences of his sin. He understood why God made a covering of animal skin and told him to offer a lamb from the flock, in anticipation of the Lamb of God who would one day pay the penalty for sin. Was Adam regenerated? Obviously not. Such a concept is only introduced in the New Testament. Yet many prior to that time knew God and looked forward to the Messiah.

Why should spiritual death to God be taken in an absolute sense, while the Christian's being dead to sin is not? There is no biblical reason for doing so. Ephesians 5:14 commands, "Awake thou that sleepest, and arise from the dead, and Christ shall give thee light." Those who are *physically* alive but spiritually dead are addressed. And that fact presents problems to the Calvinist, who claims that the spiritually dead can neither hear the gospel nor respond—yet they are commanded to arise from the dead.

Paul seems to be paraphrasing Isaiah 60:1–2, which was addressed to unbelieving and rebellious Israel. Apparently, those who are dead in sins *can* respond to Christ and be given light.

One would think that Calvinists would want to respond to Ephesians 5:14, but among the many whom I have read, not one has done so. White gives it a wide berth, as does Piper. None of the thirteen Calvinist authors of the essays that comprise *Still Sovereign* even mentions it. Not every author can cover every scripture—but for *none* of them to touch it? Isn't that odd? Even in his huge and detailed exposition of the issues on both sides, Vance is unable to quote any Calvinist concerning this scripture.

The Bible contains many difficult passages. Every passage must be interpreted in the context of the whole. For example, Jehovah's Witnesses cite "My Father is greater than I" to "prove" that Christ is not God. It sounds logical from that one verse. But when we take all of Scripture, we realize that Christ, who said, "I and my Father are one...before Abraham was, I AM, etc.," *is* God from eternity past, co-equal and co-existent with the Father and the Holy Spirit.

Likewise, we must compare scripture with scripture (the Bible is its own interpreter), as we are doing, to understand passages about Election, God's enduring vessels of wrath such as Pharaoh, His hating Esau but loving Jacob, our being dead in sins, and so forth. And to liken spiritual death to physical death does not fit the Bible as a whole.

Seeking an Understanding

Difficult passages are made plain in the light of those that are very clear. And there can be no doubt that Jesus plainly taught more than once that hearing His voice and, as a result, believing the gospel and receiving the gift of eternal life, is possible for those spiritually dead. For example, Jesus said, "The hour is coming, and now is, when the dead shall hear the voice of the Son of God: and they that hear shall live" (John 5:25).

Unquestionably, the key phrase "now is" refers to the spiritually dead being made alive through hearing and believing the gospel in Christ's day and throughout time. That fact is clear by His separate and specific reference to a later *physical* resurrection.

After declaring that the spiritually dead could hear His voice and live, Christ refers to a future day of physical resurrection, and the phrase "now is" is not included: "The hour is coming, in the which all that are in the graves shall hear his voice, and shall come forth...." Graves were not mentioned in His first statement concerning the spiritually dead hearing His voice and living. Christ refers to a future ("The hour is coming") resurrection of the physically dead coming out of their graves, some "unto the resurrection of life" and some "unto the resurrection of damnation" (John 5:28–29).

The process to which Christ first refers, whereby the spiritually dead are given life, can be ongoing only through the preaching of and believing the gospel. Surely this initial receiving of life by the spiritually dead comes as a result of faith in Christ exactly as He said:

> Verily, verily, I say unto you, He that heareth my word, and believeth on him that sent me, hath everlasting life, and shall not come into condemnation; but is passed from death unto life. (John 5:24)

All of Scripture bears witness to what Christ, the Living Word, is saying here: "faith cometh by hearing...the word of God" (Romans 10:17) and through that faith the spiritually "dead in trespasses and sins" (Ephesians 2:1) are given spiritual life, eternal life. Repeatedly we are told that he who "believeth" is given "everlasting life" through his faith, and as a result passes "from death unto life." He is not regenerated by means of God sovereignly making him spiritually alive without his believing the gospel and thereafter given faith to believe in Christ, as Calvinism asserts. No, he is regenerated as a result of putting his faith in Christ.

A Calvinist friend, to whom a preliminary copy of the manuscript of this book had been given for review, wrote in the margin, "Regeneration and salvation are distinctly different...." Yet nowhere in Scripture is that distinction made. Calvinists accuse us of confusing regeneration and salvation. There is no confusion—they are one and the same.

We've already seen that Spurgeon, like MacArthur, equated regeneration and salvation. How could one be regenerated by the Spirit of God, making one a child of God, yet still need to be saved? Surely, sovereign regeneration by the Spirit of God must be what Christ described to Nicodemus as being "born again." Yet one can believe the gospel only *after* "regeneration"? On the contrary, all the saved have been born again and all who are born again are saved—which only happens by faith. Salvation and regeneration are the same work of God.

According to Calvinism, without believing on Christ, the "elect" are regenerated. Regeneration can only mean being "born again" by the Spirit of God into the family of God. What other "regeneration" could there be? Since we are saved by faith—"by grace are ye saved through faith...

believe...and thou shalt be saved" (Ephesians 2:8, Acts 16:31)—and Calvinism says that we can't have faith until we have been regenerated—we must (according to this strange doctrine) be born again before we are saved! Though a staunch Calvinist, Dillow realizes the folly and writes, "Furthermore, the state of salvation occurs simultaneously with the exercise of this faith and does not occur before it."[32]

The "Spiritually Dead" Hear and Believe

That the unsaved, dead in trespasses and in sins, can be reasoned with and can understand and believe the gospel unto salvation is clear from many passages such as the following: "Knowing...the terror of the Lord, we persuade [unsaved] men" (2 Corinthians 5:11); "And he reasoned in the synagogue [with unregenerate men]...and persuaded the [unregenerated] Jews and Greeks [to believe]" (Acts 18:4); "he mightily convinced the [unregenerated] Jews...shewing by the scriptures that Jesus was Christ" (Acts 18:28); and so forth.

Not only these scriptures, but many more like them, clearly teach that we are to use reason and Scripture in order to convince the spiritually lost that they need a Savior. The Holy Spirit uses the persuasion of God's Word, which is "quick, and powerful, and sharper than any two-edged sword" (Hebrews 4:12), to convict the lost and bring them to Christ. To be reasoned with, persuaded, and convinced, a person must understand the arguments and believe the truth that they convey. Clearly, then, the unregenerate *can* believe on Christ prior to their regeneration—or persuading them would be a fruitless effort.

God said to the unbelieving and rebellious children of Israel, most of whom refused to respond, "Come now, and let us reason together...though your sins be as scarlet, they shall be as white as snow..." (Isaiah 1:18). If Calvinism were true, God would be wasting His time and effort reasoning with spiritually dead Israelites who could no more respond to the truth than a corpse could give itself a blood transfusion. And if the only way they could repent and believe unto eternal life was by Irresistible Grace to sovereignly regenerate them, why would He plead and warn while withholding the only means whereby those He addressed could respond?

According to Calvinism, God should have first regenerated the "elect" among Israel, and only then could He have reasoned with them to any spiritual benefit. But the Bible tells us otherwise.

From these few scriptures that we have considered, as well as from many similar passages in the Bible, one would *never* conclude that God overwhelms elect sinners with Irresistible Grace to regenerate them first and then gives them faith to believe. On the contrary, He calls upon them to repent and sends His prophets to warn and persuade them.

The very fact that Paul, Apollos, and the other early evangelists expended themselves in persuading men to believe the gospel is completely contrary to the concept of Total Depravity, Irresistible Grace, and regeneration before faith. Obviously, Paul was not aware of the principles Calvin would extract from his epistles 1,500 years later. Nor, apparently, was Jesus, for He kept urging the unregenerate to come to Him, and from the cross, asked His Father to forgive the very rebels who crucified and mocked Him.

"Limited" Irresistible Grace?

Even if we assume, for sake of argument, that grace *could* be irresistible, the Calvinist's grace could hardly be called *grace* for another reason: it is only for the elect. Yes, being sovereign, God can do as He pleases. He could damn everyone and no one could complain, for that is what we deserve. He is not obligated to save anyone.

But sovereignty is not a total description of God. Numerous passages have already been cited describing God as infinite in love, mercy, and grace toward all, and not willing that any perish. Calvinism, however, limits God's grace and mercy. Christ was asked whether few would be saved, and He stated that indeed there would be few (Matthew 7:13–14; Luke 13:23–28)—not because God limits His grace, but because so few are willing to repent and believe the gospel; indeed, Christ continually urged men to enter the path to eternal life.

One would think that these passages where Christ says that few will be saved would be favorites for Calvinists, especially Matthew 7:14 and Luke 13:23. Yet in searching many books by Calvinists, this author has been unable to find even one reference to these verses. Why? Because they contradict Calvinism. Christ very clearly puts upon the unregenerate the responsibility of entering the kingdom. "Enter ye in at the strait gate... strait is the gate, and narrow is the way, which leadeth unto life, and few there be that find it" (Matthew 7:14).

Enter? Find? These are very un-Calvinistic terms! Why would Christ give such a warning if one could only come into the kingdom through having been predestined to salvation and sovereignly regenerated, without any understanding, repentance, or faith? A. T. Pierson said it well:

> Insofar as any human being sins for himself, he must believe for himself.... Boasting is excluded. I have only to believe...to take Jesus as Saviour...to accept the white robe of His perfect righteousness, which is "unto all and upon all...that believe." [Romans 3:22][33]

Why aren't more saved? The Bible says it is because so few are willing to come as repentant sinners and enter in at the narrow gate of faith in Christ alone. Refusing to allow man a free will, Calvinism insists that so few are saved because God only loves, cares for, and saves a few, though He could save all—indeed, that saving so few is to God's greater glory. Calvin has earlier been quoted:

> We shall never be clearly persuaded, as we ought to be, that our salvation flows from the wellspring of God's free mercy until we come to know his eternal election, which illumines God's grace by this contrast: that he...gives to some what he denies to others.[34]

Here we gain further insight into Calvin's strange thinking: God illumines His grace by not extending it to multitudes! Somehow, by *limiting* His grace, God enlarges our appreciation of the wellspring from which His mercy flows! And we are to praise Him all the more because He gives to only some that which He could extend to all? This is Calvinism. Boettner reminds us that "if any are saved God must choose out those who shall be the objects of His grace."[35]

Imagine a man in a barge, surrounded by a thousand desperate people who have no life jackets and who can keep themselves afloat in the icy water for only a few more minutes. This man has the means of saving every one of them from a watery grave, and more than enough room and complete provisions on the barge for them all. He plucks only 150 from certain death, leaving the rest to drown because it pleases him to do so.

The next day, would the newspapers have banner headlines praising this man for being so kind, gracious, and merciful because he rescued 150 and left 850 to die—or even if he rescued 850 and left to their fate only 150, whom he could have saved? Hardly. By the conscience God has given to even the "totally depraved" and spiritually dead children of Adam, everyone would condemn such despicable behavior. No one with any sense of the morals that God has imprinted upon every conscience could praise such a man for leaving *anyone* to drown whom he could have saved.

Yet we are supposed to believe that God refrains from rescuing millions, and perhaps billions, whom He just as well could have saved? And we are to praise Him all the more for having limited His love, mercy, and grace? Such is the teaching of Calvinism!

The Libel Against God Clearly Stated

W. J. Seaton says, without any apparent sense of irony or shame, "If God alone can save, and if *all* are not saved, then the conclusion must be that God has not chosen to save all."[36] Pink argues that to claim that the purpose of Christ's death was to provide salvation for all "is to undermine the very foundations of our faith."[37]

What "faith" is that? How did Augustine and Calvin dare to so malign the heavenly Father, who the Bible assures us is infinitely more loving, merciful, kind, and gracious than any human could ever be? Calvinism has reduced God's love and compassion to a lower standard than even the ungodly set for one another.

Piper ends one of his most important books, in which he attempts to justify the reprobating God of Calvinism, with this exhortation to the elect readers: "We will entrust ourselves to mercy alone. In the hope of glory we will extend this mercy to others that they may see our good deeds and give glory to our Father in heaven."[38] Why should the elect's good deeds cause those who have been predestined to eternal doom to give glory to Calvinism's God, who closed the door of salvation to them? The God-given conscience is offended at the Calvinists' rejoicing in their election, with no word of sympathy for those who will spend eternity in utter anguish and for whom, from the beginning, there was never any hope. And how could they be concerned for those for whom God has no concern?

As for mercy, only if one is absolutely certain that he is among the elect (and how can any Calvinist be certain?) dare he trust himself to the "mercy" of this otherwise unmerciful God. For the non-elect there is no real mercy, for any blessings in this life are nullified by an eternity of torment. Nor need the Calvinist be merciful, except (like his God) toward those to whom it "pleases" him to be merciful.

John MacArthur writes an entire book[39] attempting to prove that God is loving and merciful toward those whom He has predestined to eternal torment, because He gives to them sunshine and rain and temporal blessings in this brief life. Only a Calvinist could possibly think in such terms! Would we commend the grace and love of a mass murderer who always gives a hearty meal to his victims just before he tortures and kills them? Ah, but God is sovereign and the clay can't complain about what the potter has made of it.

On the contrary, we are not mere lumps of clay but creatures made in the image of God and to whom He has lovingly promised salvation if we will but believe. Calvinism's God offends the conscience that the God of the Bible has put within all mankind, tramples upon the very compassion with which the One who *is love* has imbued even the ungodly, and manifests a lower standard of behavior toward multitudes than He requires of us toward our enemies. Something isn't right!

The real issue is not God's sovereignty, to which all agree. The issue is God's mercy and grace motivated by love. Calvinism's *limited* and *irresistible* "grace" is no grace at all.

---

1. John Calvin, *Acts of the Council of Trent: With the Antidote*, ed. and trans. Henry Beveridge (1851); in *Selected Works of John Calvin: Tracts and Letters*, 7 vols., ed. Henry Beveridge and Jules Bonnet (Grand Rapids, MI: Baker Books, 1983), 3:111.
2. James R. White, *The Potter's Freedom* (Amityville, NY: Calvary Press Publishing, 2000), 247.
3. Arthur W. Pink, *The Sovereignty of God* (Grand Rapids, MI: Baker Book House, 2nd prtg. 1986), 12.
4. Pink, *Sovereignty*, 144.
5. David J. Engelsma, *Hyper-Calvinism and the Call of the Gospel* (Grandville, MI: Reformed Free Publishing Association, 1980), 53.
6. Paul K. Jewett, *Election and Predestination* (Grand Rapids, MI: Wm B. Eerdmans Publishing Co., 1985 ed.), 3–4.
7. John Piper, *The Justification of God: An Exegetical and Theological Study of Romans 9:1–23* (Grand Rapids, MI: Baker Books, 2000), 179.
8. J. I. Packer, "The Love of God: Universal and Particular," in *Still Sovereign,* ed. Thomas R. Schreiner and Bruce A. Ware (Grand Rapids, MI: Baker Books, 2000), 283–84.
9. Edwin H. Palmer, *the five points of calvinism* (Grand Rapids, MI: Baker Books, enlarged ed., 20th prtg. 1999), 95, 124–25.
10. White, *Potter's*, 137.
11. Piper, *Justification*, 82–83.
12. John Piper and Pastoral Staff, "TULIP: What We Believe about the Five Points of Calvinism: Position Paper of the Pastoral Staff" (Minneapolis, MN: Desiring God Ministries, 1997), 3.
13. John Piper, *The Legacy of Sovereign Joy: God's Triumphant Grace in the Lives of Augustine, Luther, and Calvin* (Wheaton, IL: Crossway Books, 2000), 18.

14. Ibid., 38.

15. Ibid., 24–25.

16. Ibid., 32–35.

17. Ibid., 34–38.

18. R. C. Sproul, *Faith Alone: The Evangelical Doctrine of Justification* (Grand Rapids, MI: Baker Books, 1995), 26.

19. Ibid., 23.

20. Robert A. Morey, *Studies in the Atonement* (Southbridge, MA: Crowne Publications, 1989), 82.

21. R. C. Sproul, *The Holiness of God* (Carol Stream, IL: Tyndale House Publishers, Inc., 1993 ed.), 144.

22. Dick Sanford, *Predestination and Election*, ed. John R. Cross (self-published monograph, n. d.), 3.

23. White, *Potter's*, 100.

24. Ibid., 105.

25. Robert L. Dabney, *The Five Points of Calvinism* (Harrisburg, VA: Sprinkle Publications, 1992), 35.

26. Piper, *Justification*, 178, note 31.

27. Donald J. Westblade, "Divine Election in the Pauline Literature." In *Still Sovereign*, ed. Thomas R. Schreiner and Bruce A. Ware (Grand Rapids, MI: Baker Books, 2000), 72–73.

28. Packer, *"Love,"* 283.

29. Thomas R. Schreiner, "Does Scripture Teach Prevenient Grace in the Wesleyan Sense?" in Schreiner and Ware, *Still*, 231.

30. White, *Potter's*, 101.

31. Palmer, *five points*, 27.

32. Joseph C. Dillow, *The Reign of the Servant Kings: A Study of Eternal Security and the Final Significance of Man* (Haysville, NC: Schoettle Publishing Co., 2nd ed. 1993), 287.

33. Arthur T. Pierson, *The Believer's Life: Its Past, Present, and Future Tenses* (London: Morgan and Scott, 1905), 20, 33.

34. John Calvin, *Institutes of the Christian Religion*, trans. Henry Beveridge (Grand Rapids, MI: Wm. B. Eerdmans Publishing Company, 1998 ed.), III: xxi, 1.

35. Loraine Boettner, *The Reformed Doctrine of Predestination* (Phillipsburg, NJ: Presbyterian and Reformed Publishing Co.), 1932, 95.

36. W. J. Seaton, *The Five Points of Calvinism* (Carlisle, Pa: The Banner of Truth Trust, 1970), 12.

37. Pink, *Sovereignty*, 260.

38. Piper, *Justification*, 220.

39. John MacArthur, Jr., *The Love of God* (Dallas, TX: Word Publishing, 1996).

CHAPTER 25

Grace and Human Responsibility

IN ADDITION to the many scriptures already discussed, Calvinists have a number of other favorites that they cite in support of TULIP, and especially of Irresistible Grace. A sufficient number of these will be presented herein to allow Calvinist leaders to put forth their best arguments.

A passage used most frequently and with the greatest confidence is John 6:37,44: "All that the Father giveth me shall come to me.... No man can come to me, except the Father...draw him...." Note the enthusiasm with which White "proves" his thesis from this portion of God's Word:

> If believing that man is "so dead" in sin that he is incapable of coming to Christ on his own is "extreme Calvinism," then the Lord Jesus beat Calvin to the punch by 1500 years with His preaching in the synagogue recorded in John 6. Here we have the Lord teaching almost everything Norman Geisler identifies as "extreme Calvinism." Jesus teaches that God is sovereign and acts independently of the "free choices" of men. He likewise teaches that man is incapable of saving faith outside of the enablement of the Father. He then limits this drawing to the same individuals given by the Father to the Son. He then teaches irresistible grace *on the elect* (not on the "willing") when He affirms that *all* those who are given to Him *will* come to Him. John 6:37–45 is the clearest exposition of what [Geisler] calls "extreme Calvinism" in the Bible.
>
> There is good reason why [Geisler] stumbles at this point: there is no meaningful non-Reformed exegesis of the passage available....

> Let us listen to Jesus teach "extreme Calvinism" almost 1500 years before Calvin was born...."All that the Father gives me will come to me...." The action of giving by the Father *comes before* the action of coming to Christ by the individual. And since *all* those so given *infallibly come*, we have here both unconditional election and irresistible grace...in the space of nine words...!
>
> Since the action of coming is dependent upon the action of giving, we can see that it is simply not exegetically possible [to deny that] God's giving results in man's coming. Salvation is of the Lord....[1]

"Unconditional election and irresistible grace" are found in this passage? Yarbrough,[2] Piper,[3] D. A. Carson,[4] and J. I. Packer[5] (among others) also think so. However, the words "unconditional," "irresistible," and "grace" are not there—nor can they be found anywhere in the Bible. And God "limits this drawing to those given by the Father to the Son"? That is not what Christ says. Whatever Christ means, it must be in agreement with the message of God's entire Word—and both Unconditional Election and Irresistible Grace contradict the entire tenor of Scripture.

Of course, the "enablement" of God is essential not just for coming to Christ but for *anything* a saved or even unsaved man does—even to draw a breath. *Enablement*, however, is far from *irresistible enforcement causing* man's action. Yet Yarbrough asserts, "whoever comes to the Son does so as the result of the Father's forceful attraction."[6] Forceful? Where does one find such teaching in this passage?

Sproul insists that a "crucial point of dispute between Rome and the Reformation [by this he means Calvinism]...was the efficacy of divine grace. Is grace irresistible and efficacious on its own, or is it resistible and dependent on human cooperation?" Claiming that it is irresistible, he quotes Thomas Aquinas for support. But Aquinas is ambivalent: "divine help...the help of God...the help of grace, etc."[7] To help someone is not to irresistibly force them. We help people do what they desire to do; without such desire on their part, such "help" would be coercion!

A Troubling Tendency

Attention has already been called to a troubling apparent lack of sympathy for the lost among Calvinists. And how could it be otherwise? They wouldn't dare to have sympathy for those whom God has been pleased to predestine to eternal doom.

Such a theory logically leads to apathy toward evangelism, though many Calvinists do not succumb to the practical consequences of their belief. Custance reasons, "If Election guarantees the salvation of all that are predestined to be saved, why should we be bothered with evangelism...? What possible difference can it make whether we speak to men or not?"[8] He is right.

It would only be reasonable for a Calvinist to think, "I'm one of the elect. Let those whom God has damned be damned; there's nothing I can do for them. To be concerned would be to complain against God for predestining them to their just fate." But the conscience God has placed within even the ungodly condemns such an attitude.

Yet God himself does not love the lost enough to save them all? He lacks sufficient mercy for the lost to give them the faith to believe unto salvation—and is even glorified in sovereignly damning so many and saving so few? Is this the biblical God?

Morey writes approvingly, "Calvin taught that God loved the elect and planned their holiness and salvation while...He hated the reprobate and planned their sin and damnation."[9] "Planned" even *their sin*? Yes, even "the mistake of a typist"—that's Calvinism! If that is the God of the Bible, Calvinism is true. If not, Calvinism ought to be condemned for its misrepresentation of God.

The Overwhelming Testimony of Scripture

Literally hundreds of scriptures express God's genuine concern for rebellious Israel. He sends His prophets to plead with them to repent so He will not have to punish them. Surely, Paul reflects God's heart in his desire to suffer even eternal damnation if that would rescue his brethren, the Jews, from hell. He has an equal passion for the salvation of Gentiles—a selfless passion, which could only come from the indwelling Holy Spirit. The Lord Jesus Christ wept over Jerusalem, identifying Himself as Yahweh, the One who has wept over His rebellious children (Isaiah 1:1–9) for centuries.

We have heard Jesus call out to *whosoever* was weary, burdened or thirsty, "Come unto me." We have heard our Lord repeatedly declare that *whosoever* would believe on Him would be saved. And we have seen the many scriptures which offer salvation to the whole world and declare that God wants all mankind to be saved, that He gave His Son for the salvation of the whole world, that He is not willing that any should perish, and that Christ died for the sins of all.

To annul this clear teaching of Scripture, the Calvinist changes "world" to "elect" in twenty scriptures. He changes "whosoever" and "all" into "elect" at least sixteen times each. In addition, he turns the phrase "every man" into "elect" six times and "everyone" into "elect" three times. In no case is there anything in the text to justify substituting "elect." The change has been made for one reason only: to support Calvinism! Thus, when Christ says He would draw "all men" to Himself (John 12:32), the Calvinist claims, "The 'all' plainly refers to all of God's *elect.*"[10] *Plainly*? Only if one is a Calvinist.

One would think that the overwhelming testimony of Scripture that God *is love,* that He is ever merciful to all and wants all to come to the knowledge of the truth, would be accepted gratefully and joyfully by all of Christ's true followers, and that this good news would be proclaimed to the world as Christ commanded. Instead, we have seen that in those places where God's desire for the salvation of all mankind is clearly stated, Calvinists still insist that God has chosen to save only a select number. Great effort is made in order to deny what is so clearly affirmed of God's undeserved and unlimited love for all.

One must interpret passages such as "All that the Father giveth me shall come to me" (John 6:37) and "no man can come to me, except the Father…draw him" (John 6:44) in harmony with the overall message of God's love for everyone. Yet Piper goes to great lengths to "show from Scripture that the simultaneous existence of God's will for 'all persons to be saved' (1 Timothy 2:4) and his will to elect unconditionally those who will actually be saved [John 6:37 is among verses referenced] is not a sign of divine schizophrenia or exegetical confusion."[11] In fact, this is a hopeless contradiction unless one recognises man's God-given power of choice.

Consider Christ's words: "All that the Father giveth me shall come to me" does not say that "all that the Father draws shall come to me." Nor does "No man can come to me, except the Father...draw him" say that all that the Father draws come to Christ. And surely "I will raise him up at the last day" (John 6:40,44,54) refers to those who actually come to Christ, and not all who are drawn—certainly not those who are drawn and then "draw back unto perdition" (Hebrews 10:39). Let us accept what Christ actually says.

The Calvinist's Best Foot Forward

In defending our God's honor and character, great care is being taken to accurately understand Calvinism. So let us carefully consider White's arguments as he develops them from John 6:37–45, a scripture that he calls "the clearest exposition of what [critics] call 'extreme Calvinism.'" White writes:

> Literally Jesus says, "No man is able to come to me." These are words of *incapacity* and they are placed in a universal context. All men...lack the ability to come to Christ in and of themselves.... That is Paul's "dead in sin" (Ephesians 2:1) and "unable to please God" (Romans 8:8). It is the Reformed doctrine of total depravity: man's inability [here being] taught by the Lord who knows the hearts of all men....
>
> All men would be left in the hopeless position of "unable to come" *unless* God acts, and He does by drawing [some but not all] men unto Christ.... No man can "will" to come to Christ outside of this divine drawing.... Reformed scholars assert that the ones who are drawn are the ones who are given by the Father to the Son: i.e., the elect....
>
> It cannot be asserted that...the Father is drawing *every single individual human being* [or] universalism [everyone is saved] would be the result, for *all* who are drawn are likewise *raised up* at the last day.[12]

Where in this passage does Jesus mention "total depravity" or "dead in sin" or "*incapacity*" or "unable to please God" or anything about an "elect"? None of these Calvinist theories is there—nor is any part of TULIP even implied. Jesus does not say that the drawing must be limited to the elect, or universalism would be the result. Nor does He say that the drawing is *irresistible* or *unconditional.* Yet Sproul says "draw" means to "compel,"[13] and Pink insists it means "impel."[14] Yarbrough writes, "It is hard to imagine a more explicit description of the Lord's selective and effectual drawing activity."[15]

On the contrary, those ideas are imposed upon the text because Calvinism requires them. They are not stated by Christ.

Christ does *not* say that everyone who is drawn will actually come to Him and be saved. Yet White is joined by a host of others who consider this to be one of the premier "predestination passages"[16] and a proof text for Irresistible Grace. Vance cites no less than thirteen authors of that persuasion.[17] Schreiner and Ware also claim that "the one who is drawn is also raised up on the last day."[18] Yet Christ clearly says it is those who actually come to Him whom He will raise up at the last day. Calvinists read into Christ's words what isn't there. He actually said:

> 1. All that the Father giveth me [not all He draws] shall come to me;
> 2. and him that cometh to me [not everyone the Father draws] I will in no wise cast out.
> 3. And this is the Father's will...that of all which he giveth me [not all whom He draws] I should lose nothing, but should raise it up again at the last day.
> 4. Every one which seeth the Son, and believeth on him [not all who are drawn], may have everlasting life: and I will raise him up....
> 5. No man can come to me, except the Father which hath sent me draw him [all who come have been drawn—not all who are drawn come]: and I will raise him up at the last day [all who will be raised up have been drawn, but not all who have been drawn will be raised up].

Read the entire text again carefully (John 6:35–65). Christ does not say that all whom the Father *draws,* but all whom He *gives* to the Son, will come to Him, and He will lose none of them whom the Father gives Him; they will all be raised at the last day. Of whom is Christ speaking? We have seen that the Bible teaches that in God's foreknowledge He knew who would believe and who would reject the gospel. The former are those whom the Father has given to the Son. There is nothing here about causing a select number to believe unto salvation and choosing not to save the rest of mankind.

Christ says that no one can come to Him unless the Father draws him. But He doesn't say that everyone whom the Father draws actually comes to the Son and is saved. All Scripture testifies to a genuine desire on God's part for all to be saved. Salvation has been procured by Christ and is genuinely offered to whosoever will believe—but not everyone believes. God's sincere desire for all to be saved is stated so often and clearly by prophets, Christ, and His apostles that we dare not see a contrary interpretation in this passage.

The element of the Father "drawing" is mentioned by Christ only in this one passage. On the other hand, the promise is encountered repeatedly throughout John's gospel "that whosoever believeth in him should not perish.... He that believeth on the Son hath everlasting life...he that believeth not the Son shall not see life.... If any man thirst, let him come unto me, and drink," etc. (John 3:16–17, 36; 7:37).

Christ's statement is clear that not everyone who is *drawn*, but "everyone which *seeth* the Son, and *believeth* on him may have everlasting life..." (John 6:40). In this passage we encounter not Unconditional Election or Irresistible Grace but human responsibility.

The Burden of Proof

Without question, Scripture repeatedly presents God's love, compassion, and concern for all Israel and the whole world to be saved. Nor is there any doubt that He offers salvation to all in the clearest language possible. In contrast, not one scripture can be produced where any of the tenets of Calvinism is clearly stated. The burden of proof is upon the Calvinist to show where the Bible clearly teaches his doctrine. Yet even in this passage, which White calls "the clearest exposition of Calvinism," the theory is not plainly stated but must be read into it.

Indisputably, the phrases represented by the first four letters in the acronym TULIP never appear in the Bible. That fact speaks volumes. Never does the Bible say that men are by nature incapable of believing the gospel or of seeking God. Never does it say that a select group is chosen unconditionally to salvation, or that grace is irresistible, or that Christ died only for an elect. Never is sovereign regeneration taught as preceding faith in Christ. *The Calvinist cannot produce for any part of TULIP a clear, unambiguous statement from any part of Scripture!* But we can show hundreds of passages that refute TULIP.

Never does Scripture declare that God desires billions to perish and that it is His good pleasure (and even to His glory) to withhold from them salvation. Never is God's love limited to a select group whom alone He desires to save. In contrast to a few verses that Calvinists must strain to support TULIP, hundreds proclaim plainly God's love and desire for the salvation of all.

The burden of proof is on the Calvinist to show clearly from the Bible that his doctrine is true—and he cannot do it.

Those Who "Draw Back Unto Perdition"

Even in this passage about the Father drawing, there is nothing to indicate that only certain ones are drawn or that the drawing is irresistible or without the willing desire of the one being drawn. Moreover, to "draw" someone in the ordinary sense of that word doesn't mean they will necessarily come all the way, nor is there anything in either the Greek or the context to suggest, much less to demand, that conclusion.

Hundreds of times throughout the Old Testament, God calls through His prophets to Israel, to the hungry and thirsty, to all who will repent, to turn to Him, to seek Him, to "taste and see that the Lord is good" (Psalm 34:8). Surely He is seeking to "draw" them to Himself. *Not once* is there any suggestion that God will irresistibly cause anyone to come to Him, much less that He would do this for less than all. And so it is all through the New Testament. The call is given to "whosoever will" again and again. The invitation is open to all who are willing. For the Calvinist to attempt to make John 6 the exception that supports TULIP is to pervert the clear message of the totality of Scripture.

Contrary to the eisegesis forced upon this text to produce an irresistible drawing unto Christ (which He never taught), many souls are drawn partway to Christ by the Father and then turn back: "If any man draw back, my soul shall have no pleasure in him. But we are not of them who draw back unto perdition [Greek, *apoleia*]; but of them that believe to the saving of the soul" (Hebrews 10:38–39).

The same Greek word, *apoleia,* is found eight times in the New Testament. It is often translated "perdition," and in each case means eternal damnation. Piper acknowledges that "Most commentators agree that...[*apoleia*] indicates clearly the eternal perdition...."[19] Consider the following: "judgment and perdition of ungodly men" (2 Peter 3:7); "And the beast...goeth into perdition" (Revelation 17:11). Clearly, those who "draw back unto perdition" cannot be among Calvinism's elect since the elect cannot lose their salvation and be damned. Yet those who "draw back" must have been *drawn* to some extent. Otherwise, to "draw *back*" would be meaningless.

White avoids Hebrews 10:38–39. So do Pink, Sproul, Piper, and a host of other Calvinists, at least in their books that we have been able to peruse. In his exhaustive treatment, Vance is unable to quote a single Calvinist commenting on this passage.

One of many similar letters I have received declared, "You make God out to be a heavenly wimp who would sure like to save folks, but He just can't do it unless they cooperate. But the God of the Bible is mighty to save, and He does it in spite of the proud, stubborn, self-righteous will of fallen sinners!"

So God could *cause* anyone and *everyone* to believe the gospel and irresistibly draw them to heaven—but He only does this for a select number? This is Calvinism—whether one calls it "moderate" or "extreme"! It has been imposed upon the Bible in violation of the entire tenor of Scripture from Genesis to Revelation. It is a libel upon the character of God, a denial of the nature of love, and an offense to the conscience which God has placed in the heart of every man.

Unquestionably, salvation is a gift of God's love. Neither a gift, nor love, as God has designed them and as the Bible presents them, can be forced upon the unwilling, not even by God. This does not indicate any weakness in God, much less make of Him a "wimp," but simply reflects the nature of love and a gift, as we have amply shown.

That man may rebel against God, disobey His laws, and refuse God's offer of the gift of His grace does not in the least demean God's sovereignty. In fact, in His sovereignty He has ordained that love and a gift would require a choice, and He makes that clear in His Word. Another letter argued similarly:

> You say God loves every person in the world and it is His will that each one be saved.... To even think that God sovereignly allows man to thwart His divine will is heretical, demeaning to God's greatness and a fabulous invention of the mind to accommodate your bias. God controls every animal, every person and all events.... Your views, dear brother, make God's will subordinate to man's will, and represent God's plan of salvation as a failure since all men are not saved....[20]

Those who maintain this position could hardly have thought it through very carefully. We've noted the obvious: If God controls every person and event, then rape, murder, and all crime and wars and suffering must be His doing according to His will—clearly not the case. In the *counsel* of His will He *allows* that which is not His perfect will in order to give man the power of choice. Evil is surely the opposite of God's will. Therefore, we can be certain that it is not God's will for evil to reign on earth. Satan is the god of this world, and "the whole world lieth in wickedness [i.e., in the wicked one, Satan]" (1 John 5:19). God allows this state of affairs only for a time.

Without the power of choice, we could not love God or one another. Man has been given the awesome responsibility to choose for himself. Sadly, most choose evil over good and self instead of God. He does not force salvation upon man any more than He forces anyone to obey the Ten Commandments.

Is It All a Charade?

The Calvinist claims that God, in His sovereignty (if He so desired), *could* stop all sin and cause everyone always to keep the Ten Commandments perfectly. This would be possible only if man had no free will. If that were true, however, what would be the point of giving the Law? God could have controlled human thoughts, words, and deeds so that without even knowing the Law, everyone would do exactly what the Law required.

Incredibly, Calvinism teaches that God gave the Ten Commandments, caused man to break them, then damned him for doing so. The Bible is thereby turned into a charade, man into a puppet, and God into a monster whom the atheist rightly rejects.

There can be no doubt, however, that man, not God, is the cause of evil on earth, having selfishly and foolishly chosen to oppose God's will. Nor can it be doubted that God's Spirit has written His laws in every conscience and seeks to draw all men unto Christ. Yet, sadly, even those to whom God has revealed Himself in great power and miracles have often rebelled and gone to hell.

God said of Israel, "The Lord thy God hath chosen thee to be a special people unto himself...because the Lord loved you..." (Deuteronomy 7:6–8). Similar statements are made throughout the Old Testament, God even calling Israel His wife. Again, "When Israel was a child, then I loved him.... I drew them with...bands of love.... My people are bent to backsliding from me..." (Hosea 11:1–8). All Israel was drawn—many drew back.

Israel is called God's elect in both Old and New Testaments (Isaiah 45:4; 65:9,22; Matthew 24:31, etc.). There is no question that God chose Israel, called her, and drew her with "bands of love" (Hosea 11:4) unto Himself. Yet most Israelites went into idolatry, refused to repent, and were surely not among the redeemed. God had to say repeatedly, "my people have forgotten me days without number" (Jeremiah 2:32); "they have burned incense to vanity" (18:15).

Many who are drawn to the Lord refuse to believe on Him unto salvation. Christ said, "For many are called, but few are chosen" (Matthew

20:16; 22:14). And even some who are chosen are not willing to fulfill their calling but betray the One who they claimed was their Lord. Jesus said, "Have not I chosen you twelve, and one of you is a devil? He spake of Judas Iscariot..." (John 6:70–71).

Jesus called Judas, drew him, and chose him to be a disciple. Judas followed Jesus with the other disciples, called Jesus "Lord," and went forth with the other disciples "to preach the kingdom of God, and to heal the sick" (Luke 9:2). But Judas was like those who will say, "Lord, Lord, have we not prophesied in thy name?...cast out devils?...done many wonderful works?" and yet Jesus will say to them, "I never knew you: depart from me" (Matthew 7:22–23). These have not *lost* their salvation, since they were never saved. "I *never* knew you: depart from me!" will be Christ's pronouncement upon those who were drawn to Him but never came all the way to know Him as Savior and Lord.

Except the Father Draw Him: What Does that Mean?

No one naturally seeks the Lord; we all seek our own selfish desires, and no one can come to Christ except the Father draw him. But the Holy Spirit is in the world to convict all of their sin and need (John 16:8–11), the gospel is being preached, the Father is drawing everyone (even through the witness of creation and conscience). Sadly, many like Judas come partway, even seem to be disciples, then draw back unto perdition.

Jesus did not and could not teach an irresistible drawing in this passage or elsewhere, because it would have contradicted the rest of Scripture. Throughout her troubled history, God sought to draw Israel through weeping prophets. At times she heeded, but the next generation "drew back unto perdition." His dealings with Israel offer proof of God's desire for the salvation of all mankind, all of whom He draws—though few respond.

Yes, Christ clearly said, "No man can come to me, except the Father... draw him." White claims that statement indicates a total incapacity on man's part to come to Christ—that man can't cooperate in any way but must be irresistibly drawn without faith or consent. That's not being drawn but propelled against one's will.

Eisegetical Illusion

To support his assertions, White quotes Calvin, to whom he refers with great admiration. Apparently, Calvin's tyrannical rule of Geneva, where he even resorted to torture of those who disagreed with him, gives no cause for suspecting Calvin's understanding of and fidelity to Scripture.

In fact, such behavior, so completely contrary to the Spirit of Christ and God's Word, is a compelling indication that Calvin's understanding of God's sovereignty, mercy, and love was flawed. As the Apostle John writes, "He that saith he abideth in him ought himself also so to walk [conduct himself], even as he [Christ] walked" (1 John 2:6). That standard applies to every Christian everywhere at every time in history—and at times, Calvin acted so far from it that no excuse can justify his behavior.

Yet apparently oblivious to the historic facts, reflecting an admiration common among Calvinists, White writes:

> John Calvin is admitted, even by his foes, to have been a tremendous exegete of Scripture. Fair and insightful, Calvin's commentaries continue to this day to have great usefulness and benefit to the student of Scripture. Here are his comments on John 6:44:
>
> "To come to Christ being here used metaphorically for believing, the Evangelist, in order to carry out the metaphor in the apposite clause, says that those persons are drawn whose understanding God enlightens, and whose hearts he bends and forms to the obedience of Christ...hence it follows that all are not drawn, but that God bestows this grace on those whom he has elected.
>
> "True, indeed, as to the kind of drawing, it is not violent, so as to compel men by external force [such as Calvin himself used!]; but still it is a powerful impulse of the Holy Spirit, which makes men willing who formerly were unwilling and reluctant. It is a false and profane assertion, therefore, that none are drawn but those who are willing to be drawn, as if man made himself obedient to God by his own efforts...."[21]

Calvin was right that Christ uses "coming to Him" for "believing on Him." Schreiner and Ware write, "The 'coming' of John 6:37 is synonymous with 'believing.' That the words *coming* and *believing* are different ways of describing the same reality is confirmed by what Jesus says in John 6:35, 'I am the bread of life: he that cometh to me shall never hunger, and he that believeth on me shall never thirst.'"[22]

Once again we see that faith in Christ through the gospel precedes, and is, the condition of the new birth and salvation (1 Corinthians 4:15). Faith is not bestowed after one has been regenerated. The fact that *coming* is the same as *believing* also contradicts Unconditional Election and Irresistible Grace, for which "coming" must be without faith, as though a dead man were being carried. Yes, the Father draws men to Christ—but unless they truly believe in Him, they have not "come" all the way but have drawn back unto perdition.

---

1. James R. White, *The Potter's Freedom* (Amityville, NY: Calvary Press Publishing, 2000), 155–56.
2. Robert W. Yarbrough, "Divine Election in the Gospel of John." In *Still Sovereign: Contemporary Perspectives on Election, Foreknowledge, and Grace*, ed. Thomas R. Schreiner and Bruce A. Ware (Grand Rapids, MI: Baker Books, 2000), 50–51.
3. John Piper, "Are There Two Wills In God?" In Schreiner and Ware, *Still*, 107.
4. D. A. Carson, "Reflections on Assurance," *Westminster Theological Journal*, Vol. 54.
5. J. I. Packer, "The Love of God: Universal and Particular." In *Still*, 283.
6. Yarbrough, "Divine." In *Still*, 50.
7. R. C. Sproul, *Faith Alone: The Evangelical Doctrine of Justification* (Grand Rapids, MI: Baker Books, 1995), 137–38.
8. Arthur C. Custance, *The Sovereignty of Grace* (Phillipsburg, NJ: Presbyterian and Reformed Publishing Co., 1979), 277.
9. Robert A. Morey, *Studies in the Atonement* (Southbridge, MA: Crowne Publications, 1989), 296.
10. Arthur W. Pink, *Exposition of the Gospel of John* (Grand Rapids, MI: Zondervan Publishing House, 1975), 682.
11. Piper, *"Two Wills."* In *Still*, 107.
12. White, *Potter's*, 158–60.
13. R. C. Sproul, *Chosen by God* (Carol Stream, IL: Tyndale House Publishers, Inc., 1986), 69.
14. Pink, *Exposition*, 338.
15. Yarbrough, "Divine." In *Still*, 51.
16. D. A. Carson, *Divine Sovereignty and Human Responsibility* (Atlanta, GA: John Knox Press, 1981), 174.
17. Laurence M. Vance, *The Other Side of Calvinism* (Pensacola, FL: Vance Publications, rev. ed. 1999), 508.
18. Schreiner and Ware, Introduction to *Still Sovereign*, 15.
19. John Piper, *The Justification of God: An Exegetical and Theological Study of Romans 9:1–23* (Grand Rapids, MI: Baker Books, 2000), 201.
20. To Dave Hunt, n. d., received September 10, 2000. On file.
21. John Calvin, *Commentary on the Gospel of John, The Comprehensive John Calvin Collection* (Ages Digital Library, 1998); cited in White, op. cit., 161.
22. Schreiner and Ware, *Still*, 14.

CHAPTER

26

Calvin's Errors Are Serious

JOHN CALVIN BELIEVED and practiced a number of things that many of those who call themselves Calvinists today would consider seriously wrong, if not heresy. For example (as we have seen), he dogmat-ically affirmed the efficacy of infant baptism to effect forgiveness of sins and entrance into the Kingdom. And in spite of his quarrel with Rome, he taught that being baptized by a Roman Catholic priest (done to Calvin as an infant) was efficacious for eternity. The priest could even be a rank unbeliever.

Had he not maintained this Roman Catholic false doctrine, Calvin would have had to submit to rebaptism, which was repugnant to him. He derided the Anabaptists for opposing infant baptism. Their valid, biblical reason—that an infant has not believed in Christ—was scorned by Calvin, and his wrath and that of the other Reformers came upon the Anabaptists. These true evangelicals were persecuted and martyred by both Catholics and Protestants for being baptized by immersion after they were saved by grace alone through faith alone in Christ alone.

Rejection of infant baptism was one of the two charges for which Servetus (prosecuted by Calvin the lawyer) was burned at the stake. Calvin wrote, "One should not be content with simply killing such people, but should burn them cruelly."[1] [See Chapter 5 under the subheading "The Torture and Burning of Servetus" for additional context.]

Calvin promotes the error of baptismal regeneration, of salvation by "some secret method...of regenerating" without "the hearing of faith [of the gospel]," that children of the elect are automatically children of God, and of equating circumcision with baptism: "The promise...is one in both [circumcision and baptism]...forgiveness of sins, and eternal life... i.e., regeneration.... Hence we may conclude, that...baptism has been substituted for circumcision, and performs the same office."[2]

Infant Baptism and Circumcision

Nothing more than this section of his *Institutes* is needed to disqualify Calvin as a sound teacher of Scripture and to call into question his entire concept of salvation. His sacramentalism mimics Roman Catholicism:

> We have...a spiritual promise given to the fathers in circumcision, similar to that which is given to us in baptism...the forgiveness of sins and the mortification of the flesh...baptism representing to us the very thing which circumcision signified to the Jews....
>
> We confess, indeed, that the word of the Lord is the only seed of spiritual regeneration; but we deny...that, therefore, the power of God cannot regenerate infants.... But *faith*, they say, *cometh by hearing*, the use of which infants have not yet obtained....
>
> Let God, then, be demanded why he ordered circumcision to be performed on the bodies of infants...by baptism we are ingrafted into the body of Christ (1 Cor xii.13) [Therefore] infants...are to be baptised....
>
> See the violent onset which they make...on the bulwarks of our faith.... For...children...[of] Christians, as they are immediately on their birth received by God as heirs of the covenant, are also to be admitted to baptism.[3]

This same baptismal regeneration, contempt for believers' baptism, and blindness concerning the difference between circumcision and baptism remains among many Calvinists today. Under the heading, "Infant Baptism," in his Geneva Study Bible, R. C. Sproul echoes Calvin:

> Historic Reformed [Calvinist] theology contests the view that only adult, believer's baptism is true baptism, and it rejects the exclusion of believers' children from the visible community of faith.... Rather, the scriptural case for baptizing believers' infants rests on the parallel between Old Testament circumcision and New Testament baptism as signs and seals of the covenant of grace.[4]

On the contrary, baptism belongs to the new covenant and is only upon confession of faith in Christ (Acts 8:37); circumcision was under the old covenant and without faith—and neither one saves the soul. Moreover, not only did circumcision *not* effect regeneration, forgiveness of sins, or salvation, it couldn't even be a symbol thereof, as T. A. McMahon reminds us, being only for males.[5] How could women be saved? And it was for *all* male descendants of Abraham. Even Ishmael, a rank unbeliever, was circumcised—as were millions of Jews.

If, as Calvin taught, circumcision effects "forgiveness of sins, and eternal life...i.e., regeneration,"[6] how could Jews who were circumcised be lost; and why did Paul cry out to God "for Israel...that they might be saved" (Romans 10:1)? Why was he so concerned for the salvation of circumcised Jews that he said, "I could wish that myself were accursed from Christ for my brethren, my kinsmen according to the flesh: who are Israelites..." (Romans 9:1-4)? Clearly, circumcision did not provide "forgiveness of sins and eternal life"—nor does baptism!

Was Calvin Really the Great Exegete?

Calvin's arguments reflect a bias in favor of the sacramentalism he learned as a Roman Catholic from Augustine, which he elaborated upon and thereafter was compelled to defend. His logic often betrays a spiritual immaturity. Incredibly, Calvin argued:

> Such in the present day are our Catabaptists, who deny that we are duly baptised, because we were baptised in the Papacy by wicked men and idolaters.... Against these absurdities we shall be sufficiently fortified if we reflect that by baptism we were initiated...into the name of the Father, and the Son, and the Holy Spirit; and, therefore, that baptism is not of man, but of God, by whomsoever it may have been administered [if clergy].
>
> Be it that those who baptised us were most ignorant of God and all piety, or were despisers, still they did not baptise us into... their ignorance or sacrilege, but into the faith of Jesus Christ, because the name they invoked was not their own but God's.... But if baptism was of God, it certainly included in it the promise of forgiveness of sin, mortification of the flesh, quickening of the Spirit, and communion with Christ.[7]

In Calvinism, the physical act of baptism has spiritual power and imparts regeneration. To be baptized by Roman Catholic priests who were not even Christians, but promoted a false gospel, was acceptable to Calvin because they used the name of God when they administered it! Even to be baptized by *despisers* of Christ and God would bring the "promise of forgiveness of sin..." so long as they were "part of the ministerial office."

Incredibly, though a major figure in the Protestant Reformation, Calvin honored Rome's corrupt and unsaved priests as God's ministers! Yet he condemned and persecuted those who came out of that Antichrist system through faith in Christ for being subsequently baptized as believers according to God's holy Word.

Calvin taught that only the clergy, whether Roman Catholic or Protestant, could baptize or administer the Lord's Supper:

> It...is improper for private individuals to take upon themselves the administration of baptism; for it, as well as the dispensation of the Supper, is part of the ministerial office. For Christ did not give command to any man or woman whatever to baptise, but to those whom he had appointed apostles.[8]

Thus, Calvin also accepted Rome's claim that her bishops were the successors of the twelve Apostles, and from them her priests received divine authority. And he was a leader of the Reformation? Contrary to what Calvin taught about an exclusive "ministerial office," our Lord Jesus Christ clearly commanded the original disciples to make disciples and to teach every disciple they won to Him through the gospel to "observe all things whatsoever I have commanded you" (Matthew 28:20).

Tolerating Calvin's Errors

Obviously, "all things" meant that each new disciple made by the original disciples was to make disciples, baptize them, and teach them to do likewise. Every true Christian today is a disciple of a disciple of a disciple all the way back to the original disciples—each one having taught the new disciples that they, too, must observe *all things* Christ commanded the original twelve. Were the twelve commanded to baptize and to minister the Lord's Supper? Then so is every true Christian as a successor of the Apostles!

Here we have proof enough that all believers in Christ are qualified to do whatever the original disciples did, including ministering baptism and the Lord's Supper. Christ's own words effectively destroy the fiction of a special clergy class lording it over a laity. One would think that this "great exegete" could see that fact clearly from the Great Commission, but he didn't. This elementary error was the basis of the popish power Calvin wielded in oppressing the citizens of Geneva.

Worse yet, how could the priests and bishops of the Roman Catholic Church, who were not even saved but believed and taught a false salvation through works and ritual, qualify as the successors to the Apostles? And how could Calvinist ministers, who disagreed so markedly with Rome on the gospel, nevertheless be co-successors, sharing with Roman Catholic clergy this exclusive right to baptize and administer the Eucharist? Calvin's "brilliant exegesis" led him into grave error and contradictions so blatant that one wonders how today's Calvinists can overlook or tolerate them.

Furthermore, Calvin also taught that there was no difference between the baptism practiced by John the Baptist and the baptism Christ commanded His disciples to perform: "I grant that John's was a true baptism, and one and the same with the baptism of Christ...the ministry of John was the very same as that which was afterwards delegated to the apostles."[9] That is so clearly wrong that we need not discuss it. John's baptism "unto repentance" (Matthew 3:11) had nothing to do with the believer's identification with Christ in His death, burial, and resurrection, as is the case with the baptism Christ told His disciples to practice.

The fact that Paul considered John's baptism different and inappropriate for believers in Christ (Acts 19:1–6) is explained away by Calvin with the fantastic idea that these hadn't received John's baptism,[10] even though, in response to Paul's question, "Unto what then were you baptized?", they replied, "Unto John's baptism."

It seems that Calvinists are willing to tolerate a great deal of error taught by John Calvin and still consider him to be one of the greatest exegetes in history. From a careful study of what Calvin taught in his *Institutes*, however, we have a far different opinion.

That Calvin was wrong on so many other points ought to ease the pain of having to admit that perhaps he was also wrong on TULIP. Yet the high regard in which Calvin is held apparently prevents this simple admission of serious error on his part.

Finding the "Unavailable" Exegesis

There is no question that the Calvinist interpretation of John 6:37–45 is contrary to the entire tenor of Scripture. Let us examine it, too, in this specific context. In John 6:65, Jesus uses slightly different language in saying the same thing: "no man can come unto me, except it were *given* [Greek, *didomi*] unto him of my Father." Note this is not a giving of the sinner to the Son, but a giving to the sinner (given *him*), making it possible for him to come to Christ.

Surely, it is justifiable to take what He says in verse 65 as at least a *possible* indication of what Christ meant by the Father drawing: i.e., that the Father *gives* the opportunity to come. Indeed, we have an abundance of scriptures indicating that this opportunity is given to the whole world through the gospel. This simple understanding adequately refutes White's claim that "there is no meaningful non-Reformed exegesis of the passage available." Certainly this is at least a *possible* one.

In fact, we find that the very same Greek word (*didomi*) is used for "given" multiple times in the New Testament in a way that allows a distinctly non-Calvinist interpretation of Christ's words here, and which is also consistent with the overall biblical emphasis upon God's love and mercy. For example, Paul uses *didomi* when he says that God "giveth to all life, and breath, and all things" (Acts 17:25). Some of the many other places where *didomi* is used to indicate something given by God, and which men can either receive or reject, obey or disobey, and which involves their cooperation are as follows:

- **The law was given by Moses...(John 1:17).** *No one is forced to obey, although there are serious consequences for disobedience.*
- **[I] would have given thee living water (John 4:10).** *The water would not be forced upon her against her will. She would have to want it and willingly drink it.*
- **I have given them thy word...(John 17:14).** *The disciples had to willingly receive the Word and obedience thereto was by their choice—it wasn't forced upon them.*
- **The cup which my Father hath given me, shall I not drink it? (John 18:11).** *Jesus pleaded with the Father that if salvation could come to mankind any other way to spare Him this cup. However, He drank it out of obedience to the Father and love for us.*
- **Through the grace given unto me...(Romans 12:3; 15:15; Galatians 2:9, etc.).** *Paul uses this expression with this same Greek word a number of times. This is not Calvinism's mythical Irresistible Grace. God's grace was not imposed upon him so that he could not disobey or fail to fulfill all God's will, or did not need to cooperate in the fulfillment thereof.*

Surely, all of these usages (and others like them) give us ample reason for the very non-Reformed exegesis that White says is not "available." The Father draws the lost to Christ by giving (*didomi*) to them the opportunity to believe. The giving of those who believe to the Son is of another nature. And those who are drawn by the Father must, in response to the Father's drawing, "see" Him with the eyes of faith and believe on Him to be saved. The giving of the redeemed by the Father to the Son is something else—a special blessing for those who believe.

Christ is saying that we cannot demand salvation—it must be given to us from God. Salvation involves a new birth, and no man can regenerate himself into God's family; that privilege can only be given of God and only God has the power to effect it by His Holy Spirit. In all of this, however, there is neither rational nor biblical basis for believing that God only grants this for a select group and withholds it from the rest of mankind, or that He irresistibly forces it upon anyone.

Christ does not say that the Father forcefully pulls or drags or irresistibly compels anyone to come to Him. In fact, Christ gives every indication that there is definite responsibility on the part of those who are being drawn to believe in Him: "He that believeth on me shall never thirst.... Ye also have seen me, and believe not" (John 6:35–36); "Ye will not come to me, that ye might have life" (John 5:40). Not "Ye *cannot* because my Father will not draw you," but "ye *will not.*"

Instead, the Calvinist view of "draw him" renders "come to me" meaningless, absolving the sinner of any responsibility to come, repent, or believe. One cannot be held responsible for what one cannot do. As we have more than amply documented, Calvinism teaches that the sinner is dead and *cannot* respond unless God first of all regenerates him through Irresistible Grace and then causes him to believe. Nowhere can such teaching be found in Scripture—and certainly not in this passage.

Jesus said, "My Father giveth you the true bread from heaven" (John 6:32). There is no indication of force-feeding. In fact, Christ says, "I am the bread of life: he that cometh to me shall never hunger; and he that believeth on me shall never thirst.... This is the will of him that sent me, that every one which seeth the Son, and believeth on him, may have everlasting life... he that believeth on me hath everlasting life" (John 6:35,40,47). He goes on to say, "I am the living bread which came down from heaven: if any man eat of this bread, he shall live for ever..." (verse 51).

The metaphor Christ chose of eating and drinking contradicts Calvinism. It is clear from this entire passage that eating and drinking

Christ's body and blood is a metaphor for believing on Him, as Schreiner and Ware admit: "To come to Jesus is to satisfy one's hunger and to believe in him is to quench one's thirst."[11] Although the Calvinist tries to say that the faith to believe is given by God in order to *cause* the elect to believe, that idea hardly fits the analogy of eating and drinking. Surely it is the responsibility of the one to whom the Father gives the "bread of life" willingly to eat it. There is no hint that the bread of life is force-fed to the elect through Irresistible Grace.

Human Responsibility

Christ's words, "No man can come to me except the Father draw him," are not the same as White's interpretive "No man is *able* to come to me." Christ is not denying either the necessity or capability on man's part of active acquiescence and faith. The Father alone can *draw*, but men must *come* to Christ as this grace is *given* to them of the Father. And hundreds of passages tell us that this giving (*didomi*) is a gift of God's love, and like the giving of the Son to die for our sins, is for the whole world. Such an understanding is consistent with Scripture's repeated invitations to come—invitations that would be meaningless without a definite responsibility on man's part *and ability* to "come" when he is "drawn." Man has a choice to make: to come or not to come, to eat and drink of Christ or of the things of this world and Satan.

Yes, the Bible says that "there is none that seeketh after God" (Romans 3:11). But that is only one side, and the Bible makes it clear that this statement does *not* mean, as Calvinism insists, that no man is *able* to seek. It is not that man lacks the ability to seek God or that God holds back the essential grace for coming. The problem is that man, in and of himself, lacks the desire to seek God. Blinded by sin and obsessed with self, man seeks everything except God (including false gods he finds more appealing) until, by the Holy Spirit, convicted of sin and convinced of his need of a Savior, he is drawn to Christ.

In infinite love and boundless grace, God continually encourages man to seek Him. Though many, perhaps the vast majority (broad is the road to destruction), reject the wooing of the Holy Spirit and Christ's call to come to Him, many do respond to this call in repentance toward God and faith in our Lord Jesus Christ, the message that Paul preached (Acts 20:21). That is why Paul expended himself—preaching the gospel in the attempt to *persuade* men (2 Corinthians 5:11) to come to Christ—and we should also.

Men are responsible to respond to conscience, to the gospel, and to the striving of the Holy Spirit in their lives (Genesis 6:3). Nor can we as believers avoid our responsibility to obey Christ's command to preach the gospel and to do so in the power of the Holy Spirit and with sincere conviction and persuasion. Paul and Barnabas "so spake, that a great multitude both of the Jews and also of the Greeks believed" (Acts 14:1). So must we, "as the oracles of God" (1 Peter 4:11).

The Universal Thirst that Only God Can Quench

David said, "When thou saidst, Seek ye my face; my heart said unto thee, Thy face, Lord, will I seek" (Psalm 27:8). The sons of Korah sang, "As the hart panteth after the water brooks, so panteth my soul after thee, O God" (Psalm 42:1). Other scriptures could be quoted in the same vein. Not just an elect, but all men in all times and places (and that includes even the wicked and unrighteous, which we all are by nature) are exhorted thus:

> Seek ye the Lord while he may be found, call ye upon him while he is near: let the wicked forsake his way, and the unrighteous man his thoughts: and let him return unto the Lord, and he will have mercy upon him; and to our God, for he will abundantly pardon. (Isaiah 55:6–7)
> God that made the world...hath made of one blood all nations of men for to dwell on all the face of the earth...that they should seek the Lord, if haply they might...find him, though he be not far from every one of us....(Acts 17:24–27)

The Calvinist interpretation of John 6, in its attempt to prove Limited Atonement and Irresistible Grace, makes such scriptures as the above meaningless. There is no way that "wicked...unrighteous...all nations of men" can be turned into the "elect"! Unquestionably, the Bible teaches human responsibility to believe in and seek the Lord. It does not teach that only an elect group are irresistibly made to come to God and to Christ without any willingness or desire on their part. Christ's invitation, "Come unto me," surely means that, though man would not come of his own accord without the Father drawing him, yet when the Father through the Holy Spirit draws men to Christ they are able as moral agents to yield and to come by a genuine act of faith and volition—or to resist and not come.

Why would God urge to seek Him, and Christ invite to come to Him, men who, if Calvinism is true, are totally depraved and dead in sin to the extent that they can't even hear His voice or make a move toward Him? Indeed, if Calvinism were true, why would Christ even say "come unto me and drink" to *anyone*? That invitation wouldn't be appropriate for the elect, since their coming is only by the Father irresistibly drawing them. Nor would it be appropriate for the non-elect, because there is no way they could come even if they had the desire.

The extreme view that interprets human depravity and being dead in sin to mean that the natural man cannot seek after and find God is repudiated by literally hundreds of Bible verses. The few places where it says man doesn't seek God are far outweighed by the scores of passages that encourage seekers after God. Here are just a few:

- Seek the Lord...seek his face continually. (1 Chronicles 16:11)
- If ye seek him, he will be found of you.... (2 Chronicles 15:2)
- Thou, Lord, hast not forsaken them that seek thee. (Psalm 9:10)
- They shall praise the Lord that seek him.... (Psalm 22:26)
- They that seek the Lord shall not want any good thing. (Psalm 34:10)
- Let all those that seek thee rejoice and be glad.... (Psalm 40:16)
- Let not those that seek thee be confounded.... (Psalm 69:6)
- They that seek the Lord understand all.... (Proverbs 28:5)
- For it is time to seek the Lord.... (Hosea 10:12)
- Seek ye the Lord, all ye meek of the earth.... (Zephaniah 2:3)

If men not only *do* not, but *cannot,* seek God unless He causes them to do so with Irresistible Grace, what do all these passages, and scores more like them, mean? That unregenerate man can be motivated to seek after and even to find God is clear from many scriptures. God urges unbelieving and rebellious Israel, "And ye shall seek me, and find me, when ye shall search for me with all your heart" (Jeremiah 29:13). *Irresistibly drawn* without any understanding? No—"He that cometh to God must believe that he is, and that he is a rewarder of them that diligently seek him" (Hebrews 11:6).

More Contradictions

Calvin himself at times contradicted his own theories. He taught that all men "are born and live for the express purpose of learning to know God" and therefore "it is clear that all those who do not direct the whole thoughts and actions of their lives to this end fail to fulfill the law of their being."[12] In this instance, Calvin was agreeing with what the Bible says—but he was contradicting Calvinism. How could the very "law of their being" compel all mankind to seek God, when they are unable to do so? It would make sense for men to be *unwilling* to fulfill the "law" of their being, but to be *unable* to do so would indict the Creator.

Having acknowledged the fact that God made man to seek, to find, and to know Him, how could Calvin believe in Total Depravity? Would God have made all men for the very purpose of seeking after and knowing Him, as Paul plainly said on Mars' Hill (Acts 17:26–28), and at the same time neglect to provide the very grace they need for that seeking and knowing? And why would God predestine to damnation before their birth multitudes of those He would bring into the world "for the express purpose of learning to know" Him?

Calvin further contradicted himself and Scripture with the added argument that when men "do think of God it is against their will; never approaching him without being dragged into his presence, and when there, instead of the voluntary fear flowing from reverence of the divine majesty, feeling only that forced and servile fear which divine judgment extorts...which, while they dread, they at the same time also hate."[13] This horrible, unbiblical picture spawned the idea of Irresistible Grace.

What about the elect? Were they not once totally depraved, yet have been drawn to God? And what of the many scriptures (some of which we have quoted) testifying to the many who took pleasure in seeking God? Where does it ever say that Enoch (who walked with God) or Abraham (the friend of God) or Moses (who spoke with God face to face) or David (whose psalms testify to a perpetual seeking after and thirst for God) or Daniel (for whom time with God in prayer was so precious that the threat of being thrown into the lions' den could not cause him to give it up), et al., were irresistibly drawn by God, who changed their wills without willing cooperation on their part? We are told that "Daniel purposed in his heart" (Daniel 1:8)—not that he was regenerated and then given the faith and desire to seek God.

The Bible contains abundant testimony to the fact that men can be drawn to God and do indeed eagerly come and fall down and worship Him. But even if the picture of totally depraved mankind that Calvin paints were true, wouldn't that be all the more reason for a God who *is* love to extend His grace to all mankind in order to fulfill the purpose for which even Calvin admits He created them? The Calvinist interpretation of John 6 undermines hundreds of other scriptures.

Calvinists seem far too eager to embrace a few verses that say man *doesn't* seek the Lord, and too reluctant to accept the far greater number of verses that urge man to seek God and that tell of the many who found and love Him. Sadly, the God of Calvinism is very selective with love and grace and takes pleasure in damning billions. In defense of God's true character, we insist again that such is *not* the God of the Bible.

---

1. Roland Bainton, *Michel Servet, hérétique et martyr* (Geneva: Droz, 1953), 152-153; letter of February 26, 1533, now lost.
2. John Calvin, *Institutes of the Christian Religion*, trans. Henry Beveridge (Grand Rapids, MI: Wm B. Eerdmans Publishing Co., 1998 ed.), IV: xvi, 4.
3. Ibid., xv, 22; xvi, 3, 4, 8, 10, 17-32.
4. *New Geneva Study Bible*, 38.
5. T.A. McMahon, in an unrecorded interview.
6. Calvin, *Institutes*, IV: xvi, 4.
7. Ibid., xv, 16–17.
8. Ibid., 20.
9. Ibid., 18.
10. Ibid.
11. Thomas R. Schreiner and Bruce A. Ware, eds., *Still Sovereign: Contemporary Perspectives on Election, Foreknowledge and Grace*, (Grand Rapids, MI: Baker Books, 1995), 14.
12. Calvin, *Institutes*, I: iii, 3.
13. Ibid., I: iv, 4.

CHAPTER 27

Persuasion, the Gospel, and God

A THOROUGH EXAMINATION of the passage in John 6, which is extolled as the clearest presentation of Calvinism in Scripture, fails to uncover any support for TULIP. But if Calvinism were actually true, then Jesus would indeed have been "taunting and mocking"[1] the Jews exactly as Luther approvingly believed He did. According to Luther and Calvin, Christ said something like this to the Jews:

> You must believe on Me as the bread of God come down from heaven to give life unto the world. But you lack the ability to believe unto salvation, and My Father is only going to give that ability to some of you.
>
> By "world," of course, I really mean "elect." Though no one recognizes that yet, one day it will be revealed through a system called Calvinism.
>
> You must by faith eat My flesh and drink My blood [i.e., believe that I, as God, became a real flesh-and-blood man to die for your sins, fulfilling the Levitical sacrifices which the priests ate]. If you don't believe on Me, you will perish in your sins. Of course, you can't believe on me unless my Father causes you to, and He gives that grace to only a select number.
>
> You naively think the gospel is a real offer of salvation, but in fact, it is intended the better to damn you. You couldn't believe on Me if you tried.
>
> Come, you wretches, come. These are the terms. But you are all so totally depraved that you can't come to Me except My Father regenerates you and gives you the faith to believe. And

> He has already decided in a past eternity (for reasons hidden in His will and to His glory) that He will only do that for some but not all of you. But you are all held accountable anyway. Yes, He could cause all of you to believe on Me, but it is His good pleasure to rescue only some from hell. And don't think I'm going to die needlessly for those of you whom My Father has predestined to eternal destruction—that would be a waste of My blood. I will die only for the sins of the elect.

What love is this? Some Calvinists willingly admit that the real issue is "whether…God *desires* the salvation of all men."[2] Most Calvinists insist that God has no such desire. Incredibly, MacArthur says God *desires* the salvation of all but *decrees* the salvation of only some [3]—though He can do anything He decrees. Others say that God has two wills, one to save all and the other to damn multitudes—and the latter somehow overcomes the former. Zealously defending God's sovereignty, Calvinism reproaches His character.

If God *could* by His power bend anyone and everyone's heart "to the obedience of Christ" without any desire on their part, why doesn't He do it for all? And why didn't He do this for Adam and Eve at the very beginning, and thereafter for all their descendants? Why needlessly create sin and foreordain man to be its slave, bringing the horror of evil and suffering that would plague billions—and then save only *some* when *all* could be rescued? Why would God *cause* Adam and Eve and all mankind to sin, and then punish them for doing what He caused them to do? This is *not* what the Bible teaches (and conscience rises up against it), but this *is* Calvinism.

In support of this abhorrent doctrine, Calvin quotes Augustine: "Wherefore, it cannot be doubted that the will of God (who hath done whatever he pleased in heaven and in earth...) cannot be resisted by the human will...."[4] So in breaking the Ten Commandments, men are not resisting God's will but fulfilling it! This unbiblical belief created the appalling dogma that everything happening on earth, including all wickedness—even of the grossest nature—is willed by God. How could it be otherwise, if man can do nothing contrary to God's will? Thus Calvinism leads to fatalism, from which come both predestination to damnation and Irresistible Grace. It makes nonsense of the prayer "Thy will be done in earth, as it is in heaven" (Matthew 6:10), if God is the cause of all, as Calvinists insist.

Calvinism and Evangelism

If grace truly is irresistible, if only those elected by God to salvation can be saved, if no one can believe the gospel until regenerated by God and thereafter given the faith to believe, would it not be vain to attempt to persuade anyone to embrace the gospel—or for those who hear to voluntarily believe in Christ? Since there is nothing one can do to change one's eternal destiny (if among the elect, nothing can keep one out of heaven; if not, nothing can be done to escape hell) shouldn't one just let the inevitable take its course? Although many Calvinists would object to this view, inevitably, this is the practical conclusion to which that fatalistic dogma leads. After all (they say), regeneration takes place sovereignly without any faith on the part of the recipient—or even knowledge of its occurrence.

Yet Calvinists, like Spurgeon, often contradict themselves out of a sincere concern for souls that conflicts with TULIP. At times, D. James Kennedy, founder of Evangelism Explosion, makes it sound as though salvation is available to all and even that faith precedes regeneration: "Place your trust in [Christ]. Ask Him to come in and be born in you today."[5] Likewise, contrary to his professed Calvinism, Spurgeon taught that "soul-winning is the chief business of the Christian...."[6]

But soul-winning is an oxymoron if Calvinism is true. The eternal destiny of every person has already been pre-determined, so *winning* is impossible. Yet Kennedy trains others to evangelize—and in the process, further contradicts Calvinism: "For if it is true that we must be born again, then it is also true that we *may* be born again.... That, my friends, is the *good news*."[7] Does he seriously mean that salvation for the elect alone is *good news* for *everyone?* Doesn't such language mock the non-elect?

In attempting to show that evangelism has some place in Calvinism, Boettner declared that every preacher should "pray for them [to whom he presents the gospel] that they may each be among the elect."[8] But since the number and identity of the elect is already determined, isn't such a prayer in vain? Indeed, what is the point of either praying or preaching, if it is not the gospel but sovereign regeneration that brings men to Christ, and the fate of each has been predestined from a past eternity?

As for Kennedy's "*good*" news, are those who have been predestined to eternal torment expected to rejoice that their doom is sealed and there is nothing that can be done to change it? Can he and other evangelistically inclined Calvinists seriously think their practice matches their belief?

In disagreeing with Hoeksema, another Calvinist rightly points out that "for them [the elect] alone the gospel is good news."[9]

Many Calvinists are convinced, and logically so, "that the doctrines of grace are contrary to soul winning."[10] Engelsma callously declares that the call of the gospel "does not express God's love for them [the non-elect]" nor is it "a saving purpose. On the contrary, it is his purpose to render them inexcusable and to harden them."[11] No wonder that by their own admission so many Calvinists lack the Apostle Paul's zeal for winning the lost. Vance quotes a Sovereign Grace Baptist leader who admits that:

> Our preachers are not soul winning men. We do not have soul winning members...we almost never give any instructions on why and how to win souls. We do not really work at soul winning in our churches.[12]

But this is Calvinism. Why "work at soul winning"? There is no *winning* those whose eternal destiny has already been decided. Sproul insists, "Those whom [the Father] regenerates come to Christ. Without regeneration no one will ever come to Christ. With regeneration no one will ever reject him."[13] Evangelism, then, has little significance. James E. Adams declares: "Repentance and faith are the acts of *regenerated* men, not of men *dead in sins.*"[14] Contradicting his quote above, Boettner says, "Only those who are quickened (made spiritually alive) by the Holy Spirit ever have that will [to come to Christ]."[15]

We have already asked: If God is able to regenerate totally depraved sinners, why couldn't He cause the elect to live perfect lives after He has regenerated them? Why doesn't God's Irresistible Grace that is so powerful toward sinners create perfect obedience after they are saved? Why is grace irresistible for lost sinners, bending their wills to His, but not for saved sinners who so often fail to do His will? Something is wrong with this theory!

Another Favorite Verse

John 1:13 is cited by Calvinists as proof that man can have no part whatsoever in his salvation, not even in believing the gospel (hence the necessity of Irresistible Grace): "Which were born, not of blood, nor of the will of the flesh, nor of the will of man, but of God." Van Baren writes, "It is only by the irresistible grace of God that one is born again."[16] In spite of saying that the will plays an important part in salvation, Spurgeon declared, "It is utterly impossible that human language could have put a stronger negative on the vainglorious claims of the human will than this passage does...."[17]

Since a baby has nothing to do with its birth, Calvinists reason that neither can the sinner have anything to do with being regenerated. That spiritual birth is nothing at all like physical birth, however, is a major point of this very passage: "not of blood...flesh...will of man." Palmer even reasons that because an unborn baby doesn't exist, neither does an unsaved person: "a nonbeing does not exist and therefore can have no desires to go to Christ."[18] Neither can it sin or reject Christ or have the least need of being regenerated, if it "does not exist." But how can it be said that those who are not yet "born again" don't even exist?!

Calvin said "infants...are saved...regenerated by the Lord,"[19] even though too young to understand the gospel.[20] Garrett declares, "John the Baptist was born again while in his mother's womb."[21] In fact, the new birth was not experienced by Old Testament saints. Furthermore, it comes only by believing "the word of God...which by the gospel is preached" (1 Peter 1:23–25)—hardly possible for infants, much less for a fetus.

Palmer continues his unbiblical reasoning: "A baby never desires or decides...[or] contributes one iota toward his own birth.... In a similar fashion, the unbeliever cannot take one step toward his rebirth."[22] Even such a firm Calvinist as Pink points out the fallacy: "Regeneration is not the creating of a person which hitherto had no existence, but the renewing and restoring of a person whom sin had unfitted for communion with God...."[23] Vance explains the obvious contradictions inherent in this theory:

> Is a baby responsible for any of its actions before it is born? If not, then [by this reasoning] neither would an unsaved man be responsible for any of his [so he could hardly be a sinner].[24]

The Simplicity of What John Says

John 1:11–13 simply states that flesh and blood have no relationship to the new birth, which is spiritual and completely unrelated to physical birth. Treating the two as analogous was the very mistake Nicodemus made: "How can a man be born when he is old? Can he enter the second time into his mother's womb, and be born" (John 3:4)? Christ makes a clear distinction: "That which is born of the flesh is flesh; and that which is born of the Spirit is spirit" (John 3:6). These are two different births, and any seeming similarities are only superficial and cannot become the basis of sound conclusions.

John also explains that the new birth—which Christ tells Nicodemus is essential for entering the kingdom of God (John 3:3,5)—does not come by man's will but by the will of God. Man did not conceive of the new birth nor can he effect it by his efforts. Nor does the non-Calvinist believe that he can. Yet we are accused of that. Bishop imagines he is refuting the non-Calvinist when he declares that the sinner "cannot renew his own will, change his own heart, nor regenerate his bad nature."[25] Of course not.

How does maintaining that we must believe the gospel to be born again suggest that we can regenerate ourselves? It doesn't.

Of course, only God can regenerate a sinner. But verse 12 declares that God regenerates only those who receive Christ and believe on His name. Yet this verse is commonly overlooked or even avoided by most Calvinists, who reason from verse 13 alone with no regard for content.

Is the new birth imposed upon man by a sovereign God's irresistible grace? Certainly not! It comes by faith in Christ. Moreover, dozens of passages declare that eternal life is a gift from God to be received by "whosoever believeth." Even Calvin said, "Now it may be asked how men receive the salvation offered to them by the hand of God? I reply, by faith."[26] Yet non-Calvinists are criticized for saying the same.

Staggering Deductions

Commenting on John 1:12–13, Calvin links it quite biblically and logically with James 1:18 ("Of his own will begat he us with the word of truth..."). Clearly James, like John, is saying that regeneration was God's idea, "of his own will," and that He effects it ("begat he us"). James likewise confirms Peter's declaration that we are born again by "the word of truth," i.e., through believing the gospel of Jesus Christ—impossible for infants, and something that baptism cannot effect, even in adults. Calvin himself acknowledges that faith in the "word of truth" is essential to salvation—then contradicts himself:

> We confess, indeed, that the word of the Lord is the only seed of spiritual regeneration; but we deny the inference that, therefore, the power of God cannot regenerate infants.... But *faith*, they say, *cometh by hearing*, the use of which infants have not yet obtained.... But they observe not that where the apostle makes hearing the beginning of faith, he is...not laying down an invariable rule....[27]

There is nothing about *beginning* of faith or "invariable rule." The "word of truth" by which we are born again *is* invariable. Moreover, if hearing the "word of the Lord" is the beginning of faith, then an infant, baptized or not, hasn't even begun to possess what Calvin admits is "the only seed of spiritual regeneration."

Calvin retained throughout his life the unbiblical view of baptism, which, as a devout Roman Catholic, he learned from Augustine. As a result of that error, baptism became a substitute for the faith in Christ through the gospel, which Christ and His apostles declare so plainly is essential to salvation or the new birth. His own baptism as an infant was the only "born again" experience we know of for John Calvin.

Calvin's unbiblical ideas led to another astonishing heresy: children of believers are automatically among the elect and thus already regenerated from the womb. That false assurance has probably led multitudes astray! Millions are baptized, confirmed, married, and buried by state churches across Europe—and that is all they know of God and Christ. Listen to Calvin:

> Hence it follows, that the children of believers are not baptised, in order that...they may then, for the first time, become children of God, but rather are received into the Church by a formal sign, because in virtue of the promise, they previously belonged to the body of Christ.[28]

Following Calvin, the Counter-Remonstrance declared that "the children of believers, as long as they do not manifest the contrary, are to be reckoned among God's elect."[29] So a well-behaved baby, toddler, or young child of believing parents is automatically a regenerated child of God without understanding or believing the gospel! Behavior rather than faith in Christ becomes the Calvinist's assurance of salvation—another deadly error, considering the undeniable capacity of many unsaved to live seemingly good lives.

What might "manifest the contrary" mean? And whatever it means, suppose this contrary manifestation didn't show itself for many years? Prior to that time, the person would have been one of the elect but after wrong behavior would no longer be? Could one of the "elect" be lost? And how could behavior either confirm or undo God's election from eternity past? Thus we see again why the fifth point is called "Perseverance of the *Saints,*" and not "The Keeping Power of *God,*"— and why this last of Calvinism's five points, contrary to what one expects, breeds uncertainty instead of eternal security, a fact that will become even clearer in chapter 30.

If a child of one of the "elect" is by that fact alone also among the elect, then his or her children would also be among the elect—and grandchildren, great-grandchildren, great-great grandchildren, and so forth, endlessly. Is not this the logical conclusion to which Calvin's teaching inevitably leads? Why don't leading Calvinists today, instead of highly praising Calvin's *Institutes*, warn of his errors?

Although the belief that children of the elect are themselves elect might be compared to the belief that young children who die prior to reaching an understanding of the gospel are covered by the blood of Christ and taken to heaven, there is a grave difference between the two concepts. The former ultimately involves those who, rather than having been taken to heaven in infancy, continue to live into adulthood. Why should the Calvinist youth, when he comes of age, be challenged to believe the gospel, inasmuch as both by birth and infant baptism he has been declared to be one of the elect?

Later, confirmation merely reinforces confidence in what infant baptism—or being born into a Calvinist family—already allegedly accomplished. Indeed, what need is there to preach the gospel to *anyone,* since the elect are regenerated without it and the non-elect cannot believe it? To defend his dogmas, Calvin managed to rationalize an interpretation of John 1:13 and James 1:18 that actually contradicts both:

> Hence it follows, first, that faith...is the fruit of spiritual regeneration; for the Evangelist affirms that no man can believe, unless he be begotten of God; and therefore faith is a heavenly gift. It follows, secondly, that faith is not bare or cold knowledge, since no man can believe who has not been renewed [reborn] by the Spirit of God.[30]

On the contrary, verse 12 clearly states that those who *receive* Christ and *believe on His name* are as a result given authority to *become* the sons of God. Faith in Christ clearly precedes and is essential for the new birth. Far from teaching that "no man can believe, unless he be begotten of God," both James and John teach the opposite: it is through believing "the word of truth" that one is regenerated. It couldn't be said more clearly that receiving Christ and believing on His name are required by God for Him to regenerate the sinner.

Calvin contradicted himself on this subject as on others: "It is said that believers, in embracing Christ, are 'born, not of blood, nor of the will of the flesh, nor of the will of man, but of God' (John 1:13)...."[31]

Here he clearly admits the biblical order: one embraces (i.e., believes in) Christ and, as a result of this faith, is born of God, i.e., regenerated. In this same section of his *Institutes*, however, he again refers to regeneration as "preceding faith."

Directly Contradicting Scripture

How can Calvinists claim that these verses teach that one must be born again *before* one can believe on and receive Christ? They teach the opposite! From this unbiblical twisting of Scripture flows the doctrine of Irresistible Grace: God must irresistibly regenerate the elect before they can even believe on Christ.

Calvinists make some surprising deductions from John 1:13, such as that "man does not have a free will when it comes to the matter of salvation."[32] Pink insists, "In and of himself the natural man has power to reject Christ; but...not the power to receive Christ."[33] Palmer asserts, "Only when the Holy Spirit regenerates man and makes him alive spiritually can man have faith in Christ and be saved."[34] Custance declares, "What could possibly be a plainer statement than this of the fact that salvation is conferred upon a select number who are conceived by the Holy Spirit and born again by the will of God alone?"[35] Yet each of these statements contradicts the passage, which clearly says that those who have "received him...[and] believe on his name...become the sons of God [being]...born... of God" (1:12–13).

Vance provides astounding quotes from Calvinists contradicting John 1:11-13:

- A person is regenerated before he believes.[36]
- A man is not saved because he believes in Christ; he believes in Christ because he is saved.[37]
- A man is not regenerated because he has first believed in Christ, but he believes in Christ because he has been regenerated.[38]
- We do not believe in order to be born again; we are born again in order that we may believe.[39]
- Being quickened and renewed by the Holy Spirit, [man] is thereby enabled...to embrace the grace offered and conveyed in it.[40]

Read John 1:11–13 and James 1:18. Meditate upon these passages and pray about them. Such statements as the above, which are integral parts of Calvinism, contradict God's Word. They are not derived from but are imposed upon Scripture. Bob Thompson challenges any Calvinist "to point to one instance in the Bible where God implanted His Holy Spirit in...an individual *before* he or she took God at His Word and was saved...."[41]

It is no coincidence that most Calvinists avoid John 1:12. No reference is made to it in the 600 pages of the *Selected Writings of John Knox*,[42] and Pink avoids it in *The Sovereignty of God*. Piper makes two oblique references to it in *The Justification of God*, but without substantive comment.[43] Not one of the thirteen authors in *Still Sovereign: Contemporary Perspectives on Election, Foreknowledge and Grace* confronts it. To his credit, White gives it four and one-half pages[44] because Norm Geisler mentions it in his book, *Chosen But Free* (Bethany House, 1999), and White's book was written specifically as a rebuttal to Geisler.

White attempts a response to Geisler's statement that "verse 12 [John 1:12] makes it plain that the means by which this new birth is obtained is by [*sic*] 'all who receive him [Christ]'."[45] Geisler means that verse 12 gives the qualification ("as many as received him...who believe on his name") for receiving the new birth mentioned in verse 13, and that the new birth is totally "of God." This is what verse 12 clearly says.

Confusing Man's Faith with God's Work

The problem in White's response is simple and twofold: 1) He introduces (without any biblical support) the favorite argument about faith being impossible without the new birth. That assertion is not only contrary to this passage but also to the numerous passages calling upon the unregenerate to believe and offering salvation through faith; and 2) He fails to distinguish between man's believing and God's regenerating. Neither Geisler nor anyone else critical of the Calvinist interpretation of John 1:13 imagines that man's faith *causes* regeneration. Thus the Calvinist is arguing against something his critics don't even espouse.

Jesus tells Nicodemus that he must be born of the Spirit of God. He makes it equally clear that man must believe in order to be saved: "that whosoever believeth in him should not perish, but have everlasting life.... He that believeth...is not condemned: but he that believeth not is condemned already..." (John 3:16,18). And as we've seen, salvation and the new birth are one and the same. Yet White proceeds to demolish the same old straw man:

> Nothing is said in the text that the new birth is "received" by an "act of free will." In fact, *the exact opposite is stated clearly*, "the ones born *not* of the will of man...." It is an amazing example of how preconceived notions can be read into a text that CBF [Geisler's *Chosen But Free*] can say the text makes the new birth dependent upon an act of the "free will" when the text says the opposite.
>
> [Furthermore], if a person can have saving faith without the new birth, then *what does the new birth accomplish?* Evidently one does not need the new birth to obey God's commands or have saving faith.[46]

White confuses what man must do (believe) with what God does (regenerate). That the new birth is "not of the will of man, but of God" does not deny that man must believe for God to effect this work in him. Man's faith in Christ no more causes the new birth than faith causes forgiveness of sins and reconciliation to God. Forgiveness of sins, the new birth into God's family, and the many other blessings we have in Christ are all the work of God—but they are only bestowed on those who believe. Believing did not *create* these blessings; it merely fulfilled God's condition for receiving them. Yes, regeneration is not by man's fleshly will but is all of God; however, God regenerates only those who have received and believed on Christ, as the passage clearly states.

Unquestionably, not only James 1:18 ("begat he us with the word of truth") but numerous other passages teach that believing "the word of truth" is essential for and must precede the new birth. The gospel is the specific "word of truth" that must be believed for the new birth to occur: "Believe on the Lord Jesus Christ, and thou shalt be saved" (Acts 16:31). Peter puts it succinctly: "Being born again...by the word of God…which by the gospel is preached unto you" (1 Peter 1:23, 25). Believing the gospel is the means God uses to effect the new birth—thus faith cannot be imparted by God *after* regeneration, as Calvinism insists.

In response to Nicodemus's question about how a man can be born again into God's kingdom, Christ explains that He is going to be "lifted up" for sin upon the cross like the brazen serpent in the wilderness, "that whosoever believeth in him should not perish, but have everlasting life" (John 3:15–16). Salvation is not of works, but by faith: "But to him that worketh not, but believeth on him that justifieth the ungodly, his faith is counted for righteousness" (Romans 4:5). As Paul repeatedly says, the sinner is "justified by faith" (Romans 5:1).

The sinner must hear and believe the gospel *before* regeneration, not after it. That is why we must preach the gospel and seek, like Paul, to persuade men. Calvin reversed the biblical order, as do his followers today, declaring that no one can believe the gospel until he has first been regenerated. As Spurgeon said, however, one who has been regenerated has no need of the gospel, being saved already.

Is Faith, or Salvation, the Gift of God?

More than one of the critical letters I received charged me with ignorance on this count: "You don't seem to understand that *faith itself* is a God-given gift." That faith is a gift is a major foundational principal of Calvinism. The favorite passage offered as proof is Ephesians 2:8–10. Mathison says, "Saving faith is a gift of God, a result of the regenerating work of the Holy Spirit."[47] Storms claims, "Numerous texts assert that such [saving] faith is God's own gracious gift (see especially Ephesians 2:8–9...)."[48] Clark declares:

> A dead man cannot...exercise faith in Jesus Christ. Faith is an activity of spiritual life, and without the life there can be no activity. Furthermore, faith...does not come by any independent decision. The Scripture is explicit, plain, and unmistakable: "For by grace are ye saved through faith, and that not of yourselves, it is the gift of God" (Ephesians 2:8). Look at the words again, "It is the gift of God." If God does not give a man faith, no amount of will power and decision can manufacture it for him.[49]

On the contrary, the subject of the preceding seven verses is *salvation*, not faith. Verse 8 then declares concerning salvation, "by grace are ye saved...it [obviously salvation] is the gift of God." It is not saving faith, but *being saved* that is God's gift. We are repeatedly told that eternal life is "the gift of God" (Romans 6:23; see also John 4:10; Romans 5:18; Hebrews 6:4, etc.). No less definitive, as Calvin admitted and then tried to deny, is the statement that "faith comes by hearing and hearing by the Word of God." There is no biblical basis for suggesting that God gives saving faith to a select group and withholds it from others.

Furthermore, the construction of the Greek in Ephesians 2:8–10 makes it impossible for faith to be the gift. Such is the verdict of many Greek authorities, including Alford,[50] F. F. Bruce, A. T. Robertson,[51] W. E. Vine, Scofield, and others.[52] Vance notes that "A witness to the truth of Scripture against the Calvinist 'faith-gift' interpretation can be found in the Greek grammarians." He lists W. Robertson Nicoll,[53] Kenneth S. Wuest,[54] Marvin R. Vincent,[55] and others.[56]

Among the reasons the experts cite is the fact that the word *faith* is a feminine noun, while the demonstrative pronoun *that* ("and that not of yourselves, *it is* the gift") is neuter and thus could not refer to faith. Nor will the grammar, as W. G. MacDonald says, "permit 'faith' to be the antecedent of 'it.'"[57] Of course, "it is" is not in the Greek but was added for clarity by the KJV translators and thus is italicized. Nor does it require a knowledge of Greek, but simply paying attention to the entire context of Ephesians 2:8–10, to realize that salvation, not faith, is "the gift of God"—as all of Scripture testifies.

A number of other Greek authorities could be cited to that effect. Though a Calvinist, F. F. Bruce explains, "The fact that the demonstrative pronoun 'that' is neuter in Greek (*touto*), whereas 'faith' is a feminine noun (*pistis*), combines with other considerations to suggest that it is the whole concept of salvation by grace through faith that is described as the gift of God. This, incidentally, was Calvin's interpretation."[58] Calvin himself acknowledged, "But they commonly misinterpret this text, and restrict the word 'gift' to faith alone. But Paul...does not mean that faith is the gift of God, but that salvation is given to us by God...."[59] Thus White and other zealous Calvinists who today insist that faith is the gift are contradicting not only the Greek construction but John Calvin himself.

We Must Believe—God Doesn't Believe for Us

Furthermore, even if saving faith were the gift (which it could not be), there is nothing in Ephesians 2 (or anywhere else) to indicate that it is irresistibly implanted by God only after He has sovereignly regenerated the totally depraved sinner. Indeed, that very passage says we are "saved, through faith"; i.e., faith is the *means* of our salvation/regeneration—not something that follows it.

That saving faith is not only by God's enabling but is something man is responsible for is made clear from many scriptures. When we are told, "Believe on the Lord Jesus Christ" (Acts 16:31) or "have faith in God" (Mark 11:22) there is no suggestion that God will regenerate the unregenerate and then give him that faith; rather, believing is something man is expected to do. When Jesus said, "O ye of *little faith*" (Matthew 6:30; 8:26; 16:8; Luke 12:28), He was not putting the blame upon His Father for giving the disciples so little faith, but upon them for not believing.

When He said, "I have not seen so *great faith*...in Israel" (Matthew 8:10; Luke 7:9) he was crediting the centurion with that faith as his own—not as a gift from God.

For Peter to speak of "the trial of *your faith*" (1 Peter 1:7) would be meaningless if faith were a gift of God. The purpose of the gospel is to bring men into "the faith" (Jude 3), making it their own. Believing the gospel and God's Word is something we must do—God doesn't believe for us.

The epistles use the phrase "*your faith*" 22 times. Paul writes, "*your faith* is spoken of throughout the whole world" (Romans 1:8); "when *your faith* is increased" (2 Corinthians 10:15); "I heard of *your faith* in the Lord Jesus" (Ephesians 1:15); "we heard of *your faith* in Christ Jesus" (Colossians 1:4), and so forth. In the story of the man "sick of the palsy" brought to Jesus by friends, Jesus, "seeing *their faith*," forgave him his sins and healed him (Matthew 9:2; Mark 2:5; Luke 5:20). There is no indication that these men had been regenerated and faith given to them as a gift from God. We are told that "the just shall live by *his faith*" (Habakkuk 2:4). Of the person who "worketh not, but believeth" we are told "*his faith* is counted for righteousness" (Romans 4:5).

That believing God through His Word is man's responsibility is either taught directly or clearly implied in numerous passages from Genesis to Revelation. Calvinists reject the entire message of the Bible when they attempt to interpret a verse here or there to read that faith is God's responsibility to be given as a gift to man.

The Biblical Order: Faith Brings Salvation

In fact, John 1:12 is only one of many verses that make it clear that God effects the new birth/regeneration only in those who believe on Christ. Beside the verses already quoted proving that salvation is by faith in Christ, there are many others.

For example, Galatians 3:14 declares that we "receive the promise of the Spirit *through faith*"; and verse 26 says, "ye are all the children of God *by faith* in Christ Jesus." Likewise, Paul tells the Ephesian believers, "In whom ye also trusted, after that ye heard the word of truth, the gospel of your salvation: in whom also *after that ye believed*, ye were sealed with that holy Spirit of promise, which is the earnest of our inheritance..." (Ephesians 1:13–14). It could not be stated more clearly that a permanent relationship with the Holy Spirit begins only *after believing the gospel.* No wonder White and other Calvinists avoid this scripture as well.

Consider Christ's own words, "that every one which seeth the Son, and believeth on him, may have everlasting life" (John 6:40). It is evident that seeing the Son and believing on Him precede receiving eternal life. Calvin turned it around to say that everyone who is elected and sovereignly given everlasting life by Irresistible Grace will then see the Son and believe on Him. Numerous verses disprove Calvin's reversal of the biblical order.

Jesus said, "He that heareth my word, and believeth on him that sent me, hath everlasting life" (John 5:24). Again, hearing and believing precede receiving eternal life, which comes through the new birth. Surely no one could be regenerated by the Holy Spirit without receiving simultaneously the gift of eternal life—so how could regeneration come before faith? Galatians 3:22 presents the same truth: "But the scripture hath concluded all under sin, that the promise by faith of Jesus Christ might be given to them that believe." The promised new birth and eternal life are given "by faith...to them that believe." Clearly, faith precedes the new birth.

Indisputably, salvation comes by faith. But if regeneration sovereignly comes without and before faith, then the elect, as we have already shown, are regenerated without being saved. To maintain that unbiblical theory, the Calvinist argues that salvation and regeneration are two distinct events, regeneration coming first by God's sovereign act without any faith, then the gift of faith is given so that the person can believe the gospel unto salvation. We have already seen that such an idea was rejected by Spurgeon: "a man who is regenerated...is saved already...it is...ridiculous...to preach Christ to him."[60]

But that raises another problem: How could anyone be sovereignly regenerated by God without being born again of the Spirit? Surely regeneration must be synonymous with the new birth. But if Calvinism is true, there must be *two* new births—one that *precedes* faith and another that comes by believing the gospel unto the new birth (and salvation) that Jesus explained to Nicodemus.

To Whom Is Salvation Offered?

We have already noted that the Old Testament lays the foundation for the New. Specifically, God's provisions for Israel looked forward to Christ and the salvation He would procure for the world of sinners. For example: "For even Christ our passover is sacrificed for us" (1 Corinthians 5:7). Unquestionably, the provision of the Passover was for every person in

Israel without exception: "they shall take to them every man a lamb...the whole assembly of the congregation of Israel shall kill it in the evening... and the children of Israel...did as the Lord had commanded Moses..." (Exodus 12:3, 6, 28).

The manna, also, was for *every* Israelite. And that, too, was a picture of Christ, "the true bread from heaven...that bread of life" (John 6:32, 48, etc.). Of the manna, we are told: "Gather of it every man...take ye every man...and they gathered every man according to his eating" (Exodus 16:16-18). Every Israelite gathered and ate and for 40 years lived on the manna God provided—but most of them were ultimately lost. So the fact that God provided for all did not guarantee salvation to all. Individual faith was required. God did not gather the manna, much less eat it for each of these. Again, we see human responsibility, which pictures individual faith.

Every Israelite was "baptized unto Moses in the cloud and in the sea; and did *all* eat the same spiritual meat [manna]; and did *all* drink the same spiritual drink: for they drank of that spiritual Rock that followed them: and that Rock was Christ." Yet "many of them...were overthrown in the wilderness" (1 Corinthians 10:2-5). *Baptized* and *ate* and *drank of Christ*—yet lost? There is no escaping the fact that God's salvation was graciously provided for *every* Israelite. Israel as a whole is called, "Israel mine elect" (Isaiah 45:4)—yet most of them perished eternally.

The Calvinist has only two choices. He must either accept the possibility of true believers falling away from the faith, or he must admit that salvation is offered to all and that it is effective only for those who believe. Nowhere in any of these Old Testament types is there even a hint of a select group among the Israelites who were elected to salvation, sovereignly regenerated, and then given faith to believe. No wonder Calvinist apologists give these Old Testament types of Christ a wide berth.

The Sabbath pictured the eternal "rest for the people of God" (Hebrews 4:9), found in Christ alone. No Israelite was exempt from any of the Ten Commandments, which included, "Remember the Sabbath day, to keep it holy" (Exodus 20:8), "abide ye every man in his place" (16:29). Nor does the rejection of Christ and the salvation in Him dilute God's sovereignty or His sacrifice for all upon the Cross, any more than does mankind's universal refusal to keep the Ten Commandments.

The Serpent and Christ

No picture of the Cross in the Old Testament life of Israel is more insightful than the incident of the "fiery serpents" that bit the people in judgment for their sin, and the provision God made to heal all who would believe and look: "And the Lord said unto Moses, Make thee a fiery serpent [of brass], and set it upon a pole: and it shall come to pass, that every one that is bitten, when he looketh upon it, shall live. And Moses made a serpent of brass, and put it upon a pole, and it came to pass, that if a serpent had bitten any man, when he beheld the serpent of brass, he lived" (Numbers 21:8-9).

The serpents were a picture of the deadly bite of sin on the entire human race without exception. Just as healing was for "every one...bitten" by a fiery serpent, we can only conclude that healing is for everyone bitten by the "serpent" of sin. And as none is exempt from sin, so none has been left without the remedy God has provided in Christ.

Christ himself pointed to this incident as a picture of His being lifted up on the Cross. The lifting up of the brazen likeness of the serpent foretold one of the most amazing aspects of the Cross—and one most difficult to comprehend. Christ would become the very thing that had "bitten" the human race: "For he hath made him to be sin for us, [He] who knew no sin; that we might be made the righteousness of God in him" (2 Corinthians 5:21).

Calvinists avoid all of these examples that pointed forward to Christ, because they were so clearly for *all of Israel*, showing that the sacrifice of Christ is for *all the world*. As surely as every provision was for each and every Israelite, so surely do we know that many if not most Israelites were eternally lost—in spite of God's provision for them in so many ways.

One will search books by Calvinists long and hard to find any reference to these passages. White avoids them in his book *The Potter's Freedom*. And in my debate with him in book form, *Debating Calvinism: Five Points, Two Views*, he refused to respond to any of these powerful pictures that I pointed out from the Old Testament—even daring to declare that they were "irrelevant." And that included the brazen serpent![61]

John says of Jesus, "In him was life; and the life was the light of men... the true Light, which lighteth every man that cometh into the world" (John 1:4,9). Once again, the words "every man" tell us clearly that the unregenerated can be given the light of the gospel. "I am the light of the *world*:" said Jesus. "He that followeth me shall not walk in darkness, but shall have the light of life" (John 8:12). White has no comment on these verses in his book, nor upon other similar passages such as John 16:8, where Jesus said that when the Holy Spirit came, He would "reprove the *world* of sin, righteousness and judgment." Many other verses could be cited in the same vein, which Calvinists also avoid.

---

1. Martin Luther, *The Bondage of the Will,* J. I. Packer and O. R. Johnston, translator (Grand Rapids, MI: Fleming H. Revell, 1999), 153.
2. John Murray and Ned B. Stonehouse, *The Free Offer of the Gospel* (n. p., n. d.), 3.
3. John MacArthur, Author and General Editor, *The MacArthur Study Bible* (Nashville, TN: Word Publishing, 1997), 1862.
4. John Calvin, *Institutes of the Christian Religion*, trans. Henry Beveridge (Grand Rapids, MI: Wm B. Eerdmans Publishing Co., 1998 ed.), III: xxiii, 14.
5. D. James Kennedy, *Why I Believe* (Dallas, TX: Word Publishing, 1980), 140.
6. Charles Haddon Spurgeon, *The Soul Winner* (Grand Rapids, MI: Wm B. Eerdmans Publishing Co., 1963), 15.
7. Kennedy, *Believe*, 138.
8. Loraine Boettner, *The Reformed Doctrine of Predestination* (Phillipsburg, NJ: Presbyterian and Reformed Publishing Co., 1932), 285.
9. James Daane, *The Freedom of God* (Grand Rapids, MI: Wm B. Eerdmans Publishing Co., 1973), 24.
10. Joseph M. Wilson, "Soul Winning," *The Baptist Examiner*, February 15, 1992, 1.
11. David J. Engelsma, *Hyper-Calvinism and the Call of the Gospel* (Grandville, MI: Reformed Free Publishing Association, 1980), 17–18.
12. Wilson, "Soul," 1–2; cited in Laurence M. Vance, *The Other Side of Calvinism* (Pensacola, FL: Vance Publications, rev. ed. 1999), 542.
13. R. C. Sproul, *Chosen by God* (Carol Stream, IL: Tyndale House Publishers, Inc., 1986), 125.
14. James E. Adams, *Decisional Regeneration* (McDonough, GA: Free Grace Publications, 1972), 12.
15. Boettner, *Reformed*, 11.
16. Gise J. Van Baren, "Irresistible Grace," in Herman Hanko, Homer C. Hoeksema, and Gise J. Van Baren, *The Five Points of Calvinism* (Grandville, MI: Reformed Free Publishing Association, 1976), 77.
17. Charles Haddon Spurgeon, "God's Will and Man's Will," No. 442 (Newington: Metropolitan Tabernacle; sermon delivered Sunday morning, March 30, 1862).
18. Edwin H. Palmer, *the five points of calvinism* (Grand Rapids, MI: Baker Books, enlarged ed., 20th prtg., 1999), 17.
19. Calvin, *Institutes*, IV: xvi, 16–19.
20. Ibid.
21. Eddie K. Garrett, "The Purpose of the Gospel" *(The Hardshell Baptist*, December 1990, 4); cited in Vance, *Other Side*, 525.
22. Palmer, *five points*, 17.

23. Arthur W. Pink, *The Doctrine of Salvation* (Grand Rapids, MI: Baker Book House, 1975), 26–27.
24. Vance, *Other Side*, 522.
25. George S. Bishop, *The Doctrines of Grace* (Grand Rapids, MI: Baker Book House, 1977), 146.
26. John Calvin, *Calvin's New Testament Commentaries* (Grand Rapids, MI: Wm B. Eerdmans Publishing Co., 1994), 11:144.
27. Calvin, *Institutes*, IV: xvi, 18.
28. Calvin, *Institutes*, IV: xvi, 18–21; IV: xv, 22.
29. Vance, *Other Side*, 151–52.
30. John Calvin, *Commentary on the Gospel According to John* (Grand Rapids, MI: Baker Book House, 1984), 43; cited in James R. White, *The Potter's Freedom* (Amityville, NY: Calvary Press Publishing, 2000), 183.
31. Calvin, *Institutes*, II: ii,19.
32. Manford E. Kober, *Divine Election or Human Effort?* (n. p., n. d.), 31; cited in Vance, *Other Side*, 216.
33. Arthur W. Pink, *The Sovereignty of God* (Grand Rapids, MI: Baker Book House, 2nd prtg. 1986 ed.), 128.
34. Palmer, *five points*, 27.
35. Arthur C. Custance, *The Sovereignty of Grace* (Phillipsburg, NJ: Presbyterian and Reformed Publishing Co., 1979), 188.
36. W. E. Best, *Simple Faith (A Misnomer)* (Houston, TX: W. E. Best Book Missionary Trust, 1993), 34.
37. Boettner, *Reformed*, 101.
38. Arthur W. Pink, *The Holy Spirit* (Grand Rapids,MI: Baker Book House, 1978), 55.
39. Grover E. Gunn, *The Doctrines of Grace* (Memphis, TN: Footstool Publications, 1987), 8.
40. Westminster Confession of Faith (London: n. p., 1643), Chapter X.
41. Bob Thompson, "The 5 Points of Calvin's Doctrine of Predestination" (self-published monograph, 4056 Skyline Rd., Carlsbad CA 92008, n. d.), 6.
42. John Knox, *Selected Writings of John Knox* (Dallas, TX: Presbyterian Heritage Publications, 1995).
43. John Piper, *The Justification of God: An Exegetical and Theological Study of Romans 9:1–23* (Grand Rapids, MI: Baker Books, 2000), 31, note 154.
44. James R. White, *The Potter's Freedom: A Defense of the Reformation and a Rebuttal of Norman Geisler's Chosen But Free* (Amityville, NY: Calvary Press Publishing, 2000), 182–86.
45. Cited in White, *Potter's*, without footnote reference.
46. Ibid., 185.
47. Keith A. Mathison, *Dispensationalism: Rightly Dividing the People of God?* (Phillipsburg, NJ: Presbyterian and Reformed Publishing Co., 1995), 99.
48. C. Samuel Storms, "Prayer and Evangelism under God's Sovereignty;" in Thomas R. Schreiner and Bruce A. Ware, eds., *The Grace of God, The Bondage of the Will* (Grand Rapids, MI: Baker Books, 1995), 221.
49. Gordon H. Clark, *Predestination* (Phillipsburg, NJ: Presbyterian and Reformed Publishing Co., 1987), 102; cited in Vance, *Other Side*, 515–16.
50. Henry Alford, *The New Testament for English Readers* (Grand Rapids,MI: Baker Book House, 1983), 3:216.

51. Archibald Thomas Robertson, *Word Pictures in the New Testament* (New York: Harper and Bros., 1930), 4:525.
52. Cited in Samuel Fisk, *Divine Sovereignty and Human Freedom* (Neptune, NJ: Loizeaux Brothers, 1973), 32–36.
53. W. Robertson Nicoll, ed., *The Expositor's Greek Testament* (Grand Rapids, MI: Wm B. Eerdmans Publishing Co., n. d.), 3:289.
54. Kenneth S. Wuest, *Ephesians and Colossians in the Greek New Testament* (Grand Rapids, MI: Wm B. Eerdmans Publishing Co., 1953), 69.
55. Marvin R. Vincent, *Word Studies in the New Testament* (New York: Charles Scribner's Sons, 1924), 3:376.
56. Vance, *Other Side*, 517.
57. MacDonald, W. G., *Grace Unlimited,* ed. Clark H. Pinnock (Bloomington, MD: Bethany Fellowship, Inc., 1976), 87; quoted in Samuel Fisk, *Calvinistic Paths Retraced* (Raleigh, NC: Biblical Evangelism Press, 1985), 22.
58. F. F. Bruce, *The Epistles to the Colossians, to Philemon, and to the Ephesians* (Grand Rapids, MI: Wm B. Eerdmans Publishing Co., 1984), 220–21.
59. John Calvin, *Calvin's New Testament Commentaries* (Grand Rapids, MI: Wm B. Eerdmans Publishing Co., 1994), 11:145.
60. C. H. Spurgeon, "The Warrant of Faith" (Pasadena, TX: Pilgrim Publications, 1978), 3. [one-sermon booklet from 63-volume set].
61. Dave Hunt & James White, *Debating Calvinism: five points, two views* (Sisters, Oregon: Multnomah Publishers, 2004), 277.

CHAPTER

28

When Is "Love" Not Love?

IN A RADIO DISCUSSION with James White, I referred to Christ's weeping over Jerusalem. I pointed to His expression of desire ("how often would I") and His lament over Jerusalem's hard-hearted response ("ye would not") as proof of His sincere offer of grace, and of man's right and ability to receive or reject salvation:

> O Jerusalem, Jerusalem, thou that killest the prophets, and stonest them which are sent unto thee, how often would I have gathered thy children together, even as a hen gathereth her chickens under her wings, and ye would not! (Matthew 23:37)

White countered that Christ was not weeping over Jerusalem and that the ones He wanted to gather were Jerusalem's children, not the religious leaders who rejected Him. "Ye would not," he insisted, expressed the attitude of the rabbis, not of Jerusalem's "children" whom He wanted to gather under His care.

This argument, however, is of no help to White or other Calvinists who use it. Very few if any of Jerusalem's "children," any more than her leaders, ever believed on Christ. Therefore, even if Christ only meant the children, He was expressing a desire for the salvation of many who were never saved.

Did Christ Really Weep Over Jerusalem?

Here is one more example of the way in which Calvinists must twist Scripture in defending their strange doctrine. In fact, the expression, "children of Jerusalem" or "children of Israel," etc., is used throughout Scripture to indicate "the people" of a city or country or race—*never* its non-adults. When only the young children are meant, the context always makes that fact clear, as "the wives also and the children rejoiced..." (Nehemiah 12:43).

The expression, "children of Israel" is found 644 times, "children of Ammon" 89 times, "children of Benjamin" 36 times, "children of God" 10 times, and *not once* in those 779 instances is the reference to non-adults! The specific phrase, "children of Jerusalem," is used in Joel 3:6 for the "inhabitants of Jerusalem"—exactly as Christ meant in His lament. Among many similar references to "children" and "Jerusalem" (*none* of which means its non-adults exclusively) we find:

> And in Jerusalem dwelt of the children of Judah, and of the children of Benjamin, and of the children of Ephraim, and Manasseh... (1 Chronicles 9:3); the children of Judah and Jerusalem (2 Chronicles 28:10); And the children of Israel that were present at Jerusalem (2 Chronicles 30:21); all the children of the captivity, that they should gather themselves together unto Jerusalem (Ezra 10:7); children of the province...that...came again to Jerusalem (Nehemiah 7:6); Jerusalem...thy children have forsaken me...and assembled themselves by troops in the harlots' houses.... Every one neighed after his neighbour's wife.... Saith the Lord: and shall not my soul be avenged on such a nation as this? (Jeremiah 5:1-9); etc.

There are numerous other similar references, all of which clearly refer to the *inhabitants* of Jerusalem or some other city or country and *none* of which refers exclusively to non-adults. In His great love, Christ is clearly pleading with Israel—as He has through His prophets for centuries, and as He still pleads with the world for which He died.

Disagreement in the Ranks

Not only is White's argument (which is used by many Calvinists) both irrational and unbiblical, but even some Calvinist leaders disagree with it. John MacArthur, Jr., recognizes that Christ is expressing the same desire for the salvation of all the inhabitants of Jerusalem that He has expressed for centuries as the God of Israel through His prophets.[1] He declares that "Jesus weeps over the city of Jerusalem...we cannot escape the conclusion that God's benevolent, merciful love is unlimited in extent.... Luke 19:41-44 gives an even more detailed picture of Christ's sorrow over the city...."[2] And MacArthur even suggests that "the city of Jerusalem [represents] the Israelite Nation."[3]

Luther also declared, "In Christ, God comes seeking the salvation of all men; He offers Himself to all; He weeps over Jerusalem because Jerusalem rejects Him.... Here God incarnate says: 'I would, and thou wouldest not.' God incarnate...was sent for this purpose, to will, say, do, suffer and offer to all men, all that is necessary for salvation albeit he offends many who, being abandoned or hardened by God's secret will of Majesty...do not receive him...."[4]

In a further contradiction of his affirmation at other times of Limited Atonement, Spurgeon also applied Christ's words both to all of Jerusalem and to all sinners:

> In Christ's name I have wept over you as the Saviour did, and used his words on his behalf, "O Jerusalem, Jerusalem, how often would I have gathered thy children together as a hen gathereth her chickens under her wings, and ye would not...." Oh! God does plead with... everyone of you, "Repent, and be converted for the remission of your sins...." And with divine love he woos you...crying, "Come unto me...."
>
> "No," says one strong-doctrine man, "God never invites all men to himself...." Stop, sir.... Did you ever read... "My oxen and my fatlings are killed, and all things are ready; come unto the marriage. And they that were bidden *would not come*...." Now if the invitation is...made [only] to the man who will accept it, how can that parable be true? The fact is...the invitation is free.... "*Whosoever will*, let him come...."
>
> Now...some of you [may] say that I was...Arminian at the end. I care not. I beg of you to...turn unto the Lord with all your hearts.[5]

Spurgeon makes an excellent point. Christ likens the kingdom of God to a supper to which men are invited (Luke 14:15-24). In the parable, there is no question that a bona fide invitation was extended, nor that many if not most of those sincerely invited refused and even scorned the invitation and suffered the Lord's wrath: "For I say unto you, That none of those men which were bidden shall taste of my supper" (v. 24).

The problem for the Calvinist is to explain how God can sincerely invite into His kingdom those for whom Christ did not die, whom He has not elected to salvation, whom He has from a past eternity predestined to eternal torment and who can't accept because He withholds from them the grace they need—then punish them for not responding to His "invitation." How, indeed! And why does He send his servants to "compel" those "in highways and hedges...to come in, that my house may be filled" (v. 23), if regeneration is a sovereign act of God without human response? And if faith is a gift and grace is irresistible, how could the elect refuse the earnest invitation? Spurgeon leaves these questions unanswered, knowing he will be accused of being "Arminian at the end."

Nor have we found any Calvinist who attempts to answer Spurgeon. The only reasonable and biblical response is to abandon Calvinism, which Spurgeon would not do, although he continued to contradict it in his preaching. And for pointing out these contradictions, I am criticized for allegedly misquoting and misrepresenting Spurgeon.

Contradictions, Contradictions....

Calvinists speak out of both sides of their mouths in order to avoid the valid charge that Calvinism denies God's love for all mankind. Those who try to separate themselves from what they call "extreme Calvinism," or "hyper-Calvinism," go to great lengths to make it appear that Calvinism's God truly loves all. As already noted, John MacArthur spends an entire book in that vain attempt.[6] There is no escaping the fact that his book, which purports to show that God loves all, basically says the opposite.

MacArthur makes it clear that though God supposedly loves everyone, He never intended to save everyone, claiming that had He done so, all would have been saved. No place is allowed for anyone to accept or to reject a genuine offer of the gospel by his own choice. He thus falls into inescapable contradictions. For example, MacArthur condemns those who "deny that God loves everyone,"[7] but what he calls God's "love" for the non-elect is not love at all! He confesses that "to abandon logic is to become irrational, and true Christianity is not irrational."[8] Yet he argues irrationally that loving "the elect in a special way reserved only for them... does not make His love for the rest of humanity any less real."[9]

He has just declared that "God chose...unto salvation...certain individuals and passed over others, and He made that choice in eternity past... without regard to anything He foresaw in the elect; simply according to the good pleasure of his will and to the praise of the glory of his grace...(Ephesians 1:5-6)." In his next breath, however, he admits, "It seems reasonable to assume that if God loved everyone, He would have chosen everyone unto salvation.... It is folly to think that God loves all alike, or that He is compelled by some rule of fairness to love everyone equally."[10]

On the contrary, "degrees of love" cannot explain the difference between predestining a select group to heaven and the rest to hell, though all could have been received into heaven! It is *not love at all* to predestine to hell *any* who could have been saved! So MacArthur attempts a further "explanation:"

> God's love for the reprobate is not a love of value; it is the love of pity...a love of compassion...of sorrow...of pathos...the same deep sense of compassion and pity we have when we see a scab-ridden derelict lying in the gutter...a genuine, well-meant, compassionate, sympathetic love....[11]

Here we see the depths of complete irrationality into which the Calvinist falls in trying to balance on the tight rope of "God loves all but not in the same way"!

Kinds or *Aspects* of Love?

One is aghast at such astonishing statements. God has genuine "compassionate, sympathetic love" for those whom He has predestined to eternal torment, whom He could save but never intended to, and for whom Christ did not die? Words seem to have a different meaning for the Calvinist than for the ordinary person who understands love and sympathy by the God-given conscience, of which the Calvinist seems bereft!

Genuine compassion for a derelict would not just leave him there but would do all that could be done to rescue him. Otherwise it is not the compassion of the good Samaritan who cared for the derelict (Luke 10:33-35) but the hypocrisy of the priest and Levite who "passed by on the other side" (Luke 10:31-32) and left the robbed and wounded victim to die—and worse, predestined that condition. The "love" MacArthur attributes to God is like that of those condemned by James who say to one naked and starving, "Depart in peace, be ye warmed and filled," but give him nothing (James 2:15-16).

God through the Apostle James condemns such double-speak, yet God himself is guilty of such hypocrisy? MacArthur attempts to escape the conscience by suggesting that "in some sense God loves His enemies,"[12] and by hiding behind the idea of "two aspects of God's love—His universal love for all humanity and His particular love for the elect [which] must not be confounded."[13] But an "aspect" of love, whatever that might mean, must still be *love*—and it is not love of any kind, nor is it any aspect thereof, to predestine to damnation any who could just as well have been saved!

Luther tries to defend the same contradiction. Having declared that Christ came to "offer to all men all that is necessary for salvation," he adds that "the will of Majesty purposely leaves and reprobates some to perish. Nor is it for us to ask why...."[14] *Why?* There is no answer to this blatant contradiction—and to hide behind mystery is irresponsible!

All that is necessary? Then all would be saved! What an uncalvinistic statement, yet Spurgeon agreed. How could anyone disagree, since this is what God himself declared: "What could have been done more to my vineyard [Israel], that I have not done in it? Wherefore, when I looked that it should bring forth grapes, brought it forth wild grapes (Isaiah 5:3-4)?

Here is the message of the entire Bible: God himself says He has done all He could in providing salvation, which He offers freely in His love and grace to all mankind—but it can't be forced upon anyone; it must be received by faith in His promise. God is genuinely mourning over Israel!

What more could God have done? That question is mockery if Calvinism is true! He could have predestined them to salvation, extended Irresistible Grace, sovereignly regenerated them, and given them faith to believe the gospel—if this is imposed by sovereign will, with no choice by man required.

The only way that God could have done all He could, yet men remain unsaved, is if man may choose to accept or reject the salvation He offers. That conclusion is inescapable—but that biblical logic cannot be acknowledged, for it would destroy Calvinism.

This passage in Isaiah 5 is generally given a wide berth by Calvinist apologists. White avoids it. MacArthur attempts to support his misrepresentation of God's love with an equally mistaken statement from 17th-century Calvinist pastor and writer Andrew Fuller: "Likewise God gave no effectual grace to those who are accused of bringing forth wild grapes instead of grapes; yet *He looked for* and asked what He could have done more for His vineyard that He had not done (Isaiah 5:4)."[15] Well, He could have given "effectual grace"! Except that this term isn't biblical but is an invention of Calvinists to support their theory.

How can it be rationally said that God "offers all that is necessary to salvation" to those whom He "purposely leaves and reprobates...to perish"?

The conflict would be resolved, the contradiction disappear, the misrepresentation of God be erased, and God's love be vindicated by the simple admission that man has a God-given genuine power of choice. But the Calvinist cannot admit to that fact—nor could Luther, after writing an entire book against free will.

Christ Is Speaking as the God of Israel

How do we understand Christ's lament over Jerusalem? From comparing the gospel accounts, we know that Jesus had just made His triumphal entry into Jerusalem and was in the temple when He made the statement in Matthew 23. Luke specifically declares that as He rode into the city on the colt of an ass He wept as He beheld Jerusalem from a vantage point:

> And when he was come near, he beheld the city, and wept over it, saying, If thou hadst known, even thou, at least in this thy day, the things which belong unto thy peace! but now they are hid from thine eyes. For...thine enemies shall...lay thee even with the ground, and thy children within thee...because thou knewest not the time of thy visitation. (Luke 19:41–44)

There is no doubt that Christ wept over the city of Jerusalem as He looked upon it. Nor can there be any doubt that when in the temple He lamented, "O Jerusalem, Jerusalem," He was referring to the city and all of its inhabitants down through history, not to any certain segment of the population. "Thy children" could only mean the inhabitants of Jerusalem, not the babes and youth. To suggest, as White stated in a letter, that "those who were 'unwilling' were not those Jesus sought to gather" does violence to what Jesus says: "How often would I...but ye would not." He is specifically saying that He wanted to gather them, but they were unwilling. As He had so often as Yahweh in the past and now as their Messiah come in the flesh, He is addressing the inhabitants of Jerusalem as that city's children: "Return, ye backsliding children..." (Jeremiah 3:22). Non-adults only were addressed? Hardly.

Furthermore, Christ's very words, "How often would I," were a direct claim to deity, a claim that White, in his zeal to defend Calvinism, misses completely. Christ is claiming multiple prior pleadings over Jerusalem, yet no such instances are recorded in the gospel accounts during His incarnation. Unquestionably, Christ is presenting Himself as the God of Israel who had sent His prophets generation after generation to warn the inhabitants of Jerusalem, often called "the children of Israel...the children of Judah," that if they did not repent, His wrath would be poured out upon them.

Many passages could be quoted, each of which by itself could explain Christ's statement. Here are but a few of such lamentations and warnings from God at the mouth of only one of His prophets, Jeremiah. Only in this context, and as the God of Israel, is there justification for Christ to use the words "how *often* would I...but ye would not."

> Go and cry in the ears of Jerusalem...Thus saith the Lord; I remember thee, the kindness of thy youth, the love of thine espousals, when thou wentest after me in the wilderness.... Israel was holiness unto the Lord...[but] my people have...forsaken me.... My bowels, my bowels! I am pained at my very heart...O my soul, the sound...of war. Destruction upon destruction.... For my people is foolish, they have not known me; they are sottish children.... Woe unto thee, O Jerusalem! wilt thou not be made clean? I spake unto you, rising up early and speaking, but ye heard not; and I called you, but ye answered not.... I have even sent unto you all my servants the prophets, daily rising up early and sending them: yet they hearkened not unto me.... Thus saith the Lord of hosts, the God of Israel; Behold, I will bring evil upon this place...because they have forsaken me...and have burned incense...unto other gods...and have filled this place with the blood of innocents; they have built also the high places of Baal, to burn their sons with fire for burnt offerings unto Baal.... I will make this city desolate...because of all the houses upon whose roofs they have burned incense unto all the host of heaven, and have poured out drink offerings unto other gods. For this city hath been to me as a provocation of mine anger and of my fury from the day that they built it even unto this day...because of all the evil of the children of Israel and of the children of Judah... they, their kings, their princes, their priests, and their prophets, and the men of Judah, and the inhabitants of Jerusalem.... Though I taught them, rising up early and teaching them, yet they have not hearkened to receive instruction. (Jeremiah 2:2–3,13; 4:19–22; 7:13, 25–26; 13:27; 19:3–13; 32:31–33; etc.)

If these and hundreds of similar declarations from the prophets, echoed by Christ, do not express a genuine loving concern on God's part for Israel to repent so that His wrath need not be poured out upon her, then words have no meaning. Such sincere concern in the face of Israel's refusal to repent completely refutes TULIP. Otherwise, God's pleadings and warnings are a sham.

If men are totally depraved (as by the Calvinist definition), then there is no point in God's pleading with them. If only a few are among the elect and God is not sincerely offering salvation, but withholds the Irresistible Grace without which they cannot repent, then hundreds of pages in the Bible are a farce, the pretended pleadings from a Calvinist God who has no real love except for the elect, and no intention of helping those over whom He supposedly weeps. To support TULIP from the Bible, the Calvinist must do violence to Scripture.

Is There a Real Battle for Souls?

Paul tells us that Satan, "the god of this world hath blinded the minds of them which believe not, lest the light of the glorious gospel of Christ... should shine unto them" (2 Corinthians 4:4). Why would it be necessary for Satan to blind the totally depraved who are as spiritually blind as one could be? Indeed, they are *dead*, and dead men can't see. Calvinism makes this passage (and many others) meaningless.

As for the elect, if, as Calvinism declares, they are sovereignly regenerated and by Irresistible Grace given the faith to believe, and nothing can prevent them from hearing and believing the gospel, it would be impossible for Satan to blind them and therefore, there would be no point in his even trying. And since the non-elect are already damned, there would be no real battle between God and Satan for souls, no real conflict within the human heart, the whole thing having already been decided by God with nothing Satan or man could do to change that fact. Paul would have been wasting his time disputing and persuading—and the same would be true of our seeking to win to Christ those whom God has predestined to hell.

Calvinism, if it were true, would make a joke of the Bible's warnings about Satan. God's withholding Irresistible Grace does a better job of damning souls than Satan ever could. That enemy of souls could go on a long vacation. Yet the Bible declares, "Your adversary the devil, as a roaring lion, walketh about, seeking whom he may devour" (1 Peter 5:8); "The great dragon...that old serpent, called the Devil, and Satan... deceiveth the whole world" (Revelation 12:9).

"As many as received him..." sounds as though the volitional act of receiving is required on the part of the convicted sinner. Eternal life is a free gift. A gift cannot be merited, earned, or paid for in any way, but it *must* be received. Surely, to "receive" requires some acquiescence on the part of the recipient. Anything imposed upon someone by a grace that is "irresistible" is not a gift received.

Indeed, how can grace be irresistible? The very term "irresistible grace" is self-contradictory. How can it be an act of "grace" to impart to someone something the person neither believes nor desires? "God doesn't force anyone," says the Calvinist. Then what does "irresistible" mean? "God is just removing their resistance," is the reply. *Irresistibly* removing it? If it is not against their will, why must it be irresistible?

Would that not fill heaven with those who had been unwilling to believe in Christ, to love God, or even to be there, but who had been irresistibly *made* willing? "Not so," counters the Calvinist, in defense of his theory. "God through Irresistible Grace has wrought a regenerative transformation so that those thus blessed truly love God from their hearts."

But if this could be done for the elect, it could be done for all mankind. How could the infinite love of God leave anyone out? That brings us back to the compelling question: What love is this that loves so few? And why would the God of love and truth plead with those whom He had already predestined to doom to repent and believe the gospel? Calvinism turns most of the Bible into a pretense, a mere charade.

Luther's Astonishing "Answer"

In his debate with Luther, Erasmus argued that God's pleadings with a man to repent, who could not do so, would be like asking someone whose hands were tied to use them. Luther countered that God, by calling us to do what we can't do, is "trying us, that by His law He may bring us to a knowledge of our impotence, if we are His friends...[and] deservedly taunting and mocking us, if we are His proud enemies."[16] He argued that Erasmus might just as well conclude from "'If thou wilt keep the commandments, they shall preserve thee'...therefore, man is able to keep the commandments."[17]

Luther seemed to have forgotten that even unsaved men keep at least much of the Law most of the time. Even Calvin himself admitted that "total depravity" doesn't mean man is necessarily as wicked as he could be. Both Scripture and experience prove that all men do some good; and some "totally depraved" men at times exceed in goodness the behavior of some apparently genuine Christians.

Furthermore, to show man his impotence to keep the Law *is* to taunt him unless there is a remedy available. That remedy is the gospel, which requires that I come to Christ in faith, believing on Him as the One who paid the penalty for my sins. Nor does the fact that I cannot perfectly keep the Law prove in the least that I cannot come to Christ and believe on Him and receive by faith the benefit of His payment for my breach of the Law. Here is the classic distinction between works and faith. And if my only hope is sovereign regeneration by God, and He for His good pleasure will not grant it to me, what is the point of showing me my hopelessness?

Paul declares that "the law was our schoolmaster to bring us unto Christ" (Galatians 3:24). To the Calvinist, "us" refers to the elect. Yet even they were unregenerate before coming to Christ. If being "dead in trespasses and in sins" means that man is morally a corpse, how could the Law bring *anyone* to Christ? This is not the Father irresistibly dragging the elect to Christ and sovereignly regenerating and then giving them faith to believe. This is the Law working upon the conscience like a "schoolmaster." How could the Law affect the conscience of "moral corpses"?

If men could not keep even one commandment for one moment, then the Law would not only be a mockery but to no purpose. But if unregenerate man (as is the case) does understand the Law, keeps it at least some of the time, and has a guilty conscience for breaking it, then how can he morally be a corpse? And if unregenerate man can choose to obey or disobey the Law, why cannot he choose to believe the gospel—and where does the Bible say that he can't? It doesn't.

That Inescapable Will Again!

It is interesting to see how The Canons of Dort handle this problem. The fact that man has a will with which he could make moral choices is admitted, but it became depraved by the fall. As a consequence, man is supposedly impotent to respond to the gospel. The Holy Spirit must therefore sovereignly regenerate him in order to "heal" that deficiency:

> But as man by the fall did not cease to be a creature, endowed with understanding and will, nor did sin which pervaded the whole race of mankind, deprive him of the human nature, but brought upon him depravity and spiritual death; so also the grace of regeneration does not treat men as senseless stocks and blocks, nor takes away their will and its properties, neither does violence thereto; but spiritually quickens, heals, corrects, and at the same time sweetly and powerfully ends it; that where carnal rebellion and resistance formerly prevailed, a ready and sincere spiritual obedience begins to reign; in which the true and spiritual restoration and freedom of our will consist.[18]

Dort offers a strange solution: "the grace of regeneration...spiritually quickens, heals, corrects, and at the same time sweetly and powerfully ends [the will]...." What an odd "healing" that puts an *end* to what it "heals"! Why wasn't this "ready and sincere spiritual obedience" implanted in Adam and Eve? And now that the elect have this new will through regeneration, why don't they always obey God perfectly?

The reason can only be that a "will" is *no will* unless the person whose will it is wills with it. The will can be used for good or evil. The will cannot be denied or dismissed. Calvin and Luther tried to explain it away, but that is not possible. The will is one of the subjects most frequently referred to in the Bible. Unregenerate men are repeatedly called upon to exercise the will in choosing to obey God.

Even the regenerated have a fleshly will that, despite Dort, apparently wasn't *ended* at the new birth: "For the flesh lusteth against the Spirit, and the Spirit against the flesh: and these are contrary the one to the other..." (Galatians 5:17).

As we have seen, the words "will," "willing," "free-will," "freewill," "free will," along with related expressions such as "voluntary," "choose," etc., are found nearly 4,000 times in Scripture. The requirement of willing obedience is a theme that runs all through the Bible: "If ye be willing and obedient..." (Isaiah 1:19), "If thou believest with all thine heart" (Acts 8:37), etc.

God does not impose Himself upon us. He wants our hearts, and the very concept of "heart" used all through Scripture is meaningless without free will.

"Where Is Boasting Then?"

The Calvinist counters that if man could choose whether or not to believe the gospel, he could boast that he had contributed to his salvation. And it is asserted that man's will is not free to act in that manner. In declaring that "of the great body of mankind some should be predestined to salvation, and others to destruction,"[19] Calvin argues that there is "no other means of humbling us as we ought, or making us feel how much we are bound to him [Christ].... It is plain how greatly ignorance of this principle detracts from the glory of God, and impairs true humility."[20]

On the contrary, Paul says that since all we can do is to *believe*, there is nothing to boast about. "Where is boasting then?" asks Paul. "It is excluded," he declares definitively, "by...faith" (Romans 3:27). So rather than faith giving cause for boasting, it is the very reason why there can be no boasting. Once again, Calvin is seen to be in direct opposition to Scripture. Nevertheless, Palmer insists that "Calvin simply expounded the Bible...[he] uncovered truths that had been in the Bible all the time."[21]

A Calvinist author declares, "If God only saves people who of their own supposed free will accept Jesus, then they merit salvation. They *deserve* to be saved.... The notion of free will exalts man because man elects God and God only ratifies man's choice."[22] Again, the necessity to defend Calvinism drives its defenders into irrationality.

To accept salvation by faith no more means that the person who does so has thereby merited that gift of God's grace than the acceptance of a free meal and a night's lodging by a destitute person means that he or she has thereby merited this charity. "*Deserve to be saved*"? The mere acceptance of a gift does not mean that the person *deserves* it. "God only ratifies man's choice"? No, it is God who sets the terms of salvation, which man must accept to be saved—and if he doesn't, he is lost eternally. And *that* brings merit to man and basis to boast? Hardly.

There is great confusion on this matter of the will because there is no escaping the fact that, as Spurgeon admitted, "Man's will has its proper place in the matter of salvation.... When a man receives the Divine Grace of Christ, he does not receive it against his will.... Nor again, mark you, is the will taken away. For God does not come and convert the intelligent free agent into a machine."[23]

In the same sermon, however, Spurgeon denounces the idea that man can choose whether to believe in Christ or not as making "the purpose of God in the great plan of salvation entirely contingent [upon man's will]." His objection is to man's "coming to God [being] the result of his unassisted nature."[24] Not *unassisted* by God's grace and Holy Spirit conviction, of course. But man's will must still make its own choice, or God has not won the heart.

Who would say that man can come to God "unassisted" by the Holy Spirit? Not even the rankest Arminian! But Calvinism makes that false charge against those who disagree with its extremism. Indeed, to insist that unbelieving man must first be regenerated and irresistibly *caused* to come takes "grace" far beyond man's being assisted [i.e., drawn by God through the conviction and power of the Holy Spirit and the Word]. That word "irresistible" associated with grace creates the problem, because it allows no willingness or faith on man's part. And that libels God, as we have stated repeatedly. If man is totally incapable of believing and must be irresistibly dragged to Christ, then surely it denies God's love to declare that He will not to do this for *all mankind.*

Man Is Meaningless Without a Will

There is no escaping the fact that the will is essential in any meaningful relationship between man and man, or between man and God. After denouncing "free will," Spurgeon contradicts himself again, ending that sermon by quoting, "Whosoever will, let him come, and take the water of life freely."[25] Unless one can say yes or no to the offer of salvation, it could not be a gift of God's love. Nor does God ratify man's choice; man either accepts on God's terms the free gift of salvation—or he doesn't. Thus, all who will spend eternity in the Lake of Fire will be there by their own choice. They cannot say, as Calvinism does, that it was God who sent them there.

Is it not foolish to suggest that receiving a gift means that we *deserve* it? Calvinism denies the very distinction the Bible makes: "For the wages of sin is death; but the gift of God is eternal life through Jesus Christ our Lord" (Romans 6:23). Wages are earned, but a gift cannot be earned or merited; thus receiving a gift provides no cause for boasting.

We are commanded to come to the Lord Jesus Christ, believing in Him as our Savior, but that does not mean that anyone is forced to do so. And, yes, the Father draws us. But without our willingness, for Him to irresistibly cause us to believe in and receive Him would not be a gift received, nor would it establish a love relationship between us and God, either on His side or ours.

A drowning man who allows himself to be rescued has nothing to boast about, nor can he take any credit for his rescue. So it is with the lost sinner who allows Christ to rescue him: he has nothing to boast of, for he has contributed nothing to his salvation.

Calvinism, as we have seen, makes nonsense of such scriptures as "he that winneth souls is wise...they that turn many to righteousness...we persuade men" (Proverbs 11:30; Daniel 12:3; 2 Corinthians 5:11). To win someone over to believe in Christ requires persuasion. This is the job of the Holy Spirit through the gospel, and He graciously uses human instruments to present the gospel. Our hearts are won as the Father draws us and as Christ's love arouses a response of love within us: "We love him, because he first loved us" (1 John 4:19)—not because He *caused* us to do so by changing our wills.

Commissioned by God to Persuade Men

Calvinism denies that there is any winning or any persuading—salvation comes by sovereign regeneration and Irresistible Grace imposed. If one must be regenerated and then made to believe, the gospel would have no part in the new birth, preaching it would be pointless, there would be no persuading the unregenerate sinner, and it would be a waste of time to attempt to do so. Yet Paul expended himself for Christ doing exactly that: disputing and persuading in the attempt to win people to Christ.

As soon as he was converted, Paul "confounded the Jews...at Damascus, proving that this is very Christ..." (Acts 9:22). Everywhere he went, Paul "disputed...in the synagogue...and in the market daily..." (Acts 17:17). The last chapter of Acts tells us that even while under house arrest in Rome, Paul was still at it: "...there came many to him...to whom he expounded... persuading them concerning Jesus..." (Acts 28:23).

Paul said, "I am made all things to all men, that I might by all means save some" (1 Corinthians 9:22). Through his powerful preaching of the gospel, he won many to Christ wherever he went. There is not a word about Irresistible Grace regenerating the sinners to whom Paul preached and God then giving them faith. *Never* is there even a hint of this process! The consistent tone of Scripture is clear. The Calvinist must search diligently to find a passage here and there that he can "interpret" to seemingly support TULIP.

Paul wrote to the Thessalonian believers: "For our gospel came not unto you in word only, but also in power, and in the Holy Ghost, and in much assurance; as ye know what manner of men we were among you for your sake" (1 Thessalonians 1:5). The Holy Spirit brought conviction and assurance *through the gospel preached,* and the lives Paul and his companions lived before them were part of that conviction. Why all of this explanation, if God sovereignly regenerates and then irresistibly imparts "faith"? Calvinism just doesn't fit the diligent and fruitful preaching of the gospel by the Apostles to sinners from city to city—nor Christ's command for us to do likewise.

Through the Word of God preached by Paul and Barnabas, Jews and Greeks were *persuaded* to believe, and as a result of that belief in Christ, they were regenerated. Paul said to those at Corinth whom he had won to Christ, "for in Christ Jesus I have begotten you *through the gospel*" (1 Corinthians 4:15). Clearly, their acceptance of the gospel that Paul preached brought about their regeneration. TULIP denies this clear biblical pattern.

Palmer reasons, "Only when the Holy Spirit regenerates man and makes him alive spiritually can man have faith in Christ and be saved."[26]

Paul's Fervent Preaching and Example

Empowered by the Holy Spirit, Paul diligently persuaded multitudes by the preaching of the gospel. To this he devoted his life: "Knowing, therefore the terror of the Lord, we persuade men" (2 Corinthians 5:11). Where did Paul get this notion, so contrary to Calvinism, that men had to be *persuaded* to believe the gospel? He received this clear understanding from Christ himself. When Christ appeared to Paul on the road to Damascus, He sent him to Jews and Gentiles

> ...to open their eyes, and to turn them from darkness to light, and from the power of Satan unto God, that they may receive forgiveness of sins, and inheritance among them which are sanctified by faith.... (Acts 26:18)

What would be the need of Paul opening men's eyes and turning them from darkness to light through the Spirit-empowered preaching of the gospel if it all happens through sovereign regeneration, with Irresistible Grace and faith imposed as a result? Calvinism is refuted by the very commission Christ conferred upon Paul and the other Apostles. In relating this encounter with Christ to King Agrippa, Paul declared:

> I was not disobedient...but shewed first unto them of Damascus, and at Jerusalem, and throughout all the coasts of Judaea, and then to the Gentiles, that they should repent and turn to God.... I continue unto this day, witnessing both to small and great, saying none other things than those which the prophets and Moses did say.... (Acts 26:19–23)

In spite of his staunch support for Calvinism at times, what Spurgeon said at other times undermined it. As though he rejected Irresistible Grace and upheld free will, just as he rejected regeneration without faith and before salvation, Spurgeon argued:

> Now, Brethren, how is your heart and my heart changed in any matter? Why, the instrument generally is *persuasion*. A friend sets before us a truth we did not know before. He pleads with us. Puts

> it in a new light and then we say, "Now, I see that," and our hearts are changed towards the thing.... The Spirit makes a revelation of the Truth of God to the soul, whereby it sees things in a different light from what it ever did before. And then the will cheerfully bows that neck which once was stiff as iron and wears the yoke which once it despised....
>
> Yet, mark, the will is not gone.... If you are *willing*, depend upon it that God is willing. Soul, if you are anxious after Christ, He is more anxious after you.... Let your willingness to come to Christ be a hopeful sign and symptom.

As we have already noted, he ended the sermon with, "It is not of him that wills, nor of him that runs, but of God that shows mercy. Yet—'whosoever will, let him come, and take the water of life freely.'"[27]

The Bottom Line

In a personal letter accompanied by some of his writings, author and apologist Rob Zins states, "The Word of God teaches that all men are responsible before God and *accountable*. That all men are equally 'unable' to please God is also undeniable. But, inability does not diminish responsibility." God's *love* seems to be forgotten. Zins goes on to argue:

> To say that God "allows it" but does not "will it" but *lets* it take place, puts you in no better position than the Calvinist who says that God *could* give irresistible grace to all but does not want to do so. How is it that one can feel better about God *allowing* corruption, abortion, murder and lust, when He *could* stop it...?[28]

We've covered this already. Yes, God *could* stop all evil immediately (by wiping out mankind), but God gave man the genuine power of choice so that he could receive God's love and love Him in return. The cessation of sin could come only by destroying the human race as He once did by the flood. However, in His grace and love He allowed Noah and his family to survive. Sadly, through them sin survived and grew into the horror we see occurring daily. The God of the Bible, however, has a loving solution for sin for all who will believe the gospel and receive the Lord Jesus Christ as Savior.

Calvinism, on the other hand, claims that God *could* rescue everyone from hell by imposing His will upon them—which He does for the elect only. He *could* deliver everyone from all suffering and disease and death—but foreordained the wickedness rampant today. He *could have* left this world a paradise without sin ever invading it, because man has no real choice under Calvinism, and therefore, God himself is even the author of evil.

There is a huge difference between Calvinism's view of God, sin, and salvation—and that which we present herein as the biblical teaching. The difference is "Calvinism's love," which isn't love at all.

This teaching, that "God," being the cause of even the typist's error, could have a world without any sin or suffering or death, but for His own good pleasure chose the world of rampant evil and suffering as it is today, is a libel upon God's character. At the root of this libel is a denial of God's sincere love for man.

The issue we have been dealing with is very simple: Which God is the biblical One—the God of Calvinism, or the God of love who is not willing that any perish, but has given them the right to choose? There is no question which God rings true to the conscience that is given even to the unsaved. And this is the God of the Bible.

Man is a created being. As such, he is necessarily less than his Creator. That being the case, man can only make less-than-perfect choices. The amount and degree of evil on this earth will be limited only by man's imagination and the extent to which constituted authority controls human behavior. As Paul foretold, so it has happened: "But evil men and seducers shall wax worse and worse, deceiving, and being deceived" (2 Timothy 3:13). Nor is that condition what God desires for man, but contrary to His will, though He allows it.

God Contrasted with False Gods

Suffering and rampant evil are the fault of man's willful choices, which have corrupted everything he touches. Sin, suffering, and death are not God's doing or desire, nor anything God could stop without destroying the world—which He will do one day: "the heavens shall pass away with a great noise, and the elements shall melt with fervent heat, the earth also and the works that are therein shall be burned up.... Nevertheless we, according to his promise, look for a new heavens and a new earth, wherein dwelleth righteousness" (2 Peter 3:10–13).

Until then, God "is longsuffering to us-ward, not willing that any should perish" (2 Peter 3:9). God himself has come as a man to pay the infinite penalty demanded by His infinite justice for the sins of the whole world (1 John 2:2). He offers pardon to all and sends forth the gospel of salvation to "whosoever will believe."

Men are responsible for their sin and for their eternal destiny, because salvation is offered to all as a free gift and all have the ability either to receive it or to reject it. Calvinism insists that man has no such capability, yet he is responsible anyway. To hold someone responsible for failing to do what he cannot do would be like saying that a baby is responsible to run the 100–meter high hurdles in world-record time.

How can a just God hold sinners responsible to repent and believe in Christ, when He withholds from them the essential ability to do so? The very sense of justice that God himself has instilled in human conscience cries out against such a travesty! And here we confront once again the real issue: God's holy, just, merciful, and loving character is maligned by Calvinism's misrepresentation.

Zins quotes R. L. Dabney to the effect "that the absence of volition in God to save all does not imply a lack of love. God has true love which is constrained by consistent and holy reasons known only to Himself."[29] Such rationalizations fail because genuine love never fails. There are no "holy reasons" why God could not do for the reprobate what He does for the elect! There is no whitewashing Calvinism's God from His failure to rescue those whom He could rescue. Nor can this evident lack of love and compassion be excused due to "reasons known only to Himself." The so-called hyper-Calvinist frankly admits these simple facts; the self-professed "moderates" deny them.

The Bible contrasts the truth, purity, love, and mercy of the true God with the capricious destructiveness of pagan gods. In the process, the prophets appeal to our reason and to the conscience God has given us. Baal is exposed as a false god not worthy of worship because of its demand that children be sacrificed in the sacred fires on its altars. Can Baal be excused by "reasons known only to himself"? Would the true God, for reasons known only to Himself, cause billions to burn eternally in the Lake of Fire, whom He *could* deliver as He delivered the elect? Never!

It is legitimate to appeal to conscience and reason in exposing false gods. Surely no lesser standard should be applied to the true God. Therefore, any supposed deity that is less gracious, less loving, less kind, and less merciful than man's conscience tells him he must be cannot be the true God. To attribute to Him *any* lack of love and mercy is surely to misrepresent the God revealed in the Bible.

1. John MacArthur, Author and General Editor, *The MacArthur Study Bible* (Nashville, TN: Word Publishing, 1997), 1437-1438.
2. John MacArthur, *The Love of God* (Dallas, TX: Word Publishing, 1996), 111-112, 121.
3. MacArthur, *Love*, 134.
4. Cited by J. I. Packer and O. R. Johnston in their "Historical and Theological Introduction" to Luther, *Bondage,* 56.
5. Excerpted from *The New Park Street Pulpit*, "Sovereign Grace and Man's Responsibility," a sermon by C. H. Spurgeon delivered August 1, 1858 at the Music Hall, Royal Surrey Gardens.
6. MacArthur, *Love*.
7. Ibid., 101.
8. Ibid., 102.
9. Ibid., 16.
10. Ibid., 12-13.
11. Ibid., 120.
12. Ibid., 103.
13. Ibid., 95.
14. Cited by J. I. Packer and O. R. Johnston in their "Historical and Theological Introduction" to Luther, *Bondage, 56.*
15. MacArthur, *Love*, 196.
16. Martin Luther, *The Bondage of the Will*, trans. J. I. Packer and O. R. Johnston (Grand Rapids, MI: Fleming H. Revell, 1957, 11th prtg. 1999), 153.
17. Ibid., 154.
18. Canons of Dort (Dordrecht, Holland, 1619), sec. III/IV, para.16; cited in Vance, *Other Side*, 619.
19. Calvin, *Institutes*, III:xxi,1.
20. Ibid.
21. Palmer, foreword to *five points*, 2.
22. Wm. Oosterman, "Take a Long Look at the Doctrine of Election" (Ottawa, Canada: The Lord's Library Publications, n. d.), 3. Available from Westboro Baptist Church, Ottawa.
23. Charles Haddon Spurgeon, "God's Will and Man's Will," No. 442 (Newington: Metropolitan Tabernacle; sermon delivered Sunday morning, March 30, 1862).
24. Ibid.
25. Ibid.
26. Palmer, *five points,* 27.
27. Spurgeon, "God's Will."
28. Robert M. Zins to Dave Hunt, August 23, 2000. On file.
29. Ibid.

CHAPTER

29

Perseverance of the Saints

BEFORE BEGINNING what turned into an urgent and in-depth study of Calvinism, I had thought that I was at least a one-point Calvinist. Surely my belief in eternal security—the assurance of living eternally in God's presence through being redeemed by Christ and kept secure in Him—must be the same as Calvinism's Perseverance of the Saints. That turned out, however, not to be the case, and I was surprised to discover why.

Biblical assurance of salvation does not depend upon one's performance, but upon the gospel truth that Christ died for the sins of the world, and upon His promise that whosoever believes in Him receives the free and unconditional gift of eternal life.

In contrast, the Calvinist's assurance is in God's having predestined him to eternal life as one of the elect. Coppes insists that "God's answer to doubt...the only proper fount of assurance of salvation...of getting to heaven (glorification) is the doctrine of predestination."[1] That view has serious problems, as we shall see. How does the Calvinist know he is one of the elect who have been predestined? His performance plays a large part in helping him to know whether or not he is among that select group.

In contrast, my faith, hope, trust, and confidence is in my Savior the Lord Jesus Christ, who paid on the Cross the full penalty for my sins. Therefore, according to His promise, which I have believed, my sins are forgiven. I have been born again into God's family as His dear child. Heaven is my eternal home. My hope is in Christ alone.

Christ calls, "Come unto me, all ye that labour and are heavy laden, and I will give you rest" (Matthew 11:28). Laden with sin, I came to Him and, as He promised, found eternal rest in Him alone. Christ guarantees, "him that cometh to me I will in no wise cast out" (John 6:37). I came to Him by faith in His Word and He will never cast me out—i.e., I can never be lost. My assurance is in His promise and keeping power, not in my efforts or performance. He said, "I give unto them [my sheep] eternal life; and they shall never perish" (John 10:28). It would be strange "eternal life" indeed if it were mine today by His gracious gift and taken away by His judgment tomorrow.

Yet many professing Christians (including many Five-Point Calvinists who believe in Perseverance of the Saints) are troubled with doubts concerning their salvation. Doubts even assail leading Calvinists.

Zane C. Hodges points out that "The result of this theology is disastrous. Since, according to Puritan belief, the genuineness of a man's faith can only be determined by the life that follows it, assurance of salvation becomes impossible at the moment of conversion."[2] And, one might add, at any time thereafter as well, if one's life ever fails to meet the biblical standard.

Piper and his staff write, "[W]e must also own up to the fact that our final salvation is made contingent upon the subsequent obedience which comes from faith."[3] Small comfort or assurance in *my* ability to obey! Indeed, the fifth point *is* called perseverance *of the saints*, putting the burden on me. No wonder, then, as R. T. Kendall has commented, that "nearly all of the Puritan 'divines' went through great doubt and despair on their deathbeds as they realized their lives did not give perfect evidence that they were elect."[4]

Arminius, on the other hand, contrary to the false label attached to him by his enemies, had perfect assurance. He confidently declared that the believer can "depart out of this life...to appear before the throne of grace, without any anxious fear...."[5]

An Endemic Uncertainty of Salvation

Oddly, the reason for such uncertainty among Calvinists is found where one would expect assurance—in the "P" of TULIP: Perseverance of the *Saints*. Clearly, the emphasis is upon the *believer's* faithfulness in persevering—not upon God's keeping power.

Strangely enough, certainty of salvation and confidence of one's eternal destiny are not to be found in the fifth point of Calvinism where one would expect it. Nor can they be found in the other four points. Although many Calvinists would deny it, uncertainty as to one's ultimate salvation is, in fact, built into the very fabric of Calvinism itself.

Congdon writes, "*Absolute assurance of salvation is impossible in Classical Calvinism...*[emphasis his]. Understand why: Since works are an *inevitable* outcome of 'true' salvation, one can only know he or she is saved by the presence of good works. But since no one is perfect...any assurance is at best imperfect as well. Therefore, you may *think* you believed in Jesus Christ, may *think* you had saving faith, but be sadly mistaken...and because unsaved, be totally blind to the fact you are unsaved...! R. C. Sproul...in an article entitled 'Assurance of Salvation,' writes: 'There are people in this world who are not saved, but who are convinced that they are....'

"When our assurance of salvation is based *at all* on our works, we can never have absolute assurance...! But does Scripture discourage giving objective assurance of salvation? Hardly! On the contrary, the Lord Jesus (John 5:24), Paul (Romans 8:38–39), and John (1 John 5:11–13) have no qualms about offering absolute, objective assurance of salvation. Furthermore, works are *never* included as a requirement for assurance."[6]

Bob Wilkin of Grace Evangelical Society reports what he heard at Sproul's Ligonier National Conference (with about 5,000 present), June 15–17, 2000 in Orlando, Florida:

> John Piper...described himself as "a seven point Calvinist"...[and said] that no Christian can be sure he is a true believer; hence there is an ongoing need to be dedicated to the Lord and deny ourselves so that we might make it. [We must endure to the end in faith if we are to be saved.[7]]
>
> This struck me as odd, since there was so much emphasis on the sovereignty of God in this conference. Yet when it comes right down to it, within a Reformed perspective God uses fear of hell to motivate Christians to live for Him.
>
> My heart is heavy as I write this from Orlando. I feel such a burden for the people here. Why? Because their theology makes assurance impossible. It [lack of assurance] permeated the whole conference.[8]

What a commentary, that lack of assurance of salvation permeated the Ligonier National Conference featuring major Calvinist speakers! Why should that be? Because the Calvinist cannot rely upon Christ's promise of eternal life in the gospel (since that promise is for the elect alone), his security lies in being one of the elect—but how can he be certain that he is? Piper writes, "We believe in eternal security...the eternal security of the elect."[9] And there one confronts a serious problem: How can any Calvinist be certain that he is among that select company predestined for heaven?

He can't. There is not a verse in the Bible telling anyone how to be certain that he is among the elect.

Though Christ commanded that the gospel be preached to every person living in the entire world, the Calvinist says it is effective for only the elect. Others can *imagine* they believe the gospel, but not having been sovereignly regenerated, their faith is not from God and will not save. As Sproul and his fellow editors declare, "The fruit of regeneration is faith. Regeneration precedes faith."[10]

Indeed, the gospel offers false hope to the non-elect and, in fact, condemns them. Thus, believing the gospel is of no value unless one has first been sovereignly regenerated by God without faith, having been predestined to salvation. Yet predestination was determined by God in eternity past and, as Packer writes, "decreed by his counsel secret to us"[11]—so how can that doctrine give assurance to anyone today? Who can know that he is among the secretly predestined elect?

No wonder, then, that many Calvinists are plagued by doubts concerning their salvation. When facing such doubts, VanOverloop gives the cheering advice to "wait prayerfully for a season of richer grace."[12] Otis, on the other hand, suggests that "One of the proofs that we are genuinely saved is that our faith will persevere to the end of our lives."[13] But what if doubts come, such as confronted "nearly all of the Puritan 'divines'"?

Disagreement on a Vital Point

Admittedly, there is no general agreement on this point. Many Calvinists do affirm that believing the gospel brings assurance. In a Calvinist symposium, the essay on assurance by D. A. Carson, which attempts to give a balanced biblical view, does not offer any typical Calvinist arguments for Perseverance of the Saints at all and comes to no definitive conclusion.[14] As we have seen, Calvin taught that being born into a Calvinist family automatically made the child one of the elect, as did infant baptism, so long as one believed in its efficacy. Thus, while believing the gospel is no sure way to be saved, believing in one's infant baptism is.

Sproul declares, "Infants can be born again, although the faith they exercise cannot be as visible as that of adults."[15] Infants have *faith* in Christ—it is just less visible? Does Sproul or any other Calvinist really believe that?

For the Calvinist, moreover, seeking assurance that one's faith is genuine raises further difficulties, because faith is a gift from God and has nothing to do with man's volition. But how can one know whether one's faith is a gift from God, or originates in his own mind and will?

Dillow quotes Dabney that each one must examine his faith, because it is possible to have a false faith. This only raises further questions. Would God give false faith? Calvin said He would and does. So if God gives true faith to some and false faith to others, how could one know whether the faith he thinks he has is genuine? Who could stand up to a delusion from God? And how would infants examine their "faith"?

Yet Boettner carries on at length about faith being the assurance that one is among the elect, and he argues that since faith "is not given to any but the elect only, the person who knows that he has this faith can be assured that he is among the elect."[16] But what about the false faith and assurance that Calvin says God gives to the non-elect, the better to damn them? The *Geneva Study Bible* makes no mention of that problem and even suggests that John wrote his first epistle "to assure those who have believed that they actually possess the priceless gift [of eternal life]."[17] How can leading Calvinists be so ignorant of what John Calvin taught?

Attempting to fortify his argument from a different angle, Boettner writes, "Every person who loves God and has a true desire for salvation in Christ is among the elect, for the non-elect never have this love or this desire."[18] By that standard, however, the Christians in the church at Ephesus would have doubted their salvation because they no longer had that fervent love (Revelation 2:4–5)—yet there is no suggestion that they were not true Christians.

The Puritans struggled with this very question. Dillow accuses Dabney of vainly trying to defend an "issue which dominated three hundred years of English Puritan debate"[19]—considerable dissension indeed, and on a very key point. Arminius, however, declared, "[M]y opinion is, that it is possible for him who believes in Jesus Christ to be certain...that he is a son of God, and stands in the grace of Jesus Christ."[20]

Dillow, though a staunch Calvinist, disagrees that faith must be examined. He argues, "The Bible never raises this issue.... Does a man struggle to know if he loves his child...? We know we have believed aright if we have believed according to biblical truth.... The issue is not a rational examination of our faith...[but] a rational examination of the object of faith, Jesus Christ, and the gospel offer."[21] He goes on to accuse fellow Calvinists of being taken up with preserving a dogma:

> Finally, the Bible explicitly and implicitly affirms that assurance is part of saving faith.... "Faith is the assurance of things hoped for" (Hebrews 11:1). But in addition, the scores of passages which tell

> us that "whosoever believes has eternal life" surely imply that a person who has believed has eternal life.... Belief and assurance are so obviously inseparable that only the interest of preserving the Experimental Predestinarian doctrine of perseverance can justify their division.[22]

Uncomfortable with Jesus?

Following Calvin's teaching, however, like the Jehovah's Witnesses and Mormons, many Calvinists believe that the only way to make one's "calling and election sure" (2 Peter 1:10) is not through faith but through good works. Oddly, although the first four points of Calvinism insist that man can do nothing, the fifth depends, in the view of many, upon human effort. Boettner quotes Warfield: "It is idle to seek assurance of election outside of holiness of life."[23] Likewise, Charles Hodge declares, "The only evidence of our election...[and] perseverance, is a patient continuance in well-doing."[24]

But finding assurance in one's works always leaves questions unanswered in view of the undeniable fact, which we have commented upon earlier, that the apparent good works of the unsaved sometimes put professed Christians to shame. Furthermore, one's performance could be excellent most of one's life, but if failure comes at some point, one has lost performance-based assurance. R. C. Sproul expressed that very concern for his own salvation:

> A while back I had one of those moments of acute self-awareness...and suddenly the question hit me: "R. C., what if you are not one of the redeemed? What if your destiny is not heaven after all, but hell?" Let me tell you that I was flooded in my body with a chill that went from my head to the bottom of my spine. I was terrified.
>
> I tried to grab hold of myself. I thought, "Well, it's a good sign that I'm worried about this. Only true Christians really care about salvation." But then I began to take stock of my life, and I looked at my performance. My sins came pouring into my mind, and the more I looked at myself, the worse I felt. I thought, "Maybe it's really true. Maybe I'm not saved after all."
>
> I went to my room and began to read the Bible. On my knees I said, "Well, here I am. I can't point to my obedience. There's nothing I can offer.... I knew that some people only flee to the Cross to escape hell.... I could not be sure about my own heart

> and motivation. Then I remembered John 6:68.... Peter was also uncomfortable, but he realized that being uncomfortable with Jesus was better than any other option![25]

Uncomfortable with Jesus?! Where is the comfort and assurance in that? Couldn't a Muslim obtain similar assurance through being *uncomfortable* with Muhammad and the Qur'an, or a Mormon through being uncomfortable with Joseph Smith? Why is it better to be uncomfortable with Jesus than with Buddha? Where does the Bible suggest, much less commend, being *uncomfortable* with Jesus? Nor is that taught in this passage. This idea seems all the more pitiful, coming from a Christian leader and theologian as his assurance that he is one of the elect!

There is no escaping the necessity of evidence, and solid faith based upon it, which the Bible and the Holy Spirit provide in abundance to the believer. Peter could not understand what Christ meant about eating His body and drinking His blood. But that did not change the fact that he knew that Jesus was the Messiah. The important statement from Peter was "Thou hast the words of eternal life. And we believe and are sure that thou art that Christ, the Son of the living God" (John 6:68–69).

Such faith, however, is not sufficient to give the Calvinist assurance. It would still leave him uncomfortable because the non-elect often think they believe in Christ. According to Calvin, God even helps them with this delusion. Where is that in the Bible?

We have every reason to be very comfortable with Jesus—and this is one of the great blessings and part of the joy of our salvation. We have absolute proof that the Bible is God's Word, that Jesus is the Christ, that the gospel is true, and we have the witness of the Holy Spirit within. The Bible gives absolute assurance: "These things have I written unto you that believe in the name of the Son of God; that ye may know that ye have eternal life..." (1 John 5:13). That assurance, according to this scripture and many others, is for all those who simply believe in Christ. There is no other basis for assurance of sins forgiven and eternal life.

Why doesn't Sproul rely upon such promises? Because, for a Calvinist, the question is not whether one has believed the gospel but whether one, from eternity past, was predestined by God to be among the elect—and that is an elusive question, as many a Calvinist has discovered to his dismay.

The Gospel: God's Power unto Salvation

In the following pages, the question of assurance will be illustrated (compositely as we have heard it related by a number of people) through a fictitious couple whom we shall call Al and Jan. They've been married almost ten years and have two children. A devout Roman Catholic all of his life, with two brothers who are priests and a sister who is a nun, Al became a Christian a few months after his marriage. After six weeks of struggling to resolve the obvious contradictions between the Catholicism he had known all his life and his growing understanding of what the Bible teaches, Al left that Church, was baptized as a believer, and has been ostracized by his devoutly Catholic family ever since.

Jan, on the other hand, was a typical New Ager who had absolutely rejected absolutes and was open to anything—except, of course, biblical Christianity, which she disliked for being "too narrow." It seemed like a glorious miracle to both of them when Al was able to lead Jan to Christ about six months after his own conversion.

For nearly eight years Al was happy in the faith, witnessing to friends and family and seeing some come to Christ. He was crystal clear on the gospel and the basis of his salvation. There was no doubt in his mind that he had been convicted of sin, of righteousness, and of judgment to come by the Holy Spirit (as all the world is, according to John 16:7–11). Having believed the gospel that Christ died for his sins and that "whosoever believeth on him should not perish, but have everlasting life," Al had placed his faith in the Lord Jesus Christ as his Savior.

At least he was sure at the time that he had believed on the Lord Jesus Christ exactly as Paul exhorted the Philippian jailor, "Believe on the Lord Jesus Christ, and thou shalt be saved" (Acts 16:30–31). As a result (or so it had seemed to him), his life was changed, and this was the testimony he had enthusiastically shared publicly in church and in witnessing to individuals.

From the beginning of his new life in Christ, Al had had a hunger for God's Word as his spiritual food. He had read his Bible regularly with great interest and enjoyment. He and Jan had become part of a seemingly vibrant fellowship of Bible-believing Christians and had rejoiced together in their new life in Christ. Then something happened—a sad tale I've been told by a surprising number of people, that we come to now through Al and Jan.

---

1. Leonard J. Coppes, *Are Five Points Enough? The Ten Points of Calvinism* (Denver, CO: self-published, 1980), 25, 27.
2. Zane C. Hodges, author's preface to *The Gospel Under Siege* (Dallas, TX: Kerugma, Inc., 2nd ed. 1992), vi.
3. John Piper and Pastoral Staff, "TULIP: What We Believe about the Five Points of Calvinism: Position Paper of the Pastoral Staff" (Minneapolis, MN: Desiring God Ministries, 1997) 25.
4. R. T. Kendall, *Calvin and English Calvinism to 1649* (Oxford: Oxford University Press, 1979), 2; cited without page number by Bob Wilkin, "Ligonier National Conference" (*The Grace Report*, July 2000).
5. Jacobus Arminius, *The Works of James Arminius*, trans. James and William Nichols (Grand Rapids,MI: Baker Book House, 1986), 1:667; cited in Laurence M. Vance, *The Other Side of Calvinism* (Pensacola, FL: Vance Publications, rev. ed. 1999), 591.
6. Philip F. Congdon, "Soteriological Implications of Five-point Calvinism," *Journal of the Grace Evangelical Society*, Autumn 1995, 8:15, 55–68.
7. Piper and Staff, TULIP, 23.
8. Wilkin, "Ligonier," 1–2.
9. Piper and Staff, TULIP, 24.
10. *New Geneva Study Bible*, "Regeneration: The New Birth" (Nashville, TN: Thomas Nelson Publishers, 1995), 1664.
11. J. I. Packer, "The Love of God: Universal and Particular." In *Still Sovereign: Contemporary Perspectives on Election, Foreknowledge and Grace*, ed. Thomas R. Schreiner and Bruce A. Ware (Grand Rapids, MI: Baker Books, 2000), 281.
12. Ronald VanOverloop, "Calvinism and Missions: Pt. 2, Unconditional Election" (Grandville, MI: Standard Bearer, January 15, 1993), 185; cited in Vance, *Other Side*, 403.
13. John M. Otis, *Who is the Genuine Christian?* (n. p., n. d.), 39; cited in Vance, *Other Side*, 595.
14. D. A. Carson, "Reflections on Assurance." In Schreiner and Ware, *Still*, 247–48.
15. *New Geneva Study Bible*, 1664.
16. Loraine Boettner, *The Reformed Doctrine of Predestination* (Phillipsburg, NJ: Presbyterian and Reformed Publishing Co., 1932), 308.
17. *New Geneva Study Bible* (marginal note commenting upon 1 John 5:13), 1993.
18. Boettner, *Reformed*, 309.
19. Joseph C. Dillow, *The Reign of the Servant Kings: A Study of Eternal Security and the Final Significance of Man* (Haysville, NC: Schoettle Publishing Co., 2nd ed. 1993), 192–93.
20. Arminius, *Works*, 1:667.
21. Dillow, *Reign*, 193.
22. Ibid., 291.
23. Boettner, *Reformed*, 309.
24. Charles Hodge, *A Commentary on Romans* (Carlisle, PA: The Banner of Truth Trust, 1972), 292.
25. R. C. Sproul, "Assurance of Salvation," *Tabletalk*, Ligonier Ministries, Inc., November 1989, 20.

CHAPTER

30

A Calvinist's Honest Doubts

AL COULD NOT have been happier. He and Jan were more in love than ever with one another and with the Lord. Their children were growing in Christ as the family studied the Word of God and prayed together in their daily devotions, and in the exuberant fellowship of other children at their dynamic church. The only dark shadow was the continued rejection of Al's attempts to witness for his Lord to his Roman Catholic family, and the continued tension that dampened family get-togethers. And then, another disturbing influence invaded their lives, this time from a completely unexpected source.

Almost unnoticed, Calvinism was introduced into a small men's Bible study group that Al attended. Lively discussions followed, which he found intriguing and intellectually challenging. At about the same time, Calvinistic doctrines crept into the pastor's sermons with increasing frequency and fervency. Although the pastor didn't insist (as some Calvinist pastors do) that every church member be a Calvinist, a number of families left the church in protest over the new emphasis. They felt they were no longer receiving the well-rounded biblical exegesis that had attracted them in the first place. Instead, the pastor seemed to bring an unbalanced emphasis upon God's sovereignty into everything he taught—though, of course, he didn't think so. After all, he was only presenting what the Bible said, though with a different understanding than his sermons had reflected in previous years. It proved to be true once again, as William MacDonald, author of more than 80 books in 100 languages, has stated:

> It is the practice of many Calvinists to press their views relentlessly upon others, even if it leads to church division.... This "theological grid" or system becomes the main emphasis of their conversation, preaching, public prayers and ministry. Other issues seem to pale in comparison. The *system* itself is only a deduction they make from certain verses and is not directly taught in Scripture.[1]

Al was intrigued and swept along with the pastor's new insights. This was the man who had led him to Christ and discipled him, and now Al was eager to follow him into what seemed to be a deeper understanding of biblical truth. Jan, however, was not happy with the implication that God didn't love everyone and had predestined multitudes to eternal suffering, and that Christ had not died for all mankind. She considered such teaching to be directly in conflict both with her conscience and with what the Bible clearly declared. She knew, however, that Al was happy and seemed to be studying his Bible more diligently than ever, so she kept her misgivings to herself.

Enter a Troubling Uncertainty

Seeing his interest, the pastor lent Al some books and tapes by John MacArthur, John Piper, R. C. Sproul, and others. Al began listening to Sproul's daily Calvinist teaching on radio and bought a copy of the *Geneva Study Bible*. Its notes convinced him that Calvinism was the faith of the Reformation and the true gospel. Gradually the new "truth" began to make more sense, and Al became convinced that what he was learning followed logically from God's sovereignty, a teaching he could now see was neglected among most Christians.

Al became obsessed with God's absolute sovereignty and was greatly influenced by a book by Bruce Milne, in which its author said that God's will "is the final cause of all things...and even the smallest details of life. God reigns in his universe...."[2] Only later would he learn that these words were an echo from John Calvin in his *Institutes*. Of course, the premier writer on sovereignty was A. W. Pink, and it wasn't long before Al was immersed in Pink's *The Sovereignty of God* at the recommendation of friends.

It bothered Al at first to think that God had sovereignly ordained everything, even having "decreed from all eternity that Judas should betray the Lord Jesus."[3] Pink explained that "God does not *produce* the sinful dispositions of any of His creatures.... He is neither the Author nor the Approver of sin."[4] Al pondered that idea at length. He was troubled by the teaching that God's sovereignty meant that He controlled and literally *caused* everything, and yet that man was to blame for the sin God caused him to commit. The pastor explained that some things "couldn't be reconciled."

The more Al read, the more the whole matter of man's will became an enigma. He was especially puzzled by seemingly contradictory statements on that subject by a number of Calvinist authors. Pink, for example, rejected the very idea of free will,[5] a concept that he denounced repeatedly. Yet in order to encourage the study of "the deeper things of God [i.e., Calvinism]," he declared, "it is still true that 'Where there's a will, there's a way'...."[6] If God had to make the elect willing to be saved because they had no will, why did their will have any role to play? Such questions bothered Al only briefly and were soon forgotten in the excitement of discovering so much about the Reformation and the creeds it had produced, which he had never known.

Growing Confusion

In order to share his new "faith" with Jan, and to bring her along this inspiring path of learning with him, Al immersed himself in a detailed study of each of the five points of TULIP. And that turned out to be the start of a downward slide in his faith. Beginning with a deepening understanding of the doctrine of Total Depravity, doubts began to disturb the security Al had once known in Christ. How could he be sure he was truly saved? After all, as a totally depraved person he couldn't possibly have believed in Christ with saving faith unless God had first sovereignly regenerated him. Looking back on his conversion, Al tried to assure himself that that was what had actually happened, even though he didn't remember it that way.

Well, of course, he must have been sovereignly regenerated. That was the only way he could have believed the gospel. All the Calvinists were very firm on that point. But how could he be sure? After all, regeneration had to happen without his knowledge and before he believed the gospel and was saved. How could he be certain that something he wasn't even aware of when it happened had actually occurred?

If Christ's promise in John 3:16 "that whosoever believeth in him should not perish, but have everlasting life" was a genuine offer to the entire world (as he had once thought but no longer believed), then he could have assurance by simply believing. But if "whosoever" really meant "the elect" and if salvation was restricted to them, his only assurance would be in *knowing* he was among the elect. Was he or wasn't He? That question began to trouble him day and night. He couldn't escape the fear this uncertainty aroused.

First John 5:10–13 ("These things have I written unto you that believe on the name of the Son of God; that ye may know that ye have eternal life...") had once given him great comfort. He had often used the passage to lead others to confident assurance in Christ. Now, however, with his new understanding, Al was convinced that John was writing to the elect; and if he wasn't really one of the elect, then his believing would be in vain.

Yet all through this epistle, over and over again, it was "believe and have eternal life"—and nothing about being one of the elect. Al took that problem to the pastor, who explained that John was writing *to* the elect, so he didn't need to keep reminding them of who they were. Of course.

Al could not, however, escape a host of questions that kept coming back to haunt him. The Bible clearly said that faith came by hearing the Word of God, and one certainly couldn't hear the Word without faith to believe. But the totally depraved couldn't have faith until they were regenerated and given that faith from God. Yet one had to have faith to believe the gospel in order to be saved. So how could one be regenerated before believing and being saved? It was an impossible conundrum.

What "Regeneration" Was This?

There was a brief and heated dispute among his Calvinist friends at the men's Bible study group when Al raised this troubling question. Various Calvinist authors were consulted, along with the *Geneva Study Bible*, which they all read daily, devouring the notes. There was no question: it was not just a consensus among Calvinist authorities, but unanimous, that regeneration had to precede faith. Before the evening was over, Al was accused of having Arminian tendencies, which he denied, of course, but remained uncertain.

Al became convinced that his doubts had to be an attack from Satan. Could this be what Paul wrote about in Ephesians 6? Al turned there and only became more bewildered when he came to these words: "Above all, taking the shield of faith, wherewith ye shall be able to quench all the fiery darts of the wicked" (Ephesians 6:16). *Taking* the shield of faith?

Why would *taking* be necessary if faith were a gift from God, sovereignly bestowed?

There was no unanimity in the discussion group when this question came up a few days later. Al thought that *taking* the shield of faith indicated that faith must involve volition on man's part. Some argued that this was written to believers, and that of course we had responsibility to believe after we were regenerated.

"But isn't it only *after* we've been sovereignly regenerated that God gives us the faith to believe?" asked Al. "Why is that initial faith *without* volition, but afterwards it's different? Wouldn't a faith given sovereignly by God be better than a faith for which we are responsible?"

The lengthy discussion that evening ended without a consensus or further accusations about "an Arminian tendency." Now Al was not the only one having doubts.

A Victim of Subtle Deception?

Al went back over some of the Calvinist authors he had earlier found so helpful. Now their words only added to his confusion and doubts about his own salvation. Some emphasized Total Depravity to such an extent that the unsaved were incapable of even understanding the gospel. Others, however, like James White, said that the non-elect could understand it but not believe it unto salvation, without the faith God gives. Most agreed that the unregenerate could not believe unto salvation. White made that as clear as anyone:

> It is *not* the Reformed position that spiritual death means "the elimination of all human ability to understand or respond to God." Unregenerate man is...simply incapable [of] submit[ting] himself to that gospel.[7]

Reading those words really bothered Al. If while remaining a spiritually dead lost soul he *could* have understood the gospel, then what he'd thought was faith could have been purely humanistic consent without salvation! How would he know the difference? He had been sure he had understood the gospel and had believed it. But if he had only understood it as a spiritually dead and totally depraved sinner, and not as one who had been regenerated and given faith by God, he would still be lost!

Once happy and fruitful in the Lord, now Al could no longer be certain that his repentance and what he had thought was faith in Christ for salvation had not been purely human emotions. Indeed, that had to be the case unless God had first regenerated him without any act of faith on his part. But that wasn't how he remembered it happening, and he couldn't talk himself into pretending that he had been regenerated prior to what he had always referred to as his conversion.

The Impact of "Unconditional Election"

Al realized that if he had been elected unto salvation, it could only have been unconditionally and thus completely apart from any "faith" he could have placed in Christ. That faith had to be given to him *after* he was saved and could not have involved any volitional belief on his part. But that didn't fit what he remembered.

Looking back on what he had once thought was a clear memory of responding to the gospel by simply believing in Christ, his confusion only grew. He remembered the night he was saved (or thought he got saved). It was as if a light had gone on when the pastor who had led him to Christ quoted Romans 1:16: "For I am not ashamed of the gospel of Christ: for it is the power of God unto salvation to every one that believeth." A lifetime of sacraments, confession, penance, prayers to Mary, and wearing of medals and scapulars, suddenly was revealed as useless. The *gospel* was God's means of saving souls, and all he had to do was believe. He had believed the gospel, knew he was saved, and never had a doubt about his salvation for eight happy years.

Al had even presented that same gospel to others, believing it was God's power unto salvation if they would but believe. Now he knew that he had been spreading an Arminian lie, which had deceived him into imagining he was saved. And to think that he had deceived others as well! Of course, if they were among the elect, they were saved—and if not, they were doomed, no matter what they believed.

How mistaken he had been to imagine that the gospel was an offer to *him*. What *presumption* on his part at the time! That was the tragic result of hearing the gospel from a non-Calvinist—and now he was *paying the price*. So were those to whom he had passed this misunderstanding in the days when he had been under the delusion that "*whosoever* believeth in him should not perish" meant salvation was an offer to be accepted by anyone who was willing under the conviction of the Holy Spirit.

His pastor tried to encourage Al to believe that his doubts were good—that they helped him obey Peter's admonition to "[G]ive diligence to make your calling and election sure: for if ye do these things, ye shall never fall..." (2 Peter 1:10).

"But how can I make an election 'sure' that I don't have, if I'm not one of the elect?" Al asked in desperation.

"I've seen your works, Al," came the reassuring response. "There are several in our church that you led to Christ."

"Led to Christ? Isn't that an Arminian idea?" Al blurted out in despair. "What do you mean, *led* to Christ! The elect don't need to be led to Christ but are sovereignly regenerated without any understanding or faith on their part—and the non-elect *can't* be led to Christ. How could you have offered me the gift of salvation through the gospel without knowing I was one of the elect?"

"I wasn't a Calvinist then," replied the pastor awkwardly. "Anyway, since we don't know who the elect are, we preach the gospel to all and leave it to the Lord."

"If no one knows who the elect are," demanded Al earnestly, "then how can I know I'm one of the elect? That's what's bothering me! Peter says to make our election sure, but how can I do that when I can't be sure I'm elected?"

"You've got the fruits…,"the pastor began, but Al looked at his watch, muttered an excuse and headed for the door, shaking his head in confusion.

"Limited Atonement" Adds to His Despair

The third point of Calvinism, Limited Atonement, further undermined the simple faith Al had once had in Christ. At the moment when he had thought he got saved, he had believed that Christ died "for all...for the ungodly...for sinners...for every man," and thus for *him*. He had thought that Christ's sacrifice on the cross was the propitiation "for the sins of the whole world" and thus it had paid the penalty for his sins. How easily he had been deceived by an Arminian delusion!

It had finally become the "truth" to Al that Christ's blood was shed for only the elect; otherwise, some of it would have been wasted. Multitudes were already in hell before Christ died. Certainly His blood was not shed for *them*! How could it have been?

Al wondered how he could ever have dared to imagine that Christ had died for *him*! The very idea must have come from his own pride. Honesty forced Al to admit that he'd never had any proof that he was one of the elect for whom Christ had died. Nor could he imagine how he could ever hope to find such proof.

Al had offered the "good news" of the gospel to friends and relatives and acquaintances. He had told many, with great zeal and confidence, "Christ died for *you*! How can you reject Him when you realize that He loves *you* so much that He came all the way from heaven to pay the full penalty for *your sins* so that He could rescue *you* from hell? If you were the only person on earth, Christ would have died for *you*!"

Now Al trembled to think how many he had deceived. But what could he do about it? He had no way of knowing which ones were not part of the elect. And even if he did, what would be the point of telling them they had a false faith? They were predestined to eternal torment whether they "believed" in Christ or not.

Leading others to Christ had once given Al great joy and satisfaction, knowing he would meet them in heaven. Now he knew that the gospel he had preached was a lie that had led many astray, imagining that Christ had died for them. How many he had deceived, he couldn't know, but at least they weren't any *worse* off than before.

Al was now in great despair not only for himself but also for those whom he surely had led astray. Formerly, it had brought him great joy that he had become fruitful for Christ in winning a number of people to his Lord. Now he knows there is no such thing as "winning people to Christ." It is a delusion of human pride to think that anyone can say "yes" or "no" to God! Whether one will be saved or lost has all been decided by God an eternity ago, and nothing can change that fact. John Piper waxed so enthusiastic about God's sovereignty and the great comfort and joy it brought; Al had rejoiced over his books. Now God's sovereignty—at least His predestining just the elect to heaven—brought only despair to Al.

"Irresistible Grace"—the Final Blow

The fourth point, Irresistible Grace, had once brought great comfort. Learning that even the faith to believe was all of God had at first seemed so humbling. Now it troubled him deeply. Looking back on his "conversion" as he remembered it, Al could find nothing "irresistible" about his salvation.

Leading up to his "conversion," he had agonizingly weighed the choice between a few more years of sinful enjoyment, or eternal bliss with Christ. In fact, he had procrastinated after he knew the gospel. Then an auto "accident," which the doctors said he shouldn't have survived, became what he had often referred to thereafter as his "wake-up call." In the hospital, as the man who was now his pastor had presented the gospel, Al had "given his heart to the Lord," as he had heard it so often expressed. He had believed on Christ and knew he had passed from death to life because of Christ's promise.

That was then—but this was now. Now he knew it all had been a fleshly or even satanic delusion. Yes, he had been absolutely convinced that the gospel was true, and he knew he needed a Savior. He had believed with all his heart that only through Christ's having paid the penalty for his sins could he be saved from God's just judgment. But now he knew that even those who were doomed for eternity could come to such rational conclusions and think they had believed in Christ.

No, he had no proof that Christ had died for *him*—that he was one of the elect. Even less did he have any indication that he had been drawn to Christ by the Father's "irresistible grace." Even now he wanted to believe, wanted to be saved. He felt that he loved Christ for having died in his place. But it had to be wishful thinking of a totally depraved mind, because he could not identify any time when he could have been sovereignly regenerated prior to what he had thought was his conversion. It simply hadn't happened—he was now sure of that!

Turning to Calvin for Help

That he had read some though not all of that imposing and intellectually challenging volume, Calvin's *Institutes of the Christian Religion,* had once given Al considerable pride. One of the things that had first attracted him to Calvinism was the fact that so many of its adherents seemed to be more intelligent than ordinary Christians. They especially gave that impression when they talked about election. He enjoyed the company of the elect, and there was an exhilarating sense of camaraderie in knowing that others didn't understand the truth discovered by Augustine and passed on to Calvin.

Now he turned to the *Institutes* for comfort, hoping that Calvin would offer something to quell his rising doubts. Instead, he was horrified. The answers Calvin gave to his questions seemed to credit God with working an almost fiendish deception upon the reprobate, "enlightening some with a present sense of grace, which afterwards proves evanescent."[8] Al was shocked that God would intentionally deceive sincere seekers, and wondered why he hadn't noticed such statements before. (Of course, there were no "sincere seekers"—that idea was just another Satanic delusion.)

The deception Calvin attributed to God sounded almost diabolical, leaving Al severely shaken: "There is nothing to prevent his [God's] giving some a slight knowledge of his gospel, and imbuing others thoroughly... the light which glimmers in the reprobate is afterward quenched...."[9]

So the totally depraved, dead-in-trespasses-and-sins moral corpses are not *completely* "dead" but able to have "a slight knowledge" of the gospel, a light God gives them that glimmers and then is quenched, while unable to understand enough to be saved! That was *diabolical.* Yet it rang true to his own experience. How else could he explain that he had once been so sure of his salvation but was now in despair?

Al desperately searched the Bible but could not find any statement about such a difference between the elect and non-elect, especially that in order to deceive them, a false light was given to those whom God had predestined to damnation. Wasn't Satan the one who deceived those who didn't believe, to blind them to the light of the gospel? He read John 1:9 again. It seemed to say that Jesus Christ was "the true Light, which lighteth every man that cometh into the world." He searched Pink's *The Sovereignty of God,* White's *The Potter's Freedom*, Piper's *The Justification of God*, and the works of other Calvinist authors, but none of them addressed this important verse. Why was it avoided? At last he found where Schreiner dealt with it in detail. Al was excited to read, "This illumination...makes it possible for men and women to choose salvation."[10] Reading on, however, enthusiasm turned to despair. Schreiner was giving John Wesley's view and went on to debunk it. The light of Christ shines upon all men only to reveal "the moral and spiritual state" of each heart, not to reveal Christ to them.[11] That certainly agreed with Calvin.

It seemed that Calvin was saying that God not only predestined multitudes to eternal doom and there was nothing they could do about it, but He deliberately deceived some of them into imagining that they were truly saved when they weren't! Al could not remember anything in the Bible that would support such doctrine, and noticed that Calvin didn't give any biblical references to back up what he said. With horror, Al read what now seemed to be sadistic reasoning:

> [E]xperience shows that the reprobate are sometimes affected in a way similar to the elect, that even in their own judgment there is no difference between them.... Not that they truly perceive the power of spiritual grace and the sure light of faith; but the Lord the better to convict them, and leave them without excuse, instills

> into their minds such a sense of his goodness as can be felt without the Spirit of adoption.
>
> Still...the reprobate believe God to be propitious to them, inasmuch as they accept the gift of reconciliation, though confusedly and without due discernment.... Nor do I even deny that God illumines their minds to this extent, that they recognize his grace; but that conviction he distinguishes from the peculiar testimony which he gives to his elect in this respect, that the reprobate never obtain to the full result or to fruition. When he shows himself propitious to them, it is not as if he had truly rescued them from death, and taken them under his protection. He only gives them a manifestation of his present mercy. In the elect alone he implants the living root of faith, so that they persevere even to the end.[12]

What "God" Is This!

What could Calvin possibly have meant by "present mercy"? No matter how "merciful" God was to these poor souls in this life, could it be called "mercy" at all if its ultimate end was destruction? Was it not cynical to call temporary favor "mercy" upon those predestined for eternal damnation? Who could believe in such a God! Al found himself wrestling with thoughts of atheism and only with great effort suppressed such rebellion.

Luther, too, in *The Bondage of the Will*, seemed to present a "God" who was just as sadistic, "deservedly taunting and mocking"[13] the lost by calling upon them to come to Christ when they couldn't without the help He refused to give them! It is one thing to mock those who, having been given a genuine choice, have willfully rejected salvation and have persisted in their attempt to dethrone God. It is something else for Calvin's and Luther's God, having created man without the possibility of repenting and believing the gospel, then to mock him in the doom to which he has been predestined.

Al could not equate such deceit with the loving, gracious, merciful God of the Bible. But this was the God of Augustine, the premier "saint" of Roman Catholicism, to whom not only Calvin and Luther looked as their mentor but whom so many leading evangelicals praised highly. He was further shaken by this statement in a book he was reading: "The Reformation was essentially a revival of Augustinianism and through it evangelical Christianity again came into its own."[14] To learn that Augustine was the founder of Calvinism and "evangelical Christianity" shook him, as a former Catholic, to the core.

What was the truth after all?

Searching for assurance, Al found where Calvin explained that his teaching that some are predestined to salvation and others to destruction was "the only sure ground of confidence [that one was truly saved]," a confidence that only the elect possess.[15] Al thought and prayed about that, but could not see how the belief that God had predestined some to heaven and others to hell could give anyone confidence that he was chosen for heaven. Was he blind, totally reprobate, and unable to see the truth?

His inability to make sense of Calvin seemed to be the final confirmation that he was eternally lost without any hope. The only encouragement he received during those dark days came from the Westminster Confession: "True believers may have the assurance of their salvation divers ways shaken, diminished, and intermitted...by God's withdrawing the light of his countenance, and suffering even such as fear him to walk in darkness and to have no light...."[16] That seemed to bring a glimmer of renewed hope, but he couldn't find the biblical basis for true believers lacking the very assurance that the Bible promises to simple faith.

Then a friend gave him a book that he said had resolved all of his questions. It was *The Reformed Doctrine of Predestination* by Loraine Boettner. The back cover declared it to be "One of the most thorough and convincing statements on predestination to have appeared in any language...the authoritative work in this field."[17] Al began to read it with high hopes. Instead, the book shook him further. The recommendation by *Christianity Today* that "The chapter on Calvinism in history will prove illuminating to many"[18] caused him to read that part first.

Al was immediately troubled by Boettner's admission that early Christian leaders would have rejected Calvinism's view of predestination and that "This cardinal truth of Christianity was first clearly seen by Augustine...."[19] He knew very well that Augustine was responsible for most of Catholicism's doctrines and practices. A recent newspaper article told that the Pope and the Roman Catholic Church had just held some kind of commemorative observance in which this "Saint" had been hailed as the "Doctor of the Church." How could Calvinism be a "cardinal truth of Christianity" if for centuries Christian leaders believed the opposite, until Augustine, the greatest Roman Catholic, "discovered" it?

Is There No Way of Escape?

During the nearly twenty-five years that he had been a Catholic, Al had trusted the Church and its sacraments for his eternal destiny. Of course, under that system of works, rituals, medals, scapulars, and intervention of the "saints," he never could be sure he was saved. The longing for assurance had been a key factor in causing him even to consider listening to what he had been taught from childhood were Protestant heresies.

And now, in his despair, he considered turning back to Rome, even though he knew he'd find even less assurance there than in Calvinism. His former Church had taught him that one never could be sure of getting to heaven; in fact, it was a sin to claim such confidence. He vaguely remembered the anathema pronounced by the Council of Trent upon those who commit the sin of presumption by saying they *know* they are saved and will never be lost.

Now Al understood at last why Cardinal O'Connor declared:

> Church teaching is that I don't know, at any given moment, what my eternal future will be. I can hope, pray, do my very best—but I still don't *know*. Pope John Paul II doesn't *know* absolutely that he will go to heaven, nor does Mother Teresa of Calcutta, unless either has had a special divine revelation.[20]

That was what he needed—a special revelation from God! How else could one be certain, either as a Catholic or as a Calvinist, of being predestined to persevere to the end? Paul had exhorted the Corinthians, "Examine yourselves, whether ye be in the faith; prove your own selves" (2 Corinthians 13:5). Al had thought that was a call to examine his heart to make certain that his faith in Christ was sincere and being lived out in his life through the guidance and empowering of God: "...work out your own salvation with fear and trembling. For it is God which worketh in you both to will and to do of his good pleasure" (Philippians 2:12–13).

But a Calvinist author whom he had read argued from that Scripture, "'It is God who works in you both to will and do.' If this is true after conversion, when I am made free in Christ, it must be even more so before conversion when I am a slave to sin."[21] No further proof was needed of sovereign election. It is God who does all. Then what good would self-examination do? It would never reveal whether one was among the elect. He needed a special revelation from God—but how long must he wait to know it would never come?

"Hyper-Calvinism?" What's That?

Al took his confusion back to his pastor again. They had a long talk, which seemed to get nowhere. The pastor could see that Al was near despair. Putting his hand on Al's shoulder, he suggested, "Let's get on our knees and pray about this, Al."

Both of them prayed earnestly that God would clear away all doubts and confusion by His sovereign grace. As they rose from their knees, the pastor went to a bookshelf, pulled out a book, and handed it to Al. It was a well-worn copy of John MacArthur Jr.'s fairly new book, *The Love of God.*

"Don't rush—give it back when you've finished it," he told Al. "I think you've fallen into 'hyper-Calvinism.' This will help."

"Hyper-Calvinism? What do you mean?"

"Well, sometimes it's hard to tell the difference. I guess I'm to blame for leading you into it. I've emphasized Unconditional Election and Limited Atonement—maybe a little too much—without enough of God's love for the world...."

"*God's love for the world*? What are you talking about? You can't mean *everybody*...!"

"Well, that's the difference between hyper-Calvinism and the more moderate position that Dr. MacArthur takes in this book. God really does love everybody, and John 3:16 pretty much means what we all used to think it meant...."

"Pretty much...?"

"Well, God does want everybody to be saved...."

"What are you saying?" Al interrupted sharply. "You sound like an Arminian! You know Christ did not die for everybody! Is that what MacArthur says?"

"Of course not! You know he affirms Limited Atonement. Still...he shows conclusively that, contrary to hyper-Calvinism, God has a sincere desire for everyone to be saved...!"

"A sincere desire to save those He has predestined to the Lake of Fire...? That's not what you taught me and it doesn't make sense. Are you pulling my leg?"

"Please. MacArthur proves that God genuinely loves even the reprobate...but with a *different kind* of love than He has for the elect."

"*Different kind of love*? Isn't love of any kind still love?"

"Well, there *are* different *kinds* of love...J. I. Packer says the same, and so does Piper...love for wife, friend, neighbor, even enemy.... MacArthur frankly admits that 'the universal love of God is hard to reconcile with the doctrine of election....'"[22]

"*Universal love...*? Now you *are* pulling my leg!"

"Look, just take this book and read it carefully. It will answer your questions...."

Where's the Difference?

The next evening after supper, instead of going to the men's Bible study that lately didn't seem to be getting anywhere, Al stayed home and began reading the new book with high hopes. The more he read, the more confused he became.

First of all, what MacArthur—and now apparently his pastor—identified as hyper-Calvinism sounded to Al like the very Calvinism he had been taught by the pastor and had learned from books he'd been reading by leading Calvinist authors—and that included Calvin himself. Certainly both moderate and hyper-Calvinists embraced all five points, including limited atonement. Then what was the difference?

Al finally concluded that "hypers" denied that God loves everyone. To them, "For God so loved the world" didn't mean every person "without exception, but without distinction" (a mystifying phrase he now realized he'd been rather proud to interject into discussions with non-Calvinists)—all *kinds* of people that comprised the elect, but not every individual in every kind. But in this book, MacArthur claimed that God loved *everybody*—even the reprobate—and that this was what classic Calvinists had always believed: "The fact that some sinners are not elected to salvation is no proof that God's attitude toward them is utterly devoid of sincere love.... He loves the elect in a special way reserved only for them. But that does not make His love for the rest of humanity any less real."[23]

So God has (or had) a *real* love for those He never intended to save? "What nonsense!" Al muttered, beginning to feel angry. "Why not admit the truth?"

As he read, Al highlighted all the places in the book where it seemed to him that MacArthur contradicted himself, most of which the pastor himself had already highlighted, though apparently in approval. Al showed the pastor the contradictions the next time they got together for their weekly discipleship session.

"I think MacArthur is playing a semantic game," complained Al. "He believes the same thing the so-called hyper-Calvinists believe, but he isn't as honest about admitting it! He covers it up with talk about God loving everyone, but that traps him in serious contradictions!"

"How can you say that, Al? He spends an entire book showing from Scripture that God loves all mankind...."

"Yes, and that's the problem! *Loves everyone*? But is it *really* love? Look here: 'He loves the elect in a special way reserved only for them. But that does not make His love for the rest of humanity any less real.'"[24]

"Yes, that's what I believe. So...?"

"Is it *real love* to predestine someone to eternal torment who *could* have been saved?"

"Well, God isn't under any obligation to love everyone alike," protested the pastor. "He must be as free as we are to love different people in different ways!"

"It's not a question of *obligation*," persisted Al. "I didn't ask whether God was *obligated* to love everyone. Of course, He isn't—not by any law. He makes the laws. But isn't love His very essence? He *is* love. So His very nature compels Him to love everyone...."

"But not alike in the same way!" interrupted the pastor. "There are different kinds of love. My love for my wife and children is different from my love for my neighbor...."

"I'm not trying to be argumentative. God knows I'd like to get this settled. I'm to love my neighbor as myself. But forgetting that high standard...would it be *any kind of love* for me to set my neighbor's house on fire?"

"Of course not," came the instant and firm reply.

Contradictions...and Double Talk

"Then how can it be love for God to predestine multitudes to the Lake of Fire for eternity? That's double talk!"

"No it isn't. You forget that these are sinners. They deserve it. They hate God, have rebelled against Him...would tear Him from His throne if they could...! God has to vindicate His justice."

"But aren't all men equally guilty and deserving of eternal punishment? If God's justice allowed Him to save the elect, how could it prevent Him from saving all the rest of mankind? His justice has been satisfied in Christ—only for the elect, of course. But couldn't God just as well have chosen to elect everyone, to have Christ die for all mankind, and to sovereignly regenerate and provide all with faith to believe?"

"But that wasn't His plan..." the pastor protested.

"*Plan*? That's the whole point. He *could have* included all in that plan. So how is it love for God to exclude *any* that He could save?"

"That's exactly what MacArthur explains. Let me see that book." The pastor thumbed through it rapidly like someone who had read it several times. "Look here," he said at last: "'Surely His pleading with the lost, His offers of mercy to the reprobate, and the call of the gospel to all who hear are all sincere expressions of the heart of a loving God [who] tenderly calls sinners to turn from their evil ways and live. He offers the water of life to all (Isaiah 55:1; Revelation 22:17).... Reformed theologians have always affirmed the love of God for all sinners...because the Father loves the human race, and wishes that they should not perish.' Then MacArthur quotes Calvin, who said the same of John 3:16, that Christ 'employed the universal term *whosoever*, both to invite all indiscriminately to partake of life, and to cut off every excuse from unbelievers.'"[25]

Al gave his pastor a long, hard look of disbelief. "That's more double talk...and it convinces *you*? I've read the book. I know what MacArthur says. Turn the page.... Here, let me have it. Look at the end of this quote. Calvin says, 'but the elect alone are they whose eyes God opens....'"

"Of course. If God really wanted everyone to be saved then they all would be. So...?"

"You don't see the contradiction? God invites *everyone* to salvation—including those for whom Christ didn't die and whom He has already from a past eternity determined not to save and has predestined to eternal torment? Surely MacArthur can't be serious! And you think this makes sense?

"Just because it seems a contradiction to us...," the pastor began lamely, but Al cut him off.

"You know very well," interrupted Al impatiently, "that you told me many times that Calvinism teaches that God really doesn't want everyone to be saved. He only opens the eyes of the elect! You just said that if He did, everyone *would* be saved.

"Come on, Pastor! That's like issuing a general invitation for everyone in our church to come to my house for dinner but only telling a select group where I live and keeping my address secret from the rest. Of course, my Calvinist friends stick up for me and insist that I really want everyone to come, even though I make it impossible for most people to find me. That's double talk! And it's like that all through this book! I don't know what to believe any more. I want to believe the Bible—but I've lost confidence in it because so many bright men like Sproul, Packer, Piper, and MacArthur claim to find justification in it for the most blatant contradictions."

It wasn't a pleasant scene. The argument became intense, with the pastor defending MacArthur, and Al acrimoniously and impatiently insisting that the contradiction was shamefully obvious and that it formed the very basis of Calvinism. Finally he apologized to the pastor for becoming angry. He regretted having started the argument as he left the church and headed to work.

Stifling a Most Troubling Thought

Al had a difficult time all day trying to keep his mind on his job. Cutting through the semantic talk about God loving *everyone*, the truth was that whatever *kind* of love Calvinism credited God with toward the non-elect, it wasn't genuine enough to really desire their salvation. And that meant it wasn't love at all, in spite of MacArthur and Piper writing entire books to try to prove that "offering" salvation to those whom God has specifically excluded from salvation is sincere and loving.

It made Al angry every time he thought of the hypocrisy of "moderate" Calvinists claiming that God sincerely loved those He had predestined to eternal torment when He *could* have included them among the elect just as well as others. Those they criticized as hyper-Calvinists were simply honest enough to admit the truth. Even if God's "common grace" gave the entire world to someone He *could* have saved but instead consigned to eternal flames...there was no way to call that *love*!

Well, this was a general flaw in Calvinism that he had never seen before. Now it was clear. What "God" was this that the Calvinists of all kinds believed in? Al could believe in such a God no longer. Was he becoming an atheist? He knew that couldn't be right—but the temptation to reject God altogether took hold of him and was frightening.

After his conversion Al had become a strong believer in the necessity of apologetics. Reared in Roman Catholic schools, he had been taught that evolution was true. In university, a debate about evolution between a Christian geneticist and a professor in the same field first started him on an investigation that ultimately played a vital role in his conversion to Christ. He had carefully weighed a great deal of evidence and found that it all pointed to the validity of the Bible and Christianity.

As a Calvinist, however, he had lost his interest in apologetics. Some of his Calvinist friends from the study group were heavily into apologetics—

but what was the point? The elect needed no evidence or persuasion, and it would do the non-elect no good. For a time, he felt somewhat confused and even guilty over his change of mind, but that dissipated when a fellow Calvinist (who had been in it longer than he) pointed out from Calvin's *Institutes* where such an attitude was justified.

Calvin's Weakness as an Apologist

It would, of course, be consistent with Calvinism to view evidence and reason as of little if any value in establishing faith. After all, faith is a gift of God given only to the elect after their regeneration. Indeed, why should a Calvinist be concerned (though Al noted that many, inconsistently, were) to offer evidence to the ungodly for the existence of God, and that the Bible is true in every word? The totally depraved cannot be swayed by truth, while the elect don't need such persuasion—since they are sovereignly without any faith regenerated in order to cause them to believe—and evidence has nothing to do with that fact. No wonder Calvin had so little use for evidence and proof:

> The prophets and apostles...dwell [not] on reasons; but they appeal to the sacred name of God, in order that the whole world may be compelled to submission.... If, then, we would...save [ourselves] from...uncertainty, from wavering, and even stumbling... our conviction of the truth of Scripture must be derived from a higher source than human conjectures…namely, the secret testimony of the Spirit.... It is preposterous to attempt, by discussion, to rear up a full faith in Scripture....
>
> Profane men...insist to have it proved by reason that Moses and the prophets were divinely inspired. But I answer, that the testimony of the Spirit is superior to reason. For as God alone can properly bear witness to his own words, so these words will not obtain full credit in the hearts of men, until they are sealed by the inward testimony of the Spirit.... Let it therefore be held as fixed, that...scripture, carrying its own evidence along with it, deigns not to submit to proofs and arguments, but owes the full conviction with which we ought to receive it to the testimony of the Spirit.... We ask not for proofs or probabilities.…
>
> Such, then, is a conviction which asks not for reasons; such, a knowledge which accords with the highest reason, namely, knowledge in which the mind rests more firmly and securely than in any reasons...the conviction which revelation from heaven alone

> can produce...the only true faith is that which the Spirit of God seals on our hearts....
>
> This singular privilege God bestows on his elect only, whom he separates from the rest of mankind...if at any time, then, we are troubled at the small number of those who believe, let us...call to mind that none comprehend the mysteries of God save those to whom it is given.[26]

It seemed biblical and reasonable to Al that the subjective witness of the Holy Spirit was supported by objective proof. The Bible is filled with evidence. The prophets, Apostles, and Christ himself applied such proof to persuade unbelievers to believe in God and to strengthen the faith of believers. Surely, solid proof ought to be used in presenting the gospel and in reinforcing the assurance of believers.

But what was the point, if the elect alone are given saving faith and that without any evidence but as a result of sovereign regeneration? Then why did Paul and the apostles, following Christ's example, devote themselves to *proving* the gospel (Acts 1:3; 9:22, 29; 10:43; 13:26-41; 17:2-3, 17-31; 18:9-11, 28, etc.)?

Al realized that Muslims could testify to most of what Calvin said about the inner witness of the Spirit. They need no proof, because they have an inner conviction that Allah inspired Muhammad. Internal and external evidence, however, reveals that the Qur'an is not true and that Muhammad was a false prophet. Mormons, too, are able to hold fast to their "faith" in spite of the total lack of evidence for the Book of Mormon (indeed, much evidence refutes it, such as the video *DNA vs. The Book of Mormon*), because its validity was supposedly verified to them by God through a "burning in the bosom." Such is the secret "faith" of every convinced cult member.

Having belittled proofs, Calvin did go on to offer some, but they were generally weak and hardly sufficient to convince an intelligent skeptic. They involved the majesty of language and sublime truths set forth in Scripture more than evidences for its inspiration. He did touch briefly on a few prophecies, but they were of the kind which were fulfilled in short order, such as the restoration of the children of Israel under Cyrus. The most powerful prophecies fulfilled in Israel throughout history and in the coming of her Messiah were almost completely neglected—the former, no doubt, because of the rejection of Israel as God's people, which Luther and Calvin carried over from their Catholicism.

Calvin did spend several chapters speaking of the evidences that God exists, that the Bible is the Word of God, and that God is the only true God, in contrast to the false gods of the heathen. But why do this if it isn't important? The elect surely don't need any proof. Moreover, the proofs he offered were weak and superficial and would carry little weight with any intelligent skeptic. So many others have written apologetics that are far superior to Calvin's that he wasted his time.

We do not minimize the witness of the Holy Spirit within the believer. However, the Bible offers proof upon proof, as did the Apostles and prophets. We have the prophecies fulfilled, the historical evidence, and the scientific and logical evidence. These are important in establishing the Word of God and the gospel it contains as the truth of God. Paul told Titus that an elder should "be able by sound doctrine both to exhort and to convince the gainsayers" (Titus 1:9).

Al had not entirely lost his interest in apologetics, but it seemed of little value in light of his new understanding. Furthermore, he found no hope of apologetics ever being able to prove that he was one of the elect. In fact, there was no way that apologetics could establish the truth of election—much less determine the identity of the elect. That realization troubled him greatly.

---

1. William MacDonald to Dave Hunt (marginal note in review copy). On file.
2. Bruce Milne, *Know the Truth* (Downer's Grove, IL: InterVarsity, n. d.), 66.
3. Arthur W. Pink, *The Sovereignty of God* (Grand Rapids,MI: Baker Book House, 4th ed., 2nd prtg. 1986), 155.
4. Ibid., 156.
5. Ibid., 1.
6. Pink, foreword to 1st ed. 1918, *Sovereignty*.
7. James R. White, *The Potter's Freedom* (Amityville, NY: Calvary Press Publishing, 2000), 100–101.
8. John Calvin, *Institutes of the Christian Religion*, trans. Henry Beveridge (Grand Rapids, MI: Wm. Eerdmans Publishing Company, 1998 ed.), III: ii, 11.
9. Ibid., III: ii, 12.
10. Thomas R. Schreiner, "Does Scripture Teach Prevenient Grace in the Wesleyan Sense," in *Still Sovereign*, 237.
11. Ibid., 240.
12. Calvin, *Institutes*, III: ii, 11–12.

13. Martin Luther, *The Bondage of the Will*, trans. J. I. Packer and O. R. Johnston (Grand Rapids, MI: Fleming H. Revell, 1957, 11th prtg. 1999), 153.
14. Loraine Boettner, *The Reformed Doctrine of Predestination* (Phillipsburg, NJ: Presbyterian and Reformed Publishing Co., 1932), 367.
15. Calvin, *Institutes*, III: xxi, 1.
16. Westminster Confession of Faith (London: n. p., 1643), XVIII: iv.
17. Boettner, *Reformed*, back cover.
18. Ibid.
19. Boettner, *Reformed*, 365.
20. Sam Howe Verhovek, "Cardinal Defends a Jailed Bishop Who Warned Cuomo on Abortion," *The New York Times*, February 1, 1990, A1, B4.
21. Wm. Oosterman, "Take a Long Look at the Doctrine of Election" (Ottawa, Canada: The Lord's Library Publications, n. d.), 7. Available from Westboro Baptist Church, Ottawa.
22. John MacArthur, *The Love of God* (Dallas, TX: Word Publishing, 1996), 110.
23. Ibid., 14-16.
24. Ibid., 16.
25. Ibid., 17-18.
26. Calvin, *Institutes*, 71–73.

CHAPTER

31

Resting in God's Love

THE MORE DEEPLY Al studied the subject of assurance, the more confused he became at the frequent contradictions among Calvinists. He read where John MacArthur said that "those whose faith is genuine will prove their salvation is secure by persevering to the end in the way of righteousness."[1] But Joseph Dillow, in a book that had been highly recommended to him by his pastor as giving the clearest word on assurance of salvation, criticized MacArthur and (with many quotations from Calvin to support him) declared that "Saving faith in Calvin and in the New Testament is a passive thing located in the mind."[2] In that case, it would be independent of any works.

Calvin argued that "If we are in communion with Christ, we have proof sufficiently clear and strong that we are written in the Book of Life."[3] But considering the deceitfulness of every human heart, how could we possibly be sure that we were in communion with Christ—and what about all the other things Calvin said about false assurance in contradiction to this statement? Al was now exactly where Calvin had said he would be: "All who do not know that they are the peculiar people of God must be wretched from perpetual trepidation."[4] So his wretchedness was, after all, to be endless?

Al's confusion only grew (but with it a glimmer of hope) when he read the admission from Gerstner that those who think they have full assurance that they are saved "ground themselves in the faulty definitions of saving faith which we received from the first Reformers. They...defined saving faith as a belief that 'Christ has saved *me*,' making the assurance of hope its necessary essence. Now, the later Reformers...have subjected this view to searching examination, and rejected it (as does the Westminster Assembly) on scriptural grounds."[5] That could only mean that Al's former assurance of salvation had actually been in agreement with the early Reformers, and it was the later ones who retreated from that position! Whom should he believe—and why such disagreement among Calvinists?

Al wondered how he had missed the fact that so many Calvinists seemed to insist that assurance was *impossible*. Kenneth Gentry wrote, "Assurance is subjective.... Dabney rightfully notes that [absolute assurance] requires a revelation beyond the Scripture because the Bible does not specifically speak to the individual in question. Nowhere in the Bible do we learn...that Ken Gentry is among the elect."[6] Al was badly shaken. From Gentry's article and similar statements from other leading Calvinists, was he to conclude that Calvinism actually opposed the assurance he was seeking? That seemed to be what Walter Chantry was saying:

> Few seem to appreciate the doubts of professing Christians who question whether they have been born again. They have no doubt that God will keep His promises but they wonder whether they have properly fulfilled the conditions for being heirs to those promises.... They are asking a legitimate question, "Have we believed and repented? Are we the recipients of God's grace...?" Since we read of self-deceived hypocrites like Judas, it is an imperative question. "What must I do to be saved?" is an altogether different question from, "How do I know I've done that?" You can answer the first confidently. Only the Spirit may answer the last with certainty.[7]

Al was not only confused but also deeply troubled by the very selectiveness of leading Calvinist apologists, which he began to notice and which we have documented in earlier chapters. In his zeal to deny that volition had anything to do with faith, and to show that it was entirely a mental attitude produced by the Holy Spirit without man's will, Dillow cited Ephesians 6:23 ("Peace be to the brethren, and love with faith, from God the Father and the Lord Jesus Christ")[8] but neglected to mention 6:16 ("Above all, taking the shield of faith..."). Since "taking" surely was something we must do, so believing must be our responsibility as well. But that contradicted the very sovereignty Dillow was declaring. No wonder he hadn't mentioned this verse!

Al found little comfort from his Calvinist friends. They had their own doubts, which they generally denied, only admitting them in rare moments of candor. It was all sovereignty with no part for man to play at all—except that one had to persevere to the end and demonstrate it in one's life. And Al knew he was failing that test.

A friend had given Al an article by R. C. Sproul titled "Assurance of Salvation." Al had read it eagerly, hoping for help, only to come across this troubling statement: "There are people in this world who are not saved, but who are convinced that they are...."[9]

That seemed to describe the very false assurance he once had. Now he knew better. The more he researched, the more convinced he became that assurance of heaven was beyond his reach. And to his surprise, Al was discovering that uncertainty of salvation was rather common among Calvinists. A statement by I. Howard Marshall seemed to go right through his heart, because it was so true of his own situation: "Whoever said, 'the Calvinist knows that he cannot fall from salvation but does not know whether he has got it,' had it summed up nicely."[10] Was Calvinism itself, then, the root of his doubts?

The more Al read, the more confused he became. Dillow went on and on about the faith that brings assurance[11] until it became far too complex theologically for the Philippian jailor to have known what Paul meant when he said, "Believe on the Lord Jesus Christ and thou shalt be saved" (Acts 16:31). But could it really be as simple as Paul's bare statement?

The Central Issue: God's Love

Al's troubled countenance and increasing moodiness finally provoked Jan to break her silence. "Let me get this straight," she began. "The God you now believe in—"

"What do you mean, 'the God I now believe in'?" Al interjected testily. "He's the same God I always believed in and the One you believe in too!"

"Really? I listen carefully to Pastor Jim...and I'm not the only one with the same concerns. The God of the Bible that I believe in (and you used to) loves the whole world and wants everyone saved. He gives us all the right to choose—so it's not His doing if anyone goes to hell...."

"That's *your* interpretation," interrupted Al. He couldn't let Jan know his doubts.

"Let me finish, please...? Your *new* God gives no one a choice. He regenerates certain elect ones against their will, and—"

"That's not true!" Al shot back quickly. "He makes us willing by changing our hearts."

"Were *you* willing to be regenerated?"

"I didn't know I was being regenerated." Those words slipped out before Al knew it. He had to continue. "That has to come first before anyone can believe the gospel. We're regenerated and then given faith—"

"Exactly what I said. Your will was set against God. Out of the blue He regenerated you. If that isn't against your will...."

"Well...I'll have to think about that."

"You didn't have a choice. He just elected you."

"Grace has to be *irresistible,* because no one wants it. You think a sovereign God is going to let man have the last word! Then He's not sovereign! The God I believe in isn't going to let puny man frustrate His purposes! You don't understand sovereignty...God doesn't share His throne!"

"Sovereignty, foreknowledge, free will...Calvinists make it all so complicated," countered Jan. "But the Bible is simple enough for a child to understand. The real issue is love—and that clarifies everything. You actually believe that God who *is* love only loves certain ones and predestines the rest to eternal damnation? What love is this?"

"Well...the Bible does teach election. You admit that...."

"Forget election for the moment—"

"It's in the Bible, for heaven's sake! How can you forget it?"

"I mean that's too complicated. There's something simpler—God's love. I can't believe that the God I know sends anyone to hell that He could rescue!"

"It doesn't make *me* comfortable, either. But the Bible teaches this is God's good pleasure."

"*Where* does the Bible say that! My Bible says that God has no pleasure in the destruction of the wicked but wants all to be saved. Al, I love you but I can't go along with this. That's not the God of love I know and read of in the Bible. I think the Calvinism you and Pastor are into misrepresents God. But I don't want to discuss it—we just argue."

"We're not arguing, Jan. This is important. I've been studying this for months."

"Al, I admire you for the effort you've put into it. But it takes no study to see that God loves the whole world so much that He sent His Son to die for everyone's sins, so *that 'the world through him might be saved.'* And that's just one verse."

"*World* there doesn't mean every individual but all *kinds* of people that make up humanity—the elect," Al countered. "You just don't understand. A little more study...."

"Don't you think I've been studying too? I know enough verses to tell me that Calvinism libels the God who Paul said wants 'all men to be saved' (1 Timothy 2:4) and Peter said 'is not willing that any should perish' (2 Peter 3:9)."

"*All men* means all classes. Paul says, 'Kings...all that are in authority...' in 1 Timothy 2:2. He's saying there are all classes in the elect. If you'd let me explain—"

"Please, Al, don't complicate the Bible. When it says God loves the whole world and doesn't want any to perish, why work so hard to make it say *elect*?" Jan shrugged her shoulders helplessly. "You go ahead and study Calvinism. I'll stick with my simple faith, and let's not argue about it."

"We're not arguing—just discussing."

But Jan had turned to the kitchen sink and was busying herself cleaning up the dinner dishes, humming, "Blessed assurance, Jesus is mine...."

Hell: Whose Choice?

It was deeply troubling to Al (though he wasn't ready to admit it to Jan) that, in spite of the Bible's presentation from Genesis to Revelation of God's love, grace, and mercy to all, Calvinism portrayed God as pleased to damn billions. At one time, this view had seemed the only way to uphold God's sovereignty, but now he wondered whether an overemphasis upon sovereignty had diminished God's love. He read where White said:

> We know, naturally, that we are to have God's glory as our highest goal, our highest priority. So it should not be at all surprising that the most profound answer Scripture gives to the question of "what's it all about" is that it is about God's glory. *All* of salvation results in the praise of the glory of *His* grace.[12]

Those were nice words to which a few months earlier Al would have assented without much thought. Now he wondered how predestining multitudes to eternal torment could be to the glory of God's grace—and how even the salvation of the elect could glorify God if He could have done the same for all, but didn't.

Jan's words from months earlier came back to haunt him: "The Bible teaches that those in hell will be there because, although God didn't want them to go there and lovingly provided and freely offered full salvation, they rejected it."

To say that God's sovereignty would be denied if man had a choice no longer seemed quite as foolproof as it once had. Couldn't God make a sovereign decision to allow man free will? Al began cautiously to read some critics of Calvinism and came across the following, which seemed to make a lot of sense:

> What takes the greater power (omnipotence): to create beings who have no ability to choose—who are mere pawns on God's cosmic chessboard—or to create beings who have the freedom to accept or reject God's salvation? I submit, the latter.... Would a God who ordained the existence of immortal beings without making any provision for them to escape eternal torment be a cruel being? What kind of God would call on mankind to "believe and be saved" when He knows they cannot [and] what kind of relationship is there between God and people who could never choose Him—but are "irresistibly" called...? For these and other reasons I question the idea that individual unconditional election and five-point Calvinism best reflect the attributes of God. A God who sovereignly offers salvation to all through His elect Savior reflects both power and love.[13]

Perseverance of the Saints?

Al continued wrestling with the matter of assurance. Even aside from the question of whether he was one of the elect, he was still confused about whether his experience of trusting Christ was biblical. Reading again James White's *The Potter's Freedom*, he came across the statement once more upon which Calvinists were in almost 100 percent agreement: "[S]omething must happen *before* a person can 'hear' or believe in Christ: and that is the work of God in regenerating the natural man and bringing him to spiritual life."[14] That certainly hadn't been the sequence of events in his coming to Christ, as he remembered it. He had thought that he had been regenerated (born again) *following* his faith in Christ and as a *result* of believing the gospel.

But much like White, Jonathan Edwards also taught that there had to be "the principle of holiness that precedes faith...the alteration made in the heart of the sinner before there can be action [i.e., faith in Christ]."[15] Going back in his memory to that decisive night, Al could not see how that could have been the case.

Al was listening to a tape by John Armstrong, a man he greatly admired as a leading Calvinist, and was shocked to hear him say, "I was asked the question about a year ago by a group of pastors in Pennsylvania...'What do you think is the one doctrine that is the most destructive in the life of the church...today?' And I said, the doctrine of Eternal Security."[16]

Al couldn't believe his ears. He had to rewind the tape and listen to it two more times. Sure enough, he'd heard it right the first time. So the worst thing possible was to have assurance of salvation? Armstrong seemed to explain why any apparent assurance could only be false: "God justifies, but man must have faith and he must obey...(Romans 2:13–14). When it says the one who obeys the law is justified, it means exactly that. That is not a hypothetical verse, ladies and gentlemen, the way many Protestants have read it. And when James 2:13–14 says, 'The doers of the law shall be justified,' it means the doers of the law shall be justified. That's why Paul and James are not in conflict.... Let me suggest...[also] Ephesians 2:8–10.... We are saved unto good works. They're necessary consequential works. Without them there is no salvation. Right?"[17]

No wonder there could be no assurance of salvation: it depended upon our keeping the law! The Bible says no one has kept the law, so who could be saved? Al was devastated. Was Armstrong right or was Dillow? Yet both of them not only contradicted one another but themselves as well. On the same tape, Armstrong said that man had no will, that Luther's *Bondage of the Will* was what the Reformation was all about, and that even the faith to believe was a gift of God. So how could it be man's responsibility to believe and keep the law? Al was bewildered. Nor did it help when Armstrong gave his antidote: "Perseverance, and here's the point, is the necessary attribute of justification."[18]

Perseverance? That sure put the burden on him. Did he just need to *persevere*? What good would that do if he wasn't among the elect?

Perseverance was everything for some Calvinists, but not for others. Whom should Al believe? And how could a failure to persevere after the fact prove that one had not been saved in the first place? Why, that would mean that one could *never* be sure he had ever been saved until he died and thus knew whether he had truly persevered to the end! Al had once been so happy with the fifth point of Calvinism because he thought it meant that God would do the persevering: "For it is God which worketh in you both to will and to do of his good pleasure" (Philippians 2:13). Now he discovered that the persevering in good works and keeping the law was up to him, and he knew that he couldn't do it—certainly not if he wasn't one of the elect. That was the question that tortured him.

Why hadn't he noticed earlier this emphasis upon *one's own* perseverance? Al knew that his "performance" had deteriorated lately, and that meant that his perseverance in the faith was far from what it ought to be. That he was plagued by doubts was further proof that he was not persevering. And the doubts only grew the more he studied the writings of leading Calvinists, ancient or modern. Could it be Calvinism itself that fostered the doubts? Perhaps Calvin was admitting this when he wrote:

> For there is scarcely a mind in which the thought does not sometimes rise, Whence your salvation but from the election of God? But what proof have you of your election? When once this thought has taken possession of any individual, it keeps him perpetually miserable, subjects him to dire torment, or throws him into a state of complete stupor.... Therefore, as we dread shipwreck, we must avoid this rock, which is fatal to every one who strikes upon it....[19]

Al was devastated. To try to be sure you're one of the elect would be *fatal*? Wait a minute! Wasn't it Calvinism's doctrine of election that had caused his uncertainty? Non-Calvinists had no such doubts. If he abandoned this doctrine would he find peace?

More and More Unanswered Questions

Al began cautiously to ask Christian friends how they *knew* they were saved. The Calvinists said they were among the elect and had the works to prove it, though at times they weren't especially comfortable with their performance. The non-Calvinists simply replied that they had believed the gospel. Christ had promised eternal life to all who would come to Him in faith, and that was good enough for them.

The more Al studied, the more the troubling questions mounted. If man is totally depraved by nature, how can he aspire to and even do good deeds? But he does. If Total Depravity isn't total in that regard, then why is it total when it comes to believing the gospel? Why would God repeatedly appeal to men to repent if they couldn't? Why send His prophets day after day, year after year, pleading with unregenerate Israel, if they were predestined to rebel and go to hell? If Grace was Irresistible, why not just impart it to everyone? Wouldn't love do that?

Everyone? It always came back to Jan's main complaint—how could God who *is* love allow *anyone* to perish whom He could save? Even worse, how could the God of all grace (1 Peter 5:10) and mercy will anyone's destruction? He had never admitted it to Jan, but that question had long troubled him, and now was beginning to push everything else into the background. Jan's earnest query haunted him: "*What love is this?*"

Somehow, a little booklet by Spurgeon fell into Al's hands, and he was excited to read that even that great preacher and staunch Calvinist admitted that he'd had no perception at the time of his conversion that God had sovereignly regenerated him, nor could he imagine at what point that could have happened. Spurgeon confessed, "When I was coming to Christ, I thought I was doing it all myself—I sought the Lord earnestly...." It was not until some time later that he realized that "God was at the bottom of it all.... He was the Author of my faith, and so the whole doctrine of grace opened up to me...."[20] He closed his sermon declaring that those Christians who are most pious, reverent, and devoted to the Lord "believe that they are saved by Grace, without works, through faith, and that not of themselves, it is the gift of God."[21] That sounded like his non-Calvinist friends and the way he had believed before becoming a Calvinist!

To God Be the Glory!

Al remembered that before he'd become a Calvinist he had praised God for being the Author of salvation and the Savior of sinners, had given all credit and glory to Him, and had understood very clearly that he would never have sought Him had God not moved upon him by His Spirit to do so. But he had also been certain that it was his responsibility to respond in faith from his heart. Surely, for man to respond to God by gratefully receiving the gift of salvation would not nullify anything Spurgeon said. And how could it challenge God's sovereignty for man to receive gratefully what God offered while giving God all the glory?

Jan, in fact, had some time previously suggested, "It seems to me that my praise and gratitude to the Lord is more genuine and more glorifying to God than any Calvinist's."

"How can you say that?" Al had protested.

"Because my gratitude and praise comes from my heart. I wasn't programmed to accept Christ—"

"*Programmed*? No Calvinist teaches that!"

"You don't call it that, but you were totally opposed to God and instead of your heart being won to Christ by His love and grace and mercy, you were *made* to believe—"

"Not *made* to believe," Al interrupted impatiently. *When would she ever understand?* "Our wills are changed graciously!"

"Okay, you were *caused* to believe. Al, you can't get around the fact that God did something to your will so that you believed what you formerly didn't believe. And it didn't come about by any conviction on your part, any understanding, any faith on your part. I've been reading some of those Calvinist books you've got."

Like every other argument—yes, that's what they had become—this one, too, ended with neither of them giving any ground. But Al was increasingly shaken in his confidence that Calvinism was the truth of God. Most troubling had been the realization that his uncertainty seemed to arise out of Calvinism itself. No wonder Calvin had voiced so many warnings about doubts:

> Among the temptations with which Satan assaults believers, none is greater or more perilous, than when disquieting them with doubts as to their election, he at the same time stimulates them with a depraved desire of inquiring after it out of the proper way...I mean when puny man endeavors to penetrate to the hidden recesses of the divine wisdom...in order that he may understand what final determination God has made with regard to him.[22]

So it wasn't proper to want to know God's "final determination... with regard to him"? But there was nothing so important! It seemed that Calvin kept contradicting himself. Sometimes he even seemed to say that we should just trust God for our election: "Our confidence ought to go no farther than the word...."[23] Al realized that if he did that he would turn from Calvinism, back to simple faith in the gospel. Perhaps, thought Al in despair, he ought to go back even before what he had thought was his conversion and return to the Church of his upbringing.

Desperation—and Enlightenment

Al began to think more seriously of returning to Catholicism. Embarrassed and uncertain, he went back to his old parish and found that a new priest who didn't know him was in charge. That made it easier. In the process of telling the new man that he wanted to explore possibly returning to

Roman Catholicism, somehow the name of Calvin came up. In the next fifteen minutes, to his utter amazement, Al discovered that this priest knew even more about Calvinism than did Pastor Jim.

A well-worn copy of Calvin's *Institutes of the Christian Religion* was pulled from a shelf and the priest began to read a section he was sure would settle any question in Al's mind of returning to the true Church. Al almost jumped up and shouted, "Hallelujah!" when what Calvin had said about baptism was read to him. He could hardly believe his ears that, according to Calvin, his baptism as a baby into the Roman Catholic Church had made him one of the elect. All he had to do was to believe the promise inherent in his Catholic baptism!

Al was ecstatic. The Catholic Church had done more for him than he had known. So he was one of the elect after all: Calvin himself had said it! All Al needed to do was to trust his baptism.

But this new assurance lasted for only a few days. Was his faith to be in his baptism as an infant too young to understand anything, and at the hands of a Catholic priest, who himself taught and practiced a false salvation? Was that really the biblical foundation of eternal salvation? Well, Calvin had said so.

What about the true gospel he had believed, "the power of God unto salvation," and as a result had been born again? If being baptized as a baby when he didn't even know what was happening had made him a child of God, as Calvin had insisted, even to the persecution of those who disagreed, then what was the point of his believing the gospel? No, he couldn't accept that, even if Calvin had declared it. Al had finally come to a fish in the Calvinism pond too large to swallow.

Now he faced new doubts: If Calvin had been so wrong about infant baptism—and there was no doubt that like Luther he had been—maybe the rest of his teaching was equally false. Why should he believe TULIP at all? It seemed impossible that Calvin could have ever written such heresy as he had about baptism—yes, heresy; there was no other name for it—but the priest had shown it to him right there in the *Institutes*, and Al had looked it up for himself when he got home.

A Forgotten Challenge

Al turned again to his collection of Calvinist writers and began going through their books and listening to their tapes once more, hoping to find the elusive answer he'd been seeking. Tucked inside one of the books, he found a letter received from a concerned friend a few months after he'd become a Calvinist. Now the forgotten and important role it had played in contributing to his doubts flooded his memory. He read it again carefully and thoughtfully:

> As for the doctrine of election humbling you, have you ever considered how you know you are one of the elect? Calvin literally said that God causes some of the non-elect to imagine they have believed and are among the elect, the better to judge them. Is that the God you now believe in? Are you sure you aren't just imagining you are one of the elect?
>
> What qualifies you to be one of the elect? Calvin said there was no reason for God to choose you except that it pleased Him to do so. He also says that it pleased and glorified Him to predestine billions to burn in an eternal hell. Doesn't that bother you? Do you want to accept grace from *that* "God"? I think that's a libel on God's character!

There was more to it—a host of verses (which Al knew very well by now) declaring that God was not willing that any perish, that He wanted all to know the truth and to be set free, that Christ came to seek and to save sinners, not *some* sinners, etc. Al folded the letter thoughtfully and carefully put it back in the book. Originally it had made him so angry that he hadn't answered it. He must reply at last—and much differently from the way he would have responded before. But he didn't want Jan to see the letter or his reply—at least not yet.

The Turning Point

Pondering that letter and how to answer it, Al was struck with the compelling fact that his wife, whom he had "led to the Lord," had the very assurance of salvation that he was seeking. From the very first, when he had been intrigued by Calvinism's intellectual appeal, she had tried to avoid discussing the subject whenever he had brought it up. All she would say was that she was resting in Christ's love and promise and that the gospel couldn't be as complicated as having to change the obvious meaning of words into something else to make God less loving than what the Bible said He was.

What the Bible said! Those words suddenly took on a new meaning and became his deliverance. Getting back to the Bible was the turning point. Al stopped listening to and reading Calvinist and non-Calvinist experts and began to seriously study the Bible itself. It felt as if a burden had rolled off his shoulders just to be able to take the words of Scripture for what they said, rather than having to change them to fit Calvinism.

Among the last issues he wrestled with was Christ's statement, "Ye have not chosen me, but I have chosen you" (John 15:16). In pondering those words, Al realized he was complicating something that was rather simple. Christ was saying nothing more than any employer could say to each employee—that the employer's choosing was decisive. The employee could not force the employer to hire him; but neither could the employer force someone to work for him. Though the employer was completely in charge, the employee had to consent to being hired.

Likewise, we can't force Christ to choose us. He is under no obligation to us; salvation is alone by His grace and mercy and love. But our faith is essential. Salvation is only for those who believe in and receive Christ.

Al took up his remaining doubts with his pastor. They had some long discussions, and in spite of the pastor's efforts to keep him in the fold, Al's faith in Calvinism had been too badly eroded, while his confidence in the simple gospel was slowly being restored. Finally, only one problem remained which he had to wrestle with on his knees: there was no question that the Bible stated quite clearly that God blinded people's eyes to the gospel. How could that be reconciled with the infinite love that Al now believed God had for all without discrimination?

Calvinism's Last Stand

A favorite scripture of Calvinists, and one to which White gives considerable attention[24] is John's comment: "Therefore they could not believe, because that Esaias said again, He hath blinded their eyes, and hardened their heart" (John 12:39–40). White also quotes John 8:34–48, "Why do you not understand what I am saying? It is because you cannot hear My word...." He then declares:

> Again the Reformed and biblical view of man is presented with force: Jesus teaches that the Jews *cannot* (there's that word of *inability* again) hear His word and do *not* understand what He is saying...they lack the spiritual ability to appraise spiritual truths.[25]

Far from proving Total Depravity, however, and thus the necessity of Irresistible Grace, Al could now see that these passages proved the opposite. If the unregenerate Jews were totally depraved and dead in sins as Calvinism defines it, unable in that condition to see or believe, surely God would not have needed to blind their eyes and harden their hearts. The fact that God finds it necessary to blind and harden anyone would seem to be proof that unregenerate men are able to understand and believe the gospel after all.

But why would a loving God deliberately blind the eyes of the lost whom He loves to prevent them from believing the gospel? This seemed especially puzzling to Al in view of God's continual lamentations over Israel for her refusal to obey, and His repeated expressions of desire to forgive and to bless her.

Since Israel was already in rebellion against God, why would He further harden hearts? There would have to be a good reason for doing this, a reason that would not diminish God's love and mercy; a reason that must apply equally to the Jews in Isaiah's day and yet speak prophetically of those in Christ's day. What could that be?

Inspired of God, Israel's prophets laid out her sin, rebellion, and stubbornness. For example, God through Isaiah laments, "Hear, O heavens, and give ear, O earth:... I have nourished and brought up children, and they have rebelled against me" (Isaiah 1:2). God knew their hard hearts and that there was no point in pleading with them further. But He was going to use them to fulfill His purposes declared by His prophets, just as He used Pharaoh.

God would send His Son to reveal His great love, to open the eyes of the blind, heal the sick, raise the dead, feed the hungry, offer Himself to Israel as their Messiah, weep over Jerusalem here on earth as He had done repeatedly from heaven through His prophets in ages past, and die for their sins and for the sins of the world. He would not allow that purpose to be frustrated by a momentary sentimentality on the part of the Jews that might cause them, while still rejecting Him, not to insist upon the cross.

They were going to cry, "Away with Him, crucify Him!" This was what their hard hearts really wanted. And to make certain that they did not relent at the last minute out of humanistic pity, God hardened their hearts and blinded their eyes. So Peter could say, "Him, being delivered by the determinate counsel and foreknowledge of God, ye have taken, and by wicked hands have crucified and slain" (Acts 2:23).

Al could see a similar example in the blindness that will be given to those left behind at the Rapture who have heard and rejected the gospel. Paul states specifically, "And *for this cause* God shall send them strong delusion, that they should believe a lie: that they all might be damned..." (2 Thessalonians 2:10–12). For *what* cause? Because "they received not the love of the truth, that they might be saved...who believed not the truth, but had pleasure in unrighteousness." God would help them to believe the lie their already hardened hearts wanted to believe.

Here we see not a God who arbitrarily blinds people so they can't be saved, but a loving God who is also perfectly just in giving unrepentant rebels the desire of their hearts, which leads to their damnation. They rejected the truth, so God helps them to persist in that rejection. Nor would He need to blind them if they were totally depraved as Calvinism defines it.

Yes, "the natural man receiveth not the things of the Spirit of God...neither can he know them, because they are spiritually discerned [i.e., revealed alone by the Holy Spirit]" (1 Corinthians 2:14). But there Paul is not referring to the gospel that is to be preached "to every creature" (Mark 16:15). He is addressing believers and referring to "the hidden wisdom...the deep things of God," which are only revealed by the Spirit of God to those who are indwelt by and walking in obedience to the Holy Spirit.

The Final Question

Pastor Jim, concerned about Al's weakening confidence in Calvinism, had challenged him: "If you are going to return to the belief that you had the ability to say yes to God in believing the gospel, how can you be sure that some time you may not decide to say no to God—even in eternity in heaven?" Zins expresses that problem as well as anyone:

> It is ironic that many...who adamantly argue that God forces no one to come to Him have no problem believing that God forces those who have come to Him *to stay with Him*. For most evangelicals, free will mysteriously disappears after one chooses salvation...."God will not make you come, but He will make you stay," might be their theological sentiment.[26]

Al asked Jan about this, and her reply was as simple as the Bible itself: "Why would I ever want to give up heaven? There would be nothing to tempt me away from our Lord, who is so wonderful that nothing could!"

"How can you be so sure," persisted Al? "Satan was the most beautiful, powerful, intelligent being ever created. All he knew was the presence of God—yet he rebelled!"

Jan was thoughtful for a moment. Finally she said, "Yeah, but he was never redeemed…never bought with the blood of Christ…. He had no basis for loving God, no gratitude to Christ for dying in his place…."

"So you think gratitude will keep a person from sinning?" cut in Al.

"There won't be any temptation to sin, no reason…it wouldn't make sense."

Al was not trying to argue, to put her down. "But who tempted Satan? What was his reason? It was pride. Couldn't those in heaven be tempted to pride if they had a free will?"

"Al, you keep bringing up Satan. I don't know anything about him… and I don't think we're supposed to speculate about him and his demons. That has nothing to do with us. We are entirely different beings."

She paused again thoughtfully, then continued. "In Romans 7, Paul says, 'the flesh lusts against the Spirit, and the Spirit against the flesh…the two are contrary, so you can't do what you would.' He describes this inner conflict as the reason why a Christian sins, if they do, and then he cries out, 'O wretched man that I am, who will deliver me from this body of death?'—and adds, 'I thank God, through Jesus Christ.' He must be saying that the resurrection, delivering us from these bodies of sin, suffering and death, is going to solve that problem…."

Al was thinking silently. "That's a good point," he conceded at last. "I guess Satan's example doesn't have much to do with what Christians will experience in heaven. You're right, he was never born again, certainly not indwelt with the Holy Spirit."

After a long, thoughtful silence, he added, "Look, I'm not just trying to argue, as I admit has been the case too often in the past. This is a real problem and I'm looking for honest answers. I want to know the truth…but if we still have free will in heaven, I don't see how…." His words trailed off into a frustrated silence.

Jan gave him a long look of understanding and sympathy. "You really want to know the truth? Jesus said, 'Thy word is truth…I am the truth… the resurrection and the life.' He promised believers eternal life…that we would never perish. I believe Him. That's all I need to know…it's that simple." She smiled lovingly and went back to ironing Al's shirts.

A few days later, it suddenly hit Al like light from heaven that his eternal security as saved by grace depended entirely upon God and not upon himself. Neither salvation nor the assurance thereof is by works, nor can works be a sign of the reality of one's salvation or the means of providing assurance. Even the apparent working of miracles, casting out of demons, and prophesying in Christ's name are no proof that one belongs to Him, as Christ himself solemnly declared:

> Not every one that saith unto me, Lord, Lord, shall enter into the kingdom of heaven; but he that doeth the will of my Father which is in heaven. Many will say to me in that day, Lord, Lord, have we not prophesied in thy name? and in thy name have cast out devils? and in thy name done many wonderful works? And then will I profess unto them, I never knew you: depart from me, ye that work iniquity. (Matthew 7:21–23)

On the other hand, there could be in the life of a particular person not one good work to indicate the reality of salvation, yet that person could be truly saved and thus elected of God to the blessings He has planned for the redeemed of all ages. All of one's works could be consumed in the fire of God's testing of motives and deeds, yet that person not be lost, according to Paul, in spite of no outward evidence of salvation:

> Every man's work shall be...revealed by fire; and the fire shall try every man's work of what sort it is. If any man's work abide... he shall receive a reward. If any man's work shall be burned, he shall suffer loss: but he himself shall be saved; yet so as by fire. (1 Corinthians 3:11–15)

Paul, of course, was speaking of those who are truly saved through faith in Christ. Al could now see his problem clearly: not one verse in the Bible tells how to know one has been elected. If being one of the elect is the basis for assurance of salvation, then there can be no assurance.

But one had to be *certain* about eternity! Yet Calvinists couldn't agree among themselves on the answer to what was obviously the most crucial question. Al decided at last that he was finished with that theory.

Assurance for Eternity

Biblical assurance of eternal life in heaven with Christ rests alone upon His promises, the promises of the Bible, and upon the foreknowledge, predestination/election, and keeping power of God. Christ said, "Come unto me," and we came. The gospel says, "Believe on the Lord Jesus Christ and thou shalt be saved," and we believed. Christ and His Word promise the following:

- Elect according to the foreknowledge of God the Father, through sanctification of the Spirit, unto obedience and sprinkling of the blood of Jesus Christ.... (1 Peter 1:2)
- According as he hath chosen us in him before the foundation of the world...having predestinated us unto the adoption of children by Jesus Christ to himself, according to the good pleasure of his will.... In whom we have redemption through his blood, the forgiveness of sins, according to the riches of his grace.... (Ephesians 1:4–7)
- For whom he did foreknow, he also did predestinate to be conformed to the image of his Son.... Whom he did predestinate, them he also called: and whom he called, them he also justified: and whom he justified, them he also glorified. (Romans 8:29–30)
- But as many as received him, to them gave he power to become the sons of GOD, even to them that believe on his name: which were born [again], not of blood, nor of the will of the flesh, nor of the will of man, but of God. (John 1:12–13)
- For God sent not his Son into the world to condemn the world; but that the world through him might be saved. He that believeth on him is not condemned: but he that believeth not is condemned already.... He that believeth on the Son hath everlasting life.... (John 3:17–18, 36)
- And this is the record, that God hath given to us eternal life, and this life is in his Son. He that hath the Son hath life; and he that hath not the Son of God hath not life. These things have I written unto you that believe on the name of the Son of God; that ye may know that ye have eternal life.... (1 John 5:11–13)
- Verily, verily, I say unto you, He that heareth my word, and believeth on him that sent me, hath everlasting life, and shall not come into condemnation; but is passed from death unto life. (John 5:24)

We believed, were saved "according to the promise of life which is in Christ Jesus" (2 Timothy 1:1), and are simply resting in His abundant promises that "whosoever believeth in him should not perish, but have everlasting life" (John 3:16). By simple faith in God's promise (the God who cannot lie), the believer knows that he has passed from death to life and will never perish—and he has been given the witness of the Holy Spirit within: "He that believeth on the Son of God hath the witness in himself..." (1 John 5:10). And "the Spirit itself beareth witness with our spirit, that we are the children of God:...heirs of God, and joint-heirs with Christ..." (Romans 8:16–17).

Having "heard the word of truth, the gospel of [our] salvation: in whom also after that [we] believed, [we] were sealed with that holy Spirit of promise, which is the earnest of our inheritance until the redemption of the purchased possession..." (Ephesians 1:13–14). Those who believe on Christ know they are saved and will never perish, because God cannot lie. Our trust is in Him for now and eternity.

Paul said, "I know whom I have believed, and am persuaded that he is able to keep that which I have committed unto him against that day" (2 Timothy 1:12). We, too, have believed and know the One in whom we are eternally secure. We, too, are fully persuaded that "the God and Father of our Lord Jesus Christ...according to his abundant mercy hath begotten us again unto a lively hope by the resurrection of Jesus Christ from the dead, to an inheritance incorruptible, and undefiled, and that fadeth not away, reserved in heaven for [us], who are kept by the power of God through faith unto salvation ready to be revealed in the last time" (1 Peter 1:3–5).

We have the many infallible proofs of prophecy fulfilled in Israel (and still being fulfilled before our eyes), and those that promised in detail the coming of the Messiah—prophesies that have without question been fulfilled in the life, death, and resurrection of our Lord and Savior Jesus Christ. We have the historical proofs, the archaeological proofs, the scientific proofs, and the internal proofs that the Bible is God's Word. The Bible offers a true and infallible testimony of the creation of this earth, the fall of Adam and Eve, the redemption through Christ's blood poured out in death upon the cross, of His soon return for His bride, and of His Second Coming to rescue Israel and to establish His millennial kingdom, when He will rule with a rod of iron over the nations from His father David's throne in Jerusalem—and of the coming new heavens and new earth.

We simply believe God's Word in all things, and we are therefore certain that we are saved and that He is coming back to take us to His Father's house of many mansions to fulfill His promise "that where I am, there ye may be also" (John 14:1–3). As Paul said, "...and so shall we ever be with the Lord. Wherefore comfort one another with these words" (1 Thessalonians 4:17–18).

---

1. John F. MacArthur, Jr., *The Gospel According to Jesus* (Academie Books, Grand Rapids, MI: Zondervan Publishing House, 1988), 98.
2. Joseph C. Dillow, *The Reign of the Servant Kings: A Study of Eternal Security and the Final Significance of Man* (Haysville, NC: Schoettle Publishing Co., 2nd ed. 1993), 253.
3. John Calvin, *Institutes of the Christian Religion*, trans. Henry Beveridge (Grand Rapids, MI: Wm. B. Eerdmans Publishing Company, 1998 ed.), III: xxiv, 5.
4. Ibid., III: xxi, 1.
5. *Discussions by Robert L. Dabney*, ed. C. R. Vaughn (Richmond, VA: Presbyterian Committee of Publication, 1890), 1:183.
6. Kenneth Gentry, "Assurance and Lordship Salvation: The Dispensational Concern" (*Dispensationalism in Transition*, September 1993); quoted by Robert N. Wilkin, "When Assurance Is Not Assurance," *Journal of the Grace Evangelical Society*, Autumn 1997, 10:19, 27–34.
7. Walter D. Chantry, *Today's Gospel: Authentic or Synthetic?* (Carlisle, PA: The Banner of Truth Trust, 1970), 75–76.
8. Dillow, *Reign*, 280.
9. Cited in Philip F. Congdon, "Soteriological Implications of Five-point Calvinism," *Journal of the Grace Evangelical Society*, Autumn 1995, 8:15, 55–68.
10. Howard Marshall; cited in D. A. Carson, "Reflections on Christian Assurance," *Westminster Theological Journal*, 54:1,24.
11. Dillow, *Reign*, 272–91.
12. James R. White, *The Potter's Freedom* (Amityville, NY: Calvary Press Publishing, 2000), 178.
13. Congdon, "Implications," 8:15, 56–57.
14. White, *Potter's*, 112–13.
15. John Armstrong, "Reflections from Jonathan Edwards on the Current Debate over Justification by Faith Alone" (quoted in speech given at Annapolis 2000: A Passion for Truth conference, sponsored by Jonathan Edwards Institute, PO Box 2410, Princeton NJ 08543). For more information on Jonathan Edwards's view on justification, contact Grace Evangelical Society, (972) 257–1160.
16. Ibid.
17. Ibid.
18. Ibid.
19. Calvin, *Institutes*, III: xxiv, 4.
20. Charles Haddon Spurgeon, "A Defense of Calvinism," single-sermon booklet (Edmonton, AB: Still Waters Revival Books, n. d.), 3–4.
21. Ibid., 22.
22. Calvin, *Institutes.*
23. Ibid., III: xxiv, 3.
24. White, *Potter's*, 105–109.
25. Ibid., 112–14.
26. Robert M. Zins, "A Believer's Guide to 2nd Peter 3:9" (self-published monograph, n. d.), 3.

A Final Word

MY HEART HAS BEEN BROKEN by Calvinism's misrepresentation of the God of the Bible, whom I love with all my heart, and for the excuse this has given atheists not to believe in Him. My sincere and earnest desire in writing this book has been to defend God's character against the libel that denies His love for all and insists that He does not make salvation available to all because He does not want all to be saved. It is my prayer that readers will recognize that Christian authors and leaders, ancient or modern and no matter how well respected, are all fallible and that God's Word is our only authority.

God's Word declares that the gospel, which is "the power of God unto salvation to *every one that believeth*" (Romans 1: 16), is "good tidings of great joy," not just to certain elect, but "to *all* people" (Luke 2:10). Sadly, the insistence that only a select group have been elected to salvation is *not* "good tidings of great joy to all people"! How can such a doctrine be biblical?

It is my prayer that Calvinist readers who may have gotten this far have been fully persuaded to misrepresent no longer the God of love as having predestinated multitudes to eternal doom while withholding from them any opportunity to understand and believe the gospel. How many unbelievers have rejected God because of this deplorable distortion we do not know—but may that excuse be denied every reader from this time forth! And may believers, in confidence that the gospel is indeed glad tidings for *all* people, take God's good news to the whole world!

Bibliography

Acts, An Introduction and Commentary. Tyndale New Testament Commentaries. Downer's Grove, IL: InterVarsity Press, 1974.

Adams, James E. *Decisional Regeneration.* McDonough, GA: Free Grace Publications, 1972.

Adams, Jay E. *Competent to Counsel.* Grand Rapids, MI: Baker Book House, 1970.

A Faith to Confess: The Baptist Confession of Faith of 1689, Rewritten in Modern English. Carey Publications, 1986.

A Short Explanation of Dr. Martin Luther's Small Catechism: A Handbook of Christian Doctrine. St. Louis, MO: Concordia Publishing House, 1971 ed.

Alford, Henry. *The New Testament for English Readers.* Grand Rapids, MI: Baker Book House, 1983.

Allen, J. W. *History of Political Thought in the Sixteenth Century.* London, 1951.

Amédée, Roget. *L'Église et l'État a Genève du temps de Calvin. Étude d'histoire politico-ecclésiastique.* Geneva: J. Jullien, 1867.

Anderson, Sir Robert. *The Bible or the Church?* London: Pickering and Inglis, 2nd ed., n. d.

"Arminian / Calvinist Response." In *SBC Life*, August 1995.

Arminius, Jacobus. *The Works of James Arminius.* Translated by James and William Nichols. Grand Rapids, MI: Baker Book House, 1986.

Armstrong, John. "Reflections from Jonathan Edwards on the Current Debate over Justification by Faith Alone." Quoted in speech given at Annapolis 2000: A Passion for Truth conference. Sponsored by Jonathan Edwards Institute, PO Box 2410, Princeton, NJ 08543. For more information on Jonathan Edwards's view on justification, contact Grace Evangelical Society, (972) 257–1160.

Augustine, *On the Gift of Perseverance.* http://whitefield.freeservices.com/augustine06.html.

———. *A Treatment on the Soul and its Origins.* n. p., n. d.

———. *The City of God.* Translated by Marcus Dods. In *Great Books of the Western World.* Robert Maynard Hutchins and Mortimer J. Adler, eds. Encyclopaedia Brittanica, Inc., 1952.

———. *The Confessions.* In *Great Books of the Western World,* Robert Maynard Hutchins and Mortimer J. Adler, eds. Translated by Edward Bouverie Pusey. Encyclopaedia Brittanica, Inc., 1952.

Bainton, Roland. *Hunted Heretic: The Life of Michael Servetus.* Boston: The Beacon Press, 1953.

———. *Michel Servet, hérétique et martyr.* Geneva: Droz, 1953.

Baker, Alvin L. *Berkouwer's Doctrine of Election: Balance or Imbalance?* Phillipsburg, NJ: Presbyterian and Reformed Publishing Co., 1981.

Baxter, Richard. *Universal Redemption of Mankind.* London, 1694.

Bayne, Jennifer L., and Sarah E. Hinlicky. "Free to be Creatures Again: How predestination descended like a dove on two unsuspecting seminarians, and *why* they are so grateful." In *Christianity Today*, October 23, 2000.

Beard, Charles. *The Reformation of the Sixteenth Century in Relation to Modern Thought and Knowledge.* London, 1885.

Beck, Frank B. *The Five Points of Calvinism.* Lithgow, Australia: Covenanter Press, 2nd Australian ed. 1986.

Berkhof, Louis. *The History of Christian Doctrines.* Grand Rapids, MI: Baker Book House, 1937.

Bertocci, Peter A. *Free Will, Responsibility, and Grace.* Nashville, TN: Abingdon Press, 1957.

Best, W. E. *Free Grace Versus Free Will.* Houston, TX: W. E. Best Books Missionary Trust, 1977.

———. *Simple Faith (A Misnomer).* Houston, TX: W. E. Best Books Missionary Trust, 1993.

Bettany, G. T. *A Popular History of the Reformation and Modern Protestantism.* London: Ward, Lock and Bowden, Ltd, 1895.

Billion, James F. *True Wisdom Has Two Sides: Calvinism—is it Biblical?* Edinburgh: Grace Mount Publishers, n. d.

Bishop, George S. *The Doctrines of Grace*. Grand Rapids, MI: Baker Book House, 1977.

Boettner, Loraine. *The Reformed Doctrine of Predestination.* Phillipsburg, NJ: Presbyterian and Reformed Publishing Co., 1932.

———. *The Reformed Faith*. Phillipsburg, NJ: Presbyterian and Reformed Publishing Co., 1983.

Bouwsma, William J. *John Calvin: A Sixteenth Century Portrait.* United Kingdom: Oxford University Press, 1988.

Breese, Dave. "The Five Points of Calvinism." Self-published paper, n. d.

Broadbent, E. H. *The Pilgrim Church*. Port Colborne, ON: Gospel Folio Press, reprint 1999.

Bronson, Charles W. *The Extent of the Atonement*. Pasadena, TX: Pilgrim Publications, 1992.

Broughton, Len G. *Salvation and the Old Theology*. London: Hodder and Stroughton, n. d.

Bruce, F. F. *The Books and the Parchments.* London: Pickering and Inglis, Ltd., 1950.

———. *The English Bible: A History of Translations*. New York: Oxford University Press, 1961.

———. *The Epistles to the Colossians, to Philemon, and to the Ephesians*. Grand Rapids, MI: Wm. B. Eerdmans Publishing Co., 1984.

———. *Light in the West*, Bk. III of *The Spreading Flame*. Grand Rapids, MI: Wm. B. Eerdmans Publishing Co., 1956.

Bryson, George L. *The Five Points of Calvinism "Weighed and Found Wanting."* Costa Mesa, CA: The Word For Today, 1996.

Buisson, Ferdinand and Sebastien Castellion. *Sa vie et son oeuvre.* Paris: Hachette, 1892.

Butterworth, Charles C. *The Literary Lineage of the King James Bible.* Philadelphia: University of Pennsylvania Press, 1941.

Cairns, Earle E. *Christianity Through the Centuries: A History of the Christian Church.* Revised and enlarged ed. Grand Rapids, MI: Zondervan Publishing, 1981.

Calvin, John. *Calvin's New Testament Commentaries*. Grand Rapids, MI: Wm. B. Eerdmans Publishing Co., 1994.

______.*Commentary on the Gospel of John, The Comprehensive John Calvin Collection.* Ages Digital Library, 1998.

———. *Institutes of the Christian Religion*. Translated by Henry Beveridge. Grand Rapids, MI: Wm. B. Eerdmans Publishing Company, 1998 ed. First published in Latin (Basel, Switzerland, 1536); later in French.

———. *John Calvin, Calvin's Calvinism*. Translated by Henry Cole. Grandville, MI: Reformed Free Publishing Association, 1987.

———. *Letters of John Calvin.* Carlisle, PA: The Banner of Truth Trust, 1980.

———. *Selected Works of John Calvin: Tracts and Letters.* Henry Beveridge and Jules Bonnet, eds. Grand Rapids, MI: Baker Books, 1983.

Canons of Dort. Dordrecht, Holland, 1619.

Carson, D. A. *Divine Sovereignty and Human Responsibility*. Atlanta, GA: John Knox Press, 1981.

———. "Reflections on Christian Assurance." In *Westminster Theological Journal,* Vol. 54.

———. *The Difficult Doctrine of the Love of God.* Wheaton, IL: Crossway Books, 2000.

Carson, John L. and David W. Hall, eds. *To Glorify and Enjoy God: A Commemoration of the 350th Anniversary of the Westminster Assembly.* Carlisle, PA: The Banner of Truth Trust, 1994.

Chafer, Lewis Sperry. *Systematic Theology*. Dallas, TX: Dallas Seminary Press, 1948.

Chantry, Walter D. *Today's Gospel: Authentic or Synthetic?* Carlisle, PA: The Banner of Truth Trust, 1970.

———. *Predestination.* Phillipsburg, NJ: Presbyterian and Reformed Publishing Co., 1987.

Christian, John T. *A History of the Baptists*. Sunday School Board of the Southern Baptist Convention, n. p., 1922.

Clark, Gordon H. *The Biblical Doctrine of Man*. Jefferson, MD: The Trinity Foundation, 1984.

Clarke, Adam. *Adam Clarke's One-Volume Commentary.* n. p.: Cook Publications, 1989.

Codex Theodosianus. n. p., July 3, A.D. 321.

Cole, C. D. *Definition of Doctrines.* Swengle, PA: Bible Truth Depot, n.d.

Cole, Steven J. *Total Depravity.* Flagstaff AZ, 1999.

Congdon, Philip F. "Soteriological Implications of Five-point Calvinism." In *Journal of the Grace Evangelical Society,* Autumn 1995.

Cook, Frederic C., ed. *The Bible Commentary.* New York: Charles Scribner Sons, 1895.

Coppes, Leonard J. *Are Five Points Enough? The Ten Points of Calvinism.* Denver CO: self-published, 1980.

Cottret, Bernard. *Calvin: A Biography.* Translated by M. Wallace McDonald. Grand Rapids, MI: William B. Eerdmans Publishing Company, 2000.

Cox, S. Raymond. "What Caused God To Choose His People?" Self-published paper, 1980.

Cross, John R. *The Stranger on the Road to Emmaus.* Olds, AB: Good Seed International, 1997.

Cunningham, William. *Historical Theology.* Edmonton, AB: Still Waters Revival Books, n. d.

———. *The Reformers and the Theology of the Reformation.* Carlisle, PA: The Banner of Truth Trust, 1967.

Curtiss, George L. *Arminianism in History.* New York: Cranston and Curts, 1894.

Custance, Arthur C. *The Sovereignty of Grace.* Phillipsburg, NJ: Presbyterian and Reformed Publishing Co., 1979.

Daane, James. *The Freedom of God.* Grand Rapids, MI: Wm. B. Eerdmans Publishing Co., 1973.

Dabney, Robert L. *Discussions by Robert L. Dabney.* C. R. Vaughn, ed. Richmond, VA: Presbyterian Committee of Publication, 1980.

———. *Systematic Theology.* Carlisle, PA: The Banner of Truth Trust, 2nd ed. 1985.

———. *The Five Points of Calvinism.* Harrisonburg, VA: Sprinkle Publications, 1992.

Dagg, John L. *Manual of Theology and Church Order*. Harrisonburg, VA: Sprinkle Publications, 1982.

d'Aubigné, J. H. Merle. *History of the Reformations of the Sixteenth Century*. London: 1846; rev. ed. by Hartland Institute, Rapidan, VA, n. d.

Davis, Jimmie B. In *The Berea Baptist Banner,* February 5, 1995.

Dillow, Joseph C. *The Reign of the Servant Kings: A Study of Eternal Security and the Final Significance of Man.* Haysville, NC: Schoettle Publishing Co., 2nd ed., 1993.

Douty, Norman F. *The Death of Christ.* Irving, TX: Williams and Watrous Publishing Company, n. d.

Duncan, Mark. *The Five Points of Christian Reconstruction from the Lips of Our Lord.* Edmonton, AB: Still Waters Revival Books, 1990.

Durant, Will. *The Story of Civilization*. New York: Simon and Schuster, 1950.

Edinburgh Encyclopedia. Scotland: n. p., n. d.

Edwards, Jonathan. *Freedom of the Will.* Paul Ramsey, ed. New Haven, CT: Yale University Press, 1957.

Ehler, Sidney Z., and John B. Morrall. *Church and State Through the Centuries: A Collection of Historic Documents and Commentaries.* London:1954.

Engelsma, David J. *A Defense of Calvinism as the Gospel.* The Evangelism Committee, Protestant Reformed Church, n. p., n. d.

———. *Hyper-Calvinism and the Call of the Gospel.* Grandville, MI: Reformed Free Publishing Association, 1980.

———. "The Death of Confessional Calvinism in Scottish Presbyterianism." In *The Standard Bearer*, December 1, 1992.

Eusebius Pamphilius of Caesaria, advisor to Constantine. *The Life of Constantine*. n. p., c. A.D. 335.

Fairbairn, Andrew M. *The Philosophy of the Christian Religion*. New York: The MacMillan Co., 1923.

Farrar, Frederic W. *A Manual of Christian Doctrine.* New York: The Alliance Press, n. d.

———. *History of Interpretation.* New York: E. P. Dutton and Co., 1886.

Fisher, George Park. *History of the Christian Church.* New York: Charles Scribner's Sons, 1902.

———. *The Reformation.* New York: Scribner, Armstrong and Co., 1873.

Fisk, Samuel. *Calvinistic Paths Retraced.* Raleigh, NC: Biblical Evangelism Press, 1985.

———. *Divine Sovereignty and Human Freedom.* Neptune, NJ: Loizeaux Brothers, 1973.

———. *Election and Predestination.* England: Penfold Book and Bible House, 1997.

Foreman, Kenneth J. *God's Will and Ours.* Richmond, VA: Outlook Publishers, 1954.

Forster, Roger T. and V. Paul Marston. *God's Strategy in Human History.* Bloomington, MN: Bethany House Publishers, 1973.

Frend, W. H. C. *The Rise of Christianity.* Philadelphia, PA: Fortress Press, 1984.

Gay, David. *Battle for the Church: 1517–1644.* Lowestoft, UK: Brachus, 1997.

Geden, Alfred S. *Comparative Religion.* London: Society for Promoting Christian Knowledge, 1917.

Geisler, Norman L. *What Augustine Says.* Grand Rapids, MI: Baker Book House, 1982.

George, Timothy. *Theology of the Reformers.* Nashville, TN: Broadman Press, 1988.

Gerstner, John H. *A Primer on Free Will.* Phillipsburg, NJ: Presbyterian and Reformed Publishing Co., 1982.

———. *Wrongly Dividing the Word of Truth: A Critique of Dispensationalism.* Brentwood, TN: Wolgemuth and Hyatt, Publishers, Inc., 1991.

Gibbon, Edward. *The History of the Decline and Fall of the Roman Empire.* New York: Modern Library, n. d.

Gill, John A. *A Body of Doctrinal and Practical Divinity*. Paris, AR: The Baptist Standard Bearer, 1987.

———. *The Cause of God and Truth*. Paris, AR: The Baptist Standard Bearer, 1992.

Good, Kenneth H. *Are Baptists Calvinists?* Rochester, NY: Backus Book Publishers, 1988.

Goold, William H., ed. *The Works of John Owen*. Carlisle, PA: The Banner of Truth Trust, reprint 1978.

Grady, William P. *Final Authority: A Christian's Guide to the King James Bible*. Knoxville, TN: Grady Publications, 1993.

Gray, James M. *Bible Problems Explained.* Grand Rapids, MI: Fleming H. Revell, 3rd. ed., 1913.

Gunn, Grover E. *The Doctrines of Grace*. Memphis, TN: Footstool Publications, 1987.

Hanko, Herman. *God's Everlasting Covenant of Grace*. Grandville, MI: Reformed Free Publishing Association, 1988.

Hanko, Herman, Homer C. Hoeksema, and Gise J. Van Baren. *The Five Points of Calvinism*. Grandville, MI: Reformed Free Publishing Association, 1976.

Harkness, Georgia. *John Calvin: The Man and His Ethics.* Nashville, TN: Abingdon Press, 1958.

Harrison, A. W. *Arminianism.* London: Duckworth, 1937.

Henderson, Henry F. *Calvin in His Letters.* London: J. M. Dent and Co., 1909.

Hobbs, Herschel H. *Fundamentals of our Faith.* Nashville: Broadman, 1960.

Hodge, A. A. *The Atonement*. Memphis, TN: Footstool Publishers, 1987.

———. *Outlines of Theology.* Grand Rapids, MI: Zondervan, 1972.

Hodge, Charles. *A Commentary on Romans*. Carlisle, PA: The Banner of Truth Trust, 1972.

———. *Systematic Theology*. Grand Rapids, MI: Wm. B. Eerdmans Publishing Co., 1986.

Hodges, Zane C. *The Gospel Under Siege.* Dallas, TX: Kerugma, Inc., 2nd ed. 1992.

———. "The New Puritanism, Parts 2 and 3: Michael S. Horton: Holy Wars With Unholy Weapons." In *Journal of the Grace Evangelical Society*, Spring 1994.

Hoeksema, Herman. *God's Eternal Good Pleasure*. Edited and revised by Homer C. Hoeksema. Grandville, MI: Reformed Free Publishing Association, 1979.

Hoeksema, Homer. *Reformed Dogmatics*. Grandville, MI: Reformed Free Publishing Association, 1966.

———. *The Voice of Our Fathers*. Grandville, MI: Reformed Free Publishing Association, 1980.

Hoitenga, Dewey J. *John Calvin and the Will: A Critique and Corrective*. Grand Rapids, MI: Baker Books, 1997.

Horne, C. Sylvester. *A Popular History of the Free Churches*. Cambridge, UK: James Clarke and Co., 1903.

Horsch, John. *History of Christianity*. Scottsdale, PA: John Horsch, 1903.

Horton, Michael Scott. *Putting Amazing Back Into Grace*. Nashville, TN: Thomas Nelson Publishers, 1991.

———, ed. *Christ the Lord: The Reformation and Lordship Salvation*. Grand Rapids, MI: Baker Book House, 1992.

Houck, Steven R. "God's Sovereignty In Salvation." The Evangelism Committee, Protestant Reformed Church, South Holland, IL, n. d.

———. *The Bondage of the Will*. Lansing, IL: Peace Protestant Reformed Church, n. d.

http://www.iclnet.org/pub/resources/text/wittenberg/wittenberg-luther.html.

Hughes, Philip. *A History of the Church*. London, 1934.

Hughes, Paul L. and James F. Larkin, eds. *Tudor Royal Proclamations*. New Haven, CT: Yale University Press, 1964.

Hulme, Edward Maslin. *The Renaissance, the Protestant Reformation, and the Catholic Revolution*. New York: The Century Company, 1920.

Hunt, Dave and James White. *Debating Calvinism: five points, two views*. Sisters, OR: Multnomah Publishers, 2004.

Hutchins, Robert Maynard and Mortimer J. Adler, eds. *Great Books of the Western World.* Chicago: Encyclopaedia Brittanica, Inc., 1952.

IFCA International. *What We Believe.* www.ifca.org.

Ironside, H. A. *Full Assurance.* Chicago: Moody Press, 1937.

———. *In the Heavenlies, Addresses on Ephesians.* Neptune, NJ: Loizeaux Brothers, 1937.

———. *Lectures on the Epistle to the Romans.* Neptune, NJ: Loizeaux Brothers, 1926.

———. *Timothy, Titus and Philemon.* Neptune, NJ: Loizeaux Brothers, Inc., 1990.

———. *What's the Answer?* Grand Rapids, MI: Zondervan, 1944.

Jewett, Paul K. *Election and Predestination.* Grand Rapids, MI: Wm. B. Eerdmans Publishing Co., 1985 ed.

John Paul II, Sovereign Pontiff. *Augustineum Hyponensem.* Apostolic Letter, August 28, 1986. Available at www.cin.org/jp2.ency/augustin.html.

Johnson, Garrett P. "The Myth of Common Grace." In *The Trinity Review,* March/April 1987.

Jones, R. Tudor. *The Great Reformation.* Downer's Grove, IL: InterVarsity Press, n. d.

Jones, William. *The History of the Christian Church.* Church History Research and Archives, 5th ed. n. p., 1983.

Kane, Michael J., Ph.D. "Letters." In *Christianity Today,* July 9, 2001.

Kennedy, D. James. *Why I Believe.* Dallas, TX: Word Publishing, 1980.

———. *Why I Am a Presbyterian.* Ft. Lauderdale, FL: Coral Ridge Ministries, n. d.

Kennedy, John W. *The Torch of the Testimony.* Jacksonville, FL: SeedSowers Christian Books Publishing House, 1963.

Keyser, Leander S. *Election and Conversion.* Burlington, IA: Lutheran Literary Board, 1914.

Knowling, R. J. *The Acts of the Apostles, The Expositor's Greek New Testament.* New York: Dodd, Meade and Co., 1900.

Knox, John. *Selected Writings of John Knox.* Dallas, TX: Presbyterian Heritage Publications, 1995.

Leith, John H. *Introduction to the Reformed Tradition.* Atlanta, GA: John Knox Press, rev. ed. 1981.

Lockyer, Herbert. *All the Doctrines of the Bible.* Grand Rapids, MI: Zondervan, 1964.

Luther, Martin. *The Bondage of the Will.* Translated by J. I. Packer and O. R. Johnston. Grand Rapids, MI: Fleming H. Revell, 1957, 11th prtg. 1999.

———. *A Short Explanation of Dr. Martin Luther's Small Catechism: A Handbook of Christian Doctrine.* St. Louis, MO: Concordia Publishing House, 1971 ed.

MacArthur, John, Jr. *Faith Works: The Gospel According to the Apostles.* Dallas, TX: Word Publishing, 1993.

———. *Saved Without A Doubt–MacArthur Study Series.* Colorado Springs, CO: Chariot Victor Publishing, 1992.

———. *The Gospel According to Jesus.* Academie Books, Grand Rapids, MI: Zondervan Publishing House, 1988.

———. *The Love of God.* Dallas, TX: Word Publishing, 1996.

———. "The Love of God, Part 5, Romans 9". Grace to You, 1995. Audiotape.

______. *The MacArthur Study Bible.* Dallas, TX: Word Publishing, 1997.

Maclaren, Alexander. *Expositions of Holy Scripture.* London: Hodder and Stoughton, n. d.

St. Justin, Martyr. *The First and Second Apologies.* Ancient Christian Writers, No. 56. New York: Paulist Press, 1997.

Mathison, Keith A. *Dispensationalism: Rightly Dividing the People of God?* Phillipsburg, NJ: Presbyterian and Reformed Publishing Co., 1995.

McGarvey, J.W. *Commentary on Acts.* Lexington, KY: Transylvania Printing and Publishing Co., 1863.

McGrath, Alister E. *A Life of John Calvin.* Cambridge, MA: Blackwell Publishers, 1990.

McNeil, John T. *Makers of the Christian Tradition*. San Francisco: Harper and Row, 1964.

———. *The History and Character of Calvinism*. Oxford: Oxford University Press, 1966.

Milman, Henry H. *History of Christianity.* New York: A. C. Armstrong and Son, 1886.

Milne, Bruce. *Know the Truth.* Downer's Grove, IL: InterVarsity Press, 1982.

Moo, Douglas. *The Epistle to the Romans*. Grand Rapids, MI: Wm. B. Eerdmans Publishing Co., 1996.

Morey, Robert A. *Studies in the Atonement.* Southbridge, MA: Crowne Publications, 1989.

Morgan, G. Campbell. *The Westminster Pulpit.* Grand Rapids, MI: Fleming H. Revell, 1954.

Morrison, James. *The Extent of the Atonement.* London: Hamilton, Adams and Co., 1882.

Mosheim, John Laurence. *An Ecclesiastical History, Ancient and Modern.* Translated by Archibald MacLaine. Cincinnati: Applegate and Co., 1854.

Morton, Carl. In *The Berea Baptist Banner*, January 5, 1995.

Muir, Edwin. *John Knox.* London, 1920.

Muller, Richard A. *Christ and the Decree.* Grand Rapids, MI: Baker Book House, 1988.

Mullins, Edgar Y. *Baptist Beliefs*. Valley Forge, PA: Judson, 4th ed. 1925.

Murray, Iain H. *The Life of John Murray.* Carlisle, PA: The Banner of Truth Trust, 1984.

———. *Spurgeon V. Hyper-Calvinism*, Carlisle, PA: The Banner of Truth Trust, 1997.

Murray, John. *Redemption Accomplished and Applied.* Grand Rapids, MI: Wm. B. Eerdmans Publishing Co., 1955.

———. *The Free Offer of the Gospel.* n. p., n. d.

Murray, John and Ned B. Stonehouse. *The Free Offer of the Gospel.* n. p., n. d.

New Geneva Study Bible. R. C. Sproul, gen. ed. Nashville, TN: Thomas Nelson Publishers, 1995.

Newman, Albert H. *A Manual of Church History.* Philadelphia, PA: American Baptist Publication Society, 1933.

Nicoll, W. Robertson, ed. *The Expositor's Greek Testament.* Grand Rapids, MI: Wm. B. Eerdmans Publishing Co., n. d.

Noll, Mark A., ed. *The Princeton Theology.* Phillipsburg, NJ: Presbyterian and Reformed Publishing Co., 1983.

North, Gary. *Dominion and Common Grace.* Tyler, TX: Institute for Christian Economics, 1987.

Oosterman, Wm. "Take a Long Look at the Doctrines of Election." Ottawa, Canada: The Lord's Library Publications, n. d. Available from Westboro Baptist Church, Ottawa.

Ostling, Richard N. "The Second Founder of the Faith." In *Time*, September 29, 1986.

Owen, John. *The Works of John Owen.* Ed. William H. Goold. Carlisle, PA: The Banner of Truth Trust, 3rd prtg., 1978.

Packer, J. I. *Evangelism and the Sovereignty of God.* Downer's Grove, IL: InterVarsity Press, 1961.

———. "The Love of God: Universal and Particular" In *Still Sovereign,* . Thomas R. Schreiner & Bruce A. Ware, eds. Grand Rapids, MI: Baker Books, 2000.

Page, T. E. *The Acts of the Apostles, Greek Text with Explanatory Notes.* New York: Macmillan and Co., 1897.

Palmer, Edwin H. *the five points of calvinism.* Grand Rapids, MI: Baker Books, enlarged ed., 20th prtg., 1999.

Pettingill, William L. *Bible Questions Answered.* Just A Word Inc., 3rd ed., 1935.

Phelps, Fred. "The Five Points of Calvinism." In *The Berea Baptist Banner,* February 5, 1990.

Pierson, Arthur T. *The Believer's Life: Its Past, Present, and Future Tenses.* London: Morgan and Scott, 1905.

Pike, Henry R. *The Other Side of John Calvin.* n. p.: Head to Heart, n. d.

Pink, Arthur W. *Exposition of the Gospel of John.* Grand Rapids, MI: Zondervan Publishing House, 1975.

———. *Gleanings in Exodus.* Chicago: Moody Press, 1981.

———. *The Doctrine of Election and Justification.* Grand Rapids, MI: Baker Book House, 1974.

———. *The Doctrine of Salvation.* Grand Rapids, MI: Baker Book House, 1975.

———. *The Holy Spirit.* Grand Rapids, MI: Baker Book House, 1978.

———. *The Sovereignty of God.* 2nd Prtg. Grand Rapids, MI: Baker Book House, 1986.

Pinnock, Clark H., ed. *Grace Unlimited.* Minneapolis, MN: Bethany Fellowship, Inc., 1976.

Piper, John. *The Justification of God: An Exegetical and Theological Study of Romans 9:1–23.* Grand Rapids, MI: Baker Books, 2000.

———. *TULIP: The Pursuit of God's Glory in Salvation.* Minneapolis, MN: Bethlehem Baptist Church, 2000.

———. "Are There Two Wills in God?" In *Still Sovereign.* Thomas R. Schreiner & Bruce A. Ware, eds. Grand Rapids, MI: Baker Books, 2000.

———. *God's Passion For His Glory*, Wheaton, IL: Crossway Books, 1998.

———. *The Legacy of Sovereign Joy: God's Triumphant Grace in the Lives of Augustine, Luther and Calvin.* Wheaton, IL: Crossway Books, 2000.

Piper, John and Pastoral Staff. "TULIP: What We Believe about the Five Points of Calvinism: Position Paper of the Pastoral Staff." Minneapolis, MN: Desiring God Ministries, 1997.

Plass, Ewald. *What Luther Says.* St. Louis, MO: Concordia Publishing House, 1987.

Pollard, Alfred W., ed. *Records of the English Bible.* Oxford: Oxford University Press, 1911.

Potter, G. R. and M. Greengrass. *John Calvin.* New York: St. Martin's Press, 1983.

Pusey, Edward B. *What Is Of Faith As To Everlasting Punishment?* England: James Parker and Co., 1881.

Rice, N. L. *God Sovereign and Man Free*. Harrisonburg, VA: Sprinkle Publications, 1985.

Robertson, Archibald Thomas. *Word Pictures in the New Testament.* New York: Harper and Bros., 1930.

Robertson, J. M. *Short History of Freethought.* London, 1914.

Robinson, H. Wheeler. *The Bible In Its Ancient and English Versions.* Oxford: Clarendon Press, 1940.

Rose, Ben Lacy. *T.U.L.I.P.: The Five Disputed Points of Calvinism.* Franklin, TN: Providence House Publishers, 1996.

Ross, Tom. *Abandoned Truth: The Doctrines of Grace.* Xenia, OH: Providence Baptist Church, 1991.

Rowley, H. H. *The Biblical Doctrine of Election*. Cambridge, UK: Lutterworth Press, 1952.

Ruckman, Peter S. *The History of the New Testament.* Pensacola: Bible Baptist Bookstore, 1982.

Rutherford, Samuel. *Letters of Samuel Rutherford.* Carlisle, PA: The Banner of Truth Trust, 1996; 1st ed. 1664.

Ryle, John C. *Expository Thoughts on the Gospel of John.* London: Wm. Hunt and Co., 1883.

Sanford, Dick. *Predestination and Election.* John R. Cross, ed. Self-published monograph, n. d.

Schaff, Philip. *History of the Christian Church.* New York: Charles Scribner, 1910; reprinted Grand Rapids, MI: Wm. B. Eerdmans Publishing Co., 1959.

———. *The Creeds of Christendom.* Grand Rapids, MI: Baker Book House, 1990.

Schreiner, Thomas R. and Bruce A. Ware, eds. *Still Sovereign: Contemporary Perspectives on Election, Foreknowledge and Grace.* Grand Rapids, MI: Baker Books, 2000.

———. *The Grace of God, The Bondage of the Will.* Grand Rapids, MI: Baker Books, 1995.

Scofield, C. I. *Scofield Bible Correspondence Course.* Chicago, IL: Moody Bible Institute, 1907.

Scott, Otto. *The Great Christian Revolution.* Windsor, NY: The Reformer Library, 1994.

Seaton, W. J. *The Five Points of Calvinism.* Carlisle, PA:The Banner of Truth Trust, 1970.

Sell, Alan P. F. *The Great Debate.* Grand Rapids, MI: Baker Book House, 1982.

Sellers, C. Norman. *Election and Perseverance.* Haysville, NC: Schoettle Publishing Co., 1987.

Shedd, William G. T. *Calvinism: Pure and Mixed.* Carlisle, PA:The Banner of Truth Trust, 1999.

———. *A History of Christian Doctrine.* New York: Charles Scribner and Co., 3rd ed. 1865.

Sheldon, Henry C. *History of Christian Doctrine.* 2nd ed. New York: Harper and Bros., 1895.

Singer, C. Gregg. *John Calvin: His Roots and Fruits.* Nashville, TN: Abingdon Press, 1989.

Smith, H. Maynard. *Pre-Reformation England.* New York: Russell and Russell, 1963.

Smith, Preserved. *The Age of the Reformation.* New York, 1920.

Souter, Alexander. *The Earliest Latin Commentaries on the Epistles of St. Paul.* n. p., 1927.

Spencer, Duane Edward. *TULIP: The Five Points of Calvinism in the Light of Scripture.* Grand Rapids, MI: Baker Book House, 1979.

Sproul, R. C. "Assurance of Salvation." *Tabletalk.* Ligonier Ministries, Inc., November 1989.

———. *Chosen by God.* Carol Stream, IL: Tyndale House Publishers, Inc., 1986.

———. *Faith Alone: The Evangelical Doctrine of Justification.* Grand Rapids, MI: Baker Books, 1995.

———. *Grace Unknown.* Grand Rapids, MI: Baker Books, 1997.

———. *The Holiness of God.* Carol Stream, IL: Tyndale House Publishers, Inc., 1993 ed.

Sproul, R. C., Jr. *Almighty Over All.* Grand Rapids, MI: Baker Book House, 1999.

———. "The Authentic Message." In *Tabletalk.* Ligonier Ministries, Inc., June 2001.

Spurgeon, Charles Haddon. "A Defense of Calvinism." Edmonton, AB: Still Waters Revival Books, n. d. Single-sermon booklet.

———. *Autobiography of Charles H. Spurgeon.* Philadelphia, PA: American Baptist Society, n. d.

———. *Free Will–A Slave.* McDonough, GA: Free Grace Publications, 1977.

———. "God's Will and Man's Will," No. 442. Newington: Metropolitan Tabernacle; sermon delivered Sunday morning, March 30, 1862.

———. *New Park Street Pulpit.* London: Passmore and Alabaster. Volume 6.

———. *Sermons of C. H. Spurgeon.* Available from Pilgrim Publications, Pasadena, TX, n. d.

———. *Spurgeon at His Best.* Tom Carter, ed. Grand Rapids, MI: Baker Book House, 1988.

———. *Spurgeon's Sermons, Vols 1 and 2.* "The Peculiar Sleep of the Beloved." Grand Rapids, MI: 1999.

———. *The Best Bread: Sermons Preached in 1887.* New York: Funk and Wagnalls, 1891.

———. *The Soul Winner.* Grand Rapids, MI: Wm. B. Eerdmans Publishing Co., 1963.

———. *The Treasury of the New Testament.* Grand Rapids, MI: Zondervan, 1950.

———, ed. *Exposition of the Doctrine of Grace.* Pasadena, CA: Pilgrim Publications, n. d.

Steele, David N. and Curtis C. Thomas. *The Five Points of Calvinism.* Phillipsburg, NJ: Presbyterian and Reformed Publishing Co., 1963.

"Straight Talk Live." KPXQ, Phoenix, AZ, August 11, 2000. Audiotape AT073, available through The Berean Call, PO Box 7019, Bend, OR 97708.

Strong, Augustus H. *Systematic Theology*. Valley Forge, PA: Judson Press, 1907.

Storms, C. Samuel. *Chosen for Life*. Grand Rapids, MI: Baker Book House, 1987.

Talbot, Kenneth G. and W. Gary Crampton. *Calvinism, Hyper-Calvinism and Arminianism*. Edmonton, AB: Still Waters Revival Books, 1990.

Telford, Andrew. *Subjects of Sovereignty*. Acworth, GA: Harvest Time Ministries, 1980.

The Opinions of the Remonstrants. Presented at Synod of Dort, Dordrecht, Holland, 1619.

The Register of the Company of Pastors of Geneva in the Time of Calvin. Translated and edited by Philip E. Hughes. Grand Rapids, MI: Wm. B. Eerdmans Publishing Co., 1966.

Thomas, W. H. Griffith. *The Principles of Theology*. London: Longmans, Green and Co., 1930.

Thompson, Bard. *Humanists and Reformers: A History of the Renaissance and Reformation*. Grand Rapids, MI: Wm. B. Eerdmans Publishing Co., 1996.

Thompson, Bob. "The 5 Points of Calvin's Doctrine of Predestination." Self-published monograph, 4056 Skyline Rd., Carlsbad CA 92008, n. d.

Torrey, Reuben A. *The Importance and Value of Proper Bible Study.* Chicago: Moody Press, 1921.

Tozer, A. W. "The Sovereignty of God." Camphill, PA: Christian Publications, 1997. Audiotape.

———. *The Knowledge of the Holy.* San Francisco: Harper & Row, 1961.

Underwood, A. C. *A History of the English Baptists.* n. p.: The Baptist Union of Great Britian and Ireland, 1947.

Unger, Merrill F. *Unger's Bible Dictionary*. Chicago: Moody Press, 1969.

Vance, Laurence M. *The Other Side of Calvinism*, rev. ed. Pensacola, FL: Vance Publications, 1999.

Verduin, Leonard. *The Reformers and Their Stepchildren.* Sarasota, FL: Christian Hymnary Publishers, 1991.

Verhovek, Sam Howe. "Cardinal Defends a Jailed Bishop Who Warned Cuomo on Abortion." In *The New York Times,* February 1, 1990.

Vincent, Marvin R. *Word Studies in the New Testament.* New York: Charles Scribner's Sons, 1924.

Voltaire. *The Works of Voltaire.* New York: E. R. Dumont, 1901.

Wallace, Ronald S. *Calvin, Geneva, and the Reformation.* Grand Rapids, MI: Baker Book House, 1990.

Walker, Williston. *John Calvin: The Organizer of Reformed Protestantism*. New York: Schocken Books, 1969.

Ware, Bruce A. "Effective Calling and Grace." In *Still Sovereign,* Thomas R. Schreiner & Bruce A. Ware, eds. Grand Rapids, MI: Baker Books, 2000.

Warfield, Benjamin B. *Calvin and Augustine.* Samuel G. Craig, ed. Phillipsburg, NJ: Presbyterian and Reformed Publishing Co., 1956.

———. "Five Common Questions on the Doctrine of Election Simply and Clearly Answered." In *The Baptist Examiner*. November 20, 1993.

Wendel, Francois. *Calvin: Origins and Development of His Religious Thought.* Grand Rapids, MI: Baker Books, 1997.

Wesley, John. *Sermons on Several Occasions.* New York: J. Emory and B. Waugh, for the Methodist Episcopal Church at the Conference Office, 14 Crosby St., 1831.

West, David S. *The Baptist Examiner,* March 18, 1989.

Westblade, Donald J. "Divine Election in the Pauline Structure." In *Still Sovereign,* Thomas R. Schreiner & Bruce A. Ware, eds. Grand Rapids, MI: Baker Books, 2000.

Westminster Confession of Faith. London, 1643.

White, James R. *The Potter's Freedom: A Defense of the Reformation and a Rebuttal of Norman Geisler's Chosen But Free*. Amityville, NY: Calvary Press Publishing, 2000.

White, W. R. *Baptist Distinctives.* n. p.: Sunday School Board, SBC, 1946.

Wilkin, Robert N. "Ligonier National Conference." In *The Grace Report,* July 2000.

———. "When Assurance Is Not Assurance." In *Journal of the Grace Evangelical Society,* Autumn 1997.

Wilmouth, David O. *The Baptist Examiner*, September 16, 1989.

Wilson, Joseph M. "How is the Atonement Limited?" In *The Baptist Examiner,* December 9, 1989.

———. "Soul Winning." In *The Baptist Examiner,* February 15, 1992.

Wright, R. K. McGregor. *No Place for Sovereignty: What's Wrong with Freewill Theism.* Downer's Grove, IL: InterVarsity Press, 1996.

Wuest, Kenneth S. *Ephesians and Colossians in the Greek New Testament*. Grand Rapids, MI: Wm. B. Eerdmans Publishing Co., 1953.

Yarbrough, Robert W. "Divine Election in the Gospel of John." In *Still Sovereign.* Thomas R. Schreiner & Bruce A. Ware, eds. Grand Rapids, MI: Baker Books, 2000.

Zanchius, Jerom. *The Doctrine of Absolute Predestination*. Translated by Augustus M. Toplady. Grand Rapids, MI: Baker Book House, 1977.

Zeller, George. "For Whom Did Christ Die?" The Middletown Bible Church, 349 East St., Middletown CT 06457, 1999.

Zins, Robert M. "A Believer's Guide to Second Peter 3:9." Self-published monograph, n. d.

Scripture Reference Index

OLD TESTAMENT

Genesis

Exodus

Leviticus

Numbers

Deuteronomy

Joshua

Judges

1 Samuel

2 Samuel

1 Kings

1 Chronicles

2 Chronicles

1 Corinthians

2 Corinthians

Galatians

Ephesians

Author/Subject Reference Index

A

B

C

D

F

G

H

I

J

N

O

R

S

V

W

Y

Z

Other Books by Dave Hunt

- The Seduction of Christianity *(with T. A. McMahon)*
- Beyond Seduction: A Return to Biblical Christianity
- When Will Jesus Come? *(formerly* How Close Are We?*)*
- Death of a Guru *(with Rabi Maharaj)*
- Whatever Happened to Heaven?
- Peace, Prosperity and the Coming Holocaust
- The Cult Explosion
- A Cup of Trembling: Jerusalem and Bible Prophecy
- Global Peace and the Rise of Antichrist
- In Defense of the Faith
- A Woman Rides the Beast: The Roman Catholic Church and the Last Days
- Mind Invaders
- Sanctuary of the Chosen
- Y2K: A Reasoned Response to Mass Hysteria
- Occult Invasion: The Subtle Seduction of the World and the Church
- The God Makers *(with Ed Decker)*
- The New Spirituality *(with T. A. McMahon)*
- An Urgent Call to a Serious Faith
- Debating Calvinism *(with James White)*
- Seeking and Finding God: In Search of the True Faith
- A Calvinist's Honest Doubts Resolved: by Reason and God's Amazing Grace
- JUDGMENT DAY! Islam, Israel, and the Nations
- Yoga and The Body of Christ: What Position Should Christians Hold?

About The Berean Call

The Berean Call (TBC) is a nonprofit,
tax-exempt corporation which exists to:

ALERT believers in Christ to unbiblical teachings and practices impacting the church

EXHORT believers to give greater heed to biblical discernment and truth regarding teachings and practices being currently promoted in the church

SUPPLY believers with teaching, information, and materials which will encourage the love of God's truth, and assist in the development of biblical discernment

MOBILIZE believers in Christ to action in obedience to the scriptural command to "earnestly contend for the faith" (Jude 3)

IMPACT the church of Jesus Christ with the necessity for trusting the Scriptures as the only rule for faith, practice, and a life pleasing to God

A free monthly newsletter, THE BEREAN CALL, *may be received by sending a request to: PO Box 7019, Bend, OR 97708; or by calling*

1-800-937-6638

To register for free email updates, to access our digital archives, and to order a variety of additional resource materials online, visit us at:

www.thebereancall.org